573
P75i

123992

DATE DUE			

IN SEARCH OF OURSELVES

An Introduction to Physical Anthropology

Second Edition

Frank E. Poirier

THE OHIO STATE UNIVERSITY

BURGESS PUBLISHING COMPANY · MINNEAPOLIS, MINNESOTA

Printed in the United States of America
Library of Congress Card Number 77-70312
ISBN 0-8087-1657-3

0 9 8 7 6 5 4 3 2 1

Credits

Cover design by Joan Gordon, layout by Mari Ansari. Art when not otherwise cited was drawn by Mary Dersch or Shirley Hoeman. The cover photograph (repeated on page 268) and the opening photo for Part I are reproduced courtesy of Richard E. Leakey, National Museums of Kenya; the opening photograph for Chapter 1 courtesy of Dennis Tasa; opening photographs for Chapter 2, Part III, Chapter 8 and pages 128-29, and Chapter 20 by Frank E. Poirier; Chapter 11 and page 183, pages 240-41 and 249 in Chapter 15 by Wendy Lawrence. Other photographs are acknowledged below under the appropriate chapter or part headings.

Figures 15-13 and 15-15 are after W. Le Gros Clark, *The Fossil Evidence for Human Evolution,* © 1955, 1964 by The University of Chicago, and Figure 15-4 is after M. D. Leakey, "Preliminary summary of the cultural material from Beds I and II, Olduvai Gorge, Tanzania," in *Background to Evolution in Africa,* edited by W. Bishop and J. Clark, © 1967 by the Wenner-Gren Foundation. Used by permission of the University of Chicago Press.

Material cited on pages 46 and 393 and Figures 16-2, 21-1, 23-5 are from *Physical Anthropology* by A. J. Kelso. Reprinted by permission of the publishers, J. B. Lippincott Company. Copyright © 1970 and 1974.

Frontispiece. Courtesy of Atomic Energy Commission.

Part II. Courtesy of the American Museum of Natural History.

Chapter 3. By permission of the trustees of the British Museum (Natural History). *Figure 3-3.* Aus dem Bilderarchiv der Österr. Nationalbibliothek.

Chapter 4. Courtesy of American Optical Co., Instrument Division, Eggert & Sugar Roads, Buffalo, N.Y. 14215. *Figure 4-2.* From C. Benjamin Meleca et al., *Bio-Learning Guide.* Burgess Publishing Company, Minneapolis, 1971. *Figure 4-3.* Courtesy of Drs. J. H. Tijo and T. T. Puck. *Figure 4-4.* From Richard E. Dickerson and Irving Geis,

(continued on page 461)

Preface

This book is about life, our collective lives: past, present, and future. An unhealthy intellectual arrogance has recently been created by our small scientific successes, our flights to the moon, medical discoveries, and our ability to create and destroy life. The finality of this last property, the ability to destroy life, emphasizes the need to replace this arrogance, this know-it-allness, with a new humility based on expanding knowledge of the complexity of life, of which we are but one part. Kierkegaard once stated that life can only be understood backward, but it must be lived forward. However, it can only be lived forward with knowledge and appreciation of the past.

In these next few pages we examine our evolutionary history, noting the major signposts along the way. Time and our own blindnesses have erased some of the signs; but the path is not yet obscure. Prepare for the journey; for some for whom this is all new, it is as rewarding and as dangerous as any new unexplored, uncharted venture.

Immodestly, this book attempts to answer the ancient Psalmist's cry, "What is Man?" What are we if not products of millions of years of evolution? How do we survive if we do not understand these millions of years and make them part of our personal litany? The late biologist Thomas Henry Huxley stated, "The question of all questions for mankind—the problem which underlies all others and which is more deeply interesting than any other—is the ascertainment of the place Man occupies in nature and his relations to the universe of things."

We are on the threshold of fantastic happenings, one of the greatest being an expansion of all forms of knowledge. We know more about ourselves than ever before, yet we occasionally seem bridled by old concepts. This book deals with some older thoughts. It also incorporates many of the newest ideas and concepts concerning our evolutionary past, with reference to fossils, modern monkeys and apes, wolves, hyenas, and elephants, among others. This book discusses our past and present population diversity. It addresses us as we live in deserts and on mountains, as we have dark or light skins, tall or short bodies. It addresses us as we are and how we were. We are fascinating creatures with a fascinating past, and we need to demand more knowledge about ourselves.

Many things were taken into consideration in producing this new edition. User suggestions inspired a good deal of rewriting and reorganization in the section on human variation. New material on Mendelian, molecular, and biochemical genetics has been added to give students a better feeling for some of the biological aspects of evolution. The discovery of new fossils in East Africa occasioned the rewriting of the section on fossil evolution. The section on primate behavior has been expanded and a chapter on evolutionary systematics added.

Users of the original edition will notice rewriting and reorganization throughout the text as well as the addition of many new tables, charts, drawings, and photographs. Photographs opening each chapter should make the book more appealing visually, and personal field notes with photographic essays will make anthropology less abstract for students. A study guide and instructor's manual have also been developed for this purpose. The bibliography has been enlarged considerably, and gender references have been removed except in direct quotations.

The objective of the book remains the same, however, namely, to provide a comprehensive review of current information on primate evolution—specifically human evolution—for students with little or no background in anthropology or biology. The attempt to integrate biology, behavior, and culture is of key importance as we look at human evolution, nonhuman primate behavior, and human diversity. I hope the readers will enjoy this introduction to physical anthropology as much as I enjoyed putting it together.

Acknowledgments

Few people can write a book or teach a course without the help of others. I wish to acknowledge the help of those many undergraduate students and teaching assistants who took the time to comment on my teaching, to provide constructive criticism, and to buoy my spirits when they were low. I am grateful to the users of the original edition as well as reviewers of drafts of the present edition for their insightful comments and suggestions. It is primarily because of their interest that much of the book has taken new form.

My family always suffers when I work hard on a project, but without their support I couldn't finish. I thank my wife Darlene and our two children, Alyson and Sevanne. Special thanks are due to the C. V. Mosby Company, St. Louis, for kindly granting permission to use material from my 1977 publication entitled *Fossil Evidence: The Human Evolutionary Journey.* I also wish to thank Drs. J. Blank, B. Gelvin, O. Oyen, J. Pritchard, P. Sciulli, T. Tripp-Reimer, and C. Weitz for their helpful criticisms. In addition, I would like to thank the following individuals at Burgess Publishing Company: Mr. G. Brahms, Mr. J. Holtmeier, and Ms. D. Stein.

Thanks are due also to all publishers and individuals that have allowed us to use photographs, drawings, and tables. Where not shown in the text credits will be found in a separate list at the end of the book.

As is perhaps true of many who have researched a topic for many years and who have had the good fortune of being able to present this research to interested audiences, be they students or others, it soon becomes difficult to differentiate your own ideas from those which you have read and which belong rightfully to others. The task of a synthesizer, to take the ideas which many have labored to produce and attempt to put them together into some comprehensive format, is fascinating. If I have succeeded in doing this, then my debt lies with so many who have worked so hard to produce the original ideas. In fact, it may be very close to the truth to state that, in what follows, there is little which is purely original with this author. I trust that I have repaid my debt for many enjoyable hours by acknowledging the sources. If I have erred even once in this process I hope I may be forgiven by the researcher whose work I have discussed. If there are places where the reader recognizes his or her own hand in what I have said I hope that I have been gracious enough to say that I acknowledge my debt. Should I have failed, I hope it is enough to say that I have attempted my best to record your achievements. I thank you for providing the material giving me the opportunity to do so. To paraphrase a line from Tennyson's *Ulysses:* This work is part of all I have read, of all those I have had the good fortune of knowing, and of all I have been privileged to see.

If I knew as much about one thing as some claim to know about many, I would be very wise indeed.

Frank E. Poirier

Contents

There is something I don't know
   that I am supposed to know.
I don't know what it is I don't know,
   and yet I am supposed to know,
and I feel I look stupid
   if I seem both not to know it
      and not know *what* it is I don't know.
Therefore I pretend I know it.
   This is nerve-racking
   since I don't know what I must pretend I know.
Therefore I pretend to know everything.

I feel you know what I am supposed to know
but you can't tell me what it is
because you don't know that I don't know what it is.

You may know what I don't know, but not
      that I don't know it, and I can't tell you.
So you will have to tell me everything.

Part One
Introduction

If today you can take a thing like evolution and make it a crime to teach it in the public schools, tomorrow you can make it a crime to teach it in the private schools. ... At the next session you may ban books and the newspaper. Soon you may set Catholic against Protestant, and Protestant against Protestant, and try to foist your own religion upon the minds of men.

After a while, your Honor, it is the setting of man against man and creed against creed, until with flying banners and beating drums we are marching backward to the glorious ages of the sixteenth century when bigots lighted fagots to burn the men who dared to bring any intelligence and enlightenment and culture to the human mind. (From C. Darrow. "Statement for the Defense from the Scopes Trial." Reprinted in L. Leakey, J. Prost, and S. Prost, eds. *Adam or Ape.* Cambridge, Mass.: Schenkman Publishing Co., Inc., 1971, p. 60.)

THE FIRST BOOK OF MOSES CALLED
GENESIS

Creation of heaven and earth,

N the beginning God created the heaven and the earth.

2 And the earth was without form, and void; and darkness *was* upon the face of the deep. And the Spirit of God moved upon the face of the waters.

of the light,

3 And God said, Let there be light: and there was light.

4 And God saw the light, that *it was* good: and God divided the light from the darkness.

5 And God called the light Day, and the darkness he called Night. And the evening and the morning were the first day.

of the firmament,

6 ¶ And God said, Let there be a firmament in the midst of the waters, and let it divide the waters from the waters.

7 And God made the firmament, and divided the waters which *were* under the firmament from the waters which *were* above the firmament: and it was so.

8 And God called the firmament Heaven. And the evening and the morning were the second day.

of the earth separated from the waters,

9 ¶ And God said, Let the waters under the heaven be gathered together unto one place, and let the dry *land* appear: and it was so.

10 And God called the dry *land* Earth; and the gathering together of the waters called he Seas: and God saw that *it was* good.

and made fruitful,

11 And God said, Let the earth bring forth grass, the herb yielding seed, *and* the fruit tree yielding fruit after his kind, whose seed *is* in itself, upon the earth: and it was so.

12 And the earth brought forth grass, *and* herb yielding seed after his kind, and the tree yielding fruit, whose seed *was* in itself, after his kind: and God saw that *it was* good.

13 And the evening and the morning were the third day.

of the sun, moon and stars,

14 ¶ And God said, Let there be lights in the firmament of the heaven to divide the day from the night; and let them be for signs, and for seasons, and for days, and years:

15 And let them be for lights in the firmament of heaven to give light upon the earth: and it was so.

16 And God made two great lights; the greater light to rule the day, and the lesser light to rule the night: *he made* the stars also.

17 And God set them in the firmament of the heaven to give light upon the earth,

18 And to rule over the day and over the night, and to divide the light from the darkness: and God saw that *it was* good.

19 And the evening and the morning were the fourth day.

of fish and fowl,

20 And God said, Let the waters bring forth abundantly the moving creature that hath life, and fowl *that* may fly above the earth in the open firmament of heaven.

21 And God created great whales, and every living creature that moveth, which the waters brought forth abundantly, after their kind, and every winged fowl after his kind: and God saw that *it was* good.

22 And God blessed them, saying, Be fruitful, and multiply, and fill the waters in the seas, and let fowl multiply in the earth.

23 And the evening and the morning were the fifth day.

of beasts and cattle,

24 ¶ And God said, Let the earth bring forth the living creature after his kind, cattle, and creeping thing, and beast of the earth after his kind: and it was so.

25 And God made the beast of the earth after his kind, and cattle after their kind, and every thing that creepeth upon the earth after his kind: and God saw that *it was* good.

of man in the image of God

26 ¶ And God said, Let us make man in our image, after our likeness: and let them have dominion over the fish of the sea, and over the fowl of the air, and over the cattle, and over all the earth, and over every creeping thing that creepeth upon the earth.

27 So God created man in his *own* image, in the image of God created he him; male and female created he them.

28 And God blessed them, and God said unto them, Be fruitful, and multiply, and replenish the earth, and subdue it: and have dominion over the fish of the sea,

Chapter 1
Brief History of Physical Anthropology

Pre-evolutionary thought was dominated by the Biblical injunction, God created heaven and earth which since remained stable. We reconstruct our history by drawing upon general reviews of the history of science. Physical anthropology is merely part of this larger process. Prior to Charles Darwin the scientific world had absorbed the thoughts of such individuals as Aristotle, da Vinci, and Linnaeus. The Darwinian evolutionary scheme altered the picture of life by allowing that change occurred and that organisms can, and do, evolve one from another.

Prior to the 1950s what became known as physical anthropology was a field of study dominated primarily by technique and lacking an integrating theoretical stance. In the early 1950s Dr. S. L. Washburn suggested a realignment of priorities and helped popularize the term "new physical anthropology" to describe a new outlook and new subject matter.

The Biblical Injunction

Until the end of the fourteenth century the written record suggests that most intellectuals accepted the Genesis version of Creation as truth.[1] Most writers of the period had a static view of life. We were God's supreme handiwork, made in His image, first appearing on the sixth day of the universe's creation, and possessing a soul which distinguished us from all other animals. Early thinkers were quick to note our bipedal, erect posture and free hands. Thomas Aquinas noted, for example, "He has reason and hands whereby he can make himself arms and clothes, and other necessaries of life, of infinite variety." Aristotle called the hand "the organ of organs."

---

[1]This written record is not a particularly accurate record of intellectual thought, remembering that so-called heretical viewpoints were often punishable by death.

3

Renaissance Thought

The rise of commercial capitalism stirred the intellectual climate of the fifteenth and sixteenth centuries. Colonial exploration led to numerous explorers' accounts attesting to the diversity of the world's cultures and peoples and, in the intellectual community, the Renaissance produced a naturalistic empiricism as opposed to the theological authoritarianism preceding it. As the theological grip began to erode, scientists dared human dissection and drew behavioral and anatomical comparisons between human and nonhuman animals.

Leonardo da Vinci was among those who led this scientific thrust.[2] His dissections and anatomical illustrations laid a base for comparative anatomy. During the early years of the sixteenth century, Vesalius taught that physicians should study the human body by dissection. He was the first to suggest such practical experience, which the Church still considered sacrilege.

Most writers in this early period considered humans distinct from, and higher creations than, the rest of the animal kingdom. Many early volumes attempting to classify the animal kingdom scientifically excluded humans from their schemes. One exception was a series of volumes by Edward Wooton entitled *De differentiis animalium*. One whole volume of this series is devoted to the human animal.

Seventeenth Century

The seventeenth century generated much discussion as to differences between the human and nonhuman animal. Pierre Charron made one of the more interesting attempts to catalogue these differences (and thus perhaps by implication show that we were God's supreme gift to the world). Of the many traits available for comparative purposes, Charron was impressed by our faculty for speech, our erect posture, our hand, the nakedness and smoothness of our skin (vide D. Morris, *The Naked Ape*), and the ability to laugh and cry. Many of these are still cited as evidence of our distinctiveness from the rest of the animal world.

One of the better-known accomplishments of this period was Edward Tyson's work in comparative primate anatomy. Tyson is the first person on record to actually dissect a chimpanzee, a cadaver of a young ape which died a few months after being shipped from Africa. In 1699, his work was published under the title of "Orangoutang, sive Homo Sylvestris: or, the Anatomy of a Pygmie compared with that of a Monkey, an Ape and a Man." Tyson found that his ape, or "pygmie" as he called it, resembled a human more closely than it resembled monkeys and other apes (Figure 1-1). He reasoned that this animal was an intermediate link between human and nonhuman primates. Despite the importance of Tyson's work, his fellow scientists did not follow it up, perhaps because, unlike the efforts of Vesalius and later Charles Darwin, Tyson's work did not stir controversy. The seventeenth-century outlook was also dominated by the concept that development was static, that species were unchanging. That is, all forms of life as

[2]Some of da Vinci's writings evidence remarkable insights. Three centuries before the mechanism of inheritance was described, da Vinci wrote: " . . . the seed of the mother has power in the embryo equally with that of the father."

Figure 1-1. Tyson's "pygmie" or "orang-outang" was actually an immature chimpanzee.

witnessed in the seventeenth century had resulted from the original creation and had always looked the same.

Eighteenth-Century Naturalism

Eighteenth-century scientific inquiry was characterized by a concept known as naturalism. This meant that humans were viewed as a natural phenomenon, as a part of the universe governed by its laws. During the eighteenth century there was a good deal of work in the areas of comparative anatomy and systematics. The human animal was now considered part of the natural order. As early as 1732, the systematist Linnaeus wrote about the relationship between the human and nonhuman primate. In the first edition of *Systema Naturae* (1735) he included the human primate in the category of "Anthropomorpha." This group included the other known primates.

Although Linnaeus appreciated the similarity between human and nonhuman primates, we do not know if he believed in what later became known as evolution. His writings are unclear on this issue as he was cautious in his expression of heresies (remember a doctrine of evolution would have been diametrically opposed to Church doctrine and could have been dangerous to anyone expressing it). In some passages he argues for the **fixity of species**[3] (i.e., Divine Creation); in

---

[3]The concept that every species was originally divinely created and that the first individual served as a model for its descendants.

others he advocates the doctrine of mutability. In some passages Linnaeus seems to have accepted the possibility that organisms change over time according to the pressures exerted by nature (such a process is now labelled adaptation and natural selection). His exact position will remain unknown.

Another eighteenth-century scientist contributing to the history of physical anthropology was not so circumspect. James Burnett, better known as Lord Monboddo, insisted that the orangutan[4] was actually a human being. "...the Orang Outangs...are of our species, and though they have made some progress in the arts of life, they have not advanced as far as to invent a language." Lest it be thought that Monboddo was simply naive, it should be mentioned that anatomically we share much with all the Great Apes (chimpanzees, gorillas, and orangutans), and Monboddo was reacting to this similarity, calling upon the little knowledge available at that time.

Erasmus Darwin (Charles Darwin's grandfather) seems to have had an evolutionary view of human development. In one of his poems he stated

Imperious man, who rules the bestial crowd,
Of language, reason, and reflection proud,
With brow erect who scorns this earthly sod,
And styles himself the image of his God:
Arose from rudiments of form and sense,
An embryon paint, or microscope lens!

Erasmus Darwin believed in the mutability of **species,** i.e., that forms could and would change in time. This belief is seen in the following quotes: "...the great globe itself, and all that it inhabit, appear to be in a perpetual state of mutation and improvement,...animals seem to have undergone great changes, as well as the inanimate parts of the earth and are probably still in a state of gradual improvement." However, despite his belief in change, Erasmus Darwin still differentiated between the human and nonhuman animal.

Nineteenth Century

The nineteenth-century scientists who probably had the greatest impact upon later scientific development were Charles Darwin and Gregor Mendel. In contrast to Darwin's work, which had an immediate impact upon the intellectual community, Mendel's discoveries of the mechanisms of inheritance languished in total obscurity only to be discovered years after his death. Some of the works of most importance to Darwin's theory are discussed in Chapter 3. Rather than presenting this material now, we shall instead discuss twentieth-century anthropology.

Twentieth Century

Twentieth-century physical anthropology underwent two distinct phases of development separated from one another by their outlook, technique, and subject matter. During the first half of the century, prior to 1951, physical anthropology was primarily a field whose outlook was

[4]An arboreal ape living in the jungles of Borneo and Sumatra. This ape is rapidly becoming extinct.

dominated by technique. This period is labelled the "romantic" phase and was dominated by a concern with measuring and describing body form. The major concerns of early twentieth-century physical anthropologists fall into two large categories called **osteometry** (measurement of defleshed bone) and **anthropometry** (study and comparison of human body measurements). Prior to the 1950s, prior to a reemphasis on evolutionary studies, physical anthropology was 80 percent measurement of bones and teeth.

Formation of racial taxonomies was a second major concern of early twentieth-century physical anthropologists. While much attention focused on fossil populations, living populations were placed into any one of a number (varying from five to several dozen) of "racial types." Early classification attempts often proceeded on the premise that some populations are more highly evolved than others. Since such classification was done primarily by European scientists, Europeans and those of European descent were commonly the apex of this scale. A scheme recognizing "higher" and "lower" races seems to have been a natural outgrowth of the colonial empire situation which it nurtured and was itself nurtured from. The era of mercantile capitalism witnessed the exploitation of native populations by white Europeans and their missionization by so-called Christian leaders.

Another characteristic of early twentieth-century physical anthropology was a heavy involvement with statistics. Some academic positions in physical anthropology, especially those on the European continent, were staffed with statisticians and biometricians lacking any biological training. This tradition, a reliance upon statistics, had the lasting effect of discrediting physical anthropology in the minds of many.

In 1951 Dr. S. L. Washburn delivered a short speech entitled "The New Physical Anthropology" and provided a major catalyst for change. In this speech, he suggested a realignment of priorities. Washburn suggested we study human populations instead of solely measuring fossil bones. Instead of sitting in laboratories poring over mathematical formulas, he suggested that physical anthropologists become field oriented, i.e., get out and work with the subjects where they are. Instead of merely measuring bone or muscle, he suggested that we concern ourselves with experimental anatomy and functional anatomical research. Washburn's speech stands as a convenient point for distinguishing the "old" from the "new" physical anthropology. It should be noted, however, that similar changes in outlook and technique characterized other scientific fields at this time as well.

Physical anthropology has metamorphized from a collecting to an experimental stage. The "new" physical anthropology is firmly based in the biological and natural sciences. In fact, physical anthropologists are often unsure of what academic department is best suited to their concerns. Many see physical anthropology as an amalgamation of such disciplines as biology, zoology, genetics, chemistry, physiology, anatomy, psychology, and still others. Physical anthropology has carved itself a niche among its better financially endowed relatives by proclaiming itself the font of knowledge about human evolution. Physical anthropologists are the interpretors and curators of human evolutionary history from the appearance of the primates approximately 60 million years ago until today.

Much of what is the "new" physical anthropology is actually a new philosophical approach to evolution. This new approach has been greatly assisted by assimilation of knowledge of population genetics, by new geological dating techniques, and by computerization of rapidly increasing reams of data. It should also be noted that physical anthropology received a boost from the "rediscovery" of Darwinian evolution. There was a movement away from mere classification of data and toward understanding the process of natural selection and adaptation as the key to understanding evolutionary change. Research interests, especially measurement of the living and nonliving form, cultivated before 1950 have not disappeared. However, they have been refined by taking into account causal relationships. To reconstruct our evolutionary history, physical anthropologists study the blood groups and chromosomes of human and nonhuman primates, the behavior as well as anatomy of the nonhuman primates, and have adopted a more comprehensive approach for interpreting fossil evidence.

These processes are discussed in the chapters that follow, which are witness to the fruitfulness of this new integrative approach, the new

---

**Table 1-1. Intellectual Influences
on Development of Physical Anthropology**

Renaissance Thought—The Fifteenth and Sixteenth Centuries

L. da Vinci	Scientific dissections and anatomical illustrations laid basis for comparative anatomy.
E. Wooton	Wrote *De differentiis animalium* which was a scientific attempt to classify the animal world. One volume of the series was devoted to the human animal.

The Seventeenth Century

P. Charron	Tried to catalogue differences between the human and nonhuman animal.
E. Tyson	Worked with comparative primate anatomy. First to dissect a chimpanzee.

The Eighteenth Century—Naturalism in Scientific Inquiry

Linnaeus	Taxonomy.
Lord Monboddo (J. Burnett)	Dissection and comparative anatomy.
E. Darwin	Natural history, defended the doctrine of the modifiability of the species.

The Nineteenth Century

C. Darwin	Promoted the theory of evolution, theory of natural selection.
G. Mendel	The father of modern genetics.

The Twentieth Century

Prior to 1951 the major concerns were measurement of the body, osteometry and anthropometry. Racial classifications consumed a good deal of the time of the anthropologists of the early 1900s, as did statistics.

The "new" physical anthropology is based upon the concept of population genetics and the synthetic theory of evolution, as well as changes in technique and outlook in other fields of scientific endeavor.

synthetic theory of evolution. The "new" physical anthropology is concerned with living populations and with physically, culturally, and behaviorally reconstructing their ancestors. The "new" physical anthropology is a field science buoyed by laboratory research. Above all, the "new" physical anthropology is a challenge—a challenge for us to reconstruct our past and thus perhaps assist in structuring the future.

We have traced the history of physical anthropology from a non-evolutionary documentation of life to an evolutionary approach for understanding life (Table 1-1). Today's physical anthropology is concerned with understanding life's diversity, especially among human and non-human primates. Today's physical anthropology is concerned with documenting and understanding primate evolution through the fossil record, through the study of nonhuman animals, and through the study of modern populations.

Bibliography

Clark, W. Le Gros. 1958. Re-orientations in physical anthropology. In *The scope of physical anthropology and its place in academic studies,* edited by D. F. Roberts and F. S. Weiner, pp. 1-6. Oxford: Church Army Press.

Morris, D. 1967. *The naked ape: a zoologist's study of the human animal.* New York: McGraw-Hill.

Morris, D., and Morris, R. 1968. *Men and apes.* New York: McGraw-Hill.

Slotkin, J. 1965. *Readings in early anthropology.* New York: Wenner-Gren Fdn.

Washburn, S. 1951. The new physical anthropology. *Transactions of N.Y. Academy of Science* 13:298.

Chapter 2
Our Place in the Animal Kingdom

Within the scientific classificatory system, we, *Homo sapiens sapiens,* occupy certain categories: Animal Kingdom, Class Mammalia, Order Primates, Suborder Anthropoidea, Family Hominidae, etc. Here we discuss our mammalian heritage by briefly tracing the evolutionary history of mammalian groups, especially placentals. Although we trace our primate origin perhaps as far back as about 60 million years ago, to the prosimians, we differ from other primates in a number of anatomical and behavioral traits. Some similarities and differences are discussed below.

As will be discussed in a later chapter, there has been an attempt to relate living forms to one another scientifically in an evolutionary sequence. This chapter discusses our, the human animal's, place within the animal kingdom. We are members of the Animal Kingdom, we belong to the Class Mammalia, to the Order Primates, and to the Genus *Homo.* In order to appreciate our relationship with the rest of the animal kingdom, and specifically to the other primates, we will briefly present some of the evidence for that relationship.

Our Place Within the Taxonomic System

A novel way of presenting our place within the animal kingdom has been suggested by Dr. B. S. Kraus (1964). Increasing numbers of individuals struggle through years of secondary and higher educational institutions to achieve the distinction of appending a set of initials after their name. Such degree initials are insignificant when we realize that from the moment of birth, without one day of schooling, each of us could legitimately print a calling card with the legend on the following page:

Adult male olive baboons.

Jane Doe, A.K., S.K.M., P.C., S.P.V., C.M., O.P., S.O.A., S.F.H., F.H., G.H., S.S., S.S.S.

We "achieve" these initials by virtue of our place within the zoological classification system. Perhaps as much as half a billion years of evolution were invested in the attainment of these honors, by which we "earned" the right to append the following "degrees" to our name:

Animal Kingdom	(A.K.)
Subkingdom Metazoa	(S.K.M.)
Phylum Chordata	(P.C.)
Subphylum Vertebrata	(S.P.V.)
Class Mammalia	(C.M.)
Order Primates	(O.P.)
Suborder Anthropoidea	(S.O.A.)
Superfamily Hominoidea	(S.F.H.)
Family Hominidae	(F.H.)
Genus Homo	(G.H.)
Species sapiens	(S.S.)
Subspecies sapiens	(S.S.S.)

Our Place Among Mammals

Rise of the Mammals—Decline of the Reptiles. Mammals are comparatively recent arrivals on this earth, appearing probably not much more than 200 million years ago. The first mammals were small and inconspicuous compared with huge dinosaurs which dominated the landscape. But the reptiles, especially the larger ones, found survival increasingly difficult. The earth was geologically restless. Mountains were rising, and this caused major changes in the earth's surface. The food supply was changing: grasses, ivies, and new types of trees were appearing. As the food supply of the larger reptiles began to shrink, reptiles became more and more restricted in distribution. Early mammals may have helped speed the process of reptilian extinction by eating their eggs.

When the huge reptiles died off they left the mammals vast evolutionary opportunities. Mammals began to move into and exploit the new, relatively unoccupied habitat. This resulted in the rapid diversification, expansion, and proliferation of members of the Class Mammalia. This process, known as **adaptive radiation,** is one of the first stages in the evolutionary adaptation of new groups. The Order Primates, the mammalian subdivision to which we belong, is one product of this evolutionary explosion.

Mammalian Traits. Only with difficulty can we differentiate the earliest mammals from their reptilian ancestors. The most significant differences between them, reproductive and physiological traits, do not fossilize. As noted in Chapter 6, four major traits differentiated early mammals from their reptilian ancestors: warm-bloodedness (or **homoiothermy,**[1] the maintenance of a constant body temperature), **heterodontism** (differentiation of teeth for different functions), reproductive economy (fewer births per parturition and a longer growth period), and **effectance motivation** (investigatory behavior not serving an immediate end, such as sexual and feeding behavior). The fossil evidence is helpful primarily in regard to the second trait, heterodontism. The oldest

[1]There is increasing evidence that dinosaurs were warm-blooded.

undoubted mammalian fossil remains are teeth, jaw fragments, and rare skulls of small, shrewlike creatures embedded in Late Triassic rocks dating to about 180-200 million years B.P. Throughout the **Tertiary** (the period of dinosaur domination), mammals remained small and inconspicuous animals, making rare fossil appearances. The earliest mammals were generally mouselike animals which fed on seeds and insects. The largest was about the size of a house cat. Most were evolutionary dead ends, failing to leave more advanced progeny. Two groups, the marsupials and placentals, arose from this primitive mammalian stock. They were ancestral to the many kinds of mammals which came to dominate a dinosaurless world. Descendants of these two groups were extraordinarily successful; they were warm-blooded and developed efficient locomotion systems.

Marsupials vs. Placentals. The Order Monotremata represents an experimental stage in early mammalian evolution. The only survivors of this very ancient stock are the duckbilled platypus and the spiny anteater, strange little animals inhabiting Australia. Although monotremes share many traits with other living mammals, they differ in one significant respect. Monotremes lay eggs like their reptilian ancestors rather than bearing their young alive as most mammals do.

Tertiary mammals gave rise to two groups: marsupial and placental mammals. These quickly expanded to dominate the landscape. Marsupials, such as the opossum and kangaroo, bear their young alive at a very early developmental stage. The young then crawl into the mother's pouch, where they continue to mature. Placental mammals develop inside the female's uterus. A special structure, the placenta, allows the developing young to be nourished directly by the mother's body. Birth is delayed until the young are relatively mature and independent. The marsupials were less successful than the placentals.

The group of placentals of most evolutionary interest with respect to primates is the *Insectivora,* or insect eaters. This group currently includes such animals as the shrew and the mole. It was from this group that the early primates, the prosimians, descended. Ancestral placental mammals were small, superficially mouselike representatives of the Order Insectivora. The order includes such creatures as modern shrews and hedgehogs. The Order Primates was either a **Paleocene** or an **Eocene** offshoot of the insectivorous stock (see Chapter 6).

The Primates

Primate Traits. Primates are a mammalian Order, the members of which typically exhibit the following traits. It must be cautioned, however, that not all members of the Order have all these traits. Furthermore, other mammalian orders possess some of these traits. For example, some marsupials possess nailed digits and prehensile (grasping) hands or feet. A number of the mammalian orders show clavicles, postorbital bars, and pectoral mammary glands.

Nails instead of claws on their digits
Prehensile hands and feet
Five fingers and five toes—a condition known as **pentadactyly**
Tendency toward complete bony enclosure of eye orbits
Forward placement of eye orbits
Opposability of the toe and/or thumb to the remaining digits

Enlarged cerebral hemispheres of the brain

One pair of mammary glands, thoracically placed

Well-developed clavicles

Reduced olfactory sense

In an evolutionary sense the primates are a good example of a diversified and successful group. Superficially, the primates do not appear to be our likely ancestors, but they were. Most common primate attributes stem from either of two factors: (1) retention of ancient or generalized vertebrate and mammalian traits, and (2) development of an **arboreal** (tree-living) adaptation (see Chapter 7). Primates are generalized, arboreal, and intelligent animals broadly distributed throughout the Old and New World tropics. The order may be subdivided into four groups: **prosimians** (the most primitive and earliest of the group), **ceboids** (New World monkeys), **cercopithecoids** (Old World monkeys), and **hominoids** (apes and humans).

And after passion and prejudice have died away, the same result will attend the teachings of the naturalist respecting that great Alps and Andes of living world-Man. Our reverence for the nobility of manhood will not be lessened by the knowledge that Man is, in substance and structure, one with the brutes; for, he alone possesses the marvellous endowment of intelligible and rational speech, whereby, in the secular period of his existence, he slowly accumulated and organised the experience which is almost wholly lost with the cessation of every individual life in other animals; so that, now, he stands raised upon it as on a mountain top, far above the level of his humble fellows, and transfigured from his grosser nature by reflecting, here and there, a ray from the infinite source of truth.[1]

[1]From T. H. Huxley, "Man's Place in Nature," reprinted in *Adam or Ape* edited by L. Leakey, J. Prost, and S. Prost (Cambridge, Mass.: Schenkman Publishing Co., 1971), p.39.

Table 2-1

Era (and duration)	Period	Estimated time since beginning of each period (in millions of years—these times vary with different investigators)	Epoch	Life
		0.11	Holocene (Recent)	*Homo sapiens sapiens,* the only species of hominids.
	Quaternary	1.8	Pleistocene	Modern species of mammals and their fore-runners; extinction of many species of large mammals; the great glaciations.

Table 2-1 continued.

Cenozoic (age of mammals; about 65 million years)		5.5	Pliocene (the beginning of this epoch is debatable)	Appearance of many of today's genera of mammals.
		23.5 -24	Miocene	Rise of modern subfamilies of mammals; spread of grassy plains; evolution of grazing animals.
	Tertiary	37-38	Oligocene	Rise of modern families of mammals.
		53-54	Eocene	Rise of modern orders and sub-orders of mammals.
		65	Paleocene	Dominance of archaic mammals.
	Cretaceous	130		Extinction of large reptiles and origin of Primates perhaps by end of period.
Mesozoic (age of reptiles; lasted about 165 million years)	Jurassic	180		Reptiles dominant; first birds; archaic mammals.
	Triassic	230		First dinosaurs, turtles, ichthyo-saurs, plesio-saurs.

*The first occurrence of microscopic marine invertebrates of a typically Pleistocene form was about either 0.8 or 1.8 million years ago and this, according to some, is the technically correct date, but the Villafranchian land animals first appeared about 3.2 million years ago and many anthropologists include all of this interval in the Pleistocene. Recently Berggren and Van Couvering have given the date for the Miocene as 23.5-5 m.y.

Adapted from *Physical Anthropology* by Gabriel Ward Lasker. Copyright © 1973 by Holt, Rinehart and Winston, Inc. Reprinted by permission of Holt, Rinehart and Winston.

The Human Primate

It is obvious that the criteria previously set forth place us in the mammalian subdivision known as the primates. Evidence for including us within the Order Primates is multifaceted, including data from such fields as anatomy, behavioral observations (often called ethology), biochemistry, genetics, embryology, growth, and the fossil record. Much of this evidence is discussed later in this book.

We Stand Alone. There are few who would question our mammalian status or that we arose from a ratlike insectivorous stock through some small forms known as prosimians. What then makes us unique from the other primates? Why are we included in a different taxonomic family than other members of the Order Primates? Evolutionarily the most significant of our uniquely human traits are: (1) a completely erect posture and habitual bipedal gait, (2) our abstract and symbolical communication known as language, (3) our capacity for abstract and symbolic thought, (4) our cultural way of life, providing as it does immense opportunities for learning. We share many behavioral traits with other primates, as a trip to the zoo will prove.

We cannot deny that other animals, particularly other primates, learn by experience or observation. Animals, including other primates, transmit learned behavior from one generation to another; this transgenerational passing of learned behavior is the basis for cultural behavior. Furthermore, some animals make and use tools—an activity once thought to be our preserve. Some animals also display behavioral patterns we readily understand. Yet, there are dramatic differences between ourselves and other members of the Order Primates. We can sit and speculate about this proposition—that is one of our unique traits.

The Contemplative Primate

While curiosity is a major trait of primates, we are perhaps the nosiest of the nosy. We climb a hill simply to see what lies beyond. Dostoevski once wrote, "Man needs the unfathomable and the infinite just as much as he does the small planet which he inhabits." As far as we now know, we alone among the primates have the capacity for self-reflection. The English author G. W. Corner writes, "After all, if he is an ape he is the only ape that is debating what kind of ape he is." We alone of all the primates have the ability to communicate about the past and plan for the future—our language allows us this unique trait. Probably we alone of all the animals have moral and philosophical ideas. The English writer Hazlitt notes, "Man is the only animal that laughs and weeps, for he is the only animal that is struck with the difference between what things are and what they ought to be."

We are undoubtedly mammals, and we are certainly primates. Unlike many other primates, however, we are completely erect, we have a bipedal gait, we have an abstract means of communication called language, and we have an elaborate cultural way of life providing almost an endless means of elaborating upon our genetic capabilities. We are the contemplative primate, the philosophical primate, the primate which ponders life and death. But we are still primates.

Bibliography

Berggren, W., and Van Couvering, J. 1974. The Late Neogene biostratigraphy, geochronology, and paleoclimatology of the last 15 million years in marine and continental sequences. *Paleography, Palaeoclimatology, Palaeoecology* 16: Nos. 1-2.

Clark, D. 1968. *Fossils, paleontology and evolution.* Dubuque: Wm. C. Brown.

Kraus, B. S. 1964. *The basis of human evolution.* New York: Harper & Row.

Laporte, L. 1968. *Ancient environments.* New York: Prentice-Hall.

Lasker, G. 1973. *Physical Anthropology.* New York: Holt, Rinehart and Winston.

McAlister, A. 1968. *The history of life.* New York: Prentice-Hall.

Romer, A. 1950. *Vertebrate paleontology.* Chicago: University of Chicago Press.

Savage, J. 1969. *Evolution.* New York: Holt, Rinehart and Winston.

Simpson, G. 1944. *The major features of evolution.* New York: Columbia University Press.

_____. 1958. *The meaning of evolution.* New York: Mentor.

Weller, J. 1969. *The course of evolution.* New York: McGraw-Hill.

Part Two
Evolutionary Theory

When I view all beings not as special creations, but as the lineal descendants of some few beings which lived long before the first bed of the Cambrian system was deposited, they seem to me to become ennobled.
Charles Darwin, *The Origin of Species*

Chapter 3
Light Thrown on Human Origins

Like most pioneers, Darwin's intellectual journey was partially charted by those preceding him: some early Greek philosophers, Francis Bacon, William Harvey, Georges Buffon, his grandfather Erasmus Darwin, Jean Baptiste de Lamarck, Thomas Malthus, and others. The Church and its spokesmen were Darwin's major protagonists. The Biblical account stated the earth was of comparatively recent origin and that God created human life in His image. There was no time, no room, in the Biblical scheme for evolutionary change. A prime requisite for Darwin's scheme was an extended time span over and above the Creation date established by Biblical scholars. This was provided in the works of such geologists as the Englishman Charles Lyell.

As is well known, Darwin's synthesis was not universally acclaimed as a scientific breakthrough. Darwin's work was not immediately accepted when it was finally published. Following is a discussion of this and other matters impinging upon Darwin's formulation of his theory. The last section of this chapter deals briefly with Mendelian genetics.

Pre-Darwinian Views (Table 3-1)

The Opposition. Charles Darwin was a pioneer, exploring the realm of thought few before dared to explore. But, he was not the first in the sense that all his thoughts were original.[1] His intellectual journey leading to the theory of evolution was not entirely uncharted. As is often true of most important generalizations, his central thesis of natural selection was not altogether new. As early as the fifth century B.C., Greek writers hinted at the principle of natural selection.

[1] In fact, Darwin often claimed no originality of his theory.

Charles Darwin, 1809-1882.

Table 3-1. Pre-Darwinian Thoughts

The following may be mentioned among pre-Darwinian students of natural science:

Francis Bacon (British, 1561-1626) was a firm Aristotelian and thought that species were immutable. He is generally credited with the revival of scientific inquiry.

William Harvey (British, 1578-1657) is often credited with the first biological experimentation and the discovery of the mechanisms of blood circulation. However, he had some forerunners in these investigations.

Georges L. L. Buffon (French, 1707-1778) was, perhaps, the first true evolutionist, suggesting, with reservations, an evolutionary process based on the inheritance of acquired characters.

Erasmus Darwin (British, 1731-1802) was Charles Darwin's grandfather. His main theses were that earth's history was longer than specified by Ussher's chronology and that all life came from a common source.

At least three different men wrote of natural selection without, however, arriving at a firm statement of its evolutionary role. *Edward Blyth* (British) thought that natural selection, by discriminating against variation, would lead to immutability of species. *Patrick Mathew's* (British) discussion of natural selection was hidden in an appendix to a treatise dealing with naval timber and architecture. The third was *Charles Wells*, a South Carolina physician, who wrote of the idea as a commonplace fact in a paper on a white female, part of whose skin resembled that of an individual of African descent.

Jean Baptiste de Lamarck (French, 1744-1829) advanced the first comprehensive theory of evolution. He invoked the inheritance of acquired characters, now referred to as Lamarckism, although he was not the first believer in it. The usual example of Lamarckism is the giraffe, whose ancestor was assumed to have acquired its long neck by stretching to reach upper leaves on a tree and to have transmitted the acquired length to its progeny. It is more likely that giraffes with longer necks could obtain more food and thereby had an advantage over others, enabling them to leave more offspring. We know now that if their long necks were even in part hereditary, their offspring, more numerous than those of the others, would receive genetic instructions for the formation of longer necks. Thus, the average neck length of the next generation would be increased through a cumulative process we now label *natural selection*.

Thomas R. Malthus (British, 1766-1834) suggested in his "Essay on the Principle of Population" that humans multiply geometrically while means of subsistence do not. Although Darwin credited reading of this essay with generating in his mind the notion that an average individual produces more offspring than can survive, thus permitting selection to occur, there is evidence that Darwin formulated the principle of natural selection before reading Malthus. He had read Blyth, Mathew, and Wells.

Georges Cuvier (French, 1769-1832) was a defender of special creation and Lamarck's opponent in the evolutionary debate of the day. He recognized that fossils were extinct forms of life, following the discovery in 1790 by an English surveyor, William Smith, that different layers of rock contain different kinds of fossils. But his explanation was the theory of *catastrophism,* that is, that in the past, life on earth was destroyed several times, as in the Biblical account of the flood, and then created anew.

Charles Lyell (British, 1797-1875) countered catastrophism with the theory of uniformitarianism, which held that historical changes on earth were not due to a series of catastrophes but to the same gradual changes as may be observed today. This was an important cornerstone of evolutionary thought.

Adapted from I. M. Lerner, *Heredity, Evolution and Society,* p. 28. W. H. Freeman and Company, San Francisco, 1968.

Darwin planted his ideas in fertile intellectual soil and they grew. He marshalled overwhelming amounts of convincing evidence; his ideas ignited a fire utterly destroying or badly charring most intellectual edifices erected prior to 1859. The firemen who were rushed to extinguish Darwin's intellectual ideas (Creationists, for example), did not succeed. The fact of evolution is, however, still not universally accepted,[2] though Darwinism has become the central and fundamental component of scientific logic.

Greek Philosophies. Elements of the concept of gradual change, i.e., that life is not ordainly fixed and inextricably immutable, can be found in ancient Persian and Greek writings. The Greeks proceeded in their rationale from *a priori* grounds, from observation by unaided eye, logical arguments, and so-called common sense. Greek philosophical writings dating from the sixth century B.C. contain speculations about life originating in the sea. There are mythical ideas about the adaptive changes involved in the transition from an aquatic to a terrestrial existence. At least one Greek philosopher stated that fossils were animal remains. The Greek views of change, the crux of evolutionary theory, ranged from the idea that change is merely a sensory illusion to the notion that everything is always in a state of flux. Some fifth century B.C. writings contained a vague notion of organic evolution. These writings held that living things arose by fortuitous combinations of parts and that bad combinations did not survive. This is the germ of the principle of natural selection.

Aristotle (383-322 B.C.) probably provided the most important early scientific influence. Aristotle was the father of Western natural history, but he was a teleologist, a believer in intelligent design and in the idea that nature's processes are directed toward certain ends. Aristotle argued that there was a natural scale of organisms ascending to the development of humans; this concept was later labelled by such writers as Descartes as the "Great Chain of Being." However, Aristotle's views and his classification of plants and animals were basically non-evolutionary, and in many ways his authority long inhibited development of evolutionary ideas. Little can be said of post-Aristotelian thought, for medieval scholastic philosophers contributed mostly to metaphysics and to moral philosophy. Some in this group established the notion that conditions of life were immutable, unchangeable, and the world was thought to be static from the moment of creation.

Nineteenth-Century Thinkers Precedent to Darwin. A most important element for Darwin's scheme, an expanded time span, was

---

[2]The most recent example of this is the downgrading of Darwin's theory in new science textbooks for 3.3 million elementary school children in California. This is based on the argument that Christians (especially of the Creationist school) are deprived of "equal time" in the science textbooks. Recent litigation in Arkansas struck from that state's legal code an injunction against teaching evolution.

Times have changed these legal proceedings. There is nothing in the California situation which equals H. L. Mencken's record of the Scopes trial based on events recorded outside the courthouse in Dayton, Tennessee. Mencken wrote:

There was a friar wearing a sandwich sign announcing that he was the Bible champion of the world. There was a Seventh-day Adventist arguing that Clarence Darrow (Scopes's lawyer) was the beast with seven heads and ten horns described in Revelation XIII, and that the end of the world was at hand. There was an evangelist made up like Andy Gump, with the news that atheists in Cincinnati were preparing to descend upon Dayton, hang the eminent Judge Raulston, and burn the town.

established by workers in other fields, especially geology. Prior to the work of such geologists as J. Hutton and C. Lyell, the world was considered to be approximately 6000 years old. The Biblical scholar James Ussher, Archbishop of Armagh, computed from the named generations recorded in the Bible and arrived at a date of 4004 B.C. for the creation. Reverend Dr. John Lightfoot, vice-chancellor of Cambridge University, added that "…heaven and earth, centre and circumference were created all together in the same instant, and clouds full of water. This work took place and man was created by the Trinity on October 23, 4004 B.C. at nine o'clock in the morning."

Usually long periods of time are necessary for evolutionary change. The theological limit of 4004 years was hardly enough time and was presented as strong contrary evidence to evolutionary change. The establishment of a suitable time frame was left to the geologists, many of whom were strictly non-evolutionary in orientation. One of the best known geologists was the French scholar Cuvier, a younger contemporary of Lamarck. Cuvier's scheme, known as **catastrophism,** claimed that various geological layers were deposited as a result of a series of cataclysms which periodically overwhelmed the earth and totally destroyed life. After each cataclysm, new life blossomed forth through a series of successive creations; each successive appearance of new life witnessed an advance in complexity. Each new wave of living creatures showed a superiority of organization over their extinct predecessors. Cuvier's belief that the last of the great cataclysms was the Biblical Noachian flood meant that human remains should not be discovered in previous layers. Cuvier is credited with saying that "fossil man does not exist." Cuvier's scheme is important, for it does account for change in form. Although Cuvier recognized that change did occur, he did not recognize the fact that natural forces, the interactions between a gene pool and the environment, could account for differences in ancestral and descendant populations.

Cuvier's conception left little of substance for the budding group of scientists intent on proving that life was much older than Biblical accounts and that recent forms of life result from millenia of previous change. It was the geologist Charles Lyell who provided a time frame with which Charles Darwin and other evolutionists could work.[3] Lyell rejected Cuvier's catastrophism, substituting in its place the principle of **uniformitarianism.** This idea was first introduced by J. Hutton in 1785 and later independently developed by Lyell in his book *Principles of Geology* published in 1830. The principle of uniformitarianism simply states that geological agents operating in the present could, given enough time, have caused everything that happened in the past history of the earth. While Lyell's work provided the basis of a geological time span against which to construct an evolutionary scheme, he seems to have been disturbed by Lamarck's inclusion of humans in the evolutionary scheme. Lyell accepted the fact that species became extinct and were replaced by others, but he was uncertain as to the mechanisms. The uniformitarian view could not explain why new species developed; Lyell's critics adopted the only alternative known to them—Divine Creation. In the early decades of the eighteenth century, scien-

[3]It would be no exaggeration to say that Lyell's friendship was the most important influence in Darwin's career, and a debt he felt he could never sufficiently discharge.

tists felt obliged to have recourse to miracles which they admitted being unable to fathom, in order to account for natural phenomena.

Although a number of early scientists implied evolution in their writings, it was Jean Baptiste de Lamarck (1744-1829) who proposed a systematic theory for evolution as an explanation of life's diversity. Lamarck accepted the non-evolutionary idea that organisms could be ranked in a progressive series, with *Homo* at the apex. Lamarck considered evolution to be a constant striving, due to some inner drive for perfection, and considered deviations from this progression as due to local adaptations to specific environments.

Using an idea that had been previously suggested, Lamarck argued that an organism acquired new traits by virtue of using or not using different parts of the body and that newly acquired traits could be transmitted to the offspring. Lamarck believed that a trait, once acquired, could be passed on to subsequent generations. His scheme is known as the theory of acquired characteristics.

Lamarck's importance lies in his proposal that life is dynamic and that there is a mechanism in nature which promotes ongoing change. However, his method of change is incorrect, for acquired traits are not passed to one's offspring. You can cut off the tails of rats for untold generations but still fail to produce a generation of tailless rats. Although the details of Lamarck's scheme are incorrect, his emphasis on change gave impetus to the thoughts of others who would ultimately discover the accurate explanations for the change he proposed.

Lamarck's scheme is presented in Table 3-2.

One of the first individuals to attempt to verify a prehistoric period in hominid history was Jacques Boucher de Perthes (1788-1868). Digging on the banks of the Somme River in southwestern France, he found many stones not indigenous to the walls of the pit in which they

---

Table 3-2. Lamarckian Theory versus Modern Theory of Adaptation

---

Lamarck
Question:	What causes adaptive variations to occur?
Answer:	Fulfillment of needs by action of inner feelings, inheritance of acquired characteristics, effects of environment.

Darwin:
1st Question:	What causes variation?
Answer:	I do not know.
2nd Question:	What causes any variation that happens to be adaptive to be preserved so that it can modify the descendants of its possessors?
Answer:	Natural selection.

Today:
1st Question:	What causes heritable variation?
Answer:	Random mutation and recombination of genes.
2nd Question:	What causes any heritable variation that may become adaptive under changed conditions to be preserved until those changed conditions arise?
Answer:	Preservation of genes as recessives until, under changed conditions and after reshuffling of the gene complex, their effects may become adaptive and they become dominant as a result of natural selection.

Adapted from de Beer, 1965, p. 194.

Light Thrown on
Human Origins

were recovered. Furthermore, the stones appeared to have been intentionally shaped into obvious forms. Other observers had also witnessed such rocks and termed them "figured stones" of unknown origin or "thunder stones" cast by God to earth during thunderstorms. de Perthes was convinced that these stones were made by prehistoric populations, and he collected an immense amount of evidence in support of his theory. When he submitted his case in 1838 to various scientific groups, he was ridiculed. Not until after the publication of Darwin's work was de Perthes' theory considered possible by those daring to accept an evolutionary history.

Charles Darwin — The Human Scientist

Early Years. When a son was born to Robert and Emma Darwin on 12 February 1809 at Shrewsbury, England, few people except for close relatives and those present at the birth noticed the event. This is in sharp contrast to the mixed reaction greeting the birth of his book *On the Origin of Species by Means of Natural Selection or the Preservation of Favored Races in the Struggle for Life,* which first appeared in 1859. It is safe to say that his mother did not realize the amount of scorn which would subsequently be heaped upon Charles, her second of two boys and fifth of six children.

Even during his early years Charles Darwin seems to have been a naturalist. His father once commented, "You care for nothing but shooting, and rat-catching, and you will be a disgrace to yourself and all your family." Charles Darwin's school years were relatively uneventful; not the best of students, he passed from subject to subject, from medicine to theology, depending upon his father's wishes. He was first and foremost a naturalist. Except for some school acquaintances, Darwin considered much of his education a waste of time.

The H.M.S. Beagle. On 29 August 1831 one of Darwin's friends wrote to tell him that Captain Fitzroy from a ship the H.M.S. *Beagle* had invited a young man to sail around the world with him as a naturalist, without pay. Darwin's name was submitted to Fitzroy by a mutual friend. The files of the Admiralty contain the following letter referring to Darwin's nomination.

> 1 September 1831
>
> Captain Fitzroy:
> My dear Sir, I believe my friend Mr. Peacock of Trinity College Cambridge has succeeding in getting a "Savant" for you — a Mr. Darwin, grandson of the well known philosopher and poet — full of zeal and enterprize and having contemplated a voyage on his own account to S. America. Let me know how you like the idea that I may go or recede in time.
>
> Francis Beaufort

Darwin's father was not keen on allowing his son to accept the invitation and at first Charles refused the offer. An uncle, Josiah Wedgewood (of dinnerware fame), convinced Charles's father that such a trip would be a perfectly suitable undertaking for a fledgling clergyman. The elder Darwin reconsidered and Charles Darwin joined the ship on 24 October 1831. Due to one mishap after another the departure was postponed until 27 December 1831. During this time Darwin was convinced he had a debilitating heart disease.

Darwin's journey with Fitzroy covered five years and over 40,000 miles. His observations were reinforced by the many important books he read. One of these was Lyell's *Principles of Geology*. Darwin and another important evolutionist, Alfred R. Wallace, had also read Malthus's (1776-1834) work, "Essay on the Principles of Population." This work, which stated that world population grew at a rate faster than the methods of food production, implanted the idea of natural selection in both men's minds. The implication in Malthus's work was that there would be competition for food resources and that only the most fit would survive. Whereas Malthus was concerned only with humans, both Darwin and Wallace felt that his work had implications for all life.

Darwin's autobiography refers to events which most impressed him about his trip. The following passage enumerates four lines of evidence which led him to question and eventually reject the belief in the immutability of species with which he started his journey.

> During the voyage of the Beagle I had been deeply impressed by discovering in the Pampean formation great fossil animals covered with armor like that on the existing armadillos; secondly by the manner in which closely allied animals replace one another in proceeding southwards over the Continent; and thirdly by the South American character of most of the productions of the Galapagos archipelago, and more especially by the manner in which they differ slightly on each island of the group (from de Beer, 1965, p. 78).

The first line of evidence refers to the principle of "succession of types." In some areas species become extinct, as shown by their fossilized remains, while other, but similar, species flourish. The second line of evidence refers to the principle of "representative species," i.e., adjacent areas of a continent are inhabited by different but similar species which take each other's place. The third line of evidence concerns the resemblance of inhabitants of oceanic islands to those of the nearest mainland. For example, a few days after his initial arrival in the Galapagos Islands, Darwin's notebook records under the date 18 September 1835, "I certainly recognize South America in ornithology" (de Beer, 1965; 81). Darwin recognized the similarity between the finches in the Galapagos and those on the mainland. The fourth line of evidence concerns differences between the island inhabitants in the Galapagos archipelago. The environmental conditions of the islands are identical and, if the character of the organisms inhabiting the islands was determined by these conditions, the species of each island should have been identical. Darwin was astonished to find otherwise.

Flirting with Evolution. Darwin was confused about the creatures and plants he observed; the finches and tortoises of the Galapagos archipelago led him to write towards the end of his voyage, ". . . such facts would undermine the stability of species" (de Beer, 1965: 82). He returned to England with this heretical thought lurking in his mind. One of the first writing adventures he undertook after returning was his

Light Thrown on
Human Origins

Journal of Researches, a descriptive narrative of his trip. The work contains slight hint of the intellectual turmoil he was beginning to experience; however, a footnote written in relation to his discussion of the difference between the flora and fauna on the eastern and western Andean slopes appears to be his first veiled public admission of the possibility of the mutability of the species. Darwin wrote, "The whole reasoning, of course, is founded on the assumption of the immutability of the species. Otherwise the changes might be considered as superinduced by different circumstances in the two regions during a length of time" (de Beer, 1965: 85). As early as 1857, Darwin wrote:

> With belief of transmutation and geographical grouping we are led to endeavor to discover causes of changes, the manner of adaptation . . . instinct and structure becomes full of speculation and line of observation. . . . My theory would give zest to recent and fossil comparative anatomy; it would lead to closest examination of hybridity, to what circumstances favour crossing and what prevent it; and generation (sexual reproduction) causes of change in order to know what we have come from and to what we tend, this and direct examination of direct passages of structure in species might lead to laws of change, which would then be the main object of study, to guide our speculations with respect to past and future (de Beer, 1965: 94).

Darwin wrote in his *Autobiography* that selection was the key to the mutability of species. "I soon perceived that selection was the keystone of man's success in making useful races of plants and animals. But how selection could be applied to organisms living in a state of nature remained for some time a mystery to me" (de Beer, 1965:97). Arriving at this momentous conclusion, Darwin refused to commit himself in print for some time. He wrote in his *Autobiography,* "In June, 1842, I first allowed myself the satisfaction of writing a very brief abstract of my theory in pencil in 35 pages; and this was enlarged during the summer of 1844 into 230 pages" (de Beer, 1965: 119). This "abstract" was the first clear statement of Darwin's thoughts on evolution. A quote from Darwin's personal correspondence in 1844 notes, "If, as I believe, my theory in time be accepted even by one competent judge, it will be a considerable step in science" (de Beer, 1965: 119). On 11 January 1844, Darwin wrote his friend and intellectual co-conspirator Joseph D. Hooker, "At last the gleams of light have come, and I am almost convinced (quite contrary to the opinion I started with) that species are not (it is like confessing a murder) immutable" (de Beer, 1965: 135).

Wallace Intrudes. Darwin's tranquility was shattered on 18 June 1858 when he received a short paper from Alfred R. Wallace containing a replica of his own theory of evolution by natural selection.[4] Wallace asked Darwin to read his paper and if Darwin deemed it important, he was to send it to Lyell. Darwin was dumbstruck. This, coupled with such personal tragedies as the illness of his daughter and imminent death of his eighteen-month-old son, troubled Darwin deeply. He immediately read the paper and sent it on to Lyell with the accompanying note:

[4]Wallace's work was conducted in Southeast Asia.

The Debut of Evolutionary Theory (Figure 3-1)

After much ado by Darwin himself, including veiled threats to burn his book lest others think him a forger,[5] Hooker and Lyell prevailed on Darwin to submit a joint paper to the Linnean Society. A joint paper was presented before the Linnean Society of London on 1 July 1858 and it was published in the Society's *Journal of Proceedings* on 20 August 1858 under the title, "On the tendency of species to form varieties, and on the perpetuation of varieties and species by natural means of selection."

What effect did that paper have upon the world at that time? An idea which was to set the intellectual world ablaze attracted little attention. Darwin writes, "Our joint productions excited very little attention, and the only published notice of them which I can remember was by Professor Haughton of Dublin, whose verdict was that all new that was in them was false, and what was true was old" (de Beer, 1965: 150). The President of the Linnean Society dismally concluded at the subsequent annual meeting that, "The year ... had not, indeed, been marked by any of those striking discoveries which at once revolutionize, so to speak, the department of science on which they bear" (de Beer, 1965: 150).

On the Origin of Species

The last chapter of Darwin's triumphant book *On the Origin of Species* was finished on 19 March 1859. Darwin spent over twenty years with his labor of love; he wrote, "I am weary of my work. ... facts compel me

[5]"I would far rather burn my whole book, than that he (Wallace) or any other man should think that I had behaved in a paltry spirit ...."

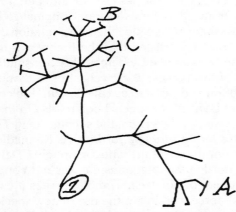

Figure 3-1. Darwin's first diagram of an evolutionary tree appeared in his "First Notebook on Transmutation of Species," 1837.

Evolution

The accompanying papers, which we have the honour of communicating to the Linnean Society, and which all relate to the same subject, viz, the Laws which affect the reproduction of varieties, races, and species, contain the results of the investigations of two indefatigable naturalists, Mr. Charles Darwin and Mr. Alfred Wallace.

The gentlemen having, independently and unknown to one another, conceived the same very ingenious theory to acount for the appearance and perpetuation of varieties and of specific forms on our planet, may both fairly claim the merit of being original thinkers in this important line of inquiry; but neither of them have published their views, though Mr. Darwin has for many years past been repeatedly urged by us to do so, and both authors having now unreservedly placed their papers in our hands, we think it would best promote the interests of science that a selection from them should be laid before the Linnean Society.

Partial contents of a letter written by Charles Lyell and Joseph D. Hooker to J. J. Bennett, Esq., Secretary of the Linnean Society, addressed 30 June 1858. As a result of this letter, Darwin and Wallace's joint paper was presented to the world.

to conclude that my brain was never formed for much thinking" (de Beer, 1965: 151). The book was magnificently conceived and written, although Darwin doubted his own abilities to communicate via the written word. Darwin's publisher was John Murray. At Darwin's urging Murray reviewed several chapters, but Murray was bewildered and skeptical of the scientific validity of the book. He thought 500 copies was the largest number which need be printed. After some delays, due to corrections and brief disagreements about the title, the book was finally published on 24 November 1859. The very day it appeared the total edition of 1250 copies was sold to booksellers; a second edition was immediately scheduled and published on 7 January 1860. When the book was published, Darwin left his home to rest after writing his "accursed book."

An insightful discussion of Darwin's book will be found in a recently published book, *Human Variation in Space and Time*, by K. Kennedy (1976). Kennedy points out that *On the Origin of Species* is a composite of two complementary theories, only one of which was original to Darwin. The idea that each species was not independently created and had descended from other forms was not original to Darwin. During Darwin's time this theory was called the transmutation doctrine. Darwin built upon this idea and insisted that the theory was incomplete until some mechanism was applied whereby this transmutation occurred. The delineation of this process, the mechanism of change, was Darwin's original contribution and came to be called natural selection.

The full title of Darwin's historical book reads *On the Origin of Species by Means of Natural Selection,* the subtitle being *The Preservation of Favored Races in the Struggle for Life.* As Kennedy notes, the title manifests the major theme of the writer's thoughts. Darwin was discussing "species," not higher categories; he was not concerned with the origins and antiquity of life itself. The title makes it clear that Darwin saw a "selective" force working in the rise of new species and that this was a "natural" mechanism quite unlike the artificial breeding practiced by horticulturists or in animal husbandry. The subtitle notes that during the "struggle" for life certain individuals are favored by their possession of adaptive traits and will succeed in reproducing themselves. Others less well adapted will die off or leave fewer progeny (a process eventually labelled differential reproduction), thus reducing their contribution to succeeding generations. Darwin's book is thus important for accounting for how the evolutionary process operates, as well as for its vast compilation of data documenting the fact of evolution.

Interestingly, while Darwin's book received much scorn, he neglected to make much mention of the possibilities of human evolution. Admittedly very little was known about fossil human remains at that time,[6] but Darwin neglected the subject of human evolution as ". . . so surrounded with prejudices." The subject of human evolution, however, received discreet recognition in the Conclusion: "When the views entertained in this volume on the origin of species, or when analagous views are generally admitted," among the accruing benefits will be that, "light will be thrown on the origin of man and his history." For some, the light subsequently thrown on the subject has tended to be blinding.

The Reactions. The publication of Darwin's work received mixed reaction (Figures 3-2 and 3-3). The biologist Huxley wrote, "How extremely stupid not to have thought of that" (de Beer, 1965: 156). Battles raged over Darwin's work and the famous Huxley (pro) and Bishop

[6]A brief note of what was known appeared in his subsequent book, *Descent of Man*.

Figure 3-2. In 1871, a cruel caricature in *The Hornet* labeled Darwin "a venerable orang-outang" and cited his contribution of "unnatural history."

Figure 3-3. An 1882 issue of the Viennese magazine *Kikeriki* published a cartoon of monkeys mourning the death of Charles Darwin. The monkeys moan, Now that our benefactor has passed away, who will be our defender and champion our cause?

Wilberforce (con) debate typifies some of the scene. Especially poignant is Wilberforce's remark to Huxley as to whether he (Huxley) claimed his descent from a monkey through his grandmother or grandfather? Huxley's reply, recalled in a letter to a friend, included such remarks as ". . . would I rather have a miserable ape for a grandfather, or a man highly endowed by nature and possessed of great means and influence, and yet who employs these faculties and that influence for the mere purpose of introducing ridicule into a grave scientific discussion! I unhesitatingly affirmed my preference for the ape" (de Beer, 1965: 166). The Huxley vs. Wilberforce debate was a microcosm of the debate pitting the non-evolutionists, who were backed by the Church, against the early evolutionists.

Darwin's reaction to the barrage was one of measured restraint. His feelings are perhaps best measured in a letter which he wrote on 15 May 1860:

> They may all attack me to their hearts content. I am not case-hardened. As for the old fogies in Cambridge, it really signifies nothing. I look on their attacks as a proof that our work is worth the doing. It makes me resolve to buckle on my armour. I see plainly that it will be a long uphill fight. But think of Lyell's progress with Geology. One thing I see plainly, that without Lyell's years, Huxley's, and Carpenter's aid, my book would have been a mere flash in the pan. But if we all stick to it, we shall surely gain the day. And I now see that the battle is worth fighting (de Beer, 1965: 159).

Darwin's Death. Darwin died of a heart attack on 19 April 1882, at the age of 73. Darwin's family wished him buried in the village of Downe; however, twenty members of Parliament, four of them fellows of the Royal Society, wrote the Dean of Westminster and suggested that Darwin be buried at Westminster Abbey. The funeral occurred on 26 April; the pallbearers included Darwin's intimate friends: Hooker, Huxley, Wallace, and other luminaries. Foreign diplomats were received from France, Germany, Italy, Spain, Russia, and America. An anthem was composed for the occasion and Beethoven's "Funeral's March" was played. Darwin lay near the graves of Newton, Faraday, and his old friend Lyell. Burial in Westminster was the only national honor Britain bestowed upon one of her most illustrious native sons. Even the Beatles received higher acclaim in their heyday; John, Paul, Ringo and George, O.B.E.

Although certain aspects of Darwin's scheme are found in the writings of scholars preceding him, Darwin's contribution reigns supreme. Charles Darwin's principal contribution to modern evolutionary theory was his insistence that natural selection was the guiding force in evolutionary change. He insisted on natural selection as the mechanism which could account for diversity and change. Although other mechanisms were proposed, such as Lamarck's theory of acquired characteristics, these were of little scientific value. Darwin's principal failure, if he can be faulted for not having knowledge hardly available to him, was that he did not know the means whereby adaptive traits were generationally transmitted. He had no knowledge of the law of genetic inheritance.

Early Concepts of Human Heredity

In the past, a number of concepts of human heredity, which now seem naive, were considered. One of these early attempts at explaining family resemblances was called the blending theory; it implied that the human child was an intermediate between maternal and paternal traits. This notion, although still believed by many people, is now known to be incorrect, for hereditary material maintains its integrity generationally— it does not blend or mix.

Charles Darwin believed, as did Lamarck, that acquired traits could be transmitted from parent to offspring. Darwin thought that particles in the body were influenced by the activities of the organisms. These particles traveled to the reproductive system through the circulatory system and modified the sex cells in such a way that acquired traits could be passed to the next generation. This theory of heredity, known as pangenesis, has also been discarded because it lacked scientific support.

Gregor Mendel

During the nineteenth century a number of scientists turned their attention to studies of small animals and the plant world. One such researcher was an Austrian monk, Gregor Mendel (1822-1884) who, while experimenting in a monastery garden in the 1860s, determined the principles of heredity. Although his studies remained undiscovered until the turn of the century, his ideas were a benchmark in modern biological sciences.

In 1868 Mendel was elected abbot of his monastery and had to relinquish his teaching position as well as the time which he had available for conducting his research. Although he assumed he would be able to return to his work, the crush of his administrative duties never permitted him to do so. His work did not become generally known until 1900, sixteen years after his death.

Mendel realized that a trait must be carefully and precisely defined if its inheritance is to be understood. The best traits for study, therefore, are those which are either present or completely absent. Mendel chose seven contrasting pairs of traits: endosperm color (yellow or green), stature (tall or dwarf), shape of the ripe seed (smooth or wrinkled), seed-coat color (gray or white), pod shape (smooth or constricted), pod color (green or yellow), and position of blossoms (axial or terminal). He observed each plant separately and kept the generations separate. The results of the experiments were quantified and expressed as ratios. A large sample was used to reduce or eliminate chance error.

Mendel performed a number of different experiments with his peas. In the first experiment he worked only with true-breeding plants. These plants had been bred only with others of the same kind and showed the same traits generationally. Mendel crossed plants which produced yellow seeds with plants which produced only green seeds; this was the parental or P_1 generation. Those plants grown from seeds produced by the P_1 generation were labelled the first filial, or F_1 generation. The hybrid plants, those produced by cross-pollinating parents with yellow and green seeds, revealed yellow seeds.

Hybrid plants were permitted to self-pollinate to produce the F_2, or second filial generation. Some F_2 plants showed yellow seeds and some showed green seeds. When Mendel counted the number of F_2 plants having each trait, he found that approximately ¾ of the plants bore yellow seeds and ¼ bore green seeds—a 3:1 ratio.

Although the F_1 hybrid plants bore only yellow seeds, when F_1 plants were allowed to self-pollinate some of their offspring showed green seeds. The trait seen in the hybrid is the **dominant** trait, while the other trait, which is not yet seen but which can be passed in a later cross, is termed the **recessive**. Yellow smooth seeds and tallness were the dominant traits.

Mendel was unaware of the physical or chemical realities of the hereditary mechanism, but he did develop a model to explain his results. He believed that hereditary factors for each trait are paired in each plant. These hereditary factors are particulate—they maintain their individuality by not mixing with one another. Mendel postulated two principles to explain his results, the principle of segregation and the principle of independent assortment. The principle of segregation deals with the separation of factors in the formation of sex cells. In other words, when the hybrid produces sex cells, the two units segregate, producing sex cells of two types—for example, either for yellow or green seeds. Half the sex cells carry the unit for yellow seeds, while the other half carry the unit for green seeds. With fertilization, four combinations can occur. Some new plants inherit only units for yellow or green seeds, the homozygous condition, and some plants inherit the units for both yellow and green seeds, the heterozygous state. Because the yellow-yellow, yellow-green, and green-yellow combinations produce yellow seeds, three of every four plants will produce yellow seeds, while only one in four (green-green) will produce green seeds.

Mendel also constructed experiments to study the simultaneous inheritance of more than one trait. He crossed a plant of normal stature (tall) with yellow seeds with a dwarf plant with green seeds. F_1 produced tall plants with red flowers. When F_1 hybrids were crossed, however,

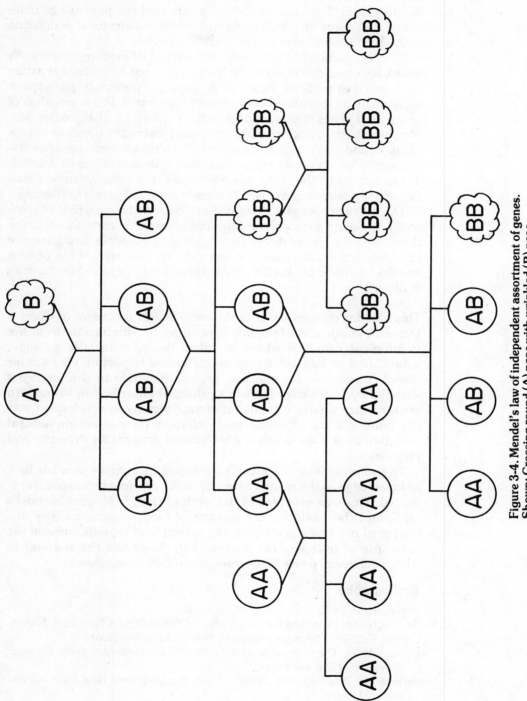

Figure 3-4. Mendel's law of independent assortment of genes.
Shown: Crossing round (A) peas with wrinkled (B) peas.

four types appeared: tall plants with yellow seeds, tall plants with green seeds, dwarf plants with yellow seeds, and dwarf plants with green seeds. The respective frequencies were 9/16, 3/16, 3/16, 1/16, or 9:3:3:1. From these results Mendel formulated the principle of independent assortment, which states that inheritance patterns of differing traits are independent of one another (Figure 3-4).

Mendel's work laid the basis for the science of modern genetics. As noted, his experiments led to the conclusions that inheritance is particulate and that particles, now called genes, are present in pairs which separate in the formation of sex cells (the **gametes**). The segregation of one pair of genes is independent of the segregation of any other pair. Mendel's discovery of two basic principles, that is, the principle of segregation and the principle of independent assortment, describes the manner in which genes are passed from one generation to another. These remain as the basic tenets of modern genetics. Mendel's laws explain the phenomenon of genetic transmission from parent to offspring.

The validity of Mendel's laws makes it possible to apply tests of probability to genetic problems and this has contributed enormously to the development of population genetics. Utilizing Mendel's principles one can identify the genotypes (the complete set of alleles) of the parents and then go on to predict the genotypes and their expected frequencies in offspring.

This chapter outlines some of the early beliefs precedent to Charles Darwin's synthesis, the major opposition to which came from the theological order. Workers in other fields, especially geology, established an expanded time span, a most important element for Darwin's scheme. Darwin was greatly indebted to the geologist Charles Lyell. Charles Darwin's principal contribution to modern evolutionary theory was his insistence that natural selection was the guiding force in evolutionary change. He insisted on natural selection as the mechanism which could account for diversity and change.

The missing link in Darwin's evolutionary scheme was his lack of knowledge of the means whereby traits are generationally transmitted. This was provided in the work of Gregor Mendel. Mendel's work laid the basis for the science of modern genetics. His discovery of two basic principles, the principle of segregation and the principle of independent assortment, describes the manner in which genes are passed from one generation to another.

Bibliography

Appleman, P. 1970. *Darwin.* New York: Norton.

Barlow, N., ed. 1958. *The autobiography of Charles Darwin.* New York: Norton.

Darwin, C. 1958. *The origin of species.* New York: Mentor Books.

———. 1965. *The expression of the emotions in man and animals.* Chicago: University of Chicago Press.

de Beer, G. 1965. *Charles Darwin: a scientific biography.* New York: Natural History Library.

Eiseley, L. 1961. *Darwin's century.* New York: Anchor Books.

———. 1970. *The firmament of time.* New York: Atheneum.

———. 1972. The intellectual antecedents of "The Descent of Man." In *Sexual selection and the descent of man, 1871-1971,* edited by B. Campbell, pp. 1-16. Chicago: Aldine.

Himmelfarb, G. 1959. *Darwin and the Darwinian revolution.* New York: Norton.

Kennedy, K. 1976. *Human variation in space and time.* Dubuque: Wm. C. Brown.

Lerner, I. 1968. *Heredity, evolution and society.* San Francisco: W. H. Freeman.

Lovejoy, A. 1936. *The great chain of being: a study of the prehistory of an idea.* New York: Harper & Row.

Moore, R. 1961. *Man, time, and fossils.* New York: Knopf.

Wilson, L. 1971. Sir Charles Lyell and the species question. *American Scientist* 59: 43-55.

Young, L., ed. 1970. *Evolution of man.* New York: Oxford University Press.

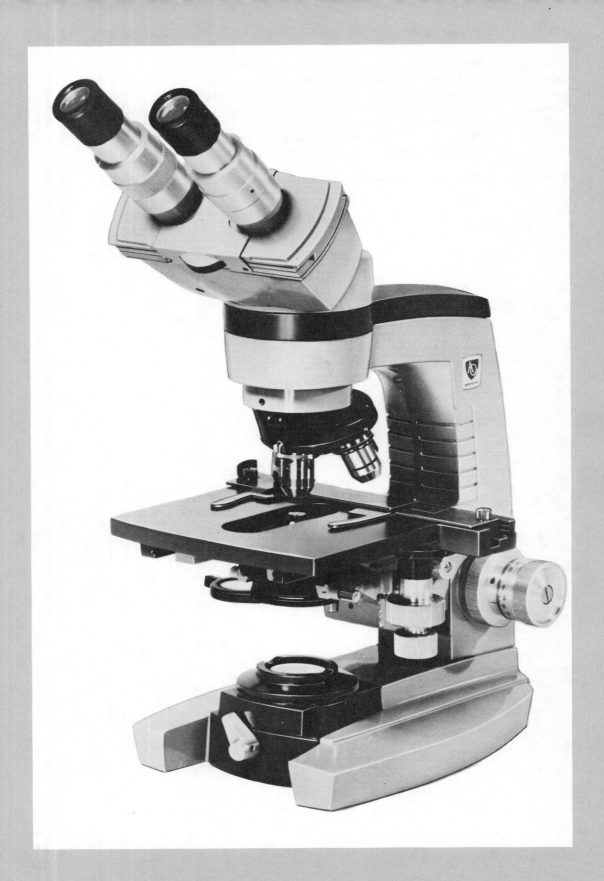

Chapter 4
Modern Evolutionary Theory

This chapter presents some of the principles of genetics and their implications for the study of human evolution. We are also concerned with defining some terminology basic to the understanding of genetics. A discussion of the molecular basis of heredity is included.

The field of genetics, especially the development of population genetics, has provided a basis for understanding human variation from an evolutionary perspective. It has also provided a clearer biological meaning to human variation than that offered by traditional racial classifications.

Population genetics is the focal point of the synthetic theory of evolution. The evolutionary process results from the culmination of four primary forces: (1) mutation, (2) recombination and genetic drift, (3) natural selection, and (4) adaptation. This chapter discusses the mechanics of these four processes and the various levels of evolutionary change, i.e., microevolution, macroevolution, megaevolution, and speciation.

It is difficult to measure gene frequency changes directly between ancestral and descendant populations. This is particularly true when one deals with the fossil record, whose story is written primarily in its skeletal remains. Evolution, as viewed in the fossil record, is primarily based upon morphological changes through time. **Morphology** is the study of the form of the organism, or of any of its parts. Analyses of morphological similarities and differences have been and always will be a basic part of evolutionary studies.

J. Buettner-Janusch (1973) has noted that the amount of attention researchers give to major problems in evolutionary biology changed as the theory of evolution became established. Once established that evolution occurred, the phylogenies of various plants and animals had to be determined. Today the process of speciation is the major concern.

Microscope.

With the establishment of genetics and genetic concepts, research focused on evolutionary rates and the process of adaptation. Today a synthetic theory of evolution states that evolution acts on variable life forms through the process of adaptation and the action of natural selection. The synthetic theory of evolution draws its information from as many scientific branches of knowledge as are applicable.

Basic Principles of Genetics

The principal unit of heredity, then, is the **gene,** which is a structure that transmits hereditary potential from one generation to another. Genes have two functions: (1) they carry hereditary information, and (2) they regulate construction of the molecules that control and form the cell. Genes are lineally ordered on a **chromosome**; the space which a gene occupies on a chromosome is known as its **locus.** There are 46 chromosomes in each human body cell (22 pairs plus one pair of sex chromosomes). A person usually contains one set of chromosomes from both the mother and father. Thus, each individual normally has a pair of genes for each locus. One *set* of chromosomes contains the **haploid** number (23) and one complete *set of pairs* of chromosomes contains the **diploid** number (46).

An individual receives one haploid set (23) of chromosomes from its mother and one haploid set (23) from its father. An offspring's genetic makeup which is inherited from its parents is its **genotype**; the outward characteristic of an organism is the **phenotype.**

The process whereby sex cells are produced is known as **meiosis** (Figure 4-1). During this process the number of chromosomes ordinarily is reduced from the diploid number found in somatic cells to the haploid number found in gametes. **Mitosis** is the cellular process resulting in two cells identical to one another and to the parental cell that has divided to produce them. All cells produced by mitosis have the diploid number of chromosomes.

Two other terms of considerable importance are **dominant** and **recessive.** Dominant **alleles** are those which are expressed in both homozygous and heterozygous combinations. Recessive alleles are expressed only when together in a **homozygous** state.

Genetic Inheritance

Each reader knows that we inherit our genetic potentialities from our parents; one member of each chromosomal pair is received from each parent. Due to the random assortment of chromosomes during meiosis, some grandparents are likely to contribute more to our chromosomal supply than others. On the average, each grandparent could be

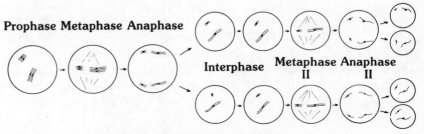

Prophase Metaphase Anaphase

Interphase   **Metaphase II**   **Anaphase II**

Figure 4-1. Meiotic cell division.

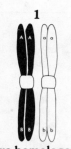
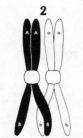
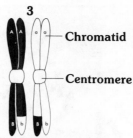

1   **2**   **3**

Chromatid

Centromere

Two homologous
double-stranded
chromosomes

During crossing-over

After crossing-over

Figure 4-2. Crossing-over between two homologous double-stranded chromosomes. (1) One chromosome bearing alleles A and B and another bearing alleles a and b lie side by side in synapsis during meiosis. (2) Breaks occur in a chromatid of each chromosome and fragments are exchanged. (3) After crossing-over, one chromatid of the first chromosome has alleles A and b; one chromatid of the second chromosome has alleles A and B.

expected to contribute one-fourth to our chromosomal supply and each great-grandparent one-eighth of an individual's chromosomal number. Tracing our ancestry back three more generations, we find 64 ancestors. However, since most of us possess only 46 chromosomes, some ancestors are obviously deleted from our genetic heritage. By **crossing over**, a process which occurs during meiosis and allows a new association of linked genes (Figure 4-2), a somewhat larger number of these ancestors may have contributed their genetic material to us. Sexual reproduction ensures that none of us can be identical with any of our ancestors. Sexual reproduction guarantees a certain amount of genetic diversity.

Human genetics is essentially concerned with ways in which our species is **polymorphic**, i.e., with understanding the genetic variability within human populations. The anthropological, in contrast to the medical, interest in human genetics focuses upon evolutionary aspects of this polymorphism. We want to know why a certain allele has a high frequency in one population and a lower frequency in another. We are interested in the adaptive efficiency of a population to survive in its environment. The interests of the physical anthropologist and the medical practitioner certainly overlap, but the medical practitioner is not much interested, from a treatment viewpoint, in the evolutionary history of certain genetic traits.

Gender Determination

An individual's gender is determined by the combination of X and Y chromosomes. The total number of human chromosomes in a typical body cell includes 44 autosomes (any chromosome that is not a sex chromosome) and either an XX combination of sex chromosomes, as in the female, or an XY combination, as in the male. Eggs produced by the female have 22 autosomes plus an X chromosome. Sperm produced by the male have 22 autosomes plus either an X or a Y chromosome. Eggs fertilized by sperm having Y chromosomes eventually develop into males (22X from mother + 22Y from father = 44XY, male), and eggs fertilized by sperm having X chromosomes become females

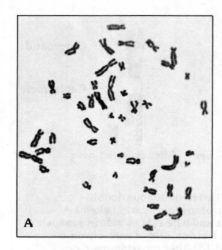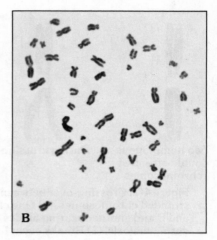

Figure 4-3. Human chromosomes. (a) Normal female cell metaphase with two X chromosomes and 44 autosomes. (B) Normal male cell metaphase with one X, a smaller Y chromosome, and 44 autosomes.

(22X from mother + 22X from father = 44XX, female). Deviations from this pattern can lead to abnormalities in constitution and behavior. About once in each 400 male births an additional X chromosome appears with the normal XY pattern. This results in a male with altered secondary sexual traits, and the condition is called Klinefelter's syndrome (44XXY). If a female lacks an X chromosome, which occurs in about one in every 3500 births, she will manifest a series of abnormalities known as Turner's syndrome (or 44XO). Such a condition also produces a somatic number of 45 instead of the normal 46 (44 + XO =45). Recently, males with the XYY condition have been described. Such individuals are often taller than the normal XY genotype, and there are claims that a few are more aggressive and show some antisocial tendencies. However, the behavioral propensities supposedly related to this genotype have been questioned.

Besides determining gender, the X and Y chromosomes differ in structure and in composition of the genes. Genes on the X chromosome are not generally matched by corresponding genes on the Y chromosome in humans. Thus, in human males, genes on the X chromosome can express themselves without influence from genes on the Y chromosome. Even recessive genes on the X chromosome are free to express themselves in the human male (XY) in the absence of any interfering genes on the Y chromosome.

It should be noted that the well-known genes that have been identified as occurring on the X chromosome have nothing directly to do with the determination of sex. The discussion above, however, indicates why many traits are "sex-linked." Some of the better-known sex-linked traits are hemophilia (a condition in which blood does not clot normally), red-green color blindness, and G6PD deficiency (the malarial protector described in Chapter 23).

We know little about the Y chromosome's influence on inheritance in the male. However, genes carried on the Y chromosome do in some way affect the development of male traits. All individuals without the Y chromosome, such as genotypes X or XX, are female. Y-linked genes determine traits that influence growth and development to the extent that sexes are **dimorphic.**

The Molecular Basis of Heredity[1]

All substances are composed of atoms, which are the basic building blocks of matter. Atoms can be joined to form molecules, which vary greatly in size depending on the number and size of atoms involved. Molecules found in living organisms tend to be large because carbon atoms, which are the fundamental constituent of such molecules, have an electron configuration that allows them to bond easily with other atoms in a seemingly endless array of possible combinations. Remember, it is the *arrangement* of atoms in addition to the kind that is important to the end product.

The primary chemical building blocks of living creatures, wherever they are found on this planet, are
1. water
2. calcium phosphates and carbonates, and other dissolved salts
3. lipids ...
4. carbohydrates: polymers of simple sugars such as glucose
5. proteins: polymers of amino acids
6. nucleic acids: alternating sugar-phosphate polymers with side chains composed of organic nitrogen bases.

To this list should be added several small organic molecules, needed in minute amounts and often obtained from outside the organism in the form of vitamins.

Each of these major components has one or more well-defined roles. Water is the solvent medium for all chemical reactions. Calcium sulfates and phosphates are the rigid framework materials of bone, teeth, and shells. Proteins and lipids provide the more dynamic framework materials for membranes, connecting fibers, tendons, and muscle. Fats contribute mechanical protection and thermal insulation. Proteins and fats each have a second role: Fats are the main energy reservoirs in animals, and globular proteins serve as enzymes (catalysts), regulators, carriers, and recognition and protective molecules. Carbohydrates are the structural materials in plants; they also are the rapid-access energy-storage molecules in animals, and the only energy reservoirs in plants. Nucleic acids have a very special role: the storage and transmission of genetic information. Deoxyribonucleic acids (DNA) are the permanent repository of information in the nucleus of a cell, and ribonucleic acids (RNA) are involved in the transcription and translation machinery that interprets that information and uses it to synthesize proteins. A small cousin of nucleic acids, ATP, is the central short-term energy-storage molecule for all life processes.

DNA. The following discussion of DNA makes reference to some of the chemical components of the molecules. A clearer and more in-depth discussion can be found in almost any introductory chemistry text. For our purposes, it is important to remember the significance of the genetic information storage ability of the DNA molecule and its ability to repli-

---

[1]The second and third paragraphs of this section are reprinted with permission from Richard E. Dickerson and Irving Geis, *Chemistry, Matter, and the Universe: An Integrated Approach to General Chemistry,* copyright © 1976 by W. A. Benjamin, Inc., Menlo Park, California.

cate itself so as to become two identical molecules. During replication, the bonds joining the complementary pairs are broken and the molecule comes apart. For it to function in heredity, the DNA molecule must have a way of storing information. The "blueprint" for a specific protein is located within the nucleus of the cell—in the DNA molecule. However, actual protein formation by the joining of specific amino acids in a specific sequence takes place outside the nucleus. DNA may be visualized as a set of coded instructions in the purine and pyrimidine sequences which specifies the sequence of amino acids to be joined together to form a polypeptide chain. The question now is, how does DNA code for a particular amino acid? Once the structure of the DNA molecule was known, it was quickly suggested that what is called a "three-letter, nonoverlapping code" was sufficient as a genetic code. Such a code means that nucleotides, taken in groups of threes (called triplets), can provide 64 ($4 \times 4 \times 4$) different combinations. That the code is nonoverlapping means that these codons, units of three nucleotides, are read as having a beginning and an end. Two triplets (U-A-A and U-A-G) code for no amino acid. These "nonsense" triplets appear to be the genetic equivalent of a punctuation, i.e., periods. These triplets terminate the synthesis of messenger RNA on the DNA template. Since 64 possibilities leads to only 20 separate results, several codons must specify the same amino acid. For this reason, the genetic code is labelled a "degenerate" code (Williams, 1973).

Messenger RNA carries information from the DNA in the nucleus. Messenger RNA is copied from a sequence of base pairs of the DNA molecule. As a particular segment of DNA containing the code for a particular polypeptide chain unwinds, it leaves a series of bases on the DNA chain exposed. Nucleotide units of RNA found in the nucleus are attracted to the complementary bases on one of the DNA chains. After the nucleotide units are in place, they link together and leave the DNA molecule as a unit, called messenger RNA or mRNA.

Small, spherical bodies known as ribosomes are found within the cell cytoplasm on a membrane known as the endoplasmic reticulum, and it is here that protein synthesis occurs. Another form of RNA, ribosomal RNA, or rRNA, is found within the ribosome. Transfer, or tRNA, is a clover-shaped ribonucleic acid containing three bases which form an anticode for a particular amino acid. If the mRNA code is ACG (adenine-cytosine-guanine), then the tRNA code consists of the complementary bases of UGC (uracil-guanine-cytosine). The tRNA lines up opposite the appropriate **codon** on the mRNA molecule which is attached to the ribosomes.[2] After the amino acids are joined, they link together by means of peptide bonds and the polypeptide chain moves away from the mRNA and tRNA (Figure 4-4).

Mutations. It should be remembered that some mutations involve mistakes at some point in the DNA molecule; these are the so-called point mutations. Point mutations may result from mistakes in the replication process of DNA molecules. Once an alteration has occurred, it would be the basis for the replication of further DNA with the same mistake.

The mistakes noted above are not all bad. In fact, mutations are a vital part of the evolutionary process. Most offspring produced by a

[2]An amino acid is determined by specific three-base units called codons.

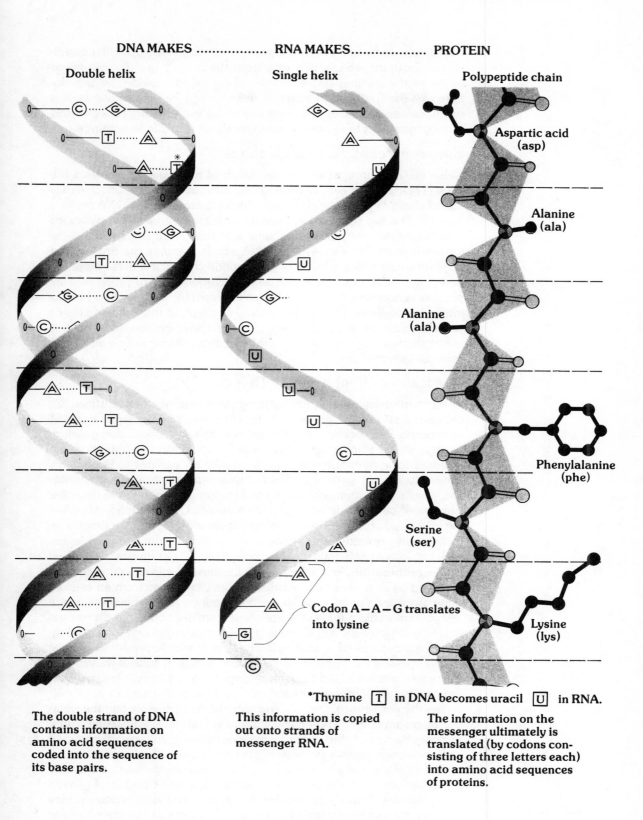

DNA MAKES .... **RNA MAKES** .... **PROTEIN**

Double helix

Single helix

Polypeptide chain

Aspartic acid (asp)

Alanine (ala)

Alanine (ala)

Phenylalanine (phe)

Serine (ser)

Codon A — A — G translates into lysine

Lysine (lys)

*Thymine T in DNA becomes uracil U in RNA.

The double strand of DNA contains information on amino acid sequences coded into the sequence of its base pairs.

This information is copied out onto strands of messenger RNA.

The information on the messenger ultimately is translated (by codons consisting of three letters each) into amino acid sequences of proteins.

Figure 4-4.

population are usually well adapted to existing environmental conditions. Those individuals that vary from the genetic norm might fail to adapt to the existing system, while others might provide the population with the flexibility to adapt to threatening altered conditions. It is this necessary flexibility that is the key to the evolutionary process—this slightly imperfect hereditary machinery that allows life to continue.

Summary of Molecular Genetics

Kelso (1974) summarizes his discussion of molecular genetics as follows: (1) DNA is the genetic material. (2) DNA consists of a long, helically coiled chain of paired nucleotides which separate during DNA replication. (3) The two surfaces exposed by replication serve as templates for construction of two identical chains and thus fulfill the structural requirements of mitosis. (4) It is DNA which specifies the amino acid sequence in the biosynthesis of polypeptide chains. It is these polypeptide chains which compose the primary components of proteins. This process is accomplished by DNA making mRNA, which, when passed into the cytoplasm, directs the activity of tRNA at the cellular sites of protein synthesis, the ribosomes. (5) DNA specifications are coded in triplet sequences of nucleotides that specify particular amino acids and form the genetic code.

The Basis of Evolutionary Theory

The evolutionary process results from the action of: (1) **mutation,** (2) **recombination and genetic drift,** (3) **natural selection,** and (4) **adaptation.** The focal point of the modern theory is population genetics. An essential feature of any "successful" population (a population not doomed to imminent extinction) is population variability. Population variability, i.e., the genetic and phenotypic differences within a population, results from mutation and recombination. Mutation is the exclusive supplier of new and different genetic material. Once mutation supplies the raw goods to the population, recombination distributes them. Recombination spreads mutant (new) genes throughout the population and develops new genetic combinations from old genotypes.

Recombination. From the material discussed earlier in this chapter it should be clear that new genetic combinations arise from an existing gene pool by the process of recombination. Recombination is the distribution vehicle for genes and gene combinations; it is the means whereby a population maintains genetic variability. One of the long-range advantages of sexual reproduction is that it produces genetic variability within a population by mixing genes of both parents. This process is accomplished through meiosis followed by fertilization. During meiosis the chromosomes divide so that one strand of each pair enters the sex cells (gametes). The gamete thus has only half the number of chromosomes. When the gamete is united in fertilization with a gamete from the other parent, it again gains a full complement of chromosomes. In this process of reshuffling, a cell may receive two copies of the same allele or a copy from each of two alleles. Asexual reproduction, on the other hand, provides a limited number of genetic combinations. Barring continuing favorable mutation, asexual reproduction will eventually lead to extinction, as long as the environment does not remain fixed.

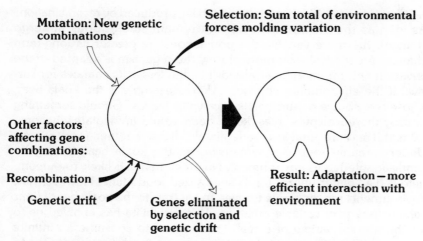

Figure 4-5. Representation of the evolutionary process.

Population variability (the infinite variety of possible genetic combinations) is the stuff of which evolution is made. Recombination enhances the effects of mutation by assembling a broad spectrum of gene combinations upon which natural selection acts. Recombination provides the genetic variability that is worked upon by the various forces producing evolutionary change.

Table 4-1. Marketing Chart.

Product: Evolutionary Change

Manufacturer: Mutation

Raw Product: New gene or genetic combinations

Means of Distribution: Recombination

Test Market: The econiche

Packaging of Product: The population

Consumer Advocate: Natural selection

Final Product: Adaptive change

Product's Advantages over Previous Brands:
Better means of coping with the environment

Product Durability: Useful until the
environment changes

Safety Warning: A combination of too many
mutations or retention of the wrong
mutation can be lethal

Savage (1969:45) sums up the importance of recombination to the evolutionary process as follows:

A single mutational change may be lost or passed on without great impact on a population, but if its effect is modified and enhanced by recombination an unending contribution to variation is begun. Variation is the raw material for evolutionary change; recombination is its principal source. Mutation alone has relatively little effect on variation without the pervasive impact of recombination.

What is the significance of the variability produced by recombination? As long as the environment doesn't remain stable (does undergo change), the more variable the population, the greater its long-term chances for survival. The more closely the organism is adapted to the environment, the more specialized it is, the lesser its chances for survival if the environment changes. A good example is the koala bear, whose sole source of nutrition is eucalyptus leaves.[3] Should something destroy the eucalyptus trees, koala bears would immediately become extinct. They are unable to adequately digest another food source. Under carefully controlled circumstances the koala bear is magnificently adapted to its environment. No other animal is likely to outcompete it (i.e., better utilize) for its specialized food niche. However, few environments remain stable forever. In contrast to the koala bear *Homo sapiens* is a very variable creature. This variability has enabled us to inhabit a great variety of climatic niches and to consume an infinite variety of foods. Theoretically at least, we are much better adapted to face some catastrophic event than the poor eucalyptus-leaf eater.

Genetic Component of Variability. Stini (1975) provides a clear discussion of the importance of population variability in terms of its evolutionary importance. Among humans, for example, there are estimates of upward of 20,000 loci, or gene pairs, per individual. Since these are reassorted independently of each other during sexual reproduction, the number of gene combinations or genotypes in our species is very large, especially if we assume that there is variability at a number of these loci. "If we combine the observation of these mechanisms for the production of genotypic variability, mechanisms strongly dependent upon the process of sexual reproduction...we may reasonably infer that the maintenance of variability enhances the survivorship of the species" (Stini, 1975:2).

Some alleles are dominant over others and prevent the expression of recessive traits in the heterozygous condition. This allows some genetic traits which are potentially harmful to be carried from generation to generation and to be maintained within the gene pool. In this manner, new recessive mutations stand a better chance of remaining within the gene pool than if exposed to natural selection each time they appear.

Besides the fact that recessive mutations are retained within the population, other mechanisms, such as segregation and recombination, preserve genetic variability within the species. Added to this is the possibility of pleiotrophy, whereby a gene at one locus influences more than one trait, and contemporary sexually-reproducing populations possess a number of mechanisms, i.e., social regulations governing marital or breeding combinations, for generating infinite variety. Thus, even though mutations are rare, numbering from one out of every 100,000 to one out of every million gametes, species are capable of meeting environmental changes with some individuals genetically capable of coping.

Natural Selection. Charles Darwin's prime contribution to evolutionary theory was the idea of natural selection as the guiding force

[3]These leaves are awful to the human taste. They are quite oily and tough. In connection with my research on Indian monkeys, I ate such leaves to see why the monkeys avoided them. If the leaves tasted as awful to the monkeys as they did to me, I understand. The eucalyptus connoisseur, the koala bear, definitely would disagree.

of evolution. Darwin's original ideas were rather unsophisticated. He saw the evolutionary process as the struggle for existence between individual organisms. This generated the now famous phrase, "Survival of the fittest," which was not Darwin's phraseology but that of the English social philosopher Herbert Spencer. The phrase stuck, and the outlook engendered a "survival of the fittest" ideology. Some have used this ideology to justify social inequities, unethical mercantile practices, aggression, colonialism, racism, and overzealous missionization. This is a gross misuse of Darwinian theory. Obviously, evolutionary theory did not always work on the side of the angels, nor are all its believers angels.

Darwin's concept of natural selection may be paraphrased as:

1. Individuals differ among themselves.
2. Individual differences are partially determined by hereditarily transmissible factors. (Darwin was ignorant of the means whereby this was accomplished.)
3. Whenever these differences involved fitness, the traits of the more fit individuals will be increasingly represented in succeeding generations.

Genetic fitness refers to an organism's ability to adapt to the environment and subsequent success in leaving fertile surviving offspring. The more genetically fit, the better an organism's ability to transmit its genes. A trait which does not affect one's reproductive success is not considered evolutionarily significant.

Changes in characteristics of successive generations are partly determined by the inequities of the reproductive rates of individuals of different hereditary endowments. This is known as differential reproduction. In time, the genetic complements of the more fit individuals will prevail. One of the means whereby various genotypes, e.g., genetic components, remain in a population is through their visible expression, which is referred to as the phenotype, the visible expression, of the genes. Mating preference related to outward preference is called sexual selection. Darwin placed a great reliance upon sexual selection as a factor which determined a population's outward appearance, and after some delay modern geneticists have again begun to accept this as a strong possibility. An example of sexual selection is the choice of mates culturally termed desirable. (More on this aspect in Chapter 24.)

Natural selection produces evolutionary change by favoring the differential reproduction of genes best adapted to a certain environment. It should be borne in mind that natural selection does not directly encourage specific genes or gene combinations but works through the intermediary of their expression, e.g., selection works upon the physical and behavioral expressions of the genes. Natural selection alone cannot account for evolutionary change because selection does not produce genetic change. However, once change has occurred, natural selection acts to encourage some genes and/or gene combinations over others through reproductive advantage.[4] Natural selection encourages those genes or gene combinations which assure the highest level of adaptive efficiency between the population and the environ-

[4]As we will see in Chapter 22, natural selection has acted to preserve certain body traits in one environment and other traits in other environments.

ment. For example, natural selection favors those koala bears whose genes and/or gene combinations allow for the most efficient mastication (chewing) and digestion of eucalyptus leaves. Individuals who get the most food and leave the most offspring with the least amount of energy expenditure are selected for. The less well-adapted organisms normally have less chance to leave a substantial number of offspring, or under severe limitations the organism dies. Although we refer to individual organisms, evolution works on populations. The population, not the individual, counts evolutionarily.

Since it favors and encourages gene combinations, natural selection is the artist, the creative force, in evolution. Selection has been the principal force operating over millions of years to facilitate the development of new adaptations to the world's diverse environments. Natural selection is responsible for the evolution of the present diversity of life. Because the environment is seldom stable but undergoes rather continual change, the nature of selection also fluctuates and what may be adaptive today may be madadaptive tomorrow. This, again, points out the importance of maintaining population variability. It should also be noted that the working of natural selection is somewhat contradictory in the sense that natural selection simultaneously selects against variation while it confers an advantage to those members of the species which are the most variable. It could be said that evolutionarily successful species consist of forms which have been selected as a result of their capacity for variability. Evolution is a meaningless concept unless one views the process in the environmental context (including the cultural milieu of humans). The forces of selection channel variation along particular lines of environmental stability.

The major features of natural selection may be summarized as follows:
1. Selection is the sum total of environmental factors favoring differential reproduction within a population.
2. The environment operates as the selective force in this process, favoring variants best adapted to meet a set of environmental particulars and removing those less well adapted.
3. Natural selection favors traits bringing an organism into an effective adaptive relationship with the environment.
4. Natural selection results in a reduction of variation due to the "weeding out" of less well-adapted forms.

Natural selection is like a good stockbroker, selecting from among the many stocks those likely to yield the highest return. Traits which are selected for or against are neither good nor bad; they are merely adaptive or nonadaptive. There is increasing evidence, however, that this is not an all or none proposition, for some traits may be of neutral value.

We must note that natural selection is not just a process that eliminates traits, genes, from a population. Natural selection is positive differential reproduction. The reproductive capacity of certain genotypes is higher than the capacity of others. Individuals whose genotypes allow them to produce more viable offspring are said to enjoy the advantages of positive differential reproduction.

Adaptation. Adaptation is the end result of natural selection. Adaptation is the result of natural selection acting upon a variable gene pool to produce a population which efficiently interacts with its environment. The end product of evolutionary change is the establishment of organisms that function more efficiently in certain environmental situations than their predecessors. Any characteristic (behavioral or morphological) advantageous to an organism's coping with its environment is said to be adaptive.

Biological adaptations can occur in various ways; some are permanent, i.e., they represent changes in the genetic structure of the population. According to scientists favoring this definition, adaptation has not occurred unless a population has experienced some alteration of gene frequencies. On the other hand, adjustments which occur within an individual's lifetime (acclimatizations) and which are not acquired specifically through inheritance or transmitted to succeeding generations fail to qualify as evolutionary adaptations. By excluding adjustments not directly reflecting an altered genetic constitution, a rigidly genetic definition of adaptation places the term within an evolutionary perspective. Wallace and Srb (1964) have said that "adaptation is evolution."

The process of adaptation includes movement into an econiche or adaptive zone. This is comprised of the physical and biotic environment. The physical environment is composed of physical and chemical factors (i.e., the air which is breathed, water, and soil components). The biotic environment includes faunal and floral components. Habitation of an econiche is not a haphazard process as organisms must adapt to their total surroundings, including all existing foods, competitors and enemies, and all forms of life affecting the given organism in any way. Furthermore, the adaptive zones change; the course of the adaptive history of any group may be seen as a shifting series of adaptive zones. The order in which organisms move into a niche influences their use of that niche. The first organisms moving into a new niche theoretically have that whole niche open to them because of lack of competition. Subsequent inhabitants, in order to reduce competition, usually occupy successively narrower portions and they tend to be more specialized than previous inhabitants. The narrower the niche, the less variable the population and the greater the chances of extinction.

Levels of Evolutionary Change (Figure 4-6)

Evolutionary rates are dissimilar and dependent upon many factors, e.g., type of habitat, generation time, and number of offspring. Furthermore, as G. Simpson (1951, 1953) has often noted, a group of organisms can go through stages of differing evolutionary speed.[5] One type of evolutionary change is referred to as **microevolution,** which involves the small changes within a potentially continuous population responsible for differences arising between related populations. An example of microevolution among *Homo sapiens* would be worldwide variations in skin pigmentation. Another example would be the great array of domestic breeds of dog. In contrast to microevolutionary changes which do not isolate breeding populations from one another, **macroevolutionary** changes involve the rise and divergence of discontinuous groups. The large-scale evolution studied by the paleontologist in the

---

[5]For example, it has been suggested that the speed of human evolution was quite slow for the first few million years of the Lower Pleistocene. However, the rate greatly accelerated during the much shorter time span of the Middle and Upper Pleistocene. Culture seems to have been the catalyst.

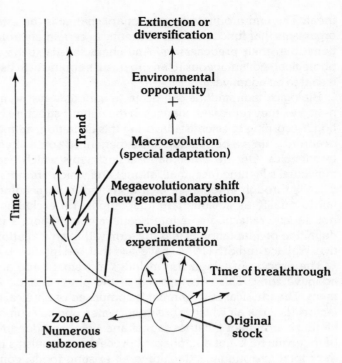

Figure 4-6. The process of evolution above the species level.

fossil record is due to macroevolutionary processes. The major differentiation between macro- and **megaevolutionary** change is that the latter normally occurs in small rapidly evolving populations moving into new habitats. Megaevolution (or quantum evolution) is a temporary phenomenon characteristic of populations in temporary states of disequilibrium. Both these processes result in genetic discontinuity, speciation, and the production of new forms. The concept of speciation is discussed in the next chapter.

The basic structure of the gene is composed of a pair of long polypeptide chains known as DNA. Information is carried from the nucleus by messenger RNA. Genes are lineally ordered on a chromosome, each occupying a space called the locus. Alternate forms of a gene at a locus are called alleles. If the alleles at a locus are the same this is the homozygous condition. If the alleles at a locus are different this is the heterozygous condition. The visible expression of the genotype is known as the phenotype.

New genetic combinations are introduced into populations through random mutations. The useful, i.e., adaptive, mutations increase an organism's chance of survival. They are then distributed throughout the population. Evolution, through natural selection, leads to an improvement of the adaptive relations between organisms and their environment.

Evolutionary rates are dissimilar and a population may pass through stages of differing evolutionary rates. Small changes within potentially continuous populations are referred to as microevolution. Larger changes, those which result in the isolation of breeding populations, are referred to as macroevolutionary or megaevolutionary changes. These latter processes are usually differentiated by speed: megaevolutionary changes are considered to occur faster and usually in small populations moving into new habitat.

Bibliography

Beadle, G., and Beadle, M. 1966. *The language of life.* Garden City, N.J.: Doubleday.

Bodmer, W., and Cavalli-Sforza, L. 1976. *Genetics, evolution and man.* San Francisco: W.H. Freeman.

Buettner-Janusch, J. 1973. *Physical anthropology: a perspective.* New York: Wiley.

Burns, G. 1972. *The science of genetics.* New York: Macmillan.

Cavalli-Sforza, L., and Bodmer, W. 1971. *The genetics of human populations.* San Francisco: W.H. Freeman.

Crow, J. 1976. *Genetics notes,* 7th ed. Minneapolis: Burgess.

Fisher, R. 1958. *The genetical theory of natural selection.* New York: Dover.

Grant, V. 1963. *The origin of adaptations.* New York: Columbia University Press.

Kelso, A. 1970, 1974. *Physical anthropology.* Philadelphia: Lippincott.

King, J., and Jukes, T. 1969. Non-Darwinian evolution. *Science* 164:788-97.

Lerner, I. 1968. *Heredity, evolution and society.* San Francisco: W.H. Freeman.

Levine, R. 1968. *Genetics.* New York: Holt, Rinehart and Winston.

McKusick, V. 1969. *Human genetics.* Englewood Cliffs, N.J.: Prentice-Hall.

Markert, C.; Shaklee, J.; and Whitt, G. 1975. Evolution of a gene. *Science* 189:102-14.

Mayr, E. 1974. Behavior programs and evolutionary strategies. *American Scientist* 62:650-59.

Merrell, D. 1962. *Evolution and genetics.* New York: Holt, Rinehart and Winston.

Moody, P. 1967. *Genetics of man.* New York: Norton.

Peters, J., ed. 1959. *Classic papers in genetics.* Englewood Cliffs, N.J.: Prentice-Hall.

Papazian, J. 1967. *Modern genetics.* New York: Norton.

Rensch, B. 1959. *Evolution above the species level.* New York: Columbia University Press.

Ross, H. 1966. *Understanding evolution.* Englewood Cliffs, N.J.: Prentice-Hall.

Salthe, S. 1972. *Evolutionary biology.* New York: Holt, Rinehart and Winston.

Savage, J. 1969. *Evolution.* New York: Holt, Rinehart and Winston.

Simpson, G. 1951. *The meaning of evolution.* New York: Mentor.

————. 1953. *The major features of evolution.* New York: Columbia University Press.

Sinnott, E.; Dunn, L.; and Dobzhansky, T. 1958. *Principles of genetics.* New York: McGraw-Hill.

Smith, J. 1966. *The theory of evolution.* Baltimore: Penguin.

Solbrig, O. 1966. *Evolution and systematics.* New York: Macmillan.

Stini, W. 1975. *Ecology and human adaptation.* Dubuque: Wm. C. Brown.

Volpe, E. 1967. *Understanding evolution.* Dubuque: Wm. C. Brown.

Wallace, B. 1966. *Chromosomes, giant molecules, and evolution.* New York: Norton.

Wallace, B., and Srb, A. 1964. *Adaptation.* Englewood Cliffs, N.J.: Prentice-Hall.

Williams, B. 1973. *Evolution and human origins: an introduction to physical anthropology.* New York: Harper & Row.

Chapter 5
Evolutionary Systematics

This short chapter deals with some basic concepts of modern evolutionary systematics. Here we are concerned with some principles of modern taxonomy and classification; we shall also briefly discuss some rules of nomenclature. In Chapter 9 we deal with some of the problems of classification as concerns the primate fossil record. Understanding the world of living organisms requires ordering this multiplicity of plants and animals into some sort of rational, manageable system. Consequently, systematics is as old as our desire to understand life, and the effort to understand and order the variability of life has led to the development of all branches of biology. The field of taxonomy, once concerned only with an effort to classify, has been transformed into a method of discovering and understanding nature's order.

Solbrig (1966) has estimated that so far about 1,500,000 species have been described and classified. However, of all the major plant and animal groups, only the birds with 8650 species and perhaps the gymnosperms among the plants with about 650 species have been more or less completely surveyed. Our knowledge of the kinds and numbers of all other groups is incomplete, and it has been estimated that there are more than 100,000 undescribed species of flowering plants, 20,000 species of fishes, and over 1,000,000 insects. Against this background, the primate fossil record, indeed the human fossil record with all its entanglements and taxonomic arguments, seems to be relatively complete and well understood. However, we shall soon see that as we deal with the Order Primates and especially with the Family Hominidae (of which we are part) taxonomic methodology becomes blurred and nomenclature somewhat misused.

[1]The author would like to express his gratitude to Dr. J. Buettner-Janusch for his clear treatment of this subject in his 1973 book, *Physical Anthropology.*

Carolus Linnaeus, 1707-1778.

Terminology

It is essential that we first establish definitions for a number of terms which are often misused and misunderstood. Systematics, according to Simpson (1961), deals with the scientific study of the types and diversity of living organisms and of the interrelationships among them. Systematics thus deals with the ordering of life; it is a very general and inclusive activity accepting data from any and all of the sciences. Once comparative studies have provided data concerning traits by which interrelationships may be established, a formal system of relating organisms to one another and placing them into groups, i.e., classification, is then used.

Systematics (the study of the diversity of animals and their interrelationships) and **taxonomy** (the theoretical study of how classifications are made) are two terms which are often used interchangeably although their meanings do differ. Placing living organisms into groups based on relationships between them is the act of classification. Buettner-Janusch (1973:28) states: "The subjects of classification are organisms; the subjects of taxonomies are classifications; and the subjects of systematics are everything that is relevant to the study of organisms." The assignment of names to groups of plants or animals is nomenclature.

Several Principles of Classification

The principal reason for constructing a classification is to provide a simple reference system. The present hierarchical system of classification is based upon the original eighteenth-century work of the Swedish naturalist Carolus Linnaeus. It is important to note that the Linnaean system is hierarchical, i.e., categories are based upon inclusive traits. Groups at the top (i.e., Kingdoms) are most inclusive while groups at the bottom (i.e., species) are least inclusive. Each category within the classification includes a group or groups of related organisms, the members of which are held together by shared traits. There are three basic steps in classification: (1) the delineation of the categories; (2) the establishment of relationships within and between categories; and (3) the formation of a hierarchy. These relationships are established in two ways: first, by overlapping or coincidence of dissimilar categories and, second, by subordination of some classes to others or by inclusion of one class within another (Solbrig, 1966).

The act of classifying is hampered by many problems, not the least of which is the fact that the Linnaean system was not designed to convey evolutionary information. When established the Linnaean system was thought to represent the "real world" as ordained by the Supreme Being. All forms represented in the Linnaean system were thought to be permanent and immutable results of a special creation. A number of consequences relate to the fact that the Linnaean system is non-evolutionary in orientation. The Linnaean system is so devised that the categories and taxa[2] are unable to reflect the true nature of evolutionary change, i.e., slow continuous change. The Linnaean system is able only to represent discontinuous relationships. One of the shortcomings of

[2]A taxon (plural taxa) is a group of creatures within the classificatory scheme related to one another by descent from a common ancestor; this group is distinctive enough to be given a name to differentiate it from other groups.

MAMMALIA.

ORDER I. PRIMATES.

Fore-teeth cutting; upper 4, parallel; teats 2 pectoral.

1. HOMO.

Sapiens. Diurnal; varying by education and fituation.
2. Four-footed, mute, hairy.   *Wild Man.*
3. Copper-coloured, choleric, erect.   *American.*
    Hair black, ftraight, thick; *noftrils* wide, *face* harfh; *beard* fcanty; *obftinate,* content free. *Paints* himfelf with fine red lines. *Regulated* by cuftoms.
4. Fair, fanguine, brawny.   *European.*
    Hair yellow, brown, flowing; *eyes* blue; *gentle,* acute, inventive. *Covered* with clofe veftments. *Governed* by laws.
5. Sooty, melancholy, rigid.   *Afiatic.*
    Hair black; *eyes* dark; *fevere,* haughty, covetous. *Covered* with loofe garments. *Governed* by opinions.
6. Black, phlegmatic, relaxed.   *African.*
    Hair black, frizzled; *fkin* filky; *nofe* flat; *lips* tumid; *crafty,* indolent, negligent. *Anoints* himfelf with greafe. *Governed* by caprice.

Monftrofus Varying by climate or art.
1. Small, active, timid.   *Mountaineer.*
2. Large, indolent.   *Patagonian.*
3. Lefs fertile.   *Hottentot.*
4. Beardlefs.   *American.*
5. Head conic.   *Chinefe.*
6. Head flattened.   *Canadian.*

The anatomical, phyfiological, natural, moral, civil and focial hiftories of man, are beft defcribed by their refpective writers.

Vol. I.—C   2. SIMIA.

Figure 5-1. Linnaeus's classification of the genus *Homo*.

the Linnaean system is that it is a static two-dimensional framework while evolution is dynamic and multidimensional and involves change through time. Although the Linnaean system was intended to work within a non-evolutionary framework, since the work of Darwin the zoological classificatory system has been slowly overhauled to incorporate the viewpoint that the living world is constantly changing, evolving new forms from old. With some success we have borrowed the form of the Linnaean system while changing its function.

Although various rules are used to establish categories within the classification, it must be remembered that the system is arbitrary and that the taxonomist imposes names upon the natural order for convenience. Disregarding the philosophical viewpoint with which one approaches the classificatory scheme, classification is not a real biological phenomenon; rather it is a set of analytical categories used to order data. The procedures employed in determining the taxon to which an organism belongs include a subjective element, that of weighting characters. This subjective element produces many of the problems noted throughout this book; some of the procedures employed in weighting characteristics are discussed later.

Evolutionary
Systematics

57

Rule of Nomenclature

The establishment of a name to identify a form is based upon a number of rules and is not, or should not be, a haphazard affair. A set of arbitrarily agreed-upon rules, embodied in the "codes" of nomenclature, governs the application of names. These rules have been established over a number of generations and include a combination of historical elements with practical rulings to ensure clarity and usefulness. Nomenclature is the device used to eliminate confusion and ensure one common language in biological classification.

The Law of Priority. The rules of nomenclature follow a number of precedents. The law of priority applies to all names used as of 1 January 1758. The first name (taxon) validly used after this date has priority if used correctly and proposed and published according to the rules established in the International Code of Zoological Nomenclature. Later forms given the same name are referred to as synonyms. In certain instances, the law of priority may be ignored, for example, if dropping a commonly held taxon in favor of a prior, but obscure, taxon will cause unnecessary confusion. In matters such as this, or in other instances of dispute over nomenclature, the decision is made by the International Commission on Zoological Nomenclature.

Certain conventions are followed in forming the names of some of the higher categories. This is illustrated in Table 5-1.

Table 5-1. Names of Higher Categories

Category	Suffix	Stem	Name of Higher Category
Superfamily	-oidea	Homin	Hominoidea
Family	-idae	Homin	Hominidae
Subfamily	-inae	Homin	Homininae

Occasionally, names are applied which later must be dropped or "sunk." The "sinking" of a taxonomic category may result from a number of factors, e.g., data analysis may eventually reveal that the form actually does not differ significantly from material already described. In this event the form takes the name of the original material. To take an example from the human fossil record, when Middle Pleistocene hominid material was first uncovered in China it was given the name "Sinanthropus"; however, later analysis proved that "Sinanthropus" was similar to hominid material uncovered earlier in Java, i.e., *Homo erectus.* The genus "Sinanthropus" was thus "sunk" in favor of the earlier proposed genus *Homo.*

The official name of an organism contains a number of parts, its **genus** (e.g., *Homo*) and **species** (e.g., *sapiens*) and **subspecies** (e.g., *sapiens*) if such is determined and applicable. The assignment of genus and species names follows the Linnaean system of establishing a binomial (i.e., a two-term name). It is obligatory to apply the binomial to each newly described species. Taking as an example modern hominids, the binomial reference would be *Homo* (the genus) and *sapiens* (the species), i.e., *Homo sapiens.* To differentiate modern hominids from ancestral forms we add a third modifier, the subspecific designation; thus we establish the taxon of *Homo sapiens sapiens.* The genus designation always begins with a capital letter, the species and subspecies designation with a small letter. Each binomial is unique and is not applied to another. The binomial always appears in italics; the names of taxa higher than a genus, e.g., family, are not italicized but they too begin with capital letters.

We mentioned above that the assignment of names follows a number of rules set forth in the *International Code of Zoological Nomenclature*. Besides the law of priority, there is also a rule called the *designation of types*. Whenever a new species is described a *type specimen* must be designated. The type is a particular specimen—a skull, for example—which establishes the criteria for a certain classification, and the type is the form to which all subsequent forms are compared. Types are established at the species, genus, and family levels. The type of a species is an individual specimen, for a genus the type is a species, and for a family the type is established upon a genus. The type specimen, being only one specimen, may unfortunately not be typical of the group it represents. However, it is hoped it will be! It must be remembered that type specimens of species, for example, are the real entities to which the species name is attached, but they do not and cannot represent or even typify the range of variation within the group for which they stand. When other finds of the same species are made at the same time, they are listed as referred specimens within the species "hypodigm." The hypodigm is a list of all known similar individuals (Simons, 1972).

It is most important to note that the word "type" as used in type specimen does not apply to, and must not be confused with, the typological concept of species favored by eighteenth- and nineteenth-century non-evolutionists. A characteristic of the Linnaean system is that it adhered to the Platonic concept of *eidos* (idea, type, essence). This principle was embodied in the concept of the type, the idealization of an individual as a representative of all other individuals of the species. This concept of type grew out of the belief in the immutability or fixity of the species and led to the false acceptance of the fact that a single specimen—the type—would be a sufficient sample of the species. Although Darwin recognized the importance of population variability, typological thinking did not cease until the dynamics of population genetics became known and accepted. Continued acceptance of the non-evolutionary concept of type dominated early hominid classification, however, and unfortunately still appears today. Only with the development of population genetics and the realization that populations and not individuals are the evolutionary units did systematics shift from considering individual specimens to studying series and mass samples.

The net effect of the taxonomic system is often one whereby species, once they have become established, appear almost to be fixed in their classification. It must be borne in mind, however, that a biological entity, represented by a title such as *Homo erectus*, is (or was) a dynamic, living creature; it was not a fixed type. Eventually *Homo erectus* changed to the extent that scientists who discovered the subsequent remains (i.e., the remains of *H. erectus* descendants), called them something else, i.e., *Homo sapiens*. Because *Homo erectus*, at this point in our knowledge, appears to have been our antecedent, there was a biological continuum between ourselves and them. Therefore, although scientific convention draws discrete boundaries between *Homo sapiens* and *Homo erectus*, these boundaries did not and could not have existed in biological reality.

The Species Concept

The species concept is the key in modern evolutionary biology. Most paleontologists prefer to characterize the species as an objective, non-arbitrary grouping. This is a population or group of a population of actually or potentially interbreeding animals reproductively isolated from other such groups.

Various kinds of species are recognized: species living in areas with overlapping home ranges are **sympatric. Allopatric** populations occupy separate nonoverlapping geographical areas. Some fossil populations are in the same species as living animals; however, groups whose ranges do not overlap in time are called allochronic or paleo-species.

Most material dealt with in this book is fossil material, thus we are usually referring to evolutionary species. An evolutionary species is an ancestral-descendant sequence of populations separately evolving from others (Buettner-Janusch, 1973; Simpson, 1961). Allochronic, or paleospecies, are difficult to distinguish because of the incompleteness of the fossil record. Because species change very slowly, the evidence would show slight gradual changes in the organisms, such that distinctions would be difficult to make. When a paleontologist has an intergrading series of fossils with no discontinuities, the series may be broken up for convenience.

The Process of Speciation

Reproductive isolation is the principal criterion for defining genetical species. Reproductive isolation is often synonymous with geographical isolation, which is one of the most important ways in which speciation occurs. A population which radiates into a number of different habitats, each with its own peculiarities, tends to adapt to these local conditions. Such adaptation, molded by natural selection, may eventually result in genetic differences in various local areas. Eventually the differences will magnify into speciation with its concomitant reproductive isolation.

Although geographical isolation is a major source of speciation, other factors also need to be considered. Among other important isolating mechanisms are behavioral patterns. Although behavioral isolating mechanisms (such as mating patterns) are not well-studied, there is no doubt that they do play a role in speciation. In effect any mechanisms leading to isolation and impeding gene flow between segments of a population could eventually lead to reproductive isolation and speciation; however, this is not always true. In addition to geographical and ethological isolation, there is temporal and seasonal isolation in which mating occurs at different seasons in different populations, and mechanical isolation, e.g., when, as among some insects, the morphology of the genitalia prevents copulation. Most likely, speciation within the Order Primates resulted from geographical and perhaps ethological isolation.

The BSC—biological species concept[3]—has been recently subjected to heavy criticism from certain evolutionary theorists (Ehrlich, Holm, and Parnell, 1974; Sokal and Sneath, 1963, 1973; Sokal and Crovella,

[3]Simpson does not like the term biological species concept. He notes it is a genetic based concept. To him, all species concepts are inherently biological.

1970; Sokal, 1973, for example). Some of the criticisms are as follows: (1) The BSC applies only to sexually reproducing organisms—hence biologists dealing with nonsexual organisms must use a different species criteria. This means biology has several types of "species" and this can be confusing. (2) The BSC can really only be applied to neontology since the criterion of interbreedability can never be adequately tested paleontologically. (3) Actual testing of interbreedability under *natural* conditions occurs only when populations are sympatric. If they are allopatric—if they never meet—then biologists can only assume species or subspecies status. (4) Arbitrary decisions on species status must frequently be made because biologists find a continuum or smooth, unbroken gradient between completely intersterile populations and those that are completely infertile. It is a matter of choice as to what to do with those in the middle—those with incomplete gene pool protection. (5) Much stress has been placed on the contention that the BSC is defined on one level (genetical: interbreedability) but is usually actually distinguished by phenetic (morphological) criteria. Sokal and Crovella go into elaborate detail on this point, and they note that interbreedability has never *really* been tested for any two species. If several individuals or small populations can interbreed, then decisions are made (it is assumed that other individuals or populations that *look similar to these*—phenetics— follow the same rule). Strictly speaking, interbreedability should be checked for all individuals of both groups to really test the BSC. Further, they note that phenetics is used even at the preliminary stages of deciding which groups to study. Point 5, the critics say, indicates that the BSC is really based upon morphology or phenetics regardless of what the ideal definition says.

Most of this criticism is associated with the school of numerical taxonomy, adherents of which feel that the BSC is implicitly phenetical anyway—so why not make it explicitly phenetical? This means all biologists could use the same species and more objectivity would be injected into the species-naming process. The subjectivity of the BSC bothers these critics. (Shaw [1969] has attacked the use of the species concept in paleontology. Ehrlich and Raven [1969] and Ender [1973] attack the notion that gene flow is the principal force binding a species.)

Higher Categories

A higher category includes taxa from lower levels in the Linnaean hierarchy, i.e., a genus contains various species. The fossil material deals primarily with categories on the species and genus level.

The genus is a different type of category than the species; it should contain several related species. Paleontologists generally refer to the genus as a stage arbitrarily separated from other stages in an evolving sequence. The genus is often characterized as a definite evolutionary unit, and is considered hardly more arbitrary than the species.

Extinction

The term extinction is applied to describe the disappearance of an animal group, such as a species, from the evolutionary record. A species may become extinct in three ways: First, the species may develop a lifeway such that climatic change would prevent its continued existence, as for example, the koala bear's dependence on eucalyptus leaves if such trees should no longer exist. This is an example of a negative role played by environmental selection in evolution. Second, a species may become extinct when it is consumed or destroyed by another species. Third, a species may become extinct when it is transformed into another; *e.g.,* a species may be a part of a continuous, progressive evolutionary lineage. The species of one time period in which this lineage exists is the ancestor of succeeding species in the next time period. The ancestral species becomes extinct through the processes by which it is transformed into its descendants. For example, Middle Pleistocene hominids of the species *Homo erectus* are extinct, yet they are likely ancestors to the species *Homo sapiens,* which contains some *Homo erectus* genes.

While taxonomy is a useful tool in dealing with the vast array of life, it has its limitations. One of the major stumbling blocks is the limited amount of evidence concerning fossil forms and the ignorance about the direction of evolutionary trends and rates of evolution. This lack of data creates a serious problem, since without data, weighting of characters in classification is largely subjective, and a truly evolutionary classification will never be a reality.

Because of problems mentioned here and in Chapter 9 the reader may question the validity and wisdom of attempting to classify organisms so that the classification will reflect their evolutionary relationships. However, the careful study of genetics, function, morphology, behavior, and ecological relationships, among others, can provide many clues. Even so, as the next chapters will indicate, different scientists read the available information differently. Granted, there are problems; however, as Solbrig (1966:120) states, "It should be remembered that science can at best present a statistical approximation to reality, and the best we can hope for is relative truth."

The species concept is one of the most important in modern evolutionary biology, and is essential for any discussion of systematics and taxonomy. Most paleontologists refer to the species as an objective, nonarbitrary grouping. Species living in areas with overlapping home ranges are referred to as sympatric. Allopatric populations of a species occupy separate, nonoverlapping home ranges. Groups whose ranges in time do not overlap are called allochronic species. Species differentiation is due to reproductive isolation which primarily results from geographical or behavioral isolating mechanisms.

A genus is a taxon containing various species. The genus is a different type of category than a species; it should contain several related species. The genus is often considered to be a natural unit of species closely related by descent.

Bibliography

Buettner-Janusch, J. 1973. *Physical anthropology: a perspective.* New York: Wiley.

Cain, A., and Harrison, G. 1960. Phyletic weighting. *Proceedings of the Zoological Society of London* 135:1.

Ehrlich, P. and Raven, P. 1969. Differentiation of populations. *Science* 165: 1229-32.

Ehrlich, P.; Holm, R.; and Parnell, D. 1974. *The process of evolution,* 2d ed. New York: McGraw-Hill.

Ender, J. 1973. Gene flow and population differentiation. *Science* 179:243-50.

Garn, S. 1971. The improper use of fossil nomenclature. *American Journal of Physical Anthropology* 35:217.

Huxley, J., ed. 1940. *The new systematics.* Oxford: Oxford University Press.

Mayr, E. 1969. *Principles of systematic zoology.* New York: McGraw-Hill.

Shaw, A. 1969. Adam and Eve, paleontology, and the non-objective arts. *Journal of Paleontology* 43 (September).

Simons, E. 1972. *Primate evolution.* New York: Macmillan.

Simpson, G. 1945. The principles of classification and a classification of mammals. *Bulletin of American Museum of Natural History* 85.

———. 1951. *The meaning of evolution.* New York: New American Library.

———. 1961. *Principles of animal taxonomy.* New York: Columbia University Press.

Sneath, P. and Sokal, R. 1973. *Numerical taxonomy.* San Francisco: W. H. Freeman.

Sokal, R. 1973. The species problem reconsidered. *Systematic Zoology* 22: 360-74.

Sokal, R., and Crovella, T. 1970. The biological species concept: a critical evaluation. *American Naturalist* 104: 127-53.

Sokal, R., and Sneath, P. 1963. *Principles of numerical taxonomy.* San Francisco: W. H. Freeman.

Solbrig, O. 1966. *Evolution and systematics.* New York: Macmillan.

Tobias, P. 1969. Bigeneric nomina: a proposal for modification of the rules of nomenclature. *American Journal of Physical Anthropology* 31:103.

Part Three
Reconstructing the Past:
Behavioral Studies

Many "human" interludes, flashes or episodes of behavior reminiscent of human behavior, occur in the daily lives of monkeys and apes. . . . Such similarities reflect the fact of continuity in human evolution. . . .

A great deal more could be learned from in-the-wild observations of species even more closely related to man. If ancestral hominids still roamed river valleys and savannas and coastal plains, say, bands like those whose traces are found in Bed I at the Olduvai Gorge or at Torralba-Ambrona, investigators could obtain firsthand records of early hunting methods and social organizations. In the absence of such bands, however, we ourselves can serve as subjects for research in living prehistory. We are all relics to some extent and, as such, provide a legitimate source of clues to the nature of prehistoric man. (From J. Pfeiffer, *The Emergence of Man.* New York: Harper & Row, Publishers, 1969, p. 309.)

Part Three
Reconstructing the Past:

Chapter 6
How We Know—Reconstructing the Past

This chapter would probably have seemed like a fictionalized tale to early twentieth-century anthropologists. Here and in the following chapters we review techniques and the subjects upon which much of the data presented in section II is based. We can tell much about our past from studying nonhuman primates, social carnivores, and elephants. There exist, in a greatly decimated state, populations living in much the same way our ancestors lived when they passed through the hunting-gathering stage on their way toward industrialization. We can use these sources in order to reconstruct our past.

Introduction

Lancaster (1975) notes that there are two lines of evidence which can be employed to reconstruct a species' evolutionary history. First, we have the fossil and archaeological record itself, that is, any traces of past behavior and bones of a species which have fortunately become preserved. All such relics are important clues in understanding and reconstructing what a species looked like and how it acted and lived its daily existence. This record, however, is always incomplete because it is based upon accidental preservation. More importantly, most aspects of behavior simply do not fossilize—and we are left to speculate. Vital questions about our behavior and social organization can, at best, only partially be solved by the fossil record. That we should seek this kind of information is indicative of the fact that behavioral changes, as well as anatomical changes, were important factors in our divergence from our pongid relatives.

Fortunately, there are some aids to help solve this dilemma, there are useful clues for reconstructing our behavioral past. These leads

Dr. Johanson excavating a mandible at Hadar, Ethiopia.

come from what is referred to as the *comparative method*. When we wish to understand our past we can find clues in three sources of living evidence: modern hunter-gatherers, nonhuman primates, and the social carnivores. Modern hunter-gatherers are most useful examples of a way of life which once characterized most of our evolutionary history. The **hunting-gathering** way of life differentiates us from the vegetarian nonhuman primates and the meat-eating social carnivores. Hunting and gathering was a way of life which probably characterized hominid evolution from the time of the Lower Pleistocene. Thus it is most important that we understand this way of life, and groups living today as hunter-gatherers are most important models.

The nonhuman primates provide a second source of evidence as a group of animals with which we are phylogenetically related. Generally, studies of nonhuman primates have concentrated on Old World species. Although we have not shared any genetic relationship with the Old World monkeys for more than 20 million years and diverged from the apes about 15-20 million years ago (or much less if one accepts the biochemical evidence of Sarich and Wilson),[1] this is a short period of time evolutionarily speaking. Studies of nonhuman primates are important keys in helping us understand the evolutionary background of many of our social behaviors, social systems, and the uniqueness and adaptability of some of our culturally-oriented behaviors.

The social carnivores have provided many clues to our evolutionary past, and this is referred to in Chapter 15. Since nonhuman primates are basically vegetarians or omnivores, the study of meat-eating, hunting carnivores provides insights into our way of life as we adapted to this new diet. When considering such factors as hunting methods, the size of the home range, and food-sharing behavior, we must turn to other meat-eating carnivores rather than to the nonhuman primates.

We are not going to argue that we are, or ever were, nothing more than social carnivores, or that modern nonhuman primates are a total reflection of our evolutionary past. It must be remembered that modern social carnivores and nonhuman primates have evolved, as have we, and that they can serve only as models. Furthermore, we have just as much to learn from these models when they provide us with negative answers, answers which show how different we are, as when they provide answers showing how much we have in common. If we find a behavioral characteristic differentiating us from these models, then we may be dealing with a behavior fundamental to hominid evolution. The more we know about the evolutionary history and adaptations of our phylogenetically related primate relatives and the ecologically related social carnivores, the more we learn about processes which shaped our evolutionary past. Quoting Lancaster (1975:5) "We can understand the whole of human nature if we appreciate both the ways in which we are like other forms of life and the ways in which we are unique."

Modern Hunter-Gatherers

Research Outlook. One of the most useful ways to test hypotheses about human evolution is to study modern populations living at a tech-

[1]See Chapter 13.

nological stage similar to human populations about 10,000 years B.C. Anthropologists have recently turned to modern hunting-gathering groups, not as living replicas of ancestral populations, and certainly not as living museum pieces, but as clues to a very old, basic life-style. Studies of the rapidly disappearing modern hunter-gatherers are important. A 1966 estimate notes 30,000 hunter-gatherers in a total population of 3.3 billion persons; since then the number has been further reduced. (A map showing the distribution of hunter-gatherers is found in Figure 6-1).

Past treatment of the hunter-gatherers has been deplorable. They were considered to be subhuman breeds with a lower mentality and they were missionized, dispossessed, hunted, slaughtered, fed poisoned food, and further exploited. Today we recognize such groups as remnants of what was once a vast population who by their remarkable adaptations to various environments offer many insights into our past experiences. They differ from us culturally; they live as we would probably live if we regarded nature similarly and had to adapt to similar conditions. Their societies differ technologically from ours; however,

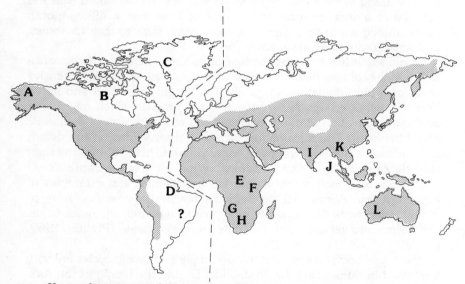

Known living sites of contemporary hunter-gatherers.

A	Eskimos, Alaska		Bantu, Angola
B	Eskimos, Northwest Territory	H	Kalahari Bushman, South Africa,
C	Eskimos, Greenland		Botswana
D	Akuri, Surinam	I	Birhar, Central India
E	Pygmies, Congo	J	Andaman Islanders, Andaman
F	Ariangulo, Tanzania		Island
	Boni, Tanzania	K	Rue, Thailand
	Sanye, Tanzania	L	Australian Aborigines, Australia
G	Koroka, Angola	?	Not verified

Figure 6-1. The world distribution of hunter-gatherers in 10,000 B.C. compared with the known living sites of contemporary hunter-gatherers. In 10,000 B.C. hunter-gatherers comprised 100 percent of the world population of 10 million. Contemporary hunter-gatherers comprise .001 percent of the 3 billion world population. Darkened areas = world distribution in 10,000 B.C. Letters = present distribution.

they offer many lessons to their more technologically advanced neighbors. A major effort is being expended towards the study of modern hunter-gatherers in this more enlightened intellectual spirit.

Besides the ever-present problem of funding anthropological research, anthropologists encounter other difficulties in studying hunter-gatherers in their natural way of life. Many governments make the hunter-gatherers' life unbearable. In 1960 visiting pediatricians from Makerere University proclaimed Hadza children among the healthiest in East Africa. However, most Hadza were recently forced to settle on a reservation where they lived in much closer contact with one another; within a year about a quarter of the children died from an epidemic.

Australian Aborigines. One of the first to attempt to study hunter-gathering peoples with this new perspective was Richard Gould (1968a, 1969), an archeologist then from the University of Hawaii. Dr. Gould worked in the Gibson Desert in western Australia with a two-family group of thirteen aborigines (three women, two men, and eight children). These were among the very few people in the world still making and using stone tools regularly.[2] Gould and his wife lived with this group and others for extended lengths of time over a fifteen-month period during which they learned the language, slept by their campsites, and walked with them in search of food.

Gould's investigation was the first of its kind, the first time a professional archaeologist had used his training in a systematic and intensive study of a hunting-gathering group. The Goulds observed and noted how aboriginal groups lived, collecting information which might bear on the interpretation of prehistoric sites and reconstruction of prehistoric social behavior. The information included observations on the details of toolmaking, hunting, camping, composition of living floors, and their very elaborate system of social behaviors, including religious practices.[3]

Gould's approach to aboriginal life has yielded vast quantities of important data. Above all it has yielded a new perspective. According to Gould, such work ". . . suggests new possibilities and analogies to us, and helps us to get unstuck for a limited range of ideas" (Pfeiffer, 1969, p.329).

Aboriginal society is close to nature; daily and yearly cycles are very important in influencing day-to-day life. During the height of the Australian summer (in December and January) a day begins just before sunup. Work (obtaining the daily sustenance) begins around six or seven, before it becomes unbearably hot. The group divides into two parties in search of food; everyone leaves camp. The women gather plant foods and may walk four or five miles with long wooden water bowls on their heads and nursing children on their hips or over their backs.

When the women are out collecting, men are hunting, which generally is a less dependable way of obtaining food in the desert. Hunting generally occurs from ambush; when possible, hunters take advantage of

Reconstructing
the Past:
Behavioral Studies

[2]A more recent example of such a group is the newly discovered Tasaday in the Philippines. Undoubtedly, our ravenous technological societies will uncover still more such groups. All efforts must be made to ensure that these highly vulnerable peoples are not prostituted to the whims of their more developed neighbors.

[3]Australian aborigines possess a complex set of religious beliefs and one of the most complex kinship systems known to modern scholars.

a water hole, hoping to ambush a thirsty emu, kangaroo, or wallaby. Women are more apt to provide the daily food (perhaps ngaru fruits, a pale green fruit the size of a small tomato) than the men. On most occasions all the men show for their efforts is a lizard or two. Roughly 60 to 70 percent of the aborigines' diet is plant food. Meat consists chiefly of lizards, rabbits, snakes, birds, and other small game.

The basis for the aborigines' remarkable adaptation to their rather harsh desert environment includes a technology familiar to a 30,000 year old toolmaker. A common aboriginal tool is the so-called "adz-flake," a thick tool with a fairly steep edge. This tool closely resembles the sort of scrapers common to many prehistoric sites, for example, the ground stone axes common to the Mesolithic about 10,000 years B.P. The aborigines use their teeth either as tools or for making some kinds of tools. The premolar teeth nibble flakes from stone; the teeth and supporting jaw structure are so strong that the aborigine can remove the top of a tin can by making successive bites along the rim. There are reasons to believe that Upper Paleolithic toolmakers similarly used their dental structure for tool manufacture.

The previous brief description of aborigine tooth use is an example of how a study of modern hunter-gatherers can also help us understand some of the morphological traits encountered in the fossil record. Since dental remains comprise a large proportion of our evidence, since a number of inferences are based upon dental wear patterns, it would be of use to note how modern populations use their teeth. For example, if the teeth are used as tools what types of wear patterns result? What types of wear patterns result from various types of diets? Can gritty diets affect the crown surfaces as is claimed for the robust variety of australopithecines? A study of dental use can also be helpful in understanding cranial morphology, e.g., does the use of the teeth as tools affect the masticatory musculature and surface features of the cranium or mandible? These questions can be raised from the fossil record and partly answered from the modern ethnographic record.

A basic implement of the aboriginal hunting kit is the spear thrower, a tool which also serves as a crude kind of archive, the closest thing to a written record among people who do not write. Decorations carved on wood have practical as well as religious and aesthetic meanings. Wavy and zigzag lines and a variety of geometric and irregular forms represent symbols of religous belief—a belief in what the aborigines call "dreamtime" when their ancestors, supernatural beings in the guise of humans and animals, rose and roamed the earth's surface and created the world.

The symbols decorating the spear throwers are personal symbols, meaning different things to different hunters. They may assist the hunter in firmly establishing in his mind the locations of sacred places and water holes upon which his life may depend. It is possible that the decorated spear throwers dating from the Magdalenian period of the Upper Paleolithic depicted similar things.

The Ainu. Another greatly reduced population is the Ainu, inhabiting Hokkaido island, Japan. Although some Ainu were still engaged in hunting-gathering until about twenty years ago, the Japanese government has been encouraging them to change their way of life since the 1880s. The government has been rather successful in forcing the Ainu to become farmers. Fortunately, a study by the Japanese anthropologist Hitoshi Watanabe (1972) and his associates has reconstructed their former way of life.

Basically, the Ainu live as our ancestors did in western Europe some 15,000 years ago. They settled in river valleys and geared their existence to nature's cycles, to the seasons and wanderings of migratory herds. The Ainu's habitat is cold and rather inhospitable at various times during the year. The manner in which the Ainu cope with the essential task of surviving in this habitat, particularly storing food for lean times and getting about in the snow, are useful examples for reconstructing the life of the European Neanderthals and Magdalenians. Based on his Ainu studies, Watanabe suggests that the Neanderthals may have only been able to follow their game across open tundra country where winds freeze and harden the snow cover. However, snowshoes, or some similar adaptation, are needed to move through the forests. That invention may not have come until the Magdalenian.

Kalahari Bushmen. A concentrated long-term effort is being expended to gather information on the Bushmen living in the Kalahari desert of Botswana. A group of Harvard scientists began the study in 1967, working under a grant from the National Institutes of Health. Approximately one-third of all existing hunter-gatherers (some 9000 persons) inhabit the Kalahari desert. The study group concentrated on the inhabitants of one small area of this 350,000 square mile expanse. The study area has a radius of less than twenty miles and is surrounded by vast stretches of waterless expanse. It includes eleven permanent water holes and wells, between 400 and 500 plant and animal species, and about 450 Bushmen.

The Harvard project investigated such topics as health, nutrition, family and group structure, child rearing, personal relationships, rituals, technology, and general ways of coping with the environment. Archaeologists with the project studied Bushman living floors, excavating them and asking explanations of what they uncovered, hoping to generate alternative interpretations for prehistoric living sites. Bushman garbage dumps were analyzed to see what kinds and amounts of accumulations were left. From this we hope to gather a clearer understanding of the many seemingly prehistoric "garbage dumps," e.g., how many people it took to accumulate the debris, how much, and what items are most likely to survive.

Much effort has been spent watching what Bushmen eat and their manner of obtaining food. Before the study it was assumed that the hunter-gatherer's life bordered on starvation and that the task of finding food was an all-consuming activity; for the Bushman, food gathering requires only a bare minimum of equipment; the basic tools include a pair of unworked hammerstones for cracking nuts and a digging stick. The most important item is the "kaross," a combination garment and receptacle made of antelope hide draped over the woman's shoulder. Into the pocket formed by draping they stuff food, such as nuts, berries, and roots, and their children.[4] Obtaining meat protein is a much harder task requiring a more complicated tool assemblage; however, the Bushman is an excellent hunter and trapper.

[4]One of the first tools which prehistoric populations developed may have been some sort of carrying device.

Richard Lee, one of the anthropologists on the project, measured the success which one group had in the food quest. Lee made a detailed twenty-eight-day study of a group averaging thirty persons. During this period, meat comprised 37 percent of the diet, mongongo nuts 33 percent, and other vegetables about 30 percent. Enough food was provided daily to ensure each group member 1.4 pounds of food, or some 2140 calories, about 154 calories more than the basic daily requirement. Furthermore, obtaining food is only a part-time job occupying from one to three days per week.[5] The rest of the week is spent resting, gossiping, and playing games. (While the four-day work week is still only an American worker's dream, a one- to three-day work week is the Bushman's reality.) It should be emphasized that these figures are from a poor year; foraging achievements would have been more remarkable in better times. This picture discounts the idea that all hunting-gathering peoples, people who own few worldly possessions, are impoverished, long-suffering, pitiful, and malnourished.

A study was made of Bushman productivity in relation to their land. With their present tools and knowledge, and at their present population level, Bushmen could not exceed a daily fuel supply of 3200 calories — no matter how hard they worked. The Bushman has achieved 60 percent of a theoretical maximum production level with few technological advantages. The Bushman model may be a reflection of basic forces and relationships encountered in the study of all communities, at all technological levels. An analysis of Bushman economics is being attempted in the hope of generating a broad mathematically based theory which can be applied to world problems far more complex than that of the Kalahari. Such a theory may permit planners to predict more precisely the impact of new programs in industry, public health, and education on the course of social development.

Studies of Bushman social behavior and organization are also being undertaken. A study is being made of the choice of living sites; hopefully we will get a clearer idea of living-floor patterns found at long-deserted sites. Lee studied the factors which force people to move from one camp to another and found that Bushman groups typically occupy a camp for weeks and months before they literally eat their way out of it. Such very basic data may help explain some of the migrations of prehistoric populations.

Summary. Answers to some of the questions we might ask about long-forgotten prehistoric peoples can possibly be answered by studying modern hunter-gatherers. Modern hunter-gatherers may provide a clue to the dynamics of the band existence of prehistoric peoples. Certainly they provide more insight than mere idle speculation. Studies of hunter-gatherers may provide clues to why our complicated lives sometimes give way; from the so-called primitive societies we may learn lessons which better enable us to cope with our technological societies.

Studies of other hunting-gathering societies have also been undertaken. One result of such studies is the establishment of the so-called

[5]Actually the figures reflect more efficiency, for the providers manage enough food for themselves plus dependents, i.e., individuals under fifteen and over sixty. These ages comprise one-third of the groups and contribute little or nothing to the larder. Furthermore, 8 percent of the 248 hunter-gatherers in the area were 60 to more than 80 years old.

"magic numbers" idea proposed about fifteen years ago by a U.C.L.A. anthropologist Dr. Joseph Birdsell (1972). Dr. Birdsell, studying rates of population growth among Australian aborigines, noted that band size ranged from twenty to fifty persons. He selected twenty-five as a representative size. Since, studies of Kalahari Bushmen and the Birhar of northern India have provided data to support the number twenty-five as being an average group size. From these figures we postulate that prehistoric populations probably averaged close to twenty-five members per band; supporting evidence comes from some prehistoric living-floors. While there is nothing absolute about this number, it may represent an equilibrium number. The number twenty-five may have something to do with the most efficient working groups of adult males and is consistent with the range of primate groups generally.

There is a second "magic number," 500, which is placed as an average for a "dialect" tribe of hunter-gatherers, that is, a group all speaking the same dialect. This is a purely human phenomenon and holds not only for aborigines but for the Shoshoni of the Great Plains and the Andaman Islanders in the Bay of Bengal. Interestingly, an architect's rule of thumb states that the capacity of an elementary school should not exceed 500 pupils if the principal expects to know them all by name.

Nonhuman Primates (Figure 6-2)

As creatures most closely related to us, nonhuman primates have been studied from various angles for many years. Most early work was bio-medical and only comparatively recently has behavioral research become a major component of nonhuman primate studies. Within the last century, largely within the past twelve to fifteen years, we have turned to the study of our primate relatives for what they may ultimately teach us about ourselves; past, present and in the future. These new findings have had an impact upon our reconstruction of hominid behavior and may ultimately alter our current behavior by offering insights into our actions.

The study of primate social behavior is one of the most rapidly growing and exciting fields in the behavioral sciences. The growth of and fascination in such studies owes much to the fact that primates, because of their special relationship to us, have attracted the attention of many disciplines — anthropology, psychiatry, psychology, biomedical fields, zoology, etc. Each discipline varies in the extent and vigor of its involvement in the study of primate social behavior and each offers something different in terms of perspective, theory, content, or method. No single discipline dominates the field. This is a mixed blessing. Primate studies provide a new approach to comparative animal behavior which cuts across traditional boundaries and accommodates many disciplines under one roof.

It is not easy to conduct a study of nonhuman primates in the natural setting. The investigator must be many things at once; psychologist, anthropologist, zoologist, botanist, geneticist, animal lover, and above all, a very patient individual. It was originally assumed that if you've seen one monkey, you've seen them all, but now we know this is a very inaccurate assumption. Our research has centered on a few primates in various parts of the world. We know something about the prosimians

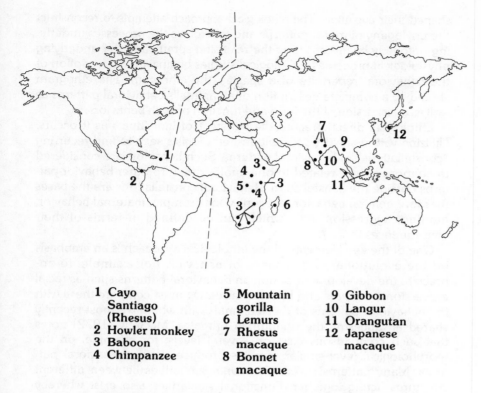

1 Cayo
  Santiago
  (Rhesus)
2 Howler monkey
3 Baboon
4 Chimpanzee

5 Mountain
  gorilla
6 Lemurs
7 Rhesus
  macaque
8 Bonnet
  macaque

9 Gibbon
10 Langur
11 Orangutan
12 Japanese
  macaque

Figure 6-2. Survey of studies of nonhuman primates.

on the island of Madagascar, a fair amount about some South American monkeys, a good bit about such Old World monkeys as baboons, macaques, and some leaf-eaters, and a fair share about apes. However, we know little or nothing about the behavior of most members of the Order Primates. We hope that the information we now have on a very few is fairly representative of some aspects of primate behavior and social organization.

The study of primate behavior is still in the gathering stage; premature theories were proposed, only to be retracted when more data accumulated or when research showed that primates differ from one another. We still propose theories, only now they are less sweeping, based on more data, and hopefully tested by field and laboratory study. Primate research follows various strategies; the least complicated treats the nonhuman primate as a human model as in biomedical research. Another approach, one with which anthropologists are more familiar, is the evolutionary-comparative perspective which uses living nonhuman primates as a means of looking into our past, for deciphering evolutionary trends in human behavior. Exercising great care, failing to fall prey to obvious conclusions, we can view living primates as prehistoric mirrors of ourselves.

Behavioral observation of the sort normally conducted by anthropologists, psychologists, and zoologists in the field is called ethology. The observer, the ethologist, searches for the functions of the observed behavior patterns trying to understand what selection pressures have shaped their evolution. The ethological approach attempts to reconstruct the phylogeny of motor patterns and to explore the processes underlying ontogeny by investigating the releasing stimuli and the underlying physiological processes. Ethological studies begin with a description of the behavioral repertoire of a species, the ethogram. The ethogram should be a complete description of an animal's behavioral patterns as well as a discussion of the form and function of such behaviors.

Ethologists directly record the behavior of individuals as it occurs. Utilizing various analytic techniques, ethologists seek to find recurring "constellations" of behavioral patterns. Such behaviors are considered to be more closely related to one another than to other behavior patterns outside the constellation. Behavioral constellations are the bases for more general behavior categories, for example, maternal behavior, hunting, aggression, etc., which can be defined in terms of their consequences.

One of the key elements of the ethological approach is an emphasis on the evolutionary significance of behavior. For example, to appreciate the development of human behavioral patterns such as facial expressions, gestures and body postures, we must compare these with the behavioral patterns of those animals with whom we most recently shared an ancestry, the nonhuman primates. McGrew (1972) notes that such comparisons exist on several levels; for example, on the morphological level similar muscles produce similar behavioral patterns. Many patterns show operational similarities between different structures acting together. Functional similarities also exist whereby interpersonal sequences of behavioral patterns may result in similar social consequences. Finally, situational similarities occur; for example, pushing and pulling commonly occur in aggressive situations. One could list a host of human and nonhuman primate behavioral patterns which are comparable.

Ethologists are also concerned with comparing the behavior of different populations of the same species. This intraspecific comparison provides an indication of the species' adaptability to different habitat requirements; such adaptability is considered important as one ascends the phylogenetic ladder.

Why Observe? The purposes of naturalistic primate studies have been consistent—to collect meaningful and accurate data which will advance our knowledge and understanding of the complex behavior of primates, including ourselves. There has been a continuity of effort to observe and describe both similarities and differences characteristic of nonhuman primates. Attempts have been made to conduct systematic studies of all observable modalities of behavior at the same time we seek plausible explanations or descriptions of behavioral determinants.

Field studies of the last few years have provided a new appreciation of the variety and complexity of primate social behavior. These investigations demonstrate the remarkable variability of social behavior. Primate studies have made major contributions to behavioral science and it is significant that the potential of scientific knowledge about primate behavior remaining to be tapped greatly exceeds that already achieved.

Field studies of monkeys and apes have added considerably to our understanding of hominid evolution. For example, Dr. Phyllis Jay (1968:487-88) has noted:

A great deal can be learned from the bones that comprise our fossil records, but the life of ancient primates comprised much more than the obvious function of these bony parts. For example, a certain kind of roughened surface on a fossilized ischium (the seat) merely indicates that the primate has ischial callosities. But by looking at how living primates with these callosities behave it is possible to infer that in all likelihood the ancient animal slept sitting up rather than on its side in a nest. This may seem trivial, but when many such clues are gathered and collated, the total picture of an animal's way of life fills in to a closer approximation of what it must have been.

Our ancestors were not the same as the living primates, but the rich variability of behavior of modern monkeys and apes makes it possible to reconstruct the most probable pattern of related forms in the past.

Studies of nonhuman primates in their habitats already have resulted in the following suggestions about what life probably was like for our ancestors (Washburn and Moore, 1974):

1. Our life was probably always social, for almost all monkeys and apes live in social groups. Social behavior seems to be deeply rooted in our evolutionary past.
2. Our daily life was restricted to a certain area. Today, primates live in limited ranges, closely coordinated with food, water, and safe sleeping areas and escape routes. The size of the range varies greatly according to the amount and distribution of resources, among other variables. As long as our ancestors were primates, they were restricted to narrow ranges. By the time they became hunters, they roamed over wider areas. This assumption is supported by the social carnivore data.
3. In many species of monkeys and apes the female is sexually receptive only during relatively short time periods. Loss of the estrous cycle, the time of sexual receptivity, may have provided an evolutionary advantage by reducing the fighting and tension that the sexual cycle often produces in nonhuman primates. Humans are the only primates that are theoretically sexually receptive twenty-four hours a day, 365 days a year.
4. In the wild monkeys rarely are observed using tools or, better stated, manipulating objects. When they do so, it is usually done to exhibit antagonism. (For a review of such tool use refer to Beck, 1975.)

Characteristics of Nonhuman Primate Societies

Most monkeys and apes live well-organized lives in social groups organized according to rules established on the basis of age, sex, and relative dominance. These groups are characterized by group cooperation, status differentiation, a rather complex communication system, and social traditions. Some nonhuman primates are **territorial** and some exhibit the rudiments of tool-using and toolmaking. Against this background, culture (the human social milieu) is clearly a greatly elaborated expression of the primate way of life. Its distinctly human hallmark is language.

Monkey and ape societies have certain unique traits differentiating them from other animal societies. For the most part, they are permanent, year-round bisexual organizations as opposed to the seasonal, sometimes unisexual groupings of many other social animals. In contrast to many other mammalian groups wherein the mother rears her young exclusively, the primate infant is raised and socialized within the stable social group (although socialization is still primarily left to the females). Social behavior is the key to understanding primate life. Because of the highly social nature of nonhuman primates we must view natural groups, as well as individuals, as the adaptive units of the species (Figure 6-3).

Social living places a premium upon learning. Many less intelligent animals, such as birds and fish, have social behaviors, but these are largely dependent on fixed and innate cues. For example, without having been taught, young herring gulls will peck at the red spot on the beak of their mother, who responds by releasing the food to the infant. On the other hand, primates respond not only to fixed cues, but to subtle variances. Since there is great individual and behavioral variability, a nonhuman primate must be flexible and discriminating in its response. One highly important adaptive trait common to nonhuman primates is their degree of flexibility and adaptability.

In a previous paper (Poirier, 1969:130-31), I noted:

Because much of primate behavior results from a sizeable learning component, and learning may not be transferable to all segments of the population, we must be prepared to find and report intertroop behavioral variability. For this reason intraspecific comparative studies are imperative before it can be stated with any degree of confidence whether a particular behavioral pattern or mode of social organization characteristic of one particular social group also typifies the genus or even the species.

And,

To understand the habitat shift which occurred in Pliocene times, we must be cognizant of the behavioral background of the higher primates. This successful habitat shift obviously involved behavioral plasticity, e.g., the ability to adapt to new surroundings, and a constant curiosity leading to the acquisition of new traits meeting the challenge of the habitat. Nonhuman primates are endowed with the ability to meet such a challenge. Behavioral flexibility ..., was probably the essential trait allowing these qualities to develop.

The importance of the fact that most primates are social animals residing in highly complex, year-around social groups of varying size and composition is crucial. The social group has long been the primate niche; indeed, the social group has long been the mammalian niche. Group characteristics vary, and the degree of sociality, dominance, sexuality, and interanimal relationships varies; however, most primates spend part of their life in close association with conspecifics (see Figure 6-3). Within the social group an animal learns to adapt to its surroundings. Differences among primate societies depend upon the species'

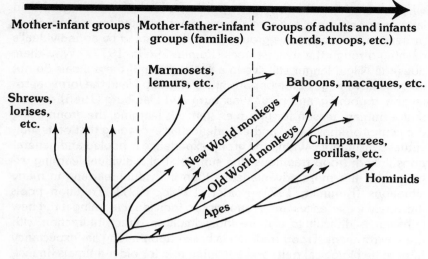

Increasing social complexity

Mother-infant groups | Mother-father-infant groups (families) | Groups of adults and infants (herds, troops, etc.)

Marmosets, lemurs, etc.

Baboons, macaques, etc.

Shrews, lorises, etc.

New World monkeys

Old World monkeys

Chimpanzees, gorillas, etc.

Apes

Hominids

Figure 6-3. Trends in primate social evolution. (This chart is incomplete and does not represent all the forms which could be listed.)

biology, and to a great extent upon the circumstances in which animals live and learn. The composition of the social group, the particular balance of interanimal relationships, constitutes the character of the social environment within which youngsters learn and mature. Because of the highly social nature of nonhuman primates we must view groups, as well as individuals, as the adaptive units of the species.

Since most primates live a rather complex social life, they must learn to adjust to one another, they must learn to get along; compared to most of the rest of the animal world primate societies may have the greatest differentiation of *learned* social roles. The primate brain is a complex and efficient learning mechanism, and Diamond and Hall (1969) specify the mammalian association cortex as the neocortex subdivision where prime evolutionary advancements have occurred. Some (e.g., Radinsky, 1975) would disagree, however. Although primate learning skills are not solely accountable by the volume of the neocortex relative to total brain volume, it is significant that the primate neocortex is proportionally larger than is true for carnivores and rodents (Harman, 1957). The complex cognitive processes and advanced learning skills are accommodated by increased cortical fissuration, increased numbers of cortical units in the cortex fine structure, and the refinement of the subcortical structure interrelating the thalmus and cortex (Norback and Moskowitz, 1963; Rumbaugh, 1970).

Social living is requisite for the young primate to perform effectively as an adult of its species. Animals with restricted social experiences, for example those raised in isolation or in unnatural conditions, exhibit some degree of social maladjustment, most especially in mothering, sexual, grooming, and aggressive behavioral patterns (Mason, 1960, 1961a,b, 1963). Laboratory studies suggest that the full development of an animal's biological potentialities requires stimulus and direction from social forces such as are usually supplied from the social group (Harlow, 1963, 1965; Mason, 1963, 1965).

While troop, or social life is important, it must be cautioned that not all primates have the "same degree" of social life. Amongst Nilgiri langurs, for example, social relations are not oriented toward individual protection by cooperative group action, but instead by an individual's dashing through the nearest trees (Poirier, 1969a, 1977).[6] Why, then, does the Nilgiri langur still live in a social group if the animals do not take full advantage of the opportunities of group life in the form of protection, grooming, and play? Washburn and Hamburg (1965) suggest that a primary reason for group existence is learning, the group being the center of knowledge and experience far exceeding that of its individual constituents. Within the group experience is pooled and generations linked; troop traditions (the sum total of individual learning experiences) are more advantageous than individual learning in many situations (Kummer, 1971; Poirier, 1972c, 1977). Tradition pools individual experiences and is superior to individual learning if the new behavior is difficult to acquire individually in direct interaction with the environment. Troop tradition is based upon a long life expectancy (a primate biological trait) and a leading role for older animals (in fact, primate societies may be viewed as gerontocracies).

Within the social context the animal is socialized, learns what foods to eat, who existing predators are, and the correct mode of behavioral interaction. Primates learn their mode of survival by living in a troop where they benefit from the shared knowledge and experience of the species (Poirier, 1970a, 1971). The primary reinforcement for all normal primate learning is the social context, the group in which the infant is born and nurtured. Even sensorimotor activities like observing, manipulating, and exploring indicative of individual independence receive some facilitation, or inhibition, from the group setting. Contrasting group social structures impose differences in learning patterns leading to individual behavior formation and imply that group modification will alter the socialization process, yielding individuals with different behaviors (Poirier, 1972; 1973b, 1977; Sugiyama, 1972).

Learning to be flexible and adaptable, learning to exist and coexist within the social context, learning one's role in the social order, is at an optimum for primates. Primates inherit an ease of learning, rather than fixed instinctive patterns; they easily, almost inevitably, learn behaviors essential for survival. Primates learn to be social, but they are so constructed that under normal circumstances learning almost always occurs (Washburn and Hamburg, 1965). Presumably in most higher mammalian systems, and particularly in primate social systems, individual behaviors are controlled by a continuous process of social learning arising from group interactional patterns. Learning to act according to social modes is extremely important, for animals whose behavioral traits do not conform sufficiently to group norms are less likely to reproduce and may be ejected. Social selection of this type apparently has a strong stabilizing influence upon the genetic basis of temperamental traits and motivational thresholds, for Crook (1970) suggests that primate societies might determine the genetic basis of individual social responses.

[6]An analogous situation is found among patas (Hall, 1968) and their social organization shows many similarities to that of the Nilgiri langur.

Learning during socialization and the emergence of one's social role has a preponderant influence in shaping individual behavior. Social conformity and the maintenance of a group structure results from the adoption of traditional behaviors characteristic of the total social system. This is primarily accomplished by three interacting groups of factors (Crook, 1970); (1) the species repertoire of biologically programmed neonate reflexes and social signals, plus innate factors affecting temperament and tendencies to learn some responses more readily than others; (2) the behavior of individuals comprising the social milieu, which partly controls the emergence of individual role playing; and (3) direct environmental effects, i.e., availability of need-reducing commodities and consequent behavioral learning that exploits the world in the manner ensuring greatest individual survival.

Brief History of Primate Studies

Pre- and Early 1900s. Perusal of the nonhuman primate behavior literature over the last forty years clearly indicates major research trends. In the late 1920s and 1930s a three month observation period was considered sufficient; now anything less than one calendar year is inadequate and even this is the minimum. During the early years, pre- and immediately post-Darwin, anecdotal accounts were given great credit. Many accepted the following account as truth. As soon as a howler monkey (a South American monkey) is wounded, so this story goes, its fellows gather round, and place their fingers in the wound,

as if they were desirous of sounding its depth. If the blood then flows in any quantity, they keep it shut up, while others get leaves, which they chew and thrust into the orifice. I can affirm having seen this circumstance several times with admiration (Zuckerman, 1963: 10).

A very readable account of the early fascination, and disgust, which humans felt towards their nonhuman primate relatives is found in Desmond and Ramona Morris's book *Men and Apes*.

Prior to the twentieth century, our knowledge of nonhuman primate behavior was anecdotal and consisted mainly of travellers' tales and miscellaneous reports. Sometimes the further from the truth, the more absurd the report, the greater credibility it seemed to have. Apart from the mythological literature surrounding some of the primates, volumes of pseudo-scientific material existed.

Dr. R. Yerkes. Due to the efforts of the late Dr. Robert M. Yerkes of Yale University, the 1920s witnessed the beginning of scientific research into nonhuman primate behavior. Yerkes never entered the jungle to study primates; he watched his chimpanzees climb trees in his backyard in New Hampshire. In 1929 the Yerkes published their important book entitled *The Great Apes: A Study of Anthropoid Life*. In this 652 page book (including the bibliography), he and his wife compiled all then-known facts about the great apes. Yerkes was amazed how little factual information existed, so in 1929 and 1930 he sent two students to Africa—Bingham to study the gorilla and Nissen to study the chimpanzee. In 1930 Yerkes opened the famed Laboratories of Primate Biology at Orange Park, Florida, which since moved to Emory University in Atlanta and has been renamed the Yerkes Regional Primate Research Center.

Dr. C. R. Carpenter. The first major breakthrough in primate field studies came in 1934 when the late Dr. C. R. Carpenter spent two years studying Central American howler monkeys on Barro Colorado Island. Barro Colorado Island (B.C.I.) is situated in the midst of Gatun Lake and was formed with the building of the Panama Canal. Carpenter's work on Barro Colorado Island stands as an early monument of scientific methodology. From here Carpenter went on to study other primates and eventually established the rhesus monkey colony at Cayo Santiago (Santiago Island) off the eastern coast of Puerto Rico. Carpenter and Yerkes were interested in primate studies for their own sake; they studied animals in their natural settings just to know something about the animals.

Sir S. Zuckerman. The English zoologist, Sir Solly Zuckerman, founded a second tradition, that of studying nonhuman primates because they can tell us something about ourselves. In 1933 Zuckerman travelled to South Africa to study chacma baboons inhabiting the cliffs near Cape Town. He also studied the hamadrayas baboons held captive in the London Zoo. His studies led him to postulate a sweeping theory of the beginning of human social behavior. Zuckerman argued that sexual behavior (the prolonged willingness on the part of the female to mate) was the original social force binding the primate social group. This theory was ultimately rejected in the late 1950s and early 1960s when it was discovered, on the basis of other baboon studies, that nonhuman primates actually partake in little sexual behavior. Furthermore, sexual behavior can actually be a disruptive force rather than a cohesive bond and in many species is seasonal and all troop members may not be involved. On the other hand, Saayman (1975) has recently resurrected Zuckerman's hypothesis. Saayman does argue for the binding force of sexual behavior. The best position presently is to recognize that there are pros and cons on both sides of the argument.

Dr. W. Köhler. During World War II, Dr. Wolfgang Köhler researched "insight learning" among chimpanzees; his are the famous experiments of chimpanzees stacking boxes to obtain bananas. Köhler began a third tradition in primate research, modern primate psychology, which studied the abilities and limitations of higher primate reasoning. As an outgrowth of this tradition, chimpanzees and gorillas were brought into one's home where their development was compared to one's own child. Such studies are recalled in C. Hayes's book *The Ape in Our House,* A. M. Hoyt's highly readable book *Toto and I: A Gorilla in the Family,*[7] the Kelloggs' book *The Ape and the Child,* and Temerlin's *Lucy: Growing Up Human.*

Japanese Colonies. Immediately following World War II Japanese primatologists developed a tradition of primate studies which changed many of our concepts about primate social organization and behavior. The Japanese established **provisioned colonies** of the indigenous Japanese macaque. Free-ranging colonies were artificially supplied food and these provisioned troops in various parts of Japan have been studied over the past twenty years.

[7]As an example of the problems one can encounter in this approach, let us refer to the episode at the Hoyt's house recounted on pp. 85 and 86.

Drs. S. Washburn and I. DeVore. In the late 1950s Dr. S. Washburn and Dr. I. DeVore travelled to East Africa to conduct a study of savanna-dwelling baboons. This study led the way in discounting Zuckerman's "sexual bond" hypothesis. Washburn and DeVore hoped they would discover something about our savanna-dwelling ancestors during the Lower Pleistocene; baboons were used as models for deciphering early hominid social behavior and organization.

Facilities for Primate Research. Primate behavior is generally studied under the following conditions: in any of the seven National Primate Research Centers,[8] in semi-natural provisioned colonies established at Cayo Santiago, Puerto Rico, or Barro Colorado, Canal Zone, in the provisioned colonies at the Japan Monkey Centre, or under strictly natural field conditions where the scientist gets whatever information can be collected. The research is determined by the type of information one wishes to gather and by one's training. Historically, psychologists have worked in laboratory conditions which allow testing of specific hypotheses in a strictly controlled environment and long-term observation of individual animals and/or problems. Work with the introduced provisioned colonies and at the Japan Monkey Centre provides access to genealogically known animals. Investigators at such facilities have kept meticulous records which supply the much needed depth perspective sorely missing from feral studies. Field-oriented scientists, anthropologists and zoologists, are most apt to work in the natural settings.

The natural setting is the appropriate situation to investigate such problems as the relationship of behavior to population pressure, predator pressure, and social structure. The laboratory is the place for answering specific questions often raised in the field, which need a controlled testing situation. Space is a major problem in the artificial colonies; crowding leads to an exaggeration of such patterns as aggression and sexual behavior—for lack of something better to do.[9] Because of an artificial food supply there is relatively unrestricted population growth and unusually large troop sizes. The provisioned colonies at Cayo Santiago and the Japan Monkey Centre have reacted to overcrowding by group fission, that is, the monkeys divide into smaller groups, usually along kinship lines. This in itself is an interesting social phenomenon.

Future Primate Studies. Future primate studies (and many now under way) will be long-range, topic oriented research projects. The one calendar year study will give way (if money becomes available) to two or three year studies by a multidisciplinary team. These studies will be more problem oriented and deal with specific topics such as socialization, adaptation to the habitat, and predator avoidance. Since it is now clear that there is much variability among free-ranging, undisturbed primate populations, and since we know there are substantial differences between and within species, we can expect that more species from a wider ecological range will be studied. There will also be

[8]Each center is primarily affiliated with at least one university. The centers include the Beaverton center, Beaverton, Oregon (University of Oregon); Davis center (University of California, Davis); New England center (Harvard University); Washington center (University of Washington); Wisconsin center (University of Wisconsin); Yerkes center (Emory University); and the Delta center (Tulane University).

[9]Can parallels be found in our crowded penal institutions or in cities?

more studies of the same species in different habitats to see what influence habitat has upon social organization and behavior. Past studies have offered leads about the future; the future will tell how true these leads have been.

Caution. Modern primates are not exact representatives of our way of life millions of years ago. Nonhuman primates have evolved. They are the end product, as are we, of millions of years of evolution. However, while there are problems with reconstructing hominid behavior patterns from nonhuman primates, the method is still very valuable. An analysis of modern monkey and ape behavior has made it possible to reconstruct some of the early stages of human development; later phases may require a different approach.

The Social Carnivores

Have you ever thought that we might learn a good deal about ourselves, about our evolutionary past, from watching the lion, tiger, hyena, or wild dog? Until recently few anthropologists and others involved with reconstructing human evolution did. A study by Dr. G. Schaller and Dr. G. Lowther of some of Africa's social carnivores changed that notion. In 1969 they published a joint article entitled "The Relevance of Carnivore Behavior to the Study of Early Hominids." While the search for clues about our past among nonhuman primates is reasonable on phylogenetic grounds, it is less so on ecological grounds. Social systems are strongly influenced by the habitats in which they appear. Monkeys and apes are essentially vegetarians living in groups confined to small ranges; however, we assume our ancestors were widely roaming hunters and gatherers for perhaps two million years of our evolutionary history. This way of life is in strong contrast to that of modern nonhuman primates. Schaller and Lowther concluded that more could be learned about the genesis of our social systems by studying phylogenetically unrelated but ecologically similar forms than by studying nonhuman primates. Social carnivores were the obvious choice. Some selective pressures influencing the social existence of social carnivores also had an effect on human societies. In Chapter 15 we follow the Schaller and Lowther approach. I refer the reader there.

Social carnivores, plus such gnawing rodents as the porcupine, are being studied in another light. Some investigators are watching what animals such as leopards eat, and are especially interested in the remains of a meal. Which bones are eaten, which are left behind, and the state of the leftovers are all important clues which allow us to decide whether bone accumulations are those of an ancient hominid or of an ancient carnivore. Porcupine burrows are being excavated in an attempt to see which bones such rodents store and how they eat these bones. The reasoning is the same—a more scientific approach to determine which are human and which are nonhuman bone accumulations. This approach provides a practical analysis of Dart's proposed australopithecine osteodontokeratic culture. Some of the questions which arise are: were the South African accumulations left by australopithecines, were they remains of a social carnivore's meal, or were they just some hungry porcupine's debris?

Other Clues — Elephants

Dr. John Eisenberg, from the Smithsonian Institute, studied the Ceylon elephant hoping to learn more about ourselves. We share with the elephant a similar life span and a record of having been able to coexist rather peacefully, at least until recently. Elephants have a basic social unit centered around a pregnant female, a female and her offspring closely associated with another female, often her mother or sister, with about the same number of offspring. Bulls (males) of twenty to thirty years live in less cohesive groups which are occasionally accompanied by one to three "satellite" males, eleven to fourteen years old. The oldest bulls, males aged forty or more, often travel alone.

During dry periods large elephant herds, some containing over 300 animals, may form loosely organized groups. Eisenberg has used this situation to test the idea that "when an animal like man or the elephant attains a certain body size and brain size, it is capable of unique memory feats" (quoted in Pfeiffer, 1972:336). Migration may mean moving over any one of a number of complicated routes, travelling long distances, and avoiding villages. This requires a considerable grasp of knowledge, of intelligence.

The elephant's environment also has a ten-year drought cycle which requires memorization of additional data which must be retained for a decade or more and then be recalled during a crisis situation. The elephant's size apparently not only provides it with predator protection; it also pays off in terms of proportionate brain size and memory capacity which permits shaping long-term survival strategies. Research on elephants may be expected to increase the understanding of the role of memory in human evolution.

The Hoyts settled in Havana, in a large house with extensive grounds. The early years were quite obviously delightful, although already, at three years of age, Toto "had the strength of a man, and the ingenuity of a dozen boys." With her growing strength, Toto was able to wreck the house. If she failed to open a door by the latch, she simply pushed, and crashed through it. Lady guests were usually terrified. So the Hoyts built Toto a special apartment in the garden, consisting of two rooms, and an outdoor enclosure covered with tropical vines for shade. A large iron bedstead, with a barred roof which could be locked on at night, was fastened to the floor, because Toto had once used the bedstead as a weapon against her keeper.

But Toto grew out of childhood, and could not control her strength. She could not understand why, when she pushed Mrs. Hoyt in play, her beloved foster mother fell backward onto the flagstones, breaking both her wrists. Toto was ashamed, and for long after the wrists were healed she took them from time to time in her hands and examined them and kissed them gently.

Powerful instincts took hold of Toto now and then, instincts to display wildly when excited, but in her human environment this was dangerous for property and persons. Toto developed hatreds of certain members of the large staff of servants and gardeners, and some of the dogs. Drastic incidents happened, and were tolerated by Mrs. Hoyt's household because of the love the Hoyts bore for Toto, and she for them.

For example, the gorilla, who by now was gigantic, pursued a terrified gardener up his ladder, so that he had to leap off. She picked up a small Japanese servant in her great arms, carried the terrified man to the top of her enclosure, and dropped him.

Tomas now had to be equipped with an electric prod, leather sheaths to protect his arms from bites, and a snake curled up in a bag around his waist, as this was the only thing that terrified Toto into submission if she was feeling rebellious. He had a wooden shield put up in Toto's room so that he could escape behind it, like a bullfighter, when Toto started throwing furniture. Tomas also had a whistle to blow when Toto went on a "spree," meaning on a destructive rampage. When he blew it, all the servants fled into the house, the doors were bolted, and the windows were fastened.

Tomas even had to surround Toto's bed with a hedge of thorn branches with a small gap through which he could drive her, sometimes with blazing rags, into her bed, while he got the roof fastened down on her. However, throughout the story runs the thread of the great affection between Toto and Mrs. Hoyt. For Toto was not always wild and rebellious. While Mr. and Mrs. Hoyt were on a holiday trip to New York, Mr. Hoyt died, and his wife, numb with grief, returned to Havana alone. When she went to see Toto, the gorilla greeted her and looked beyond her to find Mr. Hoyt. She looked puzzled. Then she took Mrs. Hoyt's hand, and gently led her into the house and through all the rooms looking for Mr. Hoyt. Not finding him, she led Maria out again, round the chicken houses and garden sheds, and finally into all the cars in the garage. At this point, Mrs. Hoyt began to weep uncontrollably. Toto gently wiped her eyes, kissed her, and embraced her.

But matters got worse. Grocery boys threw their deliveries over the wall because they were too scared to enter. Even Maria had to be prepared at all times for Toto's mood to undergo a sudden change, for without warning, the gorilla "would stand to full height and charge like an angry bull, with such speed that the only way to avoid being hit, was to fall to the ground and roll away." Sometimes she would seize Maria by the arms or part of her dress, and drag her for yards over the lawn or walk, or through a sand pile. Mrs. Hoyt and Tomas developed a technique of falling limply or of wrapping themselves around trees when out for a walk in the grounds with Toto.

Used by permission from V. Reynolds, 1967. *The Apes.* New York: E.P. Dutton and Company, Inc.

What traditionalist would have suspected that in the 1960s and 1970s in order to learn about our past we would be studying nonhuman primates, feeding leopards, crawling into hyena dens, excavating porcupine burrows, and watching elephants? It is happening and there is no telling what we may study tomorrow. We have reached the point where we are open-minded enough to try anything which may provide clues to our past. We are finally reaching the ultimate in evolutionary theory; we are using all the information at hand to reconstruct and form a theory of primate evolution.

Bibliography

Ardrey, R. 1966. *The territorial imperative.* New York: Dell.

———. 1968. *African genesis.* New York: Dell.

———. 1970. *The social contract.* New York: Atheneum.

Beck, B. 1975. Primate tool behavior. In *Socioecology and psychology of primates,* edited by R. Tuttle, pp.413-47. The Hague: Mouton.

Birdsell, J. 1972. *Human evolution.* Chicago: Rand McNally.

Carpenter, C. 1964. *Naturalistic behavior of nonhuman primates.* University Park: Pennsylvania State University Press.

Carthy, J., and Ebling, F., eds. 1964. *The natural history of aggression.* New York: Academic Press.

Chance, M., and Jolly, C. 1970. *Social groups of monkeys, apes and men.* London: Jonathan Cape.

Chapple, E. 1970. *Culture and biological man.* New York: Holt, Rinehart and Winston.

Cohen, Y., ed. 1968. *Man in adaptation—the biosocial background.* Chicago: Aldine.

Crook, J., ed. 1970. *Social behavior in birds and mammals.* New York: Academic Press.

Darling, F. 1964. *A herd of red deer.* New York: Doubleday.

Diamond, S., and Hall, W. 1969. Evolution of the neocortex. *Science* 164: 251-62.

Eibl-Eibesfeldt, I. 1970. *Ethology—the biology of behavior.* New York: Holt, Rinehart and Winston.

Eisenberg, J., and Dillon, W., eds. 1971. *Man and beast: comparative social behavior.* Washington, D.C.: Smithsonian Institution Press.

Gould, R. 1968a. *Chipping stone in the outback.* Garden City, N.Y.: Natural History Press.

———. 1968b. Living archaeology: The Ngatatjara of Western Australia. *Southwestern Journal of Anthropology,* Summer:15-26.

———. 1969. *Yiwara: Foragers of the Australian desert.* New York: Scribner.

Hahn, E. 1971. *On the side of the apes.* New York: Thomas Y. Crowell Co.

Hall, K. 1968. The behavior and ecology of the wild patas monkey, *Erythrocebus patas,* in Uganda. In *Primates: studies in adaptation and variability,* edited by P. Jay, pp.32-119. New York: Holt, Rinehart and Winston.

Harlow, H. 1963. Basic social capacity of primates. In *Primate social behavior,* edited by G. Southwick, pp.153-61. Princeton, N.J.: Van Nostrand.

———. 1966. The primate socialization motives. *Transactions and Studies of the College of Physicians of Philadelphia* 33:224-37.

Harman, P. 1957. *Paleoneurologic, neoneurologic and ontogenetic aspects of brain phylogeny.* James Arthur Lecture on the evolution of the human brain. New York: American Museum of Natural History.

Jay, P., ed. 1968. *Primates—Studies in adaptation and variability.* New York: Holt, Rinehart and Winston.

Jolly, A. 1972. *The evolution of primate behavior.* New York: Macmillan.

Knapp, P. 1964. *Expression of the emotions in man.* New York: International University Press.

Köhler, W. 1956. *The mentality of apes.* New York: Humanities Press.

Kruuk, H. 1972. *The spotted hyena.* Chicago: University of Chicago Press.

Kummer, H. 1971. *Primate societies.* Chicago: Aldine-Atherton.

Lancaster, J. 1975. *Primate behavior and the emergence of human culture.* New York: Holt, Rinehart and Winston.

Lee, R., and DeVore, I., eds. 1968. *Man the hunter.* Chicago: Aldine.

Lewis, J., and Towers, B. 1969. *Naked ape* or **Homo sapiens**? New York: Humanities Press.

Lorenz, K. 1961. *King Solomon's ring.* New York: Thomas Y. Crowell.

———. 1967. *On aggression.* New York: Harcourt, Brace & World.

McGrew, W. 1972. *An ethological study of children's behavior.* New York: Academic Press.

Mason, W. 1960. The effects of social restriction on the behavior of rhesus monkeys: I. Free social behavior. *Journal of Comparative and Physiological Psychology* 53:582-89.

_____. 1961a. The effects of social restriction on the behavior of rhesus monkeys: II. Tests of gregariousness. *Journal of Comparative and Physiological Psychology* 54: 287-96.

_____. 1961b. The effects of social restriction on the behavior of rhesus monkeys: III. Dominance tests. *Journal of Comparative and Physiological Psychology* 54: 694-99.

_____. 1963. The effects of environmental restriction on the social development of rhesus monkeys. In *Primate social behavior,* edited by C. Southwick, pp. 161-74. Princeton, N.J.: D. Van Nostrand.

_____. 1965. *The social development of monkeys and apes.* In Primate behavior, edited by I. DeVore, pp. 514-44. New York: Holt, Rinehart and Winston.

Mech, D. 1966. *The wolves of Isle Royal.* Washington, D.C.: U.S. Govt. Printing Office.

Montagu, A., ed. 1968. *Man and aggression.* New York: Oxford University Press.

Morris, D., ed. 1967. *Primate ethology.* Chicago: University of Chicago Press.

Morris, D. 1967. *The naked ape.* New York: McGraw-Hill.

_____. 1969. *The human zoo.* New York: McGraw-Hill.

Morris, D., and Morris, R. 1966. *Men and apes.* New York: McGraw-Hill.

Napier, J., and Napier, P. 1967. *A handbook of living primates.* New York: Academic Press.

Norback, C., and Maskowitz, N. 1963. The primate nervous system: functional and structural aspects of phylogeny. In *Evolutionary and genetic biology of primates,* Vol. I, edited by J. Buettner-Janusch, pp. 131-75. New York: Academic Press.

Pfeiffer, J. 1969. *The emergence of man.* New York: Harper & Row.

_____. 1972. *The emergence of man,* 2d ed. New York: Harper & Row.

Poirier, F., ed. 1972. *Primate socialization.* New York: Random House.

Poirier, F. 1968a. Analysis of a Nilgiri langur (*Presbytis johnii*) home range change. *Primates* 9:29-44.

_____. 1968b. The Nilgiri langur (*Presbytis johnii*) mother-infant dyad. *Primates* 9:45.

_____. 1969a. The Nilgiri langur troop: its composition, structure, function and change. *Folia Primatologica* 19:20.

_____. 1969b. Behavioral flexibility and intertroop variability among Nilgiri langurs of South India. *Folia Primatologica* 11:119-33.

_____. 1970a. Nilgiri langur ecology and social behavior. In *Primate behavior: developments in field and laboratory research,* Vol. 1, edited by L. Rosenblum, pp. 251-383. New York: Academic Press.

_____. 1970b. The Nilgiri langur communication matrix. *Folia Primatologica* 13:92-137.

_____. 1971. Socialization variables. Paper read at American Anthropological Association, New York.

_____. 1972. Introduction. In *Primate socialization,* edited by F. Poirier, pp. 3-29. New York: Random House.

_____. 1973a. Nilgiri langur behavior and social organization. In *Essays to the chief,* edited by F. Voget and R. Stephenson, pp. 119-34. Eugene: University of Oregon Press.

_____. 1973b. Primate socialization and learning. In *Learning and Culture,* edited by S. Kimball and J. Burnett, pp. 3-41. Seattle: University of Washington Press.

_____. 1977. *Fossil evidence: the human evolutionary journey.* St. Louis: C. V. Mosby Co.

Radinsky, L. 1975. Primate brain evolution. *American Scientist* 63:656-63.

Reynolds, V. 1967. *The apes.* New York: Dutton.

Rumbaugh, D. 1970. Learning skills of anthropoids. In *Primate behavior: developments in field and laboratory research,* Vol. I, edited by L. Rosenblum, pp. 2-70. New York: Academic Press.

Saayman, G. 1975. The influence of hormonal and ecological factors upon sexual behavior and social organization in Old World primates. In *Socioecology and psychology of primates,* edited by R. Tuttle, pp. 181-204. The Hague: Mouton.

Schaller, G. 1972. *The Serengeti lion.* Chicago: University of Chicago Press.

Schaller, G., and Lowther, G. 1969. The relevance of carnivore behavior to the study of early hominids. *Southwestern Journal of Anthropology* 25:307.

Schultz, A. 1969. *The life of primates.* New York: Universe Books.

Service, E. 1966. *The hunters.* New York: Prentice-Hall.

Sugiyama, Y. 1972. Social characteristics and socialization among wild chimpanzees. In *Primate socialization,* edited by F. Poirier, pp. 145-63. New York: Random House.

Temerlin, M. 1975. *Lucy: Growing up human.* Palo Alto, Calif.: Science and Behavior Books.

Thompson, J. 1975. A cross-species analysis of carnivore, primate and hominid behavior. *Journal of Human Evolution* 4: 113-24.

Tiger, L. 1969. *Men in groups.* New York: Vintage.

Tiger, L., and Fox, R. 1971. *The imperial animal.* New York: Holt, Rinehart and Winston.

Tuttle, R., ed. 1972. *The functional and evolutionary biology of primates.* Chicago: Aldine-Atherton.

Washburn, S., ed. 1961. *Social life of early man.* Chicago: Aldine.

Washburn, S., and DeVore, I. 1961. The social life of baboons. *Scientific American* 204:62.

Washburn, S., and Hamburg, D. 1965. Implications of primate research. In *Primate behavior,* edited by I. DeVore, pp. 607-22. New York: Holt, Rinehart and Winston.

Washburn, S., and Moore, R. 1974. *Ape into man: a study of human evolution.* Boston: Little, Brown.

Watanabe, H. 1971. *The Ainu ecosystem.* Seattle: University of Washington Press.

Yerkes, R. 1943. *Chimpanzees—a laboratory colony.* New Haven: Yale University Press.

Zuckerman, S. 1963. Human sociology and the sub-human primates. In *Primate social behavior,* edited by C. Southwick, pp. 7-16. Princeton: D. Van Nostrand.

Chapter 7
Primate Behavior—The Apes

Observers of behavior record what their subjects do—when, where, and for how long. Field observers restrict descriptions to behavior because of the difficulty of taking complex laboratory equipment into the field and because they wish to minimize disruption. The most common tools of the trade include paper and pen for taking notes (a small tape recorder or stenorette is sometimes substituted), a good pair of binoculars, and a good camera equipped with a telephoto lens. These basics, plus a good pair of legs for hiking, perseverance to sit long hours awaiting the arrival of your subjects, an open, inquisitive mind, and eighteen eyes appropriately scattered about your head for looking in all directions at once are the essentials. Under natural conditions field workers observe how animals react to changing social and environmental conditions, how they interact with each other, and how they obtain food. If social by nature, as almost all primates are, the observers attempt to describe the structure of the animal's society.

> In the jungles of Africa and Asia, hidden among cool leaves live the apes. Hard to find, harder still to observe, they lead their independent, foraging lives. Man's wars do not concern them. Each day gibbons leap among the trees, solitary orangs climb from branch to branch, groups of chimpanzees gather, and gorillas peer over giant lobelias. Theirs is a world of greens and browns, a friendly world where only Cousin Man is to be feared.[1]

Early Association and Amazement

Europeans have known some apes like the gorilla for just over a hundred years. Our early conceptions of the African apes (gorillas and

[1]Used by permission from V. Reynolds, 1967. *The Apes*. New York: E. P. Dutton and Company, Inc.

Gorilla mother and infant.

chimpanzees) range from their being regarded as subhuman animals to ferocious man-killing, man-eating, human female-ravishing beasts. These assumptions are far from true. Our association with one of the Asian apes, the gibbon, has been less dramatic and less emotional. The gibbon has always evoked amazement over its arboreal skills. The English naturalist William Charles Martin wrote the following about a female gibbon. "It is almost impossible to convey in words an idea of the quickness and graceful address of her movements; they may indeed be termed aerial as she seems merely to touch in her progress the branches among which she exhibits her evolutions." As with other apes, stories were woven around the orangutan. Seventeenth-century Europe recounted tales of male orangs lustfully and shamelessly carrying women and girls into the woods to ravish them. The Bornean translation for orangutan, "Man of the Woods," tells us something about the native feelings towards the animal.

The earliest descriptions of the African apes were derived from exaggerated tales and native folklore reported by travellers. Many explorers looked down upon the natives and used native tales or actual sightings of apes as ways to demean the natives. Two major themes emerge in the early writings: (1) that apes could walk bipedally erect, in fact they were often illustrated holding a walking stick; (2) that apes could speak if they wished.

The Chimpanzees

Early Association. Some of the first reports on chimpanzees come from anatomical treatises. The Dutch physician Tulp published an anatomical description of the chimpanzee as early as 1641 (Figure 7-1), an excerpt of which follows.

> It was in body neither fat nor graceful, but robust; yet very nimble and very active. The joints are in truth so tight: and with vast muscles attached to them: so that he dares anything; and can accomplish it. In front it is everywhere smooth; but hairy behind, and covered with black hairs. The face counterfeits man; but the nostrils are flat and bent inward, like a wrinkled, and toothless old woman (quoted in Reynolds, 1967:44).

A most fascinating report of one of the first chimpanzees to be seen by continental Europeans was published in the September 1738 edition of *The London Magazine*.

> A most surprising Creature is brought over in the Speaker, just arrived from Carolina, that was taken in a Wood at Guinea: it is a female about four foot high, shaped in every part like a Woman excepting its head, which nearly resembles the Ape: She walks upright naturally, sits down to her food, which is chiefly Greens, and feeds herself with her Hands as a human Creature. She is very fond of a Boy on board, and is observed always sorrowful at his Absence. She is cloathed with a thin Silk Vestment, and shows a great Discontent at the opening of her Gown to discover her Sex. She is the Female of the Creature, which the Angolans call Chimpanzee, or the Mockman (quoted in Reynolds, 1967:51).

Figure 7-1. Tulp's (1641) "orang-utang" is known to have been a chimpanzee.

The name "chimpanzee" is about the only part of this highly fanciful tale which modern scientific studies haven't dispelled.

Studies of wild chimpanzees actually began with the nineteenth-century work of the zoologist R. L. Garner, who chose the jungles of Gabon, West Africa, as his study area. He built a cage in the jungle from where he attempted to observe the chimpanzees. (Unfortunately he almost drowned as the cage was placed in a dry riverbed, which just happened to flood!) Garner was the first European to report what has been called the chimpanzee carnival, or "kanjo." The following quotation of his is an exquisite example of the mix between fact and fancy characterizing much of the early literature.

One of the most remarkable of all the social habits of the chimpanzee, is the *Kanjo*, as it is called in the native tongue. The word does not mean "dance" in the sense of saltatory gyrations, but implies more the idea of "carnival." It is believed that more than one family takes part in these festivities.

Here and there in the jungle is found a small spot of sonorous earth. It is irregular in shape, but is about two feet across. The surface is of clay, and is artificial. It is superimposed upon a kind of peat bed, which, being very porous, acts as a resonance cavity, and intensifies the sound. This constitutes a kind of drum. It yields rather a dead sound, but of considerable volume.

This queer drum is made by chimpanzees, who secure the clay along the bank of some stream in the vicinity. They carry it by hand, and deposit it while in a plastic state, spread it over the place selected, and let it dry. I have, in my possession, a part of one that I brought home with me from the Nkhami forest. It shows the fingerprints of the apes, which were impressed in it while the mud was yet soft.

After the drum is quite dry, the chimpanzees assemble by night in great numbers, and the carnival begins. One or two will beat violently on this dry clay, while others jump up and down in a wild and grotesque manner. Some of them utter long, rolling sounds, as if trying to sing. When one tires of beating the drum, another relieves him, and the festivities continue in this fashion for hours (quoted in Reynolds, 1967: 114-115).

Garner's work supplied little factual knowledge, but it set the tone by insisting upon an observational approach. After Dr. Yerkes established his chimpanzee colony in Florida, he sent one of his students, Henry Nissen, to West Africa to study wild chimpanzees. During the early part of 1930 Nissen collected forty-nine observation days with wild chimpanzees during which he learned many hitherto unknown facts. His study led him to question the idea that chimpanzees lived in "families" and that there was much hostility between animals of different "families."

Modern Studies

The next study of chimpanzees, which was carried out in East Africa by Adrian Kortlandt, a zoologist from Amsterdam, did not take place until 1960. His study group included animals which regularly raided a paw-paw plantation. Kortlandt spent several seasons at this plantation, observing from blinds (one of which was 80 feet high in a tree), watching chimpanzees come and go carrying their bananas and paw-paws. He notes: "On windy days the trees swayed so much that I could not use my field glasses. When a tropical thunderstorm came up unexpectedly, I could only pray that I would not be electrocuted."

Kortlandt's study dispelled the notion that chimpanzees lived in "family groups" or "harems." Instead, he found that they tended to keep together in "nursery groups" composed of mothers with their offspring. Kortlandt also distinguished other types of groups, e.g., sexual groups, consisting of adult males and childless females. This was a big step forward in understanding chimpanzee society and how it compares with our own.

One of the most interesting observations of Kortlandt's study was documentation of an experiment wherein a female chimpanzee brandished a stick and threw it at a stuffed leopard mauling a toy chimpanzee. From his zoo colony Kortlandt collected further instances of chimpanzees brandishing weapons. He witnessed them aiming and throwing sticks at snakes and at pictures of carnivores projected on zoo walls. Based on these observations, Kortlandt suggested that chimpanzees are not primarily rain-forest animals even though this is primarily where they now live. Instead, he labels them "eurytropic" animals, that is, they live in a wide variety of habitats, including dry woodland and savanna zones. These are the areas where we believe ancestral hominids first diverged from the apes.

Kortlandt continues that in this habitat, with its tall, isolated trees, ancestral chimpanzees developed their long arms as a climbing adaptation. What caused the chimpanzees to leave the plains and go into the forests? Kortlandt says our ancestors were to blame; by setting fires we eliminated the chimpanzees' food supply and drove them into humid forests where fires are unlikely. Additionally, we hunted the chimpanzees and drove them to the forest in fright. According to Kortlandt, his argument explains why chimpanzees still brandish sticks above their heads in fright or during displays. Such displays, of little use in the jungle because the sticks get caught in the low-lying limbs, were once useful in the savanna. Kortlandt also suggests that the reason chimpanzees are so frightened of us is because we once hunted them (and very unfortunately still do). Kortlandt also uses his theory to explain why chimpanzees, of all apes, are fond of meat, suggesting that chimpanzees eat meat because their ancestors were once carnivores. That is, modern chimpanzees have a latent carnivorous habit. (We will explore chimpanzee meat eating later.)

Kortlandt's theory is attractive; it seemingly explains why chimpanzees are so adaptive and intelligent. However, there is no sure way to relate tool using, meat eating, or weapon using to a remote way of life. More likely, such patterns simply reflect the wide range of chimpanzee adaptability.

In the last ten years or so, different investigators have tracked the chimpanzee about Africa. The best examples of the various studies are those by the husband and wife team Vernon and Frances Reynolds, Jane Goodall and subsequently studies by both her and Baron Hugo van Lawick, and members of the Japan Monkey Centre's Kyoto University African project. The Reynolds's study was conducted in the Budongo Forest of Uganda, Dr. Goodall's study in the Gombe Stream Reserve of Tanzania.

Goodall's African story began when she was a young secretary, fresh out of high school, to the late Dr. Louis Leakey, who observed that she showed real promise as a field researcher and offered her an opportunity to study chimpanzees if she would obtain university training. After training at Cambridge, Goodall returned to conduct her research, armed with an intense determination and affection for these animals.

Goodall's task was not an easy one. When she began her studies in the Gombe Stream Reserve, in 1960, she arose at dawn and spent the day atop a rocky hill overlooking the forests and Lake Tanganyika, where she could observe and be observed as a harmless, unassuming member of the forest community. Social acceptance by her fellow primates was long coming. Some days she spent twelve hours in the field, climbing up and down slopes and forcing her way through dense vegetation to view the chimpanzees. She often heard calls in the distance, but when she arrived at the spot the animals were long gone. During the first few months they would run from her as soon as she approached to within 500 yards. After much persistence, she began to be accepted as an unobtrusive stranger, first merely avoided but later actually accepted by the chimpanzees.

Goodall's efforts are tellingly described in Dr. David Hamburg's foreword to her book entitled *In the Shadow of Man.*

> Then, in the early 1960s, reports began trickling back from Tanganyika that a young woman named Goodall was making a sustained and courageous effort; the chimps were not cooperative. They stayed away from her, kept her at a great distance—often about five hundred yards—and threatened her if she took them by surprise. She suffered from malaria and a variety of hardships. Two years passed with only a scattering of close-range observations, and four years passed before truly abundant observations were possible. Yet she persisted—in itself one of the remarkable stories of our time. And at last the mystery of man's closest relative in nature began to yield to scientific scrutiny (p. xvi).

As of 1973 Goodall's study was in its thirteenth year. On and off during this period, various investigators from different parts of the world have worked with her or out of her camp. Her study is unique in the history of animal behavioral research not only because of the chimpanzee's special place in terms of its relationship to us, but also because Goodall learned to know the individual animals (and affectionately gave them such names as "Fifi," "Figan," "Flo," and "David Graybeard"), their personalities, and their "families" over the long period of observation. Furthermore, much of what she witnessed was documented by splendid photographs by Hugo van Lawick. Goodall's study has documented changes within the chimpanzee's life cycle (the individual growing up), she has studied individual animals in the context of their natural environment, and she conducted her study with meticulous care and affectionate concern for the animals. This is documented in her two popular books *My Friends the Wild Chimpanzees* and *In the Shadow of Man.*

The results of Goodall's study can be summarized as follows, again using Dr. Hamburg's words.

> The picture of chimpanzee life that emerges is fascinating. Here is a highly intelligent, intensely social creature capable of close and enduring attachments, yet nothing that looks quite like human love, capable of rich communication through gestures, postures, facial expressions, and sounds, yet nothing quite like human language. This is a creature who not only uses tools effectively but also *makes* tools with considerable foresight; a creature who does a little sharing of food, though much less than man; a creature gifted in the arts of bluff and intimidation, highly excitable and aggressive, capable of using weapons, yet engaging in no activity comparable to human warfare; a creature who frequently hunts and kills small animals of other species in an organized, cooperative way, and seems to have some zest for the process of hunting, killing, and eating the prey; a creature whose repertoire of acts in aggression, deference, reassurance, and greeting bear uncanny similarities to human acts in similar situations (p.xvvii).

Chimpanzees and Tools. So much has come from the Goodall studies, and from others working out of her field station, that we can only touch on the highlights. Prior to Goodall's observations, one of the major definitions of humans was that we were a toolmaker. We made tools—that separated us from the rest of the primates; this was an absolute. Then, Dr. Goodall not only saw, and photographed, chimpanzees *using* tools, she also witnessed them *making* tools. Chimpanzees use the objects of their environment as tools to a greater extent than any other living animal excepting ourselves. Numerous times chimpanzees were seen to break off grass stems or thin branches which they carried with them for short distances. These implements are poked into termite mounts to get at the termites (Figure 7-2). After termites bite the probe, the chimpanzee runs the probe across its front teeth and eats the termites. Fascinating as this may be, the chimpanzee adds more; if the probe does not fit the hole, the chimpanzee shapes it until it does; leaves are stripped from a stem to make the tool suitable for "termite fishing." The edges of wide blades of grass may be stripped to make the appropriate tool. Not only is a tool used, a tool is made. To quote Goodall:

Ardent angler, Fifi seeks an opening in a termite mound by bending low for a close look and a quick sniff. After breaking into a narrow tunnel sealed by clay, she inserts a blade of grass. Her average catch: half a dozen of the forest delicacies. Patient chimpanzees capture scores of insects at a single setting (Goodall, 1967).

Figure 7-2. A chimpanzee "termiting," i.e., poking a twig into a termite mound.

Chimpanzees have also been observed to use leaves as tools; they have been seen to chew a wad of leaves to make them more absorbent. This wad is then used as a sponge to sop up rainwater that can't be reached with the lips. The initial modification of a handful of leaves is another example of tool use. Again Goodall,

> Ingenuity provides a drink for a thirsty ape. Finding rainwater cupped in a fallen tree, but out of reach of his lips, Figan manufactures a "sponge." First he briefly chews a few leaves to increase their absorbency, then dips the crumpled greenery into the natural bowl and sucks out the liquid. By fashioning a simple tool he saves himself the bother of walking to a stream for a drink (Goodall, 1967).

Chimpanzees have been seen to use leaves to wipe the remnants of a brain from the inside of a baboon skull and to dab at a bleeding wound on the rump. They also used leaves as toilet paper in the case of diarrhea. Some chimpanzees have used leaves to wipe themselves clean of mud and sticky foods.

Chimpanzees have been seen to use stout sticks as levers to enlarge the opening of an underground bees nest. They have used sticks to pry open banana boxes stored at the observation camp, much to the chagrin of the Goodall staff. One chimp used a twig as a toothpick and one picked its nose with a piece of straw.

What differentiates chimpanzee tool use and manufacture from ours? Basically, three important things: (1) We use tools to make other tools—either chimpanzees don't, or they haven't been seen doing so. (2) We use tools much more frequently, and in more circumstances, than do chimpanzees. (3) We depend upon tools for our survival while the chimpanzee does not. It has been argued that we make tools for future use while other toolmaking animals drop the tool immediately after use. This is an interesting point, but chimpanzees have been seen to carry "termiting" sticks for rather long distances and, at times, from mound to mound, looking for a meal. We make tools for later contingencies, and we save them for long periods. The chimpanzee does not, but why should the chimpanzee store tools when sticks and grass are so prevalent? Perhaps when we began to use scarcer materials, then we began to save them for future use. If we are to keep such phrases as "man the toolmaker," it might more correctly read "man the consistent toolmaker," or "man the toolmaker, who makes tools from other tools," or "man—who saves tools for future use."

Predatory Behavior. Until rather recently it was assumed that hominids were the only predatory, carnivorous, food-sharing primates. We now know that chimpanzees not only eat meat, and much more frequently than we originally assumed, but they also hunt meat in small, organized male groups. Chimpanzees also share their kill. "The Gombe Stream chimpanzees are efficient hunters; a group of about forty individuals may catch over twenty different prey animals during one year" (van Lawick-Goodall, 1971:282). The most common prey include young bush pigs, baboons, and young or adult colobus monkeys.

A concentrated twelve-month study of chimpanzee hunting behavior has been undertaken by an anthropologist, Geza Teleki, at the Gombe Reserve. During his year's stay at Gombe, Teleki witnessed thirty episodes of predation, twelve of them successful. Interestingly, the animal most often preyed upon is another primate: leaf-eating monkey, baboon, or other forest-dwelling primate. There is no evidence that chimpanzees take or even pursue animals weighing more than twenty pounds.

Teleki isolated three major components of chimpanzee predatory behavior. The first he calls the "pursuit." The second event, the "capture," is a brief period ending with the initial dismemberment of the prey. The third and longest event, "consumption," involves highly structured activities. Once, Teleki observed a consumption period lasting nine hours and involving fifteen chimpanzees.

The pursuit phase of the hunt takes various forms, one being simple seizure of the prey. The chimpanzee takes advantage of a fortuitous situation by lunging at and grabbing the prey. Other forms of pursuit are chasing the prey, which may involve a dash of 100 yards or more, and stalking, which can last more than an hour. Both chasing and stalking seem to be premeditated. On occasion both clearly involve a strategy and maneuvers aimed at isolating or cornering the prey.

One of the major problems in interpreting these predatory episodes was to discern how they were coordinated. Gombe chimpanzees are usually very vociferous, especially during the morning and evening. That, however, is not the case when they are pursuing prey.

> Regardless of the time of day or the number of chimpanzees involved in the chase, all remain silent until the prey is captured or the attempt is broken off. This means, of course, that the hunters do not coordinate their efforts by means of vocal signals. Neither did I observe any obvious signaling gestures, although cooperation in movement and positioning was evident (Teleki, 1972:37).

We still do not know how chimpanzees coordinate their hunts; perhaps some as yet imperceptible body signals are used.

In contrast to the quiet characterizing a hunt, "the instant of acquisition is usually signaled by a sudden outburst of vocalization; the cries not only end the silence of the hunt but their volume and pitch serve to draw other chimpanzees from distances of a mile or more" (Teleki, 1973:37). Chimpanzees quickly kill their prey; if the prey is in the hunter's grasp, the chimpanzee may simply twist or bite the back of its neck. Or the chimpanzee may bang the prey's head on the ground. If more than one animal captures the prey, the prey may be literally torn apart as each captor tugs on a different limb.

Chimpanzee predatory behavior is amazing to anthropologists, who are used to considering humans as the sole predatory primate. Of equal interest is the fact that the prey is shared among fellow chimpanzees. In Teleki's words:

> Considering the length of time devoted to consumption, the small size of the prey animals, and the number of chimpanzees that congregate in sharing clusters, the conclusion is almost inescapable that social considerations and not merely nutritional ones underlie the Gombe apes' predatory behavior (40).

Chimpanzees share their meat by responding to another animal's "request." Meat can be requested in various ways; the requester can approach the possessor closely, face to face, and peer intently at the possessor for the meat. Alternatively the requester can extend a hand, open and palm up (in a begging position), holding it under the possessor's chin.

The significance of chimpanzee predatory behavior is important in understanding certain behavior traits. First, predatory behavior requires group cooperation for a common cause, obtaining meat. A second important trait is sharing the meat among one's social fellows, essentially just for the act of sharing. A third point of significance is the questions which chimpanzee predatory behavior and food sharing raise for interpreting hominid evolution. For example, could predation have developed among primates before the advent of the early hominids? If predation, cooperative hunting, and socially structured food sharing were pre-hominid traits, this would cast some doubt on some current evolutionary hypotheses. The complex of erect posture, free hands, and tool use as prerequisites to the emergence of hunting behavior would be called into question.[2] Similarly, the hypothesis that the open savanna is the habitat where hunting most likely develped must also be questioned. Actually, it is in the woodland-savanna where today one finds the highest density of mammals. One cherished belief must surely be abandoned—that is, that socially organized hunting among primates is solely a human property.

Social Organization. Through the efforts of dedicated observers, we are getting a clearer impression of chimpanzee social life and social organization. One of the most striking facts about chimpanzee social organization is the flexibility of their social life. The lack of a rigid form of organization represents a sharp contrast to the situation found among the rigidly organized savanna-dwelling baboons (discussed in the next chapter). It should be mentioned, however, that Goodall reported orally in 1975 that chimpanzees may actually recognize more rigid group boundaries than originally suggested. Furthermore, she has recorded intergroup conflicts. Forest-living chimpanzees are often found in any one of four types of bands: adult males only; mother and offspring and occasionally a few other females; adults and adolescents of both sexes, but no mothers with young; and representatives of all categories mixed together. The composition and size of these bands may change during the course of the day as individuals wander off and groups split or combine with other groups in the vicinity.

Dr. Y. Sugiyama of the Japan Monkey Centre discussed the role of flexibility within chimpanzee society in a 1972 publication. In his study, conducted in the Budongo Forest of Uganda, Dr. Sugiyama located fifty to sixty animals organized into what he called a Regional Population. Occasionally most of the chimpanzees of this population formed a party that moved together; usually, however, they formed parties of less than ten or moved alone. They also gathered into one party that subsequently divided into two or more groups. The home range of this population was surrounded by the ranges of other Regional Popula-

[2]We should mention that one of the features differentiating human from chimpanzee hunting behavior is the size of the prey. Human hunters concentrate on larger prey than do chimpanzees.

tions. These home ranges frequently overlapped, and sometimes members of one Regional Population joined with members of another. When larger groups divide, they often maintain associative and friendly contact with their rich vocal and behavioral communication. Quoting Sugiyama (pp. 159-60): "Chimpanzee society ensures the free and independent movement of each individual based on highly developed individuality without the restriction of either territoriality or hierarchy. On the other hand, a chimpanzee enjoys the benefits of group life in that it can avoid the enemy and find fruits with less effort."

Although there is a loose dominant and subordinate relationship among individuals within most primate groups, chimpanzee social life is not rigidly organized into a dominance hierarchy. A major element in rigidly hierarchical primate societies is that each animal must adjust its movements and behaviors to others in the troop. A rigidly organized social order cannot be maintained when individuals do not subordinate their personal desires for the good of troop unity or solidarity. The flexible nature of the chimpanzee social order may be one resolution of this problem. "This kind of social organization may be one of the original factors raising individuality to the level of personality. Chimpanzees have not rejected group life, but they have rejected individual uniformity and the pressure of a dominance hierarchy" (Sugiyama, 1972:160). However, as noted on the previous page, the Gombe Stream chimpanzees are now reported to be territorial, intergroup conflicts have been recorded, and the males noted to patrol territorial boundaries. These reports conflict with earlier conceptions of the Gombe chimpanzees. It may be that the Gombe Stream situation is not typical of the chimpanzee organization. In fact, it has been suggested that hunting at Gombe is due to increasing population pressure. The same might be said about the new reports of territorial behavior.

Chimpanzee social organization is flexible, and it is adaptable. Budongo chimpanzees, for example, change their behavior markedly when they approach open terrain. In the forest they are relaxed and their social organization is loose; they become tense and vigilant in open spaces, such as when crossing a road or moving into the savanna-grassland. Some of Sugiyama's co-workers, for example Itani and Suzuki (1967) and Nishida (1968), note that chimpanzees in the savanna move in structured groups more like savanna-dwelling baboons. Interestingly, the effect may also work the other way. Studies of forest-dwelling baboons suggest that they do not have hierarchies and generally live relaxed lives, more like the forest-dwelling chimpanzees with looser social structures. Forest-living baboons are also freer to move from troop to troop, and adult males do not defend the troop during emergencies, as is so true on the savanna.

Similar changes may have occurred among those primates which eventually became our ancestors. As these animals left the relative safety of the forests and trees, they may have adapted by modifying their social organizations. The once rather carefree, relatively peaceful life in the forest, with its flexible social organizations, was presented with new pressures, new dangers. The loosely knit social organizations became, in time, tightly and rigidly organized social structures.

Communicating with Chimpanzees. Because of the excitement generated by news releases in recent years concerning human-chimpanzee attempts to communicate, there will be few readers who are not aware of the efforts being made to test the language abilities of nonhuman primates (see Mounin, 1976, for an up-to-date review). Most attempts to establish a dialogue with chimpanzees have occurred with female chimpanzees, because they are considered to be more cooperative, docile, and easily managed.

The first rearing experiment with a chimpanzee was made by a Soviet scientist, N. Kohts. In 1913 she acquired a young chimpanzee, Joni, approximately two years old. She raised this animal until it was four-and-one-half years old, during which time she conducted comparable observations on her son.

Kohts's study was followed by that of the Kelloggs (Kellogg and Kellogg, 1933), who acquired a seven month old chimpanzee named Gua. They used their son Donald as a control to compare the abilities and intellectual and motor development of both infants. During early development the chimpanzee, Gua, performed better than her human male counterpart, Donald. Gua learned to react to certain words and phrases of her "parents." During the first part of the study Gua surpassed or equalled Donald in a number of test situations. However, during the last part of the study, Donald's linguistic competence overtook Gua's and he surpassed the chimpanzee in comprehension. The study ended when Gua was sixteen months old, at which time she had learned to use certain gestures consistently as communicatory signals. Although Gua did respond to human verbal communicatory signals, she was unable to duplicate them.

The next major home-rearing experiment involving a chimpanzee was made by the Hayeses (Hayes, 1952; Hayes and Nissen, 1971). The chimpanzee was named Vicki, a three-day-old female acquired from the Yerkes nursery. Vicki was raised as a human child until her death at age 6½. The Hayes's study was unique for they attempted to teach this chimpanzee to speak. The results of the Hayes's labors were not particularly noteworthy—the chimpanzee was taught to produce some hoarse sounds that the Hayeses interpreted as "momma," "cup," "pappa," and possibly the word "up." Although the Hayeses concluded that it was difficult, perhaps impossible, to teach a chimpanzee to speak, they did establish that one could communicate with the chimpanzee utilizing gestural cues.

In addition to attempting to teach Vicki to speak English, the Hayeses conducted extensive teaching and observation of their "daughter." Vicki's early development maintained the pace of a normal human child, and in some cases surpassed it—especially in terms of motor development and manipulative activities. There is some interesting evidence in the Hayes's work that Vicki recognized objects, including other chimpanzees, but she seemed to place herself in the same group as her "parents," i.e., among humans!

The Hayes's work had a strong impact and was a catalyst to a later study by two psychologists, Beatrice and Alan Gardner, at the University of Nevada. The Gardners' subject was a young female chimpanzee named Washoe. The Gardners' project called for raising their chimpanzee in a communicative environment which was amenable to the chimpanzee's natural manipulative talents. They chose American Sign Language (ASL) as their medium of communication (Gardner and Gardner, 1969, 1971).

Washoe was born in the wild and acquired by the Gardners at the age of eleven months. She was housed in a trailer in the Gardners' yard and provided with a stimulating environment which included human companions, who worked in shifts during the day. The sole means of communication between Washoe and her human companions was ASL, which was taught to Washoe by members of the research team proficient in the medium. Washoe's acquisition of ASL was evaluated either live by the staff or from film played to native "speakers" of ASL, e.g., deaf observers. The deaf observers soon were able to comprehend 90 percent of Washoe's signs.

After seven months of training Washoe acquired signs rapidly; she reliably used nouns, verbs, etc., and began to transfer sign meanings to appropriate contexts. With an increase in her vocabulary she began to put words together and form rough sentences. After thirty-six months Washoe had learned eighty-five signs; after fifty-one months her vocabulary increased to 132 signs which were consistently and correctly used. Her sentence structure resembled that of the first sentences of young children.

Soon Washoe was using signs to communicate her desires and also in "conversations" with herself. Washoe would sign when she wished to play, when she wished more food, when she wished to go into the yard, and to convey other messages.

The Gardners' experiments showed that two-way communication could be established between a human and chimpanzee if the appropriate medium was utilized. The Gardners' study was extended by one of their ex-students, Roger Fouts, who took Washoe to the Institute of Primate Studies in Norman, Oklahoma. Fouts continued to work with Washoe and he soon began to teach ASL to other chimpanzees, including two males and two females. Fouts's continuing work shows that Washoe is not a unique example of chimpanzee intelligence, or adaptability (Fouts, 1973, 1975).

Fouts reports that as of 1975 Washoe had 160 signs in her vocabulary. While the size of the vocabulary is interesting, Fouts feels it is also interesting to note the manner in which she combines the signs. Washoe combines signs and she shows a preference in her sign order which Fouts feels may be interpreted as the rudiments of syntax. She prefers the use of the pronoun sign for "you" preceding the sequence of a verb and the pronoun sign for "me."

Fouts was interested in knowing if Washoe would use her language of ASL in her communication with other chimpanzees. Washoe has used signs with other chimpanzees; unfortunately, however, the other chimpanzees at Oklahoma are either lacking training in ASL or are deficient in their ASL sign vocabulary. Even so, the investigators have noted that the chimpanzees will sign to one another in situations such as mutual comforting, eating, and general play activities such as tickling games. For example, one of the male chimpanzees, Booee, was observed to approach another male, Bruno, and ask Bruno to "tickle Booee" in signs.

The Gardners (1971) noted that Washoe not only produced signs which they had taught her, but she also produced her own signs. For example, Washoe invented her own sign for the word "bib." One of the other chimpanzees at Oklahoma, a female named Lucy, has also invented her own signs. Lucy, who is being reared in a human home, enjoys going for a walk. When she is out walking she is taken on a leash. When Lucy wishes to go out she signs "leash," which she does with a sign she invented herself—a hooking action with her extended index finger on her neck. Some of the chimpanzees at Oklahoma have also changed the grammatical function of a word; i.e., a noun was changed to an adjective. Lucy has used the sign for "dirty" in instances other than that in which she was taught. Fouts (1975) notes that she once signed "dirty cat" to a strange cat she had been aggressively interacting with. Although Lucy needs to be leashed for her enjoyable walks, she dislikes being tethered. Therefore, the leash is often signed as "dirty leash."

Two other studies were conducted on communication between humans and chimpanzees. One study was conducted in California by Ann and David Premack, two psychologists at the University of California, Santa Barbara. The communication medium in this experiment was plastic symbols of different shapes and colors (Premack, 1971a,b; Premack and Premack, 1972). These symbols were stuck to a magnetic board. The subject in this experiment was a five-year-old female named Sarah.

Sarah was taught that to receive a piece of banana, she had to place a plastic symbol onto the magnetic board. She learned this rapidly, and her vocabulary was expanded to include different color symbols for different fruits. After obtaining a competence in this series of tests, Sarah was introduced to the verb "give." After mastering the use of the verb, she was required to end a "sentence" with her name, Sarah, in order to receive her reward. Sarah was also required to master the interrogative "?", and "yes," and "no." Furthermore, Sarah mastered color names, position words such as "in," and quantifiers such as "one," "none," "all," and "several."

After eighteen months of training, the Premacks felt that Sarah had achieved a language which compared in many ways to that of a 2½ year-old child. Sarah acquired a vocabulary of 130 terms which were used correctly 75-80 percent of the time.

A later study was conducted at Yerkes Regional Primate Center, Atlanta by Dr. Duane Rumbaugh and colleagues (Rumbaugh et al., 1973). The communication medium was a computer and the subject a female chimpanzee named Lana. Lana has been taught to work a console with twenty-five keys bearing color-coded symbols which represent vocabulary terms. Lana's language has been called "Yerkish" after the name of the primate center. After six months of training Lana learned to use the computer console with facility and she now effectively communicates with her human friends. She is able to communicate her wishes by pressing the correct keys. Unless the keys are pressed in the correct order to produce a coherent sentence, Lana's request is ignored. Should she wish to request an M and M candy, she would press the keys to read "Please machine give me M and M period." Should Lana's human companions wish to communicate with Lana, they also do so through the medium of the computer console. The Yerkes experiment holds the promise of devising a language training program for helping mentally retarded human children.

Studies similar to those involved with communicating with chimpanzees have been undertaken on other great apes. Fouts (1975) did a short exploratory study with one infant male orangutan to determine if he could acquire some signs. The orangutan was able to learn a few signs (such as for drink, food, and tickle) and he combined them into two-sign combinations. One experimentor (Furness, 1916) was able to teach an orangutan two vocal words, similar to the Hayes's result with Vicki.

Work is currently being done by F. Patterson at Stanford University (from Fouts, 1975) to teach ASL to an infant gorilla. The gorilla is a nineteen month old female who has acquired and uses six signs. The gorilla also combines the sign for "more" with signs for the words "food," "drink," and "out."

These experiments have generated a good deal of scientific interest and excitement. They have enabled us to communicate more than ever before with our closest relatives in the animal kingdom. While there has been a failure to teach the chimpanzees or other great apes to speak a language, as could possibly have been predicted, these experiments do show us something of the range of ape intelligence and adaptability. It is important, however, to bear in mind that the results of all these experiments are due to humans teaching animals new techniques. The abilities witnessed in the various experiments may not be indicative of the range of abilities among wild animals. These experiments are also forcing us to rethink our definitions of what is human, as is also true of studies of chimpanzees in the wild. The gap between what it means to be human and what it means to be ape is closing. We are definitely different; however, that difference is not so much quantitative as it seems to be qualitative.

Rumbaugh et al. (1975) best sum up the philosophy of this work in a discussion of Lana's abilities.

At present, however, in the interests of remaining objective rather than fanciful, a very real temptation in this area of research, we stop well short of concluding or even suggesting that Lana has demonstrated productive language capabilities. She has, nonetheless, impressed us with her achievements, and, at times, we believe that the greatest barrier to even more rapid progress on her part is our limited understanding as to how to best convey to her what it is that we are trying to reach. She remains highly motivated and gives us reason to believe that she "enjoys" the challenge of new tasks and disdains the routine (p. 400).

The Gorilla (Figure 7-3)

Few animals have stirred public and scientific interest as the gorilla has done. Discovered over a hundred years ago, it remained a creature of mystery. The gorilla has been shot, captured, and photographed, but its reputed belligerence and remote habitat discouraged firsthand scientific study (quoted from the cover of G. Schaller's *The Mountain Gorilla: Ecology and Behavior,* 1963).

This was the dominant attitude until Dr. George Schaller made public the results of 466 hours of direct contact with mountain gorillas in

Figure 7-3. An adult gorilla standing in a bent-knee bipedal stance.

the Virunga Volcanoes region of the eastern Congo, western Uganda, and western Ruanda. A more recent study of the gorillas is being undertaken by Dianne Fossey and has been briefly reported in various issues of *National Geographic*.

Earliest Reports. The earliest report of the gorilla came in the eighteenth century. The name then given the gorilla was "Impungu," apparently a native term. The report follows:

> Of this animal there are three classes or species...This wonderful and frightful projection of nature walks upright like man; is from 7 to 9 feet high, when at maturity, thick in proportion, and amazingly strong; covered with longish hair, jet black over the body, but longer on the head; the face more like the human than the Chimpenza, but the complexion is black; and has no tail (quoted in Reynolds, 1967:53).

By the end of the eighteenth century, when the chimpanzee, orangutan, and gibbon were comparatively well known, the gorilla was still an anecdotal nightmare. A typical report, printed in an 1847 publication, is given on the next page.

> ... the *ingena*, an animal like the orangutan, but much exceeding it in size, being five feet high and four across the shoulders. Its paw was said to be even more disproportioned than its breadth, and one blow of it to be fatal. It is seen commonly by them when they travel to Kaybe, lurking in the bush to destroy passengers, and feeding principally on wild honey, which abounds. Among other of their actions ... is that of building a house in rude imitation of the natives, and sleeping outside on the roof of it (quoted in Reynolds, 1967:54).

The gorilla was not "scientifically discovered" until 1847 when it was first described on the basis of skeletal materials, primarily a skull, obtained by Dr. Thomas S. Savage. Gorillas were known from West Africa in the nineteenth century; gorillas in East Africa were first discovered by Europeans as late as 17 October 1902. The first European to report seeing an East African gorilla was a German army officer, Captain Oskar von Beringe, who lent his last name as a gorilla subspecies, *Gorilla gorilla beringei*.

The American missionary T. Savage, in the original scientific description of the gorilla, wrote the following account in the *Boston Journal of Natural History*, 1844:

> The *enge-enas* (gorillas) are exceedingly ferocious, and always offensive in their habits, never running from man as does the chimpanzee. They are objects of terror to the natives, and are never encountered by them except on the defensive. ... When the male is first seen he gives a terrific yell, that resounds far and wide through the forest. His underlip hangs over the chin, and his hairy ridge and scalp are contracted upon the brow, presenting an aspect of indescribable ferocity. He then approaches the hunter in great fury, pouring out his horrid cries in quick succession. The hunter waits until the animal grasps the barrel of his gun, and as he carries it to his mouth, he fires. Should the gun fail to go off, the barrel is crushed between the teeth, and the encounter soon proves fatal to the hunter (quoted in Reynolds, 1967:135-136).

After their discovery, a number of "great white hunters" set out for Africa to hunt the gorilla. One of the better-known hunters was Paul du Chaillu, an American trader on the West African coast who turned zoologist-explorer. He claimed to have been the first European to have hunted and killed a full-grown male gorilla. His description of the kill follows.

> His eyes began to flash fire as we stood motionless on the defensive, and the crest of short hair which stands on his forehead began to twitch rapidly up and down, while his powerful fangs were shown as he again set forth a thunderous roar. And now truly he reminded me of nothing but some hellish dream creature—a being of that hideous order, half-man half-beast, of which we find pictures by old artists in some repre-

sentations of the infernal regions. He advanced a few steps—then stopped to utter that hideous roar again—advanced again, and finally stopped when at a distance of about six yards from us. And here, just as he began another of his roars, beating his breast in rage, we fired and killed him.

With a groan which had something terribly human in it, and yet was full of brutishness, he fell forward on his face. The body shook convulsively for a few minutes, the limbs moved about in a struggling way, and then all was quiet—death had done its work, and I had leisure to examine the huge body. It proved to be five feet eight inches high, and the muscular development of the arms and breast showed what immense strength it had possessed (quoted in Reynolds, 1967:136-37).

Previous to Schaller's attempts at naturalistic studies, Garner, Akeley, and Bingham attempted to study gorillas. Their great contribution was an insistence that the gorillas were not ferocious beasts; unfortunately this message was lost. The early 1950s witnessed renewed attempts to study gorillas.

Dr. G. Schaller. The transformation of ideas about gorillas and their acceptance as nonviolent creatures is the result of Dr. Schaller's study. This study began when Schaller and his professor, Dr. John Emlen, surveyed the gorilla population at Virunga. When Emlen left, Schaller and his wife, Kay, remained behind for ten months of extensive study of ten separate gorilla groups. These ten groups included 200-odd animals who lived in the Hagenia woodland zone at about 10,000 feet. This thick mountain forest is the home of the mountain gorilla. Today some 5000 to 15,000 gorillas live here in danger of extinction. They are forced to retreat further up the mountainside as humans occupy the lower slopes and turn them over to their cattle.

Schaller's favorite study method was to habituate gorillas to his presence by slowly approaching them, alone and in full view. After a number of contacts he became accepted as an innocuous addition to the scenery. Schaller became familiar with his animals in much the same way each of us monkey and ape watchers become familiar with our subjects. Physical defects, behavioral quirks, locomotor patterns, and voice patterns are used to identify individual animals.

Schaller did not find a savage beast; he discovered a big nonaggressive vegetarian. Because they have enormous appetites, gorillas spend six to eight hours a day eating; there is little time for anything else. Gorilla aggressive behavior is very rare, and usually consists of an irritable slap or threatening stare. No fights were witnessed. Once the gorillas discovered Schaller was not dangerous, their curiosity replaced fear—they observed Schaller observing them. Even if he blundered upon the gorillas feeding, Schaller was not attacked. Unlike his predecessors, Schaller learned gorilla communicative gestures; if he frightened an animal, Schaller merely shook his head, as subordinate gorillas do, and he was ignored.

Schaller's study uncovered a host of previously unknown facts about gorillas and his work disproved many fables. Schaller found that gorillas live in fairly stable social groups, seventeen members being an average. Gorilla groups range from solitary males to groups of thirty or more animals, each containing at least one dominant silver-backed[3] male and a few younger and less dominant adult black-backed males. A group also contains a number of females and their offspring. Contacts between members of different groups are nonaggressive; animals may leave one group and simply join another.

The silver-backed male leads and controls the group; he determines when and where they should travel, and how fast. He stays behind and intimidates intruders with the famous chest-beating display: he rises on his hind feet, soundly beats his resonating chest, and throws sticks or other nearby objects into the air. The act is merely a display meant to intimidate and seldom leads to attack.

Each gorilla group wanders over its own range, which is usually ten to twelve square miles. Most of the time gorillas are quiet. They are normally quadrupedal, terrestrial, knuckle-walking animals. They usually sleep in a crudely constructed ground nest rather than in tree nests common to other apes. Schaller's study portrays the gorilla as a lazy wanderer, one who likes to doze or sunbathe in the midmorning. As Reynolds (1967:149) notes, "Perhaps the worst that can be said about the temperament of the wild gorilla is that it is morose and sullen; at best it is amiable, lovable, shy and gentle."

The Orangutan

Although the orangutan shares many traits with the other pongids, it is unique in several respects. They live in Southeast Asia, as do the gibbons; however, they are closer in size and temperament to their African relatives, the gorilla and chimpanzee. In contrast to the chimpanzee, the orangutan seems to be shy and retiring. Although they are arboreal, they move with quiet deliberation. Orangutans have always raised the primatologists' curiosity, their "odd" looks being one of the reasons. The cheeks of male orangutans bulge out in fleshy pads (Figure 7-4), unique among primates. Below this is a large air sac connecting the larynx which can be blown up like enormous goiters. This sac acts as a resonator or is involved in producing sustained sounds.[4] Orangutans in the jungle have been heard to give loud burps which may function as warning signals. While we are unsure of the evolutionary history of the male cheek pouches it may be that they are a reflection of sexual dimorphism and are actually a function of sexual selection (Horr, pers. comm.).

The name orangutan is derived from the Malay words meaning "man" and "woods"—the man of the woods. A Dutch physician noted from Java in the 1640s that "the Javanese maintain these animals can speak but refuse to do so for fear of being made to work" (Mydans: 1973:30).

Once, it is thought, there were at least 500,000 orangutans inhabiting the vast jungles from the Celebes to North China. Harrisson (1962) has suggested that in the early Christian era there were probably more orangutans than people in Borneo. A recent estimate places the current Borneo orangutan population at 9000 animals, and this low level cannot be maintained for long.

[3]So-called because of graying of the hair about the rump and up the back.
[4]The old idea that this sac was filled with air to keep an orang afloat in water is fanciful at best.

Figure 7-4. The head and upper shoulders of an adult male orangutan. Note the fleshy cheek pads.

The orangutan faces extinction due to a number of circumstances, primarily human encroachment upon its habitat. Humans have hunted orangs for food[5] and for display in zoos; however, more ominous is the human destruction of the habitat by cutting down the primary forests for farms and factories. Furthermore, humans have been intrigued by the orang's looks and captured and caged them to satisfy the human desire for amusement. Often this process involved destroying the mother to get the infant. Fortunately, the legal importation of orangs is now being limited or denied in many countries.

Preserving the Orang. The first major conservation effort was undertaken by Barbara and Tom Harrisson, who reared baby orangutans in their Sarawak home. These animals were confiscated before they were to be exported. The Harrissons established a program in which they tried to rehabilitate young orangs, eventually to be set free in their jungle habitat. The program had some success.

A new effort is underway in Sabah to rehabilitate orangs and return them to their natural habitat. The experiment is being conducted under the direction of a Ceylonese zoologist, Stanley de Silva, in the Sepilok Forest Reserve, 10,000 acres of virgin jungle located about 15 miles inland from the port of Sandakan in northern Borneo (Mydans, 1973). The program began in 1964; as of 1973, fifty-one animals had been taken into the project, all reclaimed from the native population. Some of these animals died; however, all but eight have disappeared into the forest to join their wild relatives.

[5]Cooked bones believed to belong to the orangutan have been found in Niah Cave in West Borneo from a site which dates to 35,000 years B.P.

Natural Studies. Little is currently published about orangutans living in natural conditions. A major problem with studying these animals is that they live in inaccessible swampy tropical jungles; hours or days of searching may turn up nothing. Furthermore, orangutans are primarily wandering solitary animals and it is difficult to find them; once located they are difficult to follow. However, both Schaller and Davenport, who spent short periods of time observing them, note that they can be followed without too much trouble. Their slow, precise movements make them easy targets; they seem to be too big to flee nimbly in the trees and do not run rapidly quadrupedally on the ground. Orangutans are the slowest of the apes and they seem to be too big for the trees and too arboreal for their size.

Davenport (1967) conducted a study of orangs in the State of Sabah, Borneo. He studied animals for a total of 192 animal-hours of day observation and observed the following groupings: one family group composed of two adults and a dependent infant; three of mother-child pairs, one with an independent infant and two with dependent infants; and seven of lone animals (four adults and three subadults). All these were located in primary forest; the heaviest concentration was in the Sepilok Forest Reserve, where de Silva has established the rehabilitation project.

Some of Davenport's observations follow: The type of locomotion which the orang utilizes is dependent to a great degree upon the type and structure of the vegetation. Orangs manifest a diversity of locomotor patterns: quadrupedal on the tops of branches, suspended by all fours from a branch, bipedal locomotion atop a branch, and brachiation. Regardless of the locomotor pattern, the animals were always cautious and deliberate.

In a number of instances in which Davenport witnessed the animals, resting or sleeping nests were used or made. Usually a new nest is built for nighttime sleeping. The time needed to construct a nest and the method employed depended to some extent on the site and materials available. Characteristically, all animals selected a firm branch on which smaller branches grew. Three times Davenport observed the animals building an overhead shelter to protect them from a heavy rain.

Although Davenport witnessed minimal manipulation of the environment, other than nest building, interesting examples of tool use have been reported from the de Silva project. One of the animals in the project, a female named Joan, was observed to use a dead branch as a club, as though to pound a pole into the ground. Captive orangs have been seen using tools; in fact, some argue that the orang may be the most intelligent of the apes. Orangs at the Harrissons' rehabilitation center have been seen poking into termite mounds and ant nests, sometimes with sticks. This behavior must be natural as they have had no possibility to learn it in the wild.

As is clear from this summary, much more is needed before we have a clear idea of the orang's behavior. Some preliminary reports providing such information became available in 1975 (Horr, Galdikas-Brindamour and Brindamour), and further reports from Dr. P. Rodman, Dr. D. Horr, and the Brindamours are scheduled for publication in the near future. More important still is strict adherence to a conservation program designed to save the orang from extinction.

The Gibbon (Figure 7-5)

Reports of the gibbon, the smallest of the apes, are scattered throughout the early primate literature. Early reporters were enamored with the gibbon's abilities to walk bipedally on the ground and its loud, sonorous, booming vocalizations impressed many observers. Early naturalists were also quite impressed by the fact that gibbons live in monogamous groups containing a male, female, and their nonadult offspring. The Yerkes book *The Great Apes* contains the following passage from the early field work of Dr. R. A. Spaeth on the Thailand gibbons.

> ...gibbons were for the most part in family groups...they have their young in the early summer and spring.... The gibbon has only one young a year and it takes three or four years for them to mature, so a family frequently consisted of two or more young ones in various stages of growth beside the father and mother. They hang onto the mother with an extraordinary strong grip as she swings through the trees. She appears to be not the least incommoded by the baby hanging to her and swings along as unconcernedly as though she were alone.

Figure 7-5. A gibbon hanging by its arms. Note the long arm length compared with the length of the legs.

The first full-scale investigation of wild gibbons was launched in 1937 as a joint effort of Harvard and Columbia Universities. Among its members was Dr. C. R. Carpenter, then already an experienced field investigator. He followed gibbon groups and studied their habits. He found that, when youngsters reached sexual maturity, males excluded their sons and females their daughters from the family group. Sexually mature males and females forced from the family may then form their own mated pairs with others in a similar situation.

Carpenter also found that gibbons were territorial, i.e., they defended the area in which they lived. Territorial defense does not take the form of bloody physical altercations, it is instead a battle of loud vocalizations and vigorous chases. Each group knows its territorial boundaries; if this area seems in danger of encroachment by an adjacent group, the group rushes to the spot and calls and shakes branches until the trespassers retreat. Similar observations of territorial defense have been made for other arboreal primates such as howler monkeys and langurs.

During the 1960s Carpenter's ideas were reexamined by Dr. John Ellefson. Ellefson worked in Malaysia where he studied the same species of gibbon as did Carpenter. Ellefson's few reports confirm Carpenter's observations of family groups, territorial behavior, and minimal aggression and sexual behavior. Subsequent studies by members of the Japan Monkey Centre lend further support to Carpenter's observations.

Our associations with our pongid relatives vary from one of amazement and amusement at the brachiating gibbon to one of fear of the gorilla. Of all the apes, perhaps the chimpanzee holds the greatest fascination for anthropologists. Dr. Jane Goodall's detailed chimpanzee study has revealed a number of fascinating observations. We now know that chimpanzees use and make tools. Another study by Dr. Geza Teleki has shown that chimpanzees eat meat which they hunt in small organized groups.

Two other great apes, the gorilla and orangutan, are presently less well known. Dr. George Schaller's study of the mountain gorilla has shown that instead of being brutal, ferocious animals, gorillas are gentle, giant vegetarians. Ms. Dianne Fossey's current study of lowland gorillas should add fascinating comparative data. As of this writing we know little about the Asian orangutan other than that it is in danger of extinction by human intervention.

Bibliography

Bingham, H. 1932. Gorillas in a native habitat. Washington, D.C.: Carnegie Institute of Washington.

Carpenter, C. 1940. A field study in Siam of the behaviors and social relations of the gibbon (*Hylobates lar*). *Comparative Psychological Monographs* 615.

Davenport, R. 1967. The orang-utan in Sabah. *Folia Primatologica* 5:247-63.

Ellefson, J. 1968. Territorial behavior in the common white-handed gibbon, *Hylobates lar* Linn. In *Primates: studies in adaptation and variability*, edited by P. Jay, pp. 180-200. New York: Holt, Rinehart and Winston.

Fossey, D. 1970. Making friends with mountain gorillas. *National Geographic* 137:285.

Fouts, R. 1973. Acquisition and testing of gestural signs in four young chimpanzees. *Science* 180:978-80.

———. 1975. Capacities for language in great apes. In *Sociology and psychology of primates*, edited by R. Tuttle, pp. 371-91. The Hague: Mouton.

Furness, W. 1916. Observations on the mentality of chimpanzees and orangutans. *Proceedings of the American Philosophical Society* 45:281-90.

Galdikas-Brindamour, B., and Brindamour, R. 1975. Orangutans, Indonesia's "People of the Forest." *National Geographic* 148:444-74.

Gardner, R., and Gardner, B. 1969. Teaching sign language to a chimpanzee. *Science* 165:664-72.

Gardner, B., and Gardner, R. 1971. Two-way communication with an infant chimpanzee. In *Behavior of nonhuman primates*, edited by A. Schrier and F. Stollnitz, pp. 117-84. New York: Academic Press.

Garner, R. L. 1896. *Gorillas and chimpanzees.* London: Osgood McIlvaine.

Gray, R. 1969. *The great apes.* New York: Norton.

Harrisson, B. 1962. *The orangutan.* London: Collins.

Hayes, C. 1952. *The ape in our house.* New York: Harper and Brothers.

Hayes, K., and Nissen, C. 1971. Higher mental functions of a home-raised chimpanzee. In *Behavior of nonhuman primates,* edited by A. Schrier and F. Stollnitz, pp. 60-116. New York: Academic Press.

Horr, D. 1975. The Borneo orang-utan: population structure and dynamics in relationship to ecology and reproductive strategy. In *Primate behavior: developments in field and laboratory research,* Vol. 4, edited by L. Rosenblum, pp. 307-23. New York: Academic Press.

Itani, J., and Suzuki, A. 1967. The social unit of chimpanzees. *Primates* 8:355.

Kellogg, W., and Kellogg, L. 1933. *The ape and the child.* New York: McGraw-Hill.

Köhler, W. 1956. *The mentality of apes.* New York: Humanities Press.

Kortlandt, A., and Kooij, M. 1963. Protohominid behavior in primates. *Symposium Zoological Society of London* 10:61.

Kummer, H. 1971. *Primate societies.* Chicago: Aldine-Atherton.

MacKinnon, J. 1974. *In search of the red ape.* New York: Holt, Rinehart and Winston.

Mounin, G. 1976. Language, communication, chimpanzees. *Current Anthropology* 17:1-22.

Mydans, C. 1973. Orangutans can return to the wild with some help. *Smithsonian* November:26-33.

Nishida, T. 1968. The social group of wild chimpanzees in the Mahali Mountains. *Primates* 9:167-224.

Nissen, H. W. 1932. A field study of the chimpanzee—observation of chimpanzee behaviors and environment in western French Guinea. *Comparative Psychological Monographs* 8(36):1.

Pfeiffer, J. 1972. *The emergence of man.* New York: Harper & Row.

Poirier, F. 1969. Behavioral flexibility and intertroop variability among Nilgiri langurs of South India. *Folia Primatologica* 11:119.

Premack, A., and Premack, D. 1972. Teaching language to an ape. *Scientific American* 227:92-99.

Premack, D. 1971a. Language in chimpanzee? *Science* 172:808-22.

———. 1971b. On the assessment of language competence in the chimpanzee. In *Behavior of nonhuman primates,* edited by A. Schrier and F. Stollnitz, pp. 186-228. New York: Academic Press.

Ransom, T., and Rowell, T. 1972. Early social development of feral baboons. In *Primate socialization,* edited by F. Poirier, pp. 105-45. New York: Random House.

Reynolds, V. 1965. *Budongo: A forest and its chimpanzees.* New York: Natural History Press.

———. 1967. *The apes.* New York: Harper & Row.

Rowell, T. 1966. Forest living baboons in Uganda. *Journal of Zoological Society of London* 149:344.

Rumbaugh, D.; Gill, T.; and von Glasensfeld, E. 1973. Reading and sentence completion by a chimpanzee (*Pan*). *Science* 182:731-33.

Rumbaugh, D.; Glasenfeld, E.; Gill, T.; Warner, H.; Pisani, P.; Brown, J.; and Bell, C. 1975. The language skills of a young chimpanzee in a computer-controlled training situation. In *Socioecology and psychology of primates,* edited by R. Tuttle, pp.391-403. Chicago: Aldine (Mouton World Anthropology Series).

Sarles, H. 1969. The study of language and communication across species. *Current Anthropology*, pp. 211-20.

Schaller, G. 1963. *The mountain gorilla.* Chicago: University of Chicago Press.

———. 1964. *The year of the gorilla.* Chicago: University of Chicago Press.

Sugiyama, Y. 1969. Social behavior of chimpanzees in the Budongo Forest, Uganda. *Primates* 10:197.

———. 1972. Social characteristics and socialization of wild chimpanzees. In *Primate socialization*, edited by F. Poirier, pp. 145-64. New York: Random House.

Teleki, G. 1973a. The omnivorous chimpanzee. *Scientific American* 228:33.

———. 1973b. *The predatory behavior of wild chimpanzees.* Lewisburg, Pa.: Bucknell University Press.

van Lawick-Goodall, J. 1967. *My friends the wild chimpanzees.* Washington, D.C.: National Geographic Society.

———. 1971. *In the shadow of man.* Boston: Houghton Mifflin.

Yerkes, R. 1943. *Chimpanzees—a laboratory colony.* New Haven: Yale University Press.

Yerkes, R., and Yerkes, A. 1929. *The great apes.* New Haven: Yale University Press.

Chapter 8
Primate Behavior—
The Monkeys and Prosimians

The subject of primate behavior can be presented in many ways, including the following: (1) with highlights of studies of various groups, e.g., baboon studies, macaque studies, or langur studies; (2) in terms of behavioral patterns or social structures, e.g., one-male groups, large vs. small groups, or territorial vs. nonterritorial animals; or (3) in terms of habitat, e.g., arboreal vs. terrestrial, savanna vs. forest dwellers, or diurnal vs. nocturnal animals. This chapter highlights various studies of monkeys and prosimians.

The ancient Roman Pliny provided one of the first written reports dealing with monkeys. His description of what was known about the common monkeys of his day, which he mistakenly called apes, follows. From his reference to the "dog's headed ape," it is clear that he is referring to the baboon.

> The different kinds of apes, which approach the nearest to the human figure, are distinguished from each other by the tail. Their shrewdness is quite wonderful. It is said that, imitating the hunters, they will besmear themselves with bird-lime, and put their feet into the shoes, which, as so many snares, have been prepared for them. Mucianus says, that they have even played at chess, having, by practice, learned to distinguish the different pieces, which are made of wax. He says that the species which have tails become quite melancholy when the moon is on the wane, and that they leap for joy at the time of the new moon, and adore it.... All the species of apes manifest remarkable affection for their offspring. Females, which have been domesticated, and have had young ones, carry them about and shew them to all comers, shew great delight when they

Rhesus monkey group feeding, Cayo Santiago, Puerto Rico.

Some of what Pliny records is true. Monkeys do show emotion and females take close care of their young (in most species), carrying, grooming, and embracing them. On the other hand, monkeys do not wear shoes, they do not disguise themselves with bird-lime, nor do they play chess! Some monkeys have been domesticated. In Australia a baboon drives a tractor; in South Africa a baboon helps throw the switch at a rail junction; and in Southeast Asia macaques help harvest coconuts.

Prosimians (Figure 8-1)

The suborder of Prosimii includes the families Tupaiidae, Lorisidae, Tarsiidae, and three families residing only on the island of Madagascar in the Malagasy Republic and the Comoro Islands, a French territory in the Indian Ocean—the Lemuridae, Indriidae, and Daubentoniidae. The inclusion of the Tupaiidae, the tree shrews, within the order Primates has been hotly debated. Many biologists feel that tree shrews are in fact insectivores and belong with the order Insectivora. Tree shrews do indeed have many anatomical traits possessed by members of the Insectivora such as an elongated snout, lack of nails, and lack of stereoscopic vision. Others note anatomical traits such as the relatively well-developed auditory and visual brain centers, which are more highly developed than among insectivores, as being indicative of primate heritage. Clearly, the tree shrews are not important because they are or are not primates—rather they appear to resemble a good living model of what the earliest primates looked like. They may be a form as close as we can get to the hypothetical ancestor crossing from one mode of life to another.

Members of the family Tarsiidae belong to a group known as tarsiers. These are small animals with long tails and legs and big, bulging eyes. The tarsiers are excellent leapers. They are native to Southeast Asia, strictly arboreal, are usually found in small groups or in pairs, and feed on insects and lizards. We have some preliminary field data on naturalistic behavior; however, tarsiers fare poorly in captivity.

The lorises, members of the family Lorisidae, have representatives living in both Africa and Asia. Lorises are nocturnal animals and live either solitary or pair existences. Their diet is varied and includes items such as insects, lizards, fruits, seeds, and leaves. The Asian members of the subfamily Lorisidae include the slender and slow loris; the African members are the potto and angwantibo.

The other subfamily of Lorisidae is Galaginae. This subfamily includes the galagos, some of whom are called bush babies. These are social primates, apparently territorial, and insectivorous in diet. One field study on the galagos was published in 1963 (Sauer and Sauer). The principal locomotor mode of the galagos is labelled vertical clinging and leaping, and it has been suggested by some (e.g., Napier and Walker, 1967) that this mode of locomotion was important in the evolution of bipedalism.

As already mentioned, there is a concentration of prosimians, members of the families of Lemuridae, Indriidae, and Daubentoniidae, on the island of Madagascar (Malagasy Republic). It is believed that the early ancestors of these animals have been long removed from the monkey stock and have undergone their own independent adaptive radiation into a variety of forms.

Lemurs, discussed in more detail below, belong to the family Lemuridae. While some members of the family are nocturnal and solitary, the ring-tailed lemur is diurnal and lives in social groups. The family Indriidae includes forms known as the indri, avahi, and sifaka. These are the most monkeylike of the prosimians. Little is known about the social behavior of the indri. Avahi are reputed to live in family units composed of two to four individuals. The family Daubentoniidae consists of the aye-aye. Aye-ayes are distinctive in the development of two large, chisellike teeth in the front of the jaw and an elongated nail on a long, thin, middle finger. The aye-aye is nocturnal and uses its teeth to tear open tree barks to get at grubs, which it then "spears" with its modified nail.

Some of the most primitive of the nonhuman primate social organizations are found among the Malagasy lemurs, and these social organizations provide some clues as to what some of the earliest primate social organizations may have been like. One of the Malagasy forms, *Lepilemur,* lives in individual territories (Charles-Dominique and Hladik, 1971; Hladik, 1975). This type of social organization is characteristic of that described for many other so-called solitary primitive mammals. Hladik (1975) notes that females defend these territories against other females of the species. However, a female may share her territory with one or several of her daughters for a year or two. Males have territories which extend over one or several of the female territories, and these are defended against incursion from other males. As a result some extra males, those without these territories, live outside of the nucleus of the population as peripheral males. Such males are common in most nonhuman primate species.

Figure 8-1. A lemur, a Malagasy prosimian.

A major component of the nocturnal activity of the *Lepilemur* is a motionless watching at the border of the territory. At nightfall, *Lepilemur* makes certain specific calls which function to locate the animals, and their territories, to their neighbors. Such calls, known as territorial calls, are common in all territorial nonhuman primates such as langurs, colobines, and gibbons. Hladik notes that nearby animals can probably identify one another by their calls, for there are slight differences in the calls of each animal. (I was able to notice the same thing in my field study of South Indian Nilgiri langurs. Animals had distinctive vocal patterns which served to distinguish them from one another.)

The food of this prosimian, consisting mainly of foliage and flowers, is very abundant in all parts of their territory. Hladik feels that this explains why the animals do not move much and why they spend most of their time on watch for competitors at the territorial boundaries.

Prosimian ancestry diverged from ours in the Paleocene or early Eocene, long before the evolution of higher primates. Anatomically, and in some respects behaviorally, these animals are probably closer to the common ancestor of the primate stock than more highly evolved primates. In 1863, T. H. Huxley noted, "Perhaps no order of mammals presents us with so extraordinary a series of gradations as this—leading us insensibly from the crown and summit of the animal creation down to creatures from which there is but a step, as it seems, to the lowest, smallest, and least intelligent of the placental mammals" (from Jolly, 1966:8). Interestingly, although their anatomy is primitive for a primate, their social structures resemble those of monkeys. Many lemur species have multiple male groups, and infants of either sex remain lifelong members of the bisexual social group. The bisexual, year-round, social organization appears to be an ancient primate pattern. Lemurs provide a third, independent evolutionary line to compare with New and Old World primates. When the three independent lines converge or overlap, we may have isolated a clue to the origin and nature of primate sociality.

Dr. Jolly's Studies. Dr. Alison Jolly conducted a major study of lemur behavior which was subsequently published in her 1966 book entitled *Lemur Behavior: A Madagascar Field Study.* Among the most important aspects to emerge from Jolly's study are observations of the commonality of lemur to other primate societies and of ancient traits upon which primate sociality may ultimately be based. The social Lemuroidea offer one final objection to the hypothesis that sex may be the major bonding force in primate societies, for they breed seasonally. Presumably they have always done so, for they never developed a monthly cycle. Yet they share the basic primate social order of a bisexual, year-round, lifelong social organization which must be based on cohesive forces other than permanent sexual attraction.

Jolly also suggests that the ultimate derivation of adult social behaviors may stem directly from the infant's grooming and play behavior. Momma is the infant's first, and ultimate, social mate; the mother-infant dyad may be the basis for establishing relationships vital to adult social ties.[1] If friendly social relations are derived from the mother-infant interaction, it suggests that social primates retain many infantile

[1] I have argued this point in a number of previous publications (see Poirer, 1968b, 1969a, 1970a, 1972, 1973b).

Figure 8-2. Distribution of New World primates (shaded area).

characters. (This is known as **neoteny,** the retention of infantile traits into adulthood.) The original cohesive force in primate social evolution might be an infantile or juvenile attraction to others that was retained in adulthood.

Jolly's research also points to the relationship between the development of higher levels of intelligence and social living. Primate social behavior demands learning; it also makes learning possible. There seems to be a very good relationship, a continual interaction, between intelligence and social dependence. Intelligence integrates an animal into a group (in which different animals play different roles, or the same animal plays many roles) and makes the individual more dependent on the group. This dependence, in its turn, allows and encourages increasing social intelligence. Social life may be a primate trait; but, intelligence and group dependence interrelate and reinforce each other.

New World Monkeys (Figure 8-2)

New World monkeys are arboreal animals ranging from southern Mexico south. Their arboreality indicates that much of their evolutionary history occurred in trees overlying swampy areas. Such areas afford little terrain for evolving terrestrial lifeways. Dr. Clarence Ray Carpenter was one of the first to conduct scientific studies of New World monkeys.

Some New World monkeys of the family Cebidae closely resemble the Old World monkeys, and it is difficult to believe that they are only distant relations. However, there are important cranial and dental differences. South American monkeys have three premolars while Old World monkeys have two. Another major difference is nasal shape (Figure 8-3); nostrils of New World monkeys are more widely spaced than those of Old World monkeys. Furthermore, the nostrils of New World monkeys face sideways rather than forward or down. Some New World monkeys also have prehensile tails, allowing them to use their tail like a fifth hand for grasping.

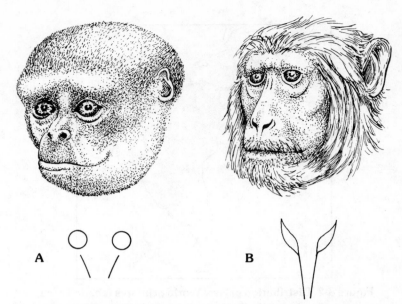

Figure 8-3. A comparison of the nose shapes of (A) New World and (B) Old World monkeys.

The Callithricidae. New World primates fall into two groups: the Callithricidae and the Cebidae. Marmosets and tamarinds are included in the Callithricidae. These are miniature monkeys, small enough to be held in one hand, and many are decorated with pompously colored patches or hair tufts. Marmosets have the generalized primate diet including insects, small vertebrates, and forest fruits. Little is known about their naturalistic behavior. They seem to live in family groups of three to eight members; however, larger groups have been observed.

Titi Monkey. The Cebidae are a large, diverse group. The most primitive member of the group is the titi (*Callicebus*) monkey, a small, thickly haired animal which quadrupedally runs and leaps through the trees. Rather recently, Dr. William Mason (1971) undertook a naturalistic study of the titi monkey. These monkeys live in pairs or small family groups averaging three to five animals. Each family recognizes a small forest area as its own domain which may be defended with vocalizations and certain postural threat gestures. Loud vocalizations emitted early in the morning seem to be spacing mechanisms signalling a group's location. The vocalizations serve to maintain group separateness. Titis form strong, long-lasting sexual bonds.

Squirrel Monkey. The familiar Central and South American squirrel monkey is a small, arboreal quadruped, with a long and thickly haired tail. Because of their size and docility, they are popular pets and often used in brain research. A number of transplanted colonies such as Florida's Monkey Jungle have been established for tourists. This colony has been studied by John and Janice Baldwin (1971) who then undertook a comparative study of squirrel monkeys in their native habitat. Such studies provide an insight into an animal's means of coping with environmental change.

Howler Monkey. Howler and spider monkeys are the best-known South American primates. The howler monkey is aptly named; it possesses a deep, booming vocalization which once heard is not soon forgotten. Howlers come in different sizes and colors; however, most are large robust prehensile-tailed monkeys with long black, brown, or copper-red hair depending upon the species. Beneath the chin a vocal apparatus, the larynx, is specialized for producing loud vocalizations. Howlers often hang or swing by their arms, somewhat reminiscent of the best Old World brachiators, the gibbons.

Howler monkeys live in groups averaging about eighteen animals; however, group sizes range from two to forty-five animals. Females usually outnumber the males, a common feature of most primate societies.[2] While most howler groups are bisexual, males occasionally live alone. Each howler group is nomadic within a fairly well-defined home range defended against intrusion by other groups. Territory is maintained by howling and shaking and breaking branches, acts which substitute for physical aggression. Howling occurs early in the morning; it is a means of locating and spacing groups and a pattern preventing intergroup contact. There is no clear pattern of male dominance and both males and females care for the young.

Spider Monkeys. Spider monkeys (Figure 8-4) are the nearest New World equivalents of gibbons. Their long arms, hooklike hands, and prehensile tail make them supreme acrobats. They are particularly

[2]The number of females to males is often expressed as the **socionomic sex ratio**. For example, 2:1 means two females for every male.

Figure 8-4. A spider moneky *(Ateles).* **Note the relatively long arms and prehensile tail draped over the upper limb.**

prized as zoo animals because of their range of acrobatic wizardry. As an animal which often sits and climbs trees in an erect position, and which often walks bipedally semi-erect, the spider monkey is getting a close look as a possible model for the development of hominid bipedalism. A number of anatomical and locomotor studies are in progress which promise to provide some interesting insights for reconstructing hominid locomotor patterns.

Dr. C. R. Carpenter made an early behavioral study of spider monkeys. Spider monkeys live in groups varying in size according to the type of habitat. Group sizes range from a small family group to large aggregations of 100 or more animals. Females outnumber males. Females with their offspring seem to form a cohesive subgroup within the larger social grouping. Male dominance behavior is evident.

Old World Monkeys (Figure 8-5)

Because they are phylogenetically closer to you and me, Old World monkeys are a source of continuing interest although few of the many different Old World monkeys have been studied. Fewer yet have been studied in detail. Major studies have been conducted on macaques, baboons, langurs or leaf-eating monkeys, and some African cercopithecines like the vervets and patas.

Macaques. This most ubiquitous laboratory primate was known for its use in biomedical and psychological testing long before anything was known about its naturalistic behavior. The first rather complete naturalistic studies of rhesus macaques were undertaken only within the last few years. Macaques are especially interesting because of their wide geographical and ecological habitation. They inhabit tropical rain forests, monsoon forests, mangrove swamps, Himalayan montane forests, and temperate forests of China and Japan. They are also found in the grasslands and dry areas of scrub in India and Ceylon. Additionally, they have been transplanted to a number of zoo colonies. Dr. Carpenter established a rhesus colony on the tiny island of Cayo Santiago, off the east coast of Puerto Rico. Macaques range from being

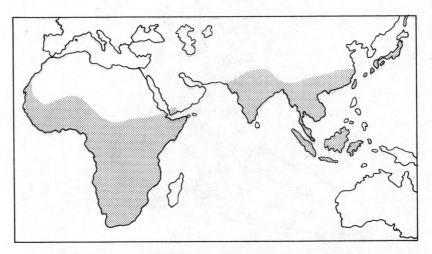

Figure 8-5. Geographical distribution of Old World monkeys (shaded areas).

January, 1966 (Ootacamund, South India)

For the first time in what seems to be ages, I am again well and ready to watch monkeys. The morning is quite chilly, it rained heavily last evening. The dew hangs heavy. The clouds roll across the sky in multiple patterns. At this altitude of 7800 feet you can almost touch and walk upon them.

I arrive at Governors Shola Forest Reserve, exhilarated to be back on my feet and hopeful that the females have not yet had the babies their stomachs seemed no longer able to hold six weeks ago. I waited impatiently to see the infants, for I badly want to study the mother-infant relationship. How will the troop's male react to the infants? Did the lowest ranking female in the dominance heirarchy give birth? What would the infants look like? What is their future as people destroy the niche? I badly wanted answers.

06:00 Clouds have settled in the valley leaving the impression of cotton snow. The bluish tint to the hills (from which they are named, the Nilgiris—the Blue Hills) is a sight through a dreamlike vapor. The scene is beyond description. I photograph this loveliness with my Nikon, but I know the pictures will not reflect what I see in my mind's eye.

I parked my jeep by a stream, which was now running rather fast. The winter monsoons (though slight this year) have been good the last few days. I walked along the stream, hoping to see, or smell, if the monkeys were recently here. I found many tracks in the mud, recognizing those of the sambar (a large deerlike creature), deer, wild boar, and leopard. Nocturnal creatures retreated for their sleep, leaving this scene to we diurnal creatures.

I walked upstream collecting new plant samples for later identification. I also collected soil samples from areas where I previously witnessed monkeys eating dirt. This earth-eating may be a response to the gastric upset common to these monkeys—so fond of lousy tasting leaves. I photographed some plants, made some new rough maps, and continued to look for the animals. I focused on the tree tops, hoping the monkeys would be sunning themselves in the few rays the sun struggled to provide. I banked on finding them in one of their favorite groups of sleeping trees within the home range. However, since I had not joined them in a while, I was unsure which one of the three areas Group A now fed and slept in. Because of the rather large size of the home range (compounded by the height dimension) I arbitrarily chose the sleeping site which seemed to be the favorite of A group, composed of 1 male and 5 females. (I assumed this to be a rather new group since infants were absent and all the females and the male were of reproductive age.) I was sorely disappointed. I sat to rest, brood, and collect some thoughts to write in my damp notebook, thankful that I long since switched to ball pen and carried spare pencils. Damp paper is a bear to write on.

At 07:15, I spotted monkeys high in an *Acacia* tree voraciously eating seeds long dismissed as inedible for my tastes. The male was absent. I waited. Then I heard his loud, booming, echoing call—his morning location to adjacent troops (in this case being three). The sound thrilled me, as usual. He leaped through the trees, crashing dead branches to the ground. He made magnificent 30 foot leaps. I knew males of adjacent troops watched as intently as I. Then silence. I approached to about 20 yards, he was nervously grinding his canines producing a squeaking noise. He defecated and urinated, as is also usual (I was glad I was not beneath him!) An erect penis indicated his tense state. I left, knowing he would soon join the females. Males of the adjacent troops then responded. The calls echoed through the forest's stillness for distances up to a mile away.

Females fed unconcerned with the male's show. Their disinterest often surprised me. Even when males of adjacent troops occasionally rushed through their troop, they fed unconcernedly. They would not be harmed, but it took me months to learn that. Then, I saw a reddish-brown bloob, two bloobs, then three. Damned, the infants were born when I was sick. The hassle with customs to get my film to record the first few days was wasted. My trip to Madras, my annoyance, a waste. I quickly put that aside when I noticed that the females left their infants. The infants screamed loudly, but their mothers were off feeding in adjacent trees. The subordinate female (she at least still looked pregnant) moved among the babies. They quieted some and briefly grappled with one another. (I later learned that Nilgiri langur females "baby sit" for one another. Surprisingly, especially in light of other primate studies, these mothers were rather lackadaisical in their maternal care.)

Day after day I watched the mothers, the infants, the male, other troops, the wild deer, boar, plants, etc. After 12 months and some 1250 hours of observation, I felt secure enough to write my doctoral dissertation and publish my data.

Excerpt of some of my field notes during my study of Nilgiri langurs.

almost completely arboreal to being almost completely terrestrial. Besides trees, they inhabit cliffs and rocky places, and in India they live in the cities, temples, and railroad stations. The major macaque groups on which we have naturalistic behavioral data are the Indian rhesus and bonnet macaques, the Japanese macaque, the "Barbary ape" or Gibraltar macaque, on the island of Gibraltar,[3] and the pig-tail macaque in Malaysia.

The rhesus is the best-known macaque (Figure 8-6). One of the first rhesus macaque studies was undertaken in the temple habitats of northern India. Indians tolerate and feed the monkeys; they are protected in the temple habitat, and many rhesus troops live permanently in various north Indian temples. The same is true of the South Indian bonnet macaque.

Provisioned Colonies—Cayo Santiago and Japan Monkey Centre. The transplanted Cayo Santiago rhesus colony is the source of longitudinal (long-term) data for approximately the past thirty years. Dr. Carpenter made the first studies of these animals in the 1940s; they have been studied regularly for the last twelve to fifteen years. The other well-known macaque group is the Japanese macaque. Some of these provisioned colonies have been the object of intensive study for the past twenty years, principally by workers from Kyoto University. The Cayo Santiago and Japanese macaque colonies have yielded very useful information, some of which has altered our conceptions of hominid evolution.

Data derived from the provisioned macaque colonies have been especially eye-opening. During the long period of observation indi-

[3]These monkeys are the charge of the British Gibraltar regiment who feed and care for them. The legend is that the British will remain on the island as long as the monkeys, and vice versa.

Figure 8-6. The rhesus macaque (*Macaca mulatta*) of India. This illustration depicts an immature animal.

vidual animals, their genealogies (traced through the female, as paternity in natural conditions is almost impossible to determine), and their individual dominance positions became known. These conditions led to such information as the fact that one's position in the social order is a reflection of the mother's position within that order,[4] that there is relatively little sexual behavior between a mother and her offspring (the basis of the incest taboo appears older than human cultural behavior),[5] that there are many behavioral differences between groups, that new behaviors can be learned and transmitted, that there are optimum group sizes (growth beyond which leads to group disintegration and increased aggression), and that there are group traditions (such as specific foods and travel routes). The complexity of primate society as revealed by these studies was quite a shock to the many scientists who believed in the very uniqueness of our cultural and social traditions. We seem to be finding the roots of many of our cultural manifestations among the behaviors and social organizations of some of the better-known and understood nonhuman primates.

The following description summarizes the major characteristics of macaque society. Macaques are very social animals; their societies are characterized among other principles by clear-cut **dominance hierarchies,** especially among males. Their societies are male dominated, but they may be female-focal. Relationships are traced through the mother, and most of the job of socializing the infant falls upon the female. The female provides group continuity. Males police the group; they minimize disruption and impose discipline upon the group. Rela-

[4]The argument here is that a dominant mother supports her infant in any altercations, thus the infant has less subordinate sessions. Furthermore, the infant learns dominance from watching its mother's behavior. Infants of dominant mothers also have more opportunity to interact with animals of high status. Finally, dominant mothers are less possessive of their infants, the infants have an opportunity for more social interaction and at earlier ages than is generally true of infants of subordinate animals (Poirier, 1970c, 1972, 1973a, 1974 discusses this at length).

[5]However, there is some information suggesting that mother-offspring matings among macaques occur more frequently than originally supposed.

PRIMATE BEHAVIOR

A. Adult female vervet (*Cercopithecus aethiops*) with young infant at her breast.

B. Subadult olive baboons (*Papio anubis*).

C. An adult male rhesus macaque (*Macaca mulatta*) threatens with a yawn. Note the canines and closed eyes.

D. A Nilgiri langur (*Presbytis johnii*) threatens with open mouth.

E. Adult capuchin monkey (*Cebus capucinus*).

F. Rhesus macaques (*Macaca mulatta*) feeding. Female in center has cheek pouches full of food.

G. Adult male patas monkey (*Erythrocebus patas*) with food in mouth.

H. Adult male vervet (*Cercopithecus aethiops*).

I. Adult male Nilgiri langur (*Presbytis johnii*) feeding. Note the leaves in mouth.

J. Young adult male rhesus macaque (*Macaca mulatta*) threatens with open mouth.

K. A juvenile bonnet macaque (*Macaca radiata*).

L. Japanese macaques (*Macaca fuscata*). Two adult females in a grooming bout. The youngster is a yearling.

tionships between animals vary and inter-animal relationships seem to be especially based upon kinship and individual personality.

The rhesus and Japanese macaque group structure is comprised of a number of subgroupings. The central part of a Japanese macaque troop is inhabited by dominant males, females and their offspring. Subordinate Japanese macaque infants have little contact with the dominant males; it is likely they will eventually leave the group. Solitary or peripheral males (animals living on the edge of the troop) are common. Subadults and young adults often spend some part of their lives outside the group either living alone or in all-male groups.

Consistent with their complex social groups, macaques have a rich communicatory network. Their gestural and vocal communicative matrix is varied and expressive. **Grooming** (picking through either your own hair or the hair of another animal) is a very common behavior pattern and many hours are spent in mutual grooming bouts. Grooming behavior serves two prime functions; it helps keep the hair or any wounds free of debris, and it helps cement social relationships. It might also be noted that the animals simply find grooming "pleasurable," as is judged by their behavior during grooming episodes.

Macaque infants and juveniles spend a good part of each day in social play, most of which occurs in subgroups composed of animals of the same age and sex. Young infant play groups are sexually integrated; however, females leave the play groups by 1½ years, at which time play is quite rough. By 1½ years males and females begin to assume different social roles. This early differentiation of social roles is in training for adult life. Young females begin to show intense interest in their newly born siblings. Females spend considerable time together; within this context young females learn the mothering role. Much of this learning is observational; however, a young female may hold, handle, and carry her siblings or other infants. Thus she practices her mothering role. This is very strong contradictory evidence to the proposition that mothering is instinctive behavior (Poirier, 1972, 1973b). (Contrary to what is commonly thought, social roles based on gender are not the sole property of the human primate.)

Baboons (Figure 8-7). Relatively speaking, the baboon is the African counterpart of the Asian and North African macaque. Baboons have been the subject of numerous behavioral studies since Washburn and DeVore's (1961) work in the late 1950s. Much has been written about baboon social life and until recently they were the model of what many knew of primate behavior. Unfortunately that clouded the picture. Original studies of savanna baboons emphasized their strong male dominance, tight troop structure, and relatively high level of aggression. More recent studies of forest-living baboons give a different perspective. Forest-living baboons have smaller groups, less male aggression, and less tightly knit groups.

Baboons are a diverse group inhabiting such vegetational zones as sub-deserts, savannas, acacia thornveld, and rain forests. Minor baboon habitats include rocky cliffs and gorges (the hamadryas baboon in Ethiopia) and seaside cliffs (the chacma baboon in South Africa). All baboons sleep in trees, excepting the hamadryas which often converge a few hundred strong to sleep on isolated rock outcrops. Their diet is

Figure 8-7. The baboon (*Papio*), an Old World monkey adapted to terrestrial quadrupedalism.

varied—baboons are omnivorous, and their diet includes fruits, grasses, seeds, roots, lizards, and occasionally other meat. There are troops in South Africa which regularly kill domestic sheep and there is a predatory East African troop.

Savanna Baboons. Savanna baboons have been studied in both East and South Africa. The most comprehensive study occurred in the Amboseli Reserve, East Africa, where baboons were observed from a Land Rover supplied with a wide range of equipment. These baboons live in closed male-dominated groups. The males play the major role in protecting the group from outside predation (e.g., by cheetahs and lions); they also police the troop by mediating dominance encounters. Grooming is a prime ameliorant of aggression and is a major form of social behavior. Sexual behavior is limited; during breeding, consort pairs (a male and female mating pair) are common on the troop's periphery. When a female enters estrus (i.e., when she is sexually receptive) she mates with many males, subordinates first. The more dominant males may mate last, when the female is at the height of estrus and is most likely to ovulate. Clues as to the state of estrus seem to be olfactory and visual; the male sniffs and visually and orally inspects the vaginal area. Since dominant males are the last to copulate with the females, they may be the most likely to pass their genes to succeeding generations. This selective mating is likely to have important effects upon subsequent generations and would justify further study.

The Gelada. The gelada *(Theropithecus gelada),* like other baboons, is a terrestrial vegetarian. The gelada mainly inhabits the Ethiopian highlands, living in troops of up to 400 animals. Geladas are beautifully adapted to their cliff habitat. During movement females and young move closest to the cliff edges where the males protect them from predatory attack. Whenever danger threatens, the whole troop moves to the cliff edge. The females and young first descend the cliff face to the ledges; the males act as a shield above them. The troop sleeps on the cliff edges.

What seems to be one large gelada troop is actually a combination of smaller one-male units. The existence of the one-male units is particularly evident during the dry season when food is scattered. At this time male bands, varying in size from four to twelve, separate from one another and forage independently. When these one-male groups rejoin they become intermixed into the larger troop; this is typical when food is plentiful. Females tend to remain closely associated with one male only and restrict their sexual activity to him. The sex ratio varies from 2.5 to 7 females for every one male.

Hamadryas Baboons. The hamadryas is a most interesting animal. The hamadryas daytime foraging unit consists of one adult male and multiple females. At night many one-adult male groups congregate at one sleeping cliff, an adaptation to the lack of sleeping facilities. The major hamadryas study was undertaken in Ethiopia by the Swiss zoologist Hans Kummer (1968) along with a colleague, F. Kurt.

The one adult male, multiple female hamadryas organization is vigorously preserved. The leader male of the "harem" group prevents mating between younger males in his group and the females. Younger males must wait until the older male gives way, or they may form their own group by "adopting" young juvenile females. These juvenile females are a few years from sexual maturity and male sexual gratification is thus delayed until later in life. The male has a specialized behavior called the neck-bite, which is used to retrieve any female who strays from his group. The male approaches the female and mouths or gums her neck. The skin is not broken. A female whose neck is bitten immediately follows a male back to her group. The male hamadryas's neck bite and the female's following response are very important communicative mechanisms, functioning to maintain the hamadryas one adult male, multiple female social unit.

The Hamadryas—A Model for Hominid Evolution. To summarize: a number of hamadryas one adult male units come together to share a single sleeping site. This group is an aggregation of familiar individuals. As a new day begins the larger group breaks into small foraging units. Because both the hamadryas and the human primate independently developed stable social units linked in large bands, the hamadryas are often seen as another model for reconstructing human evolution. Both presumably arrived at this structure when living in open country. Should the hamadryas social organization be a model for the origin of the human family? The phylogenetic gap between us and the hamadryas prevents a firm answer. Nevertheless, the hamadryas provide a measure against which hypotheses can be tested. The hamadryas model calls into question the hypothesis that permanent human sexual receptivity evolved in support of stable male-female bonds. Furthermore, the hamadryas suggest that pair bonds evolved before a sexual division of labor, contrary to the assumption that economic factors closely united the human pair.

Characteristics of Baboon Social Organization. Baboons, and to a lesser extent macaques and langurs, clearly demonstrate that social behavior and organization are influenced by the habitat. Savanna-dwelling baboons live in larger, more tightly knit groups than forest baboons. Hamadryas baboons, and to a lesser extent geladas, show a completely different social organization.

Baboon troop sizes usually vary from 8 to 200; forty to eighty animals is not an uncommon average. Females usually outnumber males by a ratio of from 4:1 to 14:1. Group dominance hierarchies are stable; the male plays a major role in maintaining group calm. Intertroop relationships are usually nonagressive; in fact, they may be amicable. Groups are largely stable and grooming seems to be an important behavior helping to maintain group stability. Play behavior is a very important element of a young baboon's life. The communication repertoire is rich in various gestural and vocal patterns.

Leaf-eaters, Langurs and Colobines. Increasingly we know more and more about this widespread Asian and African group. In Asia these monkeys are referred to as langurs, in Africa as colobus monkeys. They are primarily arboreal rain-forest dwellers and have in common their specialized stomachs, which are elaborately sacculated organs. This is their adaptation to a bulky, fibrous, extremely hard to digest leafy diet. Fruits, small insects, tree bark, and such agricultural products as potatoes and cabbages augment this diet.

North Indian Langurs. Major studies of Asian leaf-eating monkeys have occurred in India and Ceylon. Some work has also been conducted in Malaysia. The Hanuman monkey or common langur inhabiting both North and South India is the best-known Asian leaf-eater. The North Indian common langur was one of the first nonhuman primates to be studied. This study emphasized certain characteristics of North Indian langurs which were then assumed common to all leaf-eaters. For example, North Indian langurs live a very peaceful life; feeding is a major time-consuming activity. Most North Indian langurs live in bisexual groups in which females outnumber males by as much as five to one. There are multiple male groups, but there are also all-male groups and solitary males. North Indian langur groups live in home ranges which are not defended and are not therefore called territories. Altercations between animals of different groups are few.

Variations on a Theme. Subsequent studies by a number of individuals, including myself, of langur populations in South India and other parts of Asia disagreed in substantial measure with some of the above conclusions. This disagreement taught us a most important lesson, which is also applicable in reconstructing hominid evolution. One primate is not typical of all the primates; there are substantial differences, even among members of the same species. These differences are in large measure habitat-dependent.

Studies subsequent to that in North India raised a number of doubts as to the commonality of many behavioral traits. All langurs are peaceful, at least most of the time, and in comparison to more terrestrial species. However, it was discovered that in some areas these animals are also quite territorial. The same is true of the now-studied African leaf-eaters. Males, especially, guard their territories against intrusion by males of adjacent troops. Territories are maintained with loud, booming vocalizations, jumping through trees, and shaking branches. Physical contact is rare, however.

Infanticide Among Langurs. Infanticide is a very interesting behavioral pattern found among some langurs. Many langur groups are one adult male, multiple female groups. Excess males live either alone or more often in all-male (sometimes called bachelor) groups. Aggression is quite common when males of an all-male group approach and attempt to join a bisexual group. One outcome of this aggression is that all the infants of the bisexual group are killed by the new males and all males are then driven out from the group. This harsh action seems to bring the females to sexual readiness. The new male copulates with the females, ensuring that all the subsequent infants are his own. What makes this behavior so very interesting is that it appears only in some North and South Indian common langur groups and perhaps in Ceylon. The behavior is also periodic and happens about once every four years. Although we are unable to adequately interpret this phenomenon, it has been suggested that high population densities may be one cause of the aggression or that killing the infants may be a form of incest avoidance. Since the changeover occurs about once each four years and since one result of the change is that young males are driven from the troop at about sexual maturity, it is an ultimate means of avoiding mother-son, father-daughter, and brother-sister mating. This explanation is as controversial as it is intriguing.

Instances of Primate Adaptability. One result of the many baboon studies has been the documentation of a number of instances of troop-specific social traditions. Two of the most interesting examples are documentation of hunting and meat eating in an East African troop and crop-raiding in another East African troop. The hunting tradition occurs among a troop of olive baboons *(Papio anubis)* living on a farm near Gilgil, Kenya. In 1970-1971 Dr. R. Harding of the University of Pennsylvania witnessed forty-seven cases of predation during 1032 hours of observation; this was the highest rate of predation reported for any nonhuman primate. During this period the baboons in this troop preyed upon cape hares, birds, and young gazelles. All but three cases of predation witnessed resulted from adult male activity, and in all but one instance the adult male ate the meat.

In 1972-1974 Dr. Shirley Strum (1975) witnessed 100 cases of predation during 1200 hours of observation. In 1970-1971 males did 94 percent of the killing and 98 percent of the eating of prey; adult females did 6 percent of the killing and 2 percent of the eating. During 1972-1974 Strum noted that males did 61 percent of the killing, females 14 percent, juveniles 16 percent, and 9 percent of the killing was accomplished by an unidentified age group. Hence, a four-year period witnessed the spread of a troop tradition virtually throughout the age classes in this troop.

The change in participation of predatory activities altered the profile of the prey. Although the tradition had spread to new troop members, adult males were still present during 93 percent of the predatory episodes and one male ate meat in 91 percent of the recorded instances. Meat-eating and predatory activity were individual matters, and some males were more active than others. The same holds true for the females; some females were interested in the kill and others were not. Furthermore, those females who were involved in the capture of prey were not always the same females who consumed the meat. Nevertheless, the interest of some females in the capture and consumption of prey equalled that of some of the males.

During Harding's study, juvenile interest in consumption was slight; however, by 1974 juvenile interest heightened. Strum suggests that once a juvenile was successful in obtaining meat its interest in meat and participation in consumption heightened. The kill sites soon became a gathering place for youngsters and one can suggest that during this time youngsters learned to eat meat by watching the adults. Juveniles were observed to prey upon birds, hares, and even one gazelle. Infants did eat some meat; however, they didn't capture their prey. A successful relay system of capturing the prey soon became the rule.

Since meat was passed among individuals, when one animal was displaced or lost interest in the prey meat was shared by various group members. Females were observed to share meat with youngsters and some males and females shared meat with one another. This sharing of food was *only* observed during meat eating, and sharing of food between a female and a youngster was only observed in this circumstance. This observation adds credence to our suggestion made elsewhere in the book that once our ancestors began to hunt food, sharing became the rule.

One of the most important implications derived from these observations is that nonhuman primates can successfully hunt without even the rudiments of language. This is borne out by observations of predation by social carnivores and chimpanzees. Obviously hunting behavior alone was not the impetus for human language.

A further instance of the development of a troop tradition is noted in Maples's (1969) study of crop-raiding baboons in south-eastern Kenya. In contrast to savanna-living baboons, these animals have a dispersed troop structure and are quiet compared to savanna troops. Maples suggests these are adaptations to close human interaction. Confirmatory evidence for Maples's suggestion come from my own studies in South India (Poirier, 1969b, 1970a) and on St. Kitts, West Indies (Poirier, 1972b). In both India and on St. Kitts the animals not only adapted to new food sources, but to the continual harrassment of local farmers and their dogs. The potato and cauliflower were introduced to the Nilgiris in India 80-100 years ago and are now the main agricultural crops. The home range of one of the Nilgiri langur groups studied included large cultivated tracts of potato and cauliflower. Local informants related that the farms ringing the area were at most 25-30 years old. Considering that these are the sole farms in this area, this local langur population only recently adapted to this new food source.

The behavior of farm-raiding groups, both in India and on St. Kitts, as among the baboons studied by Maples, was different than that of forest groups. Because raiding usually occurs when humans are absent, these animals have marked activity peaks in the early morning and afternoon before and after the farmers have left the fields. In both the cases which I witnessed the proximity and threat of humans has altered the animal's reactions to them. This is particularly noticeable when comparing the interest and/or fright commonly shown humans in the forests.

The St. Kitts monkeys raid cultivated farm plots and sugar cane plantations. Crop raiding yields fascinating information concerning adaptive processes, for raiding consists of a number of behavioral adaptations which may have appeared in connection with the competition between human and monkey. While crop raiding is of recent origin in India, it has been established for 300 years on St. Kitts. In India, as well as on St. Kitts and in Kenya, adult males play a particular role as a look-out, as sentinel animals. Adult males in India and on St. Kitts position themselves in clear view high in trees; while farmers focus on them, other animals enter the plots and take the crops. This sentinel pattern seems to be an elaboration of the male's role.

Clearly certain behavioral and dietary patterns change in the presence of human intervention. Groups living in pockets where they are forced into continual interaction with human populations and which exploit this situation to their benefit (i.e., by crop raiding) differ behaviorally and in terms of their social organization from other members of their species.

The acceptance of the new dietary items discussed above has correlates in material published by Japanese investigators subsumed under the title "subcultural propagation." Kawamura (1959) discusses the "sweet-potato-washing sub-culture" among members of the Koshima macaque troop, Itani (1958) reports how the candy-eating habit spread among members of the Takasakiyama troop, and Yamada (1963) discusses the propagation of wheat-eating among the membership of the Minoo-B troop. Tsumori (1967) discusses the transmission of these feeding behaviors and notes that the acquisition of these new behaviors is largely determined by age and/or sex differences. The dominance and kinship relationships between the animals involved also affected the rapidity of the acceptance or rejection of a new behavioral trait.

A brief review of what has been said in the previous two chapters suggests that there are five major themes in primate social organization: dominance and dominance hierarchies, the mother-infant bond and the matrifocal social unit, the sexual bond between males and females, the separation of roles between adult and young, and the separation of roles according to gender (Lancaster, 1975). Each species, and perhaps each group within a species, has its own combination of these factors; each places different emphasis on these factors according to habitat and evolutionary-historical factors, which weave a collection of individuals into a social system. However, we must bear in mind that in primates it is the social system which enables group members to meet the demands of everyday life.

Although our discussion of primate behavior has been brief, it should now be clear that we are not primates by chance. Many of the themes binding human society are shared by our nonhuman primate relatives and many existed long before hominids appeared. Nonhuman primate social organization and behavior set the stage for the evolution of the human way of life. "By understanding the social behavior and adaptations of our closest relatives we can far better understand how and why human beings are both like and different from other primates" (Lancaster, 1975:41).

Our knowledge of the behavior and social organization of prosimians and monkeys is limited to a number of studies on a few species. Few species have been the subject of longitudinal studies or studied in varying habitats. The major prosimian habitat is the Island of Madagascar, the Malagasy Republic. Lemurs offer a

number of insights into the behavioral patterns of the most primitive, the first evolved, nonhuman primates. Many lemurs share the year-round permanent social organizations of their more highly evolved monkey and ape relatives.

New World primates are almost strictly arboreal. Anatomically and in some respects behaviorally distinct from Old World primates, New World primates have not been intensely studied. Although there is increasing interest in these animals, much work remains to be done.

The best-known Old World monkeys are some species of baboons, langurs, and macaques. Because of the establishment of such research facilities as Cayo Santiago and the Japan Monkey Centre, we have access to much longitudinal data on both rhesus and Japanese macaques, which is having a marked influence on the formulation of theories of primate behavior and human evolution. Since the early work by Sir Solly Zuckerman, baboons have been the focus of a number of studies. Baboons provide very interesting data as to the adaptations needed for coping with a savanna environment (probably that of ancestral hominids). They also tell us how a species adapts to various habitats; similar data on habitat adaptation comes from studies of Asian and African leaf-monkeys.

There is still much work to be done. Our major limitations now seem to be financial—there is a lack of funding. Future studies will be long term and problem oriented in contrast to the shorter studies of recent years.

Bibliography

Altmann, S., ed. 1967. *Social communication among primates.* Chicago: University of Chicago Press.

Altmann, S., and Altmann, J. 1970. *Baboon ecology.* Chicago: University of Chicago Press.

Baldwin, J. 1971. The social organization of a semi-free-ranging troop of squirrel monkeys (*Saimiri sciureus*). *Folia Primatologica* 14:23.

Bertrand, M. 1969. *The behavioral repertoire of the stumptail macaque.* Basel: S. Karger.

Buettner-Janusch, J., ed. 1962. *The relatives of man: modern studies of the relation of the evolution of nonhuman primates to human evolution.* New York: New York Academy of Science.

Carpenter, C. 1964. *Naturalistic behavior of nonhuman primates.* University Park: Pennsylvania State University Press.

Charles-Dominique, P., and Hladik, C. 1971. Le Lepilemur du sud de Madagascar: écologie, alimentation et vie sociale. *La Terre et la Vie* 25:3-66.

Crook, J. 1966. Gelada baboon herd structure and movement. *Sym. Zoological Society of London* 18:237.

DeVore, I., ed. 1965. *Primate behavior.* New York: Holt, Rinehart and Winston.

Dolhinow, P., ed. 1972. *Primate patterns.* New York: Holt, Rinehart and Winston.

Eimerl, S., and DeVore, I. 1965. *The primates.* New York: Time-Life Books.

Etkin, W., ed. 1967. *Social behavior from fish to man.* Chicago: Phoenix Science Series.

Hladik, C. 1975. Ecology, diet, and social patterning in Old and New World primates. In *Sociobiology and psychology of primates,* edited by R. Tuttle, pp. 3-37. The Hague: Mouton.

Itani, J. 1958. On the acquisition and propagation of a new food habit in the natural groups of the wild Japanese monkey at Takasakijama. *Primates* 1: 84-98.

Jay, P., ed. 1968. *Primates—studies in adaptation and variability.* New York: Holt, Rinehart and Winston.

Jolly, A. 1967. *Lemur behavior—a Madagascan field study.* Chicago: University of Chicago Press.

Kawamura, S. 1959. The process of subcultural propagation among Japanese macaques. *Primates* 2: 43-60.

Kummer, H. 1968. *Social organization of hamadryas baboons—a field study.* Chicago: University of Chicago Press.

Lancaster, J. 1975. *Primate behavior and the emergence of human culture.* New York: Holt, Rinehart and Winston.

Maples, W. 1969. Adaptive behavior of baboons. *American Journal of Physical Anthropology.* 31:107-11.

Mason, W. 1971. Field and laboratory studies of social organization in *Salimiri* and *Callicebus.* In *Primate behavior: developments in field and laboratory research,* Vol. 2, edited by L. Rosenblum, pp. 107-38. New York: Academic Press.

Napier, J., and Napier, P., eds. 1970. *Old World monkeys.* New York: Academic Press.

Napier, J., and Walker, A. 1967. Vertical clinging and leaping, a newly recognized category of locomotor behaviour among primates. *Folia Primatologica* 6: 180-203.

Poirier, F. 1968a. Analysis of a Nilgiri langur *(Presbytis johnii)* home range change. *Primates* 9:29-44.

———. 1968b. The Nilgiri langur *(Presbytis johnii)* mother-infant dyad. *Primates* 9:45-68.

———. 1969a. The Nilgiri langur troop: its composition, structure, function and change. *Folia Primatologica* 19:20-47.

———. 1969b. Behavioral flexibility and intertroop variability among Nilgiri langurs of South India. *Folia Primatologica* 11:119-33.

———. 1970a. Nilgiri langur ecology and social behavior. In *Primate behavior: developments in field and laboratory research,* Vol. I, edited by L. Rosen-Rosenblum, pp. 251-383. New York: Academic Press.

———. 1970b. The Nilgiri langur communication matrix. *Folia Primatologica* 13:92-137.

———. 1970c. Characteristics of the Nilgiri langur dominance structure. *Folia Primatologica* 12:161-87.

———. 1972a. Introduction. In *Primate socialization,* edited by F. Poirier, pp. 3-29. New York: Random House.

———. 1972b. The St. Kitts green monkey (*Cercopithecus aethiops sabaeus*): ecology, population dynamics, and selected behavioral traits. *Folia Primatologica* 17:20-25.

———. 1973a. Nilgiri langur behavior and social organization. In *Essays to the chief* (Essays in honor of L. Cressman), edited by F. Voget and R. Stephensen, pp. 119-34. Eugene: University of Oregon Press.

———. 1973b. Socialization and learning among nonhuman primates. In *Learning and culture,* edited by S. Kimball and J. Burnett, pp. 3-41. Seattle: University of Washington Press.

———. 1974. Colobine aggression: a review. In *Primate aggression, territoriality and zenophobia,* edited by R. Holloway, pp. 123-58. New York: Academic Press.

———. 1977. *Fossil evidence: the human evolutionary journey.* St. Louis: Mosby.

Quiatt, D., ed. 1972. *Primates on primates.* Minneapolis: Burgess.

Reynolds, V. 1967. *The apes.* New York: Harper & Row.

Sauer, F., and Sauer, E. 1963. The South-west African bush-baby of the *Galago senegalensis* group. *Journal of Southwest Africa Scientific Society* 16:5-35.

Southwick, C., ed. 1963. *Primate social behavior*. Princeton, N.J.: Van Nostrand.

Strum, S. 1975. Primate predation: interim report on the development of a tradition in a troop of olive baboons. *Science* 187: 755-57.

Tsumori, A. 1967. New acquired behavioral social interactions of Japanese monkeys. In *Social communication among primates*, edited by S. Altmann, pp. 207-21. Chicago: University of Chicago Press.

Washburn, S., and DeVore, I. 1961. *The social* life of baboons. *Scientific American* 204-62.

Washburn, S., and Moore, R. 1974. *Ape into man – a study of human evolution*. Boston: Little, Brown.

Yamada, M. 1963. A study of blood relationships in the natural society of the Japanese macaque. *Primates* 4: 43-67.

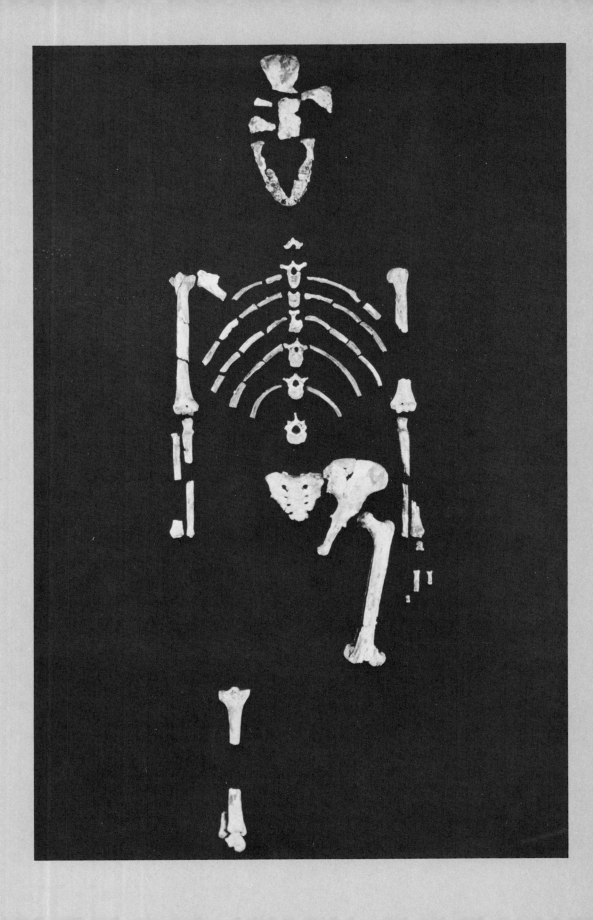

Part Four
The Fossil Record—
Recovering the Past

In anticipating the discovery of the true links between the apes and man in tropical countries, there has been a tendency to overlook the fact that, in luxuriant forests of the tropical belts, Nature was supplying . . . an easy and sluggish solution, by adaptive specialisation, of the problem of existence in creatures so well equipped mentally as living anthropoids are. For the production of man a different apprenticeship was needed to sharpen the wits and quicken the higher manifestations of intellect . . . in my opinion, Southern Africa, by providing a vast open country with occasional wooded belts and a relative scarcity of water, together with a fierce and bitter mammalian competition, furnished a laboratory such as was essential to this penultimate phase of human evolution. (From R. Dart, "*Australopithecus africanus:* The Man-Ape of South Africa." *Nature,* Vol. 115, February 1925.)

"In searching for ourselves, I find the clearest reflections in a muddy pool." (Poirier)

The skeletal remains of "Lucy" from Ethiopia.

Chapter 9
Dating Methods and the Paleontological Approach

The basic problem confronting the paleontologist is that of evaluating evolutionary changes. The paleontologist tries to establish which of a host of possible and possibly conflicting relationships is most consistent with the pattern of hominid evolution. The prime quality of evolution which emerges is that change is gradual. Beginning with this premise, there are a number of alternatives; the choice of which is most likely governed, among others, by the following propositions.

The Organization of Fossil Materials

There are four dimensions along which fossil evidence can be fruitfully compared: time, grade, line, and space (Coon, 1962). The time dimension is self-explanatory; fossil materials can't be studied, and conclusions can't be drawn, unless the material is placed within a time perspective. In primate evolution we deal with a time span of approximately 65-70 million years. In **hominid** (human) evolution the time span is approximately 15-18 million years. The space dimension deals with reconstruction of land masses. Until recently, the earth looked very different than it does today. A reconstruction of past land masses, or of water masses, helps interpret fossil distributions and migratory patterns.

Grade is an evolutionary stage or condition; a convenient reference category based upon anatomical, behavioral, and cultural evidence. Hominid evolution passed through a number of grades before *H. sapiens sapiens*. During the Miocene and Pliocene geological epochs hominids were perhaps represented by *Ramapithecus*, during the Lower Pleistocene by *Australopithecus* and *Homo*, during the Middle Pleistocene by the *Homo erectus* and *Homo sapiens*, and during the Upper

The physical anthropologist in the lab.

Pleistocene by the *Homo sapiens sapiens* grade. Hominid evolutionary grades are often defined according to the following morphological traits; brain size, skull shape, tooth size, and postcranial morphology. Morphological grades are often associated with grades on a cultural level; for example, hunting and gathering was probably the life-style of later *Australopithecus,* and big-game hunting was the life-style of *Homo erectus.* It is likely that more than one grade existed during certain time periods. For example, there is evidence that *Australopithecus* and *Homo* existed side-by-side during the Lower Pleistocene in East and South Africa and that *H. erectus* and *H. sapiens* overlapped during the Middle Pleistocene.

The evolutionary line dimension deals with evolutionary relationships within hominid grades. Herein we refer to fossil lines as forms within a grade that are more closely related to each other than they are to other lines. The Middle Pleistocene *Homo erectus* grade is represented by various lines; for example, African *H. erectus* are morphologically more alike than they are like the Asian *H. erectus* (Figure 9-1).

Establishment of Taxonomic Relationships

The various activities of paleontological research are interdependent and interrelated, yet time and human limitations make its practice multiphased and time consuming. The recovery and collection of fossils is preceded by extensive planning, geological surveys, solutions to problems specific to the locale, and so on. Because modern excavation techniques involve patient work, a relatively complete account of any fossil group must await the collection and analysis of a fairly large sample. Then follows the long and tedious task of comparing the material to other possibly related forms to establish its taxonomic affinities. Assignment of a taxonomic designation is one of the most important jobs for the paleontologist. The establishment of a taxonomic designation must solve problems of the geographical and temporal variation of related samples from other localities of known stratigraphic relationship, as well as problems of sample variation.

Pitfalls and Problems. Physical anthropologists have been notoriously bad in dealing with the classification of the Hominidae (the family of fossil and living hominids). However, there is a growing tendency to pay closer attention to principles of modern classification. Two events had special impetus in fostering this more critical attitude. One was the early dispute over the status of the Lower Pleistocene australopithecines; were they hominids (humans) or pongids (apes)? The second was exposure of the fraudulent nature of the Piltdown remains.[1] The Piltdown controversy forced many human evolutionists to take a more cautious view of the weight of interpretation and speculation based upon fragmentary fossil remains. Piltdown's unmasking forced anthropologists to the realization that hominid evolution involved relatively small and perhaps subtle morphological differences and required a more rigorous, less impressionistic approach to interpretation.

[1]For more than forty years, this odd assemblage of remains, consisting of fossilized hominid cranial fragments and an ape's mandible and canine, was the subject of controversy and speculation. The solution to the problem came when, in November 1953, it was announced that the mandible and canine were both those of a large modern ape which were remarkably faked to simulate fossilized material.

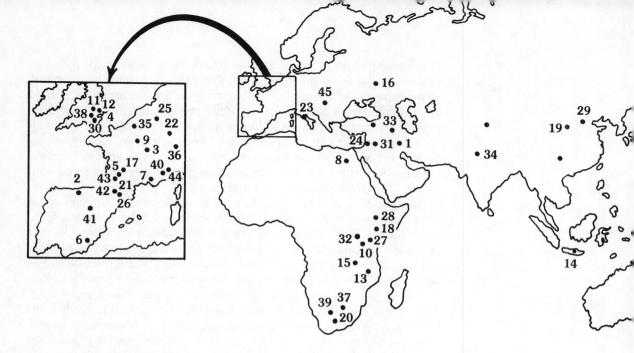

Figure 9-1. Major prehistoric sites in Europe, Africa, and Asia.

Dating of site:

   I 60 million to 4 million B.P.
  II 4 million to 1 million B.P.
 III 1 million 200,000 B.P.
 IV after 200,000 B.P.

Articles found:

A art
B bones of primates
F fire
L living floors
T tools

Key to sites on map

  1 Ali Kosh IV, L,T
  2 Altamira IV, A,T
  3 Arcy IV, B,F,L,T
  4 Clacton-on-Sea III, F,L,T
  5 Combe Grenal IV, B,F,T
  6 Cueva de Ambrosio IV, B,F,T
  7 Escale cave III, B,F,L,T
  8 Fayum depression I, B
  9 Fontainebleau IV, A,F,L,T
10 Fort Ternan I, B
11 High Lodge IV, T
12 Hoxne IV, T
13 Isimila IV, F,L,T
14 Java site III, B
15 Kalambo Falls IV, B,F,L,T
16 Kostenki IV, A,B,F,L,T
17 La Chapelle-aux-Saints IV, B,T
18 Lake Turkana site II, B,T
19 Lantian site III, B
20 Makapan II, B
21 Mas D'Azil IV, A,T
22 Mauer site III, B

23 Monte Circeo IV, B,T
24 Mt. Carmel IV, B,F,T
25 Neanderthal IV, B
26 Niaux IV, A,T
27 Olduvai Gorge II, B,L,T
28 Omo II, B,T
29 Chou Kou Tien III, B,F,T
30 Piltdown (discredited)
31 Qafzeh IV, B,F,T
32 Rusinga Island I, B
33 Shanidar cave IV, B,F,L,T
34 Siwalik Hills I, B
35 St. Acheul III, T
36 Steinheim IV, B
37 Sterkfontein II, B,T
38 Swanscombe IV, B,T
39 Taung II, B
40 Terra Amata IV, F,L,T
41 Torralba-Ambrona III, B,F,L,T
42 Tuc d'Audobert IV, A,T
43 "Valley of Caves" IV
44 Vallonet cave III, B,T
45 Vérteszöllös III, B,F,L,T

What are some of the guidelines which the scientist must follow in evaluating the fossil material? First, there should always be economy of hypotheses; all available, reliable material, and its affinities, should be embraced by a single coherent scheme. The simplest is often the correct explanation. The fraudulent nature of Piltdown was first suggested by the fact that the remains could not fit into any unitary evolutionary scheme encompassing the rest of the then known hominid remains. As it turned out, Piltdown was a cleverly produced fraud consisting of a hominid skull and pongid mandible.

Sample Size and Composition. Taxonomic relationships must be based upon well-authenticated, reliably dated, and fairly complete fossil assemblages. This criterion is often most difficult to meet. We are extremely fortunate when we find a fairly complete assemblage capable of being dated. If a new specimen is uncovered, and if the interpretation of the form is inconsistent with present taxonomic schemes, then it may be best to defer judgment until further material is uncovered. This caveat based on sample size could well be applied towards withholding judgment on such controversial forms as *Ramapithecus* and *Gigantopithecus* which are discussed in later pages. Age changes can lead to considerable modification in the structural details and proportions of the skeleton. Age changes are so marked that it would be grossly improper to compare a few measurements of the adult skull of an ancestral hominid with those of a juvenile pongid and to infer from such comparison that the former is not markedly different from the apes in general. This is particularly true in light of the **neotenous** or **paedomorphic** character of the adult hominid skull, i.e., the adult hominid skull retains numerous infantile characteristics such as a smooth brow.

Primates exhibit considerable **sexual dimorphism**, i.e., size differentiation between male and female forms which is an important consideration in interpreting fossil materials. Although there is continuing argument, some investigators have suggested that differences between the australopithecine forms, which are often used to establish separate species, may not be taxonomically relevant but may be reflections of australopithecine sexual dimorphism.

Relevant Traits. Two of the most common errors committed in assessing taxonomic affinities stem from the failure to recognize that some traits have more taxonomic relevance than others. Some traits are better differentiators of generic or family status while others may be better for specific differentiation. The principle of taxonomic relevance must be considered and may be illustrated by reference to the extinct species of *Homo erectus*. The morphological traits of the skulls and jaws of *H. erectus* are very different from those of *H. sapiens*; however, the limb skeleton is quite similar. For purposes of distinguishing the two species, the skull and jaws are relevant while the limb bones are not. In assessing the earlier representatives of the family Hominidae, skeletal characters of the pelvis and hind limbs are more important than those of the forelimbs. Unfortunately, we can't always find the most relevant morphological remains; in fact, we are lucky to find any remains whatsoever.

Mosaic Evolution. Different parts of the body evolve at different rates (Figure 9-2) and at each stage (grade) in the evolutionary scheme,

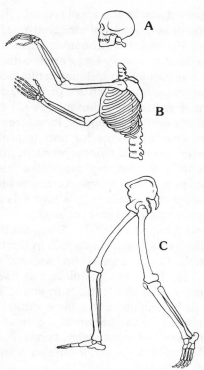

Figure 9-2. The three major body complexes: (A) the head and face;
(B) the thorax and upper limbs; and (C) the pelvis and lower limbs.

different morphological traits will be of different taxonomic value. This is due to the fact that at different points in its evolutionary history a group faces different problems of adaptation. One of the first adaptive changes made by early hominids is bipedalism. Therefore, we should expect to find that features differentiating early hominids and pongids are to be found primarily in their locomotor apparatus. A case in point is the original refusal to accept the Javan form, "Pithecanthropus," as a member of the genus *Homo*. When first uncovered, paleontologists refused to accept the contemporaneity of the femur (upper leg bone) with the skull and face, for the skull was still relatively primitive while the femur was relatively modern. A further example involves the brain of *Australopithecus*; fossilized cranial bones indicate that *Australopithecus* lacked space for either a large **cerebrum** (the part of the brain associated with learned hand movements) or for a large motor cortex. The archaeological, comparative anatomical, and fossil records all indicate that a brain of modern size and form evolved long after our ancestors were ground-living, stone-toolmaking gatherers and hunters.

Parallelism and Convergence

Similar structures, adaptive relationships, or behaviors can occur in different groups as a result of similar evolutionary opportunities. A fundamental principle of evolutionary biology is that, if there is a close similarity in the total morphological pattern of two organisms, there is also a reasonably close phylogenetic relationship. It is on this basis that relationships are formed within the fossil record. There is a problem, however, because the phenomenon of similarity may be due to parallelism or convergence. Parallelism and convergence do not necessarily imply a close phylogenetic relationship. Parallelisms are structural developments within a group which independently occur in more than one segment of that group and which are probably due to similar evolutionary conditions. For instance, Simons (1972) notes that among the primates, which are basically arboreal, long forearms have evolved a number of times as adaptations for hanging and feeding, from ancestors with shorter forearms. Convergence occurs when remotely related forms come to look alike, e.g., flipperlike fins in whales, seals, and sea cows. When two animal species or major groups that are not closely related develop similarities in adaptive relationships or structures, the two groups are said to have converged.

Clark (1967) and Simpson (1951, 1953) caution against overreliance on parallelism to explain similarities in the fossil record. If we constantly refer similarities to parallelism, we render the concept of evolution meaningless. The term parallelism is usually restricted to development of similar adaptive features in animals that are related, for example, animals belonging to the same order. Thus, parallel resemblances are probably the realization of a genetic potential present in the entire group. As will be shown later, certain New and Old World members of the Order Primates show parallel adaptations to an arboreal environment.

Dating of Fossil Materials (Figure 9-3)

Why Dating Is Important. Fossil remains must be placed within a recognized time frame so that the **osteological** (bone) evidence can be interpreted and placed within a taxonomic scheme and so that the

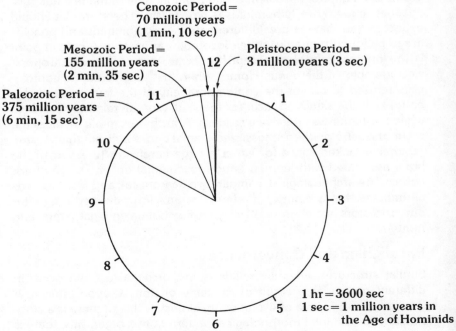

Figure 9-3. The evolutionary clock.

environmental information for a site can be correlated with the fossil remains. Rigorous dating techniques also eliminate questionable materials, like Piltdown. When considering the age of a fossil specimen answers to two important questions are sought: (1) What is the relationship of the fossil material to the geological, floral, faunal, and archaeological sequence? and (2) What is the chronological age of the specimen in years B.P. (before present)? The first query asks if the remains are contemporaneous within their context, and therefore whether the site's faunal, climatic, and archaeological information can be properly associated with the find. This procedure establishes a relative chronology. The answer to the second query provides a figure—the chronometric age of the find.

Chronologically ordering fossil remains is fundamental to understanding their evolutionary relationships and significance. To establish the contemporaneity of fossil or archaeological material with the deposit in which it lies, it must first be demonstrated that the deposit has not been disturbed. It must be shown that there is no possibility of an intrusive burial or derivation from younger or older deposits. Unless these conditions are met, all dates must be viewed as suspect. One of the excavator's major tasks is to fully document the site's condition at the time the excavated deposit was formed; photographs, maps, and charts are absolutely necessary. This phase, as much as the actual excavation, requires much time and expertise. A poorly excavated site is largely devoid of scientific value and an undated site is of questionable value and continually open to speculation.

Pleistocene Paleoclimatology and Climatic Indicators

Past climates fluctuated, and their cycles directly and indirectly affected hominid evolution. For example, the huge intermittent northern hemispheric **Pleistocene** ice sheets affected the migration patterns and subsequently the gene pools of both migratory animal populations and of populations dependent upon migratory animals as food sources. Past climatic fluctuations directly affected floral and faunal distributions, in turn influencing hominid dietary patterns. Various means have been devised to determine paleoclimates. Among these are deep sea core analysis and study of changing land and sea levels, river terraces, and African **pluvials**. All these indicators appear to be linked to the ebb and flow of the Eurasian glaciations.

Glaciations. To the average reader the Pleistocene epoch is commonly known as the "Ice Age." Glacial fluctuations were a most dramatic event of the Pleistocene epoch, influencing land and sea levels, floral and faunal distributions, and leaving conspicuous remains of their past extent. Even at their maximum, the ice sheets never covered more than one-third of the earth's surface and occurred only during one-eighth of the Pleistocene time span. However, because of their impact, glacial periods are convenient boundary markers of the Pleistocene epoch. Although there is disagreement as to why glaciations occurred, major theories lay the blame to some unusual movement or change in the earth's orbit or axis.

Glacial periods were originally defined in the Alps. Four periods were originally named and subdivided into two or more cold phases or stadials which were separated by interstadials. Glacial periods alter-

Table 9-1. Simplified Glacial Scheme.

Glacial stage	Geological stage	Cultural stage	African Pluvial Stage
Third Interglacial	Upper Pleistocene	Middle and Upper Paleolithic	Third Interpluvial
Würm glaciation			Gamblian
Riss glaciation			Kamesian
First interglacial			
Mindel glaciation	Middle Pleistocene	Lower Paleolithic	Second Interpluvial
Second interglacial			Kanjeran
Günz glaciation		Acheulian	
Villafranchian	Lower Pleistocene	Middle and Upper Paleolithic	Third Interpluvial
			Kageran

The above is a simplified version of the glacial scheme; however, many questions have been raised. Once the Pleistocene was synonomous with the Ice Age. Now a Villa-franchian stretch has been added at the beginning and this may be twice as long as the rest of the Pleistocene. In spite of new dating techniques, boundary lines are difficult to draw, especially the delineation between the Pliocene and subsequent Pleistocene. **Moreover, doubt has been cast upon the long-accepted sequence of four distinct glaciations. New work has not yet forced us to abandon them completely, but threatens to do so soon.**

nated with warm periods known as interglacials, three of which are major. Although a simplified glacial chronological scheme is presented in Table 9-1, Pleistocene chronology and climatic history is complicated. The first glacial period, the Günz, seems to have been a largely local phenomenon while the remaining three glacial periods involved extensive European ice sheets. It is difficult to correlate European glacial periods with those occurring elsewhere, but there is general consensus (which is speedily weakening) that glaciation is roughly synchronous throughout the northern hemisphere (Table 9-2).

Glaciations periodically removed large areas of northern Eurasia and North America from habitation and intermittently restricted faunal movement in some areas while encouraging it in others. Local glacial manifestations periodically created movement barriers, channeling activity along new routes or completely disallowing it. This indirectly led to establishing new life patterns which affected subsequent evolutionary history. Our knowledge of hominid evolutionary history is also affected by the fact that preexisting cultural and osteological remains

Table 9-2. Nomenclature of European and North American Pleistocene Glaciers.

Pleistocene		European	North American
Late	Fourth Glaciation	Würm	Wisconsinian
	Riss-Würm Interglacial		
	Third Glaciation	Riss	Illinoisian
	Mindel-Riss Interglacial		
Middle	Second Glaciation	Mindel	Kansan
	Günz-Mindel Interglacial		
Early	First Glaciation	Günz	Nebraskan
	Pre-First Interglacial		

Adapted from Lawrence S. Dillon, *Evolution*. St. Louis, 1973, The C. V. Mosby Company.

in glaciated areas were lost to us, as were remains deposited during glacial times. The latter were subsequently submerged during interglacial times.

Pluvials (Table 9-1). While glacials prove to be convenient markers of the European, North American, and Eurasian Pleistocene, pluvials, or periods of higher rainfall and lake levels, serve to demarcate the African Pleistocene. Since glaciers form and grow with increased precipitation, it seems reasonable to correlate high latitude glaciers with low latitude pluvials. However, despite the original enthusiasm, it has been difficult to correlate glaciations and pluvials, regardless of the fact that there is little doubt that climatic conditions favoring glaciations were directly or indirectly responsible for the pluvials. Although referring to increased precipitation, pluvials are not necessarily synonymous with the Biblical Noachian flood. Older notions of major changes accompanying the pluvials, e.g., of deserts rapidly changing to forest due to increased rainfall, are unfounded.

Floral and Faunal Indications of Pleistocene Paleoclimates

The previous information is part of a scientific armory utilized to provide climatic data. Floral and faunal remains provide climatic data; furthermore, they help place a site within a chronological sequence. Analysis of fossilized pollen, **palynology**, is one of the most valuable aids for determining past climatic conditions. When the nearly indestructible pollen granules settle to the ground they become incorporated into the deposits and are almost indefinitely preserved in the absence of lime. Since pollens of various floral species are rather individualistic and in many cases can be readily identified as to genus, pollen analysis can be applied to solving problems relating to the paleoenvironment. While pollen analysis is useful for historically reconstructing local vegetation, a major drawback is the local nature of much flora which negates cross-analysis of grains from different sites. Pollen analysis has been employed in dating and determining the environment of *Homo erectus* in China and has suggested that one of the Upper Pleistocene Iraqi Shanidar skeletons was buried on a bed of wild flowers.

Faunal Markers. Through faunal analysis, one can reconstruct paleoenvironmental conditions as fauna changes in response to climatic oscillations. There is a continual emergence and spreading of new forms and extinction of older types. The most useful mammalian groups for correlating Pleistocene deposits include the elephant, rhinoceros, bear, hyena, deer, and antelope.

Elephants are important demarcators of Pleistocene subdivisions (Table 9-3). The dating of virtually all European hominid fossiliferous sites relies on the contiguous evidence of associated fossil elephant remains. Fossil hyenas, especially *Crocuta crocuta*, have proved useful for the purposes of relative dating. The absence of the species *crocuta* from such European sites as the Mauer sands (yielding a Middle Pleistocene *H. erectus* mandible) indicates a pre-Mindel time position.

Mammalian remains also aid the dating of deposits by indicating a climatic stage. For example, in Britain it may be inferred that a hippopotamus-bearing deposit is of a different period than one con-

Dating Methods and the Paleontological Approach

151

Table 9-3. Correlation of Elephant and Hominid Remains in Europe.

Fossil hominid	Fossil elephant	Glacial period
Homo sapiens (Classic Neanderthals)	E. primigenius	Würm glaciation
Homo sapiens (Ehringsdorf, Germany)	late E. antiquus	Riss-Würm interglacial
Homo sapiens (Steinheim, Germany)	E. antiquus	Mindel-Riss interglacial
Homo erectus (Heidelberg or Mauer mandible, Germany)	E. antiquus	Günz-Mindel interglacial

taining musk-ox. African fossil mammalia have proven especially useful for inferring Pleistocene climatic stages. Fossil invertebrates, freshwater and land mollusca (e.g., snails), as well as insects, are all valuable climatic indicators.

Determining Age

This discussion deals with dating methods most useful to the paleoanthropologist. There are basically two types of dating, **relative** chronology and **chronometric** chronology. Relative dating establishes that one thing—a bone, tool, or other remains—is older or younger than something else. Relative dating arranges things in chronological order, although the total time span and interval between the things so ordered is unknown. Relative dating establishes a chronological sequence; absolute dating determines age in terms of years. Absolute dating provides the ultimate evolutionary framework; it determines the age of a specimen or source deposit and yields a numerical, chronological figure. An important element in any dating scheme is crossdating, which establishes relationships between assemblages, or significant elements therein, from various geographic locales. Crossdating ties sites into a preexisting scheme; sites must be cross-dated with other sites to establish temporal relationships.

Relative Dating

Typological and Morphological Dating. One of the first excavation procedures is to determine whether archaeological and/or osteological (bone) materials are contemporaneous with the deposit in which they lie. One must also determine the site's stratigraphy, i.e., the relative vertical placement of objects in the soil. Given an undisturbed site, materials at the lowest levels must be the oldest. In the absence of an undisturbed stratified site, other methods—typological and morphological dating—which yield far less conclusive evidence may be employed. Typological dating is based on the fact that over time manufactured objects undergo stylistic changes. On this basis it is often possible to arrange objects in a relative time sequence.

Morphological dating is conceptually related to typological dating. When material is found unaccompanied by organic material useful in age determination, or when a fossil is found lying above ground out of context, it can sometimes be dated according to its form, or morphology. Morphological dating should only be attempted when a large, well-known fossil series with a well-documented evolutionary history is available.

F-U-N Trio. A major mode of relative dating involves dating of bone either to establish the contemporaneity of various osteological remains in a deposit or of bone to the soil deposit itself. Buried bone witnesses chemical compositional changes of varying rates. The three major analytical methods of measuring this chemical change are fluorine, nitrogen, and uranium dating—often referred to as the *F-U-N trio.* These dating methods are especially important in disturbed sites where it is necessary to establish contemporaneity. The relative age of bone can be determined by comparing its chemical composition with fossil bone of known ages either from the same site or same age if they are preserved under comparable conditions.

Fluorine dating depends upon ground water seepage through bone; fluorine in the water combines with the bone's calcium to form a compound, fluorapatite. The amount of fluorapatite in various bones in a site determines their contemporaneity or lack thereof. Fluorine dating allows bones of an assemblage to be tested for stratigraphic equivalence, for contemporaneous bones should contain roughly equal amounts of fluorapatite. The most famous case of fluorine dating is the uncovering of the Piltdown hoax.

Nitrogen dating is often coupled with fluorine dating; the results complement one another. Bones accumulating little fluorine retain much nitrogen, and vice versa. Nitrogen tests are used to determine whether enough collagen (protein) degradation has occurred to attempt to radiocarbon date the bone directly. The Galley Hill material and the Piltdown fraud were fluorine and nitrogen tested before the bones themselves were finally radiocarbon dated.

The possibility of uranium dating was noted as early as 1908 when it was established that mineral phosphates, including fossil bones, contained uranium. Uranium circulating in the blood stream is fixed in the mineral matter of bone, probably through calcium replacement. The same replacement process occurs in buried bone through which ground water containing traces of uranium percolates. The longer a bone is buried, the more uranium it absorbs. Since uranium is radioactive, its content within bone can be determined by measuring radioactive deterioration. Radioactivity varies in bones from different sites, but its progressive buildup with increasing age has been established. Uranium analysis serves, as does fluorine, to distinguish between specimens which may be younger or older than the source deposit. It is superior to fluorine dating because it does not involve destruction of the bone.

The F-U-N dating trio do not permit cross-dating; their prime value lies in determining the relative ages of bone or bone objects from the same deposit. Because of the many variables, it is usually impossible to use fluorine, nitrogen, or uranium as more than a rough guide to the geological age of an isolated specimen. Ground soils vary, allowing differing amounts of percolating water through. Fluorine cross-dating is especially hampered by the fact that the amount of fluorine permeating a bone depends upon how much is present in the ground water, and this varies with the locale.

A final note on relative dating involves the use of stratigraphy to establish a chronological scheme. Simply, those materials found in the deepest soil layers are usually, but not always, the oldest. Those

Table 9-4. Radioactive Elements Useful in Establishing Mineral Ages.

Parent element	Decay product	Half-life	Remarks
Uranium 238	Lead 206	4.51 billion years	These three parent-decay prod-uct sets occur together and serve as checks on one another. Especially useful in rocks old-er than 60 million years. Un-fortunately rather rare.
Uranium 235	Lead 207	710 million years	
Thorium 232	Lead 208	13.9 billion years	
Rubidium 87	Strontium 87	50 billion years	These three sets, but particu-larly potassium-argon, are proving of great value because they are widespread in occur-rence. Used in dating rocks older than 1 million years.
Potassium 40	Argon 40	1.33 billion years	
Potassium 40	Calcium 40	1.33 billion years	
Carbon 14	Nitrogen 14	5,730 years	Useful in dating rocks and events between [50,000] and 60,000 years in the past.

Adapted from Lawrence S. Dillon, *Evolution*. St. Louis, 1973, The C. V. Mosby Company.

materials found closer to the surface are not as old. This, of course, is true only for undisturbed sites. This method is useful if no dates have been, or can be, established geologically.

Chronometric Dating (Tables 9-4, 9-5)

Chronometric dating techniques yield chronological figures and paleontologists rely heavily upon **carbon-14** or radiocarbon, **potassium argon** or K/Ar, and uranium or **fission-track** dating. The radiocarbon or C^{14} technique, devised by the physicist W. F. Libby, has been in use since 1949. Although any organic material is theoretically capable of radiocarbon dating, the best substance is charcoal; fortunately charcoal is a common organic remainder in archaeological sites, and five to ten grams of charcoal is an adequate sample. C^{14} dating is fairly sound, provided proper precautions are taken in selecting samples and ensuring that they are not contaminated by additional radiocarbon from more recent material or contaminated in the laboratory.

Table 9-5. Some Major Methods for Determining Chronometric Ages.

Time Period	Dating Method
Modern period to 2,500 B.C.	Historical documents, tree ring (dendro-chronology), glacial varve
Recent times to ca. 50,000 years B.P.	Carbon-14, amino-acid racemization
400,000-500,000 years B.P.	Various means utilized but there is no good accuracy here. Many of these dates are placed according to relative dating
500,000 years B.P. to age of earth	Potassium-argon, fission-track

(The previous table [9-4] lists the half-life of some of the major means of chronometric dating. That table also lists some of the dating methods not found in this chart which primarily lists dating modes of use in the primate fossil record.)

Adapted from Bernard G. Campbell, *Humankind Emerging*, p. 77. Copyright © 1976 by Little, Brown and Company. Reprinted by permission.

Wood charcoal is best for radiocarbon dating; burned bone is often dated but unburned bone is seldom submitted for dating although it can be dated. A fairly large sample of unburned bone is needed because it does not contain much carbon. However, unburned bone contains a substance called collagen which is rich in carbon and can be extracted and dated. A few finds have been directly radiocarbon dated but most skeletal materials are incomplete and the researchers are hesitant to destroy the amount necessary for the procedure. They rely then on radiocarbon dates of associated but more expendable materials.

C^{14} is present in the cellular structure of all plants and animals. Organisms lose C^{14} at a steady rate, but they also consume it. Plants maintain their C^{14} level through the process of oxygen exchange with the atmosphere, animals through eating plants or other animals that have eaten plants. C^{14} is maintained as long as the organism is alive; intake promptly ceases upon death, and C^{14} levels begin to disintegrate radioactively. Disintegration proceeds at a known rate, based on the C^{14} half-life of 5,730 years. By measuring the amount of C^{14} in a dead organism, it is possible to calculate the length of time in "radiocarbon years" that has elapsed since the organism died.

A radiocarbon date is expressed in terms of a date midway between two points, representing a margin of error. The limits are indicated by plus and minus signs. A typical date reads $40,000 \pm 1000$ years. Radiocarbon dating is limited to a range of approximately 50,000 to 60,000 years.; beyond this radioactivity is not accurately measured and the older the sample the greater the chance of error.

Three types of radiocarbon dating errors reduce the efficiency of the technique (Butzer, 1964): (1) statistical-mechanical errors as are indicated by the plus or minus dates, (2) errors related to the C^{14} level of the sample itself, and (3) errors related to "contamination," i.e., laboratory storage, preparation, and management. Errors relating to the C^{14} level in the sample are due to past fluctuations of C^{14} intake, and unequal C^{14} concentration in different materials, as well as from contamination. In certain times in the past some dates diverge from the true age of the sample more than at other times. When reading a C^{14} date it must be asked what is being dated, for various dates are of different reliability and not strictly comparable owing to differences in techniques and basic assumptions on the part of the laboratory doing the testing. It is thus most important to have a series of dates from any one laboratory to test for reliability. One date from one sample from one laboratory compared to one date from one sample from another laboratory is of limited value.

K/Ar. Radiocarbon dating encompasses the last stage of hominid evolutionary history, leaving approximately 95 percent of evolutionary history beyond our grasp. This huge gap is now being dated with other techniques; one such technique—potassium-argon, or K/Ar, dating—was devised by Drs. J. Evernden and G. Curtis. This technique ascertains the age of volcanic materials and other igneous rocks (rocks of volcanic origin), as well as tektites (glasslike objects probably formed during the impact of large meteorites on the earth's surface). The potassium-argon technique dates the source deposits and *not* the fossil or cultural remains themselves. Potassium-argon dating ascertains the rate of potassium and argon decay; with an upper range of 3 billion years, the procedure has been employed to date the age of the earth.

Potassium-argon has been particularly useful for dating volcanically derived East African deposits. Bed I Olduvai Gorge, Tanzania, which contains some of the early East African hominid remains, was dated by K/Ar determination. This method has also been used to help determine the age of *H. erectus* from the Trinil faunal beds in central Java.

The major drawback of K/Ar dating is the difficulty of collecting datable material; K/Ar determinations are of use primarily in volcanic areas. The scattered nature of volcanic deposits becomes extremely distressing when some areas, such as the South African australopithecine deposits, go undated because of lack of volcanic soils. Another source of concern is statistical error. So like C^{14} dates, K/Ar dates are often given within plus or minus ranges.

Fission-track. A relatively new dating technique, fission-track dating, originally developed to date manufactured glass, has recently been applied to Olduvai Bed I. The technique is fairly simple; the procedure calls for counting the number of tracks caused by spontaneous fission of uranium-238 during the lifetime of the sample. Dating depends upon the density of such tracks and the number of uranium atoms, which is found from the increase in track density produced by neutron irradiation and induced fission of uranium-235. The material used to fission-track date Olduvai Bed I consisted of specimens from the volcanic deposit used for the K/Ar date. The fission-track date was 2.0 million years plus or minus 25 percent, which compares well with the average K/Ar date of 1.8 million years. Fission-track dating is important because the possible sources of error differ from those of K/Ar. If the dates from the two different methods agree, then a fairly accurate age determination is assured.

Amino Acid Racemization. This is a chronometric dating technique recently applied to proposed early hominid materials. Technically, the process of racemization is the conversion of an optically active substance into a racemic or optically inactive substance. All amino acids do not racemize at the same rate and when considering skeletal material in the age range of 5,000 to 100,000 years aspartic acid provides the best results. This method has some advantages over radiocarbon dating in that smaller quantities are needed. Second, the practical dating range of 100,000 years is appreciably longer than the 50,000 year range of radiocarbon dating (Bada et al., 1974).

One other dating method, **paleomagnetism,** deserves mentioning as it is becoming of increasing importance in cross-checking some of our K/Ar dates. Paleomagnetic dating is based on the fact that the earth's magnetic field is continually changing, both in direction and intensity, and these changes can leave natural records. Geomagnetic polarity epochs have been established which last between 0.5 to one million years. The polarity was reversed between 0.5 million years and 2.5 million years and before 3.4 million years. It has been possible to determine the history of polarity changes over the past four million years or so with some precision and to construct what is now called "reversal chronology." Throughout the late Cenozoic the magnetic polarity has changed at fairly irregular but frequent intervals (Cox et al., 1967). Throughout this time, there has been no period longer than about

Table 9-6. Sequence of Geological Eras, Periods, Epochs[1].

Era	Period	Epoch	Time (approximate beginning in millions of years ago)
Cenozoic	Quaternary	Pleistocene	1.8
		Pliocene	5-2
		Miocene	23-24
	Tertiary	Oligocene	37-38
		Eocene	53-54
		Paleocene	65
Mesozoic	Cretaceous		130
	Jurassic		180
	Triassic		230
	Permian		235
	Carboniferous		280
	Devonian		335
Paleozoic	Silurian		375
	Ordovician		435
	Cambrian		520
Proterozoic			990
Archaeozoic			2600

[1]It is important to keep in mind that these dates vary somewhat depending upon the source.

600,000 years which has not witnessed a paleomagnetic change. The duration and frequency of events is unique for each major segment of the late Cenozoic.

Reversal chronology was first applied to East African lava; subsequently it was established that polarity stratigraphy can sometimes be determined in sediments also (Grommé and Hay, 1963; Isaac, 1967; Musset et al., 1965). Paleomagnetic dating has been applied at Olduvai (Leakey, 1975), Lake Turkana (Brock and Isaac, 1974), and the Omo (Shuey et al., 1974).

At the Omo, the unusually thick, essentially continuous deposition record provides an opportunity to examine the sequence of polarity changes over several million years. This record has then been checked against the epochs and events defined in the Magnetic Polarity Time Scale. The results have agreed in large part with those produced by the K/Ar range (Howell, 1975). On the basis of both K/Ar and paleomagnetic reversal data the Shungura Formation at Omo, the derivation of nine out of twelve hominid remains, has been given a date of 2.9 to 1 M.Y.B.P.

At Lake Turkana paleomagnetic dates at first seemed to be helpful in establishing a geophysical chronology (Brock and Isaac, 1974). However, R. Leakey (1975) reports that paleomagnetic dates are less reliable at Lake Turkana than previously thought, and feels it best to withhold judgment of these dates for the time being.

Leakey (1975) reports that a series of paleomagnetic dates is available for Bed IV. These dates have forced a revision of the dating of that bed. Based on paleomagnetic reversal, Bed IV is now considered to be not less than 700,000 years, instead of the 500,000 year date first given.

Others. Other nonradioactive chronometric dating techniques include glacial-varve counting (i.e., counting layers of soil deposition in glacier-fed lakes), tree-ring dating (or dendrochronology, counting of growth

Millions of years

			ASIA			EUROPE

EUROPE

ASIA

Pongo   Gigantopithecus   Rama-pithecus   Dryo-pithecus   Plio-pithecus

Hylobates, Symphalangus

Dryo-pithecus

AFRICA
(World-wide)

Pan   Gorilla   Homo

Australopithecus

Ramapithecus   Limnopithecus

Dryopithecus

Aegyptopithecus   Propliopithecus   Aeolopithecus

Oligopithecus

0—   PLEISTOCENE

PLIOCENE

10—   MIOCENE

20—

30—   OLIGOCENE

Table 9-7. Temporal Distribution of Hominoid Genera.

After David Pilbeam, *The Ascent of Man.* Copyright 1972 by the Macmillan Company.

rings in trees), and pottery dating techniques such as magnetic or thermoluminescent dating.

This chapter reviews some of the criteria and methods for interpreting and dating the fossil record. Without reference to a documented time span and interpretive framework, fossil remains are of limited value. As more criteria are established and as dating and interpretive techniques are further refined, we lessen the possibility of fraudulent finds such as Piltdown. New methods may eventually date currently undatable sites, e.g., the South African australopithecine remains.

The major hindrance in interpreting fossil materials is a lack of large samples wherein age and sexual differences are recognized. Until we can estimate ranges of population variability, we are faced with continual taxonomic arguments. Our most useful sites are usually chronometrically dated, either by K/Ar or potassium-argon dating for early human sites and C^{14} or radiocarbon dating for later dating.

Bibliography

Aitken, M. 1961. *Physics and archaeology.* New York: Interscience.

Bada, J.; Schroeder, R.; and Carter, G. 1974. New evidence for the antiquity of man in North America deduced from aspartic acid racemization. *Science* 184:791-93.

Brill, R.; Fleischer, R.; Price, R.; and Walker, R. 1964. The fission-track dating of man-made glasses. *Journal Glass Studies* VI:151.

Brock, A., and Isaac, G. 1974. Paleomagnetic stratigraphy and chronology of hominid-bearing sediments east of Lake Rudolf, Kenya. *Nature* 247: 344-48.

Bronowski, J., and Long, W. 1951. Statistical methods in anthropology. *Nature* 168:794.

Brothwell, D., and Higgs, E., eds. 1970. *Science in archaeology.* New York: Praeger.

Butzer, K. 1964. *Environment and archaeology, an introduction to Pleistocene geography.* Chicago: Aldine.

Cain, A., and Harrison, G. 1960. Phyletic weighting. *Proceedings of the Zoological Society of London* 135:1.

Campbell, B. 1976. *Humankind emerging.* Boston: Little, Brown.

Clark, W. Le Gros. 1964. *The fossil evidence for human evolution: an introduction to the study of paleoanthropology.* Chicago: University of Chicago Press.

Colbert, E. 1949. Some paleontological principles significant in human evolution. In *Early man in the Far East,* edited by W. W. Howells, Jr., pp. 103-47. Philadelphia: American Association of Physical Anthropologists.

Coon, C. 1962. *The origin of races.* New York: Knopf.

Cox, A.; Dalrymple, G.; and Doell, R. 1967. Reversals of the earth's magnetic field. *Scientific American* 216:44-54.

Davis, M. 1969. Palynology and environmental history during the Quaternary period. *American Scientist* 57:317.

Day, M. 1971. Postcranial remains of *Homo erectus* from Bed IV, Olduvai Gorge, Tanzania. *Nature* 232:383.

Dillon, L. 1973. *Evolution: concepts and consequences.* St. Louis: Mosby.

Dimbleby, G. 1970. Pollen analysis. In *Science in archaeology,* edited by D. Brothwell and E. Higgs, pp. 99-107. New York: Praeger.

Eckhardt, R. 1972. Population genetics and human origins. *Scientific American*, January, p. 94.

Emiliani, C. 1970. The significance of deep-sea cores. In *Science in archaeology*, edited by D. Brothwell and E. Higgs, pp. 99-107. New York: Praeger.

Fleischer, R.; Leakey, L.; Price, P.; and Walker, R. 1965. Fission-track dating of Bed I, Olduvai Gorge. *Current Anthropology* 6:389.

Garn, S. 1971. The improper use of fossil nomenclature. *American Journal of Physical Anthropology* 35:217.

Grommé, C., and Hay, R. 1963. Magnetization of basalt, Bed I, Olduvai Gorge, Tanganyika. *Nature* 200:560-61.

Harrison, G., and Weiner, J. 1963. Some considerations in the formulation of theories of human phylogeny. In *Classification and human evolution*, edited by S. L. Washburn, pp. 75-84. New York: Viking Fund Publications.

Higgs, E. 1970. Fauna. In *Science in archaeology*, edited by D. Brothwell and E. Higgs, pp. 195-96. New York: Praeger.

Holloway, R. 1972. Australopithecine endocasts, brain evolution in the Hominoidea, and a model of hominid evolution. In *The functional and evolutionary biology of primates*, edited by R. Tuttle, pp. 123-52. Chicago: University of Chicago Press.

Howell, F. 1975. An overview of the Pliocene and Earlier Pleistocene of the Lower Omo basin, Southern Ethiopia. In *Human origins: Louis Leakey and the East African evidence*, edited by G. Isaac and E. McCown, pp. 227-68. Menlo Park, Calif.: W. A. Benjamin.

Huxley, J., ed. 1940. *The new systematics*. Oxford: Oxford University Press.

Isaac, G. 1967. The stratigraphy of the Peninj Group—Early Middle Pleistocene formation west of Lake Natron, Tanzania. In *Background to evolution in Africa*, edited by W. Bishop and J. Clark. Chicago: University of Chicago Press.

Leakey, M. 1975. A summary and discussion of the archaeological evidence from Bed I and Bed II, Olduvai Gorge, Tanzania. In *Human origins: Louis Leakey and the East African evidence*, edited by G. Isaac and E. McCown, pp. 431-60. Menlo Park, Calif.: W. A. Benjamin.

Leakey, R. 1975. Evidence for an advanced Plio-Pleistocene hominid from East Rudolf. In *Human origins: Louis Leakey and the East African evidence*, edited by G. Isaac and E. McCown, pp. 343-52. Menlo Park, Calif.: W. A. Benjamin.

Libby, W. 1955. *Radiocarbon dating*. Chicago: University of Chicago Press.

Mayr, E. 1963. The taxonomic evaluation of fossil hominids. In *Classification and human evolution*, edited by S. L. Washburn, pp. 332-47. New York: Viking Fund Publications.

Musset, A.; Reilly, T.; and Raja, P. 1965. Palaeomagnetism in East Africa. In *East African Rift System: report of the Upper Mantle Committee—UNESCO seminar, Nairobi 1965*, Part II, pp. 83-94. Nairobi: University College.

Oakley, K. 1953. Dating fossil human remains. In *Anthropology today*, edited by A. Kroeber, pp. 43-56. Chicago: Aldine.

———. 1966. *Frameworks for dating fossil man*. Chicago: Aldine.

———. 1970. Analytical methods of dating bones. In *Science in archaeology*, edited by D. Brothwell and E. Higgs, pp. 23-34. New York: Praeger.

Oakley, K., and Groves, C. 1970. Piltdown man: the realization of fraudulence. *Science* 169:789.

Oakley, K., and Montagu, A. 1949. A reconsideration of the Galley Hill skeleton. *Bulletin of British Museum (Natural History) Geology* 1(2):25.

Pilbeam, D. 1972. *The ascent of man*. New York: Macmillan.

Pilbeam, D., and Simons, E. 1965. Some problems of hominid classification. *American Scientist* 53:327.

Poirier, F. 1977. *Fossil evidence: the human evolutionary journey*. St. Louis: Mosby.

Price, P., and Walker, R. 1963. A simple method of measuring low uranium concentrations in natural crystals. *Applied Physics Letters* 2:32.

Schultz, A. 1963. Age changes, sex differences, and variability as factors in the classification of primates. In *Classification and human evolution*, edited by S. Washburn, pp. 85-115. New York: Viking Fund Publications.

Shuey, R.; Brown, F.; and Cross, M. 1974. Magneto-stratigraphy of the Shungura Formation, southwestern Ethiopia; fine structure of the Lower Matuyama Polarity Epoch. *Earth and Planetary Science Letters* 23:249-60.

Simons, E. 1968a. Some fallacies in the study of hominid phylogeny. In *Perspectives on human evolution*, edited by S. Washburn and P. Jay, pp. 18-40. New York: Holt, Rinehart and Winston.

———. 1968b. Assessment of fossil hominids. *Science* 160:672.

———. 1972. *Primate evolution: an introduction to man's place in nature.* New York: Macmillan.

Simpson, G. 1945. The principles of classification and a classification of mammals. *Bulletin of American Museum of Natural History,* vol. 85.

———. 1951. *Horses.* London: Oxford University Press.

———. 1953. *The major features of evolution.* New York: Columbia University Press.

———. 1961. *Principles of animal taxonomy.* New York: Columbia University Press.

Sokol, R., and Sneath, P. 1963. *Principles of numerical taxonomy.* San Francisco: W. H. Freeman.

Washburn, S. 1967. The analysis of primate evolution, with particular reference to the origin of man. In *Ideas on human evolution*, edited by W. W. Howells, pp. 154-71. New York: Atheneum.

Weiner, J.; Oakley, K.; and Clark, W. Le Gros. 1953. The solution of the Piltdown problem. *Bulletin of British Museum* 2:139.

1. Bottom of Gorilla's foot.　　2. Back of Gorilla's hand.　　3. Orang-Outang's foot.　　4. Orang-Outang's hand.　.　5, 6, 7. Mamma, Papa, and Baby Orang-Outangs, from Borneo.
8. Bearded Saki, South America.　　9. Tartarin, North Africa.　　10. Marmoset.　　11. Male Gorilla.　　12. Proboscis Monkey, Borneo.

Chapter 10
The Primate Past

Most paleontologists are of the opinion that early primates, called prosimians, evolved from an insectivorous stock sometime during the Paleocene or the Eocene geological epoch. One viewpoint holds that early primate evolution basically occurred within an arboreal (tree living) niche as a refuge zone free from competition from insectivores generally.[1] Major early changes noted in primate evolution (i.e., dental and facial changes) were primarily associated with diet and later skeletal modifications with locomotor changes possibly associated with getting around the arboreal habitat.

Eocene prosimians evidence a number of features suggesting adjustments to getting around the arboreal habitat; some of the major changes appeared in the facial and limb skeleton. By the middle and end of the Eocene we witness the widespread extinction of many primitive primates.

Our remote prosimian ancestors were probably beady-eyed, bewhiskered, long-snouted animals looking and perhaps behaving like small rats. One view suggests that before becoming arboreal they scurried through the fallen leaves and undergrowth of the tropical forests searching for food, probably insects. Early primate evolution coincided with a time when the earth was geologically restless; the reigning reptiles, not adapted to the rapidly changing ecological conditions, became obsolete. There were violent earthquakes, volcanic eruptions, and mountains were rising; retreating waters exposed larger and larger land masses. There seems to have been an enormous expansion of the number and variety of grasses, ivy, shrubs, and trees. There may have been a sharp rise in pathogenic fungi and disease-bearing

[1]For a different viewpoint of early primate origins see M. Cartmill, *Primate Origins*, 1975.

"Remarkable Quadrumana." Drawing by Daniel Beard at the Museum of Natural History, Central Park, New York City.

insects which might have spread a major epidemic among the vulnerable reptiles.

According to one viewpoint the early primates and rodents competed intensively on the ground and in the trees. Until recently rodents had the best of the struggle; but even today rodents are represented by 3000 species and primates by about 200 species. Some early primates became terrestrially oriented and became extinct after about 10 million years; those who became arboreal fared better. Many paleontologists feel that the prosimians entered the trees as a refuge zone where competition was less intense and living more complicated. The prosimians were forced to adapt to a strange new world, a new dimension of life among the dense foliage, branches, and forest canopies.

The time of appearance, deployment, and extinction of the early primates indicates competitive relationships within the group. Rodents first appeared in the late Paleocene (60 million years ago), after which no new primate group evidenced clear rodentlike adaptations. The main spread of the rodents occurred during the Eocene and coincided with the decline and extinction of primitive primates in North America and Europe. The rodent-primate competition must have been close and crucial to their mutual evolutionary histories.

Food Habits: You Are What You Eat

Primate Diets. Major stages in primate evolution occurred within the arboreal habitat; two of the major adjustments required for arboreal life are a shift in dietary preference and habitat exploration, the latter involving structural changes in the limbs as noted during the Eocene. Most available foods within the arboreal habitat are vegetal, and most primates are essentially vegetarians, although they also consume fruits. However, many modern primates may best be described as opportunistic **omnivores**, i.e., they feed on insects and other food sources when available. Some primates have become "secondarily" carnivorous; major examples are the South African baboon and the chimpanzee. Some baboon troops prey upon sheep, monkeys, and other smaller animals; some chimpanzees have been observed to prey upon, eat, and share the remains of various monkeys and infant baboons.

Dental Traits (Figures 10-1, 10-2). Teeth form a major portion of the early primate remains. The major features distinguishing early

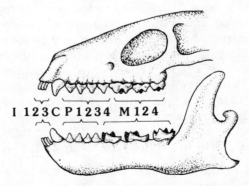

I 123 C P 1234 M 124

Figure 10-1. The dentition of an assumed early placental mammal that gave rise to the primates. I—incisors, C—canines, P—premolars, and M—molars.

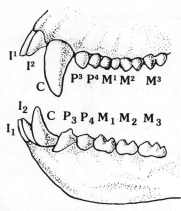

Figure 10-2. Designation of individual teeth in a catarrhine monkey _Macaca_.

prosimian dentitions reflect an important dietary shift. The change was not an absolute total shift away from an older diet; rather, it involved a relative increase in the importance of fruit, leaves, and herbaceous matter, and a decrease in feeding upon insects. Dietary changes characterizing the earliest stages of primate evolution may actually have occurred as a series of overlapping shifts. First, a large, sparsely inhabited **frugivorous-herbivorous** (fruit, bud, and leaf) niche must have been available. The changes necessary to adapt to these new foods were largely behavioral, e.g., there was a slow shift in food preference. Once a preference for, or sustained interest in, small fruits, berries, and leaves became established at the expense of a more **insectivorous** diet, selection favored populations which could most efficiently utilize these foods. Once this process was operative, a second stage was entered necessitating changes in dentition and the digestive tract.

The diet of the insectivorous stock from which the earliest primates evolved included soft-bodied invertebrates (animals lacking backbones), animals which are easily sliced and swallowed. The teeth of insectivores are characteristically tall and sharp with acute **cusps** (elevations of the tooth crown surface). Such teeth are poorly suited for masticating the rough, tough-shelled seeds or fibrous fruits found within the arboreal habitat. Early in primate evolution there was selection pressure for shorter and more bulbous (rounded) cusps and for grinding mastication of foods.

Facial, Cranial Changes. Subsequent modifications followed the basic dietary change and modification of the masticatory apparatus. A major change was reduction of the snout, probably related to a reduction in size and/or crowding of the incisors, canines, and premolars, and to an increasing reliance upon the hands for picking up objects, such as foodstuffs which were conveyed from hand to mouth. The configuration of the **zygomatic arches** (cheekbones) also changed, becoming broad and strong. This was presumably related to the increasing bulk of a stronger **masseter muscle** complex; these muscles are chiefly concerned with a grinding mode of mastication.[2] Major facial changes are noted during the Eocene with the onset of stereoscopic vision and an increasing reliance on the visual sense.

[2]If you touch your cheeks and grit your teeth, you can feel these muscles.

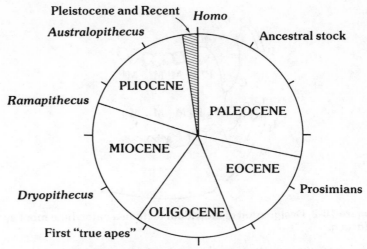

Figure 10-3. The Cenozoic clock—primate time scale.

Paleocene Primates

Some argue that the earliest evidence of this prosimian stock derives from the Middle Paleocene epoch, approximately 55 to 60 million years B.P., in North America from fossiliferous sites in Colorado, Montana, New Mexico, Wyoming, and Texas (Figure 10-3). One of the three possible Paleocene prosimian families, the Carpolestidae, exhibit the dental changes mentioned above. The family Carpolestidae (the name means fruit stealers) is based upon fossilized jaws and teeth. The teeth were presumably adapted to splitting open seeds and hard, woody stems; the second premolar is greatly enlarged and serrated (sawlike) to form a longitudinal cutting edge.

Dental patterns of these Paleocene forms suggest that many were adapting in new ways to a new diet characteristic of a group during the invasion of a new habitat. The variety of molar patterns exhibited by the Paleocene fossils indicates they were not adapted to chewing the fibrous outer body cover of animal bodies. Subsequent specializations of the incisors and canines may be related to diversified specializations of a herbivorous or frugivorous diet.

If some of the Paleocene forms are primates they are unique in the development of their incisors. The loss of piercing canines and nipping incisors for two pairs of specialized incisors indicates invasion into a broad herbivorous-frugivorous niche. The emphasis on the incisors and de-emphasis on canines indicates a general lack of predatory behavior.

One of the earliest forms designated as a possible primate is *Purgatorius* (Van Valen and Sloan, 1965). One of the later species of *Purgatorius* is based upon a sample of approximately fifty isolated teeth from a single Paleocene quarry site in Eastern Montana. While there are primate characteristics in the molar teeth, we must withhold judgment of the primate status of this form until further information is available.[3]

[3]It should be noted that some scholars feel that the Paleocene forms are not yet evolved enough to be classified as primates. If not primates, these forms are transitional between the primates and insectivores and suggest the direction which evolution was taking.

Figure 10-4. A tree shrew. Not to scale.

Trends in Eocene Evolution

The Arboreal Habitat. A second major adaptation to arboreal life was an adjustment to "getting around" in the trees, to exploiting this three-dimensional world. Major trends appear in the hands, feet, skull, and face of Eocene fossils, dating from 36 to 50 million years B.P. The Eocene epoch witnesses the maximal radiation (divergent development) of the prosimii; as many as forty-three genera and five families have been recognized. This number will likely be reduced when we learn more about population variability within the groups.

Limb Structure. Included within the general structural limb adaptations to arboreal life are grasping hands and feet equipped with nails instead of claws.[4] The hands and feet are characterized by pentadactyly (the presence of five fingers and toes) and by a grasping thumb and big toe. Using modern primates as a comparative source, it can be suggested that these contained ridged and slightly oily tactile pads on their tips.[5] Another important characteristic of the primate limb structure is retention of two separate forearm bones, the **ulna** (on the little-finger side of the arm) and the **radius** (on the thumb side). This allows for forearm rotation and greater mobility, a useful adaptation for jumping and grasping necessitated by an arboreal life.

Changes in the Skull. The Eocene witnessed major changes in the primate skull which seem adaptive for arboreal life. A major change is the reduction of the snout or nasal area and the forward rotation of the eye orbits, both of which suggest a reduction of reliance upon the **olfactory** sense (Figure 10-5). This is emphasized by the lack of a naked rhinarium (e.g., the wet nose of a dog) among most modern members. A shift in the senses meant a reorganization of the brain, for example a reduction of the olfactory and an enlargement of the visual brain centers.

Fossil evidence indicates the increasing importance of the visual sense. The suggestive evidence appears as the shifting of the orbits from a lateral to frontal position and enclosure of the eyes with a protective bone casing. Forward orbital rotation resulted in **binocular** or **stereoscopic** vision, i.e., the convergence of the two visual fields upon

[4]There are exceptions to this pattern among modern primates, e.g., the Southeast Asian tree shrew (Figure 10-4), which many reject as a primate, possesses claws on all its digits. The loris, a small Southeast Asian nocturnal form, utilizes so-called claws on its third and fourth digits for cleansing its hair of debris.

[5]Our fingerprints are derived from these ridged pads.

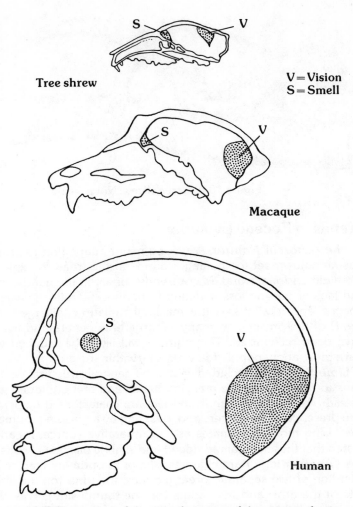

Tree shrew

V = Vision
S = Smell

Macaque

Human

Figure 10-5. Expansion of the visual centers of the primate brain.

one object. This is an adaptation to spatial orientation and may perhaps be associated with jumping from one tree limb to another. Leaping from branch to branch in search of food requires that the tree-dweller continually make distance judgments and, to the degree that visual fields overlap, image fusion and improvements of depth perception are necessary.[6]

As a result of the shift in position, the primate eye is more vulnerable than that of most terrestrial mammals whose line of sight is laterally directed. Among most prosimians the eye is protected only by a slender bar of bone. Among the Anthropoidea (suborder of Primates containing the Old and New World monkeys, apes, and humans), the entire orbit is surrounded by a ring of bone resulting in a distinct eye socket.

Two other morphological/behavioral changes appear early in primate evolution. Although there is minimal suggestive evidence, early prosimians may have possessed **ischial callosities** (a specialized skin structure present even in the fetus) which allow primates to sit on hard

[6]Misjudged leaps can result in fatal falls. Even the most accomplished arboreal primate acrobat, the gibbon, often falls from misjudged leaps or broken branches.

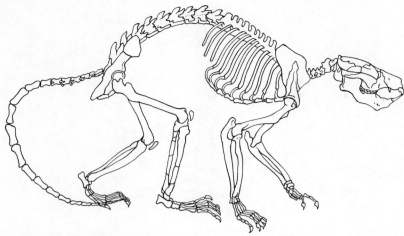

Figure 10-6. Skeletal reconstruction of *Plesiadapis* based on cranial and postcranial remains found in France and Colorado. Scale is X 0.25. *Plesiadapis* is one of the oldest possible primate fossils.

branches for endless time periods.[7, 8] Upright sitting freed the hands for other activities, such as pulling food to the mouth; such behaviors coincidentally improved hand-eye coordination. This is a **preadaptation** (a behavior or structure of value in later evolutionary stages) for tool use and bipedalism.

Evidence for these trends can be found among some Eocene prosimians. The family Adapidae, including the genera *Notharctus* from North America (Figure 10-7) and *Adapis* from France, exhibits these trends. The limb structure of Eocene forms is characterized by an opposable big toe and thumb. The snout was still quite long (resulting in a **prognathic** face), but the orbits have rotated forward indicating stereoscopic vision. Other Eocene forms show a general shortening of the snout and a forward shifting of the **foramen magnum** (the hole through which the spinal cord passes). These changes indicate an erect posture while hopping and sitting. This, coupled with forelimb shortening, suggests a locomotor pattern of hopping and climbing.

Changes in the Ear. It has recently been suggested that a major trend in early primate evolution dealt with a reorganization of the structure and function of the middle ear. This restructuring is believed to have allowed for better balance while leaping and may have enhanced the ability to make constant adjustments in body position. The argument is that the ability to determine body position is important to an animal which habitually glides, leaps, or relies occasionally, but crucially, on exacting balance. The highly advanced middle ear cavity of the

---

[7]That the lack of such structures is definitely disadvantageous is attested to by primatologists who sometimes sit on the same limbs watching the monkeys. For us, the usual result is that our legs "fall asleep." Some modern nonhuman primates lack ischial callosities.

[8]Nonhuman primates possess other adaptations for sleeping; for example, many species of monkeys sleep out on small, slender limbs where they are relatively safe from predators. Should a large-size predator attempt to climb out on the limb, the limb would shake and the monkeys would be aroused to the potential danger. Another of the sleeping adaptations is found among the apes; both chimpanzees and orangutans build nests in the sleeping trees. The gorilla also builds a nest; however, it is placed on the ground. Few trees have branches strong enough to hold a large adult gorilla for the night.

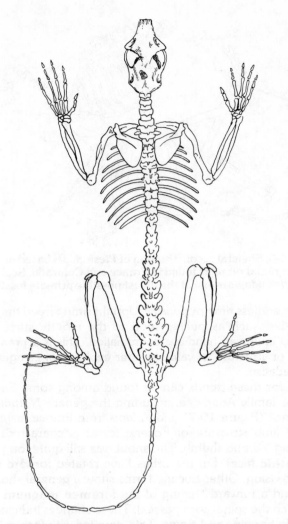

Figure 10-7. Skeleton of the Middle Eocene primate *Notharctus*. Scale is X 0.20.

Paleocene form *Plesiadapis,* especially in comparison with its relatively primitive **postcranial** (below the head) skeleton, suggests that its locomotor pattern, possibly in combination with its feeding adaptations, required a highly developed sense of balance.

An Alternate Interpretation

Arboreal Theory. The orthodox theory of early primate evolution ties our evolutionary heritage to the arboreal habitat, and has been appropriately labelled the arboreal theory. This theory was presented in one form on the previous pages and was originally propounded by the British anatomists G. Elliott Smith and F. Wood Jones. It is this arboreal theory to which many refer when attempting to explain the early primate fossil record. The major new challenge to this theory is made by Dr. M. Cartmill (1975), whose views follow this summary.

The arboreal theory of primate origins ties the major adaptations of early primates to the tree-dwelling habitat. For example, the grasping

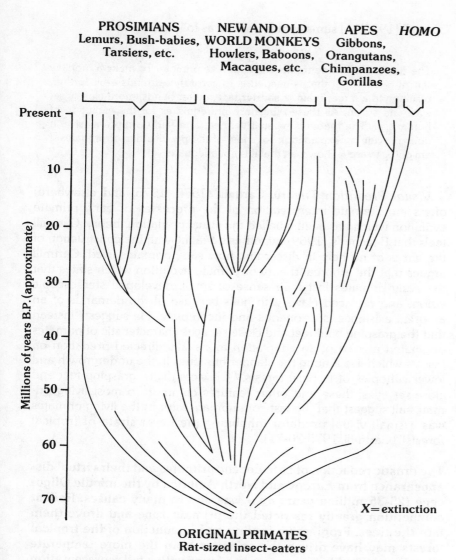

PROSIMIANS
Lemurs, Bush-babies,
Tarsiers, etc.

**NEW AND OLD
WORLD MONKEYS**
Howlers, Baboons,
Macaques, etc.

APES
Gibbons,
Orangutans,
Chimpanzees,
Gorillas

HOMO

Present

Millions of years B.P. (approximate)

10

20

30

40

50

60

70

X = extinction

ORIGINAL PRIMATES
Rat-sized insect-eaters

Figure 10-8. The primate evolutionary tree.

hands and feet are supposedly related to grasping and hanging to thin branches. Jones felt that the fore and hind limbs of the early primates had different functions and that these were of potential evolutionary significance. Jones argued that the hands were the grasping and exploratory organs while the hind limbs supported and propelled the body. These led to further anatomical and behavioral changes.

Jones argues that early in primate evolution the body posture becomes upright and the grasping hands gradually replace the jaws in obtaining food. The jaws gradually reduce in size, the face becomes smaller, and the eye orbits shift to a more forward position. These changes are accompanied by alterations in the nervous system, i.e., the olfactory sense becomes reduced in importance and the visual sense becomes elaborated. This leads to a restructuring of the brain and further anatomical changes in the facial and jaw regions.

Cartmill (1975:15) sums up this process as follows:

> The result of all these trends is a lemurlike primate. To make a monkey out of a lemur, all that is needed is to carry these trends a bit further, resulting in a larger brain, a shorter face, defter hands, more closely set eyes and so on. All these things are prerequisites for the evolution of humans. . . . The theory is persuasive, neat and fairly comprehensive. It does provide an explanation for most of the peculiarities of primates. I am going to argue, however, that it is not adequate.

Visual Predation Theory. Cartmill (1972, 1975, and elsewhere) offers an alternate interpretation of the processes of early primate evolution which has been labelled the visual predation theory. Cartmill feels that Beecher's (1969) hypothesis dealing with the construction of the ear is of no help in discerning how early primates lived. Cartmill argues that the arboreal theory of primate evolution which states that the early primates lost their sense of smell, developed stereoscopic vision, and replaced claws with nails because of the demands of an arboreal existence is erroneous and incomplete. He suggests instead that the grasping hind feet and close-set eyes characteristic of primates originated as part of an adaptation to visually directed predation on insects which live among the slender branches in the undergrowth and lower canopies of tropical forests. "Clawless digits, grasping feet and close-set eyes; these and other features common to most living primates all suggest that the last common ancestor of the living primates was a small visual predator inhabiting the lower strata of tropical forests" (Cartmill, 1975:20-21).

The drastic reduction of Late Eocene primates and their virtual disappearance from Europe and North America by the middle Oligocene (25-35 million years ago) was due to many causes. Rodent competition greatly restricted the primate zone and drove them into the trees. Progressive cooling and a reduction of the tropical forests may have driven the primates from the more temperate zone. Forms unable to compete in a fauna with a full representation of modern mammals were presumably replaced by monkeys. More progressive monkey groups were probably a decisive factor in the extinction of prosimians over large areas of Europe.

Bibliography

Barth, F. 1950. On the relationships of early primates. *American Journal of Physical Anthropology* 8:139.

Beecher, W. 1969. Possible motion detection in the vertebrate middle ear. *Bulletin Chicago Academy of Science* II:155.

Campbell, B. 1966. *Human evolution.* Chicago: Aldine.

Cartmill, M. 1972. Arboreal adaptations and the origin of the order primates. In *The functional and evolutionary biology of primates,* edited by R. Tuttle, pp. 97-122. Chicago: Aldine-Atherton.

———. 1975. *Primate origins.* Minneapolis: Burgess.

Clark, W. Le Gros. 1969. *History of the primates.* Chicago: Phoenix Books.

———. 1971. *The antecedents of man.* Chicago: Quadrangle Books.

Haines, R. 1958. Arboreal or terrestrial ancestry of placental mammals? *Quarterly Review of Biology* 33:1.

Pfeiffer, J. 1969. *The emergence of man.* New York: Harper & Row.

Simons, E. 1972. *Primate evolution: an introduction to man's place in nature.* New York: Macmillan.

Simpson, G. 1955. The Phenacolemuridae, new family of early primates. *Bulletin of American Museum of Natural History* 105:411.

Szalay, F. 1968. The beginnings of primates. *Evolution* 22(1):19.

———. 1972. Paleobiology of the earliest primates. In *The functional and evolutionary biology of primates,* edited by R. Tuttle, pp. 3-36. Chicago: Aldine-Atherton.

Van Valen, L., and Sloan, R. 1965. The earliest primates. *Science* 150:743-45.

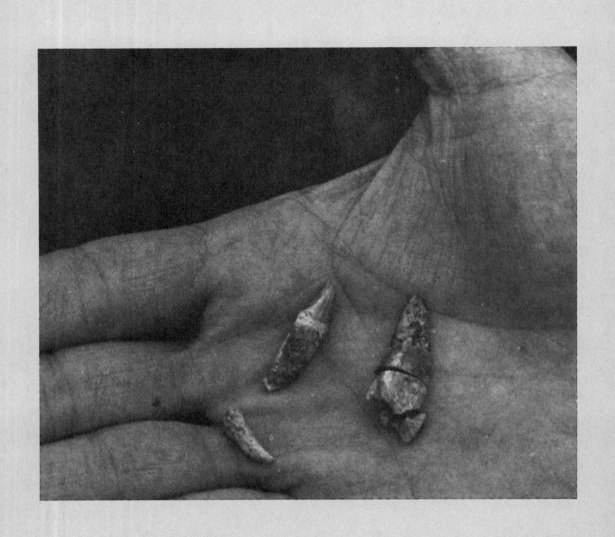

Chapter 11
Pongid Evolution

Pongid evolution commenced during the Oligocene epoch, about 35 million years ago, and reached its height during the Miocene epoch beginning about 25 million years ago. In neither geological epoch did the ancestral forms markedly resemble modern pongids other than in certain dental traits. In each period, or perhaps in both, forms existed which have been championed as direct ancestors of early hominids.

Evolution During the Oligocene — The Fayum, Egypt

Our incomplete picture of Oligocene primate evolution comes largely from the Fayum (Arabic, *El Faiyum*) region south of Cairo, Egypt, which has been dug since the early 1960s by a team led by Dr. Elwyn Simons of the Peabody Museum, Yale University.[1] Fayum deposits yield the oldest undoubted ape skeletal materials, along with fossils of long-extinct monkeys. In terms of the fossil record, monkeys and apes are generally distinguished by anatomical traits and/or complexes. Much that distinguishes them is related to differences in locomotor adaptations. For example, modern monkeys have tails and are generally quadrupedal. Modern apes lack tails and tend towards **brachiation** in the trees and **knuckle-** or **fist-walking** on the ground. The cranial capacities of apes are generally larger than those of monkeys. As we go back in time, however, the distinguishing traits become blurred. Fayum apes, for example, had relatively small brains, were arboreal quadrupeds, and some evidently still possessed tails. The dental structure of Oligocene apes, especially the molar cusp patterns, is unique to pongids.

Three genera comprise the major Fayum remains. The oldest of the materials is a form known as *Oligopithecus*. There is the very controversial *Propliopithecus*, which some once considered an ancestral

[1] However, some of the Fayum material has been available since the early 1900s.

Some teeth found at Songhor, Kenya. The tooth at the right is part of a *Dryopithecus* canine. The center tooth is a monkey canine.

Table 11-1. The Major Fayum Primates.*

Oligopithecus (Oligo = few, pithecus = ape). This is the oldest Fayum primate, dating to 32 million years B.P.

Parapithecus (para = near, pithecus = ape, i.e., near ape, ca. 30 million years B.P.).

Apidium (named after Apis, the sacred bull of Egypt, ca. 30 million years B.P.).

Parapithecus and *Apidium* are related and may have some relationship to the Italian primate known as *Oreopithecus*.

Propliopithecus (pro = before, plio = more, pithecus = ape). A very controversial form dating to about 30 million years B.P. A few once considered this an ancestral hominid.

Aegyptopithecus. A form which dates to about 28 million years B.P. *Aegyptopithecus* is related to the dryopithecines.

Aeolopithecus (named after Aeolus, god of winds). This form is considered ancestral to gibbons and dates to ca. 28 to 30 million years B.P.

*Although these names are descriptive, not all generic names are descriptive in nature.

hominid dating back 30 million years B.P., and *Aegyptopithecus* dating to 28 million years B.P., sometimes referred to as the "first true ape."[2] (See Table 11-1.)

Reconstruction of the Habitat. The excellent reconstruction of the Fayum habitat provides a rather vivid picture of the area approximately 30-35 million years ago. Although the Fayum is today desert, during the Oligocene it was a lush tropical area. Studies of fossilized seed pods, pollens, and wood have helped determine the forest's character. It was most probably a tropical gallery forest, and it is also likely that there were areas of open savanna or coastal plains.

The recovery of large quantities of fish and land vertebrates immensely helped the reconstruction. In addition to the fish bones, skeletal remains of large amphibious mammals resembling sea cows were uncovered. Reptiles were represented by land tortoises similar to those existing today in the Galapagos Islands. There is no evidence of animals related to the antelope, water buffalo, giraffe, or leopard, or any animals characteristic of modern Africa. The total Fayum assemblage indicates a warm, well-watered lowland, with vegetation-clogged rivers grading into sluggish deltaic streams and brackish estuaries which provided grazing land. The forest canopy was the environment of the Oligocene Fayum primates.

The Fossil Evidence

A large portion of the Fayum primate material consists of young animals who may have met their death due to misjudged leaps between branches overhanging the streams. An indication of their inexperience and age is evidenced by the incomplete tooth eruption of many of the jaw fragments.

Oligopithecus. The oldest and most generalized (i.e., the form most likely to be ancestral to the others) of the Fayum materials is *Oligopithecus,* an unknown form until the first excavation season in 1964. It has been dated to approximately 32 million years B.P. The material classified as *Oligopithecus* consists of a left mandibular half from which the incisors and last molar are missing. However, the **dental formula**

[2]There are also two other forms, *Parapithecus* and *Apidium,* which may be related to *Oreopithecus* found in Miocene-Pliocene deposits in Italy.

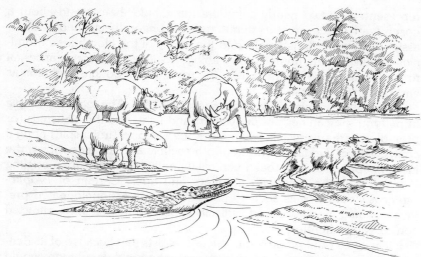

Figure 11-1. More than 30 million years ago, *Propliopithecus* may have lived in trees lining the banks of the primitive Nile River. The primitive proboscidean *Moeritherium* approaches the water from the left. The long-nosed crocodile *Tomistoma* frightens a giant dassie, *Megalphyrax*. In the background stand the great horned creatures, *Arsinoitherium*.

has been reconstructed as 2.1.2.3, that of all modern Old World higher primates—monkeys, apes, and humans. We are not certain to what forms *Oligopithecus* was ancestral, although some suggest that it may be related to Old World monkeys. According to another viewpoint the extreme primitiveness of molar crown patterns in *Oligopithecus* leads one to suspect that the find cannot be classed either as an ancestral cercopithecoid or an ancestral hominid. Thus, its ancestral position to later Fayum forms is questionable.

Propliopithecus (Figure 11-2). One of the best-known and most controversial Oligocene primates is *Propliopithecus haeckeli*, which is

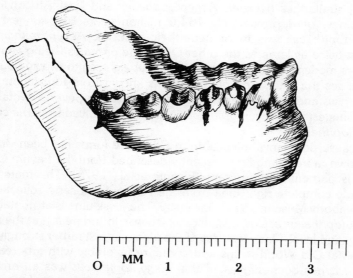

Figure 11-2. Reconstructed cast of *Propliopithecus haeckeli.*

represented by two nearly complete mandibular halves and about a dozen teeth. Because of its dental traits, *Propliopithecus* had been reassigned to a relationship close to the family of the Hominidae (hominids). Indeed, some primate paleontologists suggest that forms ancestral to the hominid line diverged from the main line of pongid evolution as early as the Oligocene.

The dental formula of *Propliopithecus* is 2.1.2.3. The teeth are simple in pattern; the canines are fairly short and light, and the bicuspids (or premolars) are unspecialized and lack the *sectorial* (unicuspid) pongid characteristic. Judging from the tooth sockets and adjacent bone, the incisors appear to have been vertically implanted rather than angling forward as is the case with monkeys and apes. Certain of *Propliopithecus's* dental traits such as the small canines, nonelongated premolars, equal molar size, and vertically implanted incisors have attracted considerable attention.

It was once thought by some paleontologists that because of its dental traits *Propliopithecus* could be an early hominid. If so, there would be little genetic relationship between humans and apes as is commonly assumed. Did the ancestral hominid line arise directly from *Propliopithecus* about 30 million years ago? We now know that *Propliopithecus's* dental characteristics are not necessarily indicative of hominid status but rather reflect its generalized nature. *Propliopithecus* may represent a small-faced arboreal ape stock, lacking large canines and slicing incisors. Since *Propliopithecus* predates *Aegyptopithecus*, a recognizable pongid, its hominid features may be due to primitiveness rather than to a direct ancestral relationship to later hominids. *Propliopithecus* is representative of an early pongid stock. Some members of this group gave rise to *Aegyptopithecus* which is ancestral to the dryopithecines, perhaps the last common stock of apes and humans.

Aegyptopithecus. *Aegyptopithecus* is dated to approximately 28 million years B.P., i.e., 8-10 million years earlier than previously known fossil ape skulls, the dryopithecines. Although incomplete, *Aegyptopithecus* is one of the best-preserved pongid fossil skulls. Numerous dental similarities between *Aegyptopithecus* and East African dryopithecines, of approximately 16-20 million years B.P., suggest that *Aegyptopithecus* was in or near their ancestry. *Aegyptopithecus* is almost twice as large as the other Oligocene primates (being about as large as modern gibbons which weigh about eighteen to twenty pounds).

Besides the skull, *Aegyptopithecus* is known from four incomplete lower jaws and half a dozen isolated upper teeth. Several dental features suggest that *Aegyptopithecus* could have evolved from the earlier *Propliopithecus*.

Because postcranial material from Oligocene forms has been virtually unknown, a new limb bone recently described from the Fayum Oligocene is particularly important (Fleagle et al., 1975). The material is a nearly complete right ulna from the Fayum Oligocene collection of the Peabody Museum, Yale University. The fossil ulna is attributable to *Aegyptopithecus zeuxis*, a skull of which was found near it at the same quarry and level. Many features of the ulna contrast rather strongly with terrestrial Old World forms and compare favorably with arboreal primates. It has been suggested that *Aegyptopithecus* was an arboreal quadruped. Morphological traits, especially characteristics of the elbow

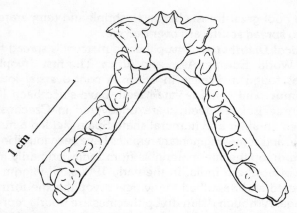

Figure 11-3. Occlusal view (from above) of *Aeolopithecus chirobates* (a possible gibbon ancestor) from Oligocene Fayum deposits.

1 cm

area, indicate that *Aegyptopithecus* was well adapted to climbing and possibly to hanging by the forelimbs. The morphological traits of the ulna support a reconstruction of locomotor behavior that could give rise to both brachiating and arboreal and terrestrial quadruped locomotion.

Morphologically and chronologically *Aegyptopithecus* could be ancestral to the Miocene dryopithecines and it may be the direct forebear of such apes as the modern chimpanzee. With *Aegyptopithecus* perhaps being representative of the oldest pongid skull, it appears that the line leading to modern apes and humans first evolved from a more generalized Old World primate. This may have occurred during the Oligocene. With respect to humans and apes, *Aegyptopithecus* is the form most likely involved in this branching. Another form, *Aeolopithecus* (Figure 11-3), is perhaps a branch leading to the gibbon and closely related siamangs. (Although their ancestry may thus be traced to Africa, modern gibbons and siamangs can only be found in Asia.) The stock from which this group evolved could be the earlier *Propliopithecus*, itself evolved from an earlier connecting link such as *Oligopithecus*.

Summary. The selective pressures of the arboreal life characteristic of millions of years ago forced a comparatively primitive primate stock in the direction of pongid evolution. For example, near the end of the Oligocene, evolutionary pressures produced a form possessing a monkey's skull and ape's teeth. This was *Aegyptopithecus*. The Fayum primates provide fossil evidence of the process of primate evolution from approximately 28-32 million years B.P. In the Fayum, in one area of forest where many rivers once entered the sea, early primate populations flourished.

Miocene Evolution — The Dryopithecines

During the Miocene there is a flowering of pongid evolution. In the Miocene, spanning an age from 18 to about 25 million years B.P., ancestral forms of modern pongids are represented in the fossil specimens known as the dryopithecines. During the Miocene the earth experienced extensive tectonic movements, great mountain ranges arose, and continents drifted apart. Volcanoes actively changed the face of the African continent and a series of geological disturbances created the Great Rift Valley. Climatic shifts occurred—as the climate continued to cool great forests began to shrink and temperate conditions began to spread southward over Europe.

Geographical Distribution. Dryopithecine material is spread throughout the Old World: Europe, Asia, and Africa. The first dryopithecine mandible was found in France in 1856. A controversial lower limb bone, the **femur,** and some isolated teeth have since been found in Germany. Three isolated teeth were uncovered in Czechoslovakia, Austria yielded an ulnar and humeral shaft, Spain yielded a number of jaws and teeth, and some fragmentary remains have been found in Turkey.

Most Asian dryopithecine material is from India, primarily from the Siwalik Hills of northern India. In the early 1900s, G. Pilgrim and G. Lewis uncovered and described many new dryopithecine forms, most of Miocene age. Although Asian dryopithecines are poorly represented outside India, the known scattered remains in the Soviet Union and China suggest that further work will reveal a wider distribution. The most extensive series of dryopithecine fossils comes from Miocene deposits in and around the Kavirondo Gulf of Lake Victoria in Kenya, East Africa. In 1931 a paleontological expedition to Kenya uncovered considerable dryopithecine material, which by 1933 was organized into three genera and species. This material includes forms considered ancestral to modern gorillas and chimpanzees. From 1939 to 1949 much additional primate material was recovered from East African Miocene deposits. These collections were reviewed in 1950 and 1951, by Sir W. E. Le Gros Clark and Dr. Louis Leakey who proposed three species of "Proconsul"[3] from the Rusinga site: "P. africanus," "P. major," and "P. nyanzae." In 1963 and 1970 new material was described from Uganda and Kenya. Taxonomically the "Proconsul" material is now generally referred to the genus *Dryopithecus.*

The East African material is definitely of Miocene age as potassium-argon reveals that the main fossiliferous zones at Rusinga are some 18 million years old. Although some specimens may date 20-22 million years B.P., most of the pongid material is probably dated to between 17.5 and 18.5 million years B.P. The Nagri faunal zone in North India is generally accepted as later Miocene or early Pliocene. Since the Nagri zone overlies the Chinji, the latter is considered to be older, perhaps of Middle Miocene dating. Dating of the Indian dryopithecines is based upon faunal associations.

Morphological Characteristics. What did the dryopithecines look like and how did they live? Much of the reconstruction is based upon the East African material from around Lake Victoria. The presence of so many animal remains in shallow-water lake deposits suggests they were vulnerable when they came to the water to drink and that they were killed there. The relative absence of limb bones may be due to the fact that, because of their high marrow content, the majority of the bones were broken and eaten by large hyenas or other carnivores. The same would account for the almost complete absence of skulls which, due to their brain content, would be liable to be eaten by larger carnivores.

[3]The name "Proconsul" was taken from a zoo chimpanzee named "Consul." "Proconsul" was considered its ancestor. The term "Proconsul" is no longer considered valid at the genus level and has been replaced by the term *Dryopithecus.* It is, however, considered by some to be a valid African subgenus.

The major available cranial material belongs to *Dryopithecus* (Pro-consul) *africanus* from East Africa. The skull is lightly built and rather small, suggesting an animal more the size of an Old World monkey (about twenty pounds) than a modern ape. Unlike modern apes, the skull lacks the heavy bone structures characteristic of the *sagittal* and *nuchal* regions. There are no heavy ridges (the *supraorbital torus*) above the eye sockets, so characteristic of modern apes and larger Old World monkeys. As is evidenced by features of an *endocranial* cast (fossilized cast of the brain), *Dryopithecus's* brain was smaller and less complex than that characteristic of most modern primates. The muzzle is rather small and narrowed in front, and the nasal aperture is monkey-like. But, all we have is one skull of one of the smaller species; other skulls may be larger and more apelike.

The limb bones are of critical importance for resolving the Hominidae and Pongidae relationship. The limbs of Miocene apes lacked many structural specializations associated with brachiation, the mode of locomotion (arm-swinging beneath branches) associated with some modern pongids.[4] The limb bones strongly suggest that the ancestral apes led a different mode of life than modern apes. Apart from the incomplete *humerus* (the arm bone) from France and from two other partial pieces, the only knowledge we have of dryopithecine forelimbs is from "Proconsul" remains in Kenya.

The humerus from Saint Gaudens, France, has been potassium-argon dated to approximately 12.5-14 million years B.P. In size and morphology it most resembles a chimpanzee humerus. Upper-limb skeletal remains from Kenya combine features typical of tree-living quadrupedal monkeys with characteristics no less distinctive of brachiating apes. However, the upper-limb structure also manifests features later seen in modern apes. *Dryopithecus* forms an important

[4]It is important to note that even though some of the modern apes, e.g., the gorilla, chimpanzee, and orangutan, spend time on the ground in various locomotor patterns, it is assumed they passed through a prior brachiating stage in their evolutionary history.

Dryopithecus
Songhor 19 May, 1975
We drive to Songhor, a *Dryopithecus* site of immense importance. The drive from Fort Ternan takes approximately 40 minutes. The security guard at the site allows us to make camp—again thanks to Richard Leakey. The Songhor site sits on the Kano Plain which itself dates to the Miocene geological epoch. The oldest date on the Kano Plain is approximately 23 million years B.P. according to potassium-argon dates on volcanically derived material. Much of the area now surrounding Songhor is largely planted over in sugar cane. In fact another near-by site, Koru, is all but erased because of cultivation.

The Songhor sites are actually a small number of hills eroded out from the action of rain. In fact, the rain-caused erosion is used to locate fossils which appear or the surface. Although no excavations are actually now in progress the guard searches for fossils twice a week. These remains are then shipped to Nairobi for scrutiny. The earth at Songhor is red, although gray ash is in evidence.

We visually search the Songhor area and see some faunal remains which have been eroded free. During our search we find (actually a better

term is "see" for Kenya's excellent tough antiquity laws forbid disturbing fossiliferous or artifactual remains at any of the national monuments. The penalty for ignoring this procedure is justifiably harsh) what appears to be a monkey molar, which I tentatively identify as a possible second mandibular molar. We also see a rodent skull and some rodent teeth. An undescribed *Dryopithecus* canine, broken in half, has recently been uncovered and awaits its delivery to Nairobi. In 1973 Peter Andrews worked at Songhor and uncovered some new dryopithecine remains.

On 20 May we get mired in thick mud as we attempt to break camp and leave Songhor for Rusinga Island. During our vigil to be "rescued" we search the areas and locate what may be another monkey tooth which was apparently dislodged during the night's heavy rain.

20 May, 1975 Rusings Island

After a few hours we are freed from the Songhor mud and proceed to drive to Rusinga. On the way we stop at Kisumu to pick up Mr. Erastro Ndere who has worked on Rusinga. We locate Ndere because of his Yale University jacket which he tells us was presented to him by Dr. David Pilbeam. Because of the late hour we spend the night in Kisumu.

On 21 May we proceed to Mbita Point where we camp and make arrangements to hire a lorry to take us across the ferry to Rusinga. On 22 May we cross the ferry, about a five minute ride, to Rusinga. Rusinga is a rather large island which rises out of Lake Victoria. The ride from the ferry landing to our first stop, the Kiahera Formation, is about 45 minutes. On the way to Kiahera we pass the memorial to the late Luo leader Mr. Tom Mboya. The Kiahera Formation contains considerable fossilized plant materials and seeds which proved most useful for determining the Miocene habitat of *Dryopithecus*.

From Kiahera we proceed to Kaswanga (also spelled Kathwanga) where the mandible of "Kenyapithecus africanus" was found washed out in 1967. At Kaswanga we find (= see) the remains of what may be monkey teeth, ungulate teeth (perhaps from a buffalo), and some fresh water snails—all useful for determining the habitat.

As at Songhor the sites at Rusinga are usually water eroded. The beds at Rusinga are lowish hills of lava flows and some sediments. The geology of the island is now readily deciphered—at least by a trained geologist. There are plentiful supplies of mica (a member of the group of mineral silicates which crystallize in monoclinic forms that separate into very thin leaves) which have caused some problem in terms of dating the deposits.

Excerpt of some of my field notes during a tour of Songhor and Rusinga Island.

link between quadrupedal monkeys and modern apes, as its generalized upper-limb structure could have provided the basis for the evolutionary development of the hominid upper-limb structure.

The fragmentary hind-limb and foot bones are of the greatest importance in reconstructing dryopithecine locomotor patterns. The hind limbs, like the forelimbs, suggest that the dryopithecines were active running and leaping creatures not particularly specialized for an arboreal life. Certain aspects of the heel suggest that the dryopithecines were capable of standing erect on the hind feet. The hind limbs provide a suitable antecedent for subsequent evolutionary developments along the divergent lines of the brachiating (arm swinging) specialization of later modern large apes and the limb structure of erect, bipedal hominids.

RUSINGA ISLAND AND SONGHOR

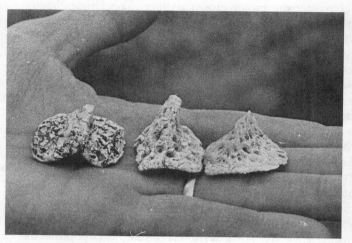

A. Crocodile plates.

B. A rodent cranium.

C. A fragmented ungulate rib, Rusinga Island.

D. A tooth lying in situ. Adjacent to the tooth is a fragmented piece of limb bone, possibly from an ungulate.

Much has been written about dryopithecine dentition, not only because teeth comprise much of the skeletal assemblage but also because of their characteristic molar crown pattern. The *Dryopithecus* Y-5 molar cusp pattern has been a hominoid trait that has persisted (with variations) for at least 20 million years.[5] Dryopithecine dentition, while typically pongidlike, shows some differences from that of modern apes. The incisors are relatively small, the tooth row tends to converge anteriorly (is wider at the back), and the upper molars show pongid traits. The canine and premolar teeth are typically apelike. When the teeth are occluded (when the upper and lower teeth contact), the canines overlap and are strongly projecting. The first lower premolar is **sectorial** (the medial surface is sheared away and thus accommodates the upper overlapping canine). The sectorial premolar may be a mechanism whereby canines maintain their sharpness and is not necessarily a response to large, overlapping canines.

Because of the pongid characteristics of the canines and premolars, some have questioned the validity of postulating a hominid derivation from a dryopithecine ancestry. The question is raised, "Is *Dryopithecus* the last common ancestor of humans and apes?" Even though dryopithecine canines are rather large and the premolar sectorial, subsequent evolutionary pressures could have reduced the canines and transformed the unicuspid, sectorial premolar to the hominid **bicuspid** (two-cusped) premolar. This viewpoint argues for a secondary reduction in canine size. As evidence, adherents of this viewpoint cite the fact that the newly erupted human canine may be quite sharply pointed and project beyond the level of adjacent teeth, and that the human canine has an unusually large root indicating some special function during its evolutionary history. They also cite fossil evidence showing a reduction in canine size between the Middle Pleistocene form *H. erectus* and modern *Homo*.

A contrary viewpoint, discussed in greater detail earlier in this chapter and in Chapter 12, argues that canine size and the sectorial premolar rule dryopithecines out of our ancestry. This viewpoint argues that canine reduction and transformation of the premolar could not have occurred. Adherents to this viewpoint suggest that we evolved from an earlier small-canine form, like *Propliopithecus*.

Habitat of the East African Forms

Africa about 20 million years ago probably had a tropical rain forest flora, with tall trees and a mulitplicity of climbers. The fauna was diverse and represented forest, marshland, and savanna forms. The area was of volcanic origin, and the slopes of the volcanoes were heavily wooded. The larger primates may have inhabited the wooded volcanic slopes, much like the present-day mountain gorilla.

Dryopithecine Phylogeny. Four species of *Dryopithecus* are most important for our understanding of hominid evolution (see Table 11-2). The largest dryopithecine, *D. major* (which was the size of a modern

[5]The Y-5 pattern is so designated because the molar surface sports five cusps separated by grooves in the form of a Y. This pattern is common to the lower molar teeth of fossil hominids. In modern hominids, however, there is frequently a reduction or absence of the fifth cusp (called the hypoconulid) and the formation of a +fissure pattern, i.e., a +4 or +5 pattern. This is especially true of the second and third molars. Morris (1970) raises some doubts as to the efficiency of using the Y-5 as a diagnostic taxonomic character.

Table 11-2. Dryopithecine Phylogenetic Relations.

D. indicus—may be ancestral to *Gigantopithecus*.

D. major—the largest dryopithecine. May be ancestral to modern gorillas.

D. africanus—may be ancestral to modern chimpanzees.

D. nyanzae—the most controversial of the dryopithecines. Some suggest it may be ancestral to subsequent hominids, i.e., *Ramapithecus*. Others suggest it may be the common ancestor to *D. africanus* and *D. major*.

large chimpanzee), may be ancestral to modern gorillas. *D. africanus,* approximately the size of a small female baboon, may be ancestral to modern chimpanzees. It has been suggested, but with lessening certainty, that hominids may have arisen from *D. nyanzae* through the intermediate stage of *Ramapithecus*. Others suggest it as the common ancestor of *D. major* and *D. africanus*.

Although dryopithecines were related to later apes, their locomotor patterns and habitat differed. Postcranial evidence suggests that *D. major* was more active and less terrestrial than living gorillas. There is nothing suggestive of a brachiating locomotor adaptation. When *D. africanus* remains are considered, this form appears ancestral to modern chimpanzees. Dentally and cranially it is possible that changes in this lineage were connected with dietary changes and related to increasing body size. Postcranial remains indicate that *D. africanus* was a small, lightly built, arboreal quadruped, yet a quadruped in which arm-swinging was becoming a major component of its locomotor capacities. In the Miocene, gorilla and chimpanzee ancestors were probably small, lightly built, and mainly arboreal creatures.

In size *D. nyanzae* is midway between *D. major* and *D. africanus*. The smallest *D. nyanzae* specimens overlap those of *D. africanus* and the largest, those of *D. major*. In overall morphology *D. nyanzae* is closest to *D. major,* although there are some dental differences. *D. nyanzae* is abundant at Rusinga, but missing from other East African sites containing *D. major*. This may be a sampling error, or it may reflect a major habitat difference between the two.

The postcranial remains, if they belong to *D. nyanzae,* indicate that, like other dryopithecines, they were relatively lightly built, actively arboreal, and quadrupedal. The postcranial remains also indicate that they were better adapted for bipedal walking than modern chimpanzees. In 1967 Dr. Leakey suggested that some postcranial remains associated with *D. nyanzae* should be attributed to *Kenyapithecus africanus*—which he considered an ancestral hominid. Many, however, disagree with his assessment. At any rate, there have been numerous suggestions that *D. nyanzae* might be close to the hominid ancestral line possibly of *Ramapithecus*. It is uncertain if *D. nyanzae* occurred early enough to occupy this position, i.e., that there was enough time for the evolutionary differentiation of *Ramapithecus's* facial and dental traits. The possible role of *D. nyanzae* in human ancestry remains intriguingly uncertain.

Dryopithecines as Hominid Ancestors

Presumably dryopithecines arose in Africa and then spread throughout the tropical rainforest then covering most of Europe and Central Asia. Paleontological evidence suggests that the radiation of the living hominids had already occurred in the Miocene. Since possible hominids (e.g., *Ramapithecus*) are known from late Miocene sites, it can be inferred that their ancestors are to be found in still earlier times. If later dryopithecines are taken as leading to the pongid line, then it is likely that the hominid line was already distinct. This could place the divergence of the ancestral hominid-pongid line somewhere about the Oligocene-Miocene border and the divergence of the chimpanzee and gorilla stock somewhat later.

The morphological variation characteristic of the dryopithecines is important; because of the variation and because of minor living habits, the genus differentiated. Some dryopithecines adapted to a life in or near the trees. These may have led to the modern chimpanzee and gorilla. Some suggest others went a different path and became hominids. The ape group eventually died out in Europe, presumably unable to adapt to shifting habitat conditions caused by slight cooling of the earth and perhaps being outcompeted for a dwindling food supply. Those in Africa survived.

The argument for a dryopithecine ancestry of hominids suggests that the line leading to hominids forever left the trees and moved into the savanna-grasslands fringing the forests. What they lacked in speed and strength was compensated for by a large brain. They were **preadapted** for terrestrial life; they had magnificent hand-eye coordination. When they became bipedal or semi-erect, their hands were freed to manipulate the environment and this eventually led to tool use. Their eyes were attuned to distinguishing things from the environment and for aiming weapons. Their brains and nervous systems were attuned to exploration. The new habitat bombarded them with new and exciting stimuli, forcing them to adapt to new conditions. They eventually became *Ramapithecus,* a hominid—or so one version of the evidence reads. However, the relationship of these forms to later apes and hominids is much in question.

Aberrant Apes?

To complete our review of pongid evolution we turn to two forms whose ancestry is unclear. At one time or another both have been considered ancestral to modern hominids, a likelihood most now reject. One of the forms, *Oreopithecus bambolii,* or the "abominable coal man," derives from coal beds of Tuscany, Italy. The other form, *Gigantopithecus,* is considered by some to be a gigantic ape from China and North India.

Oreopithecus. Oreopithecus (ore = mountain) remains come from Lower Pliocene or Upper Miocene beds in Italy dated to about 10-12 million years B.P. (Figure 11-4). Since its description in 1872, it has been labelled a hominid, pongid, or **cercopithecoid** (Old World monkey). In 1954 it was labelled a hominid, and a search was conducted for more remains. In 1958 J. Hürzeler uncovered the better part of an intact skeleton of a young adult. *Oreopithecus* has always been a taxonomic problem because it manifests characteristics intermediate between monkeys, apes, and humans. *Oreopithecus* was approximately four feet tall and weighed about eighty-eight pounds. Judging from the 1958 skeleton, it was probably the size of a medium-sized chimpanzee. The face is strikingly short (a hominid trait), resulting in projecting

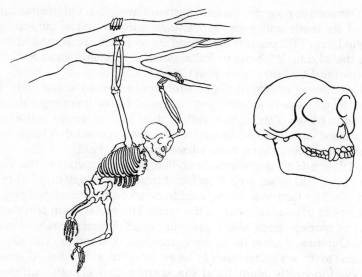

Figure 11-4. Reconstruction of *Oreopithecus* from Italy.

nasal bones which are perhaps due to crushing. Above the eyes there is a thick bony ridge and the tooth row is parallel. Both are nonhominid traits. The upper canine is short and the premolars bicuspid—hominid traits.

The postcranial remains reflect monkey and ape characteristics, but the latter predominate. The arms were longer than the legs, a condition peculiar to habitual brachiators. The relative length of the arms compared to the legs (the intermembral index) is closest to that of the knuckle-walking gorilla.

There has been continual argument about the cranial capacity of *Oreopithecus*. The cranial capacity of the 1958 form has been estimated at between 276 and 529 cubic centimeters (cc). Dr. W. Straus, who studied the material in detail, feels an average of about 400 cc is most appropriate. New estimates place a figure of 200 cc as generous but even this would be a relatively large-sized brain for a relatively short, light animal.

Although its taxonomic position is conjectural, the best estimate is that *Oreopithecus* was a somewhat aberrant brachiating ape. There is some controversial evidence in the foot and pelvis suggesting that the direct ancestors of *Oreopithecus* possessed some adaptations to erect bipedalism before adapting to an arboreal existence.

Gigantopithecus—*A Gargantuan Hominid Ancestor?* Of all fossil pongids, *Gigantopithecus* has had perhaps one of the most colorful histories; it has been called everything from an ape to a giant hominid. It has also been labelled the ancestor to the modern elusive "yeti" or abominable snowman. Early mention was made of *Gigantopithecus* by Dr. G. R. von Koenigswald in 1935 on the basis of some teeth found in a Chinese drugstore. (The Chinese were collectors of fossilized teeth and bones, referred to as "dragon bones," which were ground and mixed into aphrodisiacs and other herbal medicines.) Since, other *Gigantopithecus* remains have come from India and Kwangsi Province, China. A number of lower jaw fragments and well over 1000 isolated teeth now exist; no other skeletal parts are available. On the basis of the size of its teeth and jaws, some have judged that *Gigantopithecus* weighed over 600 pounds and stood six feet or more. It ranged in time from the Middle Pliocene in India, about 5-9 million years B.P., to approximately 500,000 years B.P. in China.

The Chinese variety of *Gigantopithecus* received attention in 1955 when the Chinese paleontologist Pei found 47 teeth among a shipment of dragon bones. Tracing the teeth to their source, a cave in the face of a limestone cliff, three additional teeth were uncovered. A large mandible and teeth were found in an adjacent farmer's field.

In 1968 a *Gigantopithecus* mandible was uncovered in the Siwalik Hills about 200 miles from New Delhi from deposits dating 5-9 million years B.P. The form was considered to be a young animal, judging from the amount of enamel wear on the teeth. The molar teeth contrast with those of modern apes, which are composed almost entirely of enamel while *Gigantopithecus* teeth are composed of dentine. The *Gigantopithecus* teeth are considered to be an adaptation to heavy chewing of abrasive foodstuffs. Mandibular shape and incisor size also support the view that *Gigantopithecus* was a heavy chewer.

Dr. C. Jolly recently attempted to explain the dental characteristics of *Gigantopithecus* by comparing its teeth with those of the gelada, *Theropithecus gelada*.[6] Jolly calls his explanation the "T-complex" hypothesis and feels that "T-complex" traits are functionally related to and are an evolutionary product of a specialized diet. This diet involves ingestion of large quantities of comparatively small, tough morsels like grass, seeds, stems, and rhizomes prepared by powerful and continuous chewing with the molar teeth. "T-complex" dental characteristics include the following: the molar teeth are high-crowned and largely composed of dentine. As the animal grows older the teeth become packed together in the jaws in a process called **mesial drift** which is associated with strenuous chewing. Other characteristics include changes in jaw structure, vertical implantation of incisors, and reduced canines.

Jolly contends that the "T-complex" is helpful in understanding human evolution. The dental complex distinguishing the gelada from the common savannah baboon reflects that distinguishing hominids from pongids (especially mesial drift, mandibular shape, vertical incisors, and small canines). Jolly argues, although not all agree with his position, that the characteristic hominid dentition arose because of the early hominid diet rather than because they learned to use tools which reduced the need for large canines. Various "T-complex" traits appear among australopithecines, especially the robust variety, and *Ramapithecus*.

The Indian and Chinese deposits allow us to reconstruct *Gigantopithecus's* life-ways. The deposits seem to have been the work of predators; the presence of wild Indian dog (dhole) remains strengthens this view, as dhole hunt and kill large animals like wild buffalo. The view of *Gigantopithecus* as a huge humanlike carnivore carrying its prey to its cave can be dismissed, for the Chinese evidence suggests that *Gigantopithecus* was the prey and not the predator. Fauna from the Indian and Chinese sites suggests that the countryside was a mixture of forest, open areas, and transitional zones.

[6]The behavior of the gelada is reported by Crook (1966).

Gigantopithecus probably originated in India and spread north and east. If the dating is correct, the Indian predates the Chinese variety by millions of years. The best candidate for an ancestral position to *Gigantopithecus* is the Indian dryopithecine, *D. indicus*. To what forms was *Gigantopithecus* ancestral? Probably none; however, Eckhardt (1972) and Robinson (1972) reopened the argument that it is on the hominid line. Most argue that *Gigantopithecus* represents a side branch in pongid evolution, a pongid line adapted to a special mode of feeding. If Jolly is right, the lineage leading to hominids independently adapted a similar mode of feeding during the first 10 million years of its evolutionary history. Dental resemblances between the two are accounted for by independent similar adaptations to similar habitats and not by a phylogenetic relationship. In the end differences rather than similarities between the forms became significant. For humans the special combination of adaptations set the stage for a second cycle of hominid evolution. For *Gigantopithecus* a parallel set of adaptations, different principally in detail and proportion, led to extinction.

Table 11-3. Summary of Important Tertiary Discoveries of Fossil Primates.

Name	Location	Time (First Appearance)	Materials Discovered
Plesiadapis	Europe, North America	Paleocene	One almost complete skull and an incomplete skeleton (Europe), several teeth and jaw fragments and an incomplete skeleton (North America).
Notharctus	North America	Eocene	Skulls, teeth, postcranial bones, and an almost complete skeleton.
Smilodectes	North America	Eocene	Several skulls and several postcranial bones.
Protoadapis	Europe	Eocene	Fragmentary mandibles.
Adapis	Europe	Eocene	Several skulls and teeth.
Necrolemur	Europe	Eocene	Several skulls and limb bones.
Parapithecus	Fayum	Oligocene	Lower jaw; though other fragments have been discovered, they are not described. Before 1960, misinterpretations were common due to the absence of the middle portion of the jawbone, which went unrecognized until then. Probably the earliest Old World monkey.
Apidium	Fayum	Oligocene	Originally a few fragments; additional material, including some juveniles, discovered recently. Perhaps a close relative of *Parapithecus*.
Propliopithecus	Fayum Kenya	Oligocene	Lower jaw and teeth. Small forms that may be ancestral to apes.

Table 11-3 continued.

Aegyptopithecus	Fayum	Oligocene	Five partial lower jaws and an almost complete skull.
Oligopithecus	Fayum	Oligocene	Left mandibular half.
Aeolopithecus	Fayum	Oligocene	Mandible.
"Limnopithecus"	East Africa	Miocene	Represented by several fragmentary remains, including limb bones. Perhaps more correctly included with *Pliopithecus.*
Proconsul	East Africa	Miocene	Considerable remains, including limb bones, a skeleton of a hand, and an almost complete skull. Probably an African member of the *Dryopithecus* group. A subgenus.
Dryopithecus	Europe, Asia, Africa	Miocene	Known mostly from a large inventory of jaws and teeth.
Mesopithecus	Europe, East Africa	Miocene	Abundant remains particularly from Greece.
Pliopithecus	Europe	Miocene	Several discoveries assigned to this genus including an almost complete skull. In the gibbon phylogeny.
"Sugrivapithecus," "Bramapithecus," "Sivapithecus," "Paleosimia"	Africa, Europe, Asia (mostly India)	Miocene	Several fragmentary upper and lower jaws and isolated teeth. Probably all of these should be included with either *Dryopithecus* or *Ramapithecus.*
Kenyapithecus	Africa	Miocene	Upper jaw fragments with one lower tooth. Possibly an African variety of *Ramapithecus.* A subgenus.
Oreopithecus	Europe	Late Miocene	Abundance of remains including an almost complete skeleton.
Ramapithecus	Originally from India. Now believed to have had wide distribution over the Old World	Late Miocene	Originally, one fragment of an upper jaw; a few other jaws and teeth have been assigned to this genus.
Gigantopithecus	India, China	Pliocene	Very large teeth and jaws, probably of an ape that is now extinct.

Adapted from *Physical Anthropology* by A. J. Kelso. Reprinted by permission of the publisher, J. B. Lippincott Company. Copyright © 1970 and 1974.

The interpretation of pongid evolution is not without controversy. Most paleontologists are unwilling to admit pongid ancestors very much prior to the early Oligocene geological epoch. Our major Oligocene evidence comes from the Egyptian Fayum as *Oligopithecus,* the oldest remains; *Parapithecus* and *Apidium; Aeolopithecus,* considered ancestral to Asian gibbons, and *Aegypto-*

pithicus, ancestral perhaps to chimpanzees. Another form, *Proplio-pithecus,* is probably an ancestral pongid; in fact it may be ancestral to *Aegyptopithecus.* Suggestions that *Propliopithecus* is an ancestral hominid are generally discounted.

Oligocene pongids are generally regarded as ancestral to Miocene dryopithecines, among whom we find ancestors of modern chimpanzees, gorillas, and possibly, orangutans. The dryopithecines were a widespread group inhabiting the then tropical forests (and possibly savanna woodlands) of Europe, Africa, and Asia. It was once widely accepted that one of the dryopithecines, perhaps *Dryopithecus nyanzae,* was an ancestral candidate to subsequent hominids. However, this is questionable.

Two controversial primates appear during the Pliocene epoch, *Gigantopithecus* in India (and later in Pleistocene China) and *Oreopithecus* in Italy. Both have at one time or another been considered hominids. *Gigantopithecus* has had a particularly colorful history as a gigantic hominid ancestor, ape ancestor, or ancestor of the abominable snowman. While most physical anthorpologists consider both forms aberrant apes, some refer *Gigantopithecus* to a hominid ancestry.

Bibliography

Ankel, F. 1972. Vertebrate morphology of fossil and extant primates. In *The functional and evolutionary biology of primates,* edited by R. Tuttle, pp. 223-40. Chicago: Aldine-Atherton.

Beadnell, H. 1905. *The topology and geology of the Fayum province of Egypt.* Cairo: Survey Department.

Bishop, W.; Miller, J.; and Fitch, F. 1969. New potassium-argon determination relevant to the Miocene fossil mammal sequence in East Africa. *American Journal of Science* 267:669.

Chesters, K. 1957. The Miocene flora of Rusinga Island, Lake Victoria, Kenya. *Paleontographica* 101:30.

Clark, W. Le Gros, and Leakey, L. 1951. *The Miocene Hominidae of East Africa.* London: British Museum (Natural History).

Crook, J. 1966. Gelada baboon herd structure and movement. *Symposium of Zoological Society of London* 18:237.

Dart, R. 1956. The myth of the bone-accumulating hyaena. *American Anthropologist* 58:40.

Eckhardt, R. 1972. Population genetics and human origins. *Scientific American,* January, p. 94.

Everden, J.; Savage, D.; Curtis, G.; and James, G. 1964. Potassium-argon dates and the Cenozoic mammalian chronology of North America. *American Journal of Science* 262:145.

Fleagle, J.; Simons, E.; and Conroy, G. 1975. Ape limb bone from the Oligocene of Egypt. *Science* 189: 135-36.

Gelvin, B. 1975. The primate os coxae and the classification of the primates. Unpublished Ph.D. dissertation, University of Missouri.

Gregory, W.; Hellman, M.; and Lewis, G. 1938. *Fossil anthropoids of the Yale-Cambridge Indian Expedition of 1935.* Carnegie Institute of Washington Publication 495:1.

Groves, C. 1967. Ecology and taxonomy of the gorilla. *Nature* 213:890.

———. 1970. *Gigantopithecus* and the mountain gorilla. *Nature* 226:973.

Jolly, C. 1970. The seed-eaters: a new model of hominid differentiation based on a baboon analogy. *Man* 5(1):1.

Kinzey, W. 1970. Rates of evolutionary change in the hominid canine teeth. *Nature* 225:296.

_____ . 1971. Evolution of the human canine tooth. *American Anthropologist* 73:680.

Kurtén, B. 1972. *Not from the apes.* New York: Pantheon.

Leakey, L. 1967. An early Miocene member of Hominidae. *Nature* 213:155.

Morris, D. 1970. On deflecting wrinkles and the *Dryopithecus* pattern in human mandibular molars. *American Journal of Physical Anthropology* 32:97.

Napier, J., and Davis, P. 1959. *The forelimb skeleton and associated remains of Proconsul africanus.* London: British Museum (Natural History).

Osborn, H. 1907. The Fayum expedition of the American Museum. *Science* 25:513.

Oxnard, C. 1967. The functional anatomy of the primate shoulder as revealed by comparative anatomical, osteometric and discriminant function techniques. *American Journal of Physical Anthropology* 26:219.

Pilbeam, D. 1967. Man's earliest ancestors. *Science Journal* 3:47.

_____ . 1968. *Tertiary Pongidae of East Africa: evolutionary relationships and taxonomy.* Bulletin 31, Peabody Museum of Natural History (Yale University.)

_____ . 1970. *Gigantopithecus* and the origins of the Hominidae. *Nature* 225:516.

_____ . 1972. *The ascent of man.* New York: Macmillan.

Pilbeam, D., and Simons, E. 1971. Humerus of *Dryopithecus* from Saint Gaudens, France. *Nature* 229:406.

_____ . 1971. A gorilla-sized ape from the Miocene of India. *Science* 173:23.

Robinson, J. 1972. *Early hominid posture and locomotion.* Chicago: University of Chicago Press.

St. Hoyme, L., and Loritzer, R. 1971. Significance of canine wear in pongid evolution. *American Journal of Physical Anthropology* 35:145.

Schaller, G. 1963. *The mountain gorilla.* Chicago: University of Chicago Press.

Simons, E. 1959. An anthropoid frontal bone from the Fayum Oligocene of Egypt: the oldest skull fragment of a higher primate. *American Museum of Natural History Novitiates* 1976:1.

_____ . 1962. Two new primate species from the African Oligocene. *Postilla* (Peabody Museum, Yale), 64:1.

_____ . 1965a. The hunt for Darwin's third ape. *Medical Opinion and Review,* Nov., p. 74.

_____ . 1965b. New fossil apes from Egypt and the initial differentiation of the Hominoidea. *Nature* 205:135.

_____ . 1967. The earliest apes. *Scientific American,* December, p. 28.

_____ . 1968. Hunting the "dawn apes" of Africa. *Discovery* 4(1):19.

_____ . 1972. *Primate evolution: an introduction to man's place in nature.* New York: Macmillan.

Simons, E., and Chopra, S. 1969. *Gigantopithecus* (Pongidae, Hominidae): a new species from North India. *Postilla* (Peabody Museum, Yale), p. 138.

Simons, E., and Pilbeam, D. 1965. Preliminary revision of the Dryopithecinae (Pongidae, Anthropoidea). *Folia Primatologica* 3:81.

Smith, E., and Pirie, P. 1973. Tooth size and body size—Is there a correlation? Paper presented to 72nd American Anthropological Association, New Orleans.

Szalay, F. 1972. Paleobiology of the earliest primates. In *The functional and evolutionary biology of primates,* edited by R. Tuttle, pp. 3-35. Chicago: Aldine-Atherton.

Tattersall, I. 1970. *Man's ancestors: An introduction to primate and human evolution.* London: John Murray.

van Couvering, J., and Miller, J. 1969. Miocene stratigraphy and age determinations, Rusinga Island, Kenya. *Nature* 22:1.

von Koenigswald, G. 1967. Miocene Cercopithecoidae and Oreopithecoidae from the Miocene of East Africa. In *Fossil vertebrates of Africa,* vol. 2, edited by L. Leakey, pp. 39-51. London: Academic Press.

Weidenreich, F. 1945. Giant early man from Java and south China. *Anthropological Papers of the American Museum of Natural History* 40:5.

Wolpoff, M. 1971. Interstitial wear. *American Journal of Physical Anthropology* 34:205.

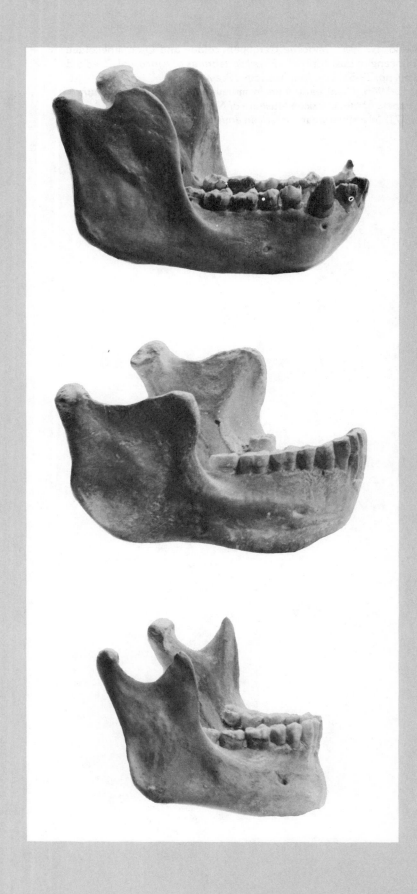

Chapter 12
Trends in Hominid Evolution

Before proceeding, we pause briefly to review six major trends apparent in hominid evolution. We are principally concerned with mechanisms resulting in size reduction and differentiation of the anterior teeth, anatomical modifications permitting postural uprightness, exploitation of the habitat, increasing brain size, tool use and manufacture, and adoption of an essentially omnivorous diet.

Trend 1: Tale of the Teeth — Reduction in Size of the Anterior Teeth

It has been argued that there was a marked reduction of the incisor, canine, and premolar teeth in *Ramapithecus* when compared to its supposed Miocene ancestor *Dryopithecus*. (The argument is, of course, superfluous if one contends that *Ramapithecus* arose from a small-canined form, such as *Propliopithecus* for example.)[1] Tool use by *Ramapithecus* is an inference largely based on what are reconstructed to be small-sized canines. The passage of time and the addition of more information led to an assault on the traditional idea that canine reduction and tool use are related. Conflicting evidence comes from unexpected sources, for if *Propliopithecus* proves to be a hominid, or close to that line, it indicates that hominids arose from small-canined forms to begin with. Other evidence arguing against the tool use-canine reduction hypothesis derives from the study of the sub-fossil form (a form recently become extinct) *Hadropithecus* (Figure 12-1) from the Malagasy Republic (Madagascar). *Hadropithecus* had

[1]Remember, our sample is so small that any discussion, no matter how tenuous, may be premature.

The Heidelberg jaw (center) is compared with the jaw of a chimpanzee (above) and that of a modern human being (below).

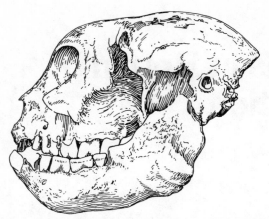

Figure 12-1. *Hadropithecus stenognathus,* **a subfossil form from the island of Madagascar.**

small canines, a most puzzling reduction given any validity to the canine reduction-tool use hypothesis. *Hadropithecus,* a clear-cut lemur in all but its chewing apparatus, could never have used tools. Yet the fact remains that it possessed small canines. Tattersall (1972), along with Every (1970), suggests that the human canine could have assumed its present size and form to complement the incisor teeth and make the biting complex at the front of the mouth more efficient.[2] The argument is still to be resolved. However, if the view of hominid evolution eventually supports a tie with forms possessing small canines, then a number of more cherished theories concerning certain aspects of hominid evolution must change.

Trend 2: Moving Erect — Skeletal and Muscular Modifications Permitting Postural Uprightness and Erect Bipedalism

Although lacking postcranial material we infer, on dental evidence (and disputed ecological evidence), that *Ramapithecus* was probably acquiring an erect posture. A number of morphological traits differentiate the hominid and pongid pelvis. Since hominid characteristics appear in a rather advanced state among the Lower Pleistocene hominids, it is assumed that they were taking place among their ancestors, presumably *Ramapithecus.*

Morphological changes permitting erect bipedalism involved a rearrangement of the pelvic structure (especially the **ilium**); shifts in the size and arrangement of **gluteal** (buttocks) muscles; and changes in the foot skeleton and its supporting musculature, all allowing the foot bones to assume full body weight and passage of the weight stress through the medial part of the foot; changes in the heel and ankle bones; and shifting in the spinal column. Correlated changes occurred in the limb structure as the upper limbs were freed from weight-bearing

[2]It should be noted that canine reduction can come about by a number of means. When large canines are not used for fighting, there is no selection pressure for them; primates living in groups in which there is minimal intragroup aggression tend to have small canines. Canine reduction is also characteristic of primates in which the canines are not specialized for some feeding behavior. Tools are behavioral substitutes for large canines, but they may not be the only ones.

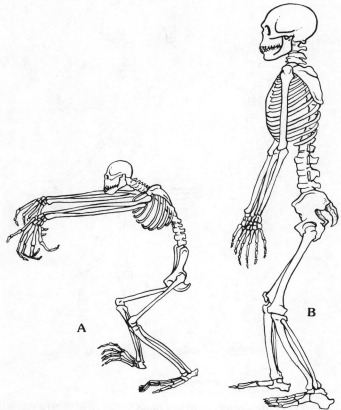

Figure 12-2. The upright posture and bipedal gait of (A) a running gibbon and (B) a walking *Homo*.

for periods of time. The lower limbs now assumed that duty. The relaxation of weight-bearing in the upper limbs led to changes in the shoulder structure. Rearrangements in the neck musculature followed changes in head balance (Figures 12-2 and 12-3).

The assumption of a bipedal posture also affects one's world view; there is the possibility that upending the body and changing the line of sight resulted in a stimuli explosion. The enrichment and proliferation of stimuli would affect the sense organs and thus the receptive organ, the brain.

Trend 3: Hominid-Land Relationship — Effective Adjustment to and an Exploitation of the Terrestrial Habitat

Behavioral as well as morphological changes were needed to cope with the terrestrial habitat. Major adjustments were probably reflected in the social group.[3] Early hominids were group-living forms, twenty-

[3]Group living is not a new adaptation. But for few exceptions, mostly nocturnal creatures, primates are group-living. In fact most mammals are group-living. However, primate groups differ from those of many other mammals in two basic features: they are year-round social groups and they are bisexual. Of all primate groups, those of the chimpanzee are probably most like those of the early hominids (van Lawick-Goodall, 1967, 1971; Sugiyama, 1972). This behavioral manifestation is consistent with their taxonomic position vis-à-vis hominids.

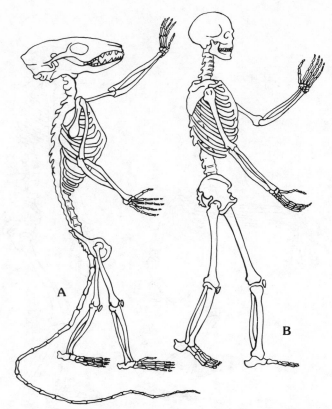

Figure 12-3. The skeletons of (A) Insectivore in an upright position and (B) Homo.

five members probably being an average, probably evidencing sexual division of labor. It has been suggested that males did most of the hunting and females collected other edibles. We can postulate that early hominid societies were probably male dominated. In most nonhuman primate societies in which there is sexual dimorphism, and in which the male is the larger of the sexes, males dominate the troop. We can assume, although we may be wrong, that the same applies for the early hominids. Among ancestral hominids the male probably led the hunt and generally determined many group activities. This is not saying that females were relegated to a peripheral role, for current evidence from comparative sources like nonhuman primates and some social carnivores suggests that these early societies were female-focal. Current nonhuman primate studies strongly suggest that females play a key role as the purveyors of troop traditions (Poirier, 1973), and are the stable element of the group. Studies of modern hunters-gatherers suggest that females play a major role as food suppliers, and that if the male hunting activity were the sole source of food, many groups would soon starve. In fact, we might argue that because of cultural biases many of our evolutionary theories are focused too strongly on the role of the male.

Most important in regard to role differentiation is the onset of the sexual division of labor. Among nonhuman primates each animal is its own separate subsistence unit. Even infants once they are weaned are dependent upon their own guile for survival as concerns food intake. Among humans, however, the weaned young are still dependent upon the adults for food. Lancaster has postulated that because of this long-term dependence on adults for nourishment, the roles of both male and female humans have greatly expanded and much of the time during the day is spent in activities which provide food for the young. "Because of the long-term dependence of children, a division of labor evolved in which the adventurous, wandering male became the hunter and the female developed the less mobile role of gatherer and mother" (Lancaster, 1975:78-79).

Because of the fact that females bear the young, and bear the major responsibility for their early care, feeding, and rearing, any sexual division of labor would be beneficial for survival of the group, and the species. Hominid females are further burdened by the fact that the human infant is born at a stage of relative immaturity and is unable to fend for itself. Furthermore, the human mother lacks the body hair (common in nonhuman primates) to which the infant can grasp and allow the mother the usual range of movement. The human mother must carry the infant. Both these conditions, relative immaturity at birth and lack of body hair, may have occurred in our early hominid ancestors, like the australopithecines. Given the long period of immaturity characteristic of the human infant, there was no other way, once hunting and gathering developed as a way of life, than for a division of labor to have occurred except between males and females.

The division of labor which developed concomitant with the hunting and gathering way of life provided a flexible system of joint dependence on plant and animal foods. The division of labor provided an efficient coping strategy quite different than that characterizing the nonhuman primates. The human hunting-gathering pattern provided great flexibility in terms of coping, for it allowed adjustments to daily, seasonal, and cyclical variations in food supplies and geographical and habitat variants. Lancaster (1975) argues that this system permitted our ancestors to cover the earth without speciating.

There is no archaeological evidence to support the contention that the early hominids and their immediate successors were characterized by a sexual division of labor. However, the adaptive advantages provided by this system suggest the likelihood that such a division existed. A division of labor may be useful in helping explain why early hominids were able to compete so successfully and establish themselves in their new habitat.

The reader is urged to read Lancaster (1975) pages 78-83 for further elaboration of this point of view.

The concept of the "home" was probably developed early in hominid evolution as an important survival mechanism. A home base provided a location where injured or sick individuals could remain and to which other group members returned at night. Among savanna-living baboons, with no home base to which they repair daily, sick or injured members must move with the troop or be left behind to die or be killed by one of the many savanna predators. A home base also became important because of the human infant's slower maturation rate (or put another way, longer growth period); extended maternal care was required to assure survival. Such care, although an imposition upon the care-taker (presumably the mother), allowed more time for infant socialization and placed a premium upon learning.

Other adaptations for effective environmental exploration involved assumption of tool use (with all its concomitant muscular and neural requirements). Tool use and terrestriality probably placed a premium on the development of an effective signalling network. Language acquisition may be a partial response to continuing pressures to effectively communicate about increasing complexities of life—how to make tools, where to find food, and so on.

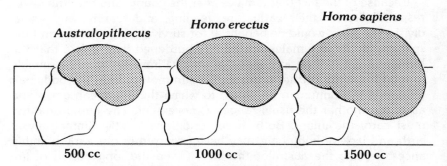

Figure 12-4. Relation of brain size to face size.

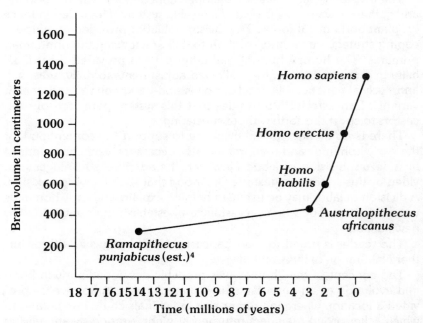

Figure 12-5. Relationship between brain volume and time in hominid evolution. The capacity of *Ramapithecus* is estimated; the temporal positions for the later species are approximate; 494 cc is the mean cranial capacity of the australopithecines.

[4]Although there is no evidence of the brain size of *Ramapithecus*, there is no reason to assume it was larger than that of modern apes. However, body weight and height are factors entering into any assessment of relative brain sizes.

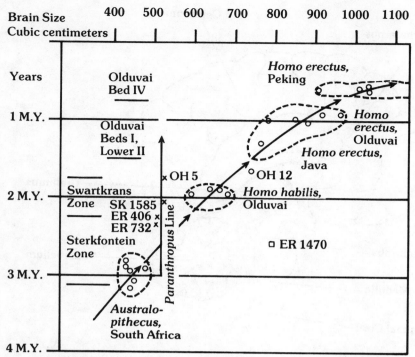

This chart illustrates the increase in brain size from *Australopithecus* through *Homo habilis* to *Homo erectus*. Individual fossils are shown as small circles. Individuals of *Paranthropus* are shown by "x" and the vertical arrow relates to them, suggesting the absence of any clear trend of increasing brain size in this lineage.

In most cases both date and brain size are estimates only. The chart is therefore not as exact as it may appear. Estimates of brain size are largely those made by Holloway and Tobias in various writings.

Figure 12-6. Increasing brain size.

Trend 4: Reign of the Brain — Increase in Brain Size

Throughout the hominid fossil record there is a trend toward increasing brain size and complexity (Figures 12-4, 12-5, 12-6). The trend was neither steady nor consistent; the increase was slight during the approximately four or more million years of *Australopithecus*, but rapid during the Middle Pleistocene with *H. erectus* and *H. sapiens*. The increase in brain size was probably related to various factors such as tool use, increasing environmental challenges, more complex social groups, and assumption of complex, organized hunting behavior.

If one takes a long-term evolutionary look, it seems that a larger brain may once have been vitally important in aiding survival in a world full of predators and devoid of controlled fire. Consequent hominid development seems to have placed decreasing importance solely on brain size and culture and social living seem to have replaced the value of a sharp mind as insurance for survival. Beyond a certain size increase, there is no evidence that further increases in brain size improve our adaptive abilities.[5] There is a shared feeling among many

[5]Furthermore, there is also no evidence that brain size always correlates with intelligence in modern *Homo*.

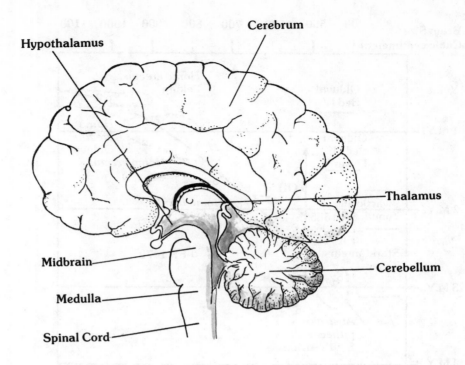

Figure 12-7. Side view of bisected modern human brain.

scientists that our brains have reached their maximum size and one may speculate that pressures will not be for larger cranial capacities but for more efficient use of the brains we now possess.

Trend 5: The Hands Work—Extensive Manipulation of Natural Objects and the Development of Motor Skills to Facilitate Toolmaking

This trend is an outgrowth of effectance motivation. Extensive manipulatory behavior was facilitated by hands freed of locomotor activities, stereoscopic vision, increasing brain size, and better hand-eye coordination. The pressures for extensive object manipulation probably derived from increasing tool use which was, in turn, related to increasing survival problems.

Trend 6: Adoption of an Omnivorous Diet and the Addition of Meat Protein to a Heretofore Largely Vegetarian Diet

Most nonhuman primates are vegetarian, although some (especially the chimpanzee) will kill and eat other vertebrates. The time when meat first assumed importance in the hominid diet is conjectural; however, we assume it was probably during the later stages of Lower Pleistocene hominid evolution. Consistent meat eating required a number of behavioral and anatomical changes. Once meat became basic to the diet, means would be developed whereby it could be most effectively obtained. Methods for carrying meat, rules of sharing, and means for cutting meat would have appeared.

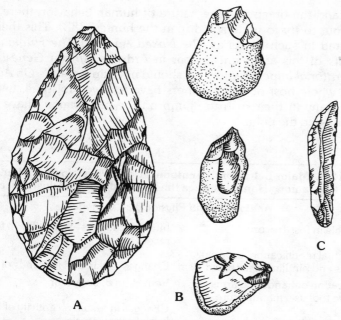

Figure 12-8. Successive levels of stone toolmaking skills. (A) Acheulean handaxe; (B) Oldowan tools, East Africa; (C) Upper Paleolithic blade implement.

A carnivorous diet, and the advent of big-game hunting, had a very marked impact upon hominid evolution. In an article entitled "The Evolution of Hunting," Washburn and Lancaster (1971) note that "the agricultural revolution, continuing into the industrial and scientific revolutions, is now freeing man from the conditions and restraints of 99 percent of his history, but the biology of our species was created in the long gathering and hunting period. To assert the biological unity of mankind is to affirm the importance of the hunting way of life.... The biology, psychology, and customs that separate us from the apes—all these we owe to the hunters of time past . . . for those who would

Table 12-1. Major Fossil Hominoids, Their Location and Dating.

Time Period	Major Forms	Location
Pleistocene	Homo, Australopithecus,[1] Gigantopithecus	Africa, Asia, Europe, later Homo found in New World and Pacific. Gigantopithecus only from Asia
Pliocene	Homo	Africa
	Australopithecus	Africa
	Gigantopithecus	Asia
	Ramapithecus	Asia, Europe, Africa
	Oreopithecus	Europe
Miocene	Dryopithecus	Africa, Asia, Europe
Oligocene	Oligopithecus	North Africa
	Propliopithecus	Africa, North Africa
	Aegyptopithecus	North Africa
	Aeolopithecus	North Africa

[1]Where listed, the genus *Australopithecus* includes both robust and gracile forms.

understand the origin and the nature of human behavior, there is no choice but to try to understand man the hunter" (83). This theme is elaborated in such books as *The Naked Ape* and *The Human Zoo*. Elements of this argument appear in Ardrey's *African Genesis* and *The Territorial Imperative* and we should not skip Lorenz's *On Aggression*. A whole host of other authors have followed this line; unfortunately, many in their rush to "jump on the bandwagon" have completely missed the point.

Table 12-2. Major Behavioral, Anatomical, and Physiological Changes among Hominids since the Hominid/Pongid Divergence.

Anatomical and Physiological Changes

A. Visible in fossil record	Inferred changes—not visible in fossil record
Postcranial modification, especially in pelvis and hindlimbs, for bipedalism	Changes in skin and in glands of skin
Modification of hands and arms for effective tool use, manufacture, and carrying	Reduction of body hair
	Changes in sexual receptivity of female, loss of estrous cycle
Brain enlargement and complexity	
Reduction of face and jaws, remodelling of face and jaws	Brain reorganization (partly seen in fossil record)
Modification of vocal tract	
	Changes related to birth process: i.e., lengthening of period of pregnancy (correlated changes, i.e., delay of maturation seen in fossil record)

Behavioral Changes

A. Visible in archaeological record	Inferred—not directly detected in archaeological record
Increasing development of and dependence upon tools	Language
Dietary changes—inclusion of meat protein and hunting behavior	Controls on emotional displays
Increasing interdependence through food sharing	Increase in cooperation and a division of labor (perhaps seen in cultural record)
Reorganization of social life around a home base	Increase in social bonding mechanisms: family, kinship, reciprocation
Larger social groups	Increase in symbolism
Dwelling structures	
Use of fire for various purposes	

In much later periods of hominid evolution we get evidence of aesthetic life, and of spiritualism.

This list is merely illustrative and while it does increase the number of categories over those included in Isaac's table many more items could be added. It might also be mentioned that more items will be added as the fossil and archaeological record of our evolutionary history increases in composition.

Adapted from Glenn Ll. Isaac, "The activities of early African hominids," in Glenn Ll. Isaac and Elizabeth R. McCown (eds.), *Human Origins: Louis Leakey and the East African Evidence,* Copyright © 1976 by W. A. Benjamin, Inc., Menlo Park, California.

Views as to the adaptive mechanisms for some of the above traits are being challenged. The classical argument linking the adoption of tool use with consequent reduction of the front teeth was challenged by the claim that *Propliopithecus* could be an Oligocene hominid already possessing small anterior teeth. Many still hold to the view, originally offered by Charles Darwin, that the adoption of tools had much to do with our subsequent evolution, for example, bipedalism. Some writers argue that once we became big-game hunters, predators, we established a behavioral pattern leading to what some consider to be our excessive aggressive behavior. There are many faults in this argument; however, it can be argued, as Washburn and Lancaster do, that much of what separates us from our pongid relatives we owe to a hunting way of life dominating much of our evolutionary history.

Bibliography

Bonin, G. von. 1963. *The evolution of the human brain.* Chicago: University of Chicago Press.

Campbell, B. 1976. *Humankind emerging.* Boston: Little, Brown.

Every, R. 1970. Sharpness of teeth in man and other primates. *Postilla* 143:1.

Howells, W. 1973. *Evolution of the genus* Homo. Reading, Mass.: Addison-Wesley.

Isaac, G. 1976. The activities of early African hominids. In *Human origins: Louis Leakey and the East African evidence*, edited by G. Isaac and E. McCown, pp. 483-514. Menlo Park, Calif.: W. A. Benjamin.

Lancaster, J. 1975. *Primate behavior and the emergence of human culture.* New York: Holt, Rinehart and Winston.

Oyen, O. 1974. *The baboon face: a different student in growth and development.* Ann Arbor, Mich.: University Microfilms.

Poirier, F. 1972. Introduction. In *Primate socialization*, edited by F. Poirier, pp. 1-28. New York: Random House.

————. 1973. Socialization and learning among nonhuman primates. In *Culture and learning*, edited by S. Kimball and J. Burnett, pp. 3-41. Seattle: University of Washington Press.

Radinski, L. 1972. Endocasts and studies of primate brain evolution. In *The functional and evolutionary biology of primates*, edited by R. Tuttle, pp. 175-84. Chicago: Aldine-Atherton.

Shapiro, J. 1971. I went to the animal fair: a review of the imperial animal. *Natural History* 80(8):90.

Sugiyama, Y. 1972. Social characteristics and socialization of wild chimpanzees. In *Primate socialization*, edited by F. Poirier, pp. 145-64. New York: Random House.

Tattersall, I. 1972. Of lemurs and men. *Natural History* 81(3):32.

Tobias, P. 1971. *The brain in hominid evolution.* New York: Columbia University Press.

van Lawick-Goodall, J. 1967. *My friends the wild chimpanzees.* Washington, D.C.: National Geographic Society.

————. 1971. *In the shadow of man.* Boston: Houghton Mifflin Co.

Washburn, S., and DeVore, I. 1961. The social life of baboons. *Scientific American*, June, p. 62.

Washburn, S., and Lancaster, C. 1971. The evolution of hunting. In *Background for man: readings in physical anthropology*, edited by P. Dolhinow and V. Sarich, pp. 386-405. Boston: Little, Brown.

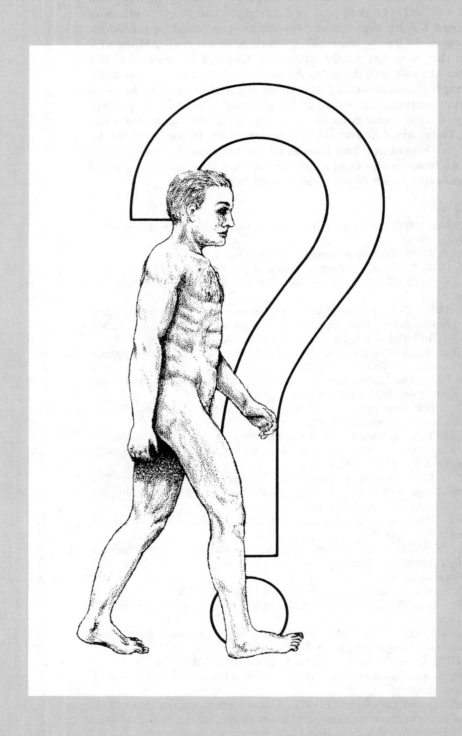

Chapter 13
Who Said It?
Alternative Viewpoints of Hominid Evolution

There is no unanimity among scholars of primate evolution, due to such factors as the scarcity and limited nature of paleontological material, the vast time spans with which we deal, and the personalities and academic backgrounds of the investigators. There is much disagreement as to the classification of various osteological remains and as to the total evolutionary scheme. This chapter reviews some theories of hominid descent: the tarsioid theory, pithecoid theory, brachiating theory (recently modified to include a knuckle or fist-walking stage), immunological theory, and finally, for diversity's sake, the aquatic idea.

Non-Anthropoid Ape Theories of Hominid Origins

The orthodox theory of hominid origins claims a particularly close relationship between hominids and pongids; it has not lacked critics, however. The French paleontologist M. Boule was one of the first to doubt a close hominid/pongid link. Boule chided anthropologists for comparing hominids with only the anthropoid apes and for regarding pongids as those primates closest to the hominid ancestry. In his discussion of the limbs, those parts of the human body which significantly differ from modern pongids, Boule emphasized that hominids approximated monkeys rather than apes. He believed that the hominid evolutionary line was independent of other primate branches, especially that leading to pongids. Boule suggested that we might be related to Old World primates at a level prior to the departure of the anthropoid ape stock, or even at the level of the divergence of New and Old World monkeys.

Tarsioid Hypothesis — F. Wood Jones. One of the best known non-anthropoid ape theories of hominid evolution is the **tarsioid** (or *tarsian*) **hypothesis** expounded by the anatomist F. Wood Jones and elaborated in his 1929 book entitled *Man's Place Among the Mammals.* The tarsioid theory vigorously denies our kinship with the anthropoids. It claims instead that our phylogenetic line stems directly from a primitive tarsioid form. Our only living near-relatives would be the form *Tarsius*, today represented by the nocturnal *Tarsius spectrum* inhabiting forested regions of Southeast Asia. If we accept F. Wood Jones's argument, then the hominid line became independent from the general primate evolutionary branch very near the base of the divergence from the mammalian stock.

The basis of the rejection of an anthropoid ape-hominid ancestry is rooted in the assumption that modern pongids are far too specialized to have given rise to hominids. Jones felt that the brachiating apes'[1] lack of a developed thumb, while we have one, and the fact that the brachiators' arms are longer than the legs, while the reverse is true in hominids, remove hominids from the anthropoid ape lineage. The tarsioid adherents contend that supporters of the anthropoid ape theory of hominid descent advocate evolutionary reversals to derive a short-armed, long-legged form with a highly developed thumb from a form with long arms, short legs, and a poorly developed thumb.

F. Wood Jones characterized the ancestral hominid stock as small, active, and agile animals which were erect and moved bipedally along the branches. Thus they were prepared for a terrestrial, bipedal life. This ancestral stock was also characterized as having large heads, small teeth, and moderately large eye orbits. If one accepts this viewpoint, then, with the possible exception of *Propliopithecus* from the Fayum in Egypt, there are no fossils in the hominid record between the Paleocene-Eocene tarsioids and the Pleistocene hominids.

Pithecoid Hypothesis — W. Straus. A widely known non-anthropoid ape theory of hominid evolution is the **pithecoid hypothesis** expounded by the anatomist W. Straus. Straus first formulated his argument in a 1949 article entitled "The Riddle of Man's Ancestry." Straus feels that the most likely evolutionary scheme should derive hominids from some sort of generalized Old World monkey, at a reasonably early date, rather than from an anthropoid ape stock. In Straus's view the major problem with the brachiator theory of hominid derivation is that it ignores a considerable number of hominid characters that can only be derived from an essentially generalized primate stock. Straus argues that the hominid phylogenetic line became independent of the Old World monkey stock prior to there being actual anthropoid apes.

Straus visualized the ancestral hominid stock as generally resembling Old World monkeys. Accordingly, the presumed earliest representatives of the hominid line may be visualized as essentially unspecialized quadrupeds, capable of both arboreal and terrestrial life, possessing expanding brains, short tails, and generalized extremities. Straus argues that they avoided specializations of brachiation (e.g., long arms, short legs, short thumbs) and early became terrestrial bipeds.

[1]This includes, besides the gibbon and orangutan, both the chimpanzee and gorilla. The latter seldom brachiates because of its large size.

This argument centers on the crucial point of whether ancestral hominids were brachiators. Straus rejects the contention that outright, habitual brachiation was a necessary prelude to hominid terrestrial bipedalism. He argues that the major features wherein hominids and pongids show special affinities are due to parallelism through the inheritance of detailed characters or genes from a common pool. That is, the shared traits do not necessarily constitute a close phyletic relationship. Straus feels that the hominid line may have diverged from the evolving Old World monkey line between 32 and 50 million years B.P., probably no later than the end of the Oligocene.

Arguments Against a Non-Anthropoid Ape Derivation

Locomotor Patterns. The major arguments against non-anthropoid ape theories of hominid evolution are based in the expanding fossil record and the fact that ancestral pongids lacked specialized adaptations for brachiation common to their modern descendants. F. Wood Jones formulated his idea when the fossil record was meager; the Fayum material was not even recovered, let alone analyzed. The same is true for the *Dryopithecus, Ramapithecus,* and *Australopithecus* material. Straus had access to more material, but *Ramapithecus* and *Australopithecus* were still being contended, as was the true nature of *Dryopithecus.* The major problem with both arguments rests on their insistence that fossil pongids were already brachiators by the time of the hominid divergence. *Dryopithecus* remains controvert this.

The East African dryopithecine fossils and the humerus from France strongly suggest that habitual brachiation developed no earlier than the later Pliocene. Prior to the Pliocene, primates revealed a variety of limb characteristics; no fossilized limb structures show more than incipient brachiation as a mode of locomotion. Brachiation is now considered to be a late secondary acquisition, occupying perhaps as little as one-fortieth of the total primate evolutionary history. Perhaps feeding at the terminal ends of branches, where competition from other primates is less severe, led to brachiation. The early anthropoid apes manifested a range of locomotor behaviors providing a more promising point of departure for the development of bipedalism than the quadrupedal monkey.

Most paleontologists reject non-anthropoid ape theories of hominid evolution. However, such theories have served a very useful function, for they have forced rethinking of the problem and caused it to be modified.

The Orthodox or Anthropoid Ape Theory of Descent

Most paleontologists subscribe to some version of the anthropoid ape theory of hominid descent. However, there is considerable controversy over how early, or late, in time hominids and pongids diverged. There is also much contention as to which fossil materials, if we now possess them, were the first hominids.

T. H. Huxley and C. Darwin. Four years after Darwin's *On the Origin of Species* appeared in 1859, T. H. Huxley published his group of essays entitled *Evidence as to Man's Place in Nature.* In these essays he argued for a close relationship between hominids and the anthropoid apes, the chimpanzee and gorilla. Although the anthropoid ape theory of human origins was vaguely perceived by certain eighteenth-century philosophers, like Buffon, Huxley seems to have been the first to express it in modern, scientific form. In his later book entitled *The Descent of Man* (1871) Darwin supported Huxley's contentions.

Sir A. Keith. The orthodox theory has had a long history and has been incorporated into many texts and popular treatises. Sir A. Keith, primarily an anatomist, produced a plausible explanation of how arm-swinging (brachiating) apes could have evolved into upright, bipedal hominids. Keith developed his thesis in a series of publications beginning in 1891. He argued that an apprenticeship of brachiating erectness, such as exhibited by modern anthropoids who habitually hang and progress by their arms, with an essentially erect trunk, was an evolutionary prelude to bipedal, terrestrial hominid erectness. Those accepting Keith's viewpoint, or something closely akin to it, claim the dryopithecines as the supposed common ancestral stock of hominids and pongids. William King Gregory contributed much to the development and popularity of this theory.

Anatomical Evidence. Serological and paleontological evidence suggests that a very early separation of the hominid line is unlikely. Our ancestors were probably behaviorally like pongids until the late Miocene or very early Pliocene; however, the approximate time of divergence of the hominid from the pongid line is currently a matter of major controversy. The Sarich and Wilson immunological viewpoint suggests a divergence on the order of 5 to 10 million years B.P. The fossil record suggests a divergence on the order of 18 to 20 million years B.P. The later the separation and the closer the relationship between hominids and African pongids, the more likely our ancestors went through a brachiating stage.

Anatomical evidence for a brachiating behavioral stage among hominid precursors lies primarily in the trunk and arms of living species. Such traits as arm length, breadth of the trunk, and shortness of the lumbar region show similarities in humans and apes. More detailed examination shows that the similarity extends to the sternum (breast bone), clavicular length (which keeps the shoulders off to the side), and many details of the bones, joints, and muscles. Hominids and pongids share major structural features of the trunk and motions making possible such actions as stretching to the side and hanging comfortably by the arms. The structure of our trunk and arms is remarkably apelike; one way of illustrating this is the facility with which one can use a human anatomical atlas to dissect a chimpanzee arm.

A Knuckle- or Fist-Walking Stage. Some anthropologists have recently modified the brachiating theory to include an intermediate stage of either **knuckle-walking** (walking on the knuckles as do chimpanzees and gorillas) or **fist-walking** (walking on the closed fist, as orangutans usually do) (Figure 13-1). Dr. S. Washburn, for example, envisions the following sequence of behavioral stages: quadruped (monkey)→ knuckle-walker (modern pongids)→biped (modern hominids) (Figure 13-2). The possibility that hominids passed through a knuckle-walking stage stems from the fact that brachiation is an infrequent behavior among our closest pongid relatives, the chimpanzee and gorilla. Recognizing this, Dr. R. Tuttle tried to ascertain if hominids were knuckle-walkers before becoming bipeds. Tuttle contends that there

The Fossil Record—
Recovering the Past

210

Figure 13-1. Fist-walking in a young orangutan compared with knuckle-walking in a young chimpanzee.

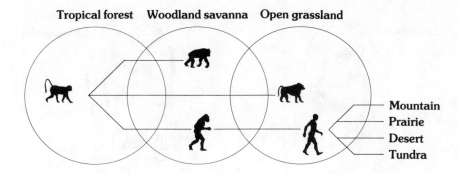

Tropical forest   Woodland savanna   Open grassland

Mountain
Prairie
Desert
Tundra

Figure 13-2. Evolution of hominid bipedalism.

are no features in the hominid hand bones evidencing a knuckle-walking stage. The earliest known hominid hand bones come from Bed I Olduvai Gorge and are dated to 1.8 million years B.P. Tuttle feels these lack evidence of a knuckle-walking stage—as do shoulder bones from the same site. The major problem is that these bones are from forms which are, minimally, the product of 10 million years of evolution since *Ramapithecus* perhaps diverged from the pongid line.

Tuttle feels that the hominid upper limbs indicate that our ancestors engaged in some form of suspensory posturing. He argues that they assumed a bipedal posture soon after coming to the ground without passing through a knuckle-walking stage. Tuttle feels that the initial divergence between hominids and pongids resulted from a differential use of the hind limbs such that the center of gravity shifted more toward the pelvis in hominid ancestors. In contrast, pongid ancestors frequently used the forelimbs in foraging and locomotion; their center of gravity remained in, or perhaps moved higher in, the chest. When the respective populations shifted to the terrestrial habitat, pongids became semierect knuckle-walkers, and hominids became bipeds.

Another advocate of an intermediate stage preceding bipedalism is Dr. Mary Marzke who suggests that hominid ancestors passed through a fist-walking rather than a knuckle-walking stage. She argues that certain traits of the human hand indicate that it was specialized for supporting the body on the back of the flexed (curled) fingers before bipedalism became the rule. She suggests that fist-walking is more advantageous for incipient tool-carriers than knuckle-walking. In fist-walking the fingers better enclose objects and bring them within the range of the thumb, which can then secure the grip. Perhaps our ancestors were more specialized fist-walkers than modern fist-walking orangutans. As does Washburn, she affirms the fact that our ancestors first went through a suspensory locomotor stage.

Washburn discounts Tuttle's argument against a knuckle-walking stage prior to erect bipedalism. The difficulty of deciding the argument rests with the fact that some anatomical adaptations to knuckle-walking occur in the ligaments. These are not likely to be determined from fossil materials.

In sum, it is still too early to say with certainty whether hominid ancestors went through a fist-walking or knuckle-walking stage, if either, before becoming bipedal.

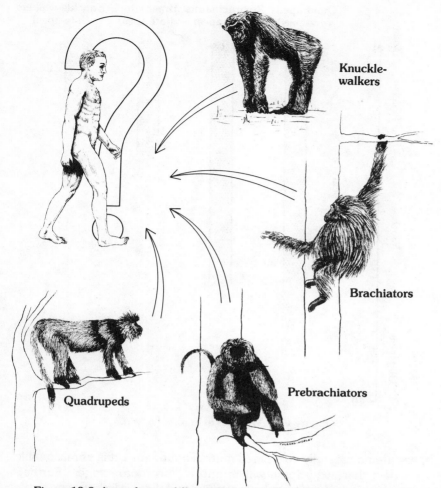

Figure 13-3. According to different theories of hominid origin, our closest relatives were quadrupedal monkeys, early prebrachiating apes, brachiating apes, or knuckle-walkers.

Figures 13-3 and 13-4 depict various theories of hominid origins and make it clear that each suggests a radically different sequence in the evolution of locomotor structure and behaviors. According to the first theory, nothing is known about human evolution during more than 30 million years, and all similarities between hominids and pongids are due to parallel evolution. According to the second theory, hominids and pongids shared an arboreal quadrupedal ancestry which evolved during the Miocene into the climbing-feeding way of life termed brachiation. Some hominids continued to share a ground-living, knuckle-walking or fist-walking adaptation, and from that point hominid ancestors first become behaviorally distinct from pongids.

We should note that the terms used to label a behavioral, locomotor stage do not represent absolute, exclusivistic categories. Animals obviously do many other things than just move quadrupedally or brachiate. For example, the knuckle-walking chimpanzee climbs, swings by its arms beneath branches (brachiates), and walks bipedally; ideally, their behavior would be characterized by a profile of all these activities. Since

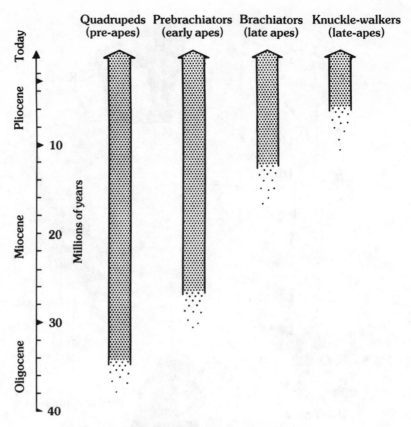

Figure 13-4. Theories of hominid origin.

there are no carefully delineated natural boundaries, it is unreasonable to expect that every fossil will fit into a "locomotor stage." Furthermore, contemporary forms have evolved and there is little reason to believe that actual ancestors were identical with any living relatives. If both fossil skeletons and data on living forms were available, there would be a greatly reduced chance of reconstruction error, but there are no living pre-brachiators with an anatomy comparable, for example, to *Dryopithecus*. Nor, for that matter, are there fossil brachiators.

Immunological Time Scale

As if things weren't bad enough for us humans, along comes a new anthropological assessment of man's relationship to the apes. We're told man and the apes may not be nearly as far apart as has been thought. Studies conducted at the University of California at Berkeley by two scientists suggest that the time of divergence by man and ape from a common ancestor they're supposed to have shared occurred only five million years ago, and not the 30 million held by some scientists. Of course, humans actually should not resent too deeply this more intimate cousinship to the ape, for the closer the scientists get man to the trees, the easier it should be to explain why he acts the way he does (from the *Austin* [Texas] *American*, 29 December 1969).

Most recently Drs. Vincent Sarich and A. Wilson raised serious questions as to the time of the separation of hominids and pongids. They originally suggested a time of divergence of approximately 4 to 5 million years B.P. as most consistent with their analytical method, termed the immunological approach. They have now pushed this back to 8-10 million years. The immunological date (or the "protein clock") provides a figure appreciably different from that of the paleontological record.

The Sarich and Wilson immunochemical approach permits precise measurements with very small amounts of antigen, the substance produced by rabbits when injected with serum from another animal. It has long been known that humans and other animals generally produce antibodies against foreign substances entering the blood stream. If human serum is injected into a rabbit, the rabbit will build up the anti-human antibodies to counteract the foreign "invader." Repeated injections strengthen the reaction. Some blood may then be drawn from the rabbit and the serum used to test the serum of other animals. As the test serum is antihuman, i.e., reacts against human serum, the closer an animal is to us, the stronger the anti reaction will be.

In many tests Sarich and Wilson injected rabbits with human albumin (a blood protein) and tested the antihuman antibody obtained against a wide variety of other primates. The albumin results were expressed in terms of ID units or "immunological distance" units. Sarich and Wilson also studied the immunological distances between primates and non-primates. By making the assumption that albumin has evolved at a constant rate in all lineages, an assumption that many reject, and that this rate can be measured, they calculated the times of divergence of various lineages. In contrast with the fossil record, Sarich and Wilson originally estimated that hominids, chimpanzees, and gorillas separated on the order of 4 million years ago, orangutans 7 million years ago, and gibbons 10 million years ago. If one accepts their data, human evolution is a very recent event.

According to the immunological approach the numerous branches of the Miocene dryopithecines left a single surviving lineage owing its unique evolutionary success to the development of brachiation. Modern hominids and pongids, as products of the adaptive radiation following this development, show similarities in basic pattern but differences in detail. The unity of the Hominoidea is based upon the relatively short time period during which a major adaptation evolved. Diversity between members is based on the relatively long time during which the lines independently evolved. The immunological approach places our ancestors as functionally monkeys until 10 to 15 million years B.P. and brachiating apes until about 6 million years B.P. At 6 million years B.P. a terrestrial adaptation began; Sarich feels that knuckle-walking would be a perfect transitional stage from full brachiation to bipedalism.

The Sarich and Wilson scheme has been attacked on a number of grounds, not the least of which is the fact that many do not fully understand the approach. Paleontologists have been in the forefront of the attack, for the Sarich and Wilson scheme makes no sense if *Ramapithecus*, dated at least 14 million years B.P., is the hominid many believe it is. Even some *Australopithecus* sites approximate the 4 mil-

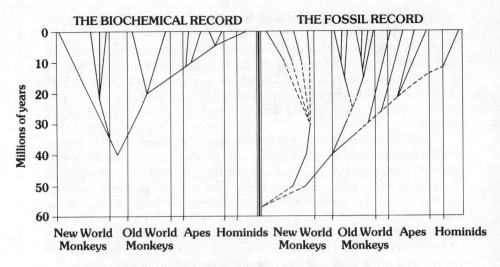

THE BIOCHEMICAL RECORD   THE FOSSIL RECORD

Millions of years

New World   Old World   Apes Hominids   New World   Old World   Apes Hominids
Monkeys   Monkeys   Monkeys   Monkeys

Figure 13-5. A comparison of two theories of the course of higher
primate evolution based on different data sources.

lion year separation date Sarich and Wilson originally postulated for
the divergence of the hominid and pongid lines.

The dating which the immunological scheme suggests is unaccept-
able to most paleontologists. There is no concrete proof that serum
albumin evolves at fixed rates; evolutionary rates could be slower or
faster at different points in time. However, there is no doubt the Sarich
and Wilson attack is an opening volley of an assault on the fossil record. If the fossil record stands, it will be further strengthened by doubts
about its validity, for it will take strengthened arguments to maintain
it (Figures 13-5 and 13-6).

The Aquatic Idea

This final suggestion is not, at least at this stage, to be taken as a
serious possibility. This idea suggests that the original terrestrial hominid went through a long aquatic stage before becoming a carnivorous
biped. Our ancestors are envisioned as moving to the tropical sea-
shores searching food. There they found shellfish and other creatures
in comparative abundance; the food supply was richer and more
attractive than that on the open plains. This form first groped around
the rock pools and shallow water; gradually they began to swim to
greater depths and dive for food. During this process they supposedly
lost their hair like other mammals who returned to the sea. Only the
head, protruding above the surface, retained a hairy coat to protect it
from the sun. When their tools (originally developed for cracking open
shells) became sufficiently advanced, they left the seashore and ven-
tured into the open plains.

This idea supposedly explains why we are so nimble in water and
why our closest relatives, the great apes, quickly drown. The aquatic
idea explains that hair on our back points diagonally backwards and
inwards toward the spine, following the direction of the flow of water
over a swimming body. Our layer of subcutaneous fat is supposedly a
compensatory insulating device.

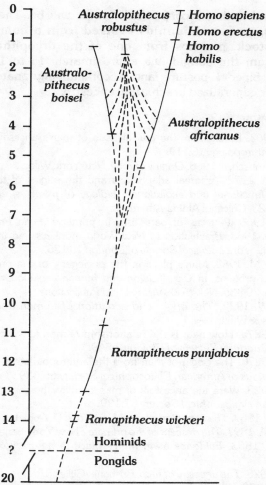

Figure 13-6. A tentative hominid evolutionary history. The solid lines represent known fossils; probable relationships are indicated by dotted lines.

A recent very delightful updating of this idea is found in Elaine Morgan's book *The Descent of Women* (1972). She argues that we were aquatic during the Pliocene as the seas provided us refuge from carnivorous predators. What is the evidence in support of this suggestion? Besides what has been mentioned above, and which could be better explained by alternate means, there is no evidence of importance to substantiate this idea. Unless some spectacular evidence is uncovered, the aquatic idea is merely an oddity.

The various suggestions mentioned are the major optional views of hominid evolutionary history. The orthodox viewpoint is that we evolved from a pongid ancestry; few support the contentions of a non-anthropoid ape hominid derivation. The brachiating theory is being questioned and modified and it may eventually include a pre-bipedal stage of fist-walking or knuckle-walking. While most paleontologists support a Miocene and Early Pliocene divergence of the hominid-pongid line, this view is challenged by Sarich and Wilson. Their views are not widely accepted and, if the paleonto-

logical and dating record stands, never will be. The orthodox view remains: modern hominids evolved from a common hominid-pongid stock, perhaps from one of the dryopithecines, and diverged from the pongid line approximately 15 to 18 million years B.P. Our bipedal posture and accompanying anatomical features reflect our generalized brachiating ancestry.

Bibliography

Avis, V. 1962. Brachiation: the crucial issue of man's ancestry. *Southwest Journal of Anthropology* 18:119.

Buettner-Janusch, J. 1966. *Origins of man.* New York: Wiley.

Cartmill, M. 1972. Arboreal adaptations and the origins of the order Primates. In *The functional and evolutionary biology of primates*, edited by R. Tuttle, pp. 97-123. Chicago: Aldine-Atherton.

Dunn, F. 1966. Patterns of parasitism in primates. *Folia Primatologica* 4:329.

Erikson, G. 1963. Brachiation in New World monkeys and in anthropoid apes. *Symposium of Zoological Society of London* 10:135.

Goodman, M. 1963. Man's place in the phylogeny of the primates as reflected in serum proteins. In *Classification and human evolution*, edited by S. Washburn, pp. 204-35. New York: Viking Fund Publications.

Gregory, W. 1922. *The origin and evolution of human dentition.* Baltimore: Williams & Wilkins.

_____. 1927a. How near is the relationship of man to the chimpanzee-gorilla stock? *Quarterly Review of Biology* 2:549.

_____. 1927b. The origin of man from the anthropoid stem—when and where? *Proceedings of American Philosophical Society* 66:439.

_____. 1928. Were the ancestors of man primitive brachiators? *Proceedings of American Philosophical Society* 67:129.

Haeckel, E. 1869. *The evolution of man.* New York: D. Appleton & Co.

Hubrecht, A. 1897. *The descent of the primates.* New York: Scribner.

Huxley, T. 1863. *Evidence as to man's place in nature.* London: Williams & Norgate.

Jones, F. 1923. *The ancestry of man.* Brisbane: Gillies.

_____. 1929. *Man's place among the mammals.* New York: Longmans, Green.

Jukes, T., and Holmquist, R. 1972. Evolutionary clock: nonconstancy of rate in different species. *Science* 177:530.

Keith, A. 1925. *The antiquity of man*, ed. 2. London: Williams & Norgate.

Klinger, H.; Hammerton, H.; Nuston, D.; and Lange, E. 1963. The chromosomes of the Hominoidea. In *Classification and human evolution*, edited by S. Washburn, pp. 235-42. New York: Viking Fund Publications.

Kohne, D. 1970. Evolution of higher organism DNA. *Quarterly Review of Biophysics* 3:327.

Lewis, O. 1972. Osteological features characterizing the wrist of monkeys and apes, with a reconsideration of this region in *Dryopithecus* (Proconsul) *africanus*. *American Journal of Physical Anthropology* 36(1):45.

Marzke, M. 1971. Origin of the human hand. *American Journal of Physical Anthropology* 34(1):61.

Morgan, E. 1972. *The descent of women.* New York: Stein & Day.

Morris, D. 1967. *The naked ape, a zoologist's study of the human animal.* New York: McGraw-Hill.

Oxnard, C. 1969. Evolution of the human shoulder: some possible pathways. *American Journal of Physical Anthropology* 30(3):319.

Pilbeam, D. 1972. *The ascent of man.* New York: Macmillan.

Poirier, F. 1977. *Fossil evidence: the human evolutionary journey.* St. Louis: Mosby.

Read, D., and Lestrel, P. 1970. Hominid phylogeny and immunology: a critical appraisal. *Science* 168:578.

Sarich, V. 1971. A molecular approach to the question of human origins. In *Background for man*, edited by P. Dolhinow and V. Sarich, pp. 60-81. Boston: Little, Brown.

————. 1972. Hominid origins revised. In *Climbing man's family tree*, edited by K. Kennedy and T. McCown, pp. 450-60. Englewood Cliffs, N.J.: Prentice-Hall.

Sarich, V., and Wilson, A. 1967. An immunological time scale for hominid evolution. *Science* 158:1200.

Schultz, A. 1936. Characters common to higher primates and characters specific for man. *Quarterly Review of Biology* 11:259.

Simons, E. 1972. *Primate evolution: an introduction to man's place in nature.* New York: Macmillan.

Straus, W. 1949. The riddle of man's ancestry. *Quarterly Review of Biology* 24:200. Reprinted in *Ideas on human evolution—selected essays*, edited by W. Howells, 1967, pp. 69-105. New York: Atheneum.

Tuttle, R. 1969. Knuckle-walking and the problem of human origins. *Science* 166:953.

Uzell, T., and Pilbeam, D. 1971. Phyletic divergence dates of hominid origins. *Science* 166:953.

Washburn, S. 1971. The study of human evolution. In *Background for man*, edited by P. Dolhinow and V. Sarich, pp. 82-117. Boston: Little, Brown.

Chapter 14
Ramapithecus—Possibly the First Hominid

In 1934, G. Edward Lewis, then a graduate student at Yale University, described a fossil primate which was found in the early 1900s in the Siwalik Hills of North India. He emphasized that the specimen, which consisted of jaw parts and teeth only, showed hominid traits; nevertheless, he cautiously classified it an anthropoid ape—christening it *Ramapithecus brevirostris.* "Rama" is a figure in Hindu mythology, "brevis" means short, and "rostric" refers to a beak or beaklike part. In other words, *Ramapithecus* had a short face.

Although a source of continuing debate, *Ramapithecus,* solely on the basis of dental remains and some jaw fragments, is often considered a Miocene-Early Pliocene hominid genus. The major *Ramapithecus* finds come from India and Fort Ternan, Kenya, East Africa. Some argue that *Ramapithecus* may be the intermediate form between an early Miocene hominid ancestor and the Lower Pleistocene hominids.

Geographical Distribution

For a while it seemed that *Ramapithecus* was a possible hominid genus restricted to India. However, in 1961 Dr. L. Leakey reported the discovery of some fossil maxillae, parts of which contained teeth, from the site at Fort Ternan, about forty miles east of Lake Victoria in Kenya. Leakey called this form "Kenyapithecus" and designated it a hominid. *Ramapithecus* remains have also been uncovered from coal beds in Hunan Province, China, the Jura mountains of southern Germany, and perhaps in north central Spain. There is also the possibility of *Ramapithecus* in Greece and Hungary (Kretzoi, 1975).[1]

[1]The reader might refer to I. Tattersall, 1975. *The Evolutionary Significance of Ramapithecus* (Minneapolis: Burgess Publishing Co.) for a fuller discussion.

Upper and lower jaw fragments of *Ramapithecus* from Fort Ternan in Kenya.

Ramapithecus in India

Dental Traits. The Indian *Ramapithecus* material is placed into one species, *R. punjabicus* (referring to the state of Punjab). Its generic status and possible acceptance as an ancestral hominid is based upon the following characteristics, most of which Lewis noted in his 1934 description. The jaws are short, small, and delicate, and the teeth are small compared to pongid teeth, approaching the hominid condition. Among the many dental traits of *Ramapithecus* common to later hominids but atypical of pongids, the following are most diagnostic: small canines, small premolars relative to the molars, and a first premolar (P-3) not markedly larger than the second premolar (P-4). The surfaces of the molars and premolars are most like those of hominids, and there is marked **interstitial wear** (wear between adjacent teeth) indicating a crowded tooth row and reduced facial **prognathism** (forward protrusion). The maxillae show an unusually deep **canine fossae** (a facial depression lateral and inferior to the nose) which again indicates facial reduction.[2] The dental arch is divergent (or **parobolic**)—the distance between the rear teeth is greater than the distance between the front teeth. In pongids, the dental arch is parallel. The canine root is ellipsoidal, a hominid trait, and there is no **canine diastema** (the gap between the canine and P³ which accommodates the overlapping canine from the opposing jaw). The chewing motion was probably rotary or sidewards, rather than up and down as in most primates (Figures 14-1 through 14-3).

Figure 14-1. *Ramapithecus* mandible and maxilla articulated.

Implications of Dental Traits. There are three major alternatives to explain such dental traits as closely packed teeth, interstitial wear, and the marked gradient of increasing wear on the chewing surfaces of the teeth from back to front: (1) Either a more abrasive diet or more powerful chewing than typical of apes promoted faster wear; (2) as in modern *Homo* the eruption sequence of *Ramapithecus's* molars extended over a longer time period; and (3) a combination of both factors. *Ramapithecus* may have had a longer growth period than typical of pongids, and judging from the degree of dental wear, it can be suggest-

[2]If you place your fingers alongside your nose, the hollow in your face, above your canines, is your canine fossa.

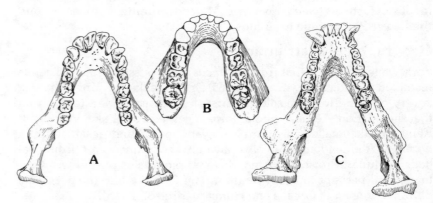

Figure 14-2. Reconstruction of the lower jaw of (B) Indian *Ramapithecus* compared with (A) large Pleistocene gelada baboon and (C) pygmy chimpanzee. Not to scale.

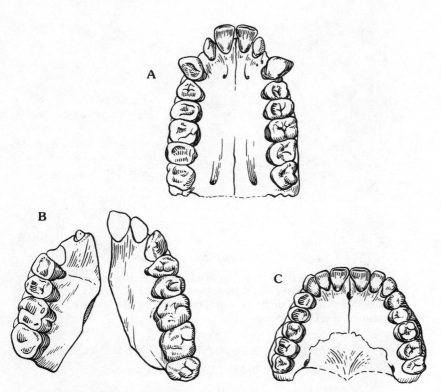

Figure 14-3. The dental arch or arcade and palate in (A) orangutan, (B) *Ramapithecus,* and (C) modern *Homo.* Not to scale.

ed that the delayed maturation characteristic of modern *Homo* was present in our early ancestors. This delay is important as it allows for a longer mother-infant dependency relationship which is a basic first step for a longer socialization period and a prerequisite for culture.

Habitat and Dating of the Indian Variety. The Indian material derives from the Chinji and Nagri formations of the Simlar and Siwalik hills, N. India. These come from the Upper Miocene and Lower Pliocene and are usually considered to date about 12-14 million years B.P. However, the material may be younger, i.e., 10-12 million years B.P.

The habitat of the Indian *Ramapithecus* has recently been the subject of debate (Figure 14-4). I. Tattersall (1969a,b, 1975) suggests that the habitat consisted of forests interspersed with broad rivers and trees. During the Nagri period, forests were more broken than during the preceding Chinji period; by the Dhok Pathan period (during the Middle Pliocene) the habitat may have been one of open prairies. Louis Leakey disputed Tattersall's interpretations and considered the faunal evidence cited by Tattersall equivocal.

Dietary Habits. Simons and Tattersall (1971), postulating from the feeding behavior of early hominids, suggest that *Ramapithecus* inhabited the forest. *Australopithecus*, the earliest of whom perhaps appeared sometime prior to 5 million years B.P., has been recovered from environments ranging from open wooded savanna to dry grassland. Yet both forms show an essentially similar feeding adaptation. "Evidently, then, early hominids, presumably the descendants of a strictly arboreal stock, were tempted to the forest floor by food items of high nutritive con-

Figure 14-4. A woodland like that in which the European and Indian *Ramapithecus* possibly lived 10 million years B.P. Giraffids (*Samotherium*) feed in the background; in the foreground are primitive deer (*Dicrocerus*).

AFRICAN *RAMAPITHECUS* = *KENYAPITHECUS* OF DR. LEAKEY

Fort Ternan 18 May, 1975 (*Ramapithecus*)

The drive to Fort Ternan from Baringo took approximately six hours over some rather rough dirt roads. In order to locate the site we stop at Fort Ternan Station, a town along the rail line. Fort Ternan Station is primarily a row of wooden frame stores. At the site we meet with the security guard Mr. Thuo who, because of Richard Leakey's kind letter of introduction, allows us to camp.

Fort Ternan site sits on a hill overlooking extensively cultivated fields of cane and corn. The original owner, Mr. Wicker, left a few years ago. It was Mr. Wicker who contacted Dr. L. Leakey and first reported the existence of fossiliferous remains. The site is an excavation in the side of the hill surrounded by a number of test pits which cut across and run up and down the hill. A fair amount of largely fragmented bone still exists in the "garbage" silt taken from the main site and the test pits.

The main site is a horse-shaped area approximately 40 feet wide at the mouth and 15 feet wide at the back. Since the hill slopes there is no average depth from the top of the hill to the floor of the excavation; however, the highest point is approximately 18 feet. Dr. Leakey's original site is now the bottom floor. The site recently dug by Peter Andrews is still covered because of the dirt falls from the hill. The *Ramapithecus* bed stands out as a clearly visible whitish-grey lens. The *Ramapithecus* bed contains considerable amounts of animal bones including elephant, lion, and antelope. This fauna is useful in reconstructing the habitat. There is a considerable amount of fossilized faunal remains scattered about the site.

At the top of the hill one can recognize a second bed. This postdates the *Ramapithecus* bed and contains considerable faunal remains. To the right of the main excavation area is another smaller excavation, from which nothing has been found.

The Fossil Record—
Recovering the Past

Excerpt of my field notes during my visit to Fort Ternan.

FORT TERNAN

A. The landscape surrounding the Fort Ternan site.

B. Looking into the Fort Ternan excavation pit.

C. The Fort Ternan excavation pit. Note the stratigraphy which is clearly visible on the wall.

D. A wall near the "Kenyapithecus" locality.

E. Fossilized faunal remains lying at the "Kenyapithecus" locality.

F. Fossilized bone at Fort Ternan. The bones are probably from the limb of an ungulate.

tent which occurred there. Primary among these would have been grains, tubers, roots, and possibly, meat. Only subsequently would hominids have moved to the forest fringes, then out into the open plains, in search initially of the same type of foodstuffs" (Simons and Tattersall, 1971:54).

Dating. The major *Ramapithecus* material outside of India derives from Africa and was uncovered by those indefatigable fossil hunters Dr. Louis and Dr. Mary Leakey. The most complete and best-dated African material is from the Fort Ternan site, dated by biotite (a common constituent of crystalline rock) collected above the layer yielding the fauna to 14 million years B.P. This date, confirmed by K/Ar analysis on different samples, places the African material within the Late Miocene. It predates the Indian material by a few million years.

Dental Traits. The Fort Ternan material consists of a left maxillary fragment with the second premolar, the first and second molar, and the roots of the third still preserved. A small upper left canine was recovered near the site. A right maxillary fragment with the first and second molars plus a mandibular second molar also come from the site. A left upper central incisor came from a few feet into the cliff at the same stratigraphic level.

Classification—Disagreement. Leakey and Simons disagreed over the classification of the Fort Ternan material. Leakey called the material *Kenyapithecus* and recognized two species; however, one form, which Leakey called *K. wickeri*, others generally include in the genus *Ramapithecus*. The other Fort Ternan form *K. africanus*, which Leakey designated a hominid, Simons feels is a pongid—one of the dryopithecines. While most agree with Simons's interpretation, Leakey felt that *K. africanus* predated *Ramapithecus* and was proof positive of the existence of a hominid line dating back at least 20 million years in East Africa.

Postcranial Material and Implications. Leakey felt that some postcranial material from the Kenya sites of Songhor and Rusinga Island might belong to *K. africanus*. These materials include heel bones, an incomplete femur, shaft of a humerus, and a tibial fragment (from the leg). At various times all this material has been attributed to one or another of the dryopithecines. However, because of their early dating, Leakey referred to them as *K. africanus,* arguing they are the oldest known examples of hominid postcranial remains. Leakey's contentions have yet to gain much credence in the scientific community.

Ramapithecus Lifeways

Dental Evidence. What can be said about *Ramapithecus* lifeways? Leaving *K. africanus* limb bones aside as dubious, the material consists only of a few jaw bones and some teeth. There is a lack of artifactual (manufactured or utilized) material. Extrapolating from the dental evidence and hypothesizing from what is known of other hominids and nonhuman primates, we can say the following: Most nonhuman primates possess large canines which may be used offensively and defensively but most often are used simply as threatening mechanisms. Many nonhuman primates have a yawning signal, the peak of which is flashing the canines, which signals tension and/or aggression. The sight of the large canines serves as a threat directed from the signaller to the re-

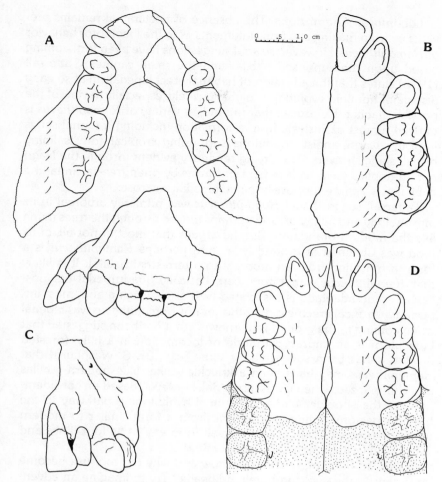

Figure 14-5. (A) *Sivapithecus alpani*—Tekkaya
(Ramapithecus?). (B) *Rudapithecus hungaricus*—
Hungary (Ramapithecus?). (C) *Rudapithecus hungari-
cus*—Kretzoi (Ramapithecus?). (D) Occlusal view of
reconstructed palate (stippled area is reconstructed).
Rudapithecus hungaris—Kretzoi (Ramapithecus?).

cipient(s). The flashing canines are an effective signal; most often
trouble is avoided and the opponent moves on.

Based upon one broken canine and some canine sockets, it is judged
that *Ramapithecus* lacked powerful, large, deep-rooted, slashing and
jabbing canines. Their canines may have approached ours in size and
had smaller and more shallow roots. Such traits have functional implications in light of comparative evidence. Simons (1964) suggests that
"these hominids were not feeding and fighting the way apes feed and
fight. They certainly could not have used their small teeth as effectively as apes in shredding plants and in aggressive displays against predators. Instead it seems likely that their hands were playing a major role
in food-getting and defense. Furthermore, the extensive use of the
hands implies that they walked upright, although we need a great deal
more evidence before we can prove that beyond doubt."

Locomotor Adaptations. The absence of postcranial remains prevents us from making any firm statements as to the locomotor behavior of *Ramapithecus*. However, several suggestions have been forthcoming based upon the supposed habitat and the small canines. Tattersall (1975) states that the adoption of habitual erect bipedalism at so early a stage of hominid evolution is highly unlikely, especially in view of the possible habitat. He argues that the Indian variety of *Ramapithecus* is derived almost exclusively from a formation including a faunal series implying warm, moist conditions supporting tropical forests lining broad, sluggish rivers. The drying tendency evident through the Nagri period implies local replacement of forests by open tree-savanna, the habitat in which we suppose hominid bipedalism arose.

Tattersall suggests that *Ramapithecus* was primarily arboreal in its morphology and behavior, and perhaps moved through the trees much like the modern orangutan. But, he argues that most, if not all, of its food was obtained at ground level, and perhaps *Ramapithecus* is a form in transition from an arboreal to a terrestrial habitat. It is likely that *Ramapithecus's* ancestors were basically quadrupedal but possessed some adaptations associated with arm-swinging and, most importantly, truncal erectness. Whether or not *Ramapithecus* was bipedal when coming to the ground is unknown, but it has been suggested that bipedalism is an impractical mode of locomotion in a hilly, forested habitat. It has been suggested by some (e.g., Dr. S. Washburn) that *Ramapithecus* may have been a knuckle-walker like modern gorillas and chimpanzees when it was terrestrial. However, based on considerations of the shoulder girdle, a minimal evolutionary pathway to the modern pectoral conditon would be from a form similar to modern orangutans which could suspend itself from any of its four limbs and which could climb using all four extremities.

Tool Use. Turning to tool use, how and why did tool use become important to the evolving hominid lineage? Try to imagine an adventurous hominid or prehominid, like *Ramapithecus* perhaps, searching the savanna for food and wandering about morphologically defenseless (without large canines and not very fleet) in a world of predators. Weapons would be most useful for self-preservation. Since some nonhuman primates use tools, there is no reason to deny such behavior to the early hominids. Chimpanzees use sticks, which they fashion as tools to extract termites from their nests; Kortlandt's work suggests that some chimpanzees may use sticks as weapons against predatory cats. Chimpanzees and gorillas wave sticks as intimidation gestures, which may provide a behavioral backgroud for using sticks and rocks to protect oneself. Modern chimpanzees seem to have the basic concept of a tool as something to be shaped for future events. Is there any reason to deny *Ramapithecus* similar ingenuity?

Evidence for Tool Use: The above speculations are based on the fossil record and primate studies. *Ramapithecus* may have used and perhaps fashioned tools; unfortunately, the possibility of finding such tools is exceedingly slim. Wood would have long decayed, and it would be practically impossible to distinguish used from unused stone. Dr. L. Leakey contends that some of the stones found in association with the Fort Ternan fossils might have been used as tools. The Fort Ternan site is well preserved as it was covered by an ash fall soon after deposi-

Table 14-1. *Ramapithecus* **Morphological Traits.**

Ramapithecus: *Considered a genus of the Hominidae distinguished by the following characters:*

Masticatory apparatus absolutely smaller and mandible shallower than that of *Australopithecus.*

Face shorter than in *Australopithecus* but not so short as in *Homo.*

Incisors and canines less reduced compared with cheek teeth than in *Australopithecus.*

Incisor procumbency considerable; maxillary canine morphologically resembling the smallest of the Indian species of *Dryopithecus*, but in size no bigger than the canine of *Australopithecus.*

Adapted from Bernard Campbell, *Human Evolution,* Aldine Publishing Company, 1966.

tion, and many bones found there are still articulated. At what may be a *living site,* Leakey found smashed antelope skulls. Since hominids eat brain, human and otherwise, the question arises, could *Ramapithecus* have smashed these skulls to extract the brain? Could the nearby smashed bones have been broken to obtain the marrow? Nearby lay a lump of lava with battered edges—could this have been used to smash the bone? It is now unlikely that this material represents tools, but, if *Ramapithecus* used the stone, it was extracting elements from the environment to use as tools. This is the first of many steps leading to modern *Homo.*[3]

Overview

Ramapithecus lived during a period of geological turbulence—land patterns were fragmenting, separating animal populations from one another. Seas were dwindling, savannas, deserts, and semi-deserts spreading, and forests shrinking. The seas, stretching from Spain to Malaysia when the primates appeared 65-70 million years ago, diminished and continued to shrink to present dimensions. This resulted in the Mediterranean, Black, Caspian, and Aral seas.

Early specimens of *Ramapithecus* may have ranged throughout the widespread Africa-to-Asia savannas. Toward the end of the Miocene the wilderness was being desiccated by declining rainfall, and a desert formed in the Middle East was probably a major barrier to migration. Conditions to the east and west were presumably different. To the east there were still unbroken regions of dense forest; forest regions remained in East Africa and in a ring around the central Congo basin. This habitat provided two major types of environment: islands of residual forests where special arboreal dwellers live today, and savanna and semiarid plains where primates, and others resided. It has been suggested that chimpanzees and gorillas evolved in the forest islands, hominids in the open plains.[4] However, early hominid ancestors, like *Ramapithecus,* may have slept in trees and perhaps used them for protection, much like modern baboons being pursued by some predator.

[3]It should be noted, however, that chimpanzees have been reported to use rocks to break open hard-shelled fruits and nuts.

[4]Kortlandt and Kooj (1963) present an interesting discussion of this point. They suggest that chimpanzees evolved first on the savanna and subsequently moved back into the forests.

Alternative Interpretations

A Small-faced Ape—Dental Hominid. With modifications, many anthropologists adhere to the view that *Ramapithecus* is a hominid, but with lingering questions; two major alternatives have been presented. First, *Ramapithecus* may be an aberrant, relatively small-faced ape morphologically resembling hominids. Second, there are not now enough pieces to judge conclusively whether *Ramapithecus* is a hominid, a difficulty often met by referring to *Ramapithecus* as a "dental hominid" since all we possess is hominid-looking dental evidence. It has also been suggested, but not widely accepted, that *Ramapithecus* may be simply a female member of *D. indicus*.

Small-Object Feeding. If Jolly's T-complex is applied to *Ramapithecus*, then *Ramapithecus* might simply be considered a savanna-adapted small-object feeder. The *Ramapithecus* dental apparatus might reflect habitat rather than phylogenetic relationships with later hominids. However, various questions have been raised about the utilitarian value of the T-complex; it is difficult to establish dietary or adaptive implications from the incidence of the T-complex in various forms.

Simons and Tattersall (1971) feel that independent support for the "small-object feeding model of hominid origins comes, surprisingly enough, from among the lemurs, generally regarded as being among the most lowly of primates" (54). The isolated Madagascar lemurs have evolved into a wide array of forms. Some of the very interesting types became extinct since the arrival of humans 1000 to 1500 years ago. *Hadropithecus* is the most advanced of these recently extinct forms.[5] Its dental traits manifest the T-complex: high-crowned, rapidly worn, and closely packed grinding teeth. Its skull, especially the facial region, is reminiscent of ours in the deep short face from front to back; it is the shortest face of any mammal other than hominids.

Ramapithecus stands alone, isolated in time. Its predecessors, perhaps a dryopithecine like its successors (the last of which may be represented by Australopithecus), are elusive. Practically nothing is known of the development of Ramapithecus from between 5 to 14 million years B.P. New evidence will appear, but conditions for fossilization are such that we should not expect too much. The world is enormous but money and personnel are scarce, fascinating as this work is.

Bibliography

Andrews, P. 1971. *Ramapithecus wickeri* mandible from Fort Ternan, Kenya. *Nature* 231:192.

Bailit, H., and Friedlaender, J. 1966. Tooth size reduction: a hominid trend. *American Anthropologist* 68:665.

Campbell, B. 1966. *Human evolution: an introduction to man's adaptations.* Chicago: Aldine.

Everden, J., and Curtis, G. 1965. The potassium-argon dating of late Cenozoic rocks in East Africa and Italy. *Current Anthropology* 6:343.

Gelvin, B. 1976. Adontometric affinities of *Ramapithecus* to extinct and extant hominoids (abstract). *American Journal of Physical Anthropology* 44(1):217.

[5]Another form, *Megaladapis,* apparently became extinct in the late 1800s. This was considered to be the "gorilla among the lemurs." It seems to have been as large as a bear cub and arboreal besides.

Goodall, J. 1965. Chimpanzees of the Gombe Stream Reserve. In *Primate behavior,* edited by I. DeVore, pp. 425-73. New York: Holt, Rinehart and Winston.

Groves, C. 1970. *Gigantopithecus* and the mountain gorilla. *Nature* 226:974.

Hrdlička, A. 1935. The Yale fossils of anthropoid apes. *American Journal of Science* 229:34.

Jones, F. Wood. 1929. *Man's place among the mammals.* Brisbane: Gilles.

Kortlandt, A., and Kooj, M. 1963. Protohominid behavior in primates (preliminary communication). *Symposium of Zoological Society of London* 10:61.

Kretzoi, M. 1975. New ramapithecines and *Pliopithecus* from the Lower Pliocene of Rudabanga in north-eastern Hungary. *Nature* 257:578-81.

Kummer, H. 1971. *Primate societies.* Chicago: Aldine.

Leakey, L. 1968. An early Miocene member of Hominidae. In *Perspectives on human evolution,* edited by S. Washburn and P. Jay, pp. 61-85. New York: Holt, Rinehart and Winston.

———. 1969. Ecology of North Indian *Ramapithecus. Nature* 223:1075.

———. 1970. Newly recognized mandible of *Ramapithecus. Nature* 225:199.

———. 1971. Bone smashing by late Miocene hominidae. In *Adam or ape,* edited by L. Leakey, J. Prost, and S. Prost, pp. 443-47. Cambridge, Mass.: Schenkman Publishing Co.

Lewis, G. 1934. Preliminary notice of the new man-like apes from India. *American Journal of Science* 27:161.

Menzel, E. 1972. Spontaneous invention of ladders in a group of young chimpanzees. *Folia Primatologica* 17(1-2):87.

Pfeiffer, J. 1969. *The emergence of man.* New York: Harper & Row.

Pilbeam, D. 1972. *The ascent of man.* New York: Macmillan.

Pilgrim, G. 1910. Notices of new mammalian genera and species from the Tertiaries of India. *Geological Survey of India Records* 40:63.

Poirier, F. 1972. Introduction. In *Primate socialization,* edited by F. Poirier, pp. 3-28. New York: Random House.

———. 1977. *Fossil evidence: the human evolutionary journey.* St. Louis: Mosby.

Prasad, K. 1969. Observations of mid-Tertiary hominids, *Sivapithecus* and *Ramapithecus. American Journal of Physical Anthropology* 31:11.

Schaller, G., and Lowther, G. 1969. The relevance of carnivore behavior to the study of early hominids. *Southwest Journal of Anthropology* 25:307.

Simons, E. 1964. On the mandible of *Ramapithecus. Proceedings of the National Academy of Sciences* 51:528.

———. 1968. A source for dental comparison of *Ramapithecus* and *Homo. South African Journal of Science* 64:92.

———. 1969. Late Miocene hominid from Fort Ternan, Kenya. *Nature* 221:448.

Simons, E., and Pilbeam, D. 1972. Hominoid paleoprimatology. In *The functional and evolutionary biology of primates,* edited by R. Tuttle, pp. 36-62. Chicago: Aldine-Atherton.

Simons, E., and Tattersall, I. 1971. Origin of the family of man. *Ventures,* Spring, pp. 47-55.

Tattersall, I. 1969a. Ecology of north Indian *Ramapithecus. Nature* 221:821.

———. 1969b. More on the ecology of north Indian *Ramapithecus. Nature* 224:821.

———. 1972. Of lemurs and men. *Natural History* 8(3):32.

———. 1975. *The evolutionary significance of* Ramapithecus. Minneapolis: Burgess.

Wolpoff, M. 1971. Interstitial wear. *American Journal of Physical Anthropology* 34:205.

Ramapithecus—
Possibly the
First Hominid

Chapter 15
Late Pliocene—Early Pleistocene Hominids

The early history of paleoanthropology is a record of frustrated, disappointed scientists speaking to a world of skeptics. In the last chapter we noted the case of G. Edward Lewis and *Ramapithecus*. In this chapter and the next we will have further evidence in the cases of Raymond Dart and *Australopithecus* and then E. Dubois and *"Pithecanthropus."*

Lower Pleistocene Africa produced a vast array of hominid fossil materials. Because of the variability within the group, a number of different taxonomic schemes have been proposed to accommodate the cultural, anatomical, and taxonomic status of this group. Various members of this group are called *Australopithecus, Paranthropus,* and *Homo.*

A Brief History—First Disbelief

Dr. R. Dart. In 1925 Dr. Raymond Dart, then professor of anatomy in Witwatersrand University in Johannesburg, South Africa, first announced the discovery of the early australopithecine material. (A number of writers colloquially refer to this group as "Dartians.") A description of Dart's findings first appeared on 7 February 1925 in the British science journal *Nature.* Dart's findings and preliminary description were based upon a skull and an associated natural endocranial cast uncovered in limestone deposits in 1924 (Figure 15-1).[1] The skull

---

[1]An endocranial cast is the mold of the interior of the braincase. An endocranial cast provides valuable evidence as to the general form and proportions of the brain, for the latter fits quite closely within the braincase. Some have tried to read too much from such casts, for example, whether the brain is supplied with enough blood and/or neurones for speech. Such an interpretation is difficult at best, and the results are almost always greeted dubiously.

Fieldwork in the Lake Turkana region, Kenya.

> ### Raymond Dart's initial discovery of the Taungs baby
> #### (Australopithecus africanus)
>
> Toward the close of 1924, Miss Josephine Salmons, student demonstrator of anatomy in the University of Witwatersrand, brought to me the fossilized skull of a cercopithecoid monkey which, through her instrumentality, was very generously loaned to the Department for description . . . this valuable fossil had been blasted out of the limestone cliff formation . . . at Taungs. . . . Important stratigraphical evidence has been forthcoming recently from this district concerning the succession of Stone Ages in South Africa . . . and the feeling was entertained that this lime deposit, like that of Broken Hill in Rhodesia, might contain fossil remains of primitive man.
>
> I immediately consulted Dr. R. B. Young, professor of geology about the discovery, and he, by a fortunate coincidence, was called down to Taungs almost synchronously to investigate geologically the lime deposits of an adjacent farm. Professor Young was enabled to inspect the site of the discovery and select further samples of fossil material for me . . . These included a natural cercopithecoid endocranial cast, a second and larger cast, and some rock fragments disclosing portions of bone.
>
> In manipulating the pieces of rock brought back by Professor Young, I found that the larger natural endocranial cast articulated exactly . . . with another piece of rock in which the broken lower and posterior margin of the left side mandible was visible. After cleaning the rock mass, the outline of the hinder and lower part of the facial skeleton came into view.
>
> Apart from this evidential completeness, the specimen is of importance because it exhibits an extinct race of apes *intermediate between living anthropoids and man.*
>
> . . . I propose tentatively, then, that a new family of Homo-simiadae be created for the reception of the group of individuals which it represents, and that the first known species of the group be designated *Australopithecus africanus,* in commemoration, first of the extreme southern and unexpected horizon of its discovery, and secondly, of the continent in which so many new and important discoveries connected with the early history of man have recently been made, thus vindicating the Darwinian claim that Africa would prove to be the cradle of mankind.

Excerpts from Dart's original report to *Nature*, February 1925, Vol. 115.

originated from a limestone cliff formation at a site variously called Taung or Taungs (Ta-ung, place of the lion) near the Botswana border of South Africa.

Dart recalls the long, tedious process of separating the fossil from its sand and limestone imprisonment as follows. "No diamond cutter ever worked more lovingly or with such care on a priceless jewel—nor, I am sure, with such inadequate tools. But on the seventy-third day, December 23, the rock parted. I could view the face from the front, although the right side was still imbedded. [The complete extraction process took four long years.] The creature which had contained this massive brain was no giant anthropoid such as a gorilla. What emerged was a baby's face, an infant with a full set of milk teeth and its permanent molars just in the process of erupting. I doubt if there was any parent prouder of his

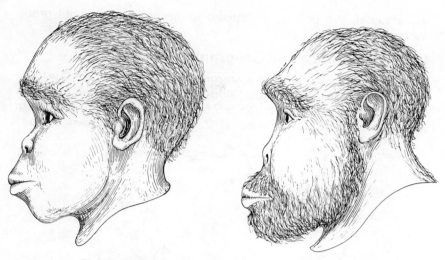

Figure 15-1. Broom's conception of the Taungs baby.

offspring than I was of my Taungs baby on that Christmas" (from Pfeiffer, 1969:63).

Dart was convinced this skull belonged to some "manlike ape," for certain facial and dental traits, as well as traits of the endocranial cast, suggested that the skull more closely approximated hominids than pongids. The paleoclimatic data suggested that the specimen lived not in the tropical forest habitats typical of pongids but in relatively dry conditions. This is now in doubt (Butzer, 1974). Dart dubbed his fossil *Australopithecus africanus* and stated that "the specimen is important because it exhibits an extinct race of apes intermediate between living anthropoids and man."

Enter Dr. R. Broom. While Dart's interpretations were being bantered about, Dr. Robert Broom who was an extremely competent and well-known paleontologist entered the scene. He travelled to Johannesburg and soon became convinced of Dart's discoveries. From deposits at Sterkfontein and Kromdraai, South Africa, he uncovered a remarkable series of australopithecine fossils, including portions of skulls, jaws, many teeth, and limb bone fragments.

Broom was into his eightieth year when he published his findings in a 1946 monograph; however, despite additional proof of Dart's suggestions and Broom's scientific caution, his work failed to carry the day. His monograph bore the impression of being hurriedly prepared —no small wonder since, at 80, Broom felt his life was short. (Actually, he died at age 85.) Broom's illustrations, freehand drawings by himself, appeared rather crude and unfinished; however, they later proved quite accurate. As has too often been true, Broom indulged himself in naming his fossils. The Sterkfontein material was allocated to the genus "Plesianthropus," although it was quite similar to *Australopithecus,* and the Kromdraai material was assigned to a new genus, "Paranthropus."

The debate over the australopithecines' taxonomic status continued into the early 1950s. As more material was uncovered, including material from new East African sites, and as more scientists reviewed

Late Pliocene—
Early Pleistocene
Hominids

the material, the position of *Australopithecus* as a hominid group became recognized.

First Appearance and Geographic Distribution

Geological Disturbances, Environmental Changes. The australopithecines (defined in the widest sense) appeared during the Middle or Late Pliocene (perhaps as much as 9 million years ago), when the earth was geologically restless (Figures 15-2, 15-3). The subsequent geologi-

Figure 15-2. Some major sites: (1) Taung, (2) Sterkfontein, (3) Swartkrans, (4) Kromdraai, (5) Makapansgat, (6) Olduvai Gorge, (7) Peninj, (8) Kanapoi, (9) Koobi Fora, (10) Omo, (11) China and (12) Java ("Meganthropus").

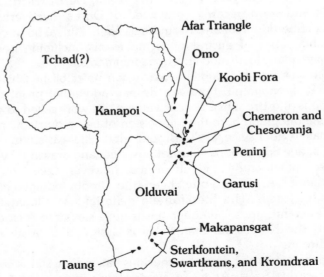

Figure 15-3. Distribution of African Lower Pleistocene sites.

cal period, the Pleistocene, was marked by periods of warm and cold weather, distinguished at the end by major swings between glaciations and interglacials. About 3.5 million years ago there were tectonic earth movements and cooling of the climate. The **Villafranchian fauna,** an important new mammalian group, first appeared in Europe, Asia, and Africa at this time.

The African Pleistocene was marked by continued shrinking of the forests and expansion of savanna grasslands. In some areas wet periods, the pluvials, alternated with the drier interpluvials. Giant earthquakes opened the cavernous Great Rift Valley in East Africa and lowered or emptied many lake beds. The southernmost part of the African continent remained stable, but the northern areas experienced convulsive changes. An example of these changes, the Great Rift Valley, extends some 4000 miles from the Zambezi River of Zambia through East Africa and Ethiopia, and as far north as the Jordan Valley. The Jordan River, Dead and Red Seas, lakes Edwards and Albert are examples of locales where water filled steep, parallel-sided valleys along rift fracture lines.

South Africa. Australopithecines were first uncovered in South Africa, primarily as a result of extensive limestone quarrying. The material comes largely from three sources: limestone quarry sites, rock pile dumps resulting from the limestone quarry operations, and fissure and cave deposits filled with sandy breccia. The five major South African australopithecine sites are located in three widely separated regions: Taung, the first find, is located in Botswana; Kromdraai, Sterkfontein, and Swartkrans are clustered within a three mile radius just north-northwest of Krugersdorf, and Makapansgat is about 165 miles north of Pretoria. It was originally assumed that Taung was in dry country, whereas the other four are well watered. These habitat differences may have existed during australopithecine times.

Because of new geomorphological studies and the reexamination of faunal remains, the Taung site has been under continual revision of late. Most significantly, Butzer (1974) has raised some serious doubts as to the habitat and the date of the Taung site. According to Butzer's recent studies, the Taung hominid is found in deposits indicating a subhumid or humid environment and not the semiarid context originally proposed. This new information raises questions about the original basis for the hypotheses concerning habitat differentiation of the robust and gracile australopithecine forms. Furthermore, the Taung specimen may actually be younger than originally assumed, and Butzer suggests the material may actually immediately predate the Middle Pleistocene. This information suggests that Taung is contemporary with or even younger than Sterkfontein and Kromdraai and not broadly contemporaneous with Sterkfontein and Makapansgat. According to Butzer 1974:384) "... the Taung hominid may postdate the arrival of true *Homo* in southern Africa, opening up a new range of problems concerning the phylogeny and ecological adaptations of the australopithecines."

Taung is a limestone plateau cut by deep cracks; animal bones have fallen into these crevices along with sand. Sterkfontein is a cave site which had a hole in the roof during australopithecine times. The three remaining sites are ordinary caves. Unlike Bed I, Olduvai, South

African sites cannot certainly be designated habitation or occupation areas. For example, both Taung and Sterkfontein seem to be refuse pits.

Dating Problems. Because all five sites were originally uncovered by quarrying operations, the remains are out of stratigraphic context, making dating a nightmare. Attempts have been made to stratify the

---

28 May Olduvai Gorge
(Australopithecus, "Zinjanthropus," Homo habilis, Homo erectus

We drove down to Olduvai from our camp at Ngorongoro Crater. The drive is dusty over dirt roads and takes about 1½ hours. The drive from the cool, cloudy, and rainy Ngorongoro Crater to the dry, dusty Olduvai Gorge is quite a change. Olduvai Gorge itself is a flat table with many side faults. The first introduction to Olduvai is the visitors gate where one contacts a guide to take you through the Gorge. We first go to the small educational building for a brief lecture and then a visit to the small museum before proceeding into the Gorge itself.

The stratigraphy at Olduvai is quite clear. Much of the area is eroded and quite water-worn. The gorge still must contain many undiscovered sites, but there are so many side faults that some of the sites will probably never be discovered. However, Dr. Mary Leakey still surveys the Gorge regularly.

The first site which we visit is the "Zinjanthropus" locality situated in a small gully. This site is identified by a stone marker, as are the other major sites at Olduvai. There are still some faunal remains scattered about the area. From here we move on to the *Homo habilis* locales, OH 7 and OH 8, found about 500 yards from the "Zinjanthropus" locale. OH 7 and 8 locales sit side-by-side in a cut. The only material left here are the markers to distinguish the sites.

From here we go on to the Stone Circle site which is now covered by a stone house to protect the site. The stone circle is laid out in a partial semi-circle with some stones from the circle piled in a corner—the remnant of the dig before it was realized what was being excavated. Approximately 15-20 feet from the stone circle is the so-called garbage pit which contains some spheroids and choppers scattered about. Many of the tools are marked with signs. Much of the bone in the garbage pit is cracked. From the highest point to the bottom of the excavation is approximately ten feet. Outside the house there is considerable quartz material, some of which looks as if it could have been fabricated.

From the Stone Circle we go on to visit some of the other sites in the Gorge. We finally move on the JK site which is where Dr. Mary Leakey excavated the foot and finger marks amidst some holes dug in the ground. Because the site has not yet been fully published, photographs are forbidden. The site is covered by a large tarpaulin, the covered area measures approximately 100 x 100 feet. We are able to see many of the footprints and the hand scrapings on the ground. There are quite a few holes dug in the ground (some of which are about 1-2 feet deep). The area at the time that *Homo erectus* visited the locale was quite muddy. The locale has good stratigraphy, and sits on a slight slope. Outside the covered area there is considerable quartz on the ground and some still in situ. Much of this material looks worked and could have been utilized as scrapers and cutting implements.

Excerpts from my field notes, May 1975.

South African sites chronologically using soil analysis and faunal and tool associations — relative dating techniques. A faunal study indicates that Taung, Sterkfontein, and Makapansgat are roughly contemporaneous or overlap in time. Swartkrans came later, after some temporal gap. The youngest site appears to be Kromdraai which could be early Middle Pleistocene. Archaeological dating suggests that the three earliest, Taung, Sterkfontein, and Makapansgat, were probably contemporaneous with the earliest hominid tool tradition, the Early Oldowan. However, as the next paragraph indicates, all this is speculative and open to many interpretations.

New evidence suggests that the South African sites may be older than usually assumed.[2] Based on a comparison with East Africa sequences, Sterkfontein may be older than 2 million years, Makapansgat may be 2.5 to 3 million years, and Swartkrans and Kromdraai may be 2 to 2.5 million years. Later South African sites may fall within the Middle Pleistocene and be contemporaneous with lower levels of Olduvai Bed II.

East Africa—Olduvai Gorge. (Figure 15-4.) Olduvai Gorge (Table 15-1), one of the major East African early hominid locales, is a well-stratified, steep-sided gorge stretching for about twenty-five miles across the Serengeti Plain in northern Tanzania not far from the Ngorongoro Crater. Olduvai Gorge is about 300 feet deep and is geologically stratified into five beds; the oldest and lowest bed, Bed I, dates from the Early Pleistocene. The earliest site in Bed I has been K/Ar dated to approximately 1.8 million years B.P.

Olduvai was "discovered" in the early 1900s, but its fossilized hominid treasures remained unknown for many years. Through the dedicated

[2]A newly announced chronology would make Makapansgat the oldest and Taung the most recent site. Makapansgat would be followed by Sterkfontein, Swartkrans, and Kromdraai.

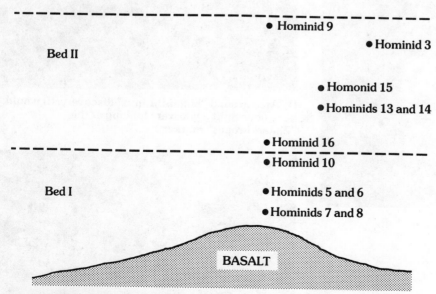

Figure 15-4. Diagrammatic representation of Olduvai Gorge Beds I and II showing the approximate placement of some of the hominids.

OLDUVAI GORGE

A. Looking into Olduvai Gorge from the Education Centre. Note the different layers of stratigraphy in the center of the picture.

B. Looking across Olduvai Gorge. Note the road in the center of the picture.

D. Area around "Zinjanthropus" discovery. (It would be to your right if you were looking at the "Zinjanthropus" marker.)

C. The marker on "Zinjanthropus" site.

E. Area around "Zinjanthropus" discovery. (It would be to your left if you were looking at the "Zinjanthropus" marker.)

F. Marker on a *Homo habilis* site. Note the fossilized faunal remains.

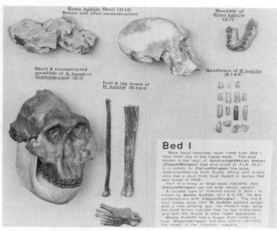

G. A display of Olduvai fossils.

H. A view of the stone circle. The rock pile at the rear is made of stones originally taken from the circle wall.

I. The remnants of part of the "garbage dump" at the stone circle (DK) site. The small horizontal markers indicate stone tools and fractured bone.

Table 15-1. Schematic Diagram of Olduvai Gorge: Dates, Beds, and Hominid Fossils.

Approximate Dating (Years B.P.)	Beds	Hominid Remains
ca. 700,000	IV	Homo erectus
	III	Homo erectus
	Upper Bed II	Homo erectus
ca. 1,700,000	Lower Bed II	Homo habilis
	I	Homo habilis
ca. 1,800,000	I	Australopithecus boisei
		H. habilis

Adapted from Mark L. Weiss and Alan E. Mann, *Human Biology and Behavior, An Anthropological Perspective,* p. 171. Copyright © by Little, Brown and Company. Reprinted by permission.

Table 15-2. Nature of Sites in Beds I and II, Olduvai.

Living floors—occupation debris found on old land surfaces, paleosoils, with vertical dimension of only a few inches (0.3 feet).

Butchering or kill sites—artifacts associated with skeleton of large mammal or group of smaller animals.

Sites with diffused material—artifacts and faunal remains found throughout site with considerable thickness of clay or fine-grained tuff.

River or stream channel sites—occupation debris incorporated in filling of former river or stream.

Data from M. Leakey, 1976.

---

efforts of the Leakeys, Olduvai Gorge has unfolded its secrets to the scientific world. (For a most insightful view of the Leakeys and their research, refer to Cole, 1975.) The Leakeys first began working at Olduvai in the early 1930s; the early years suffered from lack of funds, and the trip to Olduvai took approximately a week from Nairobi. The first important australopithecine discovery was made in July, 1959 when Dr. Mary Leakey found a bit of skull and, stuck firmly in the face of a nearby cliff, two very large premolars. It took nineteen days to free the teeth and part of the palate from the rocks.

The Omo Valley. Another very important East African site is the Omo Valley of Ethiopia. The fossil potential of the Omo Valley was first recognized in 1891, but the region is so remote that when work began in the valley supplies and personnel had to be flown in by light planes and helicopters. The first major paleontological work occurred in 1933. A detailed examination in 1966 paved the way for a systematic multidisciplinary study by the International Omo Research Expedition in 1967 and 1968 which included participants from Kenya, France, and the United States.

The Omo Valley is rapidly becoming one of the most significant hominid fossiliferous locales yet discovered. Mammalian faunal assemblages from Omo indicate that the past climate was very different than today's parched conditions. The oldest hominid remains date to approximately 4 million years B.P. by K/Ar determination. As of 1969, seventeen locales yielding hominid remains of varying ages had been uncovered.

Table 15-3. Lake Turkana Remains (1968-1973).

Skeletal remains	Number and Condition	Total
Crania	6—relatively complete	
parietal	13—fragmentary	
maxillary	5—fragmentary	24
Mandible	9—relatively complete	
	26—fragmentary	35
Clavicle		
Scapula	1—fragmentary	1
Humerus	2—relatively complete	
	5—fragmentary	7
Radius	2—fragmentary	2
Ulna	2—fragmentary	2
Pelvis		
Femur	2—relatively complete	
	14—fragmentary	16
Tibia	7—fragmentary	7
Fibula	2—fragmentary	2
Talus	3—relatively complete	
	2—fragmentary	5
Calcaneum	1—fragmentary	1
Phalanges	2—relatively complete	
	1—fragmentary	3
Metapodials	4—fragmentary	4
Isolated teeth		16

Adapted from R. Leakey and G. Isaac, "East Rudolf: An introduction to the abundance of new evidence," in Glynn Ll. Isaac and Elizabeth R. McCown (eds.), *Human Origins: Louis Leakey and the East African Evidence,* copyright © 1976 by W. A. Benjamin, Inc., Menlo Park, California.

Lake Turkana. Since 1968 a very important East African site has been located at Lake Rudolf, since renamed Lake Turkana. This site is the largest source of Late Pliocene to Early Pleistocene sites known to paleontologists. The locale is an area of approximately 1000 square kilometers (ca. 400 square miles). Although still in the early stages of excavation, numerous hominid fossils have been uncovered. A number of very early archaeological sites, with accepted stone tools and broken bones, have been located (Table 15-3). The fossiliferous beds yielded a series of comparatively well-preserved hominid crania and post-cranial bones. Although there is no detailed examination of the hominid materials, inspection shows that there is a remarkable amount of variability in size and morphology. The limb bones show contrasting robust or massive specimens and more slender ones.

The oldest fossil materials from Lake Turkana are some pig bones dated to approximately 4 million years B.P. Stone tools were found in association with one of the cranial remains. The Lake Turkana area appears to have been an occupation site, i.e., an area where hominids made tools, hunted, or scavenged. Elements of the Turkana stratigraphy overlap the upper part of the Omo sequence; faunal remains indicate an age equivalence with the lower part of the Olduvai formation. Hominid remains drawn from the Lower Pleistocene deposits appear to temporally overlap the base of the Olduvai sequence.

Homo at Lake Turkana? Richard Leakey recently announced that he had in his possession a 2.5 million year old skull belonging to the genus *Homo*. However, as discussed later, this date is now in doubt. Leakey reports that the new fragments, plus leg bones from two other specimens of the same age, came from a hillside in the Lake Turkana region. In his report given at a London scientific conference, Leakey stated, "Preliminary comparisons with other evidence indicate the new material will take a central place in rethinking and reevaluation of the evidence for the origin of *Homo sapiens,* modern man's species."

If Leakey's interpretation is correct, then the argument that modern hominids arose from *Australopithecus* is somewhat suspect. Quoting Leakey, the new material provides "clear evidence" that, rather than evolving from *Australopithecus,* "a large brained, truly upright and two-legged form of the genus *Homo* existed contemporaneously with *Australopithecus* more than 2.5 million years ago." This lends credence to his father's claim that *Homo habilis,* and not one of the australopithecines, is our direct ancestor.

Leakey's report is still too sketchy to be accepted or rejected. However, he states, "While the skull is different from our species, *Homo sapiens,* it also is different from other known forms of early man and thus does not fit into any presently held theories of human evolution."

Afar Triangle. Recent finds in the Afar Triangle of northeastern Ethiopia are most exciting. These finds are the result of an international expedition co-led by Dr. D. Johanson (U.S.A.), M. Tieb (France), and A. Asfew (Ethiopia). This expedition has unearthed a number of materials which include a complete mandible and half of a maxilla, with the teeth intact. The scientists suggest that these materials belong to the genus *Homo* and may date to three or four million years B.P. In addition to this material, the Afar group found a skull fragment and leg bones of a form which they consider to be *Australopithecus* and which dates to three million years B.P. In Johanson's words, their discovery of the form they consider *Homo* has "...in a matter of merely two days extended our knowledge of the genus *Homo* nearly 1.5 million years. All previous theories of the origin of the lineage which leads to modern man must now be totally revised."

The finds of the group at Afar lend considerable support to Richard Leakey's argument that *Homo* and *Australopithecus* coexisted at a much earlier date than originally assumed. According to Johanson the "small size of the teeth in these jawbones leads us to hypothesize that the genus *Homo* was eating meat and probably using tools, perhaps bones, to kill animals three or four million years ago." Furthermore, he states that "... there was probably some kind of social cooperation and some sort of communication system."

In late December, 1974, Johanson announced the discovery of "Lucy," a female hominid, whose bones constitute "the most complete early-man discovery ever made in Africa." "Lucy" is considered to be a small individual, about three feet, and may be an indication of the common ancestor of the genus *Homo* and the genus *Australopithecus* (Johanson, pers. comm.). Approximately 40 percent of "Lucy's" skeleton was found in the same area that yielded the jaw fragments.

A. Overview of the Hadar region, Ethiopia. It is from this area that Dr. Johanson and his co-workers found the remains of "Lucy" and other hominids, some of which they claim belong to the genus *Homo*.

B. Dr. D. Johanson excavating a mandible at Hadar.

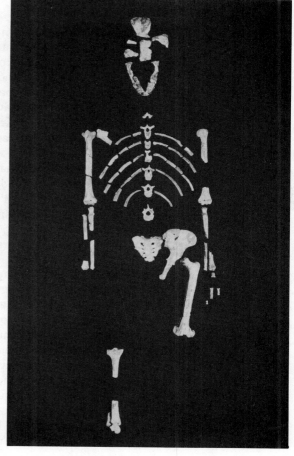

C. The skeletal remains of "Lucy" from Ethiopia.

Johanson's first finds were located 26 meters below volcanic deposits which are dated to 3.1 to 3.25 million years B.P. Since geologists are not sure how long it took these 26 meters of sediments to accumulate, the current estimate of 3.5 to 4 million years for the new finds is based partly on comparisons of animal fossils found in the area with similar faunal remains in other parts of Africa.

Johanson's finds have raised speculation as to the place of origin of the hominids. Johanson's finds come from the northeastern edge of Africa, and we know that at one time about 3 million years ago Africa and Arabia were joined. The finding of hominids at the edge of Africa raises the possibility that their origins may lie elsewhere, or, perhaps, an early migration of hominids from Africa is possible.*

At present we must withhold judgment as to the generic status of these materials and, as the researchers themselves have said, "It is certain that anthropologists from all over the world will meet these discoveries with extreme controversy and amazement."

Other Remains. Other East African australopithecine material is largely fragmentary. The Peninj mandible with all its teeth, found in the Peninj River beds near Lake Natron in Tanzania, has been dated to about 1.5 million years B.P. Some regard it as a robust australopithecine with affiliations to the Olduvai "Zinjanthropus" or South African *A. robustus* group.

In 1939 fragmentary hominid remains were uncovered at Garusi, northwest of Lake Eyasi, Tanzania, from deposits dating to the lower Omo beds. Kanapoi in northwest Kenya had yielded the distal end (elbow segment) of a humerus (Figure 15-5). Enclosing geological deposits are 2.5 to 3 millions years B.P. Another discovery at Lothagam including a piece of mandible, first molar crown, and preserved roots of the other molars has been dated to about 5 million years B.P. Extensive fossiliferous beds have been uncovered at Baringo Basin in the northern Rift Valley in Kenya where excavators recognize beds spanning from the Late Miocene to Late Pliocene, from the time of *Ramapithecus* to the earlier *Australopithecus*. Fragments of two fossil hominids from the Chemeron and Ngorora Beds have been recovered. The Chemeron material dates from 3 to 3.5 million years, the Ngorora material to around 9 millions years. Because of the time span, the Ngorora material is exciting, for it fills the gap between *Ramapithecus* and *Australopithecus*.

Lifeways

Tool Use—First Disagreement. Until recently (and there are still some lingering disbelievers) there was considerable disagreement over whether australopithecines (I use this term in the widest sense to refer to both the early *Australopithecus* and *Homo* material. The term does not apply only to the genus *Australopithecus*) made or used tools. On the pro side are stone objects found in deposits yielding australopithecine remains. Opponents argued according to anatomical considerations; it was held that the early hominid brain was too small for the necessary intellectual activity allowing the fashioning of tools from local

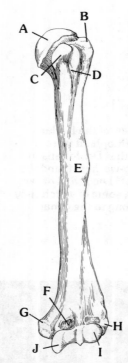

Figure 15-5. Landmarks on the modern humerus. (A) Head, (B) Greater tuberosity, (C) Lesser tuberosity, (D) Bicipital groove, (E) Deltoid tuberosity, (F) Coronoid fossa, (G) Medial epicondyle, (H) Lateral epicondyle, (I) Capitulum, (J) Trochlea.

*This information is derived from an article entitled "Digging Down to Find Man," published in *Insight* winter/spring 1975 Vol. 3 no. 2, pages 10-13.

Excerpt of some of my field notes.

objects. This notion was so solidified that when tools were recovered from Sterkfontein in 1956, they were immediately and widely attributed to more advanced hominids.

Comparative Data. The brain-size limitations argument has now been largely dismissed, directly by associated tool and early hominid remains from the same deposits and indirectly by the fact that our nearest primate relative, the chimpanzee, makes tools (Chapter 7). Chimpanzees make twig tools for probing into termite mounds in order to get the termites. They break twigs into suitable lengths and even remove side branches obstructing their probing. Some diehards refer to this as "tool modifying" and not "tool making," a distinction hardly warranted. Chimpanzees have been seen to wander from the immediate proximity of the termite mound to collect appropriate stalks, which they carry back with them; this indicates some premeditation. Tool-making for the purposes of termiting is not an instinctual pattern; it is observationally learned behavior. Tool using and termiting represent the emergence of a primitive culture, if one element of culture can be defined as "behavioral patterns transmitted by imitation or intuition." However, there is a gap between the mental ability allowing one to undertake such simple tasks that fulfill the need for some immediately visualized requirement and the conceptual capacity of the human mind allowing fabrication of implements for future contingencies.

Anatomical Considerations. Stone implements are now recognized with remains at the South African sites of Swartkrans and Sterkfontein and in East Africa at Olduvai, Omo, and Lake Turkana. The evidence suggests that the early hominid brain was capable of the

Late Pliocene—
Early Pleistocene
Hominids

Table 15-4. East African Pliocene Evidence.

The major areas yielding Pliocene sedimentary sequences in East Africa come from:

1. Lower Semliki Valley and Kaiso Areas of Lake Albert Rift.
2. Omo Valley, Lake Turkana, and southwestern areas of Lake Turkana basin.
3. Baringo Basin in the Kenya Rift.

Area	Fossil Hominid Remains
Lower Semliki Valley and Kaiso Areas of Lake Albert Rift	None as yet
Lothagam, Ekora, Kanapoi	*A. africanus* (Lothagam) *Australopithecus* (Kanapoi)
Omo	182 Hominid specimens: 161 from Shungura Formation, 21 from Usno Formation. Sample composed of 162 isolated teeth, 7 post-cranial bones, and 13 specimens representing crania, maxillae, or mandibles.
Lake Turkana	125 Hominid fossils since work began in 1969. 50 are post-cranial specimens, 16 are isolated teeth, 59 are complete or partial crania, maxillae or mandibular pieces.
Baringo Basin	Ngorora and Lukeino Formation—single molar crown Chemeron Formation—part of hominid temporal.

Data from W. Bishop, 1976.

intellectual activity needed for toolmaking and tool using. Anatomical evidence arguing for the ability of toolmaking also lies in the hand bones. Dr. John Napier (1962a and b) concluded from his study of hand bones from Bed I Olduvai that they had a "power grip," that is, the sort of grip used when wielding a hammer. They may also have had some **"precision grip,"** that is, the grip used in holding small objects by opposing the thumb and fingers to one another (Figure 15-6). (This is the grip you use when holding a pen or pencil). By practical experimentation, Napier demonstrated that the power grip was sufficient for

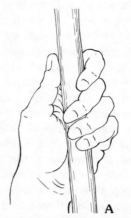

A   B

Figure 15-6. Hand grips. A. The precision grip. B. The power grip.

BARINGO BASIN

A. The dry Kapthurin River bed.

B. One of the walls lining the Kapthurin River in the area of the Chemeron Beds.

C. The area of the Chemeron Beds (which are approximately half-way up the wall). The walls are over 100 feet high.

Table 15-5. Scheme of Temporal Relationships of Late Pliocene/Pleistocene Fossiliferous Localities Yielding Hominidae in Eastern Africa.

Age m.y.	SERENGETI (Tanzania)	OMO BASIN (Ethopia)	LAKE TURKANA (Kenya)	TURKANA DISTRICT (Kenya)	BARINGO BASIN (Kenya)	KAVIRONDO GULF (Kenya)
0	MASEK BEDS IV III					
1	II	SHUNGURA FORM			CHESOWANJA	
2	I	USNO FORM	KOOBI FORA			
3			Kubi Algi Mb			KANAM
4	LAETOLIL	MURSI FORM		KANAPOI	CHEMERON	KANAM
5				upper fossil beds LOTHAGAM HILL		
6				lower fossil beds		
7						
8						

After F. C. Howell, "Pliocene/Pleistocene hominidae in Eastern Africa: Absolute and relative dates" in *Calibration of Hominid Evolution*, edited by W. Bishop and J. Miller, Scottish Academic Press, Edinburgh, 1972.

making not only the crude stone tools called **"pebble tools"** but even for making the more advanced types of **"hand axes"** similar to one of the tools recovered at Sterkfontein. However, only the precision grip could have been used on the small flakes found at Olduvai.

The Evidence. A major impediment to fully understanding the technological abilities of early hominids stems from the fact that it is hard to recognize early tools. Undoubtedly, many of the earliest tools simply involved picking some objects, a stone, bone, or stick, from the environment, using it once or twice, and discarding it. Many of the earliest examples of tools are lost to us because the utilized materials have decayed or are indistinguishable.

The chopper is a tool typically found in Lower Pleistocene sites (Figures 15-7 and 15-8). This is often a smooth, rounded cobblestone or oblong block given a rough cutting edge by knocking flakes from both sides (bifacially flaked). Most of the earliest choppers found at Olduvai are about the size of a tennis ball or slightly smaller; some tools must have been held between the thumb, ring, and index fingers and used for such purposes as preparing small pieces of plant or animal food. The Olduvai sites also contain possible bone tools; a flattened and highly polished rib from a zebra or some other horselike species may have been used to rub hides or make them smooth and pliable. A similar tool comes from Sterkfontein.

Professor Dart made a painstaking analysis of several thousand South African bone fragments; representatives from larger animals, skulls and neck vertebrae, predominate, and Dart concluded that the heads of these animals were severed before being carried off into the South African caves or rock shelters.[3] Dart suggested that many of the

[3]Dart suggests the australopithecines possessed an osteodontokeratic tool assemblage, i.e., they made tools from bone, teeth, and antlers, not only from stone.

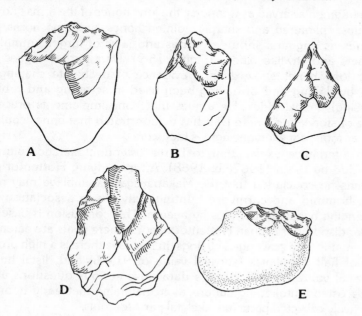

Figure 15-7. Various kinds of chopping tools from (A) Olduvai, bed I; (B and C) Olduvai, bed II; (D) Sterkfontein; and (E) the Vallonet cave, France.

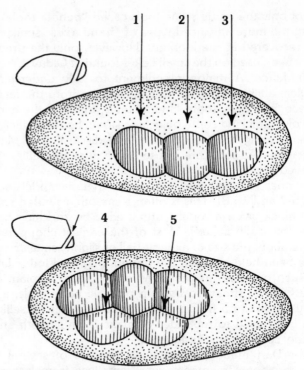

Figure 15-8. Manufacture of a pebble tool. Flakes are removed by striking a series of sharp blows (1 through 3) near the natural edge of a pebble. The pebble is turned over and blows 4 and 5 are struck on the ridges formed by the initial flaking. The resulting tool has a wavy but strong edge.

bone fragments served as weapons: the long bones of the arms and legs as clubs; splintered and sharply pointed bones, antelope horns, and canines as daggers; shoulder bones and jaws of larger animals as scrapers and sawlike blades (Figure 15-9). Dart further argues that some long bones show definite evidence of deliberate shaping for tools by flaking and of having been used in scraping and rubbing (dressing) animal hides. He argues that bone implements preceded those of stone; and where Dart has demonstrated that bones could be used as tools, not everyone agrees they were.

An alternative explanation to Dart's osteodontokeratic culture is provided by Brain (1967a,b, 1968). After studying Hottentot goat remains he concluded that the Makapansgat assemblage may result from hominid and carnivore hunting activities in association with scavenging behavior, perhaps by hyenas. This conclusion is based on similar disportions seen in Hottentot villages where goats are eaten and the remains then scavenged by dogs. In this case there is a high proportion of half mandibles (survival value of 91.4%) and distal humeri (survival value 57.3%). Brain's data raise serious questions about Dart's osteodontokeratic culture as it maintains that early hominids selectively collected particular skeletal parts for tools.

It has also been argued that the Transvaal sites were not actual hominid occupation places, but that the bone accumulations reflect passive collections by natural agencies. Hyenas have been suggested

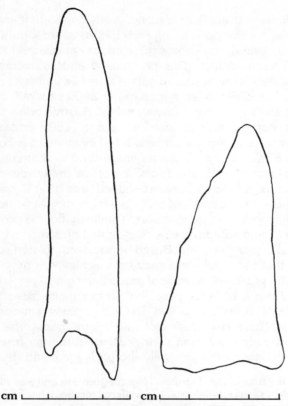

cm └─┴─┴─┴─┴─┘ cm └─┴─┴─┴─┴─┘

Figure 15-9. Representatives of Dart's osteodontokeratic culture. Bones worked to these shapes were found at Makapansgat.

as the possible collectors of the bones in the South African caves. However, Hughes's (1954, 1958) work on hyena lairs reveals that some localities lack bone, while others containing bone exhibited evidence of porcupine activity. Hughes suggested that porcupines played a role in the South African bone accumulations. However, the Swartkrans remains revealed less than 5 percent of the bones exhibiting porcupine gnawing.

Brain's (1968, 1970) study of hyena scavenging of carnivore kills notes that only minor portions of bone remained following intensive scavenging. Work in East Africa suggests that young hyenas collect bones. It is therefore possible that some of the South African bone deposits are due to hyena activities. Leopards also seem to have played some role in the bone accumulations (Brain 1968, 1970). Leopards carry their prey into trees to avoid scavenging and to consume their food leisurely. Today trees in the high veld of the Transvaal are frequently found situated near openings of dolomitic caves. If this was true in the past, some leopard prey remains may have fallen into the cave site. In fact, Brain (1970) has shown that the two puncture marks on the occipital of a partial cranium from Swartkrans (SK 54) match nicely with the mandibular canines of a fossil leopard.

Other Cultural Remains. Other evidences of cultural remains have been recovered. Volcanic dust (an excellent preservative) covers most of the **living floors** (places where objects remained in their original context) at Olduvai. A living floor is meticulously dug so that each item remains in place, for the position of each item is as important as the item itself. Once cleared, the floor is mapped and measured to ensure the location of each artifact. This painstaking and sometimes grim accumulation of data is the heart and guts of scientific endeavor.

Mary Leakey has drawn a large map of the 2400 square foot living floor where she and her husband uncovered the *Australopithecus* skull. The map illustrates the precise location of over 4000 artifacts and fossils. The core area where the artifacts are concentrated is bordered on one side by a pile of larger bone fragments and unshattered bone. Dr. Leakey sees this as a "dining room" complex, the bordering area as a garbage dump. An almost bare arc-shaped area lying between the two may have been a windbreak of branches; or, it may have served as a protective fence to keep out predators. The living floor is probably a home base; the accumulated remains suggest that hominids lived there at least seasonally over the years. Based on the accumulated remains, it is suggested that the inhabitants may have achieved a new type of social stability and possessed a sense of group belonging.

Associated Fauna. In times past, the African plains sustained an incredible fauna (Figures 15-10 and 15-11), surpassing modern-day game preserves. There is evidence of much large game; the largest creatures were the elephants and their relatives. Although resembling modern elephants, they were generally shorter legged, and their teeth

Figure 15-10. At the time of the "Dartians" Ngorongoro volcano was still a great cone, and deinotheres, antelopes, and antlered giraffes (sivatheres) roamed the Olduvai area in East Africa.

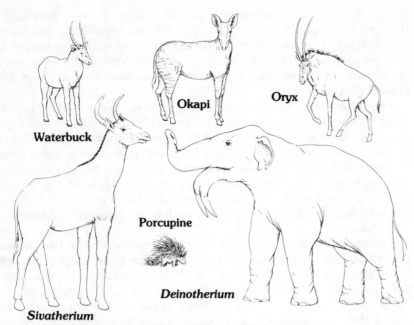

Waterbuck · **Okapi** · **Oryx**

Porcupine

Deinotherium

Sivatherium

Figure 15-11. Olduvai faunal remains.

were more primitive. One of the most remarkable forms was the deinothere or hoetusker, an elephantlike form lacking large upper tusks typical of modern elephants. Instead, its lower jaw carried two great down-curving tusks looking something like an enormous hoe; these must have been impressive creatures.

Rhinoceroses were known to the australopithecines as were horses, which included both zebralike forms and the now extinct three-toed hipparions roaming in enormous herds over the Pliocene Old World. A related extinct group was the chalicotheres—great horselike creatures with enormous claws rather than hoofs. These claws may have been fatal to many early hunters.

Giraffes, looking much like modern forms, were present, as was the enormous antlered giraffe or sivathere. Despite their massive size, there is evidence that sivatheres were attacked and killed by early hunters. Hippopotami abounded by the lakes and rivers; in the plains, bush, and forest there were various pig forms. Some of the pigs were gigantic and might have been dangerous adversaries to an unwary hominid.

Early Hominids as Prey. The early hominids possibly faced an array of carnivorous predators, the most formidable of which belonged to the cat tribe. There is no evidence of hunting dogs which, working in large packs, can overcome most wild animals. Representatives of the great cats included the leopard and lion or animals immediately ancestral to them. Among the now-extinct forms were sabre-toothed cats and the dirk-tooth, which was the size of a leopard but heavier— an agile hominid could have avoided them. Most dangerous perhaps were the lion-sized *Dinofelis* cats possessing moderately enlarged upper canines. These were probably more agile than the dirk-tooths and may have ambushed more than one hapless hominid.

If early hominids kept to open country away from thickets and if they travelled in groups, they would probably have been molested only rarely. Even when encountering a predator at close range, they might have put it to flight by using such typical primate intimidating behaviors as vocalizing, throwing objects, and shaking branches. Hominids would be most vulnerable when they came to water to drink, and present fossil accumulations suggest that our ancestors were most vulnerable exactly in such situations.

Food Sources. How did the early hominids support themselves? What did they do for food; how did they get it? The early hominids were probably hunters, gatherers, and scavengers; there is direct evidence for this lifeway in the form of large bone accumulations at some sites. Some contend that such accumulations are the work of carnivores, such as hyenas, porcupines, and leopards. In an effort to resolve this problem, carnivore food remains were studied and we can now distinguish fairly accurately between remains left by carnivore and hominid predators.

Broken bones found in such profusion in the Lower Pleistocene deposits are mostly from various kinds of antelope, both large and small. They also include bones of horses, giraffes, rhinoceroses, warthogs, baboons, and small reptilian remains and some bird skulls and egg shells. Most bones were split, perhaps to get the marrow. Dart concludes that the South African remains belong to mostly young or old creatures, that is, animals easily overpowered. However, there is evidence from Olduvai indicating that adult animals in their prime were also hunted.

It is difficult to assess the nature of food sources. Dr. J. T. Robinson (1952, 1954, 1963a and b) maintains that the robust form, the species *A. robustus,* was mainly a vegetarian. Robinson's dietary hypothesis is discussed later in this chapter. Most observers feel that the australopithecines were to some degree carnivorous; however, vegetable foods were surely incorporated in the diet.

Comparative Data—Hunting Carnivores. The manner in which meat protein was obtained has received wide attention. The easiest means of acquisition are hunting and scavenging. In a recent study, Drs. G. Schaller and G. Lowther (1969) undertook to determine early hominid hunting methods by studying the behavior of African social carnivores. The social systems of the wolf, wild dog, spotted hyena, and lion resemble those early hominids; the social carnivores hunt over large areas in search of prey. Schaller and Lowther attempted to describe some aspects of carnivore behavior bearing special relevance to the study of hominids when the latter were are a stage of cultural development lacking fire and sophisticated projectile weapons.

Social Organization—Hunting. Hunting in the open savanna implies a rather cohesive social organization; coordination and cohesion of group activities depends upon the establishment of some subtle communication system. This is not to imply that these hunters were capable of articulate speech, for there is no anatomical evidence to support this or refute it. Furthermore, social carnivores manifest various forms of cooperation, especially during hunting, without articulate speech. Even without an elaborate communicatory network and with their small brains, social carnivores use a variety of cooperative hunting techniques. The social carnivore evidence indicates that a carnivorous hominid could have used cooperative hunting techniques, like relay races to wear down the prey, driving it to members lying in ambush, and encircling and attacking it from many directions to obtain their meat. Lacking technologically advanced implements, early hominids must have hunted from ambush or by such means as driving the prey into rivers, over cliffs, or into deep mud. Most likely they used methods less dependent upon speed and physical prowess than upon group cooperative behavior.

Food Sharing. Food sharing, atypical of our primate relatives, is typical of social carnivores.[4] Some food sharing probably characterized the early hominids; males probably hunted, obtained the choice pieces, and divided the remainder among the old, infirm, females, and young. Those remaining behind probably collected roots, tubers, and berries. If data from modern hunter-gatherers is indicative these gathered foodsources, usually by females, were the dietary mainstay.

Once food sharing began, it is likely that rules governing the priority of shares appeared. The more complicated the rules and the more members with whom food had to be shared, the greater the pressures for increasing the complexity of the communicatory network. Perhaps some of the first social rules regulating human behavior stemmed from the hunting situation. While the hunting activity itself may not have required complex communicatory behavior, the rules of sharing may have and this may be one basis selecting for symbolic communication, language.[5]

How to Get By—Prey Selection. Schaller and Lowther's study suggests that the ease with which meat can be obtained varies seasonally. The four major methods for obtaining meat probably included scavenging for meat among migratory animals, driving other predators from their kills, capturing sick animals or the newborn of large mammals, and by hunting itself. Evidence from the social carnivores suggests that most prey are vulnerable animals; given a choice, weak, young, and old animals are most often taken. The hunts of early hominids must have had a relatively high rate of failure, and, as is consistent with the Olduvai and Taung remains, much of the prey must have been weak, young, or old.

Place in the Predator Hierarchy. The means whereby a hunting and scavenging hominid fit into the hunting community without extensive interspecific competition poses a problem. Our primate heritage suggests that our ancestors were diurnal and selection pressure from the primate and carnivore life-style favored a social existence. The only other diurnal social carnivore, the wild dog, hunts at dawn and dusk and takes prey under 122 pounds, leaving a niche for a social predator which hunted large animals and scavenged during the day.

Group Size. Given that there are advantages and disadvantages of group hunting, there must have been an optimum group size. Most nonhuman primates live in groups of five to 100 animals;[6] group sizes vary according to the habitat, among other factors. Terrestrial species

[4]It is important to note, however, that hunting chimpanzees do share their kill. They have a specialized begging gesture, palm up, hand outstretched, when wanting to share. See Chapter 7.

[5]However, group-hunting carnivores also share food with youngsters and others left behind, and there is no use of language.

[6]Larger groups are known. For example, artificially fed Japanese macaque troops are recorded to be as large as 750 animals.

almost always live in larger groups and groups of forest species are generally smaller than those of open-country forms. Social carnivore group sizes vary with the species and habitat.

The group sizes of contemporary hunting and gathering groups vary; the most effective social group among the African Bushmen is from three to four families to upwards of 100 people. The size and structure is flexible and the group reaches its maximum size when food is plentiful. The same is noted for the African Hadza and Mbuti Pygmy. The hunting and gathering group ranges within the confines of a circumscribed unit of relatively small size. Group size fluctuates in proportion to the amount and distribution of resources,[7] although the average size tends towards twenty-five members.[8]

Infanticide. Dr. Joseph Birdsell suggests that early hunters were dependent upon a generalized and localized fauna and flora. Modal group size probably approached twenty-five, matings were exogamous (outside the immediate group), and the groups were male dominated. When large food sources were regionally or seasonally concentrated, local groups would become larger, and the social rules would be more complex. Birdsell feels that family size was maintained with systematic female infanticide and suggests that infanticide claimed between 15 to 50 percent of the live births.

Life Span. Australopithecine life spans were short; of the gracile forms (here designated *A. africanus*) from the Transvaal caves, more than one-third (35 percent) died prior to adulthood. The robust form (*A. robustus*) from Swartkrans and Kromdraai was worse off, for well over half (75 percent) of the remains are of children and youngsters. Survivorship rates of the two species may have differed: *A. africanus* succumbed at an average of 22.9 years and *A. robustus* at an average of 18.0 years. Although *A. africanus* may have lived somewhat longer than *A. robustus* on the average, the maximum age reached by each was similar. Perhaps the robust forms at Swartkrans and Kromdraai belong to the last of their stock; their high mortality may indicate mounting environmental pressures. However, because of the small sample size Mann (1975) feels that this type of exercise is fruitless.

A Look in the Mirror

One very important fact often overlooked when discussing the Lower Pleistocene hominid morphology is the scattered nature of the remains (Table 15-6). Our interpretations are often skewed by the nature of the materials; some sites yield disproportionate remains. A statistical analysis of almost any anatomical part over the entire African sample is likely to be heavily biased by characteristics and samples from such South African sites as Swartkrans and Sterkfontein. One well-preserved skeleton could make a major difference to the composition of any of the samples. Although early hominid remains are numerous, there are parts which are poorly represented. The remains of a small number of

[7]Sugiyama (1972) notes a similar pattern of group flux among chimpanzees. When food is plentiful a number of groups gather in an area to feed; when food is scarce separate foraging groups go their own way. It is quite likely that social groups of ancestral hominids behaved accordingly.

[8]For a fuller discussion of group sizes refer to R. Lee and I. DeVore's (1968) edited book *Man the Hunter,* especially to pages 245-48.

Table 15-6. Scattered Nature of Early Hominid Remains.

Anatomical classification of remains from fourteen African sites.

	South Africa	East Africa	Total
Cranial parts	175 (17.1%)	59 (15.2%)	234 (16.6%)
Teeth	769 (75.2%)	269 (69.3%)	1038 (73.65)
Postcranial bones	78 (7.6%)	60 (15.5%)	138 (9.8%)
Grand total	1022	388	1410

Percentage frequencies of items from various anatomical parts collected from the six richest African sites (percentages are total of number of items from each site)

	Cranial Items	Teeth	Postcranial Items	Total from Site
Swartkrans	15.2	82.2	2.7	528
Sterkfontein	17.5	68.5	14.0	314
Olduvai	14.9	60.9	24.2	215
Omo	5.5	94.5	0.0	110
Makapansgat	28.0	61.0	11.0	100
Kromdraai	13.7	68.6	17.6	51
Totals	16.6	73.6	9.8	1410

List of anatomical remains from fourteen African sites

Cranial remains	calvaria
	face
	maxillae
	mandible
	endocranial cast
Dental remains	deciduous (milk) teeth
	individual maxillary and mandibular teeth
	permanent teeth
	individual maxillary and mandibular teeth
Postcranial remains	upper limb girdle—individual bones
	upper limb—individual bones
	lower limb girdle—individual bones
	lower limb—individual bones
	axial skeleton—individual bones

Used by permission from P. Tobias. 1972. In R. H. Tuttle. *The Functional and Evolutionary Biology of Primates*. Chicago: Aldine-Atherton, Inc.

well-preserved specimens often predominate; as with an iceberg, there is still so much below the surface.

Jaws and Teeth. Dental traits have received more attention than any other skeletal remains; a major reason for this is that so many teeth have been preserved. Australopithecine teeth (permanent and deciduous) are essentially hominid; the total dental pattern conforms with the family Hominidae (Figure 15-12). In all adult skeletons the dental arcade is evenly curved; there is no canine diastema. The upper incisors are small and although the canines are larger than commonly true in modern populations, they are reduced compared with pongids. The canines are not pointed; early they wear flat at the tip and do not project beyond the level of adjacent teeth. The first premolars are bicuspid. The detailed pattern of the molar cusps resembles that of subsequent hominids, *H. erectus* and *H. sapiens*.

Dentally, the early hominids are clearly distinct from pongids, but, although essentially hominid, there are some differences from the teeth

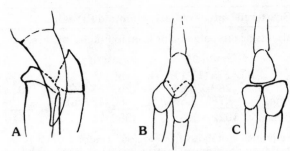

Figure 15-12. Occlusion of canines in apes and hominids. (A) An ape's upper canine overlaps and touches the lower first premolar and lower canine; in biting and chewing, it grinds a shearing edge against these teeth. (B) Initially the unworn canine in hominids (*Australopithecus* and *Homo*) overlaps the same two lower teeth, but (C) a rotary chewing motion wears the teeth down to a certain extent. Eventually, the points of all three wear, and all of them acquire smooth occlusal surfaces. Modern *Homo sapiens* generally does not chew enough to arrive at stage C, and the teeth may remain at stage B.

of *H. sapiens*. The premolar and molar teeth are large; the third lower molar commonly exceeds the length of the second. There are some other distinguishing traits, but these are evidently primitive hominid characters, for they also appear among Middle-Pleistocene *H. erectus*.

The Cranium and Face (Figures 15-13 and 15-14). The morphology and dimension of the skull first inclined anatomists and anthropologists to suggest that *Australopithecus* was an ape allied to the gorilla or chimpanzee rather than a primitive member of the Hominidae. The small braincase and massive, projecting jaws give a superficial pongid look. However, as more crania were uncovered and critically examined, this resemblance was found to be superficial.

Brain Size. At first many felt that the australopithecine cranial capacity was too small to include them within the Hominidae. The **range of variation** in australopithecine cranial capacity is from approximately 435 to 530 cc; this compares with a range of 1000 to 2000 cc for modern *Homo*. Modern chimpanzees, approximately the same size as the

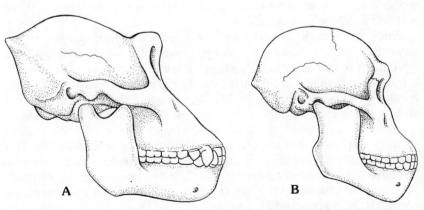

Figure 15-13. Skull of (A) a female gorilla compared with (B) a later australopithecine *(A. africanus)*.

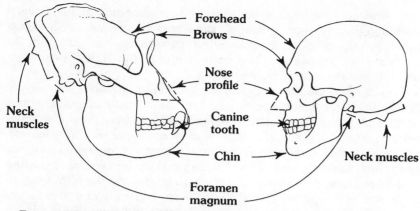

Figure 15-14. The skull of a gorilla compared with that of modern *Homo*.

early australopithecines, yield a range of 320 to 485 cc, with a mean of 394 cc for a sample of 144 individuals.

***The Skull of* A. robustus.** Reference should be made to the skulls of the robust variety of australopithecine. A major characteristic of *A. robustus* skulls is the presence of a sagittal crest, a bony ridge dissecting the midline of the top of the skull. A well-developed sagittal crest is typical of large pongids and when a crest appeared on an australopithecine skull, some assumed it was strictly comparable with the crest of pongids. However, while the robust australopithecines possess a crest, they share many cranial characteristics with the gracile australopithecines. The function of the robust australopithecine's sagittal crest is open to question, although some suggest it is related to massive chewing pressures or to a relationship of a rather small cranium and large mandible.

Hints at Posture. One of the features of the well-preserved Sterkfontein skull #5 is the height of the cranial vault over the eyes. The relative height of the australopithecine skull exceeds the range of variation in pongid skulls and comes within the hominid range. The back of the skull (the nuchal area) suggests the hominid type of head balance upon the neck, a reduction of the neck muscles and a slight facial reduction. These reflect the assumption of an erect or semi-erect posture.

Two features of the australopithecine skull—cranial height and level of the nuchal crest—are directly or indirectly related to the pose of the head upon the vertebral column. Australopithecine neck musculature was not extensively developed to support the head in relation to a forward-sloping cervical spine, as typical of modern large pongids. This, in conjunction with pelvic and limb morphology, indicates a shift toward an upright posture.

Pelvis and Limb Bones (Figure 15-15). No part of the post-cranial anatomy shows more marked contrasts between modern anthropoid apes and humans than the pelvis. A primary factor determining the evolutionary separation of the Hominidae and Pongidae was the divergent modification of the locomotor skeletons for different life styles. The pelvis of *Homo sapiens* and their ancestors became modified to accept an upright bipedal posture. If, as we suggest, these early forms are representatives of a hominid stock, then their limb and pelvic struc-

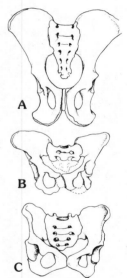

Figure 15-15. The pelvis of (A) a chimpanzee; (B) *Australopithecus*; and (C) *Homo sapiens*. All are drawn to the same scale.

Late Pliocene— Early Pleistocene Hominids

261

ture is relevant to the determination of their taxonomic status. Several australopithecine pelvic remains come from South Africa. All exhibit hominid traits although there are some significant differences from the modern hominid pelvises. The same is true of the "Lucy" pelvic material recently excavated from Ethiopia.

Functional Implications. There are two major questions we can ask: Are these characteristics meaningful in terms of the functional anatomy of the limb skeleton, and can we make inferences from these characteristics as to the manner of posture and locomotion? The answers are: (1) the morphological traits reveal much about the functional anatomy of the limb skeleton, and (2) yes, we can make inferences as to posture and locomotion. For example, the broadening of the ilium (the uppermost part of the pelvis, Figure 15-16) extends the area for attachment of the gluteal muscles utilized for balancing the trunk on the lower limbs. Other changes realigned the pelvis and corresponding muscular structure, allowing bipedal locomotion. The configuration of the australopithecine pelvis suggests they were capable of an erect posture and bipedal locomotion.

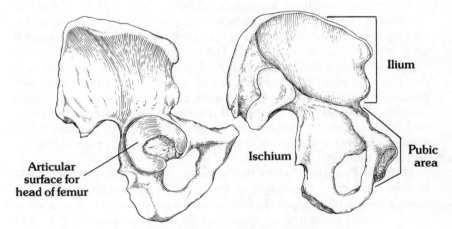

Articular surface for head of femur

Ilium

Ischium

Pubic area

Figure 15-16. Landmarks on the modern pelvis.

In a number of recent publications (i.e., 1973, 1975; Lovejoy et al., 1973) and in personal communications Dr. C. Owen Lovejoy has argued that the pelvic structure of the early hominids was better adapted to bipedalism than is the modern *Homo sapiens* pelvic structure. According to Lovejoy this is particularly true in the case of females. Given the small cranial capacities of the early hominids there would have been less conflicting pressure selecting for effective bipedalism on the one hand and a large birth canal on the other. In modern females, however, the pelvic structure is the result of adaptive pressures both for effective bipedalism and for a birth canal which can accommodate a large-brained infant. Lovejoy is of the opinion that in modern *Homo* the pressures are stronger for giving birth to large-brained infants and that the pelvic girdle adaptations for bipedalism are therefore compromised. In light of this argument the modern human male pelvis more accurately mirrors the ancestral condition than does the modern female pelvis.

> Those morphological differences between *Australopithecus* and modern man which are of mechanical significance appear to be related to the combination of a fully bipedal striding gait with different degrees of encephalization, rather than to differences in the gait pattern itself (Lovejoy et al., 1973:778).

Leg Bones. Leg bones, the **tibia** and **fibula** (Figures 15-17), uncovered at Olduvai indicate that the bipedal adaptation was well advanced in the ankle. However, it is possible that the knee joint was not fully adapted for bipedalism. The South African site at Kromdraai yielded one of the anklebones, the talus, evidencing an intermediate condition between that of *H. sapiens* and the pongids. The hominid conditions of the bone would have permitted enough stability at the ankle joint for weight-bearing in the erect posture.

The Foot (Figure 15-18). An almost complete foot skeleton, missing the toes and part of the heel, has been found at Olduvai. The foot is small and shows a remarkable anatomical resemblance to the foot of *Homo*. There is no divergence between the first and second toes typical of the pongid grasping feet. The foot does, however, differ somewhat from that of modern *Homo*, for the transmission of weight and propulsive effort through the forepart of the foot was not as fully evolved as in modern hominids. The foot bones suggest that the striding gait typical of *H. sapiens* had not evolved.

Upper Limbs (Figure 15-19). The scanty evidence indicates that the hand and upper-limb bones were not specialized for arboreal activities, as they are in modern pongids. Although little is known of the upper extremities, evidence suggests that the australopithecines possessed mobile arms and a hand with an opposable thumb capable of the finer manipulative movements needed for holding and grasping small objects. The hands could use tools, and there is no anatomical reason why they were incapable of fabricating them.

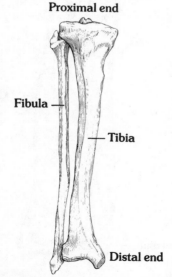

Proximal end

Fibula —

— Tibia

Distal end

Figure 15-17. Landmarks on a modern tibia and fibula.

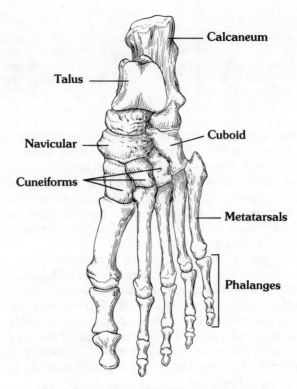

Figure 15-18. Landmarks on the modern foot.

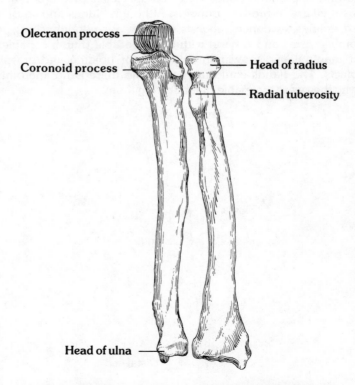

Figure 15-19. Landmarks on the modern radius and ulna.

Taxonomy

The Roots of Discord. Lower Pleistocene hominids are a morphologically diverse group, a fact indicated by the various schemes devised to accommodate them (Table 15-7). Some authorities recognize one genus *Australopithecus* containing various species. Others recognize two genera, *Australopithecus* and *Paranthropus,* with a number of species. A third group recognizes the two previous genera plus a third, the genus *Homo.* For some the only differences within the group are between robust and gracile forms, known respectively as *A. africanus* and *A. robustus.* Those recognizing the two genera of *Australopithecus* and *Paranthropus* argue that *Australopithecus* was a predatory toolmaker ancestral to *Homo; Paranthropus* was an extinct side branch of outcompeted vegetarians.[9] Those who recognize the genus *Homo* during the Lower Pleistocene argue that both *Australopithecus* and *Paranthropus* became extinct side branches leaving no progeny. Some argue that all the forms from the Lower Pleistocene should simply be placed in the genus *Homo.* Others argue that size differences within the grade do not reflect taxonomic differences but only extremes of sexual dimorphism.

One Genus **Australopithecus.** Many feel that Lower Pleistocene hominids can be accommodated within the one genus *Australopithecus* with a number of specific designations. Scientists of this persua-

[9]Dr. John Robinson (1972), the major proponent of this view, has recently suggested that the genus *Australopithecus* be dropped in favor of *Homo.* He also suggested that *Paranthropus* be included in a "parahominid" group, i.e., a group distinct from fully bipedal, erect, culture-bearing hominids.

Table 15-7. Suggested Groupings of Pliocene/Lower Pleistocene African Hominids.

	Robust Group	*Gracile Group*	Homo *Group*
Brain size	500-550 cc	450-550 cc	650-800+ cc
Dental traits	Large back teeth in relation to relatively small front teeth	Large back and front teeth	Variable; generally smaller than robust and gracile forms
Postcranial remains			Lower limbs more modern than robust forms
Locations	*A. robustus:* Swartkrans, Kromdraii *A. boisei:* Olduvai, Peninj, East Turkana, Omo, Ethiopia, Afar	*A. africanus:* Taung (?), Sterkfontein, Makapansgat, Omo (?), East Turkana (?), Ethiopia, Afar	*H. habilis:* Olduvai *Homo sp?:* Swartkrans, East Turkana, Afar triangle, Ethiopia, Laetolil
Dating	East Africa: 3,000,000-1,000,000 B.P. South Africa: no reliable dates	East Africa: 3,000,000-1,500,000 B.P. South Africa: no reliable dates	East Africa: 3,000,000-1,500,000 B.P.

Adapted from Mark. L. Weiss and Alan E. Mann, *Human Biology and Behavior, An Anthropological Perspective*, p. 189. Copyright © 1975 by Little, Brown and Company. Reprinted by permission.

sion feel that the anatomical differences are not of the same degree as those usually regarded as adequate for generic distinctions. There are differences, but such is to be expected, given the accepted time span of the group—from ca. 5 million or more years to perhaps 750,000 B.P.—and their geographical range from Ethiopia to South Africa. Such differences may only permit a broad subdivision within the two main groups. Hominids from Kromdraai, Swartkrans, Olduvai (i.e., "Zinjanthropus") and some remains from Omo and Lake Turkana appear to be larger, with more massively constructed skulls, larger jaws and teeth, and a somewhat larger cranial capacity than those from Taung, Sterkfontein, Makapansgat, Olduvai ("pre-Zinj"), and some materials from Omo and Turkana. The typical australopithecine traits are less extreme in this latter group.

One-genus adherents recognize two major species; the gracile forms are maintained in the species *A. africanus*, the robust forms in the species *A. robustus*. Of the two, *A. africanus* is smaller, lighter built, and more slender in skeletal morphology. The robust form is larger and exhibits pronounced bony ridges and crests on the skull. *A. africanus* is considered to have occurred earlier in time and be more "advanced" than *A. robustus*. However, *A. robustus* is considered to be more specialized and somewhat divergent from the main line of hominid evolution.

Dietary Hypothesis—Paranthropus vs. Australopithecus. This view was originally expounded by Dr. John Robinson who maintains that differences within the australopithecine groups warrant recognizing two genera, *Australopithecus* and *Paranthropus*.[10] Robinson feels that *Paranthropus* (which includes the robust variety) was a vegetarian and that *Australopithecus* (the gracile form) was a carnivore. The dietary habits are based upon postulated habitat differences and are reflected in dental and cranial traits. Robinson feels that *Paranthropus's* cranial architecture is related to its dental specialization.

Robinson's argument rests on the size disparity between *Paranthropus's* anterior and posterior teeth. Although many question the supposed disparity, Robinson feels the variance reflects dietary specializations. The larger canine and incisor size of the gracile form supposedly reflects its carnivorous nature, and the large molars and reduced canines and incisors of the robust form indicate its vegetarian nature. Robinson argues that *P. robustus* teeth are specialized for crushing and grinding food, supporting his contention by noting that enamel flakes were detached from the molar grinding surfaces. The enamel chipping is supposedly caused by grit adhering to the roots and tubers which supposedly formed a large portion of the *P. robustus* diet.

Robinson has unremittingly argued that something like the gracile form is the basis of later hominids. The robust form, *Paranthropus*, is a specialized offshoot which changed relatively little during its evolutionary career and eventually became extinct. The evolutionary inertia witnessed in *Paranthropus* is related to its supposedly being a nontoolmaker and probably only a nominal tool user. On the other hand, because *Australopithecus* made and used tools and most likely hunted,

[10]He (1972) recently modified this to include *Australopithecus* in the genus *Homo*.

Table 15.8.

Australopithecus: A genus of the Hominidae distinguished by the following characters:

Cranial capacity ranging from about 450 to 700 cc.

Strongly built supraorbital ridges.

A low sagittal crest in species with heavy masticatory apparatus.

Occipital condyles well behind the midpoint of the cranial length but on a transverse level with the auditory apertures.

Nuchal area of occipital bone restricted, as in *Homo.*

Consistent development of pyramidal mastoid process less striking than in *Homo.*

Jaws variable in size but often massive.

Chin absent but inner symphyseal surface relatively straight and vertical.

Dental arcade parabolic in form with no diastema.

Spatulate canines wearing down from the tip only.

Relatively large premolars and molars.

Anterior lower premolar bicuspid with subequal cusps.

Pronounced molarization of first deciduous molar.

Progressive increase in size of permanent lower molars from first to third.

Limb skeleton (so far as is known) conforming in its main features to that of modern hominids but differing in a number of details, such as smaller sacroiliac articulation and generally smaller size.

Ischial tuberosity lower than the acetabulum, unlike modern *Homo,* and oriented differently in relation to the ilium.

Adapted from Bernard Campbell, *Human Evolution,* Aldine Publishing Company, 1966.

this led to evolutionary changes culminating in *H. erectus.* The argument presumes that *Paranthropus* had an easier lot than *Australopithecus;* the struggle for existence, leaving *Paranthropus* behind in the forest, and leading to *Australopithecus'* developing on the savanna and using tools, was the stimulus leading to *Homo.*

Homo habilis. This viewpoint is most closely associated with its original proponent, Dr. Louis Leakey. In 1961 Leakey announced recovery of material from Bed I, Olduvai from a new site slightly lower than the one where the discovery of the hominid, "Zinjanthropus," had previously been announced. Leakey named his new form *Homo habilis.* Assignment of this form to the genus *Homo,* that genus to which we belong, reflects Leakey's feeling that *Homo habilis* was a precursor of modern hominids. Leakey subsequently made other finds at Olduvai which he assigned to *H. habilis.*

H. habilis has a larger brain than some of its contemporaries; its brain size has been estimated at 680 cc. It is said to have had a smoother skull, especially in comparison to robust australopithecines. The teeth are supposedly more humanlike. The modern-looking foot from Bed I is attributed to *H. habilis,* and Leakey and some others place the Bed I hand bones with the *H. habilis* type. Some material from the Omo excavations also has subsequently been assigned to *H. habilis.*

According to the supporters of *H. habilis* this form lived side-by-side with the robust australopithecines in East Africa between 1 and 2 million years B.P. Leakey argues that their head shape resembled ours, that their hands allowed manufacture of precision tools, that they walked erect, and that they built shelters. Leakey feels they represent a separate line of hominid evolution; members of this group manufactured the tools found throughout East and South African Lower Pleistocene depositions. Leakey is convinced that *H. habilis* is on the direct line to modern *Homo* and that other claimants to that position should be ignored.

Those arguing counter to Leakey and his supporters call *H. habilis* another gracile australopithecine. Some view *H. habilis* as merely an advanced member of the gracile group, a form on its way towards the next hominid evolutionary stage. A meeting of the minds is not in sight, and we must simply await further developments.

Third Hominid Model. This possibility has been proposed by Richard Leakey and some of his co-workers, and was first announced in 1972 at a meeting of the Zoological Society of London; Leakey stated, "preliminary comparisons with other evidence indicated the new material will take a central place in rethinking and re-evaluation of the evidence for the origin of *Homo sapiens,* modern man's species." Leakey's 1972 remarks were based upon materials derived from East Turkana deposits dated to approximately 2.6 million years B.P. Since the original pronouncement more materials have been described.

Leakey's original proposal for a third hominid line during the Lower Pleistocene is primarily based upon his wife's painstaking reconstruction of hundreds of skull fragments. This material is referred to as KNM (Kenya National Museum)—ER (East Rudolf) 1470. The skull fragments were found protruding from a steep slope at a level below a strata of volcanic tuff first dated at 2.6 million years B.P. Casts of the reconstructed skull yield estimates of a cranial capacity slightly over

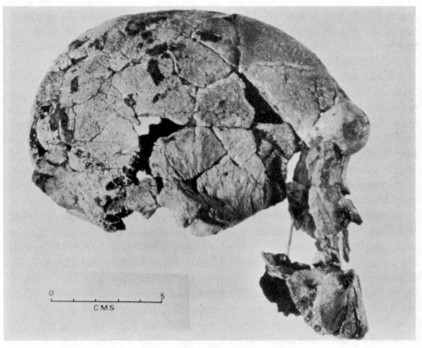

KNM-ER 1470.

800 cc, far above the *Australopithecus* range. Some, however, suggest a somewhat lower cranial capacity figure. Furthermore, the brow ridges are seen as less prominent than in *Homo erectus*. The smaller brow ridges, plus a cranial capacity overlapping the range of the early *Homo erectus*, coupled with the pre-*Homo erectus* date, throw some doubt as to the actual place of *Homo erectus* in subsequent hominid evolution. The cranial capacity of KNM-ER 1470 is larger than *Australopithecus* and *Homo habilis*, and the occiput is more rounded, the postorbital constriction is less evident, and there is no saggital cresting. It should be noted, however, that there is a robust face and palate; the teeth were also rather large.

Pebble tools and stone chips have also been recovered from the same site. The site from which the skull was uncovered, in a deposit of the same age, yielded parts of four limb bones. The limb bones are said to be morphologically consistent with an erect bipedal stance, as one would infer since the limb material discovered by Johanson from deposits of 4 million years B.P. suggest likewise.

Further discoveries from the Plio-Pleistocene sediments of East Turkana include upper and lower limb bones, several toe bones, two teeth, and a parietal fragment, plus some vertebrae and hand bones. These materials have been described by Leakey and his co-workers.

When Richard Leakey first announced the discovery of KNM-ER 1470 he stated that the new material provides "clear evidence" that, rather than evolving from *Australopithecus,* a "large brained, truly upright and two-legged form of the genus *Homo* existed contemporaneously with *Australopithecus* more than 2.5 million years ago." He further states that "while the skull is different from our species, *Homo sapiens*, it also is different from other known forms of early man and thus does not fit into any of the presently-held theories of human evolution."

There is no doubt that 1470 is different, and Leakey and his co-workers present an interesting case for other materials from East Turkana. However, are any of the anatomical features so different from corresponding parts of previously known forms that they could not fall within the range of population variability? Whatever the resolution of the problem, Leakey's new materials add more fuel to the fires of controversy, and it is becoming increasingly clear that the picture of hominid evolution is more complicated than we once thought.

Richard Leakey recently announced (*Newsweek,* 1976 and personal communication) the discovery of other remains from Lake Turkana. Included within this material is an upper part of a skull and a hipbone. Leakey feels that this skull is a "dead ringer" for 1470. If this proves true, then 1470 can no longer be dismissed as a single specimen—as a form with an abnormally large brain.

It is crucial to the maintenance of R. Leakey's scheme that there be no doubts as to the dating of ER 1470. For example, if the material should fall later in time than the australopithecine material, then this could help explain its "advanced" traits, e.g., large cranial capacity, lack of brow ridges, etc. It is of importance, therefore, that a recent dating of the Koobi Fora Formation at East Turkana conflicts with the originally published date of 2.6 million years B.P. for 1470 (Curtis et al., 1975). Some of the first to raise questions about the 2.6 million year date for the KBS tuff were paleontologists, for faunal remains from the tuff did not compare favorably with remains from other, supposedly well-calibrated localities.

Curtis et al. (1975) redated the KBS tuff using the conventional K/Ar dating method. Utilizing pumice, the investigators received an age of 1.60 plus or minus 0.05 million years for nine analyses and 1.82 plus or minus 0.04 million years on six other analyses. Although this new dating is inconclusive, as was the original date, there now seems to be further question concerning the appropriate time span, and therefore the true importance, of KNM-ER 1470. By the same token, further finds such as Dr. M. Leakey's new *Homo* lend credence to Richard Leakey's claims. Clearly, we are still unable to read and understand Lower Pleistocene hominid evolution.

In October, 1975 Dr. Mary Leakey announced the recovery of new fossils which were potassium-argon dated between 3.5 and 3.75 millions years B.P. The fossil material falls in between these two dates. The new site is approximately 25 miles south of Olduvai Gorge and has been known for some time; however, these materials are the first important hominid fossils to be recovered. In total, the material consists of jaws and teeth of eleven individuals. The two most complete remains consist of a child's mandible and the mandible of an approximately 15-year-old individual. Dr. Leakey refers this material to the genus *Homo* and notes a similarity between it and the 1470 material of her son, Richard Leakey.

Hominids Outside Africa

The early hominids may have extended beyond Africa, a possibility based on dental comparisons and jaw fragments attributed to the Javan form "Meganthropus paleojavanicus." Besides anatomical similarities, further suggestive evidence comes with redating. "Meganthropus" was originally assumed to be from the Lower Middle Pleistocene. Recently, however, the layer underlying the "Meganthropus" deposit has been dated to ca. 1.9 million years B.P., placing it within the australopithecine time span.

The early hominids existed from perhaps as far back as 8 or 9 million years to slightly under 1 million years ago, primarily in Africa. The East African forms seem to predate those in South Africa. The early hominids are a morphologically diverse group and, depending upon whose interpretation one follows, some members of the group gave rise to the next hominids, *H. erectus*. Some members of the group made and used tools, and some hunted. They lived in relatively small, bisexual, male-dominated groups, probably averaging twenty-five members.

The remarkable quantity of Lower Pleistocene materials conforms with a taxonomic position within the Hominidae and some members of the group appear to be the immediate evolutionary precursors of *H. erectus*.

Bibliography

Anonymous. 1969. History and the Omo Valley. *Nature* 223:1199.

Ashton, E. 1950. The endocranial capacities of the australopithecinae. *Proceedings of the Zoological Society of London* 120:715.

Birdsell, J. 1968. Some predictions for the Pleistocene based on equilibrium systems among recent hunter-gatherers. In *Man the hunter,* edited by R. Lee and I. DeVore, pp. 229-49. Chicago: Aldine.

Bishop, W. 1976. Pliocene problems relating to human evolution. In *Human origins: Louis Leakey and the East African evidence,* edited by G. Isaac and E. McCown, pp. 139-154. Menlo Park, Calif.: W. A. Benjamin.

Brain, C. 1957. New evidence for the correlation of the Transvaal ape-man-bearing cave deposits. *Proceedings of the Third Pan-African Congress on Pre-history,* pp. 143-48.

————. 1967a. Bone weathering and the problem of bone pseudo-tools. *South African Journal of Science* 63:97.

————. 1967b. Hottentot food remains and their bearing on the interpretation of fossil bone assemblages. *Scientific Papers Namib Desert Reserve Station* no. 32:1.

————. 1968. Who killed the Swartkrans ape-man? *South African Museums Association Bulletin* 9:127.

————. 1970. The South African australopithecine bone accumulation. *Transvaal Museum Memoir* 18.

Broom, R. 1925a. Some notes on the Taungs skull. *Nature* 115:569.

————. 1925b. On the newly discovered South African man-ape. *Natural History* 34:409.

————. 1936. A new ancestral link between ape and man. *Illustrated London News,* p.476.

Broom, R., and Robinson, J. 1949. A new type of fossil man. *Nature* 164:322.

————. 1952. Swartkrans ape-man. *Transvaal Museum Memoir* 6.

Broom, R., and Schepers, F. 1946. The South African fossil ape-men, the Australopithecinae. *Transvaal Museum Memoir* 2.

Butzer, K. 1971. Another look at the australopithecine cave breccias of the Transvaal. *American Anthropologist* 73:1197.

————. 1974. Paleoecology of South African australopithecines: Taungs revisited. *Current Anthropology* 15:367.

Campbell, B. 1968. The evolution of the human hand. In *Man in adaptation: the biosocial background,* edited by Y. Cohen, pp. 128-30. Chicago: Aldine.

————. 1966. *Human evolution: an introduction to man's adaptations.* Chicago: Aldine.

Carney, J.; Hilne, A.; Miller, J.; and Walker, A. 1971. Late australopithecine from Baringo District, Kenya. *Nature* 230:509.

Clark, W. Le Gros. 1967. *Man-apes or ape-men?* New York: Holt, Rinehart and Winston.

————. 1964. *The fossil evidence for human evolution.* Chicago: University of Chicago Press.

Cole, S. 1975. *Leakey's luck.* London: Collins.

Coon, C. 1962. *The origin of races.* New York: Alfred A. Knopf.

Curtis, G., and Evernden, J. 1962. Age of basalt underlying Bed I, Olduvai. *Nature* 115:195.

Curtis, G.; Drake, T.; and Hampel, A. 1975. Age of KBS tuff in Koobi Fora Formation, East Rudolf, Kenya. *Nature* 258:395-98.

Dart, R. 1925a. *Australopithecus africanus:* the man-ape of South Africa. *Nature* 115:195.

————. 1925b. The word "Australopithecus" and others. *Nature* 115:875.

————. 1925c. The Taungs skull. *Nature* 116:462.

————. 1926. Taungs and its significance. *Natural History* 26:315.

————. 1949. The predatory implemental technique of *Australopithecus. American Journal of Physical Anthropology* 7:1.

————. 1953. The predatory transition from ape to man. *International Anthropological and Linguistic Review* 1:201.

————. 1956. Myth of the bone-accumulating hyena. *American Anthropologist* 58:40.

————. 1957. The osteodontokeratic culture of *"Australopithecus prome-theus."* *Transvaal Museum Memoir* 10.

————. 1958. Bone tools and porcupine gnawing. *American Anthropologist* 60:715.

————. 1959. *Adventure with the missing link.* New York: Viking Press.

————. 1960. The bone tool manufacturing ability of *"Australopithecus prometheus."* *American Anthropologist* 62:134.

————. 1971. On the osteodontokeratic culture of the Australopithecinae. *Current Anthropology* 12:233.

Day, M., and Napier, J. 1964. Hominid fossils from Bed I, Olduvai Gorge, Tanganyika: fossil foot bones. *Nature* 201:969.

Day, M., and Wood, B. 1968. Functional affinities of the Olduvai hominid 8 talus. *Man* 3:440.

Esses, R., and Goodard, J. 1967. Prey selection and hunting behavior of the African wild dog. *Journal of Wildlife Management* 31:52.

Frisch, J. 1965. *Trends in the evolution of the hominid dentition.* Basel: S. Karger.

Goodall, J. 1965. Chimpanzees of the Gombe Stream Reserve. In *Primate behavior,* edited by I. DeVore, pp. 425-73. New York: Holt, Rinehart and Winston.

Gregory, W. 1949. The bearing of the Australopithecinae upon the problem of man's place in nature. *American Journal of Physical Anthropology* 7:485.

Hay, R. 1963. Stratigraphy of Beds I through IV, Olduvai Gorge, Tanganyika. *Science* 139:829.

Heiple, K., and Lovejoy, C. 1971. The distal femoral anatomy of *Australopithecus.* *American Journal of Physical Anthropology* 10:179.

Hockett, C., and Ascher, R. 1964. The human revolution. *Current Anthropology* 5:135.

Holloway, R. 1972. Australopithecine endocasts, brain evolution in the Homin-oidea, and a model of hominid evolution. In *The functional and evolutionary biology of primates,* edited by R. Tuttle, pp. 185-203. Chicago: Aldine-Atherton.

Howell, F. 1968. Omo research expedition. *Nature* 219:567.

————. 1969. Remains of hominidae from Pliocene/Pleistocene formations in the lower Omo basin, Ethopia. *Nature* 223:1234.

————. 1972. Pliocene/Pleistocene hominidae in eastern Africa: absolute and relative dates. In *Calibration of hominoid evolution,* edited by W. Bishop and J. Miller, pp. 331-68. Edinburgh: Scottish University Press.

Hughes, A. 1954. Hyenas versus Australopithecines as agents of bone accumu-lation. *American Journal of Physical Anthropology* 12:467.

————. 1958. Some ancient and modern observations on hyenas. *Koedoe* 1:105.

Isaac, G., and McCown, E., eds. 1976. *Human origins: Louis Leakey and the East African evidence.* Menlo Park, Calif.: W. A. Benjamin.

Isaac, G.; Leakey, R.; and Behrensmeyer, A. 1971. Archeological traces of early hominid activities east of Lake Rudolf, Kenya. *Science* 173:1129.

Kurtén, B. 1972. *Not from the apes.* New York: Pantheon Books.

Leakey, L. 1958. Recent discoveries at Olduvai Gorge, Tanganyika. *Nature* 181:1099.

————. 1959. A new fossil skull from Olduvai. *Nature* 184:491.

————. 1960a. The affinities of the new Olduvai australopithecine. *Nature* 186:458.

————. 1960b. Recent discoveries at Olduvai Gorge. *Nature* 188:1050.

———. 1960c. Finding the world's earliest man. *National Geographic* 118(3): 421.

———. 1963. Very early East African hominidae and their ecological setting. In *African ecology and human evolution,* edited by F. Howell and F. Bourliere, pp. 448-57. Chicago: Aldine.

———. 1965. Facts instead of dogmas in man's origin. In *The origin of man,* edited by P. DeVore, pp. 3-17. New York: Wenner-Gren Foundation.

———. 1966. *Homo habilis, Homo erectus* and the australopithecines. *Nature* 209:1279.

———. 1967. *Olduvai Gorge, Vol. 1: 1951-1961, a preliminary report on the geology and fauna.* Cambridge: Cambridge University Press.

Leakey, L.; Evernden, J.; and Curtis, G. 1961. Age of Bed I, Olduvai Gorge, Tanganyika. *Nature* 191:478.

Leakey, L.; Tobias, P.; and Napier, J. 1964. A new species of the genus *Homo* from Olduvai Gorge. *Nature* 202:7.

Leakey, M. 1971. *Olduvai Gorge, vol. 3. Excavations in Beds I and II, 1960-63.* Cambridge: Cambridge University Press.

———. 1976. A summary and discussion of the archaeological evidence from Bed I and Bed II, Olduvai Gorge, Tanzania. In *Human origins: Louis Leakey and the East African evidence,* edited by G. Isaac and E. McCown, pp. 431-60. Menlo Park, Calif.: W. A. Benjamin.

Leakey, M.; Clarke, R.; and Leakey, L. 1971. A new hominid skull from Bed I, Olduvai Gorge, Tanzania. *Nature* 232:308.

Leakey, R. 1970. In search of man's past at Lake Rudolf in Kenya. *National Geographic* 137:712.

———. 1971. Further evidence of Lower Pleistocene hominids from East Rudolf, North Kenya. *Nature* 231:241.

Leakey, R., and Isaac, G. 1972. Hominid fossils from the area east of Lake Rudolf, Kenya: photographs and a commentary on context. In *Perspectives on human evolution,* edited by S. Washburn and P. Dolhinow, pp. 129-41. New York: Holt, Rinehart and Winston.

———. 1976. East Rudolf: an introduction to the abundance of new evidence. In *Human origins: Louis Leakey and the East African evidence,* edited by G. Isaac and E. McCown, pp. 307-32. Menlo Park, Calif.: W. A. Benjamin.

Lee, R., and DeVore, I., eds. 1968. *Man the hunter.* Chicago: Aldine.

Lovejoy, C. O. 1973. The gait of australopithecines. *Yearbook of Physical Anthropology* 17:147-61.

———. 1975. Biomechanical perspectives on the lower limb of early hominids. In *Primate functional morphology and evolution,* edited by R. Tuttle, pp. 291-327. The Hague: Mouton.

Lovejoy, C. O.; Heiple, K.; and Burstein, A. 1973. The gait of *Australopithecus.* American Journal of Physical Anthropology 38:757-80.

McKinley, K. 1971. Survivorship in gracile and robust australopithecines: a demographic comparison and a proposed birth model. *American Journal of Physical Anthropology* 34:417.

Mann, A. 1975. *Paleodemographic aspects of the South African australopithecines.* Philadelphia: University of Pennsylvania Press.

Mitchell, G., and Brandt, E. 1972. Paternal behavior in primates. In *Primate socialization,* edited by F. Poirier, pp. 173-206. New York: Random House.

Napier, J. 1962a. Fossil hand bones from Olduvai Gorge. *Nature* 196:409.

———. 1962b. The evolution of the human hand. *Scientific American,* December, p. 56.

Oakley, K. 1957. Tools makyth man. *Antiquity* 31:199.

Patterson, D.; Behrensmeyer, A.; and Sill, W. 1970. Geology and fauna of a new Pliocene locality in Northwestern Kenya. *Nature* 226:918.

Patterson, D., and Howells, W. 1967. Hominid humeral fragment from the early Pleistocene of Northwestern Kenya. *Science* 156:64.

Payne, M. 1965. Preserving the treasures of Olduvai Gorge. *National Geographic* 126:194.

Pfeiffer, J. 1969. *The emergence of man.* New York: Harper & Row, Publishers.

Pilbeam, D. 1972. *The ascent of man.* New York: Macmillan Co.

Poirier, F. 1968. Analysis of a Nilgiri langur (*Presbytis johnii*) home range change. *Primates* 9:29.

———. 1969. The Nilgiri langur (*Presbytis johnii*) troop: its composition, structure, function and change. *Folia Primatologica* 10:20.

———. 1970. Nilgiri langur ecology and social behavior. In *Primate behavior: developments in field and laboratory research,* edited by L. Rosenblum, pp. 251-383. New York: Academic Press.

———. 1972a. Introduction. In *Primate socialization,* edited by F. Poirier, pp. 3-28. New York: Random House.

———. 1972b. Nilgiri langur behavior and social organization. In *Essays to the chief,* edited by F. Voget and R. Stephenson, pp. 119-34. Eugene: University of Oregon Press.

———. 1974. Colobine aggression: a review. In *Primate aggression, territoriality and xenophobia,* edited by R. Holloway, pp. 46-59. New York: Academic Press.

———. 1977. *Fossil evidence: the human evolutionary journey.* St. Louis: Mosby.

Reynolds, V. 1965. Open groups in hominid evolution. *Man* 1:441.

Robinson, J. 1952. The australopithecines and their evolutionary significance. Proceedings of Linnean Society of London 3:196.

———. 1954. The genera and species of the australopithecines. *American Journal of Physical Anthropology* 12:181.

———. 1963a. Australopithecines, culture and phylogeny. *American Journal of Physical Anthropology* 21:595.

———. 1963b. Adaptive radiation in the australopithecines and the origin of man. In *African ecology and human evolution,* edited by F. Howell and F. Bourliere, pp. 385-416. Chicago: Aldine.

———. 1966. The distinctiveness of *Homo habilis. Nature* 209:957.

———. 1972. *Early hominid posture and locomotion.* Chicago: University of Chicago Press.

Schaller, G. 1972. *The Serengeti lion: a study of predator-prey relations.* Chicago: University of Chicago Press.

Schaller, G., and Lowther, G. 1969. The relevance of carnivore behavior to the study of the early hominids. *Southwestern Journal of Anthropology* 25:307.

Stekelis, M.; Picard, L.; Schulman, N.; and Haas, G. 1960. Villafranchian deposits near Ubeidiya in the central Jordan Valley; preliminary report. *Bulletin of the Research Council of Israel* 9-G(4):175.

Sugiyama. 1972. Social characteristics and socialization of wild chimpanzees. In *Primate socialization,* edited by F. Poirier, pp. 145-63. New York: Random House.

Taieb, M.; Johanson, D.; and Coppens, Y. 1975. Expédition internationale de l'Afar, Ethiopie (3e campagne, 1974); découverte d'hominides Plio-Pléistocènes à Hadar. *Comptes rendus des séances de l'Academie des Sciences* 1297-1300.

Tobias, P. 1965. *Australopithecus, Homo habilis,* tool-using and toolmaking. *South African Archaeological Bulletin* 20:167.

————. 1966. Fossil hominid remains from Ubeidiya, Israel. *Nature* 211:130.

————. 1967. *Olduvai Gorge,* vol. 2. Cambridge: Cambridge University Press.

————. 1971. *The brain in hominid evolution.* New York: Columbia University Press.

————. 1972. Progress and problems in the study of early man in sub-Saharan Africa. In *The functional and evolutionary biology of primates,* edited by R. Tuttle, pp. 63-94. Chicago: Aldine-Atherton.

Weiss, M., and Mann, A. 1975. *Human biology and behavior: an anthropological perspective.* Boston: Little, Brown.

Wohlberg, D. 1970. The hypothesized osteodontokeratic culture of the Australopithecines: a look at the evidence and the opinions. *Current Anthropology* 11(1):3.

Wolpoff, M. 1970. The evidence for multiple hominid taxa at Swartkrans. *American Anthropologist* 72:576.

Chapter 16
Homo erectus

Homo erectus lived from approximately 250,000 or 300,000 to 700,000 to 750,000 years B.P. during the Middle Pleistocene geological epoch. A major feature of Middle Pleistocene hominid evolution is an elaboration of cultural adaptations. By the time of *Homo erectus* the story of hominid evolution is increasingly that of culture. Middle Pleistocene hominids led the same kind of hunting and gathering life characteristic of many modern populations, but their tool categories were less complex. Because of similarities to modern populations, they are included in the genus *Homo*.

Discovery of *H. erectus* Remains

E. Dubois. The first Middle Pleistocene fossil hominids appeared in 1891 when a Dutch physician Eugene Dubois reported the discovery of a skull, thigh bones, and several bone fragments from Trinil, a site on the Solo River in Central Java (Figure 16-1). Early in his career Dubois joined the Dutch Colonial Service and traveled to Java hoping to uncover the "missing link." Three years before, in 1889, the German biologist Ernst Haeckel had postulated a theoretical ancestral hominid line. Haeckel had only fragmentary information with which to work; the only well-known remains were discovered twenty years previously in the Neander valley of Germany. Haeckel suggested that the hominid line began among some extinct Miocene apes and reached *Homo sapiens* by way of an imagined group of "ape-man" (termed "Pithecanthropi") and a more advanced but speechless early hominid (termed "Alali"). He visualized the latter as the ancestral stock of modern populations.

Applying Haeckel's terminology to the bones he uncovered, Dubois established the genus "Pithecanthropus." Since the thigh bones resembled those of modern *Homo*, Dubois concluded that his "ape-man" walked erect in the fashion of *H. sapiens*. He named his genus and species "Pithecanthropus erectus," or "erect ape-man." The

Skull and restored head of "Java Man" ("Pithecanthropus erectus").

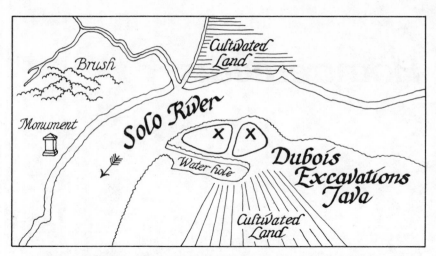

Figure 16-1. The two sites on the Solo River where Dubois found fossils of *Homo erectus* are marked on this map, based on a sketch in the Dubois family collection. The monument shown at the left was built in honor of the event.

generic name was eventually dropped and the form renamed *Homo erectus* in the 1960s. Dubois' contention that he had recovered an ancestral hominid had a poor reception at first because scientists hesitated to accept the association of an archaic skullcap with a relatively modern femur. This discouraged Dubois to the extent that he finally hid these bones, and others, beneath his dining room floor, and by the time most of the scientific world did finally accept his claims Dubois had given up and died still unconvinced of the importance of his discovery.

Other Javanese Remains. Other Javanese sites have yielded Middle Pleistocene fossil materials; between 1936 and 1939 workers identified a fossil deposit at Sangiran very similar to the fossiliferous beds at Trinil. Material from an older layer, the Djetis faunal beds, originally called "P. erectus II" was remarkedly similar to Dubois' original find. The material from the Djetis beds, "Meganthropus paleojavanicus," was discussed in the last chapter. Dating for the Trinil and Djetis faunal beds has been nettlesome. The Trinil beds are K/Ar dated to about 710,000 years and the Djetis beds about 2 million years B.P.

Chinese Remains. China has yielded fossils comparable to those from Java. In the 1920s and 1930s an international team digging at Chou Kou Tien about 25 miles from Peking uncovered the remains of approximately forty individuals associated with tools, evidence of fire, thousands of animal bones, and much fossilized pollen. The hominid remains were first put into the taxon "Sinanthropus pekinensis"; however, their similarity to the Javan hominids led to abandonment of the taxon. The material is now considered a subspecies of the Javanese *H. erectus* and is classified *H. erectus pekinensis*. The Chou Kou Tien remains consist of skullcaps, teeth, jaws, and some postcranial material; however, they lack faces, as does the Javan material. In line with their supposed date of 350,000 to 400,000 years B.P., remains from the lower cave at Chou Kou Tien are more modern looking than their Javanese cousins.

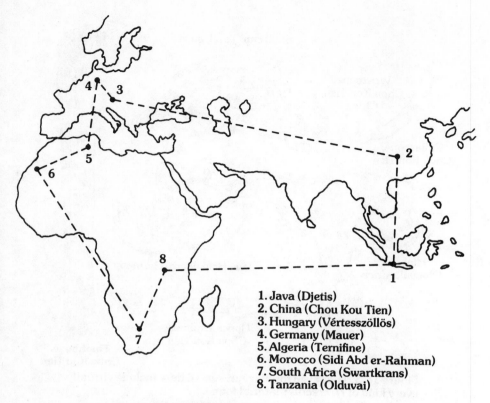

1. Java (Djetis)
2. China (Chou Kou Tien)
3. Hungary (Vértesszöllös)
4. Germany (Mauer)
5. Algeria (Ternifine)
6. Morocco (Sidi Abd er-Rahman)
7. South Africa (Swartkrans)
8. Tanzania (Olduvai)

Figure 16-2. Distribution of *Homo erectus* sites.

Other Remains. Based on remains recovered prior to World War II, with the exception of the isolated Mauer or Heidelberg jaw, the *H. erectus* population appeared to be strictly an Asian group. However, post-World War II discoveries significantly added to the picture of Middle Pleistocene hominid distribution. Remains were found in South and East Africa, Europe, Asia (Figure 16-2), and the Middle East.

Morphology (Figure 16-3)

Dental and Cranial Traits. The morphological characters of *Homo erectus* are sufficiently consistent and distinctive to justify their inclusion in the genus *Homo*; however, they differ from modern *Homo* in a number of details. The species *erectus* is characterized by a cranial capacity of between 750 and 1200 cc.[1] There is marked flattening, or **platycephaly**, of the *H. erectus* skull vault and the *erectus* face is characterized by large brow ridges above the eye orbits. Behind the brow ridges the skull is marked by postorbital constriction which in modern populations is elevated because of an increasing brain size. A sagittal ridge highlights the skull's midline; the cranial bones are thick; the nasal bones are flat and the face more prognathic than in modern populations..

The heavily built *H. erectus* mandible lacks a chin. The teeth are larger than those of modern populations and possess a well-developed

[1]The mean capacity for all twelve Asian skulls is 929 cc. Javan forms average 70 cc less, e.g., 859 cc, and the Chinese forms 114 cc more, e.g., 1043 cc.

Homo erectus

279

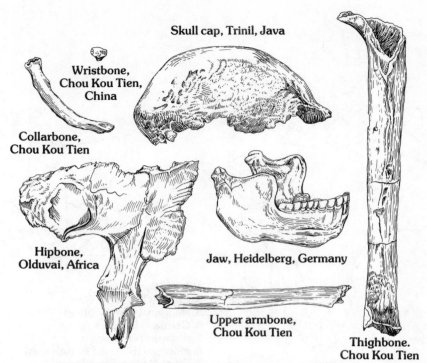

Figure 16-3. The seven fossils represented here include virtually every kind of *H. erectus* material found.

enamel ring about the base of the tooth (a basal cingulum). The canines are sometimes slightly projecting, but as among earlier hominids the dental arcade is modern and forms a parabolic arch. The limb bones are essentially modern.

Although there is a general consensus that *H. erectus* is ancestral to *H. sapiens*, this does not mean that any of the now-known *H. erectus* populations are ancestral to modern *H. sapiens*, although there is a possibility of a direct line in Africa and possibly Java. The assumption that *H. erectus* is ancestral to *H. sapiens* is based on the following criteria: (1) Morphologically *H. erectus* conforms very well with the theoretical postulates for an intermediate stage in the evolution of later hominids. (2) The existence of *H. erectus* in the early part of the Pleistocene, antedating any well-authenticated *H. sapiens*, provides it with an antiquity conforming well with its supposed phylogenetic relations. (3) Some *H. erectus* materials illustrate a satisfactorily graded series of morphological changes from one type to another.

Review of Sites

Java. Asian Middle Pleistocene sites are restricted to China and Java with the oldest known remains coming from Java. Java, among other islands of western and northern Indonesia, received invasions of Pleistocene animals from both India and China. The Djetis faunal beds are the oldest Javan beds. Besides the "Meganthropus" remains,[2] there is one specimen consisting of the back of a skull plus the palate and teeth

[2]The size of the "Meganthropus" molar teeth led F. Weidenreich to postulate that a giant race of hominids once roamed about Asia. He considered *Gigantopithecus* a member of this group.

(except the incisors) known as "Pithecanthropus IV" (or P-IV); two fragmentary mandibles; and the skullcap of an infant, called *H. modjo-kertensis*. All these fossils are probably *H. erectus*. The overlying Trinil faunal beds (the source of the original "Pithecanthropus"), contain fauna largely of South Chinese origin. As might be expected from the time separation, there are morphological differences between forms from the two beds.

The Trinil faunal beds contain examples of the earliest Javan tools, named the Patjitanian, which are crude but clearly worked flake materials. These are technically advanced over earlier tools found in Malaysia, called Anyathian, which are not associated with hominid remains.

China—Chou Kou Tien. Until recently most Chinese representatives of *H. erectus* came from Chou Kou Tien which has long been the haunt of "dragon-bone" collectors whose finds supplied many Chinese drugstores. In the early 1900s a German paleontologist, K. A. Herberer, found a human tooth in a Chinese drugstore and for the next twenty-four years various scientists, having traced the tooth back to Chou Kou Tien, worked or watched the site. In 1921 they found bits of quartz. Since animals neither eat nor use quartz, and since quartz has no business in a limestone cave, it was recognized as a tool. More quartz tools were subsequently recovered.

Human teeth were sifted from the Chou Kou Tien debris in 1923 and 1926; in 1927 the Swedish paleontologist B. Böhlin produced one more tooth. This was given to Davidson Black, professor of anatomy at Peking University, who allocated the tooth to a new hominid taxon "Sinanthropus pekinensis." That winter Black took the tooth, carried on a key chain, on world tour.

From 1927 to 1937 the site was worked under the direction of W. C. Pei and the French theologian, philosopher, and paleontologist Père Teilhard de Chardin. Before excavations were completed this team was joined by Dr. Franz Weidenreich, who subsequently described all but one of the original skulls. The Chinese government resumed work in the 1950s, recovering an additional skull in 1959.

The Chou Kou Tien *H. erectus* deposits (known as Locality 1) yielded the remains of about forty individuals, including fourteen skulls, twelve mandibles, 147 teeth, and some cranial remains. The material was mostly fragmented; however, there was enough to allow for rather complete reconstruction. Early in World War II, at the commencement of the Japanese occupation, all the skulls were mysteriously lost; nothing remains of the original material but a fine set of casts made in the basement of the University Museum in Philadelphia, a lone tooth in Sweden, and a new Chinese mandible and skull. Weidenreich also wrote a complete and fine set of detailed monographs. Recent attempts have been made to locate the "Sinanthropus" material and perhaps some of the original finds will yet be found. (Shapiro [1971] recounts attempts to relocate the material.)

Much faunal material was associated with the *H. erectus* remains; deer bones were most numerous, an indication that venison formed a substantial part of the *H. erectus* diet. Also found among the debris were numerous elephant, rhinoceros, and giant beaver remains. Quantities of broken and splintered bones indicate that they had been split for their marrow. High and low in the deposit were layers of ash and burnt bone; perhaps these were hearths where hunters sat and cooked their meat.

Scattered among the bones were evidences of a few hominid trunk and limb bones and cranial pieces. Many facial and jaw fragments were present, but these were separated from the braincase. The case has been made that Peking Man was a cannibal. If so, cannibalism then, as today, was probably ritualistic;[3] human meat was probably never an important element of the human diet.[4]

Numerous stone tools were uncovered from Locality 1 (Figure 16-4). Since there are no nearby quartz hills, the tools were either carried or traded into the cave. The characteristic tool is a pebble trimmed to make an edged blade. Many of the stone tools are large and crudely worked; few display an even, uniform edge. Some tools may have been used to work animal skins which might have been worn or used as enclosure walls to keep out the cold. *H. erectus* at Chou Kou Tien also made bone tools.

A review of *H. erectus* culture at Chou Kou Tien suggests the following: (1) Fire was a basic item, for there are substantial amounts of charcoal and burned bone. (2) The favorite food seems to have been venison; some 70 percent of the animal bones belong to deer. (3) Fruits (such as the hackberry, a relative of the wild cherry), were consumed. (4) "Peking Man" learned to live in northern temperate climatic conditions. (5) "Peking Man" was possibly a cannibal.

Lantian Material. A second important Chinese site is at Chenchiawo in Lantian District, Shensi Province, where a mandible was recovered in 1963. In 1964 at Kungwangling Hill (20 kilometers away) facial fragments, a tooth, and a good skullcap were recovered; the material apparently came from the same individual. Both sites predate Chou Kou Tien and may be contemporaneous with the Javan Djetis faunal beds. The older date of the Lantian materials is consistent with

---

[3]Among modern groups, cannibalism is usually practiced in burial rites (see Chapter 23) consuming the brain of a vanquished foe, and when food is short, such as the cases reported recently in Alaskan and South American plane crashes.

[4]Evidence supporting this is found in a 1970 article by Drs. S. Garn and W. Block entitled "Limited Nutritional Value of Cannibalism."

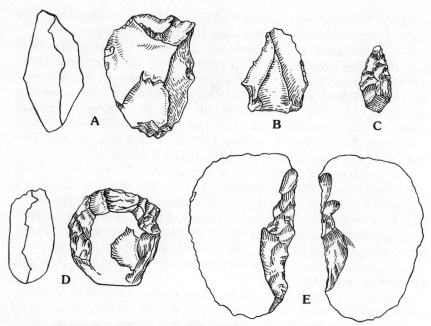

Figure 16-4. Tools from "Sinanthropus" beds at Chou Kou Tien. (A) Small chopping tool. (B) flake. (C) Point. (D) Chopper. (E) Cleaverlike tool.

their more primitive morphology; the jaw is more robust than Chou Kou Tien. In many respects the skull recalls the Djetis material—it is low and thick with massive brow ridges. The cranial capacity is approximately 780 cc, close to that of the Djetis skull. Lantian is the first fossil evidence congenitally lacking the third molar, a condition known as agenesis.

The Chinese paleontologist Dr. Woo feels that the Lantian material is of a female and is morphologically closely allied with Chou Kou Tien. However, he notes some differences, which he feels call for a new specific designation. He classifies the material "Sinanthropus lantianensis"; most other paleontologists prefer the designation *H. erectus lantianensis.*

Asian H. erectus Compared. The close phylogenetic relationship between the Javan and Chinese material is expressed by retaining all the material in the same genus and species, *Homo erectus.* The most recent Asian material is from Locality 1 at Chou Kou Tien. The major differentiating features are in the skull and teeth; the cranial capacity of "Peking Man" is larger and its teeth smaller than preceding *H. erectus* forms. Asian *H. erectus* populations did not differ postcranially, approaching modern populations in their postcranial anatomy.

All the Asian forms had equally thick skulls and all had large brow ridges. There are, however, major differences in brain size. The mean capacity of the Javan material is estimated at ca. 975 cc or slightly less; the Lantian material at 780 cc; and the Locality 1 material at 1075 cc. Because of sexual dimorphism, values for males are higher than those of females.

Europe. Until recently, European *H. erectus* populations were scarcely known, and even now we have more cultural than osteological remains. The northwest quadrant of the Old World yields most of the skeletal remains; however, there are still large, serious gaps.

Mauer Mandible. The first, and some argue only, *H. erectus* osteological remains from Europe is the Heidelberg or Mauer mandible from the Mauer sands in Germany. After a twenty-year vigil, it was uncovered in 1907 from a sandpit in the village of Mauer six miles southwest of Heidelberg. It lay seventy-eight feet below the surface in deposits dated to about 360,000 years B.P. The Mauer mandible is approximately the same age as *H. erectus* from Locality 1 at Chou Kou Tien and the *H. erectus* finds from Ternifine in North Africa.

The chinless Mauer mandible is well preserved; most of the teeth are moderately worn. The mandible is large and massive, one of the largest yet found; its most striking characteristic is the great breadth of the ascending ramus, the vertical strut of bone underlying the back of your cheekbone which carries at its posterior corner the condyle articulating the jaw with the skull. The width of the ascending ramus is undoubtedly related to mandibular length and suggests powerful, efficient jaw muscles.

Because of the large mandibular size, one might expect to find large teeth. However, while the teeth are not unduly large, they are not small and their size is not proportionate with that of the mandible. Tooth size approaches more closely that of modern rather than Asian *H. erectus* populations.

Beyond guessing that it possessed a wide, not strongly projecting face, we can't reconstruct the Heidelberg skull. Despite its large size, the jaw and teeth reflect Heidelberg's inclusion in the genus *Homo*. The Heidelberg material is most often assigned to the taxon *Homo erectus heidelbergensis*. However, some refer it to a primitive species of *H. sapiens*.

Vértesszöllös. Other possible European *H. erectus* populations have recently come to light. Sixty years after the Mauer discovery, an *occipital* bone and some deciduous teeth were uncovered from Vértesszöllös, a site dating to 400,000 years B.P. located west of Budapest, Hungary. Vértesszöllös appears to have been a campsite in a small saucer-like depression which seems to have been inhabited during the cool seasons of the year, perhaps because of its proximity to a hot spring. Many pebble tools were collected in and around the site; these pebble tools are the first undisputed early European tools. The occipital bone was recovered during dynamiting at the site, but no other skull parts were recovered. Charred bone indicates use of fire.

This material represents the oldest cranial evidence from Europe. The bone is rather thick and possesses a well-marked nuchal ridge for neck muscle insertion; nevertheless, some investigators feel that the bone represents a more advanced population than *H. erectus*. One of the cranial capacity estimates is 1400 cc, well above *H. erectus* and within the range of modern populations. Some classify the occipital bone within the species *H. sapiens*, distinguishing it as a subspecies *palaeohungaricus*, i.e., *H. s. palaeohungaricus*. This would place a progressive *H. sapiens* contemporaneously with the *H. erectus* populations of about 400,000 years ago. The possibilities are: (1) the occipital bone might represent the back of Heidelberg's head, or (2) it may represent a direct forerunner of later *H. sapiens* populations, or (3) it may be a member of that population.

Přezletice. Another European hominid fossiliferous site is Přezletice near Prague, Czechoslovakia. The site was first recognized in 1938 as a result of quarrying operations; it was excavated in the early 1960s and has yielded a tiny molar fragment and approximately fifty stone implements. On faunal comparisons, Přezletice may turn out to be one of the oldest European hominid sites. On the basis of the time period, the scanty hominid remains are referred to the *H. erectus* populations; but much more information is badly needed.

Petralona. The Petralona skull was discovered from a Greek cave (Petralona) in 1959. This skull is the first of its kind found in the Balkan peninsula. The skull, encrusted with limestone, is in an excellent state of preservation. First reports confused the skull with Neanderthal materials and it was assigned a late Pleistocene date. However, recent work on the cave's fauna indicates that it is not later than the Riss Glacial, and, in fact, may date to Pre-Mindel. If this earlier dating stands, the skull may be contemporaneous with the Heidelberg mandible (Howells, 1973).

Morphologically the skull is large; however, cranial capacity estimates are disputed. While estimates of 1440 cc and 1384 cc have been proposed, Howells (1973) feels an estimate of 1220 cc is more proper. Hemmer (1972) feels that in skull shape and brain size Petralona conforms with *H. erectus*. The skull is not yet fully cleaned and described; however, Howells (p. 78) feels that "...from its size and form it appears to rate as a moderately advanced specimen in the whole *H. erectus* spectrum, and one differing from the Olduvai and Far Eastern examples...." The Petralona skull might prove to be a most interesting specimen when fully described, for its possible early date and "advanced" features might fit well with the supposed "advanced" traits of Vértesszöllös.

New material has only recently been announced in Greece. An elephant and stone weapons dated to 700,000 years come from the sandhill plains of Kozani-Ptolemaida in northern Greece. According to the Greek anthropologist Poulianos the elephant remains were evidence of a kill. The elephant was cut in half and one half was dragged off. This is similar to the pattern to be discussed at the Torralba-Ambrona site in Spain.

In addition to various primitive stone implements, two so-called stone weapons described as looking like something between a sledge hammer and a human fist were recovered. Poulianos said there were clear signs of deliberately made hand-grips on them. The weapons were apparently used in killing animals in the hunt.

Torralba and Ambrona—Big-Game Hunters. European *Homo erectus* left substantial evidence of its cultural way of life. Major cultural remains have recently been uncovered from France and Spain; neither area, however, yields hominid skeletal remains. That *H. erectus* was pursuing a hunting way of life is evident at the Spanish sites of Torralba and Ambrona, originally uncovered in the late 1800s during laying of a pipeline. They were dug by an amateur archeologist who published a preliminary paper on the findings. Many years later Dr. F. C. Howell discovered the paper and began digging in 1961.

Ambrona Valley was part of a major animal migration route for large herds of deer, horses, and elephants. Torralba and Ambrona are open-air sites (that is, they are out in the open) which served primarily as

Homo erectus

285

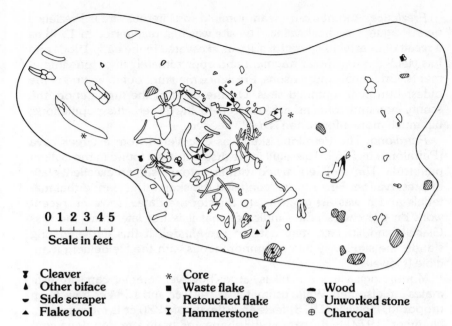

⌇ Cleaver	**✳ Core**	
▲ Other biface	**▪ Waste flake**	**⏜ Wood**
⤙ Side scraper	**• Retouched flake**	**⬙ Unworked stone**
▲ Flake tool	**⚡ Hammerstone**	**⊕ Charcoal**

Figure 16-5. The living floor at Torralba.

butchering and killing stations. Detailed stratigraphic and pollen analysis yields a date of 300,000 years B.P.—somewhat later than Chou Kou Tien. The chronological and tool record indicates that a *H. erectus* population visited this area, perhaps seasonally, to hunt game and gather plant foods (Figure 16-5).

The enormous quantity of elephant bones at Torralba and Ambrona is intriguing and suggests that these elephants were hunted and butchered at the site. The remains belong to a now extinct straight-tusked form which is somewhat larger than modern African elephants. Remains of about thirty elephants, twenty-five horses, twenty-five deer, ten wild oxen, and six rhinoceroses are concentrated in a relatively small area. One 270 square foot area contained the left side of a large adult elephant with tusks and bones in place; the head and pelvis are missing. There are also four flake tools, indicating that the elephant was butchered at the site.

Why was the elephant cut in such fashion; why was half the body missing? Perhaps the elephant was caught in a muddy swamp, struggled to get free, and when it finally fell exhausted on its side it was killed and butchered. How did the elephant get into the swamp—did it blunder in or was it herded in? Torralba lies in a steep-sided valley where the water level rises to within a few inches from the surface and where animals would be mired in mud. The terrain 300,000 years ago was even wetter. Perhaps hunting bands stood upon the high ledges overlooking the valley, following the herd movements. Perhaps a young and unwary animal wandered from the herd and found itself caught in the mud; it would be relatively easy to run down the hill and make the kill.

Possibly the hunters played an active role by driving the animals into the swamp. Howell has collected much material showing evidence of burning. Charred materials are scattered about the site and not distributed in a manner suggestive of a hearth; whoever was lighting the fires was apparently burning grass and brush over an extensive area. This evidence, plus the elephant remains in the swamps, suggest that fires were deliberately set to drive animals into the swamps. Once mired in mud they were relatively defenseless.

At Ambrona, Howell uncovered a killing and butchering site where elephant remains abound. One area included most of the skeleton of an enormous bull elephant; judging by wear on the molar teeth the animal was undoubtedly old. Its bones were distributed in an unusual manner; a tusk along with two disjointed femora and tibiae were strung together in a line. One possible explanation is that the bones served as a bridge across the muddy area to firmer ground.

There are indications of living structures at Ambrona. Workers found what may be a hearth and nearby were three grapefruit-sized stones resembling parts of a circle or stone ring. Similar stone rings come from Torralba; these might be part of a conical, tepeelike structure. Modern Eskimos build similar shelters by hanging hides from a central pole and arranging stones in a circle to hold the hides in place.

Torralba and Ambrona yielded a rich and varied tool collection indicating a wide range of daily subsistence activities (Figure 16-6). Some stone tools probably served for heavy duty chopping and hacking, others for skinning, slicing meat, and perhaps woodworking. There is also a large collection of other tools. These tools appear at an earlier time in the archaeological record than many previously expected, and they signify the early appearance of a relatively advanced technology.

There are a number of bone tools at Torralba, making it one of the very few sites where undoubted bone tools have come from a living floor. Some tools appear to be duplicates of more familiar stone implements; the function of some of these is unknown. There are also wooden tools, waterlogged implements which somehow survived in the clay, boggy deposits. Marks of use and working have also survived. A few pieces might have served as spears; these are the oldest known weapons, invented early in the history of hunting.

The high proportion of elephant bones at Torralba and Ambrona raises some intriguing questions. Why did the hunters seemingly choose elephants over other migratory animals? Was the choice motivated by a simple straightforward matter of obtaining meat, or was there something ritualistic about it? Were the elephants venerated—remember the lack of elephant heads—where are they? The few recovered cranial remains were smashed and the ten pound brain exposed; was the brain simply a delicacy, or was some ritual involved? Was the brain consumed in a religious ceremony and was there an elephant cult similar to the bear cults of certain aboriginal tribes? These questions are still to be answered.

Terra Amata. Rather recently, Henry de Lumley (1973) discovered a Middle Pleistocene site in southern France (Figure 16-7), located on a hillside on the French Riviera on a dead-end street called Terra Amata (beloved land). The site, known as Terra Amata, was uncovered during clearing for a shipyard and the construction of luxury apartments. Beginning 28 January 1966 and continuing until 5 July of the same year, 300 workers spent 40,000 manhours excavating the site. The excavated area encompasses 144 square yards and includes twenty-one separate living floors. The excavation proceeded using only

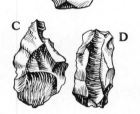

Figure 16-6. An Acheulean tool kit from Torralba, Spain, includes (A) a 10-inch quartzite cleaver, (B) a small flint cleaver, (C) a screwdriver-ended piece in chalcedony and (D) a double-edged sidescraper made of jasper.

Homo erectus

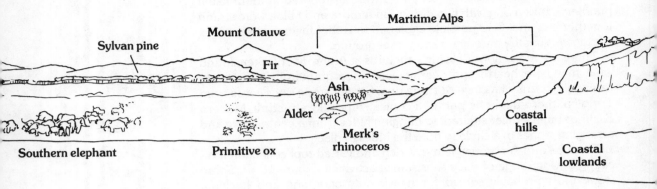

Sylvan pine

Mount Chauve

Maritime Alps

Fir

Ash

Alder

Merk's rhinoceros

Coastal hills

Southern elephant

Primitive ox

Coastal lowlands

trowels and brushes; the digging uncovered 35,000 objects, the location of each of which was plotted on 1200 charts. Casts were made of 108 square yards of living floor and the progress documented by 9000 photographs.

Superimposed living floors were uncovered in three separate locales; four are on a beach section formed by a sandbar, six on the beach, and eleven on a dune island. On the slopes of an ancient sand dune, de Lumley uncovered remains of a number of oval huts ranging from 26 to 49 feet long and 13 to 20 feet wide. They may have housed ten to twenty people. Perhaps the huts were made of sturdy branches, bent to interlock at the top, with an entrance at one end and a hole in the top for ventilation. Presumably the branches were supported by posts and rocks placed against them.

A hearth located at the center was a basic feature of each hut. These hearths are either pebble-paved or shallow pits, a foot or two in diameter, scooped from the sand. A little stone wall standing at one end of the hearth may have served as a wind screen. Areas closest to the hearths are cleared of debris, perhaps indicating that persons slept there. This practice is common among Australian aborigines and other hunting groups.

Terra Amata yielded no hominid skeletal remains; however, there are two indirect clues of the inhabitants. An imprint of a right foot, nine and a half inches long, is preserved in the sand. From the imprint the person is estimated to have been five feet, one inch tall. Another source of evidence for human habitation is fossilized feces (**coprolites**), analysis of which indicates that the sites were seasonally occupied in early summer and spring. These were seasonal camping sites, as were Torralba and Ambrona.

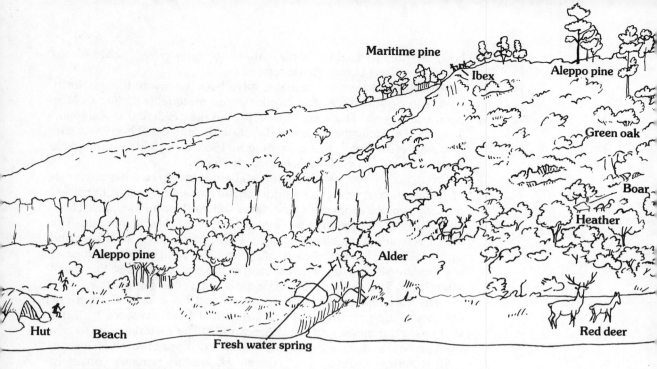

Figure 16-7. Terra Amata and its environs about 400,000 years B.P. This site was ideal for the early hunters as it had a sheltered beach with fresh water, game, and vegetation near at hand.

Animal bones uncovered at Terra Amata include bird, turtle, and eight species of mammalian skeletal remains. There is abundant evidence that the inhabitants were big-game hunters; in order of their abundance, the inhabitants preferred stag, extinct elephant, wild boar, ibex, and Merck's rhinoceros. Most remains are those of young animals who were undoubtedly easiest to bring down. There are also indications that the inhabitants ate oysters, mussels, and limpets and the presence of fish bones and vertebrae indicates that they also fished.

The Terra Amata inhabitants left many traces of their tools; most stone tools are referred to as early Acheulean. Some tools were locally manufactured; the hut floors evidencing toolmaking activity. The toolmaker's place within the hut is indicated by a patch of living floor surrounded by a litter of tool-manufacturing debris. Ground impressions may have been places where they sat, sometimes perhaps on skins.[5] There are a few bone tools; one elephant leg bone was hammered to a point. A pointed bone fragment was probably fire hardened; one end of a third fragment was smoothed by wear, while still another may have served as an awl and some fragments may have been scrapers.

Some domestic furnishings have been uncovered. Flattened limestone blocks may have provided convenient surfaces for sitting or breaking bone on. A spherical imprint in the sand, perhaps an impression of a wooden bowl, would constitute the earliest trace of a container yet uncovered. This imprint is filled with a whitish substance. In a corner, near the "bowl," excavators found lumps of the natural pigment red ocher. Some of these lumps were worn smooth and pointed like pencils at the end, indicating that they may have been used to color the

[5]At another French site, Lazaret cave, dated to approximately 130,000 years B.P., there is an indication that the inhabitants slept on seaweed beds.

Homo erectus

body in preparation for some ceremony. Similar red ocher lumps derive from later Upper Pleistocene sites.

Africa. Homo erectus remains have been uncovered from North, East, and South Africa. The North African material is limited to Morocco and Algeria. There are four Moroccan sites: Sidi Abd er-Rahman,[6] Temara (or Smuggler's Cave), Rabat, and Tangiers. The oldest site, Sidi Abd er-Rahman, was excavated in 1953 and yielded a mandible associated with an evolved Acheulean industry.

Smuggler's Cave, near Temara, is about thirty-three miles northeast of Casablanca. Among some undescribed hominid remains, there was a nearly complete mandible associated with artifacts of the final Acheulean industry. The material resembles other North African remains. The Rabat remains were blasted out in 1933; portions of the lower and upper jaws and braincase are all that remain of what was once probably a complete skull. The remains date to the end of the last European interglacial. The Tangiers material consists of a child's upper jaw.

The Ternifine remains were recovered in 1954 and 1955, from a rich site in a sandpit southeast of Oran, Algeria. Faunal evidence indicates that this is the oldest northwest African site. The material consists of a right parietal and three lower jaws resembling those of Asian *H. erectus*.

East Africa—Olduvai. East African *H. erectus* remains consist of material from Olduvai and Lake Turkana and cultural associations from Olorgesailie. Approximately fifteen to twenty feet below the sur-

[6]The word "Sidi" indicates a Muslim holy man; the site was a cemetery for Muslim holy men.

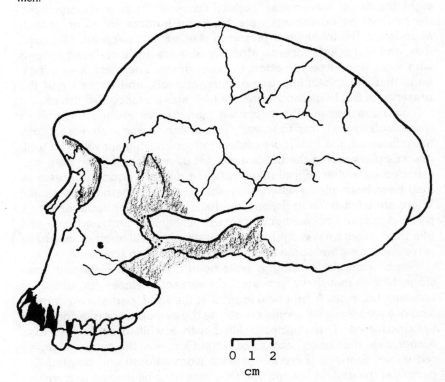

0 1 2
cm

Figure 16-8. *Homo erectus* (Lake Turkana).

face of Bed II at Olduvai, near the margin of an ancient lake, Louis Leakey recovered the skullcap of a hominid labelled Olduvai hominid 9, or "Chellean Man." Some 100 yards away lay numerous hand axes and abundant mammalian remains; the long bones were apparently split for their marrow. The remains are dated to the Middle Pleistocene. The skull resembles those from the Far East; unfortunately there is no face.

Artifactual and skeletal remains have recently been recovered from Bed IV, Olduvai. A left femoral shaft and hip bone of *H. erectus* have been found in association with an Acheulean industry. This is the first direct association at Olduvai of a well-defined tool assemblage with *H. erectus* remains. Most tools are hand axes resembling those of the Early Acheulean series of Middle Bed II. Dr. M. Leakey has recently announced a new date of 700,000 years B.P. for Bed IV.

Femoral and pelvic remains were found during the 1970 excavations. This discovery (christened Olduvai hominid 28) is of the greatest importance because it sheds light on the structure and function of Middle Pleistocene hominid lower limbs. Functionally, the alternating pelvic tilt mechanism of striding bipeds was well established during the Middle Pleistocene. The center of gravity was approximately as in modern bipeds; the weight of the upper body was transferred to the pelvis in a manner consistent with upright bipedalism. There are also indications that powerful knee extension was possible. Olduvai hominid 28 was an habitual biped; however, some have suggested that it may not have been as efficient as you and I.

Dr. Mary Leakey has recently discovered a fossilized foot print and finger marks at Olduvai dating at least 500,000 years B.P. The prints were associated with a number of shallow pits. The footprint, perhaps

Louis Leakey and the Discovery of Homo erectus at Olduvai

Another accidental discovery of the greatest importance took place in 1961—the find of remains of the same type of man as in China and Java, but twice as old in East Africa as in the Far East. This time the accident was due to an error on the part of one of my staff. The geologist working with me returned to camp one day with a draft plane table map of a certain part of the Gorge. I looked at it and said, "But you have left out one long narrow side gully." He replied, "I have not," and I said, "I am sorry, but you have; come over with me tomorrow morning and I will show you."

When we got to the long and rather grass and bush filled gully, and he had to admit that he was in error, I looked back towards our camp site and suddenly on the far side of the Gorge I saw a very small area of exposed fossil beds. . . .

Although I had explored Olduvai on foot since 1931 I knew, at once, that I had never set foot in that tiny exposure. But for the error on the part of my student which had taken me back to the point from which I saw it, I might still never have seen it. . . . As soon as we got back to camp, I went off again to locate this hidden patch of exposures, and as I walked on to it I almost trod on a half exposed fossil human skull. That was the first *Homo erectus* skull from Olduvai.

From: The UNESCO Courier, August-September, 1972. p. 29

Homo erectus

from a child's left foot, was found along with finger marks and about a dozen supposedly hand-scooped pits in the sand.

Olorgesailie Occupation Remains. From Olorgesailie, in the Rift Valley about an hour's drive from Nairobi, Leakey and Isaac discovered an extensive *H. erectus* living site. The Olorgesailie occupation areas appear to have been discrete patches of stone and bone accumulations which may have coincided with natural boundaries such as the bank of a sandy runnel or the limit of shade provided by a large tree. The inhabitants could have built shelters, e.g., hedges, which disappeared over time. Smaller occupation areas may have held four or five adults in a group; larger areas may have accommodated over twenty adults. Based on the accumulation of a ton or more of stone artifacts and **manuports** (materials carried into the site, but which do not necessarily show use), it is estimated that the sites were continuously occupied for two to three months.

The abundance and appearance of faunal remains make it obvious that the inhabitants were hunters and scavengers. Large mammalian remains predominate and there is a superabundance of a large, extinct baboon at one site. Rodent, bird, and reptilian bones are relatively scarce. Most bone material is splintered; either the inhabitants pulverized the bone or scavengers moved in after they left camp. One area appears to be a hippopotamus butchery site.

Within one oval-shaped occupation area, nineteen by thirteen meters, the excavators found 1000 kilos (2200 pounds) of stone artifacts, rubble, and unmodified cobbles. The abundance of bones of an extinct baboon attests either to continued extremely successful hunting or to a massacre of a single troop. (The present-day Hadza of Tanzania surprise a troop of sleeping baboons and club them to death.) There is scant evidence as to the hunting methods of the Olorgesailie inhabitants; however, hunters lacking such weapons as bows may have killed a large number of baboons by drugging them at a water hole.

There is no evidence of fire at Olorgesailie, as is true of all East African Middle Pleistocene sites. This may be due to the fact that charcoal is poorly preserved in well-drained soils often characteristic of open sites. In contrast with other East African sites, there is no human skeletal material.

Olorgesailie provides the following insights into Middle Pleistocene hominid social life. The inhabitants lived in groups of four to thirty adults, the smaller number probably results from temporary splitting from a relatively stable band of twenty to thirty members. The sites are either seasonal occupation grounds, or they suggest a sectional differentiation of labor. The inhabitants subsisted on hunted or scavenged food, or they partook in the systematic killing of baboons.

Richard Leakey has recently announced (*Newsweek*, 1976 and personal communication) the recovery of *Homo erectus* from Lake Turkana. The remains, the most complete *Homo erectus* skull yet discovered, was reconstructed by Dr. A. Walker of Harvard. The skull looks almost identical with *Homo erectus* from Chou Kou Tien. Quite unpredictably, however, the Lake Turkana material dates to 1.5 million years. If this older date stands, then we will certainly need a redating of the Chinese material. Furthermore, the new material suggests a far older antiquity of *Homo erectus* than usually assumed.

Hominid-Land Relationships — How to Get By

Site Distribution. The distribution of Middle Pleistocene cultural evidence suggests that major tropical African settlements were in open or lightly wooded country in close proximity to water. Asian and European sites are often in caves, suggesting a cooling of the climate and the appearance of cultural adaptations facilitating life under such conditions.

Middle Pleistocene sites take the appearance of areal tool and bone concentrations; some parts of such "cultural floors" were primarily used for toolmaking, others for butchering. Various site patterns indicate they were seasonally occupied or that several groups temporarily and contemporaneously occupied the site. The lack of appreciable thickness to the "floors" indicates their ephemeral nature.

Technology. Middle Pleistocene hunting technology shows an improvement over that of the Early Pleistocene. Small mammals are relatively scarce among the faunal remains and records of offensive weapons are meager, which may reflect a greater reliance on non-preservable implements such as wooden spears, clubs, or throwing sticks. Many stones associated with the faunal remains could have been utilized as throwing weapons. With this limited tool inventory, it is not surprising that fossils are frequently found in lake beds; perhaps a major hunting method was to kill bogged-down animals driven into swamps or lakes. Whatever the method, group hunting was well established.

Middle Pleistocene hominids occupied various habitats, ranging from African savannas and open woodlands to temperate woodlands and forest-tundra. Hominid populations were adapting by the use of fire, shelters, and probably some kind of clothing. The lack of evidence for hominid activity in tropical rainforests may be due, among other things, to poor preservation conditions.

"When *Homo erectus* Tamed Fire, He Tamed Himself"

This subtitle is from an article by J. Pfeiffer (1971) which first appeared in the *New York Times Magazine* in 1966. Fire has always had a place in our lives; as the first natural "domesticated" force, it represented a kind of biological declaration of independence. Outside Africa, fire and *H. erectus* are synonymous. With purposeful use of fire, early hominids began to shape the world according to their design; by bringing fire into their living space, *H. erectus* carved zones of light and warmth out of darkness where they enjoyed relative freedom from predation. Fire opened new living areas, lighting and warming damp, dark caves where many *H. erectus* remains occur. Fire, by changing our living habits, may have indirectly altered the brain's structure and enhanced our ability to learn and communicate. The oldest hearth remains come from the 750,000 year old Escale cave in southern France. At a depth of forty-five feet excavators uncovered proof of deliberately made fires—traces of charcoal, ash, fire-cracked stone, and five reddened hearth areas up to a yard in diameter.

Why was fire used? Fire was of minimal value while we remained in our tropical African homeland; however, as it grew colder, as we migrated north, fire may have provided warmth. Fire was probably originally obtained from such ready-made sources as volcanic eruptions, brush fires, or gas and oil seepages. Hunters may have camped near

Homo erectus

293

fire, which was a natural resource like game, water, and shelter. When they moved they may have taken smouldering embers with them; each band may have had a fire-bearer responsible for keeping the flame. From the beginning fire may have been used to keep predators away. Perhaps we became regular cave dwellers only after we learned to use fires to drive predators from the cave.

Fire for Hunting. Fire was used in hunting and Torralba strongly suggests that hunters used fire to stampede their prey. Fire may also have been used to produce more effective spears; Australian aborigines, for example, fire harden the tips of their digging sticks. Fire hardens the core and makes the outer part crumbly and easier to sharpen. A possible fire-hardened spear from Germany dates to approximately 80,000 years B.P.

Fire for Cooking. Cooking may have originated during *H. erectus* times, an assumption based upon indirect dental evidence. The molar teeth, mainly used for grinding, tended to remain large until *H. erectus* times; then they began to reduce, presumably as an indirect response to eating cooked food. Regular cooking may have helped reshape facial contours, presumably because cooked food requires less strain

---

Table 16-1.

Homo: *A genus of the Hominidae distinguished by the following characters:*

A large cranial capacity with a mean value of more than 1100 cc, a considerable range of variation, from about 700 cc to almost 2000 cc.

Masticatory apparatus variable in size but relatively smaller than the neurocranium when compared with *Australopithecus* and much reduced in modern *H. sapiens*; accompanying changes involve flattening of face.

Forward movement of occipital condyles in relation to skull as a whole.

Reduced masticatory musculature with temporal ridges never reaching the midline of the cranial vault, their height being variable.

Nuchal area relatively smaller than in *Australopithecus*, variable, and in *Homo sapiens* much reduced.

Skull more rounded, and muscular attachment areas in general variable in size but less well marked than in *Australopithecus,* and in modern *Homo* almost imperceptible.

Supraorbital torus variably developed, being enlarged in *Homo erectus,* though with reduced postorbital construction compared with *Australopithecus*; torus much reduced in some subspecies of *Homo sapiens*.

Dental arcade evenly rounded, usually with no diastema.

Mandible less deep than in *Australopithecus* but variable in its horizontal stressing, from an internal torus in *Homo erectus* to an external chin in many subspecies of *Homo sapiens*.

Canines relatively small, no overlapping after the initial stages of wear.

First lower premolar bicuspid (P3) with a reduced lingual cusp.

Molar teeth variable in size, with a relative reduction of M3.

Forelimb shorter than hindlimb.

Pollex well developed and fully opposable, so the hand is capable of a precision grip.

Hindlimb skeleton seems not to be very variable and is fully adapted to bipedal locomotion, as in modern *Homo*.

Adapted from Bernard Campbell, *Human Evolution,* Aldine Publishing Company, 1966.

Table 16-2. Brief Review of *Homo erectus* Sites (details in text)

Geographical Area	Remains*	Pleistocene Dating*
Asia		
Lantian, China	human remains	Middle Pleistocene
Java (Djetis, Trinil Faunal Beds)	human remains	Middle Pleistocene
Chou Kou Tien, China	human remains, artifacts, fire	Middle Pleistocene
India, Malaysia (?)	possibility of tools	Middle Pleistocene (?)
Africa		
Lake Turkana, Kenya	human remains	Lower Pleistocene
Olduvai Gorge, Bed IV, Tanzania	human remains, artifacts	Middle Pleistocene (?)
Omo, Ethiopia	human remains	Middle Pleistocene (?)
Olorgesailie, Kenya	artifacts, living site	Middle Pleistocene
North Africa (Morocco, Algeria, Tunisia)	human remains, artifacts	Middle Pleistocene
South Africa	human remains	Middle Pleistocene
Europe and Balkans		
Přezletice, Czechozlovakia	artifacts, human molar crown	Middle Pleistocene
Vértesszöllös, Hungary	human remains, artifacts	Middle Pleistocene
Mauer or Heidelberg, Germany	human remains	Middle Pleistocene
Petralona, Greece	human remains	Middle Pleistocene
Torralba/Ambrona, Spain	artifacts, fire, hunting	Middle Pleistocene
Terra Amata, France	artifacts, dwelling structures	Middle Pleistocene

*Rather than complicate the chart, the details of the remains, the artifacts and associated materials, and the exact dating of the materials are provided in the text.

on the jaws and supporting musculature. Jaw reduction affected skull design, the massive brow ridges reduced along with the masticatory muscles. The skull itself became thinner, which may have eased the way for brain expansion.

Results of Fire Use. Psychological changes may have accompanied the use of fire; cooking may have produced behavioral restraint, that is, control of a tendency to do things on the spur of the moment. Inhibition is a mark of evolutionary advance. Cooking of meat suggests that less food is eaten on the spot and more carried back to the camp. If the assumption that food sharing requires elaborate social rules is correct, then the more there was to share, the more rules were needed. A continuing elaboration of the communication matrix would be in order.

Fire may have helped change fundamental life rhythms; with the advent of fire perhaps we broke away from a 12-hour cycle of sleeping and waking. Preserving and feeding the fire requires a number of "anticycle" acts. Perhaps certain band members stayed awake during the night to tend the flames or aroused themselves periodically to make sure all was safe.

Introducing fire into the living spaces created a day independent of the sun's movements for light and heat; evening hours could be illumi-

Table 16-3. Middle Pleistocene Tool Assemblages from Locales in sub-Saharan Africa.

Locale	Choppers	Spheroids	Light Duty Tools	Heavy Duty Tools	Lrg. Cutting Tools	Misc.	Utilized/Modified	Total
Cornelia, S. Af.	2	3	1	1	1	–1	1	239
Amanzi, Area 2, Surface 1, S. Af.	1	–1	3		3	1	–1	1621
Kabwe, Surface 3, Zambia	1	2	4		1		–1	164
Kalambo Falls, Site B, Surface 5, Zambia	1	–1	2	1	4	–1	–1	6696
Isimilia, Lower J6, J7, Tanzania	1	–1	3	–1	3	–1	–1	1781
Isimilia, J12			1	–1	6	–1	–1	290
Isimilia, Lower H15	2		1	2	2	–1	–1	633
Olorgesailie, Land-surface 7DE/89B	1	–1	1	–1	5	–1	–1	5059
Olorgesailie, Land-surface 1	–1		6	–1	–1	–1	–1	850
Olduvai, Bed IV Site WK	1	1	1	1	3	1	2	494
Olduvai, Upper Bed II Site BK	1	2	2	–1	–1	1	–1	6801
Olduvai, Upper A Bed II Site TK, Upper	–1	3	3	–1	–1	1	–1	5180
Peninj, RHS Totals, Kenya	–1	3	1	2	3	1	–1	235
Olduvai, Middle Bed II MNK Main	2	3	1	–1	–1	1	–1	4399
Olduvai, Middle Bed II EF-HR	1	1	–1	–1	4	–1	–1	522

Legend: The numbers roughly equal the percentage of each category at the locale.

–1 under 10%; 2 20%; 3 30%; 4 40%; 5 50%; 6 60%.

Adapted from J. D. Clark, "African origins of Man the Toolmaker," in Glynn Ll. Isaac and Elizabeth R. McCown (eds.), *Human Origins: Louis Leakey and the East African Evidence*, copyright © 1976 by W. A. Benjamin, Inc., Menlo Park, California.

nated and one's attention turned to productive pursuits. Extra time could be utilized to think about complex hunting plans, migration routes, and so on. There is also the role of fire in the early religious ceremonies. Prehistoric hunters carrying torches entered the deepest cave recesses and here performed religious acts; these are recorded as early as 30,000 years B.P. Fire-obsession may be of ancient origin; fire may be a stimulant as potent as drugs in arousing visions and as such it would have served early religious functionaries.

Homo erectus cultural associations are elaborations of earlier Lower Pleistocene activities. Some morphological features distinguishing *H. erectus* from earlier hominids, e.g., changes in brain size, facial morphology, and dental structure, may be correlated with cultural elaboration. If culture is the basis of the hominid adaptation, then natural selection furthered a more efficient culture. An enlarged brain is related to increasing capacity for complex cultural skills and behavior. Cultural and physical evolution went hand-in-hand.

Unlike preceding hominids, *H. erectus* was distributed throughout the Old World. The *H. erectus* grade represents a level of cultural adaptation that allowed its possessors to expand into new once inhospitable environments. It has been suggested that because of geographical spread and because of varying environmental conditions, the origin of modern racial groups can be dated to Middle Pleistocene hominid expansion. However, this suggestion lacks proof.

H. erectus is probably the intermediate evolutionary grade between the Lower Pleistocene hominids and *H. sapiens*. Evidence in Africa and Europe shows that *H. erectus* and earlier *H. sapiens* forms were evolving contemporaneously. The best evidence suggests that *H. erectus* arose in Africa or Java. The line from *H. erectus* to *H. sapiens* is hazy, but fragments can be seen in Africa, China, and Europe. In Europe, for example, it is suggested that the Mauer jaw belonged to a representative of an *H. erectus* population which perhaps gave rise to a population such as Vértesszöllös then to Steinheim and Swanscombe. The latter two or three may be *H. sapiens* subspecies.

Bibliography

Anonymous. 1952. Early man's first fire. *Science Digest* 51:29.

Black, D. 1931. On an adolescent skull of "Sinanthropus pekinensis" in comparison with an adult skull of the same species and with other hominid skulls. *Paleontologia Sinica*, Series D7.

Brace, C. 1962. Cultural factors in the evolution of human dentition. In *Culture and the evolution of man*, edited by A. Montagu, pp. 343-54. New York: Oxford University Press.

Butzer, K. 1964. Environment and archeology. Chicago: Aldine.

Campbell, B. 1966. *Human evolution: an introduction to man's adaptations*. Chicago: Aldine.

Chance, M., and Jolly, C. 1971. *Social groups of monkeys, apes and men.* London: Jonathan Cape.

Chang, K. 1962. New evidence on fossil man in China. *Science* 136:749.

Clark, J. 1976. African origins of man the toolmaker. In *Human origins: Louis Leakey and the East African evidence,* edited by G. Isaac and E. McCown, pp. 1-53. Menlo Park: W. A. Benjamin.

Coon, C. 1962. *The origin of races.* New York: Alfred A. Knopf.

Day, M. 1971. Postcranial remains of *Homo erectus* from Bed IV, Olduvai Gorge, Tanzania. *Nature* 232:383.

de Lumley, H. 1969. A Paleolithic camp at Nice. *Scientific American,* May, p. 150.

de Lumley, H., and de Lumley, M. 1973. Pre-Neanderthal human remains from Arago Cave in southeastern France. *Yearbook of Physical Anthropology* 17:162-69.

Eiseley, L. 1954. Man the firemaker. *Scientific American,* March, p. 52.

Fejfar, O. 1969. Human remains from the early Pleistocene in Czechoslovakia. *Current Anthropology* 10:170.

Garn, S., and Block, W. 1970. The limited nutritional value of cannibalism. *American Anthropologist* 72:106.

Hemmer, F. 1972. Notes sur la position phyletique de l'homme de Petralona. *L'Anthropologe* 76:155-62.

Howell, F. 1960. European and northwest African Middle Pleistocene hominids. *Current Anthropology* 1:195.

_____. 1965. *Early man.* New York: Time-Life Books.

Howells, W. 1966. *Homo erectus. Scientific American,* May, p. 46.

_____. 1973. *Evolution of the genus Homo.* Reading, Mass.: Addison-Wesley.

Isaac, G. 1968. Traces of Pleistocene hunters: an East African example. In *Man the hunter,* edited by R. Lee and I. DeVore, pp. 258-61. Chicago: Aldine.

Jacob, T. 1967. Recent "Pithecanthropus" finds in Indonesia. *Current Anthropology* 8:501.

Kretzoi, M., and Vertés, L. 1965. Upper biharian (intermindel) pebble-industry occupation in western Hungary. *Current Anthropology* 6:74.

Kummer, H. 1971. *Primate societies.* Chicago: Aldine-Atherton.

Kurtén, B. 1972. *Not from the apes.* New York: Pantheon.

Leakey, M. 1971. Discovery of postcranial remains of *Homo erectus* and associated artifacts in bed IV at Olduvai Gorge, Tanzania. *Nature* 232:380.

Mann, A. 1971. *Homo erectus.* In *Background for man,* edited by P. Dolhinow and V. Sarich, pp. 161-81. Boston: Little, Brown.

Oakely, K. 1955. Fire as a Paleolithic tool and weapon. *Proceedings of the Prehistoric Society* 21:36.

_____. 1961. On man's use of fire, with comments on tool-making and hunting. In *Social life of early man,* edited by S. Washburn, pp. 176-93. Chicago: Aldine.

Pfeiffer, J. 1969. *The emergence of man.* New York: Harper & Row.

_____. 1971. When *Homo erectus* tamed fire he tamed himself. In *Human variation,* edited by H. Bleibtreu and J. Downs, pp. 193-203. Beverly Hills, Calif.: Glencoe Press.

Poirier, F. 1977. *Fossil evidence: the human evolutionary journey.* St. Louis: Mosby.

Sartono, S. 1972. Discovery of another hominid skull at Sangiran, central Java. *Current Anthropology* 13:124.

Sauer, C. 1961. Sedentary and mobile bents in early societies. In *Social life of early man,* edited by S. Washburn, pp. 256-66. Chicago: Aldine.

Semenov, S. 1964. *Prehistoric technology.* London: Cory, Adams and McKay.

Shapiro, H. 1971. The strange, unfinished saga of Peking man. *Natural History* 80:74.

Soriano, M. 1970. The fluoric origin of the bone lesion in the "Pithecanthropus erectus" femur. *American Journal of Physical Anthropology* 32:33.

Tobias, P. 1971. *The brain in hominid evolution.* New York: Columbia University Press.

Weidenreich, F. 1943. The skull of "Sinanthropus pekinensis." *Paleontologia Sinica,* New Series D 10.

Woo Ju-Kang. 1964. Mandible of "Sinanthropus lantianensis." *Current Anthropology* 5:98.

Chapter 17
Middle Pleistocene Hominids and the Neanderthals

When, where, and how did the transition from *H. erectus* to *H. sapiens* occur? The closer one comes in time to modern *Homo*, the easier it should be to find the answer; however, this has not been true. The ancestral line, or lines, leading to modern populations, become hazy approximately 300,000 years ago. Some of the possible genetic routes will now be discussed.

The Middle Pleistocene fossil record is rather complete both in fossil materials and conflicting interpretations. This fossil record (Table 17-1) is often divided into Second interglacial forms, including Swanscombe and Steinheim, Third interglacial forms from France, Italy, and Germany, and the Würm glacial inhabitants, the Neanderthals.

The Neanderthal's role in subsequent hominid evolutionary history has always been disputed. Some rule them out of our lineage while others make them direct ancestors; and there are other viewpoints. The argument one follows rests with one's interpretation of Second and Third interglacial fossil remains. This chapter discusses the controversy.

Second Interglacial Hominids

Swanscombe. The fossil record from approximately 200,000 to 300,000 years B.P. is rather meager. However, during the second interglacial period, about 200,000 to 250,000 years B.P., tantalizing remains appear in England and Germany. The site at Swanscombe, England, is now a gravel pit along the Thames River located not far from London. However, Swanscombe seems once to have been a favorite hunt-

Shanidar flower burial, Iraq.

Table 17-1. Middle Pleistocene Fossil Record (includes only forms discussed here).

Würm Glacial Forms

Form	Location
"Classic Neanderthals" or Western European Neanderthals	France, Spain, Southwestern Europe
Central and Eastern European Neanderthals	Czechoslovakia, Hungary
Eastern or "Progressive" Neanderthals	Israel, Lebanon, Turkey, Iraq
"Neanderthaloids"	Java, China, Borneo, Zambia, South Africa
Saccopostore	Italy
Quinzano	Italy

Third (Riss-Würm) Interglacial Forms

Fontéchevade	France
Ehringsdorf	Germany
Krapina	Yugoslavia

Second Interglacial Forms

Swanscombe	England
Steinheim	Germany
Arago	France

ing area for prehistoric populations. Several hundred thousand tools have been recovered from the site. The first hominid remains appeared one Saturday in June 1935 when a local worker uncovered an occipital bone. This began a series of lucky happenings associated with Swanscombe. A second lucky find occurred the following March 1936. This time a left partial **parietal** bone was uncovered; the fragment, against overwhelming odds, belonged with the 1935 occipital. The parietal was recovered during excavation of hundreds of tons of gravel as part of a harbor project. Nineteen years later, in 1955, a third skull fragment, the right parietal, was uncovered seventy-five feet from the original find. By remarkable coincidence, this belonged to the same individual as the two other fragments.

Deposits yielding the Swanscombe hominid remains are of Second Interglacial age. Associated faunal and archaeological materials are referred to the Mindel-Riss interglacial of the Middle Pleistocene. This dating was confirmed by fluorine analysis, making the Swanscombe material one of the best-dated fossil hominid remains.

Morphology. The three skull fragments (occipital, Figure 17-1, and two parietals) were well preserved and articulated perfectly. The cranial sutures were open, indicating an age at death of 20-25 years. The bones do not reveal any marked difference from recent *H. sapiens* skulls. The inferred cranial capacity of between 1275 and 1325 cc falls within the range of modern populations. The two major features distinguishing Swanscombe from modern skulls are its thickness (based upon forms both preceding and following it) and an indication of heavy brow ridges. However, lacking a frontal bone this cannot be confirmed.

Taxonomy. The "advanced" characteristics of Swanscombe, especially the rather modern cranial capacity, have led to some taxonomic confusion. Swanscombe represents an evolutionary advance over *H.*

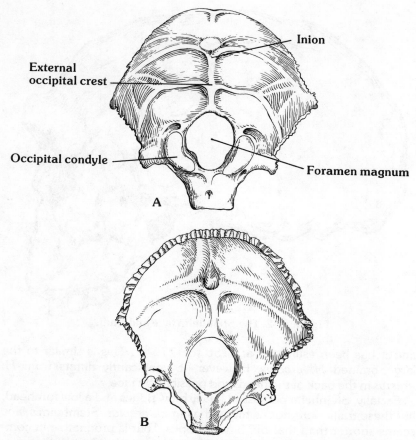

Figure 17-1. Landmarks on the modern occipital bone. (A) External view. (B) Internal view.

erectus; its large brain and the general suggestion of a rounded and expanded skull contour approach conditions of modern populations. On the other hand, the relatively low braincase height suggests that the specimen may be a less advanced form intermediate between *H. erectus* and *H. sapiens* populations. Swanscombe appears to represent a somewhat primitive variety of *H. sapiens* and is classified as *Homo sapiens swanscombensis*.

Steinheim. Swanscombe's taxonomic position is clarified somewhat by the discovery of contemporaneous material from Steinheim, north of Stuttgart, West Germany. Steinheim has been dated with great care to the Mindel-Riss interglacial, roughly 250,000 years B.P. Swanscombe and Steinheim are very similar. The Steinheim skull was alone; it lacked a mandible. Badly damaged behind the left eye, it evidenced a sizeable hole in the skull base indicating cannibalism. The skull, found in 1933, came from 25 feet deep in a gravel pit, capping a twenty-five year search by Dr. Berckhemer. The skull bones were associated with many faunal remains; no tools were recovered.

Owing to the weight of the wet earth covering it, the skull was warped and crushed; however, with some reconstruction, we can obtain an idea of what the skull and face looked like (Figure 17-2). The rear of the skull resembles Swanscombe, but the cranial capacity seems smaller

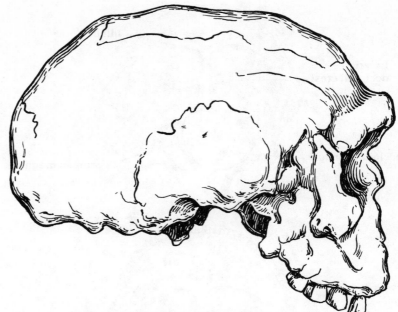

Figure 17-2. The Steinheim face and skull.

and it has been estimated at 1150 to 1175 cc. This is similar to the larger-brained *H. erectus*. However, it significantly differs from *H. erectus* in the back of the head, and possibly the face.

Facially, Steinheim possessed heavy brow ridges and a low forehead, but these traits were not as marked as in *H. erectus*. Steinheim's face seems shorter than that of "Sinanthropus," but is prognathic in comparison with modern populations. The nose is rather broad; the brow ridges, although large and heavy, were slightly separated above the nose. Although lacking front teeth, these were probably rather large, and the back teeth appear modern. The teeth are moderately **taurodont** (i.e., there is a tendency toward an enlarged pulp cavity and perhaps fusion of the molar roots). Except for taurodontism, nothing notable distinguishes Steinheim's teeth from those of modern Europeans.

Steinheim seems to be a member of an intermediate population between *H. erectus* and *H. sapiens*. Steinheim's brow ridges foreshadow those of classic Neanderthals; however, this trait does not warrant a species distinction from *H. sapiens*. The skull traits are a combination of characters conforming with modern *H. sapiens* and contrasting with the classic Neanderthals. Steinheim may be the common ancestor to both and on this accord some separate Steinheim from Swanscombe. Most classify Steinheim as *H. sapiens steinheimensis*. Taken with Swanscombe, the inference is that the evolutionary processes leading to the emergence of more modern individuals from *H. erectus* were working more swiftly on the back of the head than the face.

The derivation of Swanscombe and Steinheim is still being questioned. The most direct answer would be that they arose in Europe and are descendent from populations similar to those at Vérteszöllös. According to another theory, they were European immigrants who evolved in the Far East, perhaps from a stock like "Peking man" or else in central Asia.

Arago Cave, France. Arago Cave is located north of the Roussillon plain, at the southern tip of the Corbières mountains, near the village of Tauteval in the Pyrenees. An examination of materials from Arago occurred as early as 1963; however, it was in 1967 that undisturbed archaeological levels were reached and actual excavations began. The Arago material dates to approximately 200,000 years B.P. The presence of a large Archaic horse, a small wolf, large panther, and fragments of extinct rodents relatively date the site to the very beginning of the Riss Glaciation (de Lumley and de Lumley, 1973). The human material from Arago consists of many isolated teeth, phalanges, parietal fragments, a mandible with six teeth (Arago II), a half-mandible with five teeth (Arago XIII), and the anterior portion of an adult cranium found in 1971. This material should shed light on the taxonomic position of Swanscombe and Steinheim, and help in the reconstruction of the missing faces from European Middle Pleistocene hominids (Sullivan, 1971). According to J. Piveteau, the French paleontologist entrusted with cleaning the skull from its sandy matrix, Arago fills the gap between the Javanese *H. erectus* and European Neanderthals.

Arago is a large cave, 15 feet deep and 33 feet wide at its maximum. As early as 1838, "antediluvian" (a term used to refer to forms that preceded the presumed Biblical flood of Genesis 7) animal bones were reported from the cave. Excavation occurred in a series of layers, each defined by a set of faunal remains, tools, pollen grains, and other climatic and cultural indicators. The level most recently excavated was laid down during a dry, cold period when the cave was intermittently occupied. When it was abandoned sand blew in, covering the human relics and providing a clean floor for subsequent inhabitants. More than twenty habitation levels were laid down in the period represented by the newly discovered skull.

The de Lumleys feel that the cave was inhabited by groups of prehistoric hunters who regularly returned to establish camp. According to the de Lumleys the prehistoric hunters lived in a dimly lit area, some distance from the cave's entrance in a sandpit between a dune accumulating in the entry and another dune being formed at the rear of the cave. The habitation soils are littered with bone fragments and flint or quartz tools. In some areas the abundance and disposition of the remains suggests a tool-making work area. In other areas piles of bones more than 50 centimeters deep represent accumulating food debris. The cave also contains large stone slabs which the de Lumleys state were brought into the cave and were perhaps used to avoid sinking into the sand.

More than 100,000 artifacts have been uncovered at Arago. Most of the materials are attributed to the early Tayacian assemblage, with the exception of upper levels containing middle Acheulean tool types. Most of the Tayacian materials were made of quartz; some were made of flint and a few of quartzite. Arago Cave has yielded many pebble tools, including choppers and chopping tools. Handaxes are rare—there is less than one handaxe for 1000 retouched artifacts. Some of the smaller stone materials are comparable to specimens from Vértesszöllös.

This new material provides the first full hint of the facial appearance of pre-Neanderthal European populations. Upon complete examination, the Arago skull should help resolve the uncertainty stemming from the lack of complete European Middle Pleistocene skulls. The skull, which is still partly caked with sand, has massive brow ridges, a markedly flat forehead more horizontal than vertical (opposite the case in modern *H. sapiens*), and a narrow elongated brain case. Morphologically, the skull possesses some characteristics reminiscent of the preceding Far Eastern populations. However, the new French skull lacks the central ridge running back over the crown from the forehead, marking most *Homo erectus* skulls. Because of the absence of maxillary tooth wear the skull is thought to be that of a youth aged approximately twenty years.

The first skeletal evidence to appear was two massive teeth found protruding above the sand. Further excavation during the summers of 1969 and 1970 revealed two mandibles at approximately the same level. Neither of these apparently belongs with the skull, which lacks a mandible. The mandibles are chinless and seem to have been prognathic. The primitiveness of the mandibles is evidenced by midsection thickening (25 millimeters, almost one inch). They are considerably thicker than the older Heidelberg mandible. The heaviest of the two mandibles is thought to belong to a male, the other to a female.

The de Lumleys suggest two possibilities for the Arago cranium: (1) it appears more archaic than Neanderthals in pronounced prognathism, developed supraorbital torus, marked postorbital constriction, and frontal flattening. (2) It can be distinguished from Asian and African *H. erectus* by a shallower supratoral fossa, less postorbital constriction, and an absence of the canine fossa. Arago is less "advanced" than the Neanderthals, and its archaic features indicate it is close to the *H. erectus* evolutionary stage. Some have claimed that Arago is a new variety of hominid; however, we must await the final clearing. One thing is certain—this is a most important European fossil hominid.

Third Interglacial Forms

Preceding European "Classic Neanderthals," a number of European skeletal remains were recovered dating to the Third, or Riss-Würm interglacial. These, along with Second interglacial material from England, Germany, and France, are often referred to as pre-Mousterian (referring to the Neanderthal cultural assemblage) *H. sapiens.* Third interglacial forms come from France, Germany, and Italy. Although fragmentary, they play a major role in the taxonomic controversy as to the place of subsequent Neanderthal populations in our evolutionary history.

Fontéchevade (Figure 17-3). The Fontéchevade cave, like most French cave occupation sites, was used by a series of occupants through time. The site was excavated by Mlle. G. Henri-Martin; in 1947 she broke through the "cave floor" to find seven more meters of deposits containing tools and warm-weather fauna which belonged to the Third Interglacial period. Parts of two other skulls came from the same deposits; these included a patch from the brow area of one skull, about the size of a silver dollar, and most of the top of another, exhibiting signs of charring. Beneath this layer, Mlle. Henri-Martin found another tool assemblage but without associated skeletal remains. To establish contemporaneity of the human and nonhuman material, F, or fluorine, tests were conducted. The antiquity of the Fontéchevade skull bones seems well assured.

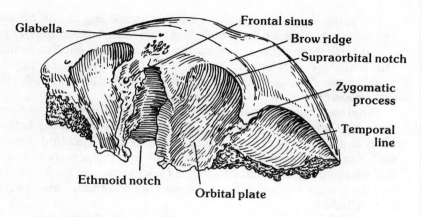

Figure 17-3. Landmarks on the modern frontal bone.

Morphology and Taxonomic Debate. A furor was caused by assertions that Fontéchevade is not demonstrably different from modern *H. sapiens,* and is more "advanced" than subsequent Neanderthals. Fontéchevade cranial capacities are estimated at about 1450 cc.[1] The most complete skull, number 2, consists of a left parietal, upper half of the right parietal, and an upper portion of the **frontal.** Many claim that enough of the frontal exists to indicate that the skull lacked the massive brow ridges supposedly characteristic of European classical Neanderthal populations. A number of paleontologists disagree, claiming that evidence for the nonexistence of ridges is inconclusive; after all, the brow ridge area is missing on the larger skull. Some charge that the smaller fragment is not from a full grown adult but from an immature individual in whom the large ridges claimed to be characteristic of European Neanderthals have not developed. The "non-brow ridge" proponents counter that the skull is from a mature individual, and, in any case, the young Neanderthal boy from Teshik-Tash (Uzbekistan, U.S.S.R.) possessed brow ridges.

Fontéchevade is distinguishable from modern populations. It most closely approaches Swanscombe in cranial thickness and in breadth across the back of the skull. There are two alternatives: (1) Fontéchevade is simply an ancestor of later European populations, or (2) it is a member of a separate evolutionary line, commonly called *Pre-sapiens,* with little genetic link to European Neanderthals.

Ehringsdorf. The Ehringsdorf skull is a Third interglacial form found in 1925 near Weimar, Germany. It comes from a depth of fifty-four feet and was associated with warm-temperature forest floral and faunal remains. The heterogeneity of the cultural and skeletal assemblages suggests to some that the remains are a mixture of several related populations but this is unlikely. The major osteological material consists of a parietal and broken faceless braincase.

[1]There are a number of problems associated with obtaining brain size estimates. Cranial capacity, for example, is only an approximation of the size of the brain. All three methods of obtaining brain size estimates, the determination of volume of a natural and an artificial brain case, and the determination of the capacity of the brain case, only provide an estimate of the volume of the space of the cranium. They do not provide an estimate of the volume of the brain itself, for the cranial cavity accommodates much more than simply brain (Tobias, 1971).

The cranial capacity was large, 1450 cc. according to one estimate. The brow ridges were heavily built, like Steinheim, but somewhat thicker and show some degree of approximation to subsequent Neanderthals. The braincase is relatively high and modern-looking. Ehringsdorf closely approximates Steinheim and Swanscombe; most consider it an archaic member of *Homo sapiens*.

Krapina. These remains come from the floor of a rock shelter in northern Croatia, Yugoslavia. The material was excavated between 1895 and 1906; the remains comprise some 649 shattered pieces of skull, skeleton, and teeth. One reason for the fragmentary remains is that excavators dynamited dangerous rock overhangs; the bones were also broken post-mortem. Some bones are charred and may be relics of cannibalism.

Over 1000 flint implements were removed from the hominid-bearing level at Krapina. The osteological material includes postcranial remains from practically every part of the body, and over 270 teeth. Five skulls are intact enough to be identified, but only three have been studied. All the adult skulls have strong brow ridge development. In some skull and jaw features these materials approximate later Neanderthal skulls, but the frontal region of some skulls closely resembles *H. sapiens*. Although their taxonomic position is uncertain, the Krapina population appears transitional between *H. sapiens* and *H. sapiens neanderthalensis*.

Quinzano and Saccopastore. These remains were found in cave deposits near Verona, Italy, and from a river deposit on the bank of a small tributary of the Tiber River just outside the walls of Rome. At Saccopastore two skulls were recovered; one found in 1929 may belong to a thirty to thirty-five year old female; the other, a "male" aged about thirty-five, was found in 1936. The "female" skull is nearly complete, but the "male" skull lacks the skullcap.

The Saccopastore skulls (now dated to the early Würm) are not large; the "female" has a cranial capacity of 1200 cc, close to the Steinheim figure. The "male" probably had a capacity close to 1300 cc. The skulls have supraorbital ridges, some cranial flattening, and a rather massive lower jaw, features which resemble subsequent Neanderthals. In other features—the position of the **foramen magnum,** rounded contour of the rear of the skull, and dental arcade—they resemble modern populations. Because of the curious combination of modern and archaic features of the Saccopastore skulls, they are often referred to as transitional. Some suggest that the skulls represent a population in an initial phase of a progressive development leading to the European Neanderthals.

Summary—Taxonomic Considerations

Second and Third interglacial fossil hominids are structurally interesting; in some respects they resemble subsequent European Neanderthals; in others they seem very modern. A number of phyletic schemes have been proposed to deal with variation within these populations. They reduce to the following: (1) These forms are simply ancestral to European Neanderthals. (2) The fossils are the basis of a separate evolutionary line with little or no genetic connection with subsequent European Neanderthals. (3) Steinheim may be ancestral to European Neanderthals while Swanscombe and Fontéchevade are the basis of a separate evolutionary line leading to modern populations. Each scheme is based upon the importance one attaches to the range of variation within these limited population samples. If the range is not great, alternative 1 is likely; however, if the range is great, alternatives 2 and 3 are more likely.

Neanderthal — How Many Evolutionary Lines?

The Problem — Fantasy, Romanticism, Truth. The so-called "Neanderthal problem" has long plagued anthropologists, and until those fairly numerous remains are arranged in some order and the temporal, geographic, and cultural boundaries delineated, confusion will reign. The appearance of what some investigators feel are more modern-looking hominids in Europe predating the European Neanderthals raised the spectre of evolutionary reversals and multiple (or **polyphyletic**) evolutionary lines. The existence of a variable Eastern European and Middle Eastern population predating and living contemporaneously with European Neanderthals complicated the picture. Finally, what many visualized as the overnight disappearance of western European Neanderthals and their replacement by anatomically modern populations smacked of catastrophism, a process akin to the Biblical flood. Fanciful notions of savage warfare between brutish Neanderthals and modern contemporaries were not uncommonly presented.

> Of all the different kinds of prehistoric peoples, certainly the one who projects the clearest image is Neanderthal man. For most of us he *is* Stone Age man, the squat, shaggy, beetle-browed fellow that inevitably comes to mind when we think of our ancient relatives. We see him standing in the mouth of a cave—stone axe in hand, a few rough furs over his shoulder, some mammoth bones piled in the background—staring out over a snow-choked landscape as he ponders the ever-present problems of the ice age and the giant cave bear (Howell, 1965:123).

Besides the romantic aspect, this image persists because there is some truth in it. Neanderthals were, in some respects, more primitive morphologically than we; sometimes they lived in caves, wore skins, and inhabited cold climates. The first fossil skull positively identified as belonging to ancient hominids was a Neanderthal; with nothing to compare it with but skulls of modern populations, scientists were struck by the divergence between them. Today the reverse is true.

Neanderthal fossil remains and their cultural assemblage (the **Mousterian,** Figure 17-4) have been traced from Near Eastern, African, Asian, and European sites. One of the problems with discerning their true nature is that we have so many Neanderthal skeletal remains, and we know so much of their culture from undisturbed cave deposits. Since we know so much, why so much trouble interpreting the data? It may be that we know too much, that is, we may be too accustomed to dealing with limited population samples.

If the concept of the Neanderthal population is to have justification, it must be limited in time, space, and culture. Most anthropologists accept the following criteria as diagnostic of this stage of hominid evo-

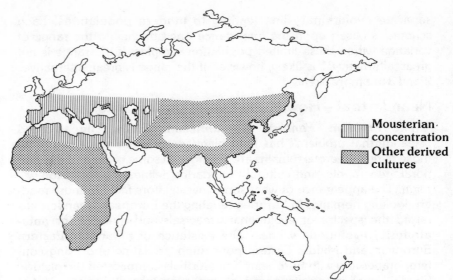

Mousterian concentration

Other derived cultures

Figure 17-4. Mousterian and derived cultures.

lution. The time span was the Early Würm or Würm I glaciation, from about 100,000 years B.P. to about 35,000 years B.P. Neanderthals inhabited Europe, West and Central Asia, the Near East, and Africa. Their culture was the Mousterian, itself a complex derivative of earlier toolmaking complexes.

Historical Overview

To appreciate some of the problems of interpretation, a word on the scientific climate of the times is needed. The discovery of the first Neanderthal remains preceded only slightly the publication of Darwin and Wallace's evolutionary theory. The remains drew more attention than they might have otherwise. People were searching for a "missing link": the Neanderthals were characterized as big, burly, and hairy, with a sloping head and back, a club-wielding creature dragging its mate to its cave by the hair.

The term "Neanderthal" itself refers to a quiet valley in the heart of western Germany which seventeenth-century Germans favored as a picnic spot. This spot was especially admired by the Düsseldorf organist and composer Joachim Neumann. He signed some of his works "Neander," the Greek translation of his name, and after his death, local inhabitants began calling the valley, then spelled "thal" in German, Neanderthal. The valley has since lent its name to a major group of human fossil remains.

The first-described Neanderthal find came from Germany in 1856. It was first mistaken for animal bones and immediately discarded, but at the last moment the owner of the excavation site saved the bones and turned them over to a local teacher. He passed them on to the anatomist Schaffhausen who termed the material "ancient," a pronouncement pleasing to the budding group of evolutionists. Anti-evolutionists, however, felt the material represented some pathological freak.

One of the most amusing of the many interpretations of the Neanderthal populations, as exemplified by the original discovery, was based on the following traits: (1) evidently the left elbow had been

The Fossil Record—
Recovering the Past

310

broken early in life and healed in such a way that movement was restricted; (2) the individual was presumed to suffer from rickets, so it was suggested that pain from the elbow and the rickets caused the person to knit its brows in a perpetual frown. A Bonn professor suggested that the bowed femurs might testify to a lifetime of horseback riding. Another suggested that the Neanderthal was a deserter from the Russian army which chased Napoleon's army back across the Rhine in 1814. More specifically the fossil was of a rickety Mongolian Cossack who crawled into the cave for refuge. Another interpretation reflected the prejudices of the nineteenth century—a French scholar referred to the form as a robust Celt resembling "a modern Irishman with low mental organization."

Further finds came to light in 1866 when a jaw accompanied by a Mousterian cultural assemblage was recovered from a Belgian cave. The associated rhinoceros, mammoth, and bear bones provided clues to the specimen's age. In 1871 Darwin described this find in *The Descent of Man*. In 1886 two additional skeletons appeared from Spy Cave in Belgium; now talk of pathological freaks was minimal.

The years prior to World War I witnessed the recovery of much European Neanderthal material, most from the Dordogne region of southwestern France. Other finds came from Spain, Italy, southeastern Europe, Russia, and Turkey. The great French paleontologist M. Boule described them in detail but erroneously noted what he considered to be their highly uniform, specialized nature. Until the 1930s it was assumed that European Neanderthals were slowly driven to extinction by subsequent populations. Then discoveries of hominid remains not quite like those of their European contemporaries, or like modern *Homo*, came to light in the Middle East mandate area of Palestine. At the same time, recovery and reexamination of Second and Third interglacial forms continued.

Classic, European or Western Neanderthals

European classic Neanderthals are limited to southwestern Europe. A number of sites are located in the sheltered and well-watered valleys of southern France and similar parts of the Iberian (Spanish) and Apennine (Italian) peninsulas, regions outside the main zone of frozen ground and tundra vegetation.[2] There was, however, at least sporadic penetration, perhaps seasonally for hunting and collecting, into adjacent areas.

Cultural Remains. The name of the Neanderthal cultural assemblage, the Mousterian, is derived from the French village of Le Moustier where the type site (the site to which others are compared) is located. The functional tool categories, scrapers, points, and knives, tell us something about the life and concerns of their manufacturers. The archaeological record from the French village of Les Eyzies reveals much about how European Neanderthals adapted to their physical surroundings. There are 200 prehistoric sites within a twenty-mile radius of Les Eyzies. Most sites are in caves, rock shelters, and open-air locations within a mile or so of well-travelled routes.

---

[2]It should be noted that the numerous remains from the area result not only from high population concentrations but also from good preservation conditions coupled with much archaeological exploration.

Neanderthals were big-game hunters and it has been suggested that animal meat provided the bulk of their caloric intake. Evidence from an open-air site such as Lebenstedt, Germany, supports the assumption that during the summer some Neanderthals followed herds of grazing animals northward into the open tundras. Some Neanderthals may have adapted to an existence of seasonal movement, following herds into the forest-tundra in winter and returning with them onto the broad tundra expanse in summer. Some members of the Neanderthal population were also sedentary; some sites in southwestern France were probably occupied year-round. It has also been suggested that the complex nature of the Mousterian assemblage in southern France precludes anything but well-established territoriality and semipermanent settlements. Migration was probably not a general pattern; perhaps it was confined to marginal populations inhabiting tundra fringes. Groups in less severe climates and where good shelter was provided basically remained sedentary. Seasonal movement seems to be a localized adaptation to certain environmental stresses.

Faunal remains associated with the Neanderthal assemblages indicate they were efficient hunters. Wooly mammoth and rhinoceros were successfully hunted; the presence of fish and fowl remains at the Lebenstedt site underscores their hunting efficiency. They overcame the great cave bear (which they seem to have worshipped), which must have been a formidable foe. The killing and eviction of the cave bear must have been a cooperative group effort. At the Drachenhöhle site (Dragon's Cave) at Mixnitz, Austria, it appears that hibernating bears, including females with young, were attacked and killed on numerous occasions.

Certain Neanderthal implements suggest use for skin-working and butchery. "Points," broad, triangular, retouched flakes, may have been tied (hafted) to a wooden spear or used as dart heads, improving the penetrating power of the plain wooden implement. Stone balls may have been used as bolas. Familiarity with fat-dressed skins could have led to the use of rawhide lashings and thongs. Neanderthals may have trapped their prey; evidence from the Shanidar Cave area in Iraq suggests that animal remains were caught by either running grazing herds over cliffs or by running them into a blind canyon and slaughtering them.

Combe Grenal is an exceptionally interesting French cave site, located in a little valley fourteen miles from Les Eyzies. It was originally dug by Dr. F. Bordes who expected to complete the excavations in short order; however, excavations covered a period of roughly eleven years. When work terminated, Combe Grenal was a huge forty-foot hole with sixty-four separate layers of geological and archaeolgical deposits. The first occupants of Combe Grenal left no fossil remains. The richest and most important layers yield an almost continuous occupation record from about 40,000 to 90,000 years B.P. Groups of thirty or forty individuals may have lived and died here over many generations.

The Combe Grenal site includes an empty grave so small that it must have contained the remains of a young child. Three smaller ceremonial pits near the grave, which are also empty, may have held meat and clothing for the dead child. Another interesting discovery is the uncovering of a posthole which may have been one of several at the cave mouth where stakes were driven into the ground to support skins or woven branches to provide shelter from wind, rain, and snow. Or, they might have supported a meat-drying rack.

Combe Grenal is especially rich in Neanderthal tools. Bordes was able to collect and classify 19,000 tools. Bordes feels that differences in manufacture reflect differences in use; he feels some tools were used to help scrape bark from narrow branches to make stakes and/or spear shafts while others were used to clean hides or make clothes. Sally and Lewis Binford have suggested that the tool types at Combe Grenal represent different everyday activities. One kit was used for "maintenance activities" such as working wood and bone—perhaps to make shafts, ax handles, tent pegs, etc. A second kit suggests activities associated with killing and butchering meat while a third kit indicated activities associated with food processing, especially meat preparation. A fourth kit was used for shredding and cutting wood and/or other plant materials; a fifth for more specialized killing and butchering.

The Binfords further tried to discern whether some of the tool kits could be associated with men's or women's tasks, speculating that since women are more likely to stay close to the base camp to care for children, they should tend to make their tools from local, readily available materials. Tools fabricated from local flint were predominantly denticulate or notched items commonly associated with food processing, which might have been woman's work. Tools generally considered to be used for hunting, for example spear points and scrapers, were made from remote sources. One implication is that the variety of materials used for hunting tools represents the fact that men were away from the base camp and had ready access to available suitable materials.

Further evidence of Neanderthal cultural ways comes from burials, and other indications of ritualistic behavior. Quoting F. C. Howell (1965:130), "In keeping with the growing complexity of his life, and the greater variety of his possessions, and his talents, Neanderthal man also apparently stood on the edge of becoming both an esthete and mystic. For the first time in human experience faint signs of decoration and artistic appreciation appear." The Neanderthals recognized death as a special social phenomenon; they buried their dead, suggesting an awareness of the transitoriness of life, and perhaps concern for the future. Burials have been found in western and eastern Europe, Iraq, and central Asia. The French sites of Le Moustier and La Ferrassi yield Neanderthal burials. At Le Moustier a young boy (between 15 and 18) was buried in a cave; he was lowered into a trench on his right side, his knees slightly drawn and his head resting on his forearm reminiscent of a sleeping position. Several stone implements and a number of charred animal bones which may be relics of a roasted meat funerary offering were also buried.

One of the most interesting of the many Neanderthal burials is Shanidar Cave, the excavation of which is described in Dr. R. Solecki's book *Shanidar: The First Flower People*. One Shanidar skeleton, no. 4, was buried on a bed of flowers[3]—the first evidence of prehistoric floral remains. The floral remains are represented by small, brightly colored

[3]Not all anthropologists accept this interpretation (see, for example, Brace, 1971).

Figure 17-5. A symbol of the cave bear cult at Drachenloch, Switzerland. A bear skull is pierced by the leg bone of a younger bear.

wild flowers which may have been woven into the branches of a pine-like shrub. Evidence of the latter is found in the soils. Mme. Leroi-Gourhan, who studied the floral remains, concluded that someone in the Last Ice Age ranged the mountainside in the mournful task of collecting floral offerings.

Another example of Neanderthal ritual practices is the Cave Bear Cult. Although probably a formidable foe, the cave bear was hunted. At the Swiss site of Drachenloch a number of bear skulls stacked in a stone chest may have been our first hunting trophies. Another cult symbol from the same site is the skull of a three year old cave bear with a leg bone of a younger animal piercing its cheek. This rests on two bones from still two other bears (Figure 17-5). A mountain cave in eastern Austria contained a rectangular vault holding seven bear skulls, all facing the entrance (Figure 17-6). There is an elaborate cave bear burial at Regourdo in southern France which includes a complete skeleton, minus the skull (which may have been stolen), stone drains, a rectangular pit covered by a flat stone slab weighing almost a ton, and the remains of more than twenty cave bears.

These findings mark a new stage in hominid evolution; life and death seemingly held new values. Burial implies concern for the individual; further evidence of concern is recovery of individuals who survived serious injuries and who must have been cared for by their contemporaries. Supportive evidence comes from Shanidar, where one individual was apparently recovering from a spear or knife wound in the ribs when he was killed by a rock fall. Another Shanidar individual had his lower right arm amputated prior to death and showed healed wounds above the eyes and right parietal. Survival from these injuries means that such individuals were possibly kept alive, nursed, and supported because of some concern for the individual. Perhaps such individuals had special knowledge of magic, rituals, or hunting techniques indicative of a more complex, extensive social organization.

Osteological Remains. The following characteristics are representative of European or Western Neanderthals. Cranial capacities were large, ranging from 1525 to 1640 cc in six male skulls and 1300 to 1425 in three females. The skulls were more capacious than those of modern populations, accommodating a larger brain than common to modern *Homo*. The skull was shaped differently; it has a lower crown and achieves its interior shape by bulging on the side and back. A fairly consistent trait is an **occipital bun**, i.e., a bony protuberance at the rear of the skull.

Figure 17-6. A representation of the Neanderthal bear ceremony.

Three major features distinguish the Neanderthal face: a receding chin, or lack thereof, large cheeks, and prominent brow ridges curving over the eyes and connected across the bridge of the nose (Figures 17-7 and 17-8). The rather large nose may be a functional adaptation to severe climates, serving perhaps to warm and moisten inhaled air, for in cold climates the brain can be endangered by inhalation of cold air. European Neanderthal jaws and teeth also manifest some distinguishing traits. The jaws are large and evidence strong muscle attachments, and certain dental traits suggest use of the teeth as tools. Neanderthal incisors are broader than those in modern populations and may have been important tools in environmental manipulation. As such, they required robust roots and supporting structures, features readily seen in the fossil record.

European Neanderthal postcranial skeletons mark them as short, powerfully built individuals just over five feet tall. Their extremities were short; the hands and fingers were short and stubby. Their feet were similar to ours, for we have a remarkably preserved Neanderthal footprint cast in the wet clay of an Italian cave. Howell (1965) suggests that a Neanderthal "would have been a formidable opponent in a college wrestling tournament." They may have weighed 160 pounds or more. It has been suggested that classic Neanderthals were incapable of erect bipedalism; however, this is based upon faulty reconstruction (Figure 17-9).

Cold Adaptations? Although it is being debated, many European Neanderthal characteristics are seen as cold adaptations. Nasal prognathism, for example, is seen as an adaptation to the cold conditions throughout southwestern Europe. The postcranial skeleton, with short,

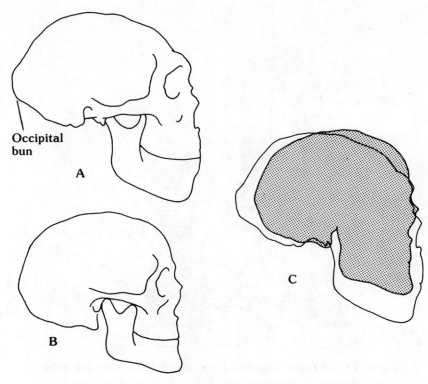

Figure 17-7. A comparison of the skulls of classic Neanderthal and modern *Homo*. (A) Classic Neanderthal. (B) Modern *H. sapiens*. (C) The two skulls compared.

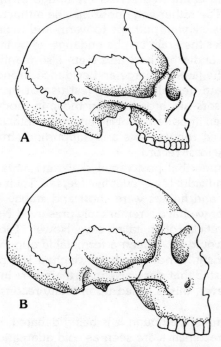

Figure 17-8. Cranial shape of (A) modern *H. sapiens* compared with (B) a western European Neanderthal.

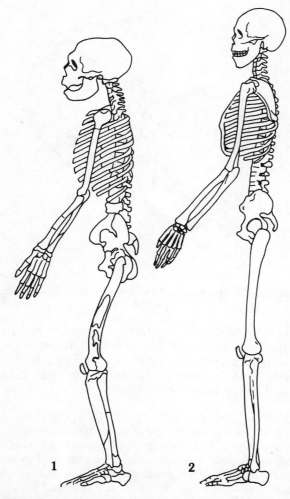

Figure 17-9. Reconstruction of the posture of a Neanderthal according to (1) Boule and (2) Weiner. Not drawn to scale. (After Boule and Vallois, 1957)

stubby limbs and phalanges, is similarly cold-adapted. There is a rough gradient of what are considered classical Neanderthal traits; the most extreme expressions are prevalent in the colder regions of Europe and tail off as you move south and east into the Middle East. Western European Neanderthal populations are most readily identified, for here climatic selection was maximized.

La Chapelle-aux-Saints: A Mistake Compounded

The La Chapelle remains and fine Mousterian tools (Figure 17-10) were recovered on 3 August 1908 from a grotto in the commune of La Chapelle-aux-Saints, in the valley of a tributary of the Dordogne river. The first written report of the find was presented to the French Academy of Sciences on 21 December 1908. The fossil material was entrusted to M. Boule for study and only now is his report being seen in proper perspective after having confused our picture of the Neanderthals for many years. Pfeiffer (1969:162) notes that the study of the

Middle Pleistocene
Hominids and the
Neanderthals

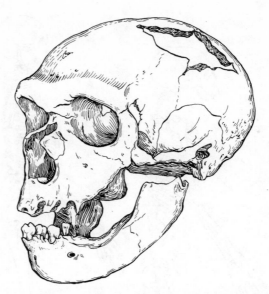

Figure 17-10. The face and skull of La Chapelle-aux-Saints.

La Chapelle remains was ". . . one of the most amazing phenomena in the history of man's efforts to downgrade his ancestors."

Boule's original report was presented orally (by E. Perrier) to the French Academy of Sciences on 14 December 1908. Excerpts of this report follow (Leakey, et al., 1971:180-81).

> The state of the cranial sutures and of the dentition proves that this skull is that of an elderly man. It strikes me first by its very considerable dimensions, keeping in mind meanwhile the small stature of its ancient possessor. Next it strikes us with its bestial appearance, or, to put it better, by the general collection of simian (ape) or pithecoid (monkey) characteristics.
>
> It seems to me no less certain that, from the collection of its characteristics, the group of Neanderthal . . . represents an inferior type closer to the apes than to any other human group.
>
> Finally, I will point out that the human group of the Middle Pleistocene, so primitive from the point of view of physical characteristics, is very primitive from an intellectual point of view.

In other places, Boule speaks about a slumped posture and supposed monkeylike arrangement of certain spinal vertebrae. He even suggests that the feet may have been grasping organs like those of apes.

As recently as 1957 this study was cited as a major source; several museums still display Neanderthals as slumped-postured brutes. La Chapelle was restudied in 1957 and this study showed that La Chapelle was hardly typical. The bones were from a rather old individual (forty or fifty years) who suffered from arthritis of the jaws, spine, and perhaps lower limbs. Any stooped appearance was caused by arthritis (Figure 17-9).

Neanderthal Health. It has been suggested that Neanderthals suffered many diseases; nearly a hundred years ago R. Virchow felt he diagnosed rickets. A recent article suggests that Neanderthals living in early Würm times suffered from a Vitamin D deficiency, but others disagree. It has also been suggested that Neanderthal skeletons were characterized by a high incidence of syphilis, of which there is no proof.

Recently there has been much discussion as to whether Neanderthals had a complex language. To quote the *New York Times* (25 April 1972), "If he tried to talk to you, his language would probably sound like a series of apelike, inarticulate grunts and noises." This is questionable. The argument that Neanderthals were incapable of much speech is based upon Boule's description of the La Chapelle-aux-Saints material and plaster casts of the same, comparative data of ape and modern human newborn, and modern adult human skulls. In addition Lieberman and Crelin made their own silicone-rubber cast reconstruction of their interpretation of a Neanderthal vocal tract. These researchers concluded that the anatomical features of adult Neanderthals show supralaryngeal vocal apparatuses similar to that of a modern human neonate. A computer program represented the supralaryngeal vocal tract by means of a series of contiguous cylindrical sections, each with a fixed area.

Lieberman and Crelin argue that Neanderthal's disappearance may have been a consequence of their linguistic, hence intellectual, failings with respect to their competitors of a more modern bearing. Some critics of this theory object to the methodology (e.g., Siegel and Carlisle, 1974). Other criticisms have also been proffered, and those interested in the debate might wish to consult Lieberman and Crelin (1974) in the *American Anthropologist.*

Central and Eastern European Neanderthals

Although less numerous than remains from western Europe, Neanderthal remains from East and Central Europe are nevertheless very important. Some argue that the sudden appearance of modern populations in western Europe supposed their origin elsewhere in the East. Fossil evidence from East and Central Europe lends some credence to this. New finds from this area have filled some of the geographical and chronological gaps in the fossil record; they have also blurred the boundary between classical European Neanderthals and fully modern *H. sapiens* populations. Major central and eastern European materials come from Czechoslovakia and Hungary. Some refer to them as transitional specimens, i.e., transitional between modern and Neanderthal populations.

Taxonomic Significance. The transitional status of this material suggests that hominid evolution in eastern and central Europe was proceeding towards modern *Homo* while classical Neanderthals were more or less isolated in western Europe. The transitional forms are important for the following reasons: (1) To varying degrees, they display many traits found in anatomically modern populations. (2) Chronologically they extend to the time period in which the oldest finds of fully modern *H. sapiens* appear. (3) Even forms designated fully modern *H. sapiens* exhibit some cultural and morphological links to the past. Such findings indicate that the appearance of *H. sapiens sapiens* in central and western Europe (and perhaps other regions) need not be explained in terms of a sudden east to west migration, but rather as local evolution in populations sharing basic traits but differing in intensity and detail. Such a situation permits relatively rapid change.

Middle Eastern or Progressive Neanderthals

Some Würm I Middle Eastern populations appear to be transitional. Some, like Quafzeh 6 and Skhūl 5, closely approach anatomically modern *Homo sapiens;* others, such as Tabūn and Shanidar I, closely approach western European classical Neanderthals save for extremes of cold adaptation. Some consider the Middle Eastern forms members of a late non-cold-adapted Neanderthal group imperceptibly grading into fully modern *H. sapiens sapiens*. The most complete finds come from Israel and Iraq; other remains come from Lebanon and Jordan. Israeli remains come from six caves: Zuttiya near the Sea of Galilee, Tabūn and Skhūl at Mount Carmel, Jebel Qafza near Nazareth, Shukba, seventeen miles northwest of Jerusalem, and Amud near Lake Tiberias. Although from the same geographical area and dating from approximately the same time period, the skulls differ from one another.

The Middle East has long been a crossroads of humanity; many consider the Middle Eastern corridor, stretching along the Mediterranean and Lebanon Mountains, as an evolutionary focal point. Many factors contributed to making the Middle East an important evolutionary pocket. Game has always been abundant, and the concentration of game seems to have produced rather heavy local human population centers. There was a climatic shift to somewhat drier conditions at approximately 40,000 to 45,000 years B.P. which led to local concentrations of grazing animals and their hunters. The richest and deepest fossil sites are in areas where vegetation and game were most abundant, e.g., in the valleys along the western slopes of the coastal ranges. Mount Carmel lies in such a valley.

Mount Carmel. Mount Carmel consists of two major sites, the Cave of et-Tabūn (Cave of the Oven) and the Cave of es-Skhūl (Cave of the Kids). A third cave, el-Wad, has yielded fragmentary remains. Mount Carmel, twelve miles from Haifa, was located as a by-product of efforts to build the port of Haifa. The Mount Carmel population lived through the last interglacial and into the first phase of the Würm glaciation. Skulls from both caves show pronounced brow ridges; however, they display a remarkable variability in the degree of development of other features typically associated with classic Neanderthals and in some respects they rather closely approximate *H. sapiens sapiens*.

et-Tabūn. Tabūn cave yielded a male mandible and a female skeleton. Tabūn woman had the low skull, arched brows, and the heavy, continuous ridges of her western European contemporaries. She lacked an occipital bun; her cranial capacity is estimated at 1270 and her mandible lacks a chin. The male mandible is large, deep, and rather square in front. Morphologically the Tabūn material falls between the central and western Neanderthals and possesses some traits seen at Skhūl. The Tabūn material may, in fact, be ancestral to Skhul.

es-Skhūl. The es-Skhūl cave site, containing ten skeletons in differing states of preservation, was one of anthropology's great finds. Originally thought to be contemporaneous to Tabūn, es-Skhūl seems to be about 10,000 years later in time and following some climatic interval which witnessed the local disappearance of hippopotamus and rhinoceros. The Tabūn group manifests some classic Neanderthal traits, but those from Skhūl show a general similarity to modern *H. sapiens*. The Skhūl braincases are similar to ours in size and shape. They are high, flat-sided, and round and lack an occipital bun. The forepart of the skull is reminiscent of earlier Neanderthals; the brows are marked, but they are not heavy or bulbous as in earlier Neanderthals. The mandible has a chin.

Interpretation of Mt. Carmel Remains. A host of explanations have been offered to explain the variation at Mt. Carmel. A recent explanation based on new dating shows that Skhūl is subsequent to Tabūn by about 10,000 years. Tabūn lived approximately 39,000 years B.P., the Skhūl population several thousand years later. We have, fairly late in time, a Neanderthal population (Tabūn) giving way to an almost modern form as typified by Skhūl (especially skull no. 5). The Skhūl remains morphologically and temporally crowd towards modern *H. sapiens*; it has been suggested that a population like Tabūn was replaced by a population like Skhul. Assuming the date at Skhūl correct, then modern populations arose from local stocks, and not necessarily in the Middle East. Transitional central and eastern European remains may be remnants of such groups.

Shanidar Cave, Iraq. Shanidar Cave is an extremely interesting Middle Eastern Würm site. Shanidar, a huge cave in the Western Zagros mountains of northern Iraq, has been occupied from early Mousterian to present times. Solecki had to ask local Kurdish inhabitants to leave the cave in order to excavate the site. Now and then, due to local earthquakes or formation of ice on the ceiling, limestone slabs plummeted from the cave roof, killing many inhabitants. Luckily for an inquisitive anthropologist, the remains of a number of victims are available for study. In 1953 Solecki uncovered a baby's skeleton, in 1957 three adult skeletons, and in 1960 three more bodies.

All the Shanidar remains lay in Mousterian culture-bearing deposits. Shanidar 1 is C-14 dated to 46,000±1500 years B.P. Shanidar 3 was perhaps a few hundred years older, Shanidar 2 and the baby were close to 60,000 years B.P. Shanidar 1 and 2 were males. Shanidar 3 appears to have been killed by a projectile point embedded in his ribs and was subsequently buried against the cave wall. Shanidar 1 met death at about age 40. His skull may prove to be one of the largest fossil skulls found—the cranial capacity is estimated at over 1700 cc. Shanidar 1 manifests signs of having come under the scalpel (probably a flint knife) of a caveman surgeon and survived an operation which removed his right arm. He was also severely wounded by blows of some sharp instrument around and above the left eye and may have been left blinded in this eye. He has a healed bone lesion from a blow on the right parietal. Despite these infirmities, which surely affected his food-getting abilities, he survived and was subsequently crushed by a slab of falling limestone, apparently while standing erect.

The flower burial was an unexpected Shanidar find. To quote Solecki (1971:250): "With the finding of flowers in association with Neanderthals, we are brought suddenly to the realization that the universality of mankind and the love of beauty go beyond the boundary of our species. No longer can we deny the early men the full range of human feelings and experience."

Middle Pleistocene
Hominids and the
Neanderthals

Shanidar flower burial.

It is difficult to generalize about the skeletal characteristics of Near Eastern and central Asia populations contemporaneous with the Neanderthals of Europe. Some specimens, for example Tabūn, Shanidar, Amud, and perhaps Teshik-Tash shared more features with western Neanderthals than did Skhūl. On the whole, however, these populations differed from western Neanderthals in their higher cranial vaults, frontal bones were less steeply inclined, and the occipital regions lacked a bun. Kennedy (1975) suggests that physical differences in the populations of the Near East and central Asia may be of the order of subspecific or racial variation. These populations may constitute one part of the species range which had more ties with the western European Neanderthals and another variety with closer ties to populations in the direct line to Upper and post-Paleolithic *H. sapiens.*

Other Forms: The Neanderthaloids

The taxonomic designation of members of this group is questionable largely because of disputed dating. Prime among this group are the Mapa skullcap from China, the Niah skull from Borneo, the Rhodesian, Florisbad, and Saldanha skulls from Africa, and the Solo skulls from

Java. Some of the skulls are anatomically modern at a time when classical and transitional Neanderthals lived in other parts of the world, while some are archaic for their supposed recent dating. The role these forms played in human evolution is likely to be questioned unless there is some way to provide concrete dates, or unless similar skulls, from dated deposits, are uncovered. At this time they remain intriguing, isolated samples.

Asian Remains. The Mapa material from China is of unknown age; it might be contemporaneous with the Neanderthals or it might be older. Morphologically it fits somewhere on the continuum between classic Neanderthals and the transitional forms further to the east and south. The Niah skull from Borneo belonging to a youth aged about 15 has been given a C-14 date of 39,000±1000 years. It is important because of its date, its anatomically modern form, and because it is in rather distinct contrast to archaic-looking but similarly dated Javan Solo remains.

African Fossils. The Rhodesian, Florisbad, and Saldanha skulls are all of questionable dating. The Rhodesian skull is unusually massive; it possesses a very strongly developed brow ridge, retreating forehead, and other archaic traits. It is intermediate between classic Neanderthals and modern *H. sapiens*, sharing traits with both. Since it was blasted from a quarry pit, the dating is unknown. The Saldanha skull from South Africa is identical to the Rhodesian. On the basis of faunal associations, the skull could be 100,000 years old; however, on the basis of associated artifactual remains it could be no more than 40,000 years old. Some feel that the Florisbad skull is a third member of the Rhodesian-Saldanha population. At first glance the skull looks primitive because of the heavy brow ridges; however, some classify it as modern *H. sapiens*. Again, dating is a problem. New studies have attempted to provide a date for the Rhodesian material. Klein's (1973) faunal

---

Table 17-2. Summary of Hominid Evolution: From late Pliocene/Pleistocene Forms Through Early *Homo sapiens*.

Approximate Dating	Fossil Forms and Location
Middle Pleistocene	
about 200,000 years B.P.	first appearance of *H. sapiens,* Europe and perhaps Africa
250,000-600,000 years B.P.	*H. erectus* in Africa, Asia, Europe
600,000-700,000 years B.P.	perhaps *A. robustus* still in Africa. *H. erectus* in Africa, Asia, Europe
Late Pliocene and Lower Pleistocene[1]	
1-2 million years B.P.	*Australopithecus* and *Homo* in Africa and perhaps Asia. Perhaps first *H. erectus* at Lake Turkana
2-3 million years B.P.	*Australopithecus* and *Homo* in Africa and perhaps Asia
3 plus million years B.P.	*Australopithecus*[2] and *Homo* in Africa

[1]*Gigantopithecus* is deleted because of its questioned status.
[2]Includes both the robust and gracile forms.

Data from B. Campbell, 1976.

studies and amino acid racemization determinations by Bada et al. (1974) suggests an age of about 100,000 years. The Omo II fossil (Day, 1965) from the Kibish formation is similar to Rhodesian and has a similar tentative date.

Summary—How Many Ancestors and Who?

The "Neanderthal problem" has circulated for years. The major questions are: (1) What is the taxonomic position of the classic or western European Neanderthals? (2) How does one interpret the variability of Würm I populations? (3) What led to the demise of western European Neanderthals? (4) In which area or areas of the world did anatomically modern populations evolve? Some answers become clearer with the recovery of new forms and the reexamination of others; other questions become harder to answer. Some of the problem is semantics.[4]

There are conflicting viewpoints as to the taxonomy of the western group. Some designate them a separate species, i.e., *H. neanderthalensis*; others include them in the species *H. sapiens* and recognize a subspecific designation, *H. sapiens neanderthalensis*. One of the major reasons for this taxonomic reshuffling is the recognition of transitional forms which cannot be assigned to either the Neanderthal or anatomically modern *H. sapiens* group. What can be said with assurance about the Würm populations? They were geographically widespread and characterized by a great deal of morphological variability. The gene pool as a whole evolved from either *H. erectus* or some very similar group. Some Würm populations (i.e., classic Neanderthals) died out, lending little of their genes to modern populations. Others, i.e., transitional forms in East and Central Europe and the Middle East, became fully modern *Homo*.

Interpretations

Neanderthal School. Various possibilities have led to various interpretations, which are illustrated in Figure 17-11. Variations of these theories are endless; they are constantly being revised and rejected. Howells (1967:241) aptly states, "... they sometimes generate more heat than light." The first-offered Neanderthal theory of unilineal evolution dates to a time when few fossils were available and dating inaccurate, or unavailable. This theory argues that modern *Homo* arose directly through a number of simple evolutionary stages including a Neanderthal phase. Dr. A. Hrdlička was the principal advocate of this theory which many reject as too simplistic. Dr. C. L. Brace has taken up the cudgels and vigorously argued that Neanderthals, as typified in western Europe, formed a large part and parcel of our genetic ancestry.

The two other points of view, the *Pre-neanderthal* and *Pre-sapiens* schools, have much in common. Both split the main stem of hominid evolution back to the time of Steinheim and Swanscombe and both

[4]Dr. C. Loring Brace, long an opponent of the theory that the Neanderthals were too primitive to be included in our ancestral lineage, notes the misusage of the term "Neanderthal." The term itself is now so familiar, specifically its implications of an archaic form, that it describes things quite unrelated to its original meaning. As Brace notes, modern writers are not adverse to referring to ultraconservatives and out-dated social attitudes as "Neanderthal," and occasionally call those with whom they disagree "Neanderthals" in thoughts or action. Similarly, "Neanderthals" in politics are regarded as human fossils, with the implication that they are outmoded and possessing long-past untenable ideas.

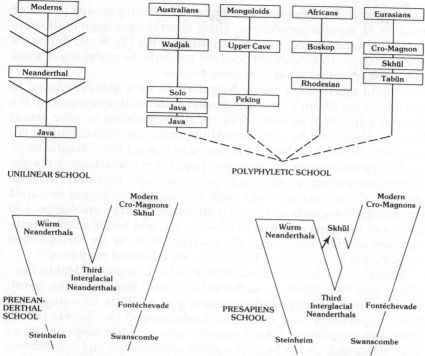

Figure 17-11. Some theories of human descent.

consider classic Neanderthals evolutionary dead ends, becoming extinct as climatic conditions to which they were adapted ameliorated. The Presapiens theory suggests that *H. sapiens* originated as a distinct, completely separate line from that leading to the Neanderthals. Both theories utilize the same evidence differently. Some adherents of the Presapiens theory split the trunk at Swanscombe and Steinheim, arguing that Steinheim led to the Neanderthals and Swanscombe, through Fontéchevade, to modern populations.

Presapiens School. The Presapiens school is rather old; it originally argued that *H. sapiens* in essentially modern form reached back into the Pleistocene as a separate evolutionary branch. Presapiens adherents feel that Fontéchevade is evidence of a long separate evolutionary history of modern *Homo*. Its major proponents today consist of some members of the paleontological schools of Italy, Germany, and France.

Preneanderthal School. Adherents of the Preneanderthal school, the viewpoint to which most subscribe, see Steinheim and Swanscombe as leading to another Third Interglacial stem (i.e., Ehringsdorf and Quinzano), of basically Neanderthal type. This group was ancestral to the western Neanderthals and to the eastern varieties, which led to modern *Homo*. In this view, there is a broad, variable population. One segment of this population is the isolated, western European, cold-adapted group (western Neanderthals); the other segment inhabited the Near East and became modern *H. sapiens*.

A Fourth Alternative? I would like to suggest that modern populations arose from a stock such as Steinheim and Swanscombe through a number of intermediate forms. While classic Neanderthals evolved isolated in a cold climate, more favorable conditions further to the east and south and the continual migration of hunting groups produced modern *H. sapiens* populations. There seem to have been *in situ* transitions of hominids and their tools throughout the Old World during the last glaciation. This viewpoint does not preclude the possibility of some classic Neanderthal genes in modern populations.

Without much doubt classic Neanderthals were greatly reduced by the end of the Würm I; however, there is evidence that segments of the general population survived. Perhaps the population became extinct through absorption by anatomically and culturally more advanced immigrants, although we have no evidence to support this. Climatic amelioration probably allowed for greater population contact along the glacial fringes; perhaps emigrating populations simply bred with the Neanderthals. Or, populations with more advanced technologies swamped the classic Neanderthals, a process known as cultural exploitation. Old tools and methods give way to newer, finer, and better adapted technologies and less technologically advanced cultures are slowly forced to extinction in contact with technologically advanced neighbors.

Where did modern *Homo sapiens* arise? In Europe, the Middle East, Africa, and Asia, for there seems to be no one area where this transition occurred—it happened in several places. What advantages did these populations have over their predecessors? Dr. Solecki (1971) offers two suggestions. One is speech—fully articulate language. It has been suggested, on the basis of a stable tool tradition and fragmentary anatomical reconstructions, that Neanderthals lacked a fully articulate, precise language. This is yet to be proven. A second cultural achievement of Upper **Paleolithic** populations subsequent to the Neanderthals may have been their ability to make notational counts, an advance enabling them to record events for the future. There is evidence of such notational sequences on engraved bones and stones. A mnemonic device which provided a reference to past and future events would grant an important economic advantage for control over one's environment and destiny.

This chapter supports the argument that there is nothing in Second and Third interglacial hominid assemblages suggestive of a modern *Homo sapiens* population preceding the Neanderthals. The evidence arguing for a separation of Steinheim and Swanscombe and for an advanced status for Fontéchevade seems dubious.

The Neanderthal controversy is unsettled. The viewpoint adopted here is that the Neanderthals are part of our evolutionary heritage, for it seems likely that we share some of our genes with the European Neanderthals. We need a clearer definition of what the term "Neanderthal" means and a closer investigation of the importance and distribution of eastern and central European "transitionals" and their tool assemblages.

Bibliography

Bada, J.; Schroeder, R.; Trotsch, R.; and Berger, R. 1974. Concordance of college-based radiocarbon and aspartic acid racemization ages. *Proceedings National Academy of Science* 71:914-17.

Bardon, L.; Bouyssonie, A.; and Bouyssonie, J. 1908. The discovery of a human Mousterian skeleton at La Chapelle-aux-Saints (Correze) (a note by the authors to the French Academy of Sciences). In *Adam or ape*, edited by L. Leakey, J. Prost, and S. Prost, pp. 177-78. Cambridge: Schenkman Publishers, 1971.

Binford, L., and Binford, S. 1966. A preliminary analysis of functional variability in the Mousterian of Levallois facies. In *Recent studies in paleoanthropology* (*American Anthropologist* special publication), pp. 238-95.

Binford, S. 1968. Early Upper Pleistocene adaptations in the Levant. *American Anthropologist* 70:707.

Bordes, F. 1972. *A tale of two caves.* New York: Harper & Row.

Boule, M., and Vallois, H. 1957. *Fossil man.* New York: Dryden Press.

Brace, C. 1962a. Cultural factors in the evolution of the human dentition. In *Culture and the evolution of man*, edited by A. Montagu, pp. 343-54. New York: Oxford University Press.

————. 1962b. Refocusing on the Neanderthal problem. *American Anthropologist* 64:729.

————. 1964. The fate of the "classic" Neanderthals: a consideration of hominid catastrophism. *Current Anthropology* 5:3.

————. 1968. Neanderthal. *Natural History* 77:38.

————. 1971. Digging Shanidar. *Natural History* 80:82.

Brace, C., and Molnar, S. 1967. Experimental studies in human tooth wear. *American Journal of Physical Anthropology* 27:213.

Brose, D., and Wolpoff, M. 1971. Early upper Paleolithic man and late Paleolithic tools. *American Anthropologist* 73:1156.

Brothwell, D. 1960. Upper Pleistocene human skull from the Niah Cave. *Sarawak Museum Journal* 9:323.

Butzer, K. 1964. *Environment and archaeology.* Chicago: Aldine.

Campbell, B. 1966. *Human evolution.* Chicago: Aldine.

————. 1976. *Humankind emerging.* Boston: Little, Brown.

Carlisle, R., and Siegel, M. 1974. Some problems in the interpretation of Neanderthal speech capabilities; a reply to Lieberman. *American Anthropologist* 76:319-23.

Clark, W. Le Gros. 1964. *Fossil evidence for human evolution.* Chicago: University of Chicago Press.

Coon, C. 1962. *The origin of races.* New York: Knopf.

Cornwell, I. 1968. *Prehistoric animals and their hunters.* New York: Praeger.

Dahlberg, A. 1963. Dental evolution and culture. *Human Biology* 35:237.

Dahlberg, A., and Carbonell, V. 1961. The dentition of the Magdalenian female from Cap Blanc, France. *Man* 61:49.

Day, M. 1965. *Guide to fossil man.* Cleveland: World Publishing.

de Lumley, H., and de Lumley, M. 1973. Pre-Neanderthal human remains from Arago Cave in southeastern France. *Yearbook of Physical Anthropology* 17:162-69.

Dupree, L.; Lattmen, L.; and Davis, R. 1970. Ghar-i-Mordeh Gusfand (Cave of the Dead Sheep): a new Mousterian locality in North Afghanistan. *Science* 167:1610.

Ewing, J. 1960. Human types and prehistoric cultures of Ksar 'Akil, Lebanon. *Fifth International Congress of Anthropological and Ethnological Sciences*, pp. 535-39.

Howell, F. 1951. The place of Neanderthal man in human evolution. *American Journal of Physical Anthropology* 9:379.

————. 1957a. Pleistocene glacial ecology and the evolution of "classical Neanderthal" man. *Quarterly Review of Biology* 32:330.

————. 1957b. Pathology and posture of Neanderthal man. *Quarterly Review of Biology* 32:360.

_____. 1960. European and Northwest African Middle Pleistocene hominids. *Current Anthropology* 1:195.

_____. 1965. *Early man.* New York: Time-Life Books.

Howells, W. 1967. *Mankind in the making.* Garden City, N.Y.: Doubleday.

Hrdlička, A. 1927. The Neanderthal phase of man. *Journal of the Royal Anthropological Institute* 57:249.

Ivanhoe, F. 1970. Was Virchow right about Neanderthal? *Nature* 227:577.

Jelinek, J. 1969. Neanderthal man and *Homo sapiens* in central and eastern Europe. *Current Anthropology* 10:475.

Keith, A. 1925. *The antiquity of man,* ed. 2. London: Williams and Norgate.

Keith, A., and McCown, T. 1939. *The stone age of Mount Carmel,* vol. 2. Oxford: Clarendon Press.

Kennedy, K. 1975. *Neanderthal man.* Minneapolis: Burgess.

Klein, R. 1969. *Man and culture in the late Pleistocene.* San Francisco: Chandler Publishing Co.

_____. 1973. Geologic antiquity of Rhodesian man. *Nature* 244:311-12.

Leakey, L.; Prost, J.; and Prost, S., eds. 1971. *Adam or ape.* Cambridge: Schenkman.

Lieberman, P., and Crelin, E. 1971. On the speech of Neanderthal Man. *Linguistic Inquiry* 2:203-22.

_____. 1974. Speech and Neanderthal Man. A reply to Carlisle and Siegel. *American Anthropologist* 76:323-25.

Lieberman, P.; Crelin, E.; and Klatt, D. 1972. Phonetic ability and related anatomy of the newborn and adult human, Neanderthal man, and the chimpanzee. *American Anthropologist* 74:287-307.

Loomis, W. 1967. Skin pigment regulation of vitamin-D biosynthesis in man. *Science* 157:503.

Luguet, G. 1930. *The art and religion of fossil man.* New Haven: Yale University Press.

Maringer, J. 1960. *The gods of prehistoric man.* London: George Weidenfeld & Nicolson.

Marschack, A. 1972. *The roots of civilization.* New York: McGraw-Hill.

Mayr, E. 1971. Was Virchow right about Neanderthal man? *Nature* 229:253.

McCown, T., and Keith, A. 1939. *The stone age of Mount Carmel,* vol. 1. The fossil human remains from the Levallois-Mousterian. Oxford: Oxford University Press.

Morant, G. 1938. The form of the Swanscombe skull. *Journal of the Royal Anthropological Institute* 68:67.

Pfeiffer, J. 1969. *The emergence of man.* New York: Harper & Row.

Poirier, F. 1972. Reply to teeth wear and culture: a survey of tooth functions among some prehistoric populations (by S. Molnar). *Current Anthropology* 13:519.

_____. 1977. *Fossil evidence: the human evolutionary journey.* St. Louis: Mosby.

Proetz, A. 1953. *Essays on the applied physiology of the nose,* ed. 2. St. Louis: Annals Publishing Co.

Sergi, S. 1967. The Neanderthal palaeanthropi in Italy. In *Selected essays 1949-61,* edited by W. Howells, pp. 500-506. New York: Atheneum.

Solecki, R. 1971. *Shanidar: the first flower people.* New York: Knopf.

Straus, W., and Cave, A. 1957. Pathology and the posture of Neanderthal man. *Quarterly Review of Biology* 32:348.

Sullivan, W. 1971. The life and times of man 200,000 years ago. *New York Times* pp. 1, 20, October 17.

Tobias, P. 1971. Human skeletal remains from the Cave of Hearths, Makapansgat, Northern Transvaal. *American Journal of Physical Anthropology* 34:335.

Vallois, H. 1952. Monophyletism and polyphyletism in man. *South African Journal of Science* 49:69.

_____. 1954. Neanderthals and presapiens. *Journal of the Royal Anthropological Institute* 84:11.

_____. 1961. The social life of early man: the evidence of skeletons. In *Social life of early man*, edited by S. Washburn, pp. 214-35. Chicago: Aldine.

Weiner, J., and Campbell, B. 1964. The taxonomic status of the Swanscombe skull. In *The Swanscombe skull*, edited by C. Overy. London: Royal Anthropological Society of Great Britain.

Wolpoff, M. 1968. Climatic influence on the skeletal nasal aperture. *American Journal of Physical Anthropology* 29:405.

_____. 1971. Vértesszöllös and the presapiens theory. *American Journal of Physical Anthropology* 35:209.

Wright, P. 1971. Syphilis and Neanderthal man. *Nature* 229:409.

Chapter 18
Appearance of Modern *Homo sapiens sapiens*

In the last chapter we traced hominid evolutionary history until approximately 40,000 years B.P. This chapter completes that history with the colonization of the New World and some of the Pacific Islands. No single Pleistocene cultural group emerges so markedly as Late Paleolithic European hunters. During this time there is a noticeable acceleration of cultural and technological innovation, and we witness the full flowering of our aesthetic senses.

Where the transition to modern *H. sapiens* occurred is still arguable. Current evidence is skewed towards Europe because this is where most work has been done. We know a lot about some European populations, especially in France, and comparatively little about those residing in other parts of the world. However, that other parts of the world were inhabited is not questioned; late Paleolithic inhabitants moved into North and South America and into Australia. During the time period from 10,000 to 40,000 years B.P. *H. sapiens* lived as small-band hunters and gatherers. They spread across the world where they encountered a variety of environmental conditions.

Evidence in Europe

We have a rather large sample of European Upper Paleolithic populations. Because of the practice of burying their dead, a number of almost complete skeletons are known. The stature of the populations varied, but the males attained a height comparable to modern males. Women seem to have been somewhat shorter. Their bones indicate a robust build, but not as robust as preceding Neanderthals. Upper Paleolithic populations had large heads (with modern cranial capacities),

Upper Paleolithic art.

wide faces, prominent chins, and high-bridged noses. Little distinguishes them from modern populations.

Distribution. The geographical distribution of these populations reveals that places too cold during the Würm I were also difficult to inhabit during the Würm II and III and subsequently. Southern France was again a favorite living spot. Like their predecessors, Upper Paleolithic populations were big-game hunters; it has been argued that this dependence on big game selected for a larger body size and larger brains. Perhaps Upper Paleolithic *Homo* was being shaped by the creatures hunted. To be a more effective hunter, they became a herd animal. "He invented crowds to become a better predator" (Pfeiffer 1969:198).

Upper Paleolithic populations learned to live sucessfully in all environments but high barren arctic regions and true deserts. Cultural and ecological adaptations to the diverse habitats are everywhere evident in housing structures and the clothes-making kits.

Dwellings. Upper Paleolithic populations inhabited a great variety of dwellings (Figure 18-1); rock shelters (i.e., rock overhangs as distinguished from deep caves) were widely used. Trees were felled and propped against the rock face, perhaps trellised by branches and skins. Large caves were inhabited; huts or tents built inside caves were heated with wood or bone fires. Where rock shelters are rare, as in central and eastern Europe, we find remains of permanent dwellings. At Pushkari, U.S.S.R., there are long-shaped huts which are sometimes sunk into the ground. One hut measures 39 × 13 feet. At the Kostenki I site there are traces of two dwellings, each 120 × 49 feet. There are also nine hearths situated on the long axis, and numerous silos of varying shapes and heights. It is unlikely that this complex was accommodated under one roof.

Tool Inventory. Upper Paleolithic populations produced a culture that, in variety and elegance, far exceeded anything of their predecessors. Upper Paleolithic groups made fine stone tools and delicately worked bone. The Eurasian Upper Paleolithic was essentially a blade-

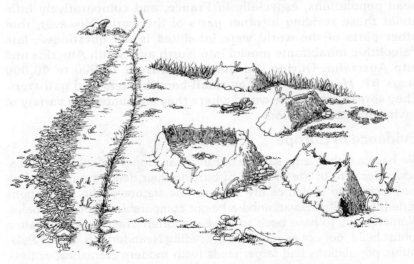

Figure 18-1. A reconstruction of the 23,000 year old Dolni Vestonice site.

tool assemblage characterized by an abundance and variety of long, parallel-sided implements called "blades." The blade-tool industry was partially devised for working bone and wood. Of the functional tool types, burins (chisel-shaped blades) were probably utilized for engraving and working wood, bone, or antler. These may have been employed as handles or shafts by scraping or shaving wood. Various types of scrapers may have been used to scrape wood or hollow out wood or bone. Laurel-leaf blades were carefully made into thin, sharp-edged knives or arrowheads, presumably used as daggers.

New Tools and Weapons. New items such as polished pins or bone or antler awls are found in Upper Paleolithic tool kits. New types of points were probably hafted to sticks. The later **Magdelanian** inventory (a cultural complex from western Europe dating from ca. 12,000 to 17,000 B.P.) included hooked rods employed as spear-throwers, barbed points and harpoons for fishing, fish-hooks, needles with eyes, bone and ivory bodkins (large-eyed blunt needles), belt-fasteners, and tools of undetermined use. Many of these tools were highly decorative, depicting hunt animals and may have served as ceremonial items.

The use of the bow and arrow is first verified for the latter part of Late Paleolithic. Some one hundred wooden arrows have been recovered at the Mesolithic Stellmoor site, a former lake near Hamburg, Germany, dating to ca. 10,500 years B.P. About 25 percent of the arrows were designed for use without a tip; one such untipped arrow was found *in situ* in a wolf vertebra. These arrows were probably fire-hardened. The flint-tipped arrows may have been used for large game only, the untipped types for smaller game.

Upper-Paleolithic Lifeways

Dietary Patterns. Upper Paleolothic economies varied according to the habitat, but these were primarily big-game hunters with hunting techniques comparable to those of preceding times. The offensive weaponry included spears, javelins, harpoons, clubs, stone missiles, bow and arrow, and boomerangs or throwing sticks. Bolas were probably slung at the legs of animals, snares and pitfalls almost certainly trapped big game, and gregarious herds were run off cliff faces. Some French and Spanish cave drawings have been interpreted as depicting snares, traps, pitfalls, and enclosures.

Although fishing long preceded Upper Paleolithic peoples, the technique underwent refinement. Harpoons and fish-gorges were used during the Upper Paleolithic. Aquatic foods may have formed a sizable part of some local diets.

Reindeer played a large role in the hunting of some later Upper Paleolithic populations. It has even been suggested (on scanty evidence) that reindeer were semidomesticated and that some form of reindeer nomadism occurred during the terminal Paleolithic. Some Upper Paleolithic sites indicate that the human inhabitants relied almost entirely on reindeer for food, accounting for upwards of 99 percent of the food requirements. The reindeer-hominid relationship seems to have been very close. Clark (1967:64) notes that "by establishing close association with a reindeer herd a group of hunters was able to secure what was in effect a walking larder and a source of supply of raw materials needed in technology."

In addition to protein, reindeer supplied their hunters with raw materials for clothing and tents, sinews for thread and line for hunting gear, bones and antlers for tools and weapons, and teeth for ornaments. There is abundant evidence of reindeer antler being fashioned into harpoons at the German sites of Schleswig-Holstein. The frequency of bone sewing needles, bodkins, and belt fasteners suggests that elaborate wearing apparel, presumably of tanned hides and furs, was common.

Group hunting economies may have been specialized for certain animals. While reindeer was certainly the most important food item in France and Germany, the woolly mammoth was important to folks farther east. Horses were locally important. If the game were seasonal migrants, their predatory hunters presumably followed the same pattern. If the gregarious herds were sedentary, semipermanent dwellings were possible.

Group Organization. Although Upper Paleolithic groups probably still lived in bands, there may have been the beginnings of larger social organizations. A tribal structure, an association of many bands cemented by marriage and economic bonds, may have been developing. Upper Paleolithic populations may have developed rituals for coming and remaining together. To reduce friction they may have elaborated upon previous social and behavioral patterns. Incest taboos and mating and kinship rules may have been formulated to create a more intricate and cohesive relationship among large numbers of individuals.

Reliance upon reindeer as a food source played a large role in sustaining the rather sizeable communities common to Upper Paleolithic populations. Some summer reindeer hunting sites cover up to five acres; the rather large continuous string of rock shelters stretching along the Dordogne River Valley may have housed communities of 300 to 900 persons. The sizeable communities probably instituted new forms of social controls to make life more bearable and organized. These societies were probably more complicated and stratified than those of their predecessors.

Despite technological achievements, Upper Paleolithic populations had high mortality rates; the mortality pattern is similar to preceding Neanderthal populations. Less than 50 percent of the seventy-six Eurasian skeletons were from individuals attaining twenty-one years of age. Only 12 percent were past age forty. Practically no female reached the ripe old age of thirty.

An Example of an Upper-Paleolithic Living Site: Kostenki-Borshevo

The Kostenki-Borshevo sites are located in the Don Valley of Russia. Human occupation layers date to 25,000 years B.P.; however, most occupation layers have a C-14 date of 12,000 to 15,000 years B.P. The last occupations are from about 11,000 years B.P.

The late Würm inhabitants of this region were successful big-game hunters who used the meat and bones of their quarry. They built rather permanent structures; the spectacular size and nature of some dwellings suggest that some settlements were rather large. Cultural activity, through trade or movement, extended over distances greater than 100 miles. Evidence for ritual practices, and perhaps religious life, is manifested in their burials and in the presence of numerous art objects.

Vast quantities of faunal remains found in association with cultural levels furnish direct evidence of subsistence patterns. The most prevalent animal remains are of large herbivores, especially horse and mammoth; wild cattle are rare and reindeer not especially abundant. Wolf and fox skeletons are the most frequent carnivore remains. While they may be remnants of a meal, it is likely they were caught for their pelts which subsequently became clothing. Furthermore, perforated canine teeth seem to have been popular decorative items. Hare remains also occur and their pelts could have been used for clothing.

The numerous habitation ruins exhibit much variability in size, shape, and state of preservation. In some cases all that remains is a large ground depression; in others there is a considerable accumulation of nearly intact mammoth bones (which may have been used in construction). Others are simply a roundish or oval area where cultural materials accumulated. The framework of these habitations was probably wood and/or bone covered with skins and hides. Most structures seem to have contained hearths and pits used either for storage or cooking.

Fire was known to the site occupants. Besides the ordinary usages of providing warmth, light, and predator protection, fire also seems to have been an important aid in artifact manufacture. It may have been used to harden spear tips, to prepare some types of flint for working by careful preheating, and to obtain (from iron ore) a red, ochreous pigment. Perhaps as part of a reburial or delayed burial ritual, this pigment was rubbed on bones of the deceased. Bone and stone artifacts comprise the most abundant tool remains; a number of these artifacts probably represent elements of weaponry. Some stone and bone points may have armed throwing or thrusting spears. A large number of different tool types were probably used to process animal remains, especially to prepare skins. A wide variety of bone implements have been recovered including possible mattocks or hoes (for digging holes), "clothes fasteners," "hairpins," and a large array of unexplainable objects. Bone was used in house construction and may have been used for fuel.

Burials. Four burials were uncovered, each associated with some kind of burial ritual. In one instance, the deceased was accompanied by a quantity of grave goods. There are burials at some sites, but none at others. Some of the Kostenki-Borshevo people may have disposed of their dead away from the living sites.

Aesthetic Life of Upper-Paleolithic Populations

One reason Upper Paleolithic populations, especially in Europe, are so vivid is because they left numerous traces of their artistic works which tell much about their daily life, ritual practices, and concerns. Upper Paleolithic populations were inclined to animal worship. They left many provocative assortments of animal bones and skulls. The Cave Bear Cult persisted through part of the Upper Paleolithic.

Cave Art. Upper Paleolithic art can be divided into two categories: chattel art, i.e., art applied to small objects normally found in archaeological deposits, and cave art, i.e., art restricted to the walls, roofs, and occasionally floors of cave and rock shelters. France alone has more than seventy cave art sites dating from 10,000 to 28,000 years B.P., most dealing with animals of the hunt. Cave art took the form of engraving and painting, either separately or together. Reliefs were made by cutting away the rock to varying depths and there are examples of doodling on clay films on cave walls, ceilings, and floors, and modelling of clay figurines. Coloring consisted of various kinds of ocher, manganese, and charcoal.

Art and Magic? Upper Paleolithic art seems strongly tied to spiritual life; much of this is placed on walls deep in relatively inaccessible caves and much is very difficult to see. The caves were probably entered by people utilizing artificial light (torches or fat-burning lamps). The French priest Henri Breuil, who devoted much of his life to the study of prehistory, noted that much of the art is in areas badly situated for viewing—in narrow niches, behind rock bumps, and sometimes in areas which must have been dangerous for both artist and viewer to enter. The art is apparently not to enhance the beholder's life but for some mysterious ritual.

Some view Upper Paleolithic art as related to the food-quest, as magical rituals bound to the hunt. Another group interprets much of the art as representative of sexual symbolism. No matter what interpretation one accepts—the time-honored theory that representations were made to gain control over the food supply by sympathetic magic, or as representing in some way the antithesis between male and female principles—much of the art is zoomorphic (i.e., concerned with animal representations). So close seems the tie between humans and animals that some are depicted as masked figures with animal heads, antlers, and skins strapped over human forms.

Upper Paleolithic art is not so much an attempt at amusement or self-expression as an adjustment to daily life. Much of the expression reflects concerns with food procurement. Many of the animal figures are painted with spears in them or marked with blows from clubs. The

Figure 18-2. A portrait of a possible Cro-Magnon sorcerer.

French cave of Font-de-Gaume has several drawings of traps or enclosures with animals suggestively caught in them. One depicts a mammoth in a pitlike trap.

Many paintings are superimposed one atop another; some of the paintings in the magnificent French cave of Lascaux are four layers deep. If these paintings are magical manifestations, i.e., a way of ensuring a good hunt, were there also magicians? There are some fifty paintings of strange-looking sorcerers, human figures clad in animal skins, sometimes wearing animal heads or horns. Many of these are depicted in the midst of a dance (Figure 18-2).

Sculpture and Engravings. Upper Paleolithic populations were also sculptors and engravers; there are incised animal outlines on cave walls, some produced in bas relief. At Cap Blanc, near Les Eyzies, there is a set of horses carved in bas relief; the natural rock curves accentuate the sides of the horses' bodies. Female statuettes of bone, stone, and ivory of varying design and merit are widely distributed throughout Europe. Their most obvious trait is emphasis on the torso, focusing on the belly, breasts, and buttocks to the exclusion of head and limbs. These resemble tiny earth goddesses or fertility figurines, and so they have been interpreted. A prime example is the so-called "Venus of Willendorf," a four inch limestone statuette, with a wavy hairdo and accentuated female curves (Figures 18-3 and 18-4).

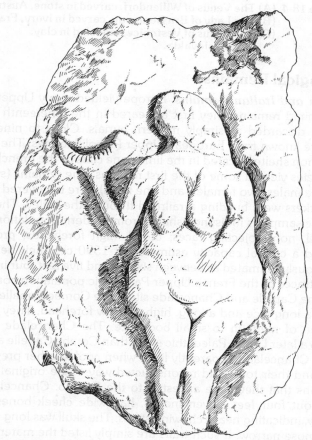

Figure 18-3. The Venus of Laussel, carved in stone, French.

Appearance of
Modern *Homo
sapiens sapiens*

337

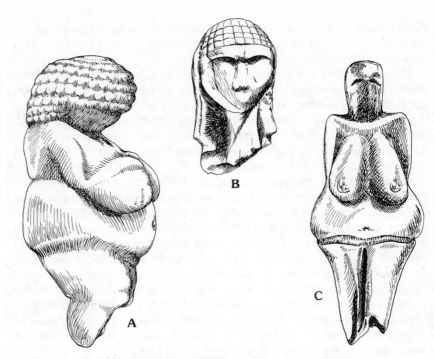

Figure 18-4. (A) The Venus of Willendorf, carved in stone, Austria.
(B) The Lady of Brassempouy, carved in ivory, France.
(C) The Venus of Vestonice, modeled in clay,
Czechoslovakia.

Osteological Remains

French and Italian Remains. Europe yielded many Upper Paleolithic hominid remains; they first appeared in the nineteenth century and were discarded as simply modern burials. Close to ninety individuals are known from European Upper Paleolithic sites. The famous Cro-Magnon shelter located in the limestone cliffs by the French village of Les Eyzies yielded some of the first remains. The remains (six skeletons: three males, two females, and one fetus) were uncovered in 1868 while workers were building a railroad through the valley. The Upper Paleolithic sample is indistinguishable from modern populations. They had small, non-projecting faces; broad, high foreheads; protruding chins; and a cranial capacity estimated at 1590 cc. Their height has been variously estimated as between six feet and five feet four inches.

Other traces of the French Upper Paleolithic population come from the Combe Capelle and Chancelade sites. The Combe Capelle individuals had a long face and a long, high, narrow forehead. They seem to have been of medium to small body size. The Chancelade remains belong to a later Upper Paleolithic stage than Combe Capelle and Cro-Magnon. Chancelade apparently lived when cool weather prevailed in Europe and their tools and reconstructed way of life originally led to suggestions that they were ancestral to the Eskimo. Chancelade was short, about four feet eleven inches, had wide cheek bones, and a heavy jaw, indicating heavy chewing stress. The skull was long and narrow, the nose narrow. If such traits are simply listed the material looks Eskimo; however, the total morphological pattern of the skull does not support this assumption. The Eskimo-like traits may simply be responses to heavy chewing stresses and to the use of the teeth as tools.

A pair of interesting skeletons, possibly a mother and teen-aged son, come from the Grotte des Enfants, one of the Grimaldi caves on the Riveria. These skeletons were originally called the "Grimaldi Negroids" because they supposedly exhibited African traits. However, the most likely explanation is that the resemblance is a coincidence due to a limited population sample and reconstruction errors.

Central European Remains. There are a host of central and eastern European representatives of Upper Paleolithic populations. Three of the major finds come from Czechoslovakia: Predmosti, Brno, and Lautsch. Predmosti is a common grave containing eighteen individuals which may date from 20,000 to 30,000 years B.P. Two other individuals were recovered at the site. Some of the skulls show primitive traits; for example there is evidence of brow ridges, which is a unique feature among Upper Paleolithic populations. The material is associated with over 1000 mammoths; obviously, the Predmosti inhabitants were big-game hunters. The Brno skull, an adult male, manifests some primitive traits. In comparison with the French remains, it had more accentuated brow ridges and other skull features resembling the classic Neanderthals.

Asian Hominid Remains—China. Asian Upper Paleolithic remains are not especially prevalent; the major material comes from Chou Kou Tien, China, and Wadjak, Java. The Chou Kou Tien remains, consisting of the skeletal parts of at least seven individuals, have been dated to approximately 10,000 years B.P. Skull fractures seem to indicate that they died an unnatural death, but while they may have been killed in a mass murder, they were not cannibalized. One of the seven was killed by an arrow or small-headed spear piercing the skull. Two of the females seem to have been killed by a stone dropped on the side of their heads. Other fragmentary materials also date to the Upper Paleolithic of China, and some argue that this material is ancestral to modern Chinese populations.

Java. Prior to his discovery of *H. erectus*, E. Dubois found two fossil skulls at Wadjak (also spelled Wajak), Java. Since the site has long been destroyed, the exact dating is unknown. For thirty years Dubois hid these skulls from the world in a newspaper-covered glass case. It was not until the 1920s that Dubois showed this material to the world.

Table 18-1. The Upper Paleolithic of Southwestern France.

Divisions of Würm Glaciation	C^{14} Dates	Cultural Tradition
Würm IV	9,500	Magdalenian
Würm III/IV	15,000 17,000	Magdalenian
Würm III	19,000 29,000	Solutrean Perigordian Aurignacian
Würm III/II	32,000	Perigordian Aurignacian
Würm II	37,000	Mousterian

Adapted from F. Bordes, 1968.

Appearance of Modern *Homo sapiens sapiens*

Africa

African Upper Paleolithic remains are scarce and much of the material, as a result of being blasted out of quarries, is of disputed dating. Most remains come from East and South Africa. A human mandible from Makapansgat, South Africa, is dated to 40,000 plus or minus 10,000 years B.P. Another South African find, the long and narrow Cape Flats skull, is from a site near Capetown. It has a cranial capacity of 1230 cc. Dr. C. Coon (1962) suggests that the skull may be ancestral to some modern black African populations; however, his evidence is questionable. A final South African skull is the Boskop braincase found in 1913. The cranial capacity of the skull is estimated between 1800 and 1900 cc. Along with other remains, known as Fish Hoek, the Boskop material is often considered ancestral to the modern South African Bushman.

There are a number of Upper Paleolithic remains from East Africa, a crossroad open to access from many directions. With marginal success, many have searched here for the origins of a number of modern populations. Rather late remains, spanning the range between 5000 and 10,000 years B.P., include material from Gamble's Cave and the Singa skull from the Sudan. The Asselar skeleton was found in 1927 in a dry Sahara river bed north of Timbuctu and was associated with remains of fresh-water molluscs, fish, crocodiles, gazelles, and antelope. A few contend that Asselar is one of the earliest representatives of modern black populations. This assumption is based upon skull shape and size, tooth dimensions, and overall skeletal size. However, such assessments, without benefit of a large population sample, are questionable.

Perhaps the best evidence for the early appearance of *Homo sapiens* in sub-Saharan Africa comes from the Omo River Valley. In 1967 R. Leakey recovered parts of three skeletons, including two broken crania and some postcranial bones, plus skull fragments of a third individual. Although this material is not fully published, the two incomplete crania have been described by Day (1969, 1971). Omo I and Omo II show some variation; however, Rightmire (1975) feels they should be grouped together for now. Omo II, which unfortunately lacks a face, is quite heavily built and has a long low cranial vault. There is a well-developed ridge of bone across the back of the occiput. Omo I is more modern in appearance; it lacks frontal flattening and has a more rounded occiput. Both skulls are fairly clear representatives of *Homo sapiens*.

The dating of this material is still questioned. Associated faunal remains may be of Middle Pleistocene derivation, and an age of 130,000 years has been obtained for the geological formation containing the crania. However, the thorium/uranium method used for the date is considered doubtful. According to Day, the Omo II cranium shows a general resemblance to the Rhodesian fossils, and Rightmire maintains some resemblance to the Florisbad material.

Australia

Dating. The colonization of Australia poses a number of problems such as when and how humans first entered Australia, with what Asian forms were they related, and what are the relationships between Australia, Tasmania, and New Guinea on the one hand, and Indonesia on the other? Lately, the dating of when humans first entered Australia has undergone considerable alteration. New discoveries suggest a much earlier colonization date than once considered.

Australia's original colonizers arrived by boat and foot via two major island routes: (1) Java and Timor, or (2) Borneo, the Celebes, and the Moluccas. The widest distance to be crossed over water was about fifty miles; this was probably managed by small rafts or boats. Which route was selected is unknown; however, there are broad anatomical relationships between modern Australian aborigines and the fossil materials from Ngandong and Wadjak, Java; Aitape, New Guinea; and Niah, Borneo. Once in Australia, humans crossed the Bass Strait and colonized Tasmania. Prior to 10,000 years B.P. a broad level causeway linked the two land masses. A period of approximately 9000 years was available to cross the 150 mile causeway. One site in Tasmania dates back to 7200 B.P.

Green Gully. Until recently only three major finds were available in Australia: Keilor, Cohuna, and Talgai. New and exciting material has recently come to light, however. One of the major new remains is the Green Gully site located two miles south of the Keilor site and nine miles northwest of Melbourne. The Green Gully bones were accidentally uncovered during a commercial excavation in August 1965. Various charcoal samples yielded dates of between 8000 and 9100 years B.P.

The Green Gully material is largely fractured and is a mixture of male and female bones. The distortion of the bones, and the mixture of male and female remains, suggest that this is not a simple burial. It is quite likely a delayed burial. The skeletal remains were buried some twelve months after death and after most flesh had rotted away. Delayed burial is still practiced by some aboriginal bands.[1]

Reconstruction of the Green Gully remains was a horrendous task. A normal skeleton contains but 236 bones—the Green Gully material consisted of 3900 pieces. Only 730 of these pieces could be identified and used for restoration. The unexpected discovery of male and female bones confused restoration. This mixture is probably due to the fact that a male and a female body were adjacently exposed awaiting their delayed burials. The bones were mixed and dispersed by predatory birds and animals. During actual burial, the mourners simply gathered the material and buried it in one grave, some two-thirds of the female and one-third of the male.

Keilor, Talgai, Cohuna. The Keilor skull has been variously dated from 7400 to 16,500 years B.P.; the later date is gaining respectability. The face is not projecting; the cranial capacity is estimated between 1464 cc to 1593 cc. It has been argued that there is a strong resemblance between this skull and the Wadjak material from Java. The Talgai skull, found in 1884, is apparently of a male, fourteen to sixteen years old. It is smaller than Keilor; the cranial capacity of 1300 cc falls within the range of modern Australian aborigines. The Cohuna skull was uncovered in 1925. The skull was mutilated; immediately after death the skull case was dislodged, apparently to get at the brain.

Lake Mungo. The most recent evidence of fossil material in Australia is also the most exciting. The new material comes from the Lake

[1]This is a good example of the strength of cultural conservatism.

Appearance of Modern *Homo sapiens sapiens*

341

Mungo area, one of a chain of lakes in southwestern New South Wales. Five shoreline sites contain evidence of prehistoric populations dating back 32,000 years B.P. One of the sites contains a human cremation; the others are typical aboriginal fireplaces. The Lake Mungo remains are among the most significant in Australian prehistory. Based on the number of teeth erupted, muscle markings on the bones, and the state of the cranial suture closure, the remains belong to a fragmented skeleton of a young, adult female. Before burial in a shallow grave, the body was burned and the charred bones extensively smashed. Reconstruction shows the female's skull to be full *H. sapiens*. Charcoal and shells near the site yield a date ranging from 30,000 to slightly older than 32,000 years B.P. The skeleton is more than 10,000 years older than any other Australian remains.

The Pleistocene presence of a late *H. sapiens* morphology in Australia has implications for Southeast Asia if the migration route for modern Australian aborigines is found there. Given the time needed for genetic infiltration and/or migration, the presence of morphologically *H. sapiens* populations in Australia by 26,000 years B.P. at the latest argues for the much earlier presence of similar people on the Southeast Asian mainland. This is supported by the morphology and probable age of the Niah skull. The Lake Mungo skeleton suggests that fully modern populations were present in South Asia perhaps earlier than elsewhere.

There is a recent report of material from Kow Swamp in Australia (Thorne and Macumber, 1972). This site is in southern Australia and has yielded skeletal material which supposedly is nine or ten thousand years old. However, it is argued that the material bears a close morphological resemblance to *Homo erectus* forms in Java rather than to modern Australian aborigines. Hulbert (1975) suggests that if this resemblance is confirmed then it may provide "...evidence that pre-*sapiens* man was capable of crossing thirty miles of water (at the least) which separated the Sahul and Sunda shelves during low-water periods. If this material is representative of pre-*sapiens* or transitional forms of *Homo sapiens*, it may also demonstrate the irregularity of the time level at which 'sapienization' took place" (p. 158).

The Americas

Dating. The date of entry into the New World has long been disputed. There is also a dispute as to how human populations arrived, i.e., by crossing the Bering Straits into Alaska and moving south, or by floating across the ocean to South America and migrating north.[2] A superabundance of caution characterized the early outlook. When the first **Folsom** point (Figure 18-5) dating from about 11,000 years B.P. was discovered in New Mexico in 1926, in association with extinct bison, it took three expeditions and discovery of several *in situ* points among faunal remains to convince many. Yet, nothing *a priori* argues against a Paleolithic entry into the New World.

The pendulum is now full swing; some, notably Dr. Louis Leakey, suggest a very old date for a New World entry. The Calico site is a very controversial site in San Bernardino County, California. This site has been subjected to much publicity and continuing intensive study, the

[2]For example, Thor Hyerdahl's Kon Tiki and more recent Ra I and II expeditions.

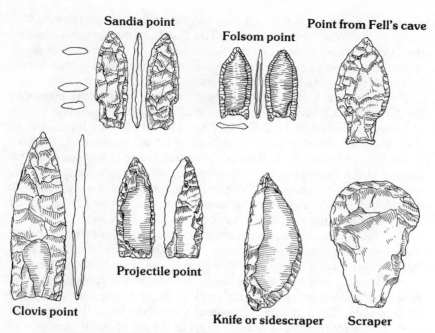

Sandia point

Folsom point

Point from Fell's cave

Projectile point

Clovis point

Knife or sidescraper

Scraper

Figure 18-5. Paleo-Indian implements from America.

results of which are contested. A major feature at Calico is a supposed hearthlike feature uncovered at a depth of ca. 22 feet. The site has been aged from 30,000 to 500,000 years B.P. The issue as to age, and in fact as to whether the supposed artifacts are fabricated or naturally flaked, is not yet resolved. However, it seems highly unlikely that the American continent was ever trodden upon by the feet of *H. erectus*, or their immediate successors.

Migration Routes—Bering Land Bridge. Most plausible theories concerning New World colonization are tied to late Pleistocene sea levels and glaciations. It is generally agreed that populations passed from the Old to the New World by way of an emergent Bering land platform and thence through central Canada and south. Since vast continental glaciers grew at the expense of sea waters, sea levels were lowest when glaciation was at its maximum. During glaciation the emergence of the Bering land platform made Alaska part of the Asian continent. North America and Asia were one, creating a Siberia-to-Alaska migration route.

The maximum depth of the Bering Strait is now 180 feet. On a clear day one can see across the Strait from the heights of Cape Prince of Wales to Cape Dezhev in Siberia. A number of small intermediate islands form stepping stones. The Wisconsin glacier which covered much of North America reached its maximum about 40,000 years ago and lowered the sea by as much as 460 feet. As the glacier grew, oceans receded and a broad highway was created at the Bering Strait. A sea-level drop of only 150 feet created a 200 mile wide corridor connecting Alaska and Siberia. A drop of 450 feet would have created a corridor 1300 miles wide for the flow of biological traffic between the joined continents.

Some argue that a smooth and unbroken land bridge wider than present-day Alaska joined the Old and New Worlds during much of the

Appearance of
Modern *Homo
sapiens sapiens*

343

Pleistocene and large animals may have crossed it during the 80,000 years of the Wisconsin glaciation. The first humans probably crossed the bridge before the end of the Wisconsin period in pursuit of game slowly spreading out of Asia into Alaska. We may yet find New World hominids back 40,000 to 50,000 years.

On the other hand, some suggest that the bridge first appeared 25,000 to 28,000 years B.P. After a period it closed and reopened again at between 8500 and 14,000 years B.P. The bridge may have opened and closed several times in conjunction with the retreats and advances of ice during deglaciation. Resolution of the dating of the opening and closing of the Bering bridge is of major importance to settling the story of New World colonization. Whatever the nature of the migration, it probably occurred as two major waves. A first wave may have moved from Asia along the Pacific shores about 40,000 years ago.

One thing we do know, humans were present in the western United States and northern South America by 15,000 B.P. at the very latest. Besides the glacial ice barrier, there seems to have been no impediment to movement in the New World. No doubt the emptiness of the American continent speeded dispersal, as did the abundance of game encountered. Eight or nine thousand years has been the estimated time for the journey from Alaska south to the tip of South America at Tierra del Fuego. The rather rapid southern extension must have meant similar rapid loss of contact between various groups, leading to cultural and genetic isolation. This could help explain the dissimilarities in modern American Indian languages.

Early Paleo-Indian Period. The easiest way to view the New World situation is to divide it into three relative periods: The Early, Middle, and Late Paleo-Indian. The most difficult period to define is the Early period, which began prior to 30,000 years ago. There are scant remains from this time, except for some flints of questionable workmanship. Sites are few, the most intriguing being Calico. Most possible Early Paleo-Indian sites do not meet the minimal criteria for inclusion as early hominid sites. Although the geological age of possible Early Paleo-Indian sites is reasonably well understood, either the association or nature of possible artifacts is questionable.

Some possible Early Paleo-Indian sites follow: The Lewisville site, near Lewisville, Texas, yielded nineteen hearths with elephant, extinct bison, horse, and camel remains, as well as those of various small animals such as a coyote, prairie dog, and rabbit. The largest hearth contained a **Clovis** point (a fairly large dartlike, grooved point, Figure 18-5) and pieces of charred wood C-14 dated at 37,000 years B.P. The date may be in error, even though a second date is similar. Clovis points from other sites consistently fall within a range of 8,000 to 15,000 years B.P. One hearth at the site is believed to have been a camel cookery. Four samples of charred bone from Santa Rosa Island, off southern California, yielded dates averaging 29,650 plus or minus 2500 years.

A rather recently described Paleo-Indian site producing a rich assemblage of Pleistocene fossils comes from the Yukon at the Old Crow River locality (Irving and Harington, 1973). A bone implement and a number of bone artifacts which were broken or considered to be otherwise modified were uncovered in 1966. Additional materials were uncovered in excavations through 1970. The single implement which can be identified is made from an excellently preserved caribou tibia. The proximal end of the tibia was chopped or broken and then whittled to a spatulate form; a regular series of notches was carved into the convex working edge to provide a row of subrectangular "teeth." Bone from the implement was dated to 27,000 +3000 −2000 years B.P. Since attempts to establish the contemporaneity of this bone to two other large mammoth fragments has proved fruitless, the dating must be considered questionable.

Recent digging along the Old Crow River at a site called Dry Creek has yielded a human jawbone with a single tooth intact dating to at least 20,000 years and bone tools dated up to 29,000 years old. Some of the implements at the site represent an Asian-Siberian stone technology and suggest the possible source of these hunters.

California yields many interesting finds. In the years between 1926 through 1929 several skeletons were excavated at two sites near La Jolla. The first site was discovered in 1926 when a steam shovel working on a development project unearthed several skeletons. These materials received little attention until Bada et al. (1974) attempted to date them using the aspartic acid racemization method. According to their analysis the material is very old. The first individual, a rib and miscellaneous rib fragments which had olivella beads cemented to them, yielded a date of 28,000 years. The second individual, found at a lower level and consisting of a frontal bone, yielded a date of 44,000 years. The last individual, a skull and mandible plus long bones and a scapula fragment, yielded a date of 48,000 years. These are the oldest dates directly obtained from New World skeletal material. Although the dating technique is new and reliability may be questioned, a control sample of material from a shell midden radiocarbon dated at from 5000 to 7500 years yielded an aspartic acid racemization date of 6000 years (Bada et al., 1974).

Middle Paleo-Indian Period. The Middle Paleo-Indian period dates from 11,500 to 28,000 years B.P. The earliest sites yield crude scrapers, flakes, and blade points. Human bones are generally lacking from the Middle Paleo-Indian period and no Middle Paleo-Indian site has yielded any quantity of cultural material. But, it seems simply a matter of time before the existence of this period is firmly established.

In 1936 a group of workers was working on a WPA project of digging a storm drain along the Los Angeles River near Los Angeles and at a depth of 12-13 feet from the surface they found a partial human cranium and seven other bone fragments. Less than two months after the original find workers discovered large animal bones in the same geological stratum as the human remains. I. A. Lopatin, of the University of Southern California, explored the area and found some teeth and bone fragments identified as belonging to an Imperial Mammoth. The site was considered to be of Pleistocene age. The cranium was so badly crushed that little could be said beyond the fact that it may be from a female (Wormington, 1957). It was impossible to date the material when first discovered because it could not be shown to be undisturbed. In recent years, however, several dating methods have been applied. Heizer and Cook's (1953) chemical components analysis of the human and mammoth bones indicated that the human bone was slightly older than that of the mammoth. There is some confusion as to a recently obtained radiocarbon date, and Stewart (1973) cites it as being less than 23,600 years. Bada et al. (1974), however, used aspartic acid racemization and found a date of 26,000 years.

In 1972, Mr. Morlin Childers of Imperial Valley Museum uncovered what may be the oldest complete New World fossil hominid. The remains come from 30 miles south of El Centro in the Yuha Desert, southern California. The fossil is christened "Yuha Man"[3] and preliminary C-14 dating suggests an age of 21,500 years B.P. The Yuha mate-

[3]An indication that most paleontologists are male is in the fact that most fossils are called "such and such" man.

The Yuha burial.

rial was found beneath a cairn of boulders and in a stratum of coarse-grained calcareous alluvium. The bones were partly covered and cemented into the material by caliche (a crust of calcium carbonate found on sandy soil in arid areas). Two samples were radiocarbon dated. The first, from caliche scraped from the bones after their excavation, yielded a date of 21,500 plus 2000 minus 1000 years. The second was on caliche scraped from one of the overlying cairn boulders and yielded a date of 22,125 plus or minus 400 years (Childers, 1974). Final evaluation of this find will have to await the release of further and more detailed information. Two possible stone tools of the type Mr. Childers labels "Ridge-back" were uncovered with the burial. I visited the area in March 1976, and it certainly looks as though the Yuha area will yield most exciting evidence of early habitation in the New World.

Other sites dating to the Middle Paleo-Indian period follow. The Tule Springs site, Nevada, yielded charcoal dated to more than 23,800 years B.P. A south-central Idaho cave yielded stone artifacts and cut bone assigned dates of 14,500 to 15,000 years B.P. A C-14 date of 13,200 plus or minus 170 years B.P. (from a charcoal sample reportedly associated with a projectile point) has been obtained from Fort Rock cave, Oregon. The Marmes rock shelter from eastern Washington, estimated between 10,800 and 13,000 years B.P., yielded the oldest firmly established date for New World skeletal material. The Midland skull from western Texas may be older, i.e., about 18,500 years B.P.

Some of the most recently discovered, and exciting, finds in the New World are from the Meadowcroft Rockshelter about 25 miles southwest of Pittsburgh. Radiocarbon dating of charcoal from the site has yielded a date of 14,225 years; an earlier attempt at dating in 1974, on two pieces of charcoal, yielded a date of 17,000 B.P. The dig, under the supervision of Dr. J. Adovasio of the University of Pittsburgh, began in 1973. The first findings from the site established it as the earliest for human habitation in the eastern United States.

The newest discoveries from Meadowcroft include more than 50 cutting tools. These artifacts, plus another 100 found in the previous excavation season, make this site the richest and most securely dated collection of tools in North and South America. Scientists in charge of the dig feel that Meadowcroft was used as a temporary shelter for wandering bands. Because of the number of projectile points, knives, and faunal and floral remains, it has been concluded that the rockshelter was continuously used until European contact.

Dr. Adovasio is hopeful that continued digging will reveal evidence of earlier settlement at Meadowcroft. Another firepit has been discovered below that yielding the 14,225 date. This site lends credence to the argument that human migration to the New World will probably date back at least to 20,000 to 30,000 years.

Mexico and South America yield a number of Middle Paleo-Indian sites. The Mexican sites near Puebla and Tlapacoya constitute some of the strongest proof of a Middle Paleo-Indian occupation. A blade and hearth have been uncovered at Tlapacoya, near Mexico City, dating to 23,150 ± 950 years B.P. and 24,000 ± 4000 years B.P., respectively. A site of questionable dating of 21,850 ± 850 years B.P. was excavated in the Valsequillo reservoir area. There is also a C-14 date of 16,375 ± 400 years B.P. from Venezuela.

Some interesting material was found in Peru in 1969 and 1970 (MacNeish, 1971) from an area near Ayacucho. All the sites from Ayacucho lie within a mountain-ringed valley, and most come from elevations of 6500 feet above sea level. The valley in which Ayacucho sits is situated some 200 miles southeast of Lima and is rich in prehistoric remains. Two of the major caves at Ayacucho are Pikimachay (Flea) Cave and Jayamachay (Pepper) Cave. Flea Cave is situated 9000 feet above sea level; the cave mouth is 40 feet high in places. The cave is 175 feet wide and 80 feet deep at the deepest end.

Excavations from the Ayacucho area reveal a series of remains representative of successive cultures in an unbroken sequence spanning an age from 20,000 B.P. to A.D. 150. This sequence documents the progression from early hunter to incipient agriculturalist to village farmer and finally to the role of subject during imperial rule. The early strata at Flea Cave reveal a succession of stone tool types that appeared about 20,000 years ago and continued until about 10,500 years ago. The oldest level from Flea Cave, zone K, revealed four crude stone tools made from volcanic tuff and a few flakes.

Late Paleo-Indian Period. The most complete evidence comes from the Late Paleo-Indian period dating from 11,500 years B.P. Such sites are common and show increasing cultural sophistication. Humans were now well established in the New World, where hunting sites and camps appear from Tierra del Fuego to Nova Scotia. The earliest part of this period is characterized by the remains of technologically advanced and highly skilled hunters utilizing a distinctive projectile point known as the Clovis point for killing mammoth and other big game. The transition from the Clovis to Folsom point about 11,000 years ago coincides with the extinction of mammoths, horses, camels, and several other members of the Pleistocene megafauna.

Clovis Points. Clovis remains predominate in the American Southwest. Clovis points take their name from an early site located between Clovis and Portales, New Mexico. Work has been conducted here since 1932. The most important discoveries date to 1936 and 1937 when artifacts were found in a sand deposit in unmistakable association with mammoth remains. Two important polished bone pieces were also found. One lay near the foreleg of one of the mammoths, the other by a tusk. Similar finds come from Alaska, California, Washington, and Florida.

Table 18-2. Appearance of *Homo sapiens* in Fossil Record (incomplete listing).

Approximate Age	Fossil Evidence
20,000–30,000 years B.P.	Modern *Homo* in Old World, New World, Pacific
35,000 years B.P.	Early appearance of modern *Homo* in Africa, Asia, Europe, and perhaps the New World
ca. 40,000 years B.P.	Skhūl
75,000–45,000 years B.P.	Solo, Broken Hill, Classic Neanderthals, Shanidar, Tabūn
150,000–100,000 years B.P.	Fontéchevade, Solo, Omo I
about 200,000 years B.P.	Steinheim, Swanscombe

Data from B. Campbell, 1976.

Folsom Points. A discovery of far-reaching impact on American archaeology was made in 1926, at a site 8 miles from Folsom, New Mexico. While excavating a fossil bison, a party uncovered two pieces of chipped flint. A third piece was later found embedded in clay surrounding an animal rib. This discovery of manufactured objects in association with the articulated bones of a long-extinct fauna, in undisturbed deposits, suggested a far greater human antiquity in North America than previously assumed. At first most rejected the evidence. After three field seasons, nineteen flakes, and proof-positive of Pleistocene geological age, the date of Folsom points gained acceptance.

Folsom points are distinctive. They are pressure flaked, about two inches in length, thin, more or less leaf-shaped, with concave bases; they evidence removal of a long flake from each side. This flake removal gives a fluted character. Grooves or channels extend from one-third to almost the whole length of the flake. Why they were fluted is debatable. However, there are three suggestions: (1) Grooves may have lightened the point so it carried further. (2) The points were grooved to facilitate hafting. (3) They were designed on the principle of the bayonet; the fluting permitted greater blood flow from the wound and faster downing of the prey. Hafting is most likely, according to some.

Since their original discovery, Folsom points, and their derivatives, have been found in many locales. These are often surface finds uncovered by wind and/or water erosion. The greatest concentration of Folsom points is in the High Plains, extending along the eastern slopes of the Rockies. Elsewhere finds are less frequent, although there are examples in Alberta and Saskatchewan, Canada. Examples of Folsom sites include the Lindenmeier and Kersey sites, Colorado; the Lubbock site, Texas, dated between 9,100 and 10,000 years B.P.; the Liscomb Bison Quarry site in Texas; and the MacHaffie site in Montana.

A number of important early finds come from South America. One of the most important is the 10,000 to 11,000 year old Fells Cave site in Tierra del Fuego, where bone and stone artifacts were found associated with skeletal remains of extinct game animals.

Where fully modern *H. sapiens* evolved is debatable, but it is likely they appeared in various places during the Upper Pleistocene. Upper Pleistocene populations were largely migrating hunters and gatherers; however, there is substantial evidence at some sites of a sedentary life-style. During the Upper Paleolithic we evidence many examples of artistic expression: cave paintings, engravings, and sculpture. Upper Paleolithic groups probably lived in larger groups than their predecessors, and their social organizations may have been more complex.

During the Upper Paleolithic, at about 30,000 years ago, populations moved into Australia which were ancestral to modern Australian aborigines. Ancestral American Indian populations moved out of Asia and entered the New World across the Bering land bridge. Although the date of entrance into the New World is debated, it is unlikely to have happened prior to 40,000 years ago.

Early New World populations were big-game hunters; in fact, they may have entered this virgin territory in pursuit of migratory game. The tool technology seems to have been "homegrown," despite some attempts to tie it to Europe.

Appearance of
Modern *Homo
sapiens sapiens*

349

Bibliography

Bada, J.; Schroeder, R.; and Carter, G. 1974. New evidence for the antiquity of man in North America deduced from aspartic acid racemization. *Science* 184:791-93.

Bada, J., and Helfman, H. 1975. Amino acid racemization dating of fossil bone. *World Archeology* 7:160-73.

Barbetti, N., and Allen, H. 1972. Prehistoric man at Lake Mungo, Australia, by 32,000 years B.P. *Nature* 240:346-48.

Birdsell, J. 1971. *Human evolution: an introduction to the new physical anthropology.* Chicago: Rand McNally.

Bordes, F. 1958. *The old Stone Age.* New York: McGraw-Hill.

Bowler, J.; Thorne, A.; and Polack, H. 1972. Pleistocene man in Australia: age and significance of Mungo skeleton. *Nature* 240(Nov.):348-50.

Brothwell, D. 1961. Upper Pleistocene human skull from Niah Caves, Sarawak. *Sarawak Museum Journal* 9:323.

Bryan, A. 1969. Early man in America and the late Pleistocene chronology of western Canada and Alaska. *Current Anthropology* 10:339.

Bushnell, G., and McBurney, C. 1959. New World origins as seen from the Old World. *Antiquity* 33:93.

Campbell, B. 1976. *Humankind emerging.* Boston: Little, Brown.

Chard, C. 1959. New World origins: a reappraisal. *Antiquity* 33:44.

Childers, W. 1974. Preliminary report on the Yuha burial, California. *Anthropological Journal of Canada* 12:1-9.

Clark, C. 1967. The stone age hunters. New York: McGraw-Hill.

Coon, C. 1962. The origin of races. New York: Knopf.

Cornwall, I. 1968. Prehistoric animals and their hunters. New York: Praeger.

Cressman, L., with collaboration of Frank C. Baker, Henry P. Hansen, Paul S. Conger, and Robert F. Heizer. 1942. *Archeological researches in the northern Great Basin.* Washington, D.C.: Carnegie Institute of Washington, Publication 538.

Day, M. 1969. Omo human skeletal remains. *Nature* 222:1135.

————. 1971. The Omo human skeletal remains. In *The origin of Homo sapiens,* edited by F. Bordes, pp. 31-35. Paris: UNESCO.

Eiseley, L. 1955. The Paleo-Indians: their survival and diffusion. In *New interpretations of aboriginal American culture history* (Anniversary volume of Anthropological Society of Washington), pp. 1-11.

Galt, J. 1970. Calico conference. *The Piltdown Newsletter* 2:1.

Griffin, J. 1960. Some prehistoric connections between Siberia and America. *Science* 131:801.

Haag, W. 1962. The Bering Strait land bridge. *Scientific American,* January, p. 112.

Haynes, C. 1969. The earliest Americans. *Science* 166:709.

Heizer, R., and Cook, S. 1953. Fluorine and other chemical tests of some North American human and animal bones. *American Journal of Physical Anthropology* 10:289-304.

Hulbert, K. 1975. Hominoid-hominid heterography and evolutionary patterns. In *Paleoanthropology, morphology, and paleoecology,* edited by R. Tuttle, pp. 153-62. The Hague: Mouton.

Irving, W., and Harington, C. 1973. Upper Pleistocene radiocarbon dated artifacts from the Northern Yukon. *Science* 179:335-40.

Jelinek, J. 1969. Neanderthal man and *Homo sapiens* in central and eastern Europe. *Current Anthropology* 10:475.

Leakey, L.; Simpson, R.; and Clements, T. 1968. Archaeological excavations in the Calico Mountains, California: preliminary report. *Science* 160:1022.

Macintosh, N. 1967. Fossil man in Australia. In *Yearbook of Physical Anthropology* 15:39.

MacNeish, R. 1971. Early man in the Andes. *Scientific American* 224:36.

Martin, N. 1967. Pleistocene overkill. In *Pleistocene extinctions: the search for a cause*, edited by P. Martin and N. Wright, pp. 75-120. New Haven: Yale University Press.

Pfeiffer, J. 1969. *The emergence of man*. New York: Harper & Row.

Poirier, F. 1977. *Fossil evidence: the human evolutionary journey*. St. Louis: Mosby.

Rightmire, P. 1975. New studies of post-Pleistocene human skeletal remains from the Rift Valley, Kenya. *American Journal of Physical Anthropology* 42:351-70.

Roberts, F. 1935. A Folsom complex: preliminary report on investigations at the Lindenmeier site in northern Colorado. *Smithsonian Miscellaneous Collections* 94.

Stewart, T. 1960. A physical anthropologist's view of the peopling of the New World. *Southwestern Journal of Anthropology* 16:259.

———. 1973. *The people of America*. New York: Scribner.

Thorne, A., and Macumber, P. 1972. Discoveries of Late Pleistocene man at Kow Swamp, Australia. *Nature* 238:316-19.

Vallois, H. 1961. The social life of early man: the evidence of skeletons. In *Social life of early man*, edited by S. Washburn, pp. 214-35. Chicago: Aldine.

Weidenreich, F. 1943. The skull of "Sinanthropus pekinensis." *Paleontologica Sineca*, New Series D 10.

Wormington, H. 1957. *Ancient man in North America*. Denver: Denver Museum of Natural History.

Chapter 19
Continuing Problems and Biological Relics

We have embarked on a long journey over time to recount an exciting tale of the attainment of our present condition. We began approximately 65 million years B.P. during the Paleocene, when hominids were an unknown among the primitive prosimian stock. During the Oligocene, as witnessed in the Egyptian Fayum, there are signs of the florescence of the pongid stock. Some contended our ancestry began 28 to 30 million years B.P. in the guise of *Propliopithecus*. Others argue that during the Miocene, hominids were still a part of a general hominoid stock known as dryopithecines. Still others argue that hominids and pongids diverged only 3 to 5 million years B.P.. Given a Miocene divergence, hominids had their day during the Upper Miocene and Lower Pliocene, perhaps as early as 15 or 16 million years B.P. Perhaps as *Ramapithecus,* the "dental hominid" of a few teeth and jaws, we roamed the widespread savanna woodlands of Africa, Asia, and possibly Europe. Lower Pleistocene hominids appeared as the australopithecines and possibly *Homo,* which were in turn followed by the Middle Pleistocene *H. erectus* and finally by *H. sapiens.*

My scheme was presented with minimal complication; however, the picture of hominid evolution is not simple. It is an abstract piece, at times a collage. The hominid evolutionary line becomes blurred in a myriad of forms, many with distinctive claims to fame. The hominid evolutionary line, or lines, resembles a three-dimensional model for which we do not presently have all the pieces, and probably never will. The present scheme has not been without its opponents, with various individuals championing different forms and theories. Some theories are plausible, others can be forthrightly rejected. Some may argue that

Polychrome cave painting representative of the Magdalenian artistic tradition of the later Upper Paleolithic period.

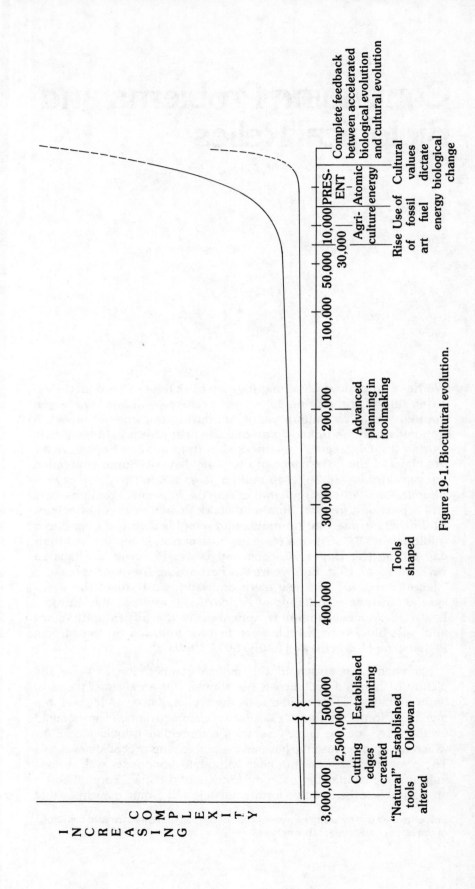

Figure 19-1. Biocultural evolution.

since questions can be raised about parts of the scheme, the scheme itself should be summarily discarded. This is the proverbial reaction of "throwing out the baby with the bath water." Current controversies, rather than negate the fact that hominid evolutionary history is closely tied to that of the other primates, only strengthen it. The schemes currently presented are not 100 percent correct, but neither are they 100 percent wrong.

Unanswered Questions Remain

The major unanswered questions are: (1) What is the date of the hominid-pongid split? (2) Is *Ramapithecus* a hominid?[1] (3) What is the true nature of Lower Pleistocene hominid evolution? (4) What is the nature of the Leakeys' new material? If they are correct, their theory makes mincemeat of classical interpretations of hominid evolution. (5) When and where did modern *H. sapiens sapiens* appear? These questions will be answered; the finds recovered in the last ten years exceed those made in the last hundred years. Possibly finds made next year may exceed those of the last ten.

Dates may change and schemes be altered, but the basic fact remains—we are and were of the primates; their evolutionary development and ours are inextricably joined. Are we simply another primate, slightly bigger than most, lacking a tail, unlike our monkey cousins, living outside nature's jungles in concrete jungles built by human hands? Or, are there major differences? We are primates and share many aspects of our behavioral and social repertoires with our relatives. However, we are also different. We are the products of a unique feedback between culture and biology (Figures 19-1 to 19-3). The feedback is manifested in anatomical, social, or technological traits usually assumed basic to hominids, i.e., large brains, symbolic speech, bipedalism, consistent tool use and modification of tools with other tools, use of fire, and life within large complex social groups.

Appearance of Major Hominid Traits. When did those traits considered so important in hominid evolution first appear? For some traits such as speech there is no answer in the early fossil record, save for educated speculation. Hints as to brain size and bipedalism are fossilized, at least since the Lower Pleistocene. Other traits such as tool use and manufacture, use of fire, evidence of big-game hunting, and larger, complex social groups can also be identified in the fossil record.

[1] It should now be clear that the term "hominid" has had different meanings to different interpreters of the fossil record and that its meaning shifts according to the time period in which the fossil form lies. The very earliest forms (i.e., *Propliopithecus* and *Ramapithecus*) are (were) given hominid status by some paleontologists by virtue of their dental traits (such as parabolic arch, short face, bicuspid premolars, non-projecting canines). Later forms, such as *Australopithecus* and *Homo*, are considered hominids on the basis of their overall morphology. In these forms, however, emphasis is placed upon locomotor adaptations (i.e., evidence for bipedalism or incipient bipedalism), cranial capacity, and dental and facial structure. To the biological traits, we often add that these are culture-bearing, tool-using and tool-manufacturing animals. However, no one claims that on this basis they are hominids or should be considered as such. One of the factors which clearly separates human from nonhuman primates is the possession of a symbolic means of communication, language. (This statement may have to be altered somewhat in light of claims that some of the fossil hominids, like Neanderthals, lacked the ability for more than rudimentary speech. However, more evidence is needed before this view can become credible.)

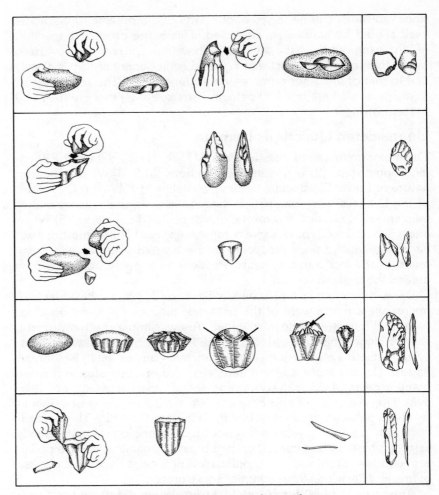

Figure 19-2. Early stone tool manufacture.

A most interesting, albeit somewhat controversial, attempt to deal with the acquisition of linguistic behavior is P. Lieberman's (1975) book *On the Origins of Language.* As noted elsewhere, Lieberman contends that present-day linguistic skills are of relatively recent origin and that many of the Neanderthal forms, as well as the earlier hominids, lacked this ability. This scheme is based upon the evolution of the bent two-tube vocal tract which is apparently an anatomical essential for enhanced linguistic ability.

According to Lieberman's scheme, as well as that of others, the first hominid "languages" probably evolved from something akin to the communication systems of modern apes: a combination of vocal, postural, and gestural signals. Lieberman argues that the australopithecines (it is unclear whether he also includes the supposed Lower Pleistocene *Homo* fossils in this group) had essentially the same supralaryngeal vocal tract as extant pongids. "The initial language of the australopithecines thus may have had a phonetic level that relied on both gestural and vocal components" (Lieberman, 1975:159). This system may have become elaborated in conjunction with such behaviors as tool using and making and social interaction. Enhanced linguis-

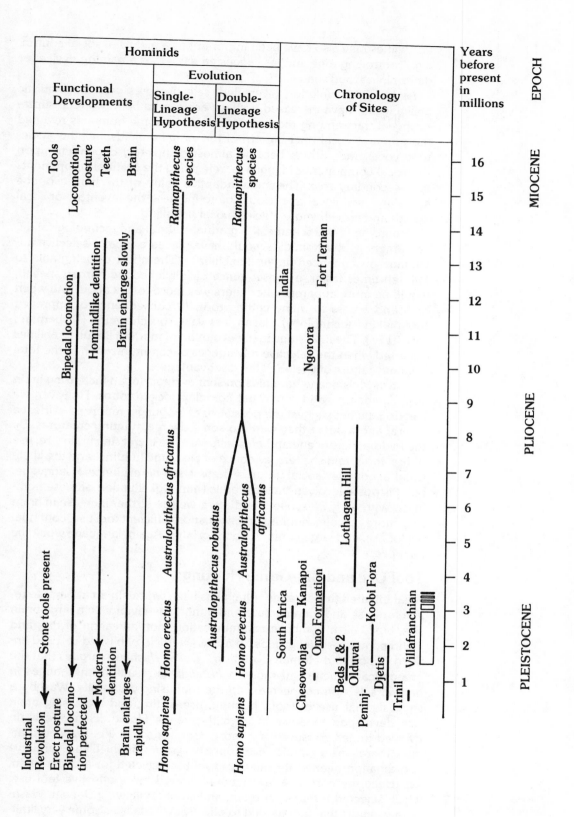

Figure 19-3. Hominid evolutionary history.

tic abilities may also have been important as a means of social control, e.g., controlling rage and, as suggested earlier, as a naming device for determining food shares.

As hominid evolution diversified, selective pressures for linguistic ability would have increased until we achieved a bent two-tube supralaryngeal tract among modern *Homo*. While some hominids retained the primitive vocal tract pattern of the early hominids, i.e., the single-tube vocal tract, others became almost completely dependent upon the vocal component of language, relegating the gestural components to a secondary role. The initial adaptive value of the bent two-tube supralaryngeal vocal tract would be to increase the inventory of vocal signals and provide more efficient vocal signalling.

According to this scheme, the gradual cultural and technological development of the hominids would have placed a greater selective advantage on enhanced linguistic abilities. "The effect of being able to talk ten times faster, a consequence of fully encoded human speech, would be more apparent when there was more to talk about and when fires and access to many cutting tools (a consequence of improved tool-making technology) placed less value on chewing" (Lieberman, 1975:177). The final stage in the evolution of modern linguistic abilities occurred when the selective advantages of communication in the total hominid culture outweighed the disadvantages.

Lower Pleistocene hominids present evidence of an increasing brain size, bipedalism, and somewhat complex social groups. However, we can do little but suggest the possibility of language, report no evidence of fire, and assume they were, to some degree, hunting creatures. By the Middle Pleistocene and *H. erectus*, we see increasing brain size, use of fire, tools, and shelters, evidence of big-game hunting, and the likelihood of complex social groups. There is still no evidence of language, but it is possible, given the economic (hunting) situation of these hominids. With early *H. sapiens*, and after, we see further increase in brain size, more complex hunting practices, more efficient tool use, continual use of fire, and large complex social groups. Again, language would be adaptive.

Tool Use and Big-Game Hunting

What initiated these trends? Much has been written in an attempt to relate tool use and manufacture and hunting behavior with a large brain size, bipedalism, symbolic communication, domestication of fire, and life in complex social groups. In a classic article published in 1960 entitled "Tools and Human Evolution," Dr. S. Washburn argues that the anatomical structure of modern *H. sapiens* results from changes in natural selection connected with the tool-using way of life. Washburn suggests that use of tools, hunting, use of fire, and increasing brain size developed together to form the genus *Homo*. Then the brain evolved under pressures of a more complex social life. Washburn argues there was a circular evolutionary system in which the hand-eye coordination needed for effective tool use selected for a larger brain, especially the cortex. A larger brain allowed more effective tool use, which selected for a larger brain, and so on. Following Darwin, Washburn suggests that tool use led to effective bipedalism. Some very limited bipedalism freed the hands from locomotor behavior so they could do other things. Hand-carried objects conveyed an advantage that led to more and more efficient bipedalism and more efficient tool use. (Doubts have been raised about parts of this scheme, especially the link between tool use and canine reduction.)

Big-game hunting has been of utmost importance to hominid evolution. *Homo erectus*, and their successors until about 6000 years ago, were primarily big-game hunters. It has been argued that our intellect, emotions, and basic social life are evolutionary products of the success of the hunting adaptation. It is argued that the success of the hunting adaptation dominated the course of human evolution for hundreds of thousands of years. Agriculture only began to replace hunting as an economically feasible pursuit about 8000 years ago. The common factors dominating our evolutionary history and producing anatomically modern *H. sapiens* were preagricultural; they occurred during the hunting stage of hominid evolution. More effective tool use, selection for developing a more complex communication system, more efficient bipedalism, beginnings of movement over large ranges (compared to other primates), cooperation, and food sharing may all be related to big-game hunting. According to Drs. Washburn and Lancaster (1968), the agricultural revolution, continuing into the industrial and scientific revolutions, only now frees us from conditions characteristic of 99 percent of our evolutionary history. Our biology as a species was created during the hunting apprenticeship; asserting the biological unity of humanity affirms the importance of the hunting way of life.

It is worthwhile to mention something about the evolution of hunting behavior as this can be reconstructed from current evidence among nonhuman primates (for details of such hunting behavior see chapters 7,8). The following information is drawn primarily from Harding (1975) and Suzuki (1975). As Harding notes, the nonhuman primate data supports observations among human groups which show that meat eating is something more than simply a way of obtaining dietary protein because meat is a high-priority item no matter what portion it comprises of the total diet (see Woodburn, 1968).

At least two nonhuman primates are known to include various portions of meat protein in their diet, the chimpanzee (Teleki, 1973; van Lawick-Goodall, 1967, 1968, 1971) and some baboon troops (Altmann and Altmann, 1970; Dart, 1963; DeVore and Washburn, 1963; Harding, 1975; Marais, 1939; Strum, 1975). This practice of catching and consuming small animals is done without any particular anatomical specializations. Nonhuman primates possess the brains for cooperative hunting, the communicative matrix to allow for group hunting (as among chimpanzees), the locomotor skills suitable for catching small prey, teeth capable of preparing meat protein, and a digestive system capable of receiving the masticated meat.

Harding notes that while it is possible to use nonhuman primate data to construct models for the evolution of human hunting behavior, these models are speculative. "The real importance of this information lies elsewhere; i.e. the demonstration that at least two species of nonhuman primates, specifically the two species most often used as hominid surrogates in theories of human evolution, have a lively interest in meat eating and an ability to acquire substantial amounts of meat blurs the line dividing human and nonhuman primate behavior. Be-

Table 19-1. Review of the Pleistocene: The glacial periods, cultural stages, and selected fossil hominids.

Geological Stage	Cultural Stage	Hominid Grade	Fossil examples
Upper Pleistocene			
Recent 10,000 yrs.	Upper Paleolithic	H. sapiens sapiens	Cro-Magnon
Würm 70,000	Mousterian	H. sapiens neanderthalensis	Neanderthals
Middle Pleistocene			
Riss-Würm interglacial (3rd interglacial forms)	Acheulian	H. sapiens	Fontéchevade Ehringsdorf Saccopastore? Quinzano
Mindel-Riss interglacial (2nd interglacial forms)	Acheulian	H. sapiens steinheimensis swanscombensis	Steinheim Swanscombe
Mindel 300,000	Acheulian	H. erectus	North Africa Arago (France) Torralba-Ambrona Terra Amata
Günz 500,000+	Early Acheulian	H. erectus	Chou Kou Tien Trinil Heidelberg Vértesszöllös Olduvai Přezletice
Lower Pleistocene			
Villafranchian	Oldowan	Australopithecus Paranthropus (?) Homo (?)	Olduvai Omo Lake Turkana Afar Triangle, Ethiopia Laetolil

cause it does so, it is less likely that predatory behavior was a major shaping force in human evolution..." (Harding, 1975:255-256). This statement is, of course, contrary to that of Washburn and Lancaster and of such popular writers as R. Ardrey and D. Morris. Harding suggests that the characteristic human diet of a mixture of meat protein and vegetable matter is probably a continuation of an ancient primate diet.

Suzuki (1975) notes that there are three factors considered fundamental for the human pattern of hunting on a large scale: (1) the ability for long distance locomotion, (2) a high level of social relationships within the group, and a division of labor, and (3) a high level of technical skills such as the making and using of tools. Chimpanzees today have the first two skills and also the ability to produce certain types of implements. Chimpanzees do share food (e.g., hunted meat) and have a flexible social organization and large-sized groups; furthermore they can and do travel long distances in order to exploit their habitat. As

Suzuki sees it, the origins of human hunting behavior are related to a developing mental organization, which preceded an erect bipedal posture. The second stage required the release of the hands, and was one of the forces leading to the evolution of bipedalism, a larger brain, and consistent tool use.

Biological Relics

Dr. David Hamburg (1963), a Stanford psychiatrist, argues that although most of us no longer live as hunters, we are still physically (and emotionally) hunter-gatherers. The point has been made that we are biologically equipped for one way of life, hunting, but live in another. Is there some link between an emotional reaction like aggression, which is most useful to a hunter, and some killing ailments of modern society, e.g., heart disease? Strong emotions mobilize cholesterol. If cholesterol plays a role in heart disease, if our way of life no longer allows an efficient release of pent-up cholesterol, and if high levels of cholesterol are bad, then the point is made: modern *H. sapiens* is not equipped for modern life but is emotionally still in the Stone Age. (This is the biological correlate to the statement that we are technologically on the moon but culturally and socially still on earth.) Hunters have little problem dissipating cholesterol which they release during the hunting process. Adrenalin buildup is also a problem; adrenalin is increased during states of high tension. The rise in adrenalin increases blood flow to the heart, lungs, and central nervous system, but decreases the flow to the abdominal organs. This is advantageous to the hunter who has the chance to dissipate the effects of increased adrenalin levels during stalking, chasing, and killing the prey. However, in a modern society which frowns upon violent outbursts, increased adrenalin and blood flow can have dire effects. We retain physiological adaptations making us effective hunters, but we have lost a major safety valve (the actual hunting behavior and its concomitants) which allows dissipation of the increased flow of cholesterol and fatty acids. Although hard physical labor helps dissipate increased adrenalin, frustrating desk jobs do not seem to do so.

There are many unanswered questions concerning the primate fossil record. Major questions deal with the taxonomic status of various forms, such as *KNM-ER 1470* and *Ramapithecus*. With luck, and much hard work, the major controversies as to primate evolution may be solved. We badly need a fuller fossil sample, representing both sexes and various ages, from certain time spans and geographical areas.

A second set of questions deals with the appearance of hominid traits like bipedalism, speech, tool use, and an increasing brain size. Unfortunately, the fossil record is not always helpful; we don't know when fully articulate speech appeared. The fossil record suggests a relationship between big-game hunting and more complex social groups, increased brain size, increased tool use, greater social coordination (and perhaps control), manipulation of fire, and increased pressures for efficient bipedalism.

Some biologists and psychiatrists working in the field of stress biology argue that emotionally and physically we remain hunters, regardless of our cultural pursuits. It is intriguing to try to relate modern ailments, like heart disease, to stresses linked to our failure to adjust to the decline of hunting and the rise of agriculture. However, the evidence is not conclusive.

Bibliography

Altmann, S., and Altmann, J. 1970. *Baboon ecology.* Basel: S. Karger.

Dart, R. 1963. Carnivorous propensities of baboons. *Symposium of Zoological Society of London* 10:49-56.

DeVore, I., and Washburn, S. 1963. Baboon ecology and human evolution. In *African ecology and human evolution,* edited by F. Howell and F. Bourliere, pp. 335-67. Viking Fund Publications in Anthropology 36. New York: Wenner-Gren Foundation.

Freud, S. 1951. *Psychopathology of everyday life.* New York: New American Library.

Hallowell, A. 1961. The protocultural foundations of human adaptation. In *Social life of early man,* edited by S. Washburn, pp. 236-55. Chicago: Aldine.

Hamburg, D. 1963. Emotions in the perspective of human evolution. In *Expression of the emotions in man,* edited by P. Knapp, pp. 300-317. New York: International Universities Press.

Harding, R. 1975. Meat-eating and hunting in baboons. In *Socioecology and psychology of primates,* edited by R. Tuttle, pp.245-58. The Hague: Mouton.

Hockett, C., and Ascher, R. 1964. The human revolution. *Current Anthropology* 5:135.

Holloway, R. 1967. Tools and teeth: some speculations regarding canine reduction. *American Anthropologist* 69:63.

Kinzey, W. 1971. Evolution of the human canine tooth. *American Anthropologist* 73:680.

Krantz, G. 1968. Brain size and hunting ability in earliest man. *Current Anthropology* 9:450.

———. 1970. On brain size and behavior in early man. *Current Anthropology* 11:176.

Laughlin, W. 1968. Hunting: an integrating biobehavior system and its evolutionary importance. In *Man the hunter,* edited by R. Lee and I. DeVore, pp. 304-20. Chicago: Aldine.

Lee, R., and DeVore, I., eds. 1968. *Man the hunter.* Chicago: Aldine.

Lieberman, P. 1975, *On the origins of language.* New York: Macmillan.

Marais, E. 1939. *My friends the baboons.* London: Methuen.

Selye, H. 1956. *The stress of life.* New York: McGraw-Hill.

Strum, S. 1975. Primate predation: interim report on the development of a tradition in a troop of olive baboons. *Science* 187:755-57.

Suzuki, A. 1975. The origin of hominid hunting: a primatological perspective. In *Socioecology and psychology of primates,* edited by R. Tuttle, pp. 259-78. The Hague: Mouton.

Teleki, G. 1973. The omnivorous chimpanzee. *Scientific American* 228:32-42.

van Lawick-Goodall, J. 1967. *My friends, the wild chimpanzees.* Washington, D.C.: National Geographic Society.

———. 1968. The behavior of free-living chimpanzees in the Gombe Stream Reserve. *Animal Behavior Monographs* 1:161-311.

———. 1971. *In the shadow of man.* London: Collins.

Washburn, S. 1959. Speculations on the interrelations of the history of tools and biological evolution. *Human Biology* 31:21.

———. 1960. Tools and human evolution. *Scientific American,* September, p. 63.

———. 1965. An ape's eye view of evolution. In *The origin of man* (Symposium transcript), edited by P. DeVore, pp. 89-96. New York: Wenner-Gren Foundation.

Washburn, S., and Lancaster, C. 1968. The evolution of hunting. In *Perspectives on human evolution*, edited by S. Washburn and P. Jay, pp. 213-30. New York: Holt, Rinehart and Winston.

Woodburn, J. 1968. An introduction to Hadza ecology. In *Man the hunter*, edited by R. Lee and I. DeVore, pp. 49-55. Chicago: Aldine.

Part Five
Human Diversity

O ne day the master potter decided it might be amusing to make men. So, he scooped up some clay, molded it into a man and put it into his kiln to bake. However, while it was baking something else attracted his attention, and he left it in the kiln too long. When he took it out, it had been blackened by the heat. Thus was born the black man. Realizing his mistake, the master potter fashioned another man and tried again. This time he took it out too soon, before it was fully baked, and thus was born the white man. Being a patient artisan, the master potter tried again. This time he was successful. There emerged from the kiln the perfectly formed, golden founder of the Chinese people. (A Chinese folk tale. From M. Klass and H. Hellman. 1971. *The Kinds of Mankind.* New York: J. P. Lippincott Company.)

"UNDERSTANDING is a thirteen-letter word—perhaps the length of the word itself keeps us apart." (Poirier)

Two classic examples of the trait of steatopygia (accumulation of fat on the buttocks).

Chapter 20
Studies of Living Populations

One way of differentiating the interests of physical anthropologists is to distinguish between what can be termed evolutionary events and what can be termed evolutionary processes. Dr. G. Simpson has discussed this dichotomy and he separates historical studies of human evolution, based mostly on morphological information, from the study of evolutionary processes, i.e., those phenomena causing evolution to occur. Evolutionary events are witnessed in the fossil record, whereas evolutionary processes such as mutation, drift, gene flow, and selection can be studied in living populations. This chapter will serve to introduce the reader to the study of evolutionary processes.

Humans as Research Subjects

Sanctions and taboos surrounding our own mating behavior effectively inhibit the required procedures for laboratory manipulation of humans. Even if this were not so, few would be interested in beginning an experiment which might not be concluded until long after the investigator's death. We are poor and impractical experimental animals for genetic studies; fortunately, however, we can obtain genetic information about ourselves without benefit of laboratory breeding stocks. By closely observing the effects of human mating, even outside the laboratory, we have added enormously to our knowledge about human genetics. Hospital records, genealogical records, and animal experimentation data have all contributed to a better understanding of human genetics.

Although we are rapidly accumulating data on human genetics, much of it is concerned with gross abnormalities and deviant genetic traits, information which is of supreme importance to the physician but not so important for the physical anthropologist. Fortunately, most

Toda men. The Toda inhabit the Nilgiri Hill region of southern India.

inborn metabolic errors are very rare. Few of us suffer from Wilson's disease resulting from the inability to synthesize the proper quantity of a blood protein called ceruloplasmin, which contains copper. If ceruloplasmin is not formed, copper atoms, ingested as normal parts of food, are deposited in the liver and brain, among other organs, producing tissue degeneration. Few of us are afflicted by **phenylketonuria,** PKU, wherein the lack of an enzyme required for normal biochemical transformations within the body leads to excretion of large amounts of phenylpyruvic acid and severe mental deficiency. Each of these afflictions results from recessive alleles.

During the past twenty or thirty years, more attention has focused on the study of genetically based traits exhibited by a proportion of humans, normal or otherwise. However, our knowledge is still woefully inadequate. It is still very difficult to design human chromosome maps, and attempts to demonstrate linkage between different genes have not been totally successful. Human genetic research is a very active field, however, and our understanding of our own complexities is rapidly increasing. Genetic engineering, i.e., the ability to correct defects on the genes or chromosomes, is not simply a future dream; it is rapidly becoming a reality. The issues to be faced in the near future will be as much moral and philosophical as scientific.

The Mendelian Population

Living human populations offer a wide range of physical characteristics worthy of investigation. The focal point of an evolutionary study, the Mendelian population, is a spatial-temporal group of interbreeding individuals sharing a common gene pool. Although the individual is indispensable to the evolutionary process as the carrier and transmitter of genetic matter and the source of all mutations, genetic changes within an individual are not looked upon by the population geneticist as constituting evolution. Through time evolutionary forces operate on a gene pool. Only populations comprise gene pools; thus populations evolve, not individuals.

Unfortunately, a population does not just present itself to the observer as "Study me, I'm a good Mendelian population." It is far easier to define a Mendelian population theoretically than to delimit it accurately from the totality of humanity. Our tendency to join other individuals and populations, for example through trade, war, migration, and travel, has usually prevented genetic isolation of any human group for extended time periods. Human populations are not totally closed genetic systems; to varying degrees their gene pools are shared by individuals from other populations. Actual populations are thus less "pure" than those found in theoretical constructs.

The Deme. Theoretically, the concept of the Mendelian population may be extended to include the entire human species; all members of our species share in the common gene pool of *Homo sapiens sapiens.* Modern *Homo* constitutes a population and can be considered the proper unit of genetic study, but only for the purpose of understanding the cohesive forces binding the total human species. Because the term "population" can refer to all of humanity, or to lesser constituent parts, the term **deme** is often substituted. A deme is a relatively self-sufficient small endogamous group (a group marrying among its members in contrast to an exogamous group which marries outside of itself) which is isolated from other such groups. Demes are the smallest basic population units studied by the population geneticist.

Obviously **panmixis** (i.e., random mating) does not occur within the total species of modern *Homo sapiens*. To the argument that populations are partially open breeding systems must be added the qualification that they are also partially closed. To the extent that one population's gene pool is closed to genes from another, they are considered genetically isolated from one another. The boundaries may be geographical or social and may be effective to varying degrees.

How to Identify the Breeding Population

An accurate definition of a human Mendelian population is complicated by the fact that one population segment in a social grouping may or may not serve as a biological breeding unit. One might mistake any American city as a Mendelian population, whereas the true structure of the city is a political unit subdivided into smaller subgroups. Some of these smaller subgroups may be distinct breeding units, but only careful preliminary demographic investigation of the structure and dynamics of a group will distinguish between social and political units and the true biological breeding units.

Identifying the Breeding Population (Figure 20-1). The population geneticist's first task before undertaking an analysis of the breeding population and the forces acting upon it is to identify and describe the breeding unit. In smaller, isolated communities—on islands for example—this is a relatively simple matter, and this is one reason why population geneticists work with such groups. In these circumstances the social rules and regulations determining mating behavior (not simply marriage, for extramarital and premarital procreation also affect the gene

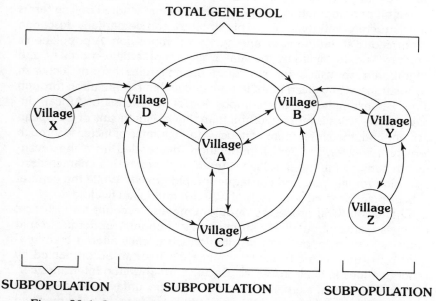

Figure 20-1. Genes are interchanged among various subpopulations within the total gene pool.

pool) must be clearly understood. To infer the composition of a gene pool at any point in time, one must first enumerate and describe the actual progenitors, that is, the parents in the population for they constitute the breeding populations. The breeding population is always smaller, often by one-third, than the total number of individuals actually living in the group. The breeding number cannot be obtained by census alone, for all individuals capable of breeding do not breed. Furthermore, the breeding population does not contain population members incapable of contributing genes to the next generation because they have either not yet achieved reproductive maturity or have passed it. The breeding population can only be defined by documenting mating behavior and by eliciting reproductive records. This is different for many reasons, not the least of which is the fact that some societies (such as the Toda of South India) recognize sociological and not biological paternity.

After completing a demographic survey and defining the breeding population, genetic analysis is still in the future. The breeding population must be further defined. To determine the ideal population, that is, a population in which there are equal possibilities of genetic influences coming from any parent, all of whom are unrelated, you must delete related individuals. Such individuals, to the extent they are related, do not reflect the size, composition, and heterozygosity of the ideal population. The actual number and type of unrelated gametes available to the next generation is less than the actual total number of gametes (related and unrelated) present. Because of the presence of related individuals, the effective breeding size of any human population is generally smaller than its actual breeding size.

Population Structure and Dynamics

Vital Processes. To understand the dynamics of genetic evolution, one must appreciate that every population has its own structure. The evolution of a population can be understood and studied only in terms of its structure and dynamics. This structure can be partially described in terms of distribution, size, and age/sex composition. A population's structure is determined by the vital processes of fertility, mortality, and migration responsible for structural dissimilarities existing between populations at any given point in time and within a population through time. For example, the age composition of Americans of African descent in the cities is more youthful than that of Americans of European descent and, therefore, more conducive to high rates of increase through fertility. Likewise, the Amish population (descended from the seventeenth-century Mennonite Jacob Amen or Ammann) is characterized by a high fertility rate and consequent rapid growth. While the general U.S. population doubled, that of the Amish multiplied fivefold.

Changes in vital processes through time also account for historical changes in the population's structure. As a country undergoes rapid industrialization, population distribution is radically altered by migration from rural to urban centers. Migration is often accompanied by other changes in vital processes. Because urbanization intensifies certain environmental elements that are, or can be, unfavorable to fertility (such as the cost of raising children), fertility tends to drop in urbanized societies. The reduction of fertility in the U.S. since 1800 has been dramatic; the average number of children dropped from seven to three or less. Pronounced changes in the vital processes of a population markedly affect its structure and gene pool. However, genetic consequences on the gene pool may not be easily detectable or predictable.

Mechanisms of Evolution Within a Population

In an earlier chapter we noted that static populations are often eventually doomed to extinction and that variability within a population is some insurance against extinction. Populations in genetic equilibrium are populations which are not evolving. In order to understand how gene pools change we will discuss a number of factors which have been identified as a source of change: mutation, gene flow, selection, and drift. Another process, that of nonrandom mating, is discussed in Chapter 24. Any circumstance which causes gene frequency changes is an important evolutionary factor.

Mutation (Table 20-1). A mutation, any change in the chemical organization of a gene or structural or numerical chromosomal changes, is the spontaneous appearance of a new gene expression. Since the stimuli activating the chemical changes in genes act randomly, mutations are considered to occur randomly. Most mutations are harmful to

Table 20-1. Human Mutation Rates for Several Traits.

Trait	Population	Mutations per Million Gametes
Autosomal Dominants		
Retinoblastoma, an eye tumor	—	15-23
Retinoblastoma	England	14
Retinoblastoma	Michigan	23
Chondrodystrophy, dwarfism	Denmark	43
Chondrodystrophy, dwarfism	Sweden	70
Palmaris longus muscle	United States "whites"	32
Palmaris longus muscle	United States Afro-Americans	7
Huntington's chorea (involuntary uncontrollable movements)	United States "whites"	5.4
Autosomal Recessives		
Infantile amaurotic idiocy, (Tay-Sachs disease)	Eastern European Jews	38
Infantile amaurotic idiocy	Japan	11
Albinism	United States "whites"	28
Albinism	Japan	28
Cystic fibrosis of pancreas	—	0.7-1.0
Phenylketonuria	United States "whites"	25
Sex Linked		
Hemophilia	—	25-32
Hemophilia	England	20
Hemophilia	Denmark	32
Muscular dystrophy	—	43-100

Adapted from Stephen Molnar, *Races, Types and Ethnic Groups: The Problem of Human Variation,* © 1975, p. 33. Reprinted by permission of Prentice-Hall Inc., Englewood Cliffs, New Jersey.

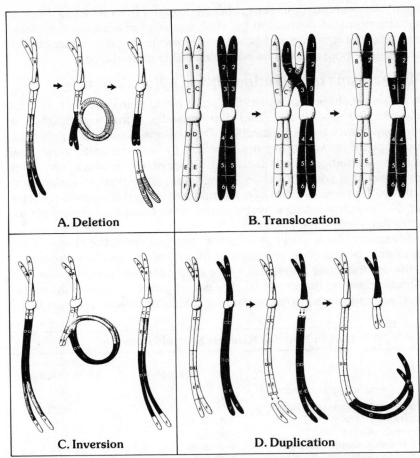

| A. Deletion | B. Translocation |
| C. Inversion | D. Duplication |

Figure 20-2. Diagrammatic representation of chromosomal aberrations. (A) Deletions occur when terminal breaks cause the loss of a segment of a chromosome. (B) Translocations occur when parts of chromosomes become detached and reunited with other non-homologous chromosomes. (C) Inversions occur when parts of chromosomes become detached and reinserted in such a way that the genes are in reverse order. (D) Duplications represent additions of chromosome parts arranged in such a way that segments are longitudinally repeated.

the organism. However, mutation, whatever the cause, is the only means whereby genetic material can be altered.

Mutations may occur either in the gene or on the chromosomes. Chromosomal mutations, which differ only in degree from gene mutations, usually involve a number of genes; if a chromosome undergoes spontaneous reorganization or modification the effect is usually more pronounced than if only a single gene mutates. Chromosomal mutations are of two types: changes in the number of chromosomes or structural changes of the chromosome itself (Figure 20-2). An example of the first type of chromosomal mutation is the condition known as aneuploidy, i.e., the addition or deletion of one or more chromosomes (Table 20-2). Structural changes include losses in the number of genes (known as deletion), addition in the number of genes (known as duplication), changes in gene arrangement such as an exchange of parts

Table 20-2. Klinefelter's Syndrome, a congenital condition resulting from nondisjunction.

Genotype	XXY
Phenotype	Male
Number of autosomes (haploid)	22
Somatic chromosome number (diploid)	47
Fertility	Neg

(translocation) and rotation of a group of genes 180 degrees on a chromosome (inversion). Any of these changes can result in death or impaired fertility.

Gene Flow, Migration, Hybridization. Gene flow, migration, or hybridization is a process whereby genes of one gene pool or population of a species are introduced into another population. The resulting process of hybridization changes the frequency of genes already existent within local populations of the species. Hybridization does not produce new genes, a process reserved to mutations. Nevertheless, gene flow can have significant effects upon the genetic makeup of a population.

Gene flow or migration is expressed as the amount of genetic mixture from two parental populations in a descendant population. The mathematical calculation is rather simple if we know the following: the frequency of the allele in the three populations (two parent and the descendant populations), the allele frequency of the population into which gene migration is considered to have occurred (one parent population), the allele frequency of the population from which the migrating genes derived (second parent population), and frequencies in the descendant population. Three assumptions are made in calculating admixture. First, the migration of genes is entirely from one population to another. Second, there is no assortative mating (see Chapter 24) with respect to the allele being considered. Third, those **zygotes** produced by the admixture of the two parental populations are fertile. If this third condition was not met, admixture could not occur. If the hybrids could not produce, there would be no gene flow from one population to another regardless of the amount of hybridization which occurred. Williams (1973) provides the following example for calculating gene flow. If population C is composed of indigenous individuals plus arrivals from population B, then m, which is the rate of gene flow, is merely the proportion of members of population C who are immigrants.

A major problem of trying to calculate gene flow under these conditions is determination of the ancestral population. The amount of the calculated admixture depends upon the frequency of the particular allele in each of the three populations. A mistake in choosing the ancestral or founder population could produce a considerable error in the calculated amount of admixture. An understanding of gene flow requires a knowledge of population structure, inbreeding, movements in and out of the population, mating practices, and the effect of other evolutionary processes on the population and any of its subunits.

The effect of gene flow as an evolutionary mechanism is quite clear. A population characterized by a particular genetic structure which mates with a group of migrants from another population, which carries a different genetic structure, will produce a population with a genetic structure different than both parents. As noted above, there are means whereby such admixture can be calculated, and although errors can occur, it is now possible to calculate the genetic effects of migration on an offspring population.

Commonly a population consists of a number of subunits which tend to mate more often within themselves. However, these subunits are linked together by regular outmating, the rate of which varies from one subunit to another. Under such conditions, no actual migration need occur for gene change to occur, and for this reason the phenomenon is labelled gene flow rather than migration.

Genetic Model of Natural Selection

Charles Darwin was unaware of the gene; he knew living beings adapted to their environment, but he was unsure of how they adapted. Genetics has provided the explanatory vehicle. Natural selection continually eliminates ill-adapted individuals; if poor adaptation results from genetic features, the deleterious allele is eventually eliminated from the breeding population. A store of hidden traits may be retained, phenotypically invisible as it were, in the recessive (not phenotypically expressed) state. The less frequent the appearance of the trait, the less often it appears, the longer its retention within the population. Heterozygosity often leads to milder and homozygosity to more severe affliction. There is a tendency for deleterious genes to be removed over time, but some ailments may not appear until past reproductive age when the gene is transmitted to succeeding generations. However, this is how a population "genetically adapts" to its surroundings.

This is the simplistic method of genetic selection. This model depends upon the assumption that a given allele produces only adaptive or nonadaptive phenotypic traits, but this is not always true. Many genetically based ailments serviced by the physician fit into this model, but many cases of genetic polymorphism which interest the anthropologist do not. The model inadequately explains these. Furthermore, some alleles may be neither adaptive or nonadaptive—they may be neutral to a certain environment.

There are many genetic differences between members of any breeding population. In but few cases is the possession of one allele rather than another at a given locus advantageous in any obvious way. Many times we don't know the selective advantage of a genetically determined trait. Some interpret this uncertainty to mean that natural selection ceases to be a factor under the conditions of modern life; but, there are other alternative explanations. One alternative is that adaptation is the sole cause of variation and that we will eventually uncover a selective advantage for every known trait. Another popular view is that many, if not most, ways in which human populations differ result from genetic drift, or chance variation. Examples uphold each argument and statistical models supporting each can be created. Neither model explains all the available data and it is quite likely that modern variability is due in part to both these factors, and many others.

From the standpoint of the gene pool, the product of natural selection is a gradual reduction of population variation to conform to the requirements of selection. From the viewpoint of selection, the only measure of fitness within a species is the number of viable offspring produced. This perspective can be understood directly on a population level. It provides an explanation for the origin of species by means of natural selection. With respect to genotype distributions, natural selection exerts its influence in the following ways, considering one locus and two alleles. Selection against: (1) one or the other homozygote, (2) one or the other homozygote and the heterozygote, (3) both homozygotes, and (4) the heterozygote (Kelso, 1974).

Differential reproduction and mortality are usually combined in one measure of selection which is the differential representation among genotypes in the offspring generation after the effects of mutation, migration, and so on are eliminated. One means of representing these differences is to let the most fit genotype or genotypes have a fitness value of unity and express the fitness of the remaining genotypes as some fraction of this. Williams (1973) provides the following example:

Genotypes	AA	Aa	aa
Fitness values	1.00	0.90	0.80

In this example the genotype Aa is intermediate in fitness between the two homozygotes. The definition of fitness, as reflected in this example, means that the ratio of Aa offspring to parents will be only 90 percent of the ratio of AA offspring to parents. The ratio of aa offspring to parents will be only 80 percent of the ratio of AA offspring to parents.

Natural Selection at the Gene Level. A new argument regarding the applicability of natural selection to evolution at the gene level has recently beset the theory of evolution. At issue is the application of Darwinian evolutionary theory to genes, the fundamental units of heredity. Some researchers now suggest that mere chance plays a bigger role in evolutionary change than previously suspected. The controversy does not threaten the basic premise of evolution, however. Scientists on both sides of the argument agree that natural selection determines most adaptations of an organism, although some question whether the same process occurs on the molecular level.

As with many other developments, this argument was born out of technological/methodological advances, in this case a process known as electrophoresis. The process of electrophoresis allows researchers to identify proteins; these are the large molecules that conduct most of the basic life processes. Electrophoresis works as follows: when a protein is placed in a gel between two electric terminals, it tends to drift toward one or the other at a speed determined by its electrical charge. The structure of a protein reflects the molecular code of the gene that originally created the protein, thus electrophoresis provides a means of identifying and analyzing individual genes.

Of late, electrophoresis has revealed a wide variation of protein structures that conduct the same tasks in different individuals of the same species. This phenomenon is known as polymorphism, and polymorphic genes are the result of mutation. Most mutations are deleterious and disappear from the gene pool. According to Darwinian evolutionary theory, all genes that survive do so because they benefit the species in some way. In recent years, however, some scientists (primarily molecular biologists) have argued that the number of genetic polymorphisms is simply too great to be accounted for in this way.

Molecular critics of the Darwinian scheme offer an alternative and suggest that many of the polymorphic forms of genes neither increase nor decrease an individual's chances of survival. Rather, they suggest, such polymorphisms are neutral and become established simply by chance. Proponents of this view are often called "neutralists." In support of their argument they suggest that rates at which similar genes evolve in different species seem to be remarkably constant—a fact they feel cannot be accounted for by natural selection. Two of the foremost proponents of this neutralist viewpoint are Dr. J. King and Dr. T. Jukes (1969).

Scientists who allow that Darwinian principles are still valid on the molecular level—often called "selectionists"—argue that this constancy is largely illusory and that Darwinian principles are still applicable on the molecular level. Studies by Dr. F. Ayala show that certain polymorphic genes appear with the same frequencies in a variety of different groups within the same species of fruit fly. Ayala argues that chance alone would not account for this (Ayala, 1974).

A third group of molecular biologists is casting doubt on the role of simple genetic mutations in major evolutionary changes. Using a method of analysis known as protein sequencing, these scientists have discovered considerable genetic similarities between living forms. For example, the proteins of humans and chimpanzees differ by no more than one percent. It has been argued, for example by Dr. A. Wilson and Dr. M. King (1975), that a small number of genes could be responsible for major evolutionary adaptations that involve shape, size, and behavior. This group of scientists has begun to assail the primate fossil record. They argue that our divergence from a common pongid ancestor occurred more recently in time than the paleontological record suggests. This is discussed more fully in Chapter 23 in the form of Sarich and Wilson's immunological approach.

Relaxed Selection and Genetic Load. The first statements on relaxed selection date to the early eugenics movement, which had an uncolorful political and social flavor. Early statements concerning relaxed selection argued for the so-called "survival of the fittest" in social terms. For example, various forms of social welfare were attacked because they supposedly preserved less fit individuals.

Genetically, however, the concept of relaxed selection is debatable. By increasing the fitness of one genotype by definition you decrease the fitness of alternatives. One can only speak of relaxed selection in terms of specific genotypes and not as an overall phenomenon. This proposition means that relaxed selection is only a change in fitness values of specific genotypes due to environmental changes. An example of this is the apparent rise in frequency of red-green color blindness. Studies suggest that the frequency of red-green color blindness is proportionate to the length of time a society has depended on hunting as a way of life (Post, 1962, 1965). Post tabulated data on populations in which red-green color blindness was investigated. He classified these populations into three groups, presumably on the basis of how long it had been since their ancestors were hunters and gatherers. Averaging the frequency of red-green color blindness in each category, he arrived at the following figures:

Economic pursuit	*Frequency of color vision defect*
Hunters and gatherers	0.020
Intermediates	0.033
Long-time agriculturists	0.080

There is the possibility that a number of rare genetic defects may increase in frequency due to relaxed selection precipitated by medical intervention. Phenylketonuria (PKU), inherited as a recessive defect in the metabolism of phenylalanine, is an example. Since in the past children with PKU seldom survived to become adults and reproduce, the condition appears to have been maintained in the population solely by mutation. In most populations the frequency of PKU is one in 10,000 or less, a gene frequency of 0.01 or less. New tests can early detect a PKU infant and a special dietary regime has been employed to try to mediate any occurrence of severe defects, often without success.

The PKU example serves to highlight a current controversy among social thinkers, namely the issue of genetic load. The issue of genetic load also serves to highlight the interaction between culture and biology and illustrates how modern culture can affect future evolutionary trends. Genetic load refers to the number of deleterious genes maintained within a population. The greater the number of deleterious genes, the heavier the genetic load. A number of geneticists feel that populations have limits as to the number of deleterious genes they can tolerate. They fear that preventing the natural death of an organism, that is, neutralizing the deleterious gene, will result in genetic weakening of the population. The issue is a moral as well as a genetic problem. Which traits do we preserve within a population and which do we permit to die out? Furthermore, what are today genetic malfunctions may tomorrow seem quite insignificant. For example, all individuals who today wear glasses for nearsightedness would, during the days of total reliance upon hunting, have been deemed genetically unfit. Imagine trying to stalk an animal which you could not see!

In many societies the problem of genetic load is met by genetic counseling. Individuals exhibiting some genetic disorder can be helped to lead a "normal" life through medical intervention, and such individuals are often advised against reproducing. Some states in the United States have on occasion taken the extreme measure of sterilizing severely mentally impaired persons to prevent them from having children, but this was often done without the consent of the individuals concerned and was therefore against the law. It should be made quite clear that genetic counseling is as much a debatable topic as is genetic load. The fear that genetic counseling could be manipulated for social, political, or economic means is quite apparent.

Inbreeding. Inbreeding and outbreeding provide major deviations from random mating. Due to the importance of animal and plant breeding in the development of population genetics, more is known about the mechanisms of inbreeding. The effects of outbreeding, however, can be assumed to be opposite those of inbreeding. An organism is considered to be inbred when its parents are related. A population is inbred when more such consanguineous mating occurs than expected under the assumptions of randomness. Inbreeding serves to increase the frequency of homozygous loci in the inbred individual or population as compared to expectation under the Castle-Hardy-Weinberg assumption.

Drift (Sampling Error). The mechanism known as genetic drift may provide a possible explanation for many of the problems in physical anthropology which deal with population relationships. When, for example, two or more populations believed to be distantly related are found to share gene frequencies, this similarity can be explained as due to genetic drift (chance). By the same token, genetic drift may be used to explain differences between populations believed on other grounds to be closely related. Thus, differences between Micronesians and Polynesians may be explained by invoking drift.

Since genetic drift is effective only in small populations, it may have played a major role in our early evolutionary stages. Genetic drift was possibly a more potent evolutionary force early in our history than it is today. While the magnitude of drift is hard to assess, it seems certain that at one time our ancestors lived in exactly the situation conducive to drift—small isolated groups. With the introduction of agriculture and sedentism, population size and density increased, thus decreasing the potential effect of drift upon subsequent evolutionary history.

In 1931 Sewall Wright, one of the founders of population genetics, developed a mathematical model dealing with the population as a finite evolutionary unit. He proposed that under certain conditions a population is subjected to special evolutionary forces which he labelled genetic drift. This process, the **Sewall Wright effect**, refers to the random fluctuation or drift of gene frequencies from generation to generation in relatively small, isolated populations. Due to drift, a number of local populations, although originally derived from the same parental population, may eventually differ from one another to varying degrees. The random nature of genetic drift places it in a different category than other evolutionary forces; for example, mutation and natural selection, which exert systematic pressures on a gene pool. Genetic drift exerts nonsystematic pressures, and gene frequency changes are indeterminate in direction. Genetic drift leads to a net loss of heterozygosity within a total population subdivided into small isolates (the so-called decay of variability).

What constitutes a small population within which drift is effective depends upon the interrelations between the number of breeding individuals, selective value of the alleles, mutation pressure, and gene flow. It is often stated that drift is effective in small populations (numbering in the hundreds) and inoperative in larger populations, but this is an oversimplification.

The measurement and demonstration of genetic drift is difficult. It is doubtful if any human population ever approximated the ideal conditions requisite for the application of mathematical models of drift. However, within limits imposed by the population, there are various means of measuring drift; one is by noting the variance in gene frequency between local populations and the offshoot and parental populations. Unless strong selection pressures account for gene frequency differences, they are probably due to drift.

Founder Principle. The **founder**, or bottleneck, principle refers to a change in the genetic composition of small breeding populations often accompanied by a reduction in total population size. The process is best defined as the total genetic impact experienced by a population due to the combined events of (1) drastic size reduction, (2) rapid expansion, and (3) relative isolation, with little genetic admixture. With all three conditions present, the effects of the original size reduction persist, and, in accumulation, shape the profile of ancestral contributions to the present gene pool.

The initial event of the founder principle, drastic size reduction, occurs in two major ways: (1) death of a large number of the population and (2) migration. In the first instance, the remaining population constitutes the "founder population" for future generations. If in the second case the net mass migration results in leaving behind only a small group, this is considered the founder population. On the other hand, if the migration consists of only a very small number of people who form a new community after leaving the majority, the emigrants are considered to be a founder population.

One oft-cited example of the founder principle is the absence of the gene for the B blood type in the ABO system among American Indians. It is quite likely that American Indian populations were descended from small groups of migratory hunters and gatherers who crossed the Bering Straits during the Late Pleistocene and migrated into the Americas to form a rather large population. The original migrants came from a population which probably had relatively low frequencies of blood group B. The founding groups of the new populations may have had no B alleles. It is also possible, however, that natural selection, working on the ABO phenotypes, was operative. This is discussed later.

Two Examples of the Founder Principle. The island population of Tristan de Cunha[1] grew from 15 to 270 between 1816 to 1961. However, this overall growth was marked by two separate major population reductions which influenced the genetic pattern of subsequent growth. The first fluctuation was due to mass migration, the second to the combined effects of a boating accident claiming most adult males and the subsequent migration of widows. The population twice passed through a "bottleneck" whereby some individuals were extracted and others left. Those who remained formed the founder population and they disproportionately contributed to the genetic structure of subsequent populations.

Our second example is the Amish living in a number of local endogamous communities ranging from 1000 to 9000 people. The focus of many genetic studies, the Amish provide a classic example of the results of inbreeding, genetic drift, and the founder effect. The present Amish population was founded by successive small waves of European immigrants between 1720 and 1850 who primarily settled in Pennsylvania, Ohio, and Indiana. Each Amish deme is descended from a very few founders, reflected in the set of relatively few family names accounting for the majority of individuals within each deme. In three demes, three different sets of eight names account for approximately 80 percent of the Amish families. Extensive genetic and demographic studies show that the limited occurrence of certain rare recessive genetic syndromes and unique gene frequency distributions are best explained by the founder effect.

In addition to having been founded by relatively few individuals, both the Amish and Tristan de Cunha populations fulfill two other conditions of the founder effect: (1) rapid expansion in relative isolation, and (2) rare interjection of genes from outside the breeding population. Tristan de Cunha's population grew from fifteen people in 1851

[1]A group name for three small islands belonging to the United Kingdom, located in the South Atlantic midway between South Africa and South America. Of the three islands only Tristan is inhabited. The island is remote and periodically evacuated because of volcanic action.

to 270 in 1961 in extreme geographical isolation, interrupted only rarely by immigration. The Amish population grew from 8200 people in 1905 to 45,000 in the 1960s and remained socially isolated.

Drift and the Founder Principle—Forces in Evolution. Both genetic drift and the founder effect may have played a role, perhaps major in some cases, in determining the composition of early hominid populations. If early hominid populations were composed of relatively small, endogamous, and geographically distributed groups, this would have affected their breeding structure. The same situation may have produced some of the population diversity we witness in the world today.

Isolated populations provide valuable information for the human geneticist in the form of aberrant gene frequencies, rare recessive diseases, and demographic data. Although unchallengeable proof of genetic drift in human populations is not readily available, isolated populations continue to be the population geneticist's laboratory.

An Example of an Isolated Community: Roman Jewish Population

An example of a study of an isolated community is provided in the data which the geneticist L. C. Dunn and his anthropologist son Stephen collected on the small Roman Jewish community.[2] The Roman Jewish community is interesting because of its long documented history and because its members have retained their group identity. If there is a cultural or social unity in Jewry as a whole or in any single community, are there also biological effects? Do traditional rules prohibiting marriage outside the Jewish community provide effective genetic isolation from surrounding non-Jewish communities? If so, if this Jewish community is genetically isolated, then we have ways of evaluating some of the biological effects of social and cultural development and thought.

Until recently the typical European Jewish social unit was a small community. In northern and eastern Europe this community is known as the Shtetl, the little town. In Italy the community is the Universita, a secular organization recognized by the state as representing the Jewish inhabitants of a town or a region. Christianity culminated in the enclosure of many Jewish communities in walled ghettos. Palestinian Jews settled in Rome in 160 B.C. Pope Paul closed this ghetto in 1554 and it remained closed for some 300 years. The intent was to isolate the Jewish community socially and reproductively. This was strengthened by prohibitions against intermarriage, curfew laws, and forbidding the employment of those of Jewish origin in Christian homes. Garibaldi's troops eventually opened the ghetto to the outside world in 1870.

The Dunns were able to identify the Roman Jewish community readily because descendants of the ancient community were recognized by a group of families with "ghetto names," a residence pattern centering in ghetto areas, and use of the community's social facilities. Marriage and birth records showed them to be families of Roman Jewish origin, marrying among themselves. This was an endogamous community numbering about 4000 persons with a high degree of reproductive isolation. The Dunns tested the blood, saliva, and urine of 700

[2]Another fascinating example is found in James Neel's (1970) article on the Yanomamo of South America entitled "Lessons from a Primitive People."

individuals, about one-fifth of the community. The following characteristics were uncovered.

1. The B blood group[3] was proportionally twice as great in the Jewish community as in the Italian Catholic community: 27 percent of the Jewish community was group B; in the Italian Catholic community the percentage was 10 or 11 percent. These percentages indicate that there was little interbreeding between the groups. If there had been interbreeding the B frequencies would tend toward similarity in both groups.

2. Some other Jewish communities showed similar high incidences of B in relation to surrounding communities, suggesting that the ancestral Jewish population showed a high percentage of group B. If so, it also suggests a retention by separate Jewish populations of an ancestral genotype.

3. Compared to other Jewish communities, the proportion of B among Roman Jews is high. This may reflect the effect of population size, i.e., we may be witnessing the effect of genetic drift.

4. One of the Rh alleles, Rh-negative, which is usually rare in Europe, is higher than in any other Jewish population. In the Roman Jewish community Rh-negative comprises 5 percent of the population. This figure is much higher than the percentage of Rh-negative in Italy generally and may be due to genetic drift.

5. The above information suggests that social isolation has had its genetic effects.

A Model Population — Castle-Hardy-Weinberg Law

A scientific study begins with some model or set of testable assumptions. Our present interest is with the distribution of alleles within a population, not simply their mode of inheritance. One assumption basic to our study of population genetics is that mating is random within a breeding population. The search for population equilibrium is based on the assumption that genetic stability is generationally maintained; this is mathematically expressed by the **Castle-Hardy-Weinberg Law**. This was formerly known as the Hardy-Weinberg Law, named after G. H. Hardy, a mathematician at Cambridge, and W. Weinberg, a professor from Germany. Hardy's paper was published in 1908, the same year in which Weinberg published his own formulations. Actually an American geneticist, W. Castle, preceded Hardy and Weinberg by five years. This law is stated in terms of allele frequencies. It is necessary to transform the data, which concern the relative proportions of different observed phenotypes, into percentages of various alleles responsible for the phenotypes.

Theoretical Assumptions. The Castle-Hardy-Weinberg Law applies the algebraic formula known as the expansion of the binomial to problems of population genetics. The formula is written as $p^2 + q^2 = 1$, or

---

[3]The blood group is determined by the presence of (1) composition differences (known as antigens) in the red blood cells and (2) substances in the serum called antibodies. Antibodies distinguish particular antigens from others in a particular way, causing agglutination of cells. Agglutination occurs when clumps of cells form islands in a preparation solution. The antigen-antibody reaction, characterized by agglutination, is widespread as a physiological defense mechanism against the effects of exposure to foreign proteins. This is the mechanism which protects against bacterial infection.

totality, the whole population. The Castle-Hardy-Weinberg Law permits prediction of gene frequencies on the basis of observed genotypes and phenotypes. To compute such frequencies, a number of assumptions must be made about the subject population.

1. It is assumed that all mating is within the population and is random with respect to the genetic differences being considered. The population's age structure is ignored and parents are assumed to be replaced by their children.
2. We assume an infinitely large population.
3. It is assumed that there are no forces of evolution existing, i.e., drift, natural selection, migration, or mutation.

The list of assumptions is such that all of them are seldom realized in a "real" population. However, the optimism underlying the use of such a set of simplifying assumptions is justified. As an example of the workings of the Castle-Hardy-Weinberg Law, we refer to a study conducted by Dr. Frederick Hulse, a physical anthropologist at the University of Arizona. With a colleague, Hulse studied the Quinault Indians (a Northwest coast group) for the incidence of the MN blood group. Hulse found that the distribution of MN was seventy-seven individuals homozygous for type M (i.e., carried only the M allele), 101 were heterozygous for MN (i.e., carried one M and one N allele), and twenty-three homozygous for N (i.e., carried only the N allele). Each individual for M and N was homozygous for these alleles. Each individual heterozygous for MN contained one M and one N allele. The total number of M alleles is $77 + 77$ (because of the homozygous state of M) $+ 101$ (one allele in the MN heterozygote) $= 255$. The total number of the N alleles is $23 + 23$ (because of the homozygous state of N) $+ 101$ (there being one N allele and one M in the MN genotype) $= 147$. The population of 201 individuals has a total of 402 alleles at this locus. To obtain the allele frequency of M, you divide 255 by 402 (402 is the total number of alleles; 255 is the total number of M alleles). The answer is 63 percent. Likewise, to obtain the allele frequency of N you divide 147 (the actual number of N alleles) by 402 (the total alleles at the locus). The answer is 37 percent. We can then decide if the Quinault are a breeding population in genetic equilibrium by applying the Castle-Hardy-Weinberg Law.

Using the formula $p^2 + 2pq + q^2 = 1$, we let p stand for the gene M and q for the gene N. Since the phenotype M is only produced in the homozygous state, by receiving M from both parents, the frequency will be $M \times M = p^2$. Likewise, N is only phenotypically expressed in the homozygous state, N results from receipt of one N allele from each parent; thus $N \times N = q^2$. The heterozygous state is produced by receiving M from one parent and N from the other; the cross-fertilization of M and N is pq. Since it is equally likely that the egg or sperm be either M or N, the equation is given as 2pq. To apply the formula we multiply $.63 \times .63$ (p^2, the percentage of M) which equals .397; we multiply $.37 \times .37$ (q^2, percentage of N) which equals .137; and then we multiply $.63 \times .37$ (pq, percentage of MN) and double it to equal .466. The total of 1.000 represents 201 individuals. Continuing, we compute the expected allele frequencies as follows: p^2 or .397 of 201 is 80 persons who are expected to have M. The observed number was 77.

The 2pq or .466 of 201 is 94 persons expected to have MN. The observed number was 101. The q^2 or .137 of 201 is 28 persons expected to have N. The observed number was 23. These values are applied to a chi-square test to determine if this tribe is in a state of equilibrium as concerns the MN blood types (see Table 20-3).

This exercise tells the investigator if the particular traits being investigated are under selective pressure or are affected by other evolutionary processes. When a population is in equilibrium for some trait, it can be assumed there is no strong positive or negative selection. Other explanations such as **genetic drift** or the **founder principle** might then be entertained. If we use the Castle-Hardy-Weinberg formula to determine if the allele for sickle-cell is in equilibrium in West Africa we

---

Table 20.3. The Castle-Hardy-Weinberg Law as Applied to the Quinault Indians.

Step 1: The incidence of MN in the real population

M:	77
MN:	101
N:	23
	201

Step 2: Computing allele frequencies

M: 77 + 77 = 154 alleles + M 101 = 255 M alleles
N: 23 + 23 = 46 alleles + N 101 = 147 N alleles

Total alleles in the population: 402

Step 3: Computing the actual allele frequencies in percentage

M: $\frac{255}{402} = 63\%$

N: $\frac{147}{402} = 37\%$

Step 4: Computing expected genotype frequencies

Using the formula $p^2 + 2pq + q^2 = 1$

we substitute $M^2 + 2MN + N^2 = 1$

Given the figures above, the formula then reads:

$p^2(.63 \times .63) + 2pq(2 \times .63 \times .37) + q^2(.37 \times .37)$

Which equals

.397 + .466 + .137 = 1.000

Step 5: Comparing the expected frequencies to the observed genotype frequencies:

Expected		*Observed*	
M:	80 persons	77 persons	
N:	28	23	
MN:	94	101	

These figures are computed by multiplying the figure 201 (the actual number of persons) with the expected allelic frequencies of each allele. Thus for M we multiply 201 with .397 (80), for N 201 with .137 (28), and MN 201 with .466 (94).

Step 6: Apply the observed frequencies to a chi-square table.

Step 7: Decide whether the population is in equilibrium or if selection is occurring for or against certain allelic expressions.

---

would find a negative answer. There is strong selection for the hetero-zygote condition because it confers protection against extreme malarial infection (see Chapter 23).

> I think about my education sometimes. I went to the University of Chicago for a while after the Second World War. I was a student in the department of anthropology. At that time, they were teaching that there was absolutely no difference between anybody. They may be teaching that still.
>
> From Kurt Vonnegut, Jr.,
> *Slaughterhouse Five or The Children's Crusade*

The basic evolutionary unit is the population. Evolutionarily the Mendelian population is the focal point of genetic studies. Because of the difficulties of working with large, relatively undefined populations, population geneticists restrict their research to small breeding units referred to as demes. A number of complicating factors impinge upon the genetic study of populations; prime among these are definition of vital processes, the Sewall Wright effect, and the founder principle.

The genetic model of natural selection is based upon a number of theoretical assumptions. One of these assumptions is that mating is random within a breeding population and that genetic stability is generationally maintained. This assumption is mathematically expressed in the Castle-Hardy-Weinberg Law. Application of this law tells the investigator whether or not the trait being studied is under selective pressure.

Gene frequencies within populations change primarily through the action of mutation, drift, flow, and selection. These mechanisms are discussed.

Bibliography

Ayala, F. 1974. Biological evolution: natural selection or random walk? *American Scientist* 62:692-701.

Ayala, F., and Anderson, W. 1973. Evidence of natural selection in molecular evolution. *Nature: New Biology* 241-274-76.

Buettner-Janusch, J. 1968. *Origins of man.* New York: Wiley.

Cavalli-Sforza, L., and Bodmer, W. 1971. *The genetics of human populations.* San Francisco: W. H. Freeman.

Crow, J. 1972. The dilemma of nearly neutral mutations: how important are they for evolution and human welfare? *J. Heredity* 63:306-16.

Dobzhansky, T. 1959. *Evolution, genetics and man.* New York: Wiley.

_____. 1962. *Mankind evolving: the evolution of the human species.* New Haven: Yale University Press.

Dubos, R. 1968. *Man adapting.* New Haven: Yale University Press.

Dunn, L. 1968. *Heredity and evolution in human populations.* New York: Atheneum.

Dunn, L., and Dobzhansky, T. 1960. *Heredity, race and society.* New York: Mentor.

Ford, E. 1965. Genetic polymorphism. Cambridge, Mass.: M.I.T. Press.

Glass, B.; Sacks, M.; Jahn, E.; and Hess, C. 1952. Genetic drift in a religious isolate; an analysis of the causes of variation in blood group and other gene frequencies in a small population. *American Naturalist* 86:145-59.

Hulse, F. 1971. *The human species.* New York: Random House.

Kelso, A. J. 1970. *Physical anthropology.* Philadelphia: Lippincott.

————. 1974. *Physical anthropology,* 2d ed. Philadelphia: Lippincott.

King, J. 1974. *The biology of race.* New York: Harcourt Brace Jovanovich.

King, J., and Jukes, T. 1969. Non-Darwinian evolution. *Science* 164:788-98.

King, M., and Wilson, A. 1975. Evolution at two levels in humans and chimpanzees. *Science* 188:107-15.

Klass, M., and Hellman, H. 1971. *The kinds of mankind.* Philadelphia: Lippincott.

Lasker, G. 1952. Mixture and genetic drift in ongoing human evolution. *American Anthropologist* 54:433.

Livingstone, F. 1967. The founder effect and deleterious genes. *American Journal of Physical Anthropology* 30:55.

Mayr, E. 1970. *Populations, species and evolution.* Cambridge, Mass.: Harvard University Press.

McKusick, V. 1969. *Human genetics.* Englewood Cliffs, N.J.: Prentice-Hall.

Molnar, S. 1975. *Races, types, and ethnic groups.* Englewood Cliffs, N.J.: Prentice-Hall.

Morris, L., ed. 1971. *Human populations, genetic variation and evolution.* San Francisco: Chandler Publishing Co.

Neel, J. 1958. The study of natural selection in primitive and civilized human populations. *Human Biology* 30:43.

————. 1970. Lessons from a "primitive" people. *Science* 170(3960):815.

Post, R. 1962. Population differences in red and green color vision deficiency: a review and a query on selection relaxation. *Eugenics Quarterly* 9:131-46.

————. 1965. Selection against "colorblindness" among "primitive" populations. *Eugenics Quarterly* 12:28-29.

Slobodkin, L. 1961. *Growth and regulation of animal populations.* New York: Holt, Rinehart and Winston.

Williams, B. 1973. *Evolution and human origins.* New York: Harper & Row.

Wright, S. 1968. Evolution and the genetics of populations. Vol. 1, *Genetic and biometric foundations.* Chicago: University of Chicago Press.

————. 1969. Evolution and the genetics of populations. Vol. 2. *The theory of gene frequencies.* Chicago: University of Chicago Press.

MAMMALIA.

ORDER I. PRIMATES.

Fore-teeth cutting; upper 4, parallel; teats 2 pectoral.

1. HOMO.

Sapiens.   Diurnal; varying by education and fituation.

2. Four-footed, mute, hairy. *Wild Man.*

3. Copper-coloured, choleric, erect. *American.*
   Hair black, ftraight, thick; *noftrils* wide, *face* harfh; *beard* fcanty; *obftinate*, content free. *Paints* himfelf with fine red lines. *Regulated* by cuftoms.

4. Fair, fanguine, brawny. *European.*
   Hair yellow, brown, flowing; *eyes* blue; *gentle*, acute, inventive. *Covered* with clofe veftments. *Governed* by laws.

5. Sooty, melancholy, rigid. *Afiatic.*
   Hair black; *eyes* dark; *fevere*, haughty, covetous. *Covered* with loofe garments. *Governed* by opinions.

6. Black, phlegmatic, relaxed. *African.*
   Hair black, frizzled; *fkin* filky; *nofe* flat; *lips* tumid; *crafty*, indolent, negligent. *Anoints* himfelf with greafe. *Governed* by caprice.

Monftrofus Varying by climate or art.

1. Small, active, timid. *Mountaineer.*
2. Large, indolent. *Patagonian.*
3. Lefs fertile. *Hottentot.*
4. Beardlefs. *American.*
5. Head conic. *Chinefe.*
6. Head flattened. *Canadian.*

The anatomical, phyfiological, natural, moral, civil and focial hiftories of man, are beft defcribed by their refpective writers.

2. SIMIA.

Chapter 21
An Outlook—
The Seeds of Controversy

Quick reference to Tables 21-1 and 21-2 shows that human populations have been the object of various means of classification. A major problem confounding the understanding of population diversity is finding a means whereby population differences can be accurately assessed, and then finding criteria which most would agree are useful. The problem of establishing meaningful criteria whereby populations can be said to differ as a result of multitudinous factors is complicated by a combination of the following: there is much disagreement as to what are "meaningful criteria" (what is meaningful to one researcher may be less so to another), there are various assessments of physical types in the folk evaluation of various cultures (the recognition of "you" and "us"), and the subject of human variation is loaded with emotionalism. Working within this framework is distressing, and many shy away.

Table 21.1. Racial Criteria Based Upon Blood Groups.

System	Gene	Caucasoid (European)	Negroid (African)	Mongoloid (Asiatic)
ABO	A_2	Moderate	Moderate	Essentially absent
	B	Low	Intermediate	High
Rh	R	Low	High	Low
	r	High	Intermediate	Essentially absent
Duffy	Ry^a	Intermediate	Low	High
	Fy	Absent	High	High
Diego	Dr^a	Absent	Absent	High
Sutter	Js^a	Absent	High	Absent

From *The Biological and Social Meaning of Race* by Richard H. Osborne. W. H. Freeman and Company. Copyright © 1971.

Linnaeus's classification of the genus *Homo*.

Table 21-2. Racial Criteria Based Upon Surface Features.

Sorting Criteria	Caucasoid	Negroid	Mongoloid
Skin color	Light brown to white, pink, or ruddy.	Dark brown to black.	Yellow or yellow-brown.
Eye color	Never black, all lighter shades.	Dark brown, all black.	Medium to dark brown.
Hair color	Rarely black, all lighter shades.	Black.	Black.
Hair form	Wavy to straight, sometimes loosely curled.	Wooly to frizzy.	Straight, coarse texture.
Nasal form	Usually high and narrow, index* under 70.	Usually low and broad, tip and alae thick, index** 85 and over.	Root very low, top short, tip and alae medium, index intermediate to Caucasoid and Negroid.
Malars (Cheek bones)	Small.	Variable, usually larger than Caucasoid.	Strong forward and lateral jut, usually covered with a flat pad.
Beard and body hair	Usually medium to heavy, highly variable.	Medium to sparse.	Less than Caucasoid or Negroid.
Membranous lip	Medium to thin, little eversion.	Usually thick, everted, marked lip seam.	Medium, variable.
Skull	Greater development of brow ridges than in Negroids and Mongoloids, large mastoid processes.	Rounded forehead, long skull, prominent occiput (back of skull).	Brow ridges poorly developed, round skull, flat occiput with marked ridge; vault (top of the skull) often with a keel.
Face	Straight face; small jaws and prominent chin; high narrow nasal bones and well-developed nasal spine.	Prognathism (forward protrusion of upper jaw), small chin, low broad basal bridge and broad nasal aperture; long narrow palate.	Malars (cheek bones) prominent; root of nose flat and broad; nasal aperture narrow, palate short and wide, lower jaw wide.
Long bones	Thick; joints large and muscle markings prominent.	Slender; shin and forearm bones long relative to upper segments.	Not remarkable; intermediate in Caucasoid and Negroid.

*As proposed by Hooton and others and customarily applied when race classification is based on surface features.
**Breadth x 100/height.
From *The Biological and Social Meaning of Race* by Richard Osborne. W. H. Freeman and Company. Copyright © 1971.

Classification Schemes[1]

Fifteenth and Sixteenth Century. During the fifteenth and sixteenth centuries efforts were made to order newly discovered human populations. Attempts were made to explain morphological diversity, especially skin color, as being related to climatic factors. Jean Bodin (1530-1596) attempted to classify humanity in the following manner:

> . . . the people of the South are of contrarie humor and disposition to them of the north: these are great and strong, they are little and weak; they of the north hot and moist, the others cold and dry; the one hath a big voyce and greene eyes, the other hath a weake voyce and black eyes; the one hath a flaxen haire and a faire skin, the other hath both haire and skin black; the one feareth cold, and the other heate.

Objective and systematic classification of natural phenomena such as plants and animals—and humans—began in the sixteenth century with the new philosophy of scientific observation and inductive reasoning under principles formulated by Francis Bacon. Previously, few classification schemes existed for any natural phenomena; the view of the world was about as subjective as Augustine's in the third century when he classified animals into three groups: helpful, hurtful, and superfluous. After Bacon, far-reaching explorations of the next two centuries from the South Pacific to the Arctic provided a vast array of hitherto unknown plants and animals. Samples and descriptions brought to Europe provided a wealth of material for scientific examination.

Seventeenth Century. During the seventeenth century the influence of the Old Testament's account of human history substantially handicapped biological research, especially that concerned with human origins. Despite this, polygenesis, i.e., the notion of multiple human origins, not necessarily related to God's creation, cautiously began to emerge. Such ideas, however, remained isolated cries in the wilderness. In 1695 an anonymous author expounded on the polygenesis viewpoint, citing as evidence cultural differences between the Old and New Worlds, geographical difficulties of migration, and floral and faunal differences between the Old and New World. Earlier investigators bold (or foolish) enough to expound heresies were burned at the stake.

Eighteenth Century. The Swedish botanist, Carolus Linnaeus, brought order to studies of the plant and animal world; in his work *Systema Naturae* he devised a hierarchical classificatory scheme for plants (1735) and animals (1758). In 1745 he proposed four living human races—Europeans, Africans, Asiatics, and American Indians—whose differentiation was largely based upon pigmentation and a subjective judgment of each group's behavioral traits.

Johann Friedrich Blumenbach (1752-1840) (Table 21-3) was the last influential eighteenth-century systematist; he might have been the first to have used comparative anatomy to study different populations. In his 1770 book, whose title is roughly translated as "The Variety of Man," he divided *Homo* into four races. In the second edition pub-

[1]For a most interesting brief review of the development of various explanations of human diversity, the reader might refer to K. A. R. Kennedy's book *Human Variation in Space and Time* (Dubuque: Wm. C. Brown Co., 1976).

Table 21.3. Early Racial Classifications.

Linneaus (1735)	Buffon (1749)
American (Reddish)	Laplander
European (White)	Tartar
Asiatic (Yellow)	South Asiatic
Negro (Black)	European
	Ethiopian
	American
Blumenbach (1781)	**Cuvier (1790)**
Caucasoid	Caucasoid
Mongoloid	Mongoloid
American Indian	Negroid
Ethiopian	
Malay	

From Stephen Molnar, *Races, Types and Ethnic Groups: The Problem of Human Variation,* © 1975, p. 7. Reprinted by permission of Prentice-Hall, Inc., Englewood Cliffs, New Jersey.

lished in 1781 he divided *Homo* into five races on the basis of head shape. His five divisions were Caucasian (a name coined on the basis of a skull from the Caucasus region which Blumenbach felt typical of this "race"), Negro, Mongol, Malayan, and American Indian; he adhered to this scheme in all subsequent works. According to this scheme, morphological differences were attributable to climate, diet, mode of life, hybrid generation, hereditary peculiarities of animals from diseased temperament and perhaps mutilations, and other factors which may contribute to differences in native varieties. Blumenbach's classification avoided Linnaeus's subjective behavioral characteristics and more or less took into account basic differences in skin pigmentation.

Why Classify? The question often arises as to why early scientists (and pseudo-scientists) and by implication their heirs apparent were interested in classifying people into races. Early scientists were concerned with cataloging the human diversity rapidly being thrust upon them by explorations, contact with others, and the age of mercantilism. When Linnaeus published his classification in the mid-eighteenth century, Europe still was dividing the legendary from the real. Many still considered the unicorn real, while orangutans and chimpanzees were considered subhuman humans. In the zoological naïveté of the time they represented human creatures whose existence was sworn to by travelers, missionaries, and traders. "Scientific" descriptions of different human groups were another way of adding to one's knowledge about the environs.

During the period between Linnaeus and Darwin, individuals were measured and described; racial groupings were created and rearranged in an endless procession of descriptive material. Behind attempts at constructing racial categories was the implicit, and sometimes explicit, belief that persistence would eventually reveal a divinely inspired pattern. An aura of theological fervor, the search for the racial holy grail, pervaded; a certain dogmatic tenor characterized this work, and still exists for some today. Many regard races as not only rigid and unchanging, but somehow preordained to exist in a "pure" and original nature. Nothing could be more inaccurate; there is not now, and probably never was, anything akin to a "pure" race. Racial formation and breakdown is a dynamic process, occurring whenever populations meet and mate with one another.

Problems with Early Attempts. Early classifiers worked in complete ignorance of what are today considered two fundamental concepts necessary for studying modern population variability—the principles of evolution and population genetics. Once we accepted our place within the evolutionary scheme, studies of population differences radically changed. Instead of seeking a divine pattern, students of human diversity asked questions like: "What is the evidence for natural selection in this group?" "What kinds of adaptations have certain populations made with their environment?" "How recent is this group's ancestry?" Within this evolutionary framework, new questions were raised and new techniques developed.

Twentieth Century. The first two or three decades of the twentieth century witnessed much interest in population diversity and human adaptation. Unfortunately early twentieth-century workers shared much of their outlook with their pre-evolutionarily oriented predecessors. Ernest A. Hooton was among the last of the physical anthropologists to present a detailed classification of living populations based upon comparative physical and pre-genetic evolutionary formulations. Hooton's sorting criteria were primarily phenotypic features, many of which continue to be used in conjunction with other criteria. (Examples of these criteria are found in Tables 21-1 and 21-2.) Hooton's scheme recognized three races—Caucasoid, Mongoloid, and Negroid—which were then divided into primary subraces and then into morphological types. This system provided for different levels of intermixture and some races were considered to be the result of intermixture with other races. Soon some proposed a blender effect—mix two parts Negroid and one part Caucasoid to produce "subtype A," or what have you. This led to some ludicrous schemes.

Individuals were first segregated one from another by measurement of phenotypic traits, outward manifestations of genetic combinations which were thought to be easily measured and described. The problem with using these traits, besides the fact that we are unsure of their genetic base, is that they don't segregate easily, making them hard to measure. Early attempts at distinguishing populations from one another were largely based on anthropometric measurements (i.e., measurements of the human body) made with the caliper (see Figure 21-1). For example, head shapes were measured and divided into three types: dolicocephalic (narrow headed), mesocephalic (medium headed), and brachycephalic (round headed), obtained by calculating a ratio of skull breadth to skull height from fixed points on the skulls. The major problem with calculating skull shape, the cephalic index, is that skull shape changes with environment and diet. In the early part of the twentieth century it was shown that head shapes of American immigrants' children differed from those of their parents. This was probably due to dietary changes.

Early students often established classifications on the basis of other readily observable traits. Prime among these was skin color, which was then measured by holding a paint chart against the skin and noting the nearest match. In addition to other invalidating points, there was a

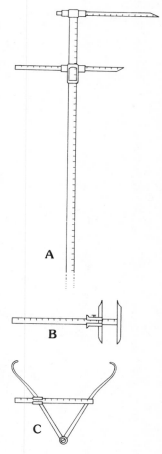

Figure 21-1. Anthropometric equipment.
(A) Anthropometer
(B) Sliding caliper
(C) Spreading caliper

lack of standardized charts. Hair form and distribution on the body were two additional traits used as an early basis for distinguishing populations.

The Present Outlook

Theoretical Stance. Hooton's scheme is still used today; however, new questions limit its value. His scheme has been greatly modified and is now part of a larger list of sorting criteria. Ideas about modern population differences have been greatly altered by the impact of population genetics. The application of population genetics and new laboratory techniques have added important dimensions towards better understanding population variability. Two ideas having the greatest impact for understanding human diversity are the genetic definition of the species and the concept that populations, not individuals, are being classified.[2] With these realizations, new questions have been raised, such as: What is the nature of the distribution of genetic traits within and between populations resulting in observed population differentiation? Which population differences are genetic, which environmental, and which result from both?

From the Linnean system to the present, using multiple techniques, all attempts to classify human populations have consistently drawn lines at major geographic boundaries. This underlines the fact that these boundaries are fundamental to human diversification. Usually the greater the geographical distance between groups, the greater the genetic distance; geographically intermediate populations tend toward genetic intermediacy. We have moved from a nonevolutionary, three-fold classification of "pure" stocks, to an evolutionarily oriented genetically based, multitudinous scheme. Today's questions—and today's answers—are different; furthermore, today's research techniques vary. However, there is one basic conclusion: the world is composed of many different human populations and our task is to find out why.

Racial Historical Approach. Various classification schemes employed to order human diversity fall into one of three approaches: the racial-historical approach, the genetic-distance approach, and the zoogeographic approach. The racial-historical approach is the oldest. It considers races fixed and unchanging entities. The primary aim of this approach is to derive a group's evolutionary history by listing certain physical traits which are then compared to other possibly related populations. Under this scheme populations are classified into pure and mixed races, the latter being formed when two or more primary races meet as a result of large-scale migrations. The racial-historical approach renders only token credit to natural selection as the source of population differentiation. Most of the credit goes to historical derivations.

Zoogeographic Approach. The zoogeographic approach attempts to integrate population genetics with evolution and classification; the major emphasis is on the relationship of physical traits to one's habitat. Adherents of this scheme are concerned with the role of environmental or geographical variation in influencing human diversity.

[2]Under the old system even individuals of the same genetic family sometimes found themselves members of different races. We now recognize that a great deal of intrapopulation variability exists; there is no "pure" racial type to which all members of one group must strictly conform.

Clinal Approach. On the opposite end of a continuum of approaches on human variation in which Hooton's typological approach represents one scheme, we have the clinal approach where attention is paid to the distribution of individual traits and gene frequencies. Since the real variation of any particular genetic trait is limited at any point in time, the distribution of identical forms can be grouped into zones and separated from other areas by boundaries determined by the ranges over which a particular trait may be found to have a common expression. This approach establishes clines, like temperature gradients on a climatic map. Adherents of this approach deny that so-called races actually exist—only clines occur. The assumptions behind the clinal approach stem from evolutionary theory and population genetics. The major cornerstones of the genetic distance or clinal approach are blood group genes and abnormal hemoglobins, and population relationships are determined according to the frequencies of shared genetic traits. Clinal analysis has several assumptions: (1) traits vary, (2) trait variations are due to systematic forces which may relate to some evolutionary mechanism, i.e., selection or migration, or to other factors, (3) the two kinds of systematic forces are, in principle, separable, and (4) trait distributions offer an alternative means of relating human diversity to evolutionary theory (Kelso, 1974).

The following chart adapted from Kelso (1974) presents four main alternatives for interpreting human diversity.

Method of Classification	Criteria Utilized	Names Applied
Typological classification	Trait clusters	Races and other "types"
Population	Mating systems, Mendelian populations	Breeding populations
Clinal Approach	Individual trait distribution	Clines
Zoogeographical approach	Population genetics, physical traits adapted to habitats	Races

Important Concepts

Polytypism and Polymorphism. The Mendelian population, a reproductive community of sexual and cross-fertilizing individuals among whom mating regularly occurs and who thus contribute to the gene pool, is the focal point for determining population affinities. *Homo sapiens sapiens* is a **polymorphic** and **polytypic** species. The term polymorphic refers to the variety of traits within a Mendelian population, e.g., skin color, body size, and body shape. Polytypic refers to the fact that *Homo sapiens sapiens* contains different varieties of traits which vary from place to place. Both these traits are natural to any species.

Homo sapiens sapiens is also considered to be panmictic, at least theoretically. In a panmictic population, gene flow is nonrestrictive; each population segment has the same or similar gene frequencies as other parts. In truth, however, restrictions exist; there are reproductive barriers. Our cultural norms are the most effective barriers to true panmixis; linguistic, cultural, or historical differences have all prevented panmixis from becoming a reality.

Race vs. No Race

The concept of race arose in mercantile Europe, when Europeans awoke with renewed awareness to the fact that many different peoples and cultures existed in various parts of the world. The race concept emerged in an effort to assimilate this new information and the term "race" was introduced into common usage and scientific taxonomies. Soon, racist ideologies evolved, as much a result of economic, social, and religious exploitation as anything. Eighteenth-century scientists debated whether races had separate origins and they argued over whether God independently created each so-called race.[3] In the nineteenth century the debate switched to the matter of equality. In the first decades of the twentieth century, especially during and immediately after World War II, most scientists and educated persons shifted to a position of equalitarianism. Now, anthropologists argue whether in fact there is such a phenomenon as race (Lieberman, 1968).

Lumpers and Splitters. The subject of population diversity, human races, elicits emotional and often passionate responses. Freed from the emotional situation, what posture should the scientist adopt? Two extreme attitudes emerge. One is to leave the problem in abeyance because of the risk that scientific findings will be prostituted to political or social ends. The alternative is to adopt a make-believe detachment. Some believe racial groups are discernable, that human races exist, that there is enough human diversity to separate populations. Others argue that racial groupings do not exist. These scientists belong to the clinist school. Clinists do not deny variability within and between populations; they simply argue that this variability is not of the magnitude to separate some populations from others. Those who believe races exist accept that clines occur; however, they maintain that it is necessary to distinguish clines between and within populations. Clinists argue that human differences result from natural selection operating within ecological zones and that such forces and zones do not coincide with population boundaries. They say that races do not exist because isolation of any group has been infrequent, and point out that populations have always interbred with one another. A crucial point in their favor is the fact that the so-called racial boundaries depend heavily on the classifier's criteria.

Both sides do agree upon a definition of a race as a population distinguishable from others on the basis of inherited physical characters. Beyond this there is disagreement as to where one group ends and another begins. The various antagonists contend over the issue of whether one can locate boundaries; the argument hinges on the significance of the gradation of genetically based physical characters. The race-exists school argues that these genetic gradations are intergradations between races. The no-race adherents, clinists, hold that the gradations are not intergradations but overlapping gradients not confined to boundaries or a particular population.

Inhabitants in different parts of the world are often visibly different; these differences are in part genetic and this is the essence of the biological conception of race. Surely, any two persons, even brothers or sisters, differ; however, racial differences are genetic differences between Mendelian populations, not between persons. Yet traits considered to

[3]The argument pitting monogenesis against polygenesis.

be racial differentiators are also traits which differ between persons. The difficulty arises when a group is given a name; at this time one is likely to assume that all individuals composing that group are alike in each trait. This is typological thinking, and modern biologists should abandon this notion.

Race Defined (Table 21-4)

What then are these so-called races and what constitutes a race? Those who believe races can be distinguished define a race as any population containing a genetic constellation differentiating it from adjacent populations. A race is characterized not so much by the absolute presence or absence of some hereditary trait, rather racial differences are compounds of individual differences. This relativity, this lack of hard and fast dichotomies in racial differences, is disappointing to adherents of old-fashioned racial typologies.

New concepts as to what constitutes a taxonomic species have had an important influence on the race concept. The lowest category generally recognized in formal zoological nomenclature is the subspecies. These are not closed breeding units, as species normally are, although they represent distinct breeding populations. Such breeding units have been reproductively isolated from one another (for whatever reason) for a sufficient time to have developed a degree of genetic sameness rendering them distinguishable from adjacent populations. Some biologists, like Ernst Mayr, consider subspecific differences to be equivalent to racial differences. One widely accepted definition for establishing races is that they are breeding populations differing in the frequency

Table 21-4. Definitions of Race.

Dobzhansky	Races are defined as populations differing in the incidence of certain genes, but actually exchanging or potentially able to exchange genes across whatever boundaries (usually geographic) separate them. (1944:252)
	Race differences are objectively ascertainable facts, the number of races we chose to recognize is a matter of convenience. (1962:266)
Hulse	...races are populations which can be readily distinguished from one another on genetic grounds alone. (1963:262)
Boyd	We may define a human race as a population which differs significantly from other human populations in regard to the frequency of one or more of the genes it possesses. It is an arbitrary matter which, and how many, gene loci we choose to consider as a significant "constellation"....(1950: 207)
Garn	At the present time there is general agreement that a race is a breeding population, largely if not entirely isolated reproductively from other breeding populations. The measure of race is thus reproductive isolation, arising commonly but not exclusively from geographical isolation. (1960:7)
Mayr	A subspecies is an aggregate of local populations of a species, inhabiting a geographic subdivision of the range of the species, and differing taxonomically from other populations of the species. (1963:348)

From Stephen Molnar, *Races, Types and Ethnic Groups: The Problem of Human Variation,* © 1975, p. 13. Reprinted by permission of Prentice-Hall, Inc., Englewood Cliffs, New Jersey.

of one or more genetic variants. Races are simply populations within which a significant number of individuals carry a particular variant of a gene, or genes, common to the population.

Except for identical twins, everyone is biologically, genetically different; this diversity must not, cannot be confused with inequality. Equality and inequality are sociological, political, economic concepts; identity and diversity are biological phenomena. Diversity is an observable fact where equality is an ethical concept. Societies may, and unfortunately many do, withhold equality from all their members, but at this stage they cannot make all their members genetically alike. It is very doubtful that this would be a good thing evolutionarily, for population diversity is our long-range adaptation for survival.

There is considerable disagreement as to an effective means of defining populations and describing population diversity. Early attempts were frustrated by the Biblical injunction that all individuals were divinely created. In the fifteenth and sixteenth centuries populations were distinguished on the basis of readily observable traits such as skin color. Certain subjective statements were made about behavior according to morphological characteristics.

During the eighteenth century the work of Carolus Linnaeus received wide attention; he proposed that there were four living human races. Blumenbach, a well-known eighteenth-century systematist, based his racial classification upon anatomy. Early twentieth-century anthropologists continued their reliance on easily measured traits and they distinguished populations on the basis of such things as head shape.

Today's theoretical outlook is different; the core of this new outlook is a reliance upon the principles of population genetics. Today we prefer to deal with genetic traits with a known mode of inheritance. Basic to the study of population diversity is the understanding that *H. sapiens sapiens* is a polymorphic, polytypic, panmictic population.

A debate rooted in social and political considerations has arisen in the study of population differences which opposes clinists to those arguing for the validity of race. Clinists contend that races can't be differentiated, that there is a continuum of traits. Those arguing for the validity of race contend that there are clear-cut population differences. Neither set of proponents equates population differences with social discriminatory injustices.

Bibliography

Anonymous. 1956. *The race question in modern science.* UNESCO Publications. New York: Morrow.

Baker, P. 1967. The biological race concept as a research tool. *American Journal of Physical Anthropology* 27:21.

Barnicot, N. 1964. Taxonomy and variation in modern man. In *The concept of race,* edited by A. Montagu, pp. 180-227. New York: Free Press.

Birdsell, J. 1972. *Human evolution.* Chicago: Rand McNally.

Bleibtreu, H., and Downs, J., eds. 1971. *Human variation: readings in physical anthropology.* Beverly Hills, Calif.: Glencoe Press.

Boyd, W. 1950. *Genetics and the races of man.* Boston: Little, Brown.

———. 1963. Genetics and the human race. *Science* 140: 1057-64.

Brace, C.; Gamble, C.; and Bond, J., eds. 1971. *Race and intelligence*. Washington, D.C.: American Anthropological Association.

Clegg, E. 1968. *The study of man*. New York: American Elsevier.

Comas, J. 1960. *Manual of physical anthropology*. Springfield, Ill.: Charles C Thomas.

Coon, C. 1962. *The origin of races*. New York: Knopf.

Coon, C.; Garn, S.; and Birdsell, J. 1950. *Races: a study of the problems of race formation in man*. Springfield, Ill.: Charles C Thomas.

Count, E. 1950. *This is race*. New York: Shuman.

Dobzhansky, T. 1944. On species and races of living and fossil man. *American Journal of Physical Anthropology* 2:252.

————. 1962. *Mankind evolving: the evolution of the human species*. New Haven and London: Yale University Press, p. 266.

————. 1968. *Science and the concept of race*. New York: Columbia University Press.

Ford, E. 1965. *Genetic polymorphism*. Cambridge, Mass.: M.I.T. Press.

Garn, S., ed. 1960. *Reading on race*. Springfield, Ill.: Charles C Thomas.

Garn, S. 1971. *Human races*. Springfield, Ill.: Charles C Thomas.

Goldsby, R. 1971. *Race and races*. New York: Random House.

Hiernaux, J. 1964. The concept of race and the taxonomy of mankind. In *The concept of race*, edited by A. Montagu, pp. 29-45. New York: Free Press.

Hulse, F. 1963. *The human species*. New York: Random House.

Kelso, A. 1970. *Physical anthropology*. Philadelphia: Lippincott.

————. 1974. *Physical anthropology*, 2d ed. Philadelphia: Lippincott.

King, J. 1971. *The biology of race*. New York: Harcourt Brace Jovanovich.

Klass, M., and Hellman, H. 1971. *The kinds of mankind*. Philadelphia: Lippincott.

Laughlin, W., and Osborne, R., eds. 1967. *Human variation and origins*. San Francisco: W. H. Freeman.

Lieberman, L. 1968. The debate over race: a study in the sociology of knowledge. Reprint from *Phylon*, the Atlanta University Review of Race and Culture. Atlanta, Georgia.

Livingstone, F. 1967. *Abnormal hemoglobins in human populations*. Chicago: Aldine.

Mayr, E. 1963. *Animal species and evolution*. Cambridge, Mass.: The Belknap Press of Harvard University.

Mead, M.; Dobzhansky, T.; Tobach, E.; and Light, R., eds. 1968. *Science and the concept of race*. New York: Columbia University Press.

Molnar, S. 1975. *Races, types, and ethnic groups*. Englewood Cliffs, N.J.: Prentice-Hall.

Montagu, A., ed. 1964. *The concept of race*. New York: Free Press.

Montagu, A. 1964. Discussions and criticism on the race concept. *Current Anthropology* 5:317.

————. 1965. *Man's most dangerous myth: the fallacy of race*. New York: Macmillan.

Osborne, R., ed. 1971 *The biological and social meaning of race*. San Francisco: Freeman.

Race, R., and Sanger, R. 1962. *Blood groups in man*. Oxford: Blackwell Scientific Publications.

Slotkin, J. 1965. *Readings in early anthropology*. New York: Wenner-Gren Foundation.

Spuhler, J., ed. 1967. *Genetic diversity and human behavior*. Chicago: Aldine.

Stanton, W. 1960. *The leopard's spots: scientific attitudes toward race in America, 1815-59*. Chicago: University of Chicago Press.

Washburn, S. 1963. The study of race. *American Anthropologist* 65:521.

————. The study of race. In *The concept of race*, edited by A. Montagu, pp. 242-60. New York: Free Press.

Weiner, J. 1971. *The natural history of man*. New York: Universe Books.

Chapter 22
Climatic Adaptations

This chapter discusses the differences between the mechanisms of adaptation, acclimation, acclimatization, and habituation. The chapter focuses on adaptations requisite for life in humid, hot environments; life on the desert; life in extreme cold; and life at high altitudes. We shall also be concerned with possible explanations for differences in skin and eye color.

Important Concepts[1]

At this point it is important to define a number of concepts applicable to the understanding of how an organism meets environmental pressures. Different processes are operable in the mechanics of adaptation, acclimation, acclimatization, and habituation.

Adaptation. The scientist trying to understand human diversity has to deal with the problem of short-term adaptation (or acclimatization) and long-term adaptations related to survival in a particular environment. Dr. Stanley Garn (1957) has stated, " . . . it is one thing to prove either logically or experimentally that a given trait may be beneficial, and another thing to demonstrate survival value." We know that individuals possess enough plasticity to adapt to new conditions in the short run, e.g., tanning in high-light conditions. However, this plasticity is very different from the adaptive capacity of individuals living in an environment over a long period of time. As an example, individuals living in low altitudes can make some of the requisite adjustments to high altitude living (such as life high in the Andes), but they will probably not be able to work and reproduce with the same efficiency as populations long-adapted to this environment. Both long- and short-term adaptations are of interest to the human biologist trying to ascertain evolutionary processes.

[1]For a fuller discussion refer to W. Stini, *Ecology and Human Adaptation*, 1975 (Dubuque: Wm. C. Brown Co., Publishers). The following discussion derives from that work.

Southern Portal, Ferrar Glacier, Antarctica.

In humans, as well as among other animals, climatic adaptations involve at least four different mechanisms: genetic changes, growth changes, physiological changes, and behavioral changes. Genetic changes are the slowest of the group, while behavioral changes are normally the most rapid. Genetic changes are intergenerational changes which occur between successive generations of a population. Growth changes refer to ontogenetic changes, i.e., relatively irreversible changes occurring within an individual's lifetime. Physiological changes are, for the most part, reversible. An example of this would be the menstrual disorders experienced by females who move from low to high altitudes and back to low altitudes.

The problem with this scheme is that genetic, growth, and physiological changes are not mutually exclusive categories. The demarcation between growth and physiological response is often hazy; the same is true for the dividing line between physiological and behavioral responses. These categories of response are sometimes designated by the terms adaptation, acclimation, acclimatization, and habituation.

Our behavioral response takes on a greater importance than is the case with any other animal. Because of our culturally patterned ways of dealing with environmental stresses, much of behavior, although capable of rapid alteration, usually manifests itself in quite stable patterns that are nongenetically generationally transmitted. This has proven to be a highly efficient means of responding to environmental stress, permitting *Homo sapiens* to explore many possibilities for moving into new environments. For this reason we inhabit a diverse array of environments. Although cultural adaptations have sometimes replaced genetic responses, the possibility of cultural adaptations to environmental stress has not totally excluded genetic adaptations. That is, there are real differences among populations in their respective abilities to adapt to certain stresses. Technological adaptation has, however, opened many areas for human habitation which might not now be available if we relied solely on biological/genetic mechanisms.

Despite methodological problems brought about by the possibility of acclimatization, cultural adaptation, and small sample sizes, there are studies whose results indicate that there are real differences in a given population's ability to adapt to certain stresses. Some of these differences are discussed below. Before we proceed, however, we should note that climatic adaptations are not clear-cut. An adaptation often carries with it some disadvantageous side effects. Adaptation is a game of probabilities, of balancing the adaptive against the nonadaptive. If the bad side effects, the detrimental nature of the adaptation, are outweighed by its good effects, we may expect that adaptation to be retained. (Balanced polymorphisms, discussed in the next chapter, are a good example of this process.)

Acclimation. Acclimation refers to short-term physiological responses to stress. These responses are relatively modest and utilize resources already present to redress stresses which lower functional efficiency. For example, some of the problems encountered in high altitudes can be corrected by acclimation. In most cases the complaints of sea-level dwellers due to high altitude stresses such as dizziness, nausea, shortness of breath, and inability to sleep subside after a few days as a result of short-term physiological adjustments. The capacity to endure new environmental stresses may be increased by repeated exposures until one attains a state resembling acclimitization.

Acclimatization. Acclimatization refers to an adjustment to a situation which lasts for a relatively extended period of time. Some acclimatization may persist for an extended period, as when one makes a permanent move to a significantly different climatic condition. Acclimatization may also occur in the short run, as when one experiences seasonal changes. In each case the changes which occur are useful for coping and they are reversible. Stini (1975:10) notes that acclimatization provides an example "of an unexpressed genotypic capacity being exploited in the face of a new set of demands and might be viewed as a temporary reordering of priorities, which may persist as long as the conditions evoking it persist."

Habituation. Short-term responses to stress might be included in the category of habituation. Habituation may be viewed as a reduction in the level of physiological responses to a stress situation. This process allows an organism to maintain a normal state despite potentially disruptive stimuli and cushions an individual from adverse secondary reactions of its own response system (Stini, 1975). Habituation may fall into two categories: "specific habituation" or "general habituation." The former refers to a process such as reduction in pain experienced in a specific region, as in chilling one finger, while "general habituation" refers to the reduction in the overall intensity of a physiological response. Using the same example, "general habituation" would refer to the reduction in the overall intensity of a physiological response, such as vasoconstriction (reduction of the blood flow) to the entire periphery while the chilling of the single finger is experienced. Habituation is concerned with preventing damage to the organism as a result of its own overreaction to stress, while acclimation refers to a graded adjustment to the stress itself.

Some General Rules of Adaptation (Table 22-1)

Allen's and Bergmann's Rules. The human body comes in various shapes and sizes. Some variation is undoubtedly due to nutrition; but some is a response to long-standing adaptations to certain habitats. Two rules, **Bergmann's rule** (formulated in 1847) and **Allen's rule** (formulated in 1877), are often used to explain the diversity in body size and shape in animals. The climatic factor in the case of both rules is cold or heat. Allen's rule, which deals with shape changes to achieve an optimal volume-to-surface ratio, states that extremities and appendages (ears, limbs, tail, fingers, and toes) tend to be shorter in colder climates. Because they expose less body surface and are closer to the body's core temperature, shorter extremities conserve heat. Longer extremities expose greater body surface and offer additional surface for dissipating heat in warm climates. Bergmann's rule, dealing with volume, states that body size tends to be greater (heavier) in cold than in warm climates. Furthermore, Bergmann's rule maintains that in warmer climates, the individual is taller. In colder climates the individual is stockier and shorter. Bergmann's rule describes the relationship between body volume and surface area. A low surface area to high body volume is efficient in heat retention, a high surface area and low body volume proportion is efficient in heat dissipation.

Table 22-1. Population Differences in Response to Heat and Cold

Sample	Results
8 Central Australian aborigines 6 Control "whites" 9 Tropical Australian aborigines	Small, important differences in temperature and metabolic responses to moderate nighttime cold while sleeping.
5 Australian "whites" 6 Central Australian aborigines	Non-aborigines maintained body heat by increased muscle movement (i.e., shivering) during sleep.
2 Unacculturated Bushmen 2 Europeans	No significant differences in response to moderate night cold.
9 Alacaluf	Marked increase in metabolic response to night cold, continued elevated BMR (basal metabolism rate).
7 Afro-American soldiers 7 "white" soldiers 6 Anaktuuk Eskimos	Systematic black-white Eskimo differences in skin temperatures and BMR during the 2-hour cold exposure.
17 "white" and 16 black volunteers matched for body size and composition	Fewer rewarming cycles and lower finger temperatures in black subjects exposed to moderate cold.
16 East Indians 16 U.S. blacks 23 Chinese 17 U.S. of European descent 8 Eskimos	Marked differences in plasma volume and blood volume for the Eskimo especially. Results of questionable value in terms of adaptive significance.
40 pairs of black and "white" soldiers matched for body composition and size	Blacks displayed higher physiological tolerance to hot, humid conditions, but less tolerance (in terms of building a heat load) in hot dry conditions.
8 African mine laborers compared with non-African "white" sample from literature	Africans had lower sweating rates, lower heart rates and lower rectal temperatures.

Adapted from Stanley M. Garn, *Human Races,* 3rd edition, 1971. Courtesy of Charles C Thomas, Publishers, Springfield, Illinois.

These rules were relatively unknown as explanatory vehicles of human diversity until 1950. Even now no one argues that these rules can be strictly applied to animal populations in all cases; however, they are possible explanatory models for various adaptive traits. For example, the short limbs and minimum surface-to-mass ratio in the Eskimo illustrate Allen's rule at one extreme. These are adaptations to conserve heat. The increased limb length and a maximum surface-to-mass ratio characteristic of the African Nuer are oft-quoted examples of Allen's rule working where heat loss is adaptive. Overall, however, there is less evidence for Allen's rule than there is for Bergmann's in human populations. There is evidence, for example, for shorter lower extremities in cold climate populations, but not especially short upper extremities.

H. sapiens sapiens have inhabited diverse habitats since their first appearance in the tropical areas of Africa and possibly Asia. Settlement in previously uninhabited areas, many of which presented new environmental pressures, required a number of new adaptations. Anatomical and physiological adaptations accompanied settlement in humid, hot climates, in dry desert conditions, in cold Arctic and semi-Arctic regions, and in areas of high altitude. What general adaptations might we expect to find in each of these different habitats? What are the adaptive pressures?

Bear in mind that the following discussion deals only with biological responses to stress. We will not deal with cultural adaptations to environmental stresses, although one factor separating us from the rest of the animal world is the fact that we have the capacity to adapt culturally to stress situations and have done so many times in our evolutionary history.

Humid, Hot Climates. A major problem of survival in the tropics is the danger of excessive salt loss through continual perspiration (itself a cooling mechanism). If the body temperature rises too high to induce perspiration, there is the possibility of death by circulatory collapse. Hot, humid climates favor individuals who can maintain a moderate work load in the water-saturated atmosphere.

Assuming long-term tropical inhabitants are the product of evolutionary adaptations to humid heat, what mechanisms are at least theoretically operative? One major adaptation would be a rise in body temperature, inducing perspiration at an earlier stage. Perspiration would induce cooling. One way in which this is accomplished is the possession of a darkly pigmented skin, for according to the laws of physics, dark colors absorb more infrared light (heat) than lighter colors. (More on this shortly.) You should ask, by raising the body temperature and perspiring earlier, isn't one risking circulatory collapse and excessive salt loss? You do slightly increase salt loss; but, on the other hand, you prevent heat exhaustion and circulatory collapse. Furthermore, the extra salt loss is not excessive and is partially offset by the possibility that long-term inhabitants adapted to these conditions can conserve water through concentrated urine and dry feces.

Adaptations to Desert Living. Adapting to desert life is essentially a compromise requiring a tolerance for midday heat and night-cold. Desert inhabitants must also be tolerant of high ultraviolet intensities without dramatically increasing heat load. At the same time they must be able to dissipate heat by perspiration while saving precious water. Assuming adaptations to desert living are not cultural, e.g., air-conditioned homes and cars, lightly colored clothing, and ready water supplies, how does nature handle the problem?

Skin Color. There are several ways to approach the multifaceted problems of desert life; many animals escape the desert heat by sleeping during the day in cool dwellings and moving about at night. The most usual human biological adaptations are a lean body build, moderation of skin color, and concentration of water loss. Modern desert dwellers tend to be leaner than inhabitants in other environments. Among the South African Bushmen, for example, there is an early loss of subcutaneous fat, which may indicate its maladaptive nature. In theory, desert dwellers should have a moderate skin color; the skin should be pigmented enough to protect deeper skin layers from damage but must not be too dark in order not to build an intolerable heat load. Extremely dark skin is disadvantageous under hot-dry conditions; for example, it was found that U.S. black soldiers fared worse in desert tests than their lighter-skinned counterparts. However, there is a lack of uniformity in skin color among desert dwellers.

Water Conservation. Another important adaptive mechanism is some means of conserving water. For example, desert-dwelling kangaroo rats minimize water loss by concentrating their urine. Human desert dwellers with the same adaptation could conserve one to two pints of water daily and, while not a big saving, it is a saving nonetheless. Preliminary tests indicate urinary disorders are less prevalent among desert dwellers than among non-desert dwellers. This may reflect the survival value of concentrated urine and be an indication that disorders causing excessive water loss are definitely nonadaptive.

Cold Adaptation. Of the climatic extremes into which *H. sapiens sapiens* moved, none is more quickly lethal (therefore more selective) than extreme cold. Winter temperatures from −40° to −90° F are reported for parts of the inhabited Arctic. Furthermore, as in the desert, some areas may be relatively warm during the day and cold at night. Adaptation to this latter situation is probably much more of a compromise than is adaptation to the extremely cold Arctic. Approximately 20 percent of the earth is below freezing (32° F); examples of groups inhabiting such areas are the Eskimo, Lapplanders, Ainu of northern Japan, Tibetan and Andean highlanders, and the Indians of Tierra del Fuego.

Failure to make the requisite adjustments to extremely cold temperatures results in many problems, including death. One of the first problems to be avoided is lowering of the body temperature to a point at which frostbite, and eventually death, occurs. Secondly, body temperatures must be maintained at relatively comfortable levels, for it would be maladaptive to shiver constantly in order to maintain body temperature. Of importance, especially in Arctic areas, is the ability to maintain skin temperatures at sufficiently high levels for normal functioning.

Peripheral Temperatures. Some of the earliest studies of cold adaptation by non-Western groups were conducted in the 1930s on the Australian aborigines. At night, the Australian aborigine sleeps nude in temperatures at or below freezing. Their only cultural acquiescence to this situation is sleeping between small fires or curling up with their dogs. (The name of the rock group The Three Dog Night means, in the aborigine experience, a rather cold night. The more dogs it takes to maintain warmth, the colder it is.) To test the aborigines' adaptation to the cold nights, some Western scientists attempted to sleep alongside them. The scientists remained awake most of the night, constantly shivering and thereby preventing sleep in anything more than fits. The aborigines' major physiological adaptation for sleeping nude on cold nights is a marked drop in **peripheral temperatures** (that is, temperatures of the hands and feet). A reduction in the temperature gradient between the body and air conserves internal body heat and prevents cooling of the limbs when in contact with the air.

Despite warm arctic clothing, certain body parts such as the hands are often exposed to high winds and extreme cold. The hands must not only be protected from freezing, they must maintain the fine manipulative skills needed for hunting, etc. It has been found that many cold-adapted peoples adapt to their environment by having high peripheral skin temperatures.

There are two fundamentally different mechanisms of cold adaptation. The first, which is characteristic of the Eskimo, increases the amount of heat near the skin by means of increased metabolic activity and peripheral blood flow. The second, which is found in Australian aborigines, is based on insulation of the vital organs. Unlike the Eskimo, the peripheral surfaces do cool, but as they do so, they further insulate the deeper organs of the chest and abdomen. Whether these different mechanisms are due to different adaptive pressures, i.e., rather continual cold for the Eskimo and primarily seasonal and night cold for aborigines, is not yet clear (Table 22-1).

Body Shape. One of the more obvious biological adaptations to cold stress is minimizing the surface area/mass ratio (e.g., by having a heavy, small squat body). This body shape, coupled with short limbs and stubby fingers and toes, has a heat-preserving potentiality. There is a reduction of heat loss through blood flow to the body peripheries as these are brought closer to the center of the body. An increased thickness of the layer of subcutaneous fat would be adaptive by acting as a heat shield and thus be energy conserving. Lastly, by raising the basal metabolism rate (BMR) to above-normal levels the conversion of food to energy is accelerated, providing more heat.

Coping with Altitude. Between 20 and 25 million persons live permanently above 10,000 feet, mainly in the Ethiopian, Andean, Caucasus, and Himalayan highlands. Studies of high altitude populations virtually provide a natural laboratory equipped with significant stresses of low humidity, low temperatures, low air pressures, high solar radiation, and often marginal diets. Large populations have resided at high altitudes for many generations.

Oxygen Debt. The main stress in altitude adaptation is that of low oxygen pressure. There is no effective economical way to lessen oxygen deficiency culturally; thus populations living at high altitudes must biologically adjust to their surroundings. The oxygen debt is usually lessened by an increased production of red blood cells and a corresponding increase in hemoglobin (the substance which colors blood red). Hemoglobin is a protein substance carrying oxygen from the lungs to the tissues and carbon dioxide from the tissues to the lungs. Any increase in number and size of the red blood cells means an increase in the ability to move oxygen about the body. Another response to high altitudes is an increase in the capillary network of alveoli, resulting in more blood contacting the alveoli of the lungs and facilitating oxygen exchange and transportation. There is also an increase in capillary pressure, shunting oxygen-carrying red blood cells faster through the body and helping prevent oxygen debt. As might also be expected, compared to lowland populations there is as much as a 15 percent increase in the total lung volume of many high altitude dwellers.

Fertility Disorders. Most factors required for high-altitude living involve oxygen exchange within the body, preventing oxygen debt, subsequent brain damage, and eventually death. However, there are some data suggesting that fertility disorders are more prevalent at high altitudes. For example, the number of miscarriages in Denver is higher than in most other parts of the United States and altitude is a likely culprit. Female visitors to altitudes above 10,000 feet often experience menstrual disorders, skipping of cycles or excessive flow. There is a tendency toward later onset of menarche (the age of first menstruation) among females native to high altitudes compared to low level inhabitants. Male visitors to high altitudes are also affected; after about two weeks the sperm level drops and becomes alkaline, there is a decrease in motility and a 40 percent increase in abnormal forms. The sperm returns to normal with return to sea level.

Altitude Sicknesses. The inability to cope with altitude, primarily because of oxygen debt, causes a number of sicknesses such as pulmonary edema and mountain sickness (also called soroche). Mountain sickness is characterized by headaches, shortness of breath, and nausea. Acute cases of mountain sickness, often called Monge's disease, are further characterized by abnormal production of red blood cells and increased pulmonary hypertension.

Inhabitants of high altitudes show three modalities of coping: (1) short-run physiological changes; (2) modifications during growth and development; and (3) modification of the population's gene pool itself, although evidence here is rather scant.

May, 1975   Climbing Mt. Kenya, Kenya

We depart our camp at Met Station which is approximately 10,200 feet at 8:15 A.M. to begin our ascent to 14,000 feet and Teleki Hut. The climb will take us up a track which leads through the Cloud Forest and the Vertical Bog. Because of the foul weather, hail and rain, because we lose the trail, and because of physical fatigue the climb takes approximately ten hours and we arrive in cold darkness.

On our way up the mountain we notice physical fatigue, due both to the strenuous nature of the hike and because of the altitude. We follow standard climbing procedures as concerns walking speed and gait and we constantly munch on our home-made gorp (a mixture of M and M's, peanuts, and dried fruits). We begin to notice after a few hours that most of us have lost our appetite (mine particularly for gorp). Clothing becomes a problem during the ascent, we turn hot and cold—not only with the weather but because of exhaustion.

Some of the problems we note when we finally reach our destination and camp within the shadow of the glacier follow. The temperature variations between the warm day sun and the night cold seem to precipitate colds in some of the party. At night we have difficulty keeping warm— even though 13 of us are squeezed within a small tin hut. Most uncomfortable is the fatigue—although some of the party are well enough to do some exploring the day after arrival. Nighttime brings its own devilish problem—the inability to sleep. Most of the party sleeps in fits, if at all. Time hangs heavily on our minds and we all hope for an early sunrise to break the fight to go to sleep. The sleep problem remains for the three nights on the mountain. Another major problem is nausea and the lack of desire to eat. Many in the party are constantly sick to their stomachs and our food rations go largely untouched. Irritability is also a problem for some—due to fatigue, lack of sleep, and nausea.

Within a day of our descent from the mountain the symptoms have alleviated, although some of the party still have troubles sleeping the first night and nausea is still with us. Within 48 hours everyone is readjusted.

Excerpt from my field notes.

Some Advantages and Disadvantages of Gross Body Size. Population variations in body size represent one of the important parameters in the study of ongoing human evolution. Considerable evidence indicates that variation in body size results from environmental and genetic factors at both the developmental and adult stages. One productive way to study possible variation in survival and mortality is under conditions of environmental stress. Poor socioeconomic conditions, because they are usually associated with limited nutritional levels, represent an environmental stress known to influence body size during growth and adolescence. A study in a "Barriada" (poor section of town) in southern Peru supports the hypothesis that a small body size is more adaptive to poor socioeconomic conditions of dietary restriction than is a large body size (Frisancho et al., 1973). This is presumably due to lower caloric or nutritional requirements for growth and maintenance of the smaller body. It is possible that the high offpsring survival effectiveness witnessed in this Barriada (as indicated by the high percent of offspring survival), which is associated with small parental body size, may reflect developmental adaptive responses to poor socioeconomic conditions in the Barriada. This particular study presents evidence of higher offspring survival associated with small parental body size; however, in order to advance these findings as an explanation of population variation in body size, further studies with larger samples are needed.

A disadvantage of a heavier body size is that it takes more calories to keep alive—Americans and Europeans in Asian prisoner-of-war camps soon learned this. Since larger body sizes usually require more calories for growth, genetically large children may be at a disadvantage when food is scarce. Famine is a most powerful selective force which would differentially eliminate massive individuals. Faced with continual caloric restriction, genetically small individuals might have more chance to mature and reproduce. It may not be mere chance that smaller peoples are often marginal in their subsistence patterns.

Climatic Correlations. Lighter weight peoples in the world tend to be found nearer the equator. Granted our migration patterns cloud the picture, nevertheless, there seems to be a correlation between mean annual temperature and body weight in a population long resident in an area. Moving southward in Europe, temperatures rise and body weight drops. The lowest average body weights (90 to 100 pounds) are associated with mean annual temperatures of 72° to 80° F; the highest average weights (in excess of 160 pounds) are associated with temperatures of 40° F and below. These correlations tend to hold true for U.S. Army inductees, for the warmer an inductee's state of origin, the greater the chances of a thinner build and lower body weight compared to those of soldiers from colder states.

Skin Pigmentation

Of all traits used to differentiate populations, none has been more misused than skin pigmentation even though it is simply another biological adaptation to environmental stress. Regardless of what some may preach, the social, economic, religious, and political values associated with one or another pigmentation are non-biologically based.

Gloger's Rule. In 1833 an ornithologist named Gloger formulated a rule now applied to help explain variation in pigmentation of the skin, hair, and eyes. Simply stated, animals living in wet tropical areas tend to be darkly pigmented, those in desert areas tend to be brown, and those in or near the Arctic tend to be lightly pigmented. This rule is generally true for *Homo*. Since we arose in tropical areas, it is conceivable that originally our skin was darkly pigmented; lightly pigmented skins may be a more recent adaptation to nontropical habitats.

Skin is composed of two layers, the outer epidermis and inner dermis. The epidermis is composed of four layers; the deeper layer, the stratum germanativum or the columnar layer, produces the **melanocytes**, amoebalike cells producing the **melanin** which gives skin its color. Above the columnar layer sits the prickle-cell layer; melanin from the melanocytes is injected into the prickle-cell layer. When this layer migrates to the skin's surface, melanin contained within the prickle-cells moves with it. Variations in skin color are not due to the number of melanocytes present; rather, skin color differences are due to the amount of melanin produced by the melanocytes. All individuals, even albinos (those lacking pigmentation in the skin, hair, and eyes) have approximately the same number of melanocytes. Other factors besides melanin affect skin color, e.g., hemoglobin gives skin a reddish tint and the pigment carotene provides an orangish or reddish color.

Many theories, each with its own proponents and merits, have been proposed to explain the distribution of different skin pigmentations. It is becoming quite obvious, however, that there are multiple causes for different skin pigmentations. Furthermore, there may be conflicting pressures on a particular skin pigmentation in any one environment.

Vitamin D Production. One of the key explanatory theories suggests a link between skin pigmentation and vitamin D production. This theory, first proposed in 1934, suggested that light skin pigmentation represents an adaptation to low levels of ultraviolet radiation (UVR) where decreased melanin is necessary for maximal usage of UVR in synthesizing vitamin D. Accordingly, light skin color, as an adaptation to vitamin D synthesis, is adaptive in northern latitudes where sunlight is minimal. Light pigmentation allows maximal UVR absorption whereas darkly pigmented skins reflect UVR. Since a vitamin D deficiency can result in rickets and scoliosis (abnormal spinal curvature), among other defects, which could interfere with the birth process, lightly pigmented individuals would be at an advantage in a low-light region because of the increased ability to absorb UVR and synthesize vitamin D. Because a darkly pigmented skin allows minimal penetration of UVR, presenting problems with bone growth, such individuals would be selected against in low UVR areas. Application of this rule to the modern situation is limited by the fact that we have vitamin-D enriched milk, bread, and other foods. If the vitamin D theory is applicable, provided vitamin D were artificially supplied, the most darkly pigmented individual today could still live in the lowest light situation and without a problem.

What is the adaptation of darkly pigmented skin? It is argued that darkly pigmented individuals are adapted to high-light conditions. While a vitamin D deficiency is harmful, too much vitamin D (hypervitaminosis D) results in failure of bone calcification and pathological calcifications. Lightly pigmented individuals may be at a disadvantage in high UVR conditions. Since darkly pigmented skins reflect UVR, darkly pigmented individuals may be selected for in high light areas.

A case of rickets in a village in Nepal. The people in this village live in very narrow huts with tiny windows. During the rainy season of 5-6 months children are always kept indoors. Rickets develop from lack of sunshine, lack of vitamins, and from improper diet.

Arguments Against the Vitamin D Theory. Selection against the dangers of rickets on the one hand and toxic doses of vitamin D on the other has been used to explain the worldwide correlation of dark skin pigmentation with proximity to the equator. Although this theory has received much attention in standard anthropology texts, it has not been accepted without argument. A recent proponent suggested that lightly pigmented individuals inhabiting high-light areas are subject to toxic doses of vitamin D. However, there are no confirmatory reports suggesting a high incidence of hypervitaminosis D in the many lightly pigmented individuals living in Arizona, South Africa, and Australia. Another problem is that vitamin D is not stable to excess doses of UVR; there may be no naturally occurring toxic dosage such as can be laboratory produced.

A second qualifying statement about the relationship of dark skin pigmentation and tropical adaptations is that darkly pigmented individuals absorb more infrared light and thus the body heats faster. Lighter pigmentations reflect more heat, as everyone who wears a white shirt during the summer knows. However, the heat-load problem, while a subsidiary effect of skin color, is apparently not the "main" selective force involved in the evolution of different skin pigmentation.

Disease Protection and Skin Injury. A second explanatory theory for skin pigmentation differences involves disease protection. Darkly pigmented tropic dwellers may reflect the selective forces of disease rather than climate. For example, darkly pigmented populations appear to have a greater resistance to certain tropical diseases such as the mosquito-borne filariasis.

A rather recent explanation proposed by Dr. Peter W. Post (1971; Post et al., 1975) attempts to link skin pigmentation differences to cold injury. Using carefully documented epidemiological studies of U.S. Army personnel during the Korean War, it was found that soldiers of African origin were more susceptible to frostbite than those of European descent. A study conducted in Norway during World War II suggests that more darkly pigmented men had a higher incidence of frostbite than lighter-pigmented individuals. Considering the rather limited range of skin color among Norwegians, this observation is interesting.

Using these data, Dr. Post studied the effects of freezing skin patches on piebald (black and white) guinea pigs. By freezing small areas of the skin at overlapping points of white and black pigmentation, he tested the differential reaction to freezing and demonstrated that lighter pigmented skins are cold adapted by virtue of experiencing less cold-induced injury. Darkly pigmented skin, on the other hand, sustained striking damage due to the freezing. These results make sense if our evolutionary past was originally tied to tropical areas, as we assume it was.

One of the oldest explanations of skin pigmentation differences links the effects of UV radiation to skin damage. Mild sunburn produces erythema (reddening) and mild discomfort. More severe sunburn involves increased sensitivity to pain, blistering, a lowered resistance to further sunburn, susceptibility to infection, damage to the vascular beds in the dermis, loss of sweating in the damaged area, and skin cancers. Even a mild sunburn can significantly reduce perspiration; in turn, this can impair an individual's ability to lose excessive heat through evaporation. Repeated sunburn would affect an individual's fitness. Although few individuals die of skin cancers, and although skin cancers usually appear past reproductive age, they could be a secondary factor producing skin pigmentation differences.

Skin pigmentation differences must be explained on the basis of selection acting on phenotypic variation leading to gene frequency changes. There was not one, but many, selective agents acting to produce the range of skin tones. Earlier selective pressures operating to produce skin pigmentation differences are either no longer important, or of reduced importance, given shelter, dietary vitamin D, central heating, and other technological changes. Most biological advantages of one or another skin pigmentation are things of the past.

Explaining differences in pigmentation acknowledges that we arose in the tropical regions of the world. As we moved north out of the tropical zones, we began to meet lower light intensities. Since darkly pigmented individuals may have experienced difficulties in such situations — perhaps from rickets and cold damage, for example — more lightly pigmented individuals may have had an advantage and may have left more surviving offspring. As we continued to move north and encountered colder conditions, where selection was stronger, we may assume that more lightly pigmented skins were selected for.

Eye Color. There is a correlation between eye and skin color, for the same genes controlling skin color may also influence eye color; this is known as a **pleiotropic** effect. Generally, there is a correlation between visible skin color and the pigment of the optic fundus. Assuming an original darkly pigmented eye color, what are the selective advantages of lightly pigmented eyes? Lightly pigmented eyes are mostly found in conjunction with light hair and fair skin, traits primarily concentrated in cloudy, foggy northwest Europe, where we consider they had a long history. We should search here for selection pressures, for there may be advantages to lightly pigmented eyes in low light intensities. Lightly pigmented eyes may be better able to distinguish distant objects more accurately in dim misty light. It has also been suggested that lightly pigmented eyes are better adapted to the light of fire embers. Since later European hominids lived, painted, and held religious ceremonies in caves, using artificial torch light, lightly pigmented eyes might have been adaptive for them.[2]

In this chapter we introduced a number of important concepts. Adaptations are long-term biological adjustments related to survival in particular environments. Acclimation refers to short-term physiological responses to stress. These responses are relatively modest. Acclimatization refers to an adjustment to a situation which lasts for a relatively longer period of time. However, acclimatization may also occur in the short run as when one experiences seasonal changes. Habituation refers to a reduction in the level of physiological responses to a stress situation. Habituation may fall into two categories: specific or general.

Anthropologists have used a number of general rules of adaptation to help explain differences in body sizes, shapes, and skin pigmentation. Allen's rule deals with extremity length in general—the colder the climate the shorter the extremities. Bergman's rule deals with body shape—the warmer the climate, the more linear the body. Gloger's rule is used as an explanatory vehicle for skin pigmentation.

Of the various climatic stresses which humans experience we have discussed some general adaptations to hot and humid climates; to desert life; to extreme cold; and high altitudes. It is important to bear in mind that adaptations to various habitats are often balanced; that is, there may be elements of both adaptive and maladaptive features of an adaptation. Skin pigmentation differences are a good example of this proposition.

It is important to bear in mind that of all animals, humans have occupied and now occupy perhaps the greatest diversity of habitats. To survive in this array of climates, we have adapted both culturally and biologically. Indeed, it is the success of our cultural adaptations which has allowed us this freedom of movement and habitation.

[2]It is interesting to note that individuals with lightly pigmented eyes seem to experience more visual problems with high light intensities, e.g., bright sun and bright artificial light glaring off glossy paper.

Bibliography

Allen, J. 1877. The influence of physical conditions in the genesis of species. *Radical Review* 1:108.

Baker, P. 1958. Racial differences in heat tolerance. *American Journal of Physical Anthropology* 16:287.

_____. 1969. Human adaptation to high altitude. *Science* 163:1149.

Baker, P., and Weiner, J., eds. 1966. *The biology of human adaptability.* London: Oxford University Press.

Barnicot, N. 1957. Human pigmentation. *Man* 57:114-20.

_____. 1959. Climatic factors in the evolution of human populations. *Cold Springs Harbor Symposia on Quantitative Biology* 24:115.

Blum, H. 1962. Does the melanin pigment of human skin have adaptive value? An essay in human ecology and the evolution of race. *Quarterly Review of Biology* 36:50-63.

_____. 1969. Is sunlight a factor in the geographical distribution of human skin color? *Geographical Review* 14(4):557-81.

Brues, A. 1959. The spearman and the archer—an essay on selection in body build. *American Anthropologist* 61:457.

Coon, C. 1962. *The origin of races.* New York: Knopf.

_____. 1965. *The living races of man.* New York: Knopf.

Coon, C.; Garn, S.; and Birdsell, J. 1950. *Races: a study of the problems of race formation in man.* Springfield, Ill.: Charles C Thomas.

Damon, A., ed. 1975. *Physiological anthropology.* New York: Oxford University Press.

Frisancho, A. 1975. Functional adaptation to high altitude hypoxia. *Science* 187:313-18.

Frisancho, A.; Sanchez, J.; Pallardel, D.; and Yanez, L. 1973. Adaptive significance of small body size under poor socio-economic conditions in southern Peru. *American Journal of Physical Anthropology* 39:255.

Frisch, R., and Revelle, R. 1969. Variations in body weights and the age of the adolescent growth spurt among Latin American and Asian populations, in relation to calorie supplies. *Human Biology* 41:185-212.

Garn, S. 1957. Race and evolution. *American Anthropologist* 59:218.

_____. 1971. *Human races.* Springfield, Ill.: Charles C Thomas.

Hiernaux, J. 1971. Ethnic differences in growth and development. In *The biological and social meaning of race,* edited by Richard H. Osborne, pp.39-55. San Francisco: W. H. Freeman.

Kelso, A. 1963. Dietary differences: a possible selective mechanism in ABO blood group frequencies. *Southwestern Lore* 29:44.

Kennedy, K. 1976. *Human variation in space and time.* Dubuque, Ia.: Wm. C. Brown.

King, J. 1970. *The biology of race.* New York: Harcourt Brace Jovanovich.

Lerner, I. 1968. *Heredity, evolution and society.* San Francisco: W. H. Freeman.

Loomis, F. 1967. Skin pigment regulation of vitamin D biosynthesis in man. *Science* 157:501-6.

Newman, R., and Munro, E. 1955. The relation of climate and body size in U.S. males. *American Journal of Physical Anthropology* 13:1.

Osborne, R., ed. 1971. *The biological and social meaning of race.* San Francisco: W. H. Freeman.

Post, P. 1971. Pigmentation and its role in human adaptation. Ph.D. dissertation, Columbia University.

Post, P.; Daniels, F.; and Binford, R. 1975. Cold injury and the evolution of "white" skin. *Human Biology* 47:65.

Roberts, D. 1953. Body weight, race and climate. *American Journal of Physical Anthropology* 11:533.

Stini, W. 1975. *Ecology and human adaptation.* Dubuque: Wm. C. Brown.

Williams, B. J. 1973. *Evolution and human origin: an introduction to physical anthropology.* New York: Harper & Row.

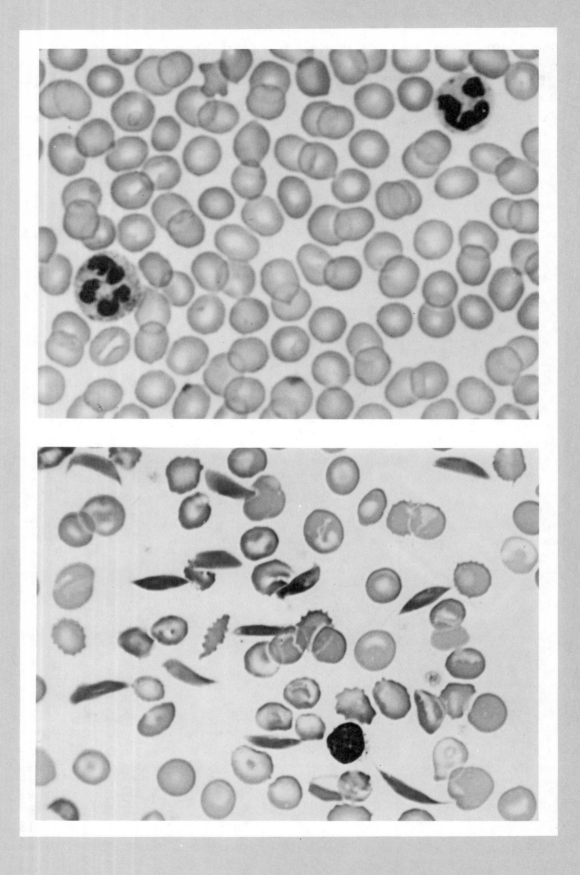

Chapter 23

The Hows and Whys of Human Diversity: Microevolutionary Studies and Human Variability

Whether or not one recognizes the term "race" as describing some actuality, such as a population exhibiting some trait(s) distinguishing it from other populations, everyone agrees that populations do differ. Some differences are easily recognizable with the naked eye, some take microscopic analysis. This chapter explores some differences and attempts to explain their occurrence. Some differences are genetically based, some are stable over time, and some change with diet and other influences. Some differences are meaningful traits distinguishing one population from another.

What follows is not by any means an exhaustive list of traits which are often used to differentiate populations one from another. Furthermore, for some of the traits listed, it is unclear which are important in terms of a population's efforts to adapt to an environment and which are of relatively recent appearance. Each anthropologist, depending upon his or her philosophical stance and training, feels that some traits are more important than others. This chapter deals with (1) those traits whose genetic inheritance is unknown or not clearly understood and (2) traits of known genetic inheritance. Among the former are body shape and size, adaptations to such habitats as deserts and high altitudes, the advantages of gross body sizes, skin and eye color (all of which are discussed in Chapter 22), and bone densities and tooth size

Photomicrographs of normal and sickled blood cells. Courtesy of Carolina Biological Supply Company.

and shape. We shall also discuss various physiological and biochemical differences between populations. In the latter category, we shall discuss blood group distributions and disease correlates, in addition to exploring the occurrence of abnormal hemoglobins, polymorphisms, and population-limited diseases.

Population Differences of Unknown Importance

Many traits appearing in various populations are of unknown adaptive value; presumably some were either once adaptive or arose in small isolated populations by drift or the founder principle (Chapter 20). Some of these traits are noted below. Some interesting differences in the size, proportions, form, and mineral content of bone have long been documented. There are population differences in the relative proportions of the limb bones, the relative lengths of the metatarsals of the feet, and in the heel bones.

Bone Densities. Recent bone density studies reveal marked population differences; the weight to volume ratio is high in African-descended populations. Members of this group seem to have a higher mineral requirement for normal growth. Dr. Stanley Garn of the University of Michigan found that total bone apposition (i.e., growth around the perimeter of the bone) is greater in American blacks than in individuals of Asian and European descent. This is true in rural undernourished areas of the South and the northern city ghettos. During the period of adult bone loss (known as osteoporosis) American black women experience fewer femoral and radial fractures than women of Asian or European descent. Such differences have practical importance, especially after age forty when progressive bone loss increases the possibility of fracture.

Dentition. Many population differences in dentition have been documented. Tooth size is variable; the largest crown sizes are found among Australian aborigines, New Guinea natives, and Pima Indians. Root length, a sexually dimorphic trait, also varies and is especially short in some Asiatic populations. Gross size differences exist in the canines, incisors, premolars, and molars. In some groups the anterior teeth are large, and in others the posterior teeth are large.

Tooth morphology also differs; for example, the rear surfaces of the upper mesial incisors of many American Indian and Asian popula-

Table 23-1. Shovel-Shape in Upper Mesial Incisors.[1]

Population	Percent Male	Percent Female
Chinese	66-89	82-94
Japanese	78	—
Mongolian	62-91	91
Eskimo	84	84
Pima Indians	96	99
Pueblo Indians	86-89	86-89
Aleut	96	—
American Negro	12	11
American White	9	8

[1]Based on Carbonell, 1963, and Comas, 1960.

From Stephen Molnar, *Races, Types and Ethnic Groups:* The Problem of Human Variation, © 1975, p. 62. Reprinted by permission of Prentice-Hall, Inc., Englewood Cliffs, New Jersey.

tions are distinctive. This is one of the many traits used to historically link American Indians with Asian populations.[1] (Table 23-1.) The number of molar cusps varies and is often reduced in Middle Eastern populations and increased in some Melanesian and Australian aborigine groups. The incidence of congenital tooth loss varies; while the last molar is rarely absent in East and West Africans, it is lacking in 12 percent of the Europeans, and in 30 percent of some American Indian, Eskimo, and Asian groups.

Physiological and Biochemical Differences

BAIB. There are population differences in urinary excretion patterns. One of the normal urinary constituents (the nonprotein amino acid B-aminoisobutyric acid) shows a most interesting individual and population variation in the amount excreted. This acid is rarely excreted in large amounts by Australian aborigines or Europeans. However, a fair proportion of Chinese and Japanese excrete high amounts of BAIB; the same is true of many American Indian groups. High levels of BAIB excretion suggest an Asian origin. However, it is not yet clear how the BAIB polymorphism is maintained, or what the population differences mean (Table 23-2).

[1]The inward folding of the incisors characteristic of shovel-shape incisors increases the chewing surfaces without increasing their breadth in relation to the size of the dental arcade. To the extent that such an increase in chewing surface is desirable and improves tooth life, shoveling is an adaptive trait. Brace (1963) has suggested that shoveling is retained in those populations where the functions of the incisor teeth have not been superseded by such factors as food preparation and cutting tools.

Table 23-2. Distribution of BAIB Excretors.

Population	Number Tested	Frequency of High Excretors
North America		
European descent		
Michigan	71	0.03
Texas	255	0.10
New York	218	0.10
New York	148	0.11
African descent		
Michigan	25	0.20
New York	38	0.15
Athabascan	25	0.56
Indians		
Apache	110	0.59
Apache	113	0.42
Eskimo	120	0.23
Chinese	33	0.45
Japanese	41	0.41
Central America		
African descent (Black Caribs)	285	0.32
Asia		
India	16	0
Thailand	13	0.46
Marshall Islands		
Rongelap	188	0.86
Utirik	18	0.83

After J. Buettner-Janusch, *The Origins of Man: Physical Anthropology*, John Wiley & Sons, 1966.

Tasters vs. Nontasters. Dietary differences have long been viewed with interest and numerous suggestions have been made that people who prefer the very hot, spicy foods differ in their taste acuity from those espousing culinary blandness. While conclusive evidence as to taste parameters is not yet available, there are some genetically determined differences in sensitivity. There are individual and population differences in the capacity to taste a laboratory-produced chemical compound known as phenylthiocarbamide, or PTC, which does not exist in nature. It was first discovered about thirty-five years ago when a chemist spilled some onto the laboratory floor. During the mopping-up he and his co-workers tasted the substance and an argument ensued as to whether it was bitter or tasteless. Since then many students in genetics and monkeys and apes in zoos have been tested. The procedure is easy; one simply slips a bit of paper treated with PTC into the mouth and waits.

The ability to taste PTC is controlled by allelic or multifactorial genes; T (for taster) is dominant, and t (for nontaster) is recessive. Those with genotypes TT and Tt are tasters. Asians and Africans have the highest percentage of tasters; Australian aborigines and some Pacific Islanders have the lowest percentage. Up to 43 percent of the population in India are nontasters.

What is the adaptive significance of being a taster or nontaster? The geographic distribution of the alleles shows no correlation with gross climatic conditions. Tasting may be nonadaptive in areas of scarce food sources where one must be able to consume anything. Since tasters probably have more food aversions than nontasters, tasting would be disadvantageous during food scarcity. There may be some disease correlates associated with tasting or nontasting. For example, one study showed that nontasters have a higher incidence of dental caries than tasters. Nontasters of European descent are more susceptible to glaucoma past age forty; they also are more susceptible to thyroid difficulties (such as goiter) than tasters. Tasters could be expected to have some advantage over nontasters in resisting nodular goiter by rejecting bitter-tasting thyroid-activity suppressors and it has been demonstrated that nontasters are more commonly victims of nodular goiter than would be expected by mere chance (Azevedo et al., 1965). While the relationship between tasting, thyroid function, and goiter is interesting, it fails to account for geographic variations in allelic frequencies.

Secretor. Some individuals show water-soluble antigens of the ABO system in their saliva and other body fluids; others have alcohol-soluble antigens, which are found on the surface of the red blood cells. Almost everyone has alcohol-soluble antigens, but some do not have the water-soluble ABO antigens, and whether they do or not is genetically determined. Those who have the water-soluble antigens are known as **secretors**, those who do not are **non-secretors**. The secretor locus segregates independently of the ABO locus and can be occupied by either of a pair of alleles, Se or se. Secretors are either SeSe or Sese, and all non-secretors are sese. Secretor is dominant to non-secretor in such a way that:

Genotype	equals	Phenotype
SeSe		secretor
Sese		secretor
sese		non-secretor

A person with one Se gene produces a water-soluble ABO substance, whereas the sese homozygote produces only an alcohol-soluble ABO substance. Because of this the ABO substance is found in many fluids of the secretor. The existence of ABO antigens outside the red blood cells was known as early as 1910, and the manner of inheritance has been known since 1932. The frequencies of Se and se were found to vary in no clear pattern.

In 1948 R. Grubb published a paper noting a relationship, a linkage, between the Lewis antigens (one member of the blood group system) and secretor. The importance of Grubb's findings are such that they provide an understanding of certain genetic principles (Kelso, 1970). It is now clear that inherited traits can no longer be thought of as distinct and separate entities; instead, they result from an interaction among the loci as well as between genetic elements and the environment. As a practical consideration for physical anthropologists this suggests that a simultaneous consideration of allelic frequencies will be more informative than a consideration of each separately.

Blood Groups and Abnormal Hemoglobins

The interest in blood groups originated from the practice of blood transfusions. Such experiments began in the seventeenth century and were frequently harmless; in a few cases, however, the recipient of the transfusion died. In 1900 Karl Landsteiner, who won a Nobel prize for his work, discovered why transfusions were fatal to some individuals. He noted that when red blood cells from some individuals are mixed with those from another individual, the cells may clump or agglutinate. Landsteiner and his students found they could group humans into four types on the basis of these agglutination reactions. The four types are explained by the presence of either or both of two substances, the A and B antigens, in the cells.

The serum known to react with a specific antigen is called an antiserum to it. A and B antigens can be identified with tests utilizing the two types of antisera containing antibodies called anti-A and anti-B. If a drop of anti-A serum is added to a drop of blood, the red cells may remain in normal suspension or they may clump together. If the blood clumps its red blood cells must contain the A antigen. If the blood reacts to anti-A but not to anti-B, it is called type A; if it reacts to anti-B but not anti-A, it is type B. If the red blood cells react to both anti-A and anti-B sera, it is called type AB, and if it reacts to neither it is called type O. (Figure 23-1, Table 23-3.)

Although it was long believed that blood groups were inherited, it was the mathematician F. Bernstein who described the mechanism. Bernstein demonstrated that blood group inheritance could be explained as due to three alleles. The genes for antigen A (designated I^A) and for B (I^B) are equally dominant; the gene for antigen O (the universal donor), designated i, is recessive. Blood group O is usually homozygous; genotypes for A and B may be either AA or OA and BB or OB (Tables 23-3, 23-4).

Anthropologists have studied blood groups and other polymorphic blood factors as a means of reconstructing the history of human populations. Although first considered a taxonomic panacea for determining racial classification, blood groups have not produced very firm results, for each blood factor calls for another hypothesis to help explain its

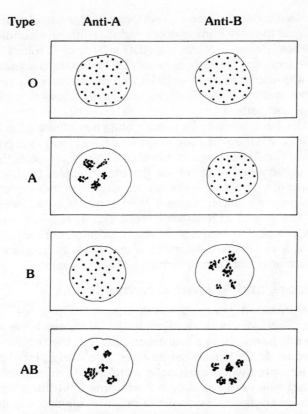

Type   Anti-A   Anti-B

O

A

B

AB

Figure 23-1. Blood type determination of the ABO system.

Table 23-3. ABO Determinations.

Genotype	Phenotype (Blood Type)	Antibodies
AA AO	A	anti-B
BB BO	B	anti-A
AB	AB	none
OO	O	anti-AB

Comparison of ABO types in families, sometimes for three generations, has shown the exact mode of inheritance. Given the parental genotypes, the probable genotypes of the children can be predicted.

	1st		2nd		3rd			
Parents	AB x OO		BB x OO		BO	x	AO	
Children	AO	BO	BO	BO	AB	AO	BO	OO

In mating 1, type O offspring are not possible, even though one parent has this blood type. Mating 2 produces only type B children. A mating of heterozygotes for type A and B produces four different blood types in their children, as shown in mating 3.

Adapted from Stephen Molnar, *Races, Types and Ethnic Groups: The Problem of Human Variation,* © 1975, p. 69. Reprinted by permission of Prentice-Hall, Inc., Englewood Cliffs, New Jersey.

Table 23-4. Matings and Offspring in Selected Blood Group Systems.

Mating	Offspring Possible phenotypes	Impossible phenotypes
ABO system*		
O X O	O	A, B, AB
O X A	O, A	B, AB
O X B	O, B	A, AB
O X AB	A, B	AB
A X A	O, A	AB
A X B	A, AB, B	none
A X AB	A, B, AB	O
B X B	O, B	A, AB
B X AB	A, B, AB	O
AB X AB	A, B, AB	O
MNs System**		
M X M	M	N, MN
M X MN	M, MN	N
M X N	MN	M, N
MN X MN	M, MN, N	none
MN X N	MN, N	M
N X N	N	M, MN

*Phenotypes defined by anti-A and anti-B antisera.
**Phenotypes defined by anti-M and anti-N antisera.

distribution. The discovery of the blood groups produced the biological version of the California Gold Rush. Anthropologists and geneticists searched the world for blood group distributions in the hope that by matching the blood groups of various populations they could discover their true relationships.

Modern blood group studies follow two paths: (1) dividing the world into more or less discrete populations and deriving blood group frequencies for each separate system. This approach is used to measure population divergence. (2) Tracing the occurrence of each blood group system in an attempt (Tables 23-5 to 23-7) to explain their distribution in terms of natural selection. The most fruitful studies have followed the second course.

Early Results of Serology. Blood groups were considered ideal study materials as they are simply inherited. Thus, they qualify as ideal traits for population comparisons. Since samples were easily obtained in most situations, they further won approval as good study materials. (I qualify this statement because there are societies in which it would be considered grossly inappropriate to take someone's blood. Although samples are not hard to obtain—you simply prick the fingertip—they are difficult to store and need refrigeration. More than one research project has been spoiled in the muggy heat of tropical areas.)

Because millions of blood types are taken each year, the investigator has a ready backlog of data. In spite of the advantages of blood grouping, early taxonomies were fanciful at best. Totally unrelated populations were linked on the basis of comparative serology. Using the **ABO** system, India and Africa were lumped together and the American Indian and the Australian aborigine were considered members of the same group. Coupled with a refinement of the system was the belated serological confirmation that the American Indian and Asiatic popula-

The Hows and Whys
of Human Diversity

Table 23-5. Frequencies of ABO Blood Groups.

| Population | Place | Number Tested | Blood-group frequency | | | |
			O	A	B	AB
Low A, virtually no B						
American Indians:						
Toba	Argentina	194	98.5	1.5	0.0	0.0
Sioux	S. Dakota	100	91.0	7.0	2.0	0.0
Moderately A, virtually no B						
Navaho	New Mexico	359	77.7	22.5	0.0	.0
Pueblo	New Mexico: Jemez, etc.	310	78.4	20.0	1.6	.0
High A, little B						
Bloods	Montana	69	17.4	81.2	0.0	1.4
Eskimo	Baffin Land	146	55.5	43.8	.0	0.7
Austr. aborigines	S. Australia	54	42.6	57.4	.0	.0
Basques	San Sebastian	91	57.2	41.7	1.1	.0
American Indians:						
Shoshone	Wyoming	60	51.6	45.0	1.6	1.6
Polynesians	Hawaii	413	36.5	60.8	2.2	0.5
Fairly high A, some B						
English	London	422	47.9	42.4	8.3	1.4
French	Paris	1,265	39.8	42.3	11.8	6.1
Armenians	From Turkey	330	27.3	53.9	12.7	6.1
Lapps	Finland	94	33.0	52.1	12.8	2.1
Melanesians	New Guinea	500	37.6	44.4	13.2	4.8
Germans	Berlin	39,174	36.5	42.5	14.5	6.5
High A and high B						
Welsh	North Towns	192	47.9	32.8	16.2	3.1
Italians	Sicily	540	45.9	33.4	17.3	3.4
Siamese	Bangkok	213	37.1	17.8	35.2	9.9
Finns	Hame	972	34.0	42.4	17.1	6.5
Germans	Danzig	1,888	33.1	41.6	18.0	7.3
Ukrainians	Kharkov	310	36.4	38.4	21.6	3.6
Asiatic Indians	Bengal	160	32.5	20.0	39.4	8.1

After William C. Boyd, "Genetics and the human race," *Science*, Vol. 140, pp. 1051-64, 7 June 1963. Copyright © 1963 by the American Association for the Advancement of Science.

tions were historically related and that Europeans were not the result of a blend between an Asiatic and Australian aborigine population. (Needless to say, this brought a sigh of relief from the stalwarts of European supremacy!)

The greatest contribution of **serology** (blood group genetics) has been not the establishment of a racial taxonomy but a more adequate basis for comparing population relationships. For populations formed by the recent interbreeding of two populations, blood groups offer the possibility of precise quantification of genetic contributions. For example, genetic studies leave no doubt about the fact that the Afro-Americans have felt at times the considerable genetic influence from American "white" populations, this often as a result of such social injustices as rape, the forced breeding of slave women, and prostitution. Blood

Table 23-6. Red Blood Cell Antigens.

There are about 80 known human red blood cell antigens grouped into several systems. Each major system is controlled by alleles at a different locus. This table summarizes the history of the discovery of the major human blood group systems.

System	Year of Discovery	Number of Antigens Known
ABO	1900	6
MNS	1927	18
P	1927	3
Rhesus	1940	17
Lutheran	1945	2
Kell-Cellano	1946	5
Lewis	1946	2
Duffy	1950	2
Kidd	1951	2
Diego	1955	1
Auberger	1961	1
Xg	1962	1
Dombruck	1965	1

In addition to antigens of the major systems, there are also antigens found only in single families (private systems) or antigens which are common to most humans (public systems).

Private Systems		Public Systems
Levay	Romunde	1
Jobbins	Chr^a	Vel
Becker	Swann (Sw^a)	Yt
Ven	Good	Gerbich
Cavaliere	Bi (Biles)	Lan
Berrens	Tr^a	Sm
Wright (Wr^a)	Webb	
Batty		

After I. M. Lerner, *Heredity, Evolution and Society*, W. H. Freeman and Company. Copyright © 1968.

Table 23-7. Major Human Blood Group Systems.

System	Antigens
ABO	A, B, AB
Lewis	Le^a, Le^b, Le^v, Le^c
MNSs	M, N, S, s
Diego	Di^a
Xg	Xg^a
P	P$_1$, P$_2$
Lutheran	Lu^a, Lu^b
Dombruck	Do^a
Kell	K, k, Kp^a, Kp^b, Js^a, Js^b
Duffy	Fy^a, Fy^b
Kidd	Jk^a, Jk^b
Yt	Yt^a, Yt^b
I	I, i
Rh	Rho (cdE), rh'' (cdE), rh' (cde)
	R$_2$(CDE) Ry(cdE), R$_1$(CD$_2$), R$_2$(cDE)

*Antigens are protein substances which cause certain cells to form antibodies, e.g., proteins which react specifically with antigen molecules and inactivate them.

Table 23-8. The ABO Blood Group and Chronic Diseases.

Disease	Mean Relative Incidence[a]	
Duodenal ulcer	1.4	O:A, B and AB
Cancer of the stomach	1.25	A:O
Pernicious anemia	1.5	A:O
Stomach ulcer	1.82	O:A, B and AB
Cancer of the pancreas	1.27	A:O and B

[a]The mean relative incidence is the ratio of, for example, O:A in diseased patients divided by O:A in a control series.

After L. Cavalli-Sforza and W. Bodmer, *The Genetics of Human Population,* W. H. Freeman and Company. Copyright © 1968; and Stephen Molnar, *Races, Types and Ethnic Groups: The Problem of Human Variation,* © 1975, p. 136. Reprinted by permission of Prentice-Hall, Inc., Englewood Cliffs, New Jersey.

groups offer help in determining population relationships; however, some blood group genes are more sensitive than others as indicators of genetic interchange. While blood group distributions are not always consistent with other forms of evidence, like the fossil record, the blood group record serves as another independent line of evidence.

An additional problem with using comparative serological data is that blood groups themselves may be subjected to selection pressures. Contrary to what was originally thought, present gene frequencies don't provide a perfect indication of what they were in the past, making present distributions of limited value in solving ancient population distributions. The fact that there is some relationship between antigens in the ABO system and illness indicates that some blood groups may have been selected for or against (Table 23-9). This would influence their current numbers. For example, individuals of group A tend to have a higher incidence of gastric cancer than those with the other ABO genotypes.

Blood Group Distributions (Table 23-10). Type O is the most common blood group in the ABO system; among American Indians generally the incidence is over 90 percent. However, there are variations; 97 percent of the Utes and only 23 percent of the Blackfoot are of type O. In much of Europe the incidence of O is between 35 and 40 percent. Among Chinese, Japanese, and many African groups O is about 30 percent.

Following O, type A is the most frequent blood group. Type A is rare in some American Indian tribes; however, in other tribes it accounts for over 75 percent of those typed. Type A is found in about 45 percent of the English population and in approximately the same proportion of Americans of Northwest European ancestry.

Blood type B is the least common of the ABO system, and has the most interesting worldwide distribution. B appears to be totally absent in North and South American Indians and is rarely found in more than 2 percent of any American Indian population, a low percentage which may be the result of intermating. B is less common than A in Europe; it is found in 9 to 25 percent of the population. The average in Europe is about 15 percent. The percentage in Asia is between 35 and 37 percent and is a bit higher in Africa. B seems to be more an Asiatic and African rather than a European type. Although it is assumed that

Table 23-9. Association Between Blood Group Phenotypes and Diseases.

Disease	Associated ABO or Secretor Phenotype	Number of Studies (where cited)	Countries (where cited)
Bronchial pneumonia	A		
Filaria parasitic infection	A		
Smallpox	A		
Staphylococci infection	A		
Streptococci infection	A and O		
Typhoid	A		
Stomach cancer	A	8	England, Scotland, U.S., Norway, Australia, Switzerland, Austria
Pernicious anemia	A	4	England, Scotland, U.S., Denmark
Diabetes mellitus	A	5	England, Scotland, Austria
Salivary gland tumors	A	2	U.S.
Cervix cancer	A	3	England, Austria, Italy, Germany
Ovarian tumors	A	1	U.S.
Cancer of pancreas	A	1	England
Influenza	probably O		
Plague	O		
Duodenal ulcer	O	8	England, Scotland, U.S.
Gastric ulcer	O	8	England, Scotland, U.S.
Adenoma of pituitary	O	1	U.S.
Rheumatic fever	excess of secretors[1]	1	England
Paralytic poliomyelitis	excess of secretors, B reduced[2]	11	England, U.S., Germany, Denmark, Italy, France

[1], [2]Evidence is inconclusive.

Adapted from J. Buettner-Janusch, *Physical Anthropology: A Perspective*, p. 428. Copyright © 1973 by John Wiley and Sons, Inc.; and Stephen Molnar, *Races, Types and Ethnic Groups: The Problem of Human Variation*, © 1975 by Prentice-Hall, Inc., Englewood Cliffs, New Jersey.

American Indians are historically related to some part of the Asian population, there is a surprising lack of evidence for that relationship in the B blood type. Again, assuming the ancestor-descendant relationship valid, B may be a relatively recent phenomenon in Asia, appearing after the colonization of the Americas; it may have been lost or selected against in the American descendants, or may be the result of the founder effect.

MNS-U System. Other blood systems are helpful in determining population relationships; one is the MNS-U system. Most of the world is equally divided between M and N, rarely is either entirely missing. M is especially high in American Indians, N is slight or missing. In contrast, the incidence of N is especially high in Australia. The percentage of N dominates M throughout the Pacific area, and the high incidence of

Table 23-10. Summary of Principal Blood Group Systems Distributions.

System	Phenotypic Frequencies
ABO (including A_1 and A_2)	O most common, over 50% of most individuals in a population. B nearly absent in American Indians and Australian aborigines. B present in up to 15% of Europe and 40% of Africa, Asia and India. A_2 limited primarily to Europe.
MNS-U	American Indians almost exclusively M, N most common in Australia and the Pacific. MS and NS absent in Australia. U-negative appears limited to Africa.
Rh (R_1, R_2, R_O, r', etc.)	Rh negative (rr) rare or absent in most of world, but found in 15% of Europeans. R_O, almost exclusively of African origin, found in 70% of Africans.
Duffy (Fy^a, Fy^b, Fy)	Most Australians and Polynesians and 90-99% of Asian populations. Duffy positive (Fy^a) 90% in India, 85-90% in American Indians, 65% in England and America, 27% in American blacks. Fy^a very low in Africa, but Fy gene is very common to about 80%.
Diego (Di^a, Di^b)	Diego-positive (Di^a) limited to American Indians 2-20% and Asians. Diego-positive is absent in Europe and Africa, and much of the Pacific and among Eskimos.
Kidd (Jk^a, Jk^b)	Jk^a, Kidd-positive, is most common in West Africa and among American blacks, 90%. Also found in American Indians, 70-90%, Europeans, ca. 70%, and is least common among Chinese, 50-55%.

Adapted from Stanley M. Garn, *Human Races,* 3rd edition, 1971. Courtesy of Charles C Thomas, Publishers, Springfield, Illinois.

N in Pacific populations sets them off from and probably precludes recent contact with America. The near absence of B separates Pacific area populations from those of Asia.

Since extreme percentages of M and N occur in populations formerly explained as having developed on the basis of admixture, it is notable that no combination of Asiatic populations could yield the current low values of both M and N common to Australian aborigines. Furthermore, no hypothetical mixture of "Causasoid" with "Negroid" could yield the nearly M-free Australian aborigine population. Either the so-called three original races, i.e., Caucasoid, Negroid, Mongoloid, never existed, or subsequent evolution altered their genetic makeup beyond recognition. The first possibility is the most likely.

The S gene was discovered in 1947 in England, where it is quite common. While the S gene is absent among Australian aborigines, it is present in New Guinea. Since there is strong fossil evidence of a relationship between the Upper Pleistocene New Guinea population (represented by the Niah skull) and the Upper Pleistocene Australian population (at Lake Mungo), it is possible that S was selected out in Australia or that it is a new arrival in New Guinea. Europeans are U positive; American blacks are about 1 percent U negative. A mismatch of positive and negative can lead to transfusion complications.

Rhesus. The Rh blood group was described in 1940 and shortly afterward the Rh system was connected with hemolytic disease of the newborn due to isoimmunization of the mother (Levine, 1943). This process occurs when an incompatible pregnancy results from an incompatible mating. The consequences of this for a population depend partly on the frequency of the Rh+ and Rh− genes, leading to the Rh-positive or Rh-negative classification. Rh incompatibility, erythroblastosis fetalis, is characterized by an excessive destruction of red blood cells and a compensatory overdevelopment of tissues in which such blood cells are formed. The skin may have a yellowish color, and the liver and spleen become enlarged.

The disease is usually due to a difference in Rh blood types between the mother and her infant. The various subtypes of the Rh factor are all inherited as dominants over the Rh-negative condition. In addition to sensitization by transfusion, an Rh-negative woman may become sensitized from an Rh-positive fetus carried in her womb. Although fetal blood does not freely cross the placenta to flow into the mother's veins, some antigen does cross, because Rh substances in the fetal red blood cells can produce antibodies in the mother's blood serum. Antibodies can be built up in the mother which may then be carried in her serum to a subsequent Rh-positive fetus where they react with the red cells to the detriment of the fetus. Interestingly, erythroblastosis fetalis apparently occurs less often when mother and father are of different ABO blood groups. Incompatibility in the ABO system appears to reduce the likelihood of erythroblastosis fetalis caused by development of Rh antibodies in the infant.

Erythroblastosis fetalis can be prevented by treating the Rh-negative mother after her first Rh-positive infant. Immediately after delivery the mother is given immunoglobulin with anti-Rh antibodies which prevent her developing them in her own serum and thus protect any future Rh-positive child. Furthermore, erythroblastosis fetalis can be treated by blood transfusions to the infant.

Most of you are aware of the fact that your blood types are given as positive (+) or negative (−). You are either rhesus positive (Rh+) or rhesus negative (Rh−). The proportion of Rh− ranges from about 12 to 15 percent in the United States and England. Among the Basques, a population primarily settled in France and Spain and who maintain considerable cultural and political autonomy, the percentage rises to 30 percent. Elsewhere the percentage of Rh− is rare.

Among Afro-Americans the incidence of Rh− is about half of what it is among Europeans. One rhesus gene, known as R_O, is common in Afro-Americans, running about 40 percent incidence. This is of some interest, for this gene appears in about 70 percent of the ancestral African populations. There appears to have been some loss of the R_O gene in New World African-derived populations. This loss may be explained in one of three ways, or as a combination of all three: (1) there is some advantage to the R_O gene in Africa, but none in the New World; (2) the separation of the African population because of the institution of slavery resulted in some drift among the New World group; (3) there may have been a dissolution of the R_O gene in the New World as a result of the inter-population matings.

Duffy. The Duffy blood group derives its name from a Mr. Duffy in whose blood the antigen was discovered in 1950. There are two forms of Duffy, a positive allele Fy^a and a negative allele Fy^b. Since Fy^a, or Duffy positive is dominant over Fy^b, or Duffy negative, there are only two phenotypes. In England 65 percent of a test population were Fy^a. This amounts to a gene frequency of 0.40. Higher frequencies appear in Pakistan and India, among New York Chinese and the Australian aborigine, and far lower percentages appear in African populations. The extreme rarity of the Fy^a type in Africa and the relatively high frequency of its appearance in Europe make the Duffy system the most sensitive measure of European admixture with Afro-American populations. The incidence of Duffy among Afro-Americans is a good sign of mating with Europeans. Apparently the home of Duffy positive is in the Pacific area and East Asia; there is a decreasing frequency both southward into the Americas and westward into Europe and Africa.

Diego. One of the most recently discovered blood groups involves a pair of genes Di^a and Di^b, and two phenotypes, positive and negative. The positive phenotype is in the minority. The Di^a gene incidence clearly separates indigenous Australian and Pacific populations from those of the American Indians and Asia. No Diego negative individuals have been found in New Guinea and among the Central Australian aborigines. Diego positive is found in about 25 percent of the Peruvian Indians.

Hemoglobins

Before discussing hemoglobin variations such as sickle-cell and thalassemia, it would be well to discuss the qualities of hemoglobin itself.[2] Hemoglobin is found within the red blood cells and functions to carry oxygen to the body's cells while it carries away carbon dioxide. Hemoglobins show a good deal of genetic variability. Hemoglobin is one of the proteins which is well enough understood so that we know its structure quite precisely. The most common adult hemoglobin molecule consists of four long amino acid chains, or, more accurately, two pairs of identical chains, two alpha and two beta. The amino acid sequences in both chains are well known. In the human fetus there is another hemoglobin named hemoglobin F. Hemoglobin F is replaced by adult hemoglobin, A, in normal individuals within two months of birth. Both hemoglobin F and hemoglobin A contain two alpha chains, but hemoglobin F contains two distinct chains in place of the two beta chains in hemoglobin A.

The most common type of hemoglobin is HbA; however, there are now over 100 known "abnormal" hemoglobins that have an hereditary basis. Hemoglobin variations can occur in three ways: (1) alterations in the normal acid sequence in either the alpha or beta chains; (2) molecular modifications of the iron-bearing structures (the hemes) which serve as sites for oxygen attachment, and (3) quantitative differences in the production of the alpha and beta chains. A change in any

[2]Three substances in the blood are known, or thought, to offer some disease resistance. These are hemoglobin, blood group antigens (or the foreign particles stimulating antibody production), and the globulins, or proteins which carry the antibodies.

of these is almost always harmful, varying in severity from mild anemias to fatal diseases.

Examples of hemoglobin variations follow in the form of a discussion of sickle-cell anemia and thalassemia.

Today malarial vectors are primarily concentrated in the New and Old World tropics. In the Old World they are spread from West Africa to Melanesia, and are especially prevalent in West African forest regions; only rarely does malaria extend into regions above 6000 feet or above the winter frost line. We would expect populations long-resident in malarial regions to have some natural protection from one of the species of *Plasmodium*. The two principal malarial adaptations of which we are aware are thalassemia, major and minor, appearing primarily in the Mediterranean area and southeast Asia, and the sickle-cell trait.

Sickle-Cell. The hereditary antimalarial defense with which most of you are familiar is sickle-cell anemia which is primarily (but not exclusively) African in its distribution (Figures 23-2, 23-3).[3] The trait receives its name from the characteristic sickle-shaped appearance of affected red blood cells when they are placed in a saline solution (Figure 23-4). Sickling is inherited as a Mendelian codominant or incomplete recessive. There are two forms: the mild sickle-cell trait (the heterozygotic state) and the severe sickle-cell disease (the homozygotic state).

A University of Michigan geneticist, Dr. James Neel, confirmed the inheritance of sickling in 1949, noting that individuals with the sickle-cell disease were invariably offspring of parents who both carried the sickle-cell trait. The homozygous individual produces the hemoglobin S which has less oxygen-carrying ability than normal hemoglobin, A. There are three genotypes—homozygous "normals" (AA), homozygous for sickle-cell disease (SS), and heterozygous for the sickle-cell trait (AS). Table 23-11 presents the genetic mechanisms for the inheritance of sickle-cell.

Adaptive Significance. In some African areas frequencies for the sickling trait vary from zero to as high as 40 percent and estimates as to the number of Americans of African origin carrying the trait range above 3 million. The disorder probably came to the United States when the first slaves were brought to Jamestown in 1619; it is now the most common hemoglobin disorder found in the United States. What is the advantage of such a trait? Since the sickle-cell disease (the homozygote) is usually lethal because of the hemoglobin's inability to hold and carry oxygen, and since there is some selection against individuals with the sickle-cell trait (the heterozygote) in non-malarial areas, some selective advantage must maintain the sickling gene. A number of workers have noted the geographical association between malaria and sickling, and postulated a heterozygous advantage. In malarial areas individual homozygous "normals" develop malaria early and many die; the survivors have impaired vitality. Individuals heterozygous for sickling have increased protection against malaria, for their collapsed cells offer the plasmodia vector less opportunity to feed and be carried in

[3]The sickling trait also occurs among Greeks and Italians, for example. Recently it was found that an individual could have both sickle-cell and thalassemia.

Table 23-11. The Adaptation of Sickle-Cell.

Let S = the sickle gene
A = the normal hemoglobin

In a West African population there are both sickling and normal genes

SS	SS	SS	Homozygous sickling
AA	AA	AA	Homozygous normal
AS	AS	AS	Heterozygous

In each generation the sickling homozygote dies of sickle-cell anemia

SS   SS   SS   These forms die because of lack of oxygen and sickle-cell anemia

The normal homozygotes also die each generation

AA   AA   AA   These forms die of malaria

The heterozygotic condition survives

AS   AS   AS   If these forms contract malaria, it is only a mild form. In malarial conditions, these individuals are selected for.

The surviving heterozygotes leave progeny which include the range of genotypes: homozygous sickler, normal, and heterozygous

SS   SS   SS   As long as malaria remains a
AA   AA   AA   selective factor, the progeny are
AS   AS   AS   subject to the same evolutionary pressures as their parents. The cycle is repeated anew.

Adapted from Stanley M. Garn, *Human Races,* 3rd edition, 1971. Courtesy of Charles C Thomas, Publishers, Springfield, Illinois.

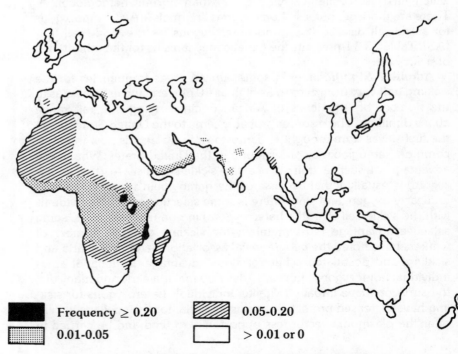

Frequency ≥ 0.20   0.05-0.20

0.01-0.05   > 0.01 or 0

Figure 23-2. The distribution of the allele for hemoglobin S in the Old World.

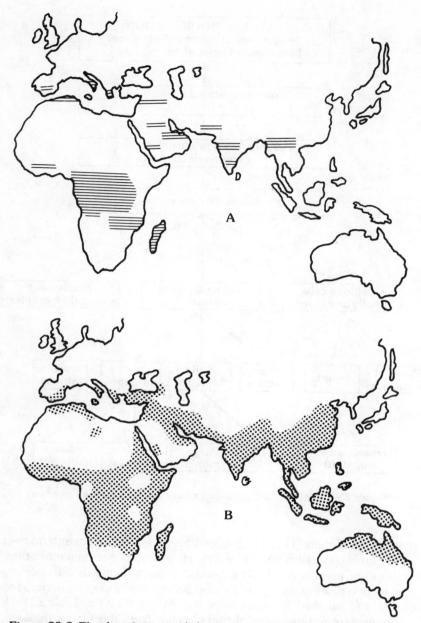

Figure 23-3. The distribution of (A) sickle cell hemoglobin and (B) falci-parum malaria.

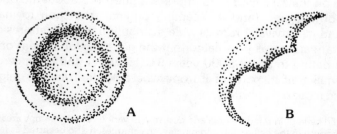

Figure 23-4. (A) A normal blood cell. (B) A sickled red blood cell.

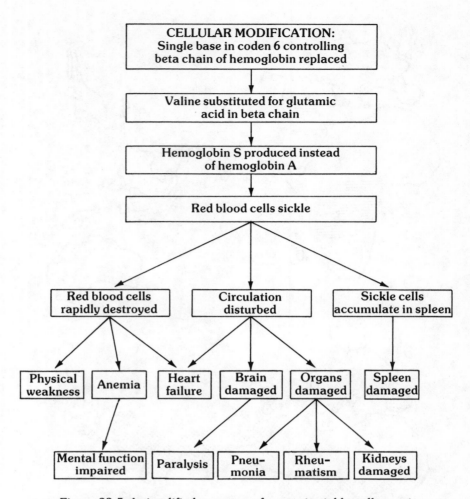

CELLULAR MODIFICATION:
Single base in coden 6 controlling
beta chain of hemoglobin replaced

Valine substituted for glutamic
acid in beta chain

Hemoglobin S produced instead
of hemoglobin A

Red blood cells sickle

Red blood cells
rapidly destroyed

Circulation
disturbed

Sickle cells
accumulate in spleen

Physical
weakness

Anemia

Heart
failure

Brain
damaged

Organs
damaged

Spleen
damaged

Mental function
impaired

Paralysis

Pneu-
monia

Rheu-
matism

Kidneys
damaged

Figure 23-5. A simplified sequence of events in sickle-cell anemia.

the red blood cells. These individuals are at a relative advantage over both homozygotes in malarial areas. However, in non-malarial areas, such as the present-day United States,[4] some individuals with sickling may be at a disadvantage, for the trait sometimes causes pain, reduced vitality, and can lead to other complications (Figure 23-5, Table 23-11).

Thalassemia. One form of thalassemia (from the Greek thalassa, the Mediterranean Sea, and haima, blood) is known as "Mediterranean thalassemia" or Cooley's Anemia (Figure 23-6). Clinical and geographical data on thalassemia raised important questions about the origin of the abnormal gene (and its seeming original restriction to malarial areas) and its survival. From its wide distribution on both shores of the Mediterranean, it was postulated that the gene was of ancient origin—perhaps dating to about 5000 years B.C. However, the absence of the thalassemia trait in parts of Europe where Mediterraneans migrated remained a puzzling mystery.

[4]It should be kept in mind that malaria occurred in various of the swampy areas in the American South in the eighteenth and nineteenth centuries. It also occurred as far north as St. Louis and Evansville as late as the 1940s.

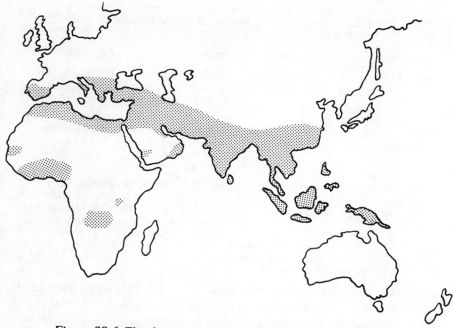

Figure 23-6. The distribution of thalassemia in the Old World.

Original explanations tried to link high regional incidences of thalassemia with increased fertility of heterozygous individuals. However, a high rate of fertility could not be found, nor could abnormally high mutation rates for the thalassemic gene. Beginning in 1950, a number of workers pointed to the correspondence of thalassemia with the distribution of malaria. In those parts of the Mediterranean where malaria was a severe year-round problem, thalassemia frequencies were the highest. The current picture, confirmed by the sickle-cell pattern, is that thalassemia provides some malarial protection.

Table 23-12 shows the mechanism whereby thalassemia works in the three genotypes: homozygous normal, homozygous for thalassemia (thalassemia major), and heterozygous for thalassemia (thalassemia minor).

G6PD. Still another gene, apparently sex-linked and carried on the X chromosome, is concerned with malarial protection. This gene controls production of a red cell enzyme called glucose-6-phosphate dehydrogenase (G6PD). Enzyme-deficient red blood cells contain very little glutathione, upon which malarial parasites depend for growth. Some plasmodia species enter and live in older red cells rather than the younger cells and since older red blood cells are normally those deficient in glutathione, the plasmodia are poorly nourished in the bloodstream of anyone having this enzyme deficiency.

The person carrying the gene is not likely to suffer, unless given certain drugs which affect the blood. The red blood cells of persons deficient in G6PD rupture when given certain drugs. One of the drugs to which the carrier is sensitive is a malarial depressant known as primaquine. Primaquine sensitivity is found in many African, Mediterranean, and Near Eastern populations and also occurs in some Southeast Asian and New Guinea groups. During World War II the wholesale ad-

Table 23-12. Thalassemia Genotypes and Clinical Picture.

Clinical status	Genotype	Clinical picture	Hemoglobins
Normal	Homozygote normal	Within normal limits for hemoglobin and cellular fragility	Normal, slight amount of fetal hemoglobin
Thalassemia minor	Heterozygote	Slight anemia, increased osmotic pressure of the red cells	Slight amount of fetal hemoglobin
Thalassemia major	Homozygote	Marked anemia, abnormal red cells fragile and increased osmotic pressure	Hemoglobin primarily of fetal type, little normal hemoglobin

From Stanley M. Garn. *Human Races*. 3rd edition, 1971, Courtesy of Charles C Thomas, Publishers, Springfield, Illinois.

ministration of primaquine as a malarial protectant adversely affected soldiers of certain genetic backgrounds. A similar problem occurs in relation to a sensitivity to the fava (*Vicia fava*) bean, commercially grown in southern Europe and the Middle East. The G6PD deficients are sensitive to the fava bean when eaten. This sensitivity is often referred to as favism.

Polymorphisms

Before discussing the evidence for the existence of polymorphisms, it would be well to briefly discuss the topic of polymorphism itself. A polymorphism can be defined as a trait which is controlled by two or more common alleles. Two types of polymorphisms are commonly recognized, transient polymorphisms and balanced polymorphisms. Transient polymorphisms are unstable systems; conversely, balanced polymorphisms are stable systems. Polymorphisms are maintained within a population by two processes: selection for the heterozygote and nonrandom mating. Commonly, selection is seen as a process which acts largely by limiting variation. In any favorable environment the prevailing conditions will create, for any gene, a favorable condition for one allele and thus either reduce the frequency of or completely eliminate its alternatives. Polymorphisms contradict this in the sense that their existence proves that two or more alleles can be found and often are found together in the same population. Furthermore, they can be found in fairly high frequencies. If selection acts to favor one allele or genotype over another, then why are polymorphisms so frequent? Balanced polymorphisms offer the heterozygote some selective advantage, that is, an equilibrium exists in which several different alternative alleles are maintained.

If the heterozygote individuals are more viable and to some extent favored over individuals who are homozygous, the population is likely to achieve a state of balanced polymorphism. Both alleles of a gene (i.e., Y and y) will be maintained within the population by selection for the survival of the Yy genotype. Since matings between two heterozygous genotypes (Yy x Yy) will produce roughly one homozygote (YY) and one homozygote (yy) for each two heterozygous (Yy) offspring, selection will continue every generation. Furthermore, depending upon the selection pressures against both homozygotes, YY and yy, there will be some ratio of Y to y in the general population which will be maintained in equilibrium. In a state of balanced polymorphism there is a ratio of Y to y at which any increase in the relative frequency of either allele will tend also to increase the force of natural selection against that allele and tend to return the ratio to its former balance.

Balanced Polymorphisms. Both thalassemia and sickle-cell anemia are examples of **balanced polymorphisms;** there is a strong selective pressure to maintain the heterozygote state in a certain proportion of the population. Thalassemic homozygotes (Th^2Th^2) die before reaching reproductive age due to severe anemia. "Normal" homozygotes, individuals without the thalassemia gene, are afflicted with malaria and frequently die early. The heterozygote is strongly selected for under such conditions. Heterozygotes experience milder forms of malaria and are not too incapacitated by the abnormal red blood cells (and consequent oxygen loss) characteristic of thalassemia. Malaria exerts strong selective pressures which help retain both "normal" and thalassemia genes within the population; selection pressure is for a balanced polymorphism.

Culture, Malaria and the Sickle-Cell Trait

The relationship between malaria and abnormal hemoglobins is quite clear in Africa and the Mediterranean; however, the existence of malaria poses a problem. Much of Africa is not naturally malarious; pre-agricultural Africa offered little to the malarial mosquito and only when rainforests were opened for agriculture did the mosquito have a chance to spread. The mosquito does not breed in the rain forest or the shaded forest floor, and malaria seems to be nonexistent in untouched African jungles. Dr. Frank Livingstone (an anthropologist at the University of Michigan) concluded that malaria is of recent origin in West Africa and appeared following the introduction of slash-and-burn (or swidden) agriculture. With the opening of the forest floor and the appearance of stagnant, unshaded pools, a whole new habitat was provided for the carrier mosquito. Agriculture made Africa malarial by providing the mosquito a place to breed; malaria spread following the spread of slash-and-burn agriculture, and S hemoglobin became adaptive in its wake. Sickling frequencies, especially in West Africa, bear out this hypothesis; pre-agricultural peoples or those recently becoming agriculturalists have the lowest incidence of sickling.

The relationship which Livingstone postulates between malaria and agriculture, with the consequent change in genetic structure, is the first concrete example of how culture can initiate genetic change. The demonstration of the mosquito-malaria relationship brought about a review of the situation in the Mediterranean. Here, human habitation did not create wet, humid, marshy areas; however, populations moved into them for the purpose of practicing lowland agriculture. Early agricultural civilizations developed along the rivers, with their seasonal floods and consequent stagnant pools and lowland marshes. Oasis villages (where malaria is a scourge) provided the basis for early stable populations; primitive means of irrigation—ditch irrigation and wheel bucket watering—caused seasonal flooding and created optimum areas for breeding malarial mosquitos. Consequent food surpluses made high population densities possible and vastly increased the numbers subjected to malarial selection.

Culture created malarial zones in Africa, and it is again changing the picture, for by the use of modern sprays, such as DDT and other mosquito sprays, technology is killing many malarial vectors. (It is also selecting for DDT-resistant strains of mosquitos.) This may again result in changed proportions of genotypes; one could expect a slow increase in the proportion of "normal" homozygotes and a slow decline in the heterozygote condition, depending upon the mosquito's adaptation.

Haptoglobins and Transferrins

Haptoglobins are serum proteins which are part of the alpha$_2$-globulins in serum. Haptoglobins can combine with free hemoglobin (that is, hemoglobin released into the plasma when a red blood cell disintegrates), and this ability prevents it from being lost through excretion in the kidneys. Three types of haptoglobin are known, each apparently under genetic control. While the occurrence of different haptoglobins varies widely, the adaptive significance of the various haptoglobins is unclear, although there may be some environmental selection.

Another type of serum protein variant is a beta-globulin fraction of serum which binds with iron. The transferrins transport iron to the tissues as needed, especially bone marrow where hemoglobin is formed. There are at least seventeen forms of transferrins and each appears to be under genetic control. Transferrin variants are arranged in three groups, TfC, TfD, and TfB.

These transferrins are distributed unevenly in populations; TfC is most common and TfB is not widely distributed. Since there may be a difference in binding capacity of the various transferrins, certain forms may be more efficient in some populations. However, as with haptoglobins, more work is needed.

Populations and Their Diseases

A brief look at Table 23-13 shows that some populations and diseases are related. Since many populations are reproductively isolated from each other and have had a somewhat separate evolutionary history, it is not surprising that we find certain diseases primarily restricted to some groups. Some diseases, rare in themselves, are also very rare in the populations exhibiting them. Population isolates like the Amish have a high frequency of rare genetic diseases due to inbreeding or random genetic drift. There are a number of diseases in which inheritance may determine susceptibility but environment determines which individuals are afflicted. Some examples are diabetes mellitus, peptic ulcers, cancers, and pulmonary tuberculosis and, if current research is correct, alcoholism, drug abuse, and schizophrenia can also be included. Mutations being what they are, no disease can be considered 100 percent population limited; the same abnormal hemoglobin protecting Italians from malaria also protects the Burmese. Furthermore, common diseases may not always indicate common ancestry.

Kuru. Kuru, limited to the Eastern highlands of New Guinea, is one of the most remarkable population-associated diseases and was un-

Table 23-13. Populations and Their Diseases.

Population	Relatively high frequency	Relatively low frequency
Ashkenazic Jews	Abetalipoproteinemia Bloom's disease Dystonia musculorum deformans Factor XI (PTA) deficiency Familial dysautonomia Gaucher's disease Niemann-Pick disease Pentosuria Spongy degeneration of brain Stub thumbs Tay-Sachs	Phenylketonuria
Mediterranean peoples (Greeks, Italians, Sephardic Jews)	Familial-Mediterranean Fever, G6PD deficiency, Hemoglobinopathies (i.e. thalassemia)	Cystic fibrosis
Africans	G6PD deficiency (African type). Hemoglobinopathies	Cystric fibrosis. Hemophilia, PKU, Wilson's disease
Japanese (Koreans)	Acatalasis Dyschromatosis universalis hereditaria, Oguchi's disease	
Chinese	Thalassemia, G6PD (Chinese type)	
Armenians	Familial Mediterranean fever	

Adapted from *The Biological and Social Meaning of Race* by Richard H. Osborne. W. H. Freeman and Company. Copyright © 1971.

known to scientists until 1953 and unstudied until 1957. In pidgin English kuru is known as "skin Guria" or shaking. Kuru is a progressive and incurable neurological disorder—the afflicted individual usually dies within a year. The first sign of the disease is incoordination; persons begin to stumble and then are unable to walk. Involuntary tremors become more common and soon the victim can't walk, sit, or speak intelligibly. The final stage comes when the victim can't swallow food, and urination and defecation are no longer controlled. The course of the disease is usually a year, but the victim may die within three months.

Kuru is limited to the Eastern New Guinea Fore and to some neighboring peoples married to Fore women. Women are more often afflicted than men, resulting in a ratio of fourteen males to every female in later life. In some Fore hamlets the kuru death rate runs as high as 50 percent.

In an effort to discover the cause of the disease, Dr. C. Gajdusek (who won a Nobel Prize in 1976 for his work) and his colleagues began a search of Fore food, water, fires, etc. No trace element or rare earth that could poison the nervous system was found and since Fore men outside the district living on government diets were afflicted, nutritional sources were ruled out. The search was narrowed to some sort of slow virus.[5] When investigators found they could produce kurulike dis-

[5]Similarly, slow viruses may be the cause of multiple sclerosis, Parkinson's disease, and amyotrophic lateral sclerosis (Lou Gehrig disease).

orders in chimpanzees inoculated with extracts of nerve tissue from kuru victims, they concluded that a virus was the cause.

How was the virus transmitted? Gajdusek suspected cannibalism as the primary means of transmission. The usual practice of cannibalism as a mourning rite had women and children disposing of the butchered bodies of dead relatives. They were thus covered with human tissue, including the brain and visceral tissue. Cannibalism was outlawed in 1957; since then the rate of kuru affliction has slowly declined.

The sex-limited nature of the disease, with females heavily predominating in terms of affliction, is due to the sexual division of labor. Dismembering a kuru victim is women's work. The familial nature of the disease is due to the fact that "one takes care of one's own." The lack of direct person-to-person transmission is explained by the fact that a slow virus is involved; the disease is infectious but not contagious. The men are aloof, engaging in cannibalism only when it is a very close relative, such as a mother. Even then they only sample muscle tissue.

Familial Mediterranean Fever. Mediterranean fever is a cyclic disease; once the symptoms have begun, they recur sporadically and unpredictably throughout life. In mild cases there is fever which lasts a day or so, joint pains, and chest and abdominal pain. In severe cases there is joint involvement, bone decalcification, and kidney insufficiency. Most afflicted individuals are not permanently or seriously impaired; however, about 10 percent of the case studies have succumbed to renal complications.

Familial Mediterranean fever arose in the Middle East and appears to be of ancient origin. The disorder has a narrow distribution among Armenians and Sephardic Jews. While its inception may be due to the founder principle, the high incidence suggests instead a heterozygote effect. The mutation may be 5000 to 6000 years old, and its concentration in the Mediterranean area suggests its origin there. The familial nature of the fever is apparent; about half of the siblings of index cases and about 50 percent of the offspring of index cases develop Mediterranean fever, suggesting a Mendelian dominant. There is a slight excess of males over females among the afflicted.

Since the gene frequency for the disorder is low—well under 0.0001—the present limits may be due to chance. However, since the fever is associated with impaired fertility and since a certain portion of the genes are removed from the population each generation due to death, the maintenance of the frequency must be explained. The fact that Ashkenazic Jews (those in Europe and North America) rarely exhibit the trait while Sephardic Jews (those in the Middle East) do requires explanation. The heterozygote may be at an advantage in the Mediterranean region but not in colder northern climates.

Tay-Sachs. Tay-Sachs is a rare disease bearing the name of its co-discoverers which is found primarily in Jewish populations. The disease is genetically determined and results in a neurological disorder that begins in infancy. The progressive nature of the disease usually results in death between ages two to four. The disease has its highest incidence in European Jewish populations, where it is a hundred times more common than in Sephardic Jews. The highest incidence is found in Jewish populations living in the provinces along the old Polish-Russian border near Vilna. Among non-Jews the incidence of the

Table 23-14. Frequency of Lactase Deficiency.[1]

Group	No. of Subjects	Percent Deficient
Afro-American	97	74% (approx.)
Batutsi (Rwanda)	12	17
Bahina (Ankole)	11	9
Australian aborigines		
Papunya (all less than 15 years old)	25	90
Maningrida (age range 6 to 48 months; mean 22 monthly)	19	80
Greenland Eskimos	32	72
American Indian (Chami, Colombia)	24	100
American Indian	3	67
Chinese	20	85
Formosa	(7)	
U.S.	(3)	
Philippines	(10)	
Baganda (Africa)	17	94
Bantu	35	89
Thai	140	97
Thai	75	100

[1]Based on McCracken, 1971.

Adapted from Stephen Molnar, *Races, Types and Ethnic Groups: The Problem of Human Variation,* © 1975, p. 87. Reprinted by permission of Prentice-Hall, Inc., Englewood Cliffs, New Jersey.

homozygote is one in about 500,000 live births. Since the disease is on the rise, there is the possibility of some selective advantage of the heterozygote; however, we don't yet know what it is.

Lactase Deficiency—No Use for Milk Sugars (Table 23-14). While many babies can drink milk, some adults cannot tolerate milk in any quantity because they lack sufficient lactase for the breakdown and absorption of lactose-milk sugar. (Lactase is an enzyme, an organic substance which accelerates chemical transformation.) If the lactase-deficient person drinks much milk, she or he gets abdominal cramps; diarrhea results and the individual is deprived of lactose as an energy source.

Lactase deficiency may be a secondary function of malnutrition and malabsorption, as in protein-calorie malnutrition. In some cases, the deficiency may result from a previously milk-free diet, which is common to many adults in the world. Or the deficiency may be congenital, genetically determined, and population-linked. In true lactase deficiency, lactose intolerance cannot be cured by improved nutrition or by gradually increasing milk intake.

Lactase deficiency is common in many parts of Asia (where there may be some biological link to the Chinese taboo on drinking milk), Africa, and in Afro-Americans. The deficiency is least common in adult Europeans and those of European ancestry. Possibly, other than traditional and economic reasons explain why milk is regarded as unfit for adults in some cultures. The deficiency seems to be both genetic and environmental in origin.

This chapter attempted to provide a picture of some population differences and their significance. We have not exhausted the traits we could list, and we are unsure about the genetics and meaning of many of them. Whatever social meaning may be inappropriately attached to some of the traits, they are, by and large, reflections of a population's past or continuing struggles to adapt.

We do not know when and where many of the population differences discussed here arose. But such differences probably do not date very far back into the fossil record and many traits useful in modern classification cannot be obtained from the fossil record.

Bibliography

Allison, A. 1954. Protection afforded by sickle-cell trait against subtertian malarial infection. *British Medical Journal* 1:290.

_____. 1955. Aspects of polymorphism in man. *Cold Springs Harbor Symposia on Quantitative Biology* 20:239.

_____. 1963. Malaria and glucose-6-phosphate dehydrogenase deficiency. *Nature* 179:609.

_____. 1964. Polymorphism and natural selection in human populations. *Cold Springs Harbor Symposia on Quantitative Biology* 29:137-49.

Allison, J., and Blumberg, B. 1959. Ability to taste phenylthiocarbamide among Alaskan Eskimos and other populations. *Human Biology* 31:352-59.

Angel, J. 1966. Porotic hyperostasis amnesias, malarias and marshes in prehistoric eastern Mediterranean. *Science* 153:760-63.

Azevedo, E.; Kreeger, H.; Mi, P.; and Morton, N. 1965. PTC taste sensitivity and endemic goiter in Brazil. *American Journal of Human Genetics* 17:87-90.

Bayless, T., and Rosenzweig, N. 1966. A social difference in incidence of lactase deficiency. *Journal of American Medical Association* 197:968.

Blumberg, B., and Gartler, S. 1961. The urinary excretion of B-aminoisobutyric acid in Pacific populations. *Human Biology* 33:355.

Boyd, W. 1950. *Genetics and the races of man.* Boston: Little, Brown.

_____. 1963. *Genetics and the human race. Science* 140:1057-64.

Brace, C. 1963. Structural reduction in evolution. *American Naturalist* 97:39-49.

Brues, A. 1963. Stochastic tests of selection in the ABO blood groups. *American Journal of Physical Anthropology* 21:287.

Buettner-Janusch, J. 1966. *Origins of man.* New York: Wiley.

_____. 1973. *Physical Anthropology: A perspective.* New York: Wiley.

Carbonell, V. 1963. Variations in the frequency of shovel-shape incisors in different populations. In *Dental anthropology,* edited by D. R. Brothwell, pp. 211-33. Elmsford, N.Y.: Pergamon.

Cavalli-Sforza, L., and Bodmer, W. 1971. *The genetics of human populations.* San Francisco: W. H. Freeman.

Coon, C.; Garn, S.; and Birdsell, J. 1950. *Races: a study of the problems of race formation in man.* Springfield, Ill. Charles C Thomas.

Damon, A. 1969. Race, ethnic group and disease. *Social Biology* 16:69.

Gajdusek, C. 1962. Kuru—an appraisal of five years of investigation. *Eugenics Quarterly* 9:69.

Gajdusek, C., and Zigas, V. 1959. Kuru. *American Journal of Medicine* 26:442.

Garn, S. 1957. Race and evolution. *American Anthropologist* 59:218.

_____. 1971. *Human races.* Springfield, Ill.: Charles C Thomas.

Giblett, E. 1969. *Genetic markers in human blood.* Philadelphia: Davis Co.

Giles, E. 1962. Favism, sex-linkage, and the Indo-European kinship system. *Southwest Journal of Anthropology* 18:286-90.

Grubb, R. 1948. Correlation between Lewis blood group and secretor character in man. *Nature* 16:933.

Harrison, G.; Weiner, J.; Tanner, J.; and Barnicot, N. 1964. *Human biology: an introduction to human evolution, variation and growth*. New York: Oxford University Press.

Johnston, F. 1973. *Microevolution of human populations*. Englewood Cliffs, N.J.: Prentice-Hall.

Kelso, A. 1963. Dietary differences: a possible selective mechanism in ABO blood group frequencies. *Southwestern Lore* 29:44.

Landsteiner, K. 1945. *The specificity of serological reactions*. Cambridge, Mass.: Harvard University Press.

Lerner, I. 1968. Heredity, evolution and society. San Francisco: W. H. Freeman.

Levine, P. 1943. Serological factors as possible causes of spontaneous abortion. *Journal of Heredity* 34:71-80.

Livingstone, F. 1958. Anthropological implications of sickle-cell gene distribution in West Africa. *American Anthropologist* 60:533.

———. 1967. *Abnormal hemoglobins in human populations*. Chicago: Aldine.

———. 1971. Malaria and human polymorphisms. *Annual Review of Genetics* 5:33-64.

McCracken, R. 1971. Lactase deficiency: an example of dietary evolution. *Current Anthropology* 12:479-500.

Molnar, S. 1975. *Races, types, and ethnic groups*. Englewood Cliffs, N.J.: Prentice-Hall.

Motulsky, A. 1960. Metabolic polymorphisms and the role of infectious diseases in human evolution. *Human Biology* 32:28.

Mourant, A. 1956. *The distribution of blood groups in animals and humans*. Springfield, Ill.: Charles C Thomas.

Myrianthopoulos, N., and Aronson, S. 1966. Population dynamics of Tay-Sachs Disease. I. Reproductive fitness and selection. *American Journal of Human Genetics* 18:313.

Neel, J. 1949. The inheritance of sickle-cell anemia. *Science* 110:64.

Osborne, R., ed. 1971. *The biological and social meaning of race*. San Francisco: W. H. Freeman.

Otten, C. 1967. On pestilence, diet, natural selection, and the distribution of microbial and human blood group antigens and antibodies. *Current Anthropology* 8:209.

Race, R., and Sanger, R. 1962. *Blood groups in man*. Oxford: Blackwell Scientific Publishers.

Rosen, A., and Scanlan, J. 1948. Favism. *New England Journal of Medicine* 239:367.

Saldanha, P., and Nacrur, J. 1963. Taste thresholds for phenylthiouria among Chilians. *American Journal of Physical Anthropology* 21:113-20.

Stini, W. 1975. Ecology and human adaptation. Dubuque: W. C. Brown.

Vogel, F. 1968. Anthropological implications of the relationship between ABO blood groups and infections. *Proceedings Eighth International Congress of Anthropological and Ethnological Sciences* 1:365-70.

Wiesenfeld, S. 1967. Sickle-cell trait in human biological and cultural evolution. *Science* 157:1134-40. Reprinted in L. Morris, ed., 1971, *Human populations, genetic variation, and evolution*, pp. 273-89. San Francisco: Chandler Publishing Co.

Williams, B. 1973. *Evolution and human origin: An introduction to physical anthropology*. New York: Harper and Row.

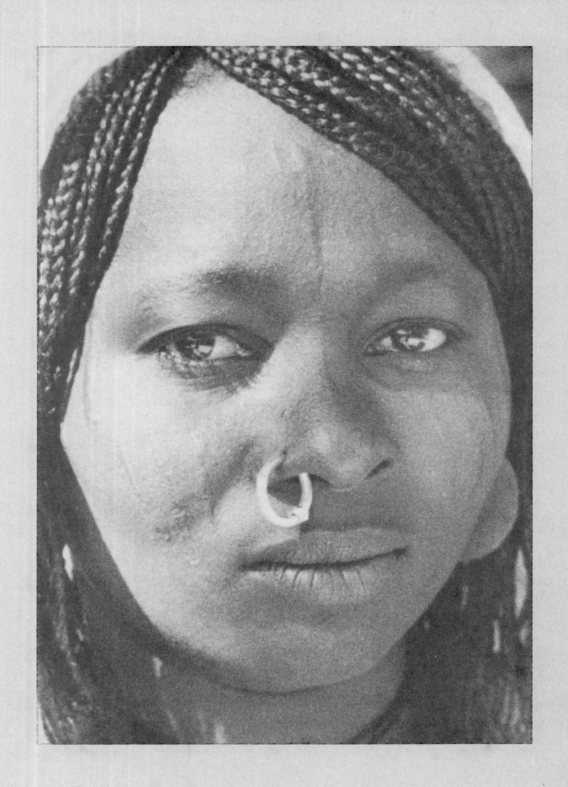

Chapter 24
Development of Human Diversity

How have population differences become established and perpetuated? Gene frequencies must alter if changes are to occur in the gene pool; this can be accomplished by migration, genetic drift, mutation, and natural selection. Once change occurs adaptation and natural selection play their role, separating adaptive from non-adaptive, or maladaptive genes. Most differences in population genotypes result from natural selection which acts by increasing the frequency of genes that improve adaptation and decreasing those lowering adaptation. Thus genotype differences are primarily adaptive responses to the environment.

The conclusion that population differences in genotypes result from natural selection must not be seen as proof that any given phenotypic characteristic is or has been adaptive to a specific environment. Most genes affect many traits, a condition known as *pleiotropy*. Even though there is a close relationship between genetic inheritance and phenotypic traits, the adaptive value of a gene need not be related to any one aspect of the phenotype to the exclusion of others.

Looking at the Fossil Record

The longer a population lives in an area, the greater the probability that any of its genetic eccentricities result from adaptation; ecologically stable populations are more likely to show genetic adaptations than ecologically unstable populations. Genetic differences are probably related to stable environmental stresses such as climate and disease rather than to the more changeable stresses produced by culture. We are, as were many of our ancestors, a geographically and ecologically diverse species. We live now, and did so in the past, in various climatic conditions; and any living thing (plant or animal) occupying an extended range is subjected to forces tending to divide it into smaller segments. Simple geographical isolation impedes **random mating** and gene flow. Among social animals, no matter how naturally and uncon-

443

sciously they may be organized, social as well as geographical barriers to mating occur. Mutations in one group do not necessarily spread to another, regardless of how potentially useful. We might expect, as a species ranges from Olduvai to Java to Chou Kou Tien and parts of Europe and North Africa, that it might begin to differentiate.

An examination of living human populations shows that we are not exempt from the normal processes of local evolutionary change. Genetic differences between groups have accumulated throughout the thousands of generations during which such groups were at least semi-isolated from each other. What is of interest is not that we share such features with other animals but that we differ in one very significant respect. Unlike many other animals which spread across the world, we did not divide into different species. One of the most widespread and evolutionarily successful members of the animal kingdom is still one species. Amongst modern human populations, none is so isolated that it is today a member of its own species; with modern transportation and the so-called "shrinking world," this is unlikely to happen in the future.

Since today we are all members of the same species, and since the hominid fossil record yields forms different from you and me, it is often assumed that population diversity postdates the appearance of modern *H. sapiens*. Undoubtedly there were differences in fossil populations. The Middle Pleistocene form *H. erectus*, scattered throughout Europe, Asia, and Africa, was perhaps as variable as modern populations. Whether these differences were such that modern populations arose directly from different Middle Pleistocene groups is debatable.

Upper Paleolithic fossil populations are often placed into various racial groups; however, European skeletal remains indicate a lack of racial divisions among them, regardless of the fact that some are called Eskimo or Negroid. Yet, European fossil populations are distinguishable from those of Asia and Africa. The Upper Paleolithic witnessed populations adapted to different environmental conditions; therefore what forces kept Upper Paleolithic populations and their predecessors from becoming different species? Obviously there was gene flow, or the situation would be very different but how much gene flow existed and how it was accomplished we don't know. A hypothesis suggesting widespread population migrations as the reason behind assumed worldwide similarities is tenuous. A more cautious view suggests that gene flow occurred by mating between adjacent groups. Judging from western technological societies, and from modern hunters and gatherers, we assume that the average distance of movement was not very great. Gene transmission was probably quite slow when walking was the only transportation available. We should not be surprised to find differences among fossil hominids; and we should expect differences among contemporaneous fossil populations from different geographic areas.

The Role of Culture

Incest Taboo. As an influence on a population's genetic composition, culture is second only to geography as an isolating factor. Although it is difficult to assess the exact role culture played in the original diversification of populations, it certainly played a potent role in later hominid evolution. The incest taboo, as a characteristic of all human societies, has served to maintain genetic lines of communication. Although what constitutes incest varies from culture to culture, the taboo usually denies sexual access to persons linguistically classified as kinsfolk. Incest laws have reduced the incidence of consanguineous mating (i.e., matings between genetically related individuals). There is probably more gene flow among adjacent hominid groups than is true for any other primate. Such mating offers an opportunity for forming new genetic combinations and increasing heterozygosity and also causes the spread of new mutations from the point of origin.

Migration. Another factor maintaining genetic communication has been the migration of hunting groups. To what extent migration occurred, and to what extent hunters from different groups passed their genes to other groups is unknown. However, we can assume that geographical barriers impeded some movement. The persistence of different tool traditions separating East Asia and the rest of the Old World suggests that there was minimal population movement between these areas. Culture again influences the direction of human evolution, for migration becomes easier as technology improves.

Assortative Mating Patterns. Culture has acted as a unifying influence in the evolution of the human species; however, particular cultures, or cultural ideals, often tend to act as divisive forces. Ideals as to what constitutes a suitable mate vary from population to population. Darwin suggested that races developed as a result of sexual selection; while this is debatable, existing differences may have been at least partially maintained in this manner. Assortative or preferential mating patterns have probably had a major role in keeping segments of populations or populations themselves genetically isolated. Preferential mating patterns refer to mate choice according to certain cultural ideals; religious ties, class or caste affiliation, and standards of beauty all affect mating patterns. The upper class American male of European background will probably marry another upper class American of European background.

Positive assortative mating patterns which refer to the mating of individuals sharing certain traits can work for or against natural selection. There is strong positive assortative mating between individuals with abnormal genetic traits. The incidence of dwarfs marrying dwarfs, for example, is probably higher than the incidence of dwarfs marrying non-dwarfs. Mating of this sort is reinforced by individuals (e.g., the blind and the deaf) attending special schools, clinics, etc.

Miss America—Cultural Ideals. As an example of these processes at work, let us take a brief look at what are considered to be "typical" American (of European descent) social ideals (Kurtz, 1971). Miss America in 1962 had measurements of 35-24-35. This was the ideal, and for some it has changed little. We tend to romanticize the Hollywood image; our ideal men should be tall and muscular, our women not too tall and well-proportioned. While there is a good deal of individual preference, the presence of the ideal can be tested by noting perceptions of one's body images. Do these images reflect cultural values? A test conducted in the early 1960s by a clinical pyschologist attempted to answer this question utilizing a young, white, middle-class student sample of eighty-nine men and eighty women. These individuals were asked to judge their own bodies according to various dimensions using a seven-point rating scale. They were asked to judge the value of their body: was it considered good or bad? How good or how bad was it to be of one body type as compared to another? They were asked to rate their body according to potency; was their body strong or weak? Finally, they were asked to rate their body in terms of activity; was their body active or passive?

The following results are noteworthy. Women tend to have global attitudes toward body shapes. Women have opinons about their bodies as good or bad, strong or weak, active or passive, and they are aware of body features in considerably greater detail than men. Could this result from the fact that our male-oriented society is far more conscious and admiring of the female than the male form? Women tend to like their own bodies more than men like their own bodies—they tend to value their bodies more.

Since muscular strength, aggression, and dominance are considered male virtues, males should rate their bodies higher in potency than do women—they do. The large mesomorphs (Charles Atlas types) liked their bodies best of all—so did the women. These men thought themselves more active and sexually potent than did men with other body builds. Large and small heavy-set men also considered their bodies potent, and men seemed to associate potency as much with sheer bulk as with physical strength.

Lean, tall women liked their bodies more than women with other types of builds. Does this reflect the TV commercial and Hollywood ideal? Broad-hipped, buxom women thought their bodies more potent, however. This may be a cross-cultural ideal, for in many cultures the buxom, large-hipped woman is often viewed as the best possible mate for producing children. Large, heavy-set women are seen as most potent, but tall, thin women felt themselves more desirable (and other women seem to agree).

Height is also important; in American society height is often associated with dominance, self-confidence, and leadership. Were we to review the history of presidential elections we would find that in most cases the taller man was the winner. Did voters respond to height in casting their votes? It is commonly said that women look up to tall men, whom they admire and consider good mates. Men see shortness as a liability, as the elevator shoe industry well knows.

This exercise reflects certain values in some segments of American society.[1] Given an equal chance, certain individuals are more apt to pass on their genes than others because of cultural conceptions of what the ideal mate should be like. Those individuals deviating too far from cultural norms have a lesser chance of passing their genes to following generations.

Other Cultural Factors. Culture influences population differences in other ways. In certain areas population increases due to food production have led to a rapid spread of contagious diseases and the eventual selection of mutations providing immunity from one disease or another. Cultural devices, such as clothing, housing, and artificial means of warmth or cooling, have permitted individuals not biologically adapted to an environment to move into it. In many cases these late arrivals have replaced biologically adapted native populations.

[1]See also Vandenberg (1972).

Diversity as an Evolutionary Episode

This paraphrase of a statement by Dr. F. Hulse (1962) implies that population differences are not eternally stable and that selection causing evolution does not occur overnight. As conditions change, new selective forces replace older ones; individuals who might once have died out are now successful. The flow of genes from one population to another may accelerate or impede any shift of gene frequencies due to local adaptations.

Discrete populations, which some call races, are simply episodes in the evolutionary history of a widespread species. Without diversification in response to existing local circumstances over a wide geographical range and through time, species cannot be considered successful. (By most measures, *Homo sapiens sapiens* has been successful, too successful in fact for most of the world's other flora and fauna. It is sobering to ponder that our successes may ultimately be the source of our doom.) Such diversification as witnssed among modern human populations is useful insurance against environmental changes bound to occur. Perhaps these environmental changes will occur at greater speeds as we continue to tamper with, and destroy, segments of the world surrounding us.

A Taxonomy

Although clines (see Chapter 21) occur, such gradations do not deny that gene clusters exist which some argue are of the magnitude to distinguish some populations from others. This does not deny that there is substantial and continuous overlap of genes from very diverse populations; but all populations are not exactly alike. We can deplore the social stigmas attached to certain groups, as any intelligent person should; but by denying that differences occur we do not reduce racial prejudices. Only major social and intellectual changes can do that and should such changes occur tomorrow, they will already be long overdue.

Geographical Race. Following the taxonomy of Dr. Stanley Garn (1971), many anthropologists recognize three major levels of racial groupings (Table 24-1), each of which may be divided into smaller units. The largest unit is a broad, geographically delimited population called a **geographical race.** Such populations coincide with major continental boundaries and their existence is largely due to such barriers. Each geographical race is a collection of populations whose similarities are due to long-continued confinement within set geographical limits. They are collections of breeding populations but are not genetically uniform units. The long-resident populations of Europe are an example of such a unit. We stress long-resident populations, for transportation, mobility, and cultural desires constantly disembark individuals whose evolutionary history is outside the sphere where they now reside.

Local Race. The second unit is the **local race,** which corresponds more closely to what we might designate as breeding populations. Local races are largely endogamous groups which are most readily identified where populations are small and there is little doubt of their limits due to geographical separation or cultural strictures on marriage and/or mating. An example of such a group is the South African Bushman. While clearly members of a geographical race which might be termed

Table 24-1. Geographical Races of *H. sapiens sapiens*

Geographical race	Geographical range
Amerindian	From Alaska, Northern Canada, throughout the Americas
Polynesian	Pacific Islands
Micronesian	Pacific Islands, limited to area from Ulithi, Palau, and Tobi to Marshall and Gilberts
Melanesian-Papuan	New Guinea and neighboring islands
Australian	Australia
Asiatic	Eastern continental Asia, Japan, Philippines, Sumatra, Borneo, Celebes, Formosa
Indian	India
European	Europe, western Asia, Middle East, Africa north of Sahara
African	Africa, south of Sahara

Local Races of H. sapiens sapiens (partial listing)

Eskimo
North American Indian
Fuegian
Ladino
Neo-Hawaiian
Negrito
Northwest European
Mediterranean
Afro-American
East African
Bantu

After Stanley M. Garn, *Human Races;* 3rd edition, 1971. Courtesy of Charles C. Thomas, Publishers, Springfield, Illinois.

African, Bushmen are more likely to marry or mate with Bushmen than Nigerians or other Africans.

Microrace. Local races may not be demonstrable in densely populated areas, yet there are biological differences between groups which are maintained by regional or cultural differences. There are large numbers of microraces in Europe; the Basques and Lapps are two examples. Other possibilities include members of small, isolated villages in which endogamy is rather strongly enforced. Microraces are the smallest races of a breeding population; population geneticists normally refer to them as demes.

Population Rise and Fall. Why some populations are more numerous than others is difficult to explain, although historical and technological factors have had an impact. Given two populations, one a subsistence group of nomadic hunters and gatherers in which numbers are limited by food resources, the other a sedentary agricultural population, we might expect that the agriculturalists will eventually outnumber the hunter-gatherers. Because of a larger potential food supply, the agriculturalists' gene pool theoretically has a greater upper limit than does the hunter-gatherer gene pool. A population which moves into a rich habitat may soon outnumber its neighbors in poorer environments. In time one set of genotypes, one gene pool, may come to dominate. Given that both populations feel their way of life is best and thus might not mate with members of the other, we could expect disproportionate growth rates. These possibilities, and many others, may have influenced the sizes of different gene pools. Many of the original factors are still at work while new possibilities constantly appear.

The scheme presented here follows the suggestion of a number of anthropologists that the roots of modern population differences are yet unknown. The distribution of modern racial groups is due partly to evolutionary forces and partly to modern technology. The picture continually changes as more and more groups come into contact; but, given the current situation, we can assume that differences will remain. Differences will be maintained, if not due to geographical barriers, then due to cultural sanctions against cross-mating.

We have little more than leads as to when modern population differences first appeared. A few anthropologists argue that this occurred early, perhaps during the Lower or Middle Pleistocene. However, most anthropologists would agree that modern differences are of rather recent origin and some give a figure of 10,000 years or so.

Culture has played a strong role in both maintaining and preventing population contact. The incest taboo and migration are two means whereby genetic intermixture is encouraged. As isolating mechanisms we might mention such cultural expressions as religion, linguistic differences, and cultural standards of beauty.

Bibliography

Chagnon, N.; Neel, J.; Weitkamp, L.; Gershowitz, H.; and Ayres, M. 1970. The influence of cultural factors on the demography and pattern of gene flow from the Makiritare to the Yanomomo Indians. *American Journal of Physical Anthropology* 32:339-50.

Coon, C. 1962. *Origin of races.* New York: Knopf.

Ehrlich, P., and Raven, P. 1969. Differentiation of populations. *Science* 165: 1228-32.

Garn, S. 1963. Culture and the direction of human evolution. *Human Biology* 35:221.

_____. 1971. *Human races.* Springfield, Ill.: Charles C Thomas.

Hulse, F. 1955. Technological advance and major racial stocks. *Human Biology* 27:184.

_____. 1962. Race as an evolutionary episode. *American Anthropologist* 64:929.

_____. 1972. *The human species.* New York: Random House.

Johnston, F. 1964. Racial taxonomies from an evolutionary perspective. *American Anthropologist* 66:822.

Kurtz, R. 1971. Body image—male and female. In *Human variation,* edited by J. Downs and H. Bleibtreu, pp. 102-106. Beverly Hills, Calif.: Glencoe.

Laughlin, W., and Osborne, R., eds. 1968. *Human variation and origins.* San Francisco: W. H. Freeman.

Mead, M.; Dobzhansky, T.; Tobach, E.; and Light, R., eds. 1968. *Science and the concept of race.* New York: Columbia University Press.

Montagu, A., ed. 1965. *The concept of race.* New York: Free Press.

Newman, M. 1963. Geographic and microgeographic races. *Current Anthropology* 4:189.

Osborne, R., ed. 1971. *The biological and social meaning of race.* San Francisco: W. H. Freeman.

Vandenberg, J. 1972. Assortative mating, or who marries whom? *Behavior Genetics* 2:127-57.

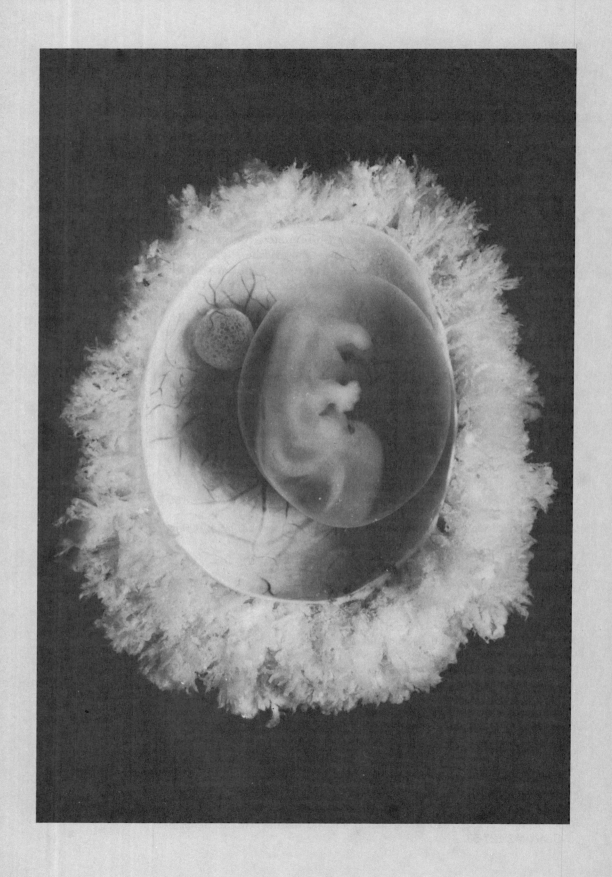

Chapter 25
Conclusion

We shall not cease from exploration,
And the end of all our exploring
Will be to arrive where we started
And know the place for the first time.
(T. S. Eliot: *"Little Gidding"*)*

We have attempted to answer some questions about our past. We began our task with a short history of physical anthropology, for the history of anything, either a people or a discipline, influences its future. Physical anthropology's past has strongly influenced its present concerns. Some physical anthropologists once argued that primate behavior was outside the anthropological purview. Further arguments are likely as other "nonrelevant," "nonanthropological" endeavors are undertaken by physical anthropologists.

For many the meat of physical anthropology is the study of fossil hominids and human diversity. It is safe to say that as these sections are here constituted, they would have been foreign to investigators only a short while ago. Time and methodologies have changed, and to be current today means to be left behind tomorrow. Surely there are few fields more exciting than physical anthropology, especially if one is interested in knowing about himself or herself.

The importance of the behavioral approach in anthropology is likely to increase. Current studies indicate several trends in behavioral evolution. How far we can carry our studies, and in which directions, is not yet clear. However, one thing is certain, in our exhausting search for new explanations we will soon be on the edges of new horizons.

*From "Little Gidding" in *Four Quartets* by T. S. Eliot, copyright, 1943, by T. S. Eliot; copyright, 1971, by Esne Valerie Eliot. Reprinted by permission of Harcourt Brace Jovanovich, Inc.

Seven-week human embryo, shown inside the amniotic cavity.

In the time when Dendid created all things,
He created the sun,
And the sun is born, and dies, and comes again;
He created the moon,
And the moon is born, and dies, and comes again;
And the stars are born, and die, and come again;
He created man,
And man is born and dies, and does not come again.
>   (Old Dinka song. From: P. Matthiessen, *The Tree Where Man Was Born*.)

Glossary

The terms defined here are italicized when first used in the text.

ABO blood groups—The originally defined blood group system.

Acheulean hand axe—Refers to Lower Paleolithic tool type from the Old World. Name derives from Saint-Acheul, France, where tools first defined.

adaptation—The means whereby an organism meets the demands of its eco-niche.

adaptive radiation—Branching out from a basic form to meet diversified ecological niches. This is a basic feature of the early evolutionary stages of new forms.

allele—Alternate form of a gene, one of a series of genes with the same locus on homologous chromosomes.

Allen's rule—The tendency for animals living in cold places to have shorter appendages than their close relatives in warmer areas.

allopatric—Species or populations inhabiting exclusive areas which are often adjacent.

anthropometry—Measurement of the human body.

arboreal—A tree-dwelling form.

autosome—Any chromosome that is not a sex chromosome.

BAIB-(Beta-aminoisobutyric acid)—An amino acid usually excreted in small amounts. Because of genetic misfunctioning some individuals often excrete larger amounts.

balanced polymorphism—Maintenance in a population of two or more alleles in such proportions that the rarest of them cannot be maintained merely by recurrent mutation.

Bergmann's rule—The tendency for animals living in colder areas to have greater body bulk than their relatives in warmer areas.

bicuspid—Having two cusps, a characteristic of $P_{\overline{3}}$, the hominid first lower premolar.

binocular (stereoscopic) vision—Ability to merge visual images from both eyes. Binocular vision allows 3-D or depth perception.

bipedal—Upright locomotion on two hind limbs.

brachiation—Locomotor mode, referring to arm swinging beneath branches.

canine diastema—Gap in the dental arcade of the mandible and maxilla to accommodate the projecting canines.

canine fossa—Anatomical term referring to the hollow in the cheekbone on either side of the nose. This is a characteristic of later hominids and appears with facial reduction.

C-14 (carbon 14)—A chronometric dating technique. Dates the time when an organism died by measuring the amount of radioactive C-14 which has disappeared.

Castle-Hardy-Weinberg Law—A law which maintains that, under random mating and free from disturbing forces, genotype frequencies will be constant in successive generations.

catarrhine—The primate group including humans, apes, and the Old World monkeys.

catastrophism—A belief that earth's history consists of series of great catastrophes. Popularized by the Frenchman G. Cuvier.

ceboids—A term referring to New World monkeys.

cell—A small, complex unit, usually with a nucleus, cytoplasm, and enclosing membrane. All plants and animals are made up of one or more cells.

centromere—Spindle-fiber attachment region of a chromosome.

cercopithecoid—Pertaining to Old World monkeys. Cercopithecoidea—superfamily of the Old World monkeys.

cerebrum—The forebrain section that functions in the maintenance of equilibrium and learned hand movements.

chromatin—A protoplasmic substance in the nucleus of living cells; chromatin forms the chromosomes and contains the genes.

chromosomes—Microscopic bodies which carry the genes that convey hereditary characteristics and are constant in number for each species.

chronometric chronology—Determination of the age, in years, of a specimen or geological formation.

clavicle—Bone connecting the sternum, or breastbone, with scapula or shoulder blade. Helps keep shoulders off the chest.

cline—Gradient in the frequency of a biological trait which is common in one area but less so in another.

Clovis point—Fairly large dart point with a groove extending up the sides, dating to about 10,000 years B.P. in the New World.

codon—A small group of chemical units, believed to be a sequence of three nucleotides, which codes the incorporation of a specific amino acid into a protein molecule during the synthesis of a protein; codons are present in DNA and RNA.

coprolites—Fossilized fecal material.

cranium—The part of the skull enclosing the brain, also called the brain case.

cranial capacity—Referring to the size of the brain. Often given in cubic centimeters (cc).

crossing over—A process inferred genetically by a new association of linked genes. It results in the exchange of segments between homologous chromosomes and therefore produces combinations differing from those characteristic of the parents.

cusp—Elevation on the crowns of the premolar and molar teeth.

DNA (deoxyribonucleic acid)—A nucleic acid based on the sugar deoxyribose. DNA is composed of sugar-phosphate chains to which organic bases are attached. DNA stores genetic information and is replicated to form two identical copies.

deciduous—Refers to the first set of temporary teeth, the "milk teeth."

deme—Usually the smallest identifiable breeding population.

dental formula—The count of the different teeth. Old World primates show a formula of 2-1-2-3: 2 incisors, 1 canine, 2 premolars, 3 molars on each half of each jaw.

dental hominid—A name commonly applied to *Ramapithecus*. The term refers to the fact that teeth are hominidlike, but judgment as to phyletic position should be reserved.

dietary hypothesis—A hypothesis proposed by Dr. John Robinson to explain the differences between *Australopithecus* and *Paranthropus*.

dimorphism—Two different forms in a group, as determined by such characters as sex, size, and coloration.

diploid number—One complete set of pairs of chromosomes (46 in humans).

diurnal—Day-living vs. nocturnal or night-living.

dominance hierarchy—A ranking of animals vis-à-vis one another.

dominant—Allele which expresses itself in the phenotype in either homozygous or heterozygous condition.

effectance motivation—Behavior, such as investigatory or play behavior, which does not serve an immediate end. An important mammalian trait.

endocranial cast—Cast of the skull interior. The cast represents the shape and, to some degree, the brain's surface.

Eocene—Second Cenozoic geological epoch.

evolution—Process of descent with modification.

extinct—A form which has died out, leaving no phyletic offspring.

F-U-N trio—A trio of methods used in relative dating: fluorine, uranium, nitrogen.

familial Mediterranean fever—A recessive periodic disease, largely restricted to persons of Eastern Mediterranean origin, which causes high fever and muscle pain. The disease is progressive and lethal.

favism—An affliction caused by sensitivity to the fava bean.

femur—Upper leg bone, the thigh bone.

fibula—The smaller of the two lower leg bones.

fission track dating—A method of dating volcanic substances. A chronometric dating method used at Olduvai, Bed I.

fist-walking—Method of locomotion common to orangutans. Walking on the clenched fist.

fixidity of species—A pre-evolutionary idea which states that forms once created don't change.

Folsom points—A cultural assemblage spread over the Great Plains area. A thin leaf-shaped blade. Dates from 10,000 to 25,000 years B.P. in the New World.

foramen magnum—Opening at base of skull through which the spinal cord passes.

founder principle—The chance effects of a small number of parents on the gene pool of their descendants.

frontal bone—The bone forming the forehead.

frugivorous—A fruit-eater.

G6PD deficiency (glucose-6-phosphate dehydrogenase)—A genetic disease which is also known as favism and primaquine sensitivity. Causes severe reaction to primaquine (a malarial drug) and the fava bean. Seems to provide some protection against certain forms of malaria.

gamete—A mature male or female reproductive cell (sperm or egg).

gene—A structure occurring at a specific point on chromosomes by which hereditary characters are transmitted and determined.

generalized—An animal, or organ, which is not specifically adapted to any given environment or task. The ability to function in a number of ways or environments.

genetic drift—Shift in allele frequencies due to chance rather than selection. May occur in small, isolated populations.

gene pool (breeding population)—The group in which most breeding occurs and within which an individual is most likely to mate.

genotype—The genetic constitution of an organism. The complete set of alleles inherited from the parents.

genus—Taxonomic category.

geographical race—A geographically delineated collection of similar races.

genotype—The genetic constitution which reacts with the environment to produce the phenotype.

Gloger's rule—The tendency for animals which live in hot, damp areas to have darkly pigmented coat colors.

gluteal muscles—The muscles of the buttocks which function in walking and extending the trunk.

graminivorous—A dietary pattern which involves the ingestion of large quantities of small, tough morsels prepared by powerful and continuous grinding.

grooming—A behavioral pattern whereby an animal picks through the hair of another animal with either or both hands and teeth (social grooming) or picks through its own hair (allogrooming).

hand axes (coup-de-poing)—A superficially flaked core-tool probably used as one of the first formal implements.

haploid number—One complete set of chromosomes (23 in humans).

herbivorous—Feeding on buds and leaves, eating vegetable matter only.

heterodontism—Differentiation of the teeth for different functions.

heterozygous—Plants or animals that have contrasting alleles at corresponding loci on homologous chromosomes and hence do not breed true to type for the particular character involved; a hybrid.

home range—The area in which an animal lives. The total geographical area covered in the normal course of events.

hominid—Any living or fossil member of the family Hominidae.

hominoids—A group including apes and humans.

homoiothermy—The maintenance of a constant body temperature. Warm-bloodedness.

homologous chromosomes—A pair of chromosomes which have identical genes or their alleles located at corresponding loci.

homozygous—Having identical alleles at the same gene locus.

humerus—The upper arm bone.

hunting and gathering—A way of life characteristic of most of hominid evolutionary history. A way of life prior to agriculture.

ilium—Uppermost part of the innominate bone.

immunological theory—A theory associated with a late divergence of the hominid-pongid lines.

incest taboo—Sexual or marriage prohibition between individuals culturally considered related.

insectivorous—feeding on insects.

interstitial wear—Wear between adjacent teeth.

ischial callosities—Hairless areas of the buttocks found on all Old World monkeys and gibbons.

karyotype—Classification of chromosome pairs according to number and pattern.

knuckle-walking—Walking on the knuckles as do modern chimpanzees and gorillas.

kuru—A progressive, incurable, and lethal neurological disease caused by a slow virus. Restricted to a New Guinea group called the Fore.

living floor—Area of intense activity within a hominid fossil site.

local race—A breeding population or population isolate. Totally or largely endogamous populations.

locus (pl., loci)—The area which a gene occupies on a chromosome.

macroevolution—Evolutionary changes resulting in the rise and divergence of discontinuous groups.

Magdalenian—The last level of the Upper Paleolithic in Europe characterized by an increase in antler and bone working.

mandible—Referring to the lower jaw.

manuports—Material carried into a hominid fossiliferous site. Often refers to unworked stone.

masseter muscle—A large muscle of the lower jaw important for mastication or chewing.

maxilla—Refers to the upper jaw.

megaevolution—Major rapid changes usually occurring in small, isolated populations.

meiosis—The process whereby sex cells are produced. All cells produced by meiosis have the haploid number of chromosomes.

melanin—Pigmented substance deposited in the skin, hair, and eyes which gives them their color.

melanocytes—Melanin-producing cells in the skin which are contained within the prickle cell layer.

Mendelian population—Genetically, a spatial-temporal group of interbreeding individuals sharing a common gene pool.

mesial drift—Movement of the teeth forward in the jaw.

microevolution—Small changes within potentially continuous populations.

Miocene—The fourth geological epoch of the Cenozoic era.

mitosis—Ordinary cell division through which a cell gives rise to two cells which are like the original and each other in chromosome composition.

MNS-U—One of the blood group systems.

modifiability of species—The concept that forms could and would change over time. In a way, the philosophical precursor to evolutionary theory.

monogenesis—Early view that all of humanity is descended from one pair of progenitors.

morphology—Refers to structure or form.

Mousterian—The cultural assemblage commonly associated with the Neanderthals.

mutant—A changed gene.

natural selection—Mechanism of evolution proposed by Charles Darwin.

neoteny (paedomorphism)—Evolutionary change in which young developmental forms persist into the maturity of adult forms.

neural—Referring to the brain structure.

nuchal crest—Crest of bone on the occipital bone to which heavy neck muscles attach.

occipital bone—Rearmost portion of skull to which the neck muscles attach.

occipital bun—Projection of bone on occipital. A characteristic of classic Neanderthals. Also occurs in some living populations.

occipital condyle—Knob or joint surface on the occipital bone with which the first vertebra articulates.

Oligocene—The third geological epoch of the Cenozoic era.

olfactory—Refers to sense of smell.

omnivorous—A method of feeding which includes ingestion of various foodstuffs. A diet not specialized for one food source.

orthagnathous—Reduction of face and jaw. Opposite of prognathous or jutting out of jaw and/or face.

orthograde—Refers to upright body posture.

osteodontokeratic culture—Dart's claim for an australopithecine bone, tooth, and antler culture.

osteological—Refers to bone material, i.e., osteological remains.

osteometry—The measurement of bone.

Paleocene—The first geological epoch of the Cenozoic era.

Paleolithic—The first 99 percent of our evolutionary history prior to the inception of agriculture.

palynology—Analysis of fossil pollens and spores. Very helpful in reconstructing paleo-ecological conditions.

panmixis—Random, nonrestricted mating within a gene pool.

parabolic dental arch—A horseshoe-shaped dental arcade between the front teeth. The human arrangement.

parallel dental arch—Tooth rows diverge anteriorly. This is primarily a nonhuman primate trait.

parietals—The bones on either side of the top of the skull.

pebble tools—Crudely worked early stone tools associated with early hominid deposits.

pentadactyly—Having five fingers and toes.

peripheral temperature—The temperatures of the digits, ears, and tail.

phenotype—The observable characteristics of an organism collectively that result from both its heredity and its environment.

phenylketonuria (PKU)—A recessive disease, due to the inability to convert phenylalanine, that causes severe mental retardation.

pithecoid theory—Associated with Dr. W. Straus. The theory states that we arose directly from monkeylike forms without passing through an ape stage.

platycephaly—Flattening of the top of the skull.

platyrrhine—Referring to New World primates.

pleiotropy—Refers to a condition whereby a single gene produces multiple phenotypic expressions.

Pleistocene—The sixth of the geological epochs of the Cenozoic era.

Pliocene—The fifth geological epoch of the Cenozoic era.

pluvials—Periods of increasing rainfall. Study of pluvials is useful for dividing the African Pleistocene.

polygenesis—The hypothesis that different human groups arose from different ancestors. The opposite of monogenesis.

polymorphism—Two or more forms maintained in a breeding population.

polyphyletic—Multiple phyletic or evolutionary lines.

polyploidy—The condition in which an organism has more than one complete set of chromosomes.

polytypic—Occurring in several readily distinguishable forms.

pongid—A term which refers to apes.

Pongidae—The pongid taxonomic family.

postcranial—All the bones below the head or cranium.

postorbital bar—Bony enclosure at the rear of the eye orbit, a diagnostic primate trait lacking in some Paleocene forms.

postorbital constriction—Constriction of the cranium behind the brow ridges.

potassium-argon (K/Ar) dating—A method of chronometric dating. The method dates volcanically derived materials.

preadaptation—A behavioral and/or morphological characteristic (determinable by hindsight only) useful for conditions in which an animal does not yet live.

precision grip—The grip used in holding small objects by opposing the thumb and forefingers.

presapiens—A theory which suggests that *H. sapiens* originated as a distinct, completely separate line from that leading to the Neanderthals.

prognathism—Forward protrusion of lower face and/or jaws.

prosimian—One of the lower primates. Member of taxonomic suborder Prosimii, which includes all fossil and living lemurs, tree shrews, lorises, and galagos.

provisioned colonies—Artificially fed primate colonies.

quadrupedal—Locomotion on all fours.

RNA (ribonucleic acid)—An essential component in all living matter, present in the cytoplasm of all cells and composed of long chains of phosphate and sugar ribose along with several bases; one form is the carrier of genetic information from the nuclear DNA and is important in the synthesis of proteins in the cell.

race—A population within a species which can be distinguished from other populations within the same species.

radius—One of the two lower arm bones.

random mating (panmixis)—System whereby matings are entirely governed by chance.

range of variation—Intra-population variability.

recessive—In genetics, an allele which is not expressed in the phenotype except when the organism is homozygous.

recombination—The process whereby units of genetic information are shuffled, giving rise to a number of different genotypes.

relative chronology—Determination of the age, in years, of a specimen or geological formation in relation to another specimen or formation.

relative dating—These dating methods establish a chronological sequence of latest to youngest.

rhesus (Rh + or Rh −)—A blood group system named after the North Indian rhesus macaque.

sagittal crest—The strut of bone across the top of the skull from front to back to which the temporalis muscles attach.

scapula—Anatomic term referring to the shoulder blade.

secretor—Individual who shows water-soluble antigens in the ABO system in the saliva and other body fluids.

sectorial premolar—A characteristic of all primate first lower premolars ($P_{\overline{3}}$) except those of hominids. The sectorial premolar accommodates the projecting canine from the opposing jaw.

selection—The differential survival of certain genotypes because they are better adapted.

serology—The comparative study of blood groups.

Sewall Wright effect—Non-directed changes in gene frequency, i.e., genetic drift.

sexual dimorphism—Marked differences in morphological characteristics of males and females.

sickle-cell anemia—A condition caused by presence of sickled red blood cells in the blood stream.

socioeconomic sex ratio—The ratio of females to males in primate groups.

somatic cells—Referring to body tissues; having two sets of chromosomes, one set normally coming from the female parent and one from the male.

speciation—An evolutionary developmental stage.

species—Total group of organisms capable of breeding and producing fertile offspring.

subspecies—A subdivision of a species, consisting of individuals in a given geographic area, which differs slightly from, but which can interbreed with, other subspecies of the same species.

supraorbital torus (brow ridges)—Development of heavy bony ridges above the eyes.

sympatric—Reproductively isolated populations inhabiting an overlapping or the same area.

systematics—Scientific study of kinds of organisms and the relationships between them.

T-complex—Dental traits which Dr. C. Jolly relates to an adaptation of a graminivorous diet.

tarsioid theory—Associated with the late Dr. F. Wood Jones. Asserts that we arose directly from a primitive tarsioid stock without passing through a monkey or ape stage.

taurodont—Term referring to enlarged molar root cavity and perhaps fusion of the molar roots.

taxonomy—Science of the classification of living forms in a manner best suited to show their genetic relationship to each other.

Tay-Sachs—Genetic neurological disease, limited primarily to those of European Jewish ancestry, that begins in infancy. Usually leads to early death.

territory—That part of the home range which is defended against others.

Tertiary—The earlier period of Cenozoic. Includes the Paleocene through Pliocene epochs.

thalassemia—An inherited anemia. Its presence in some malarial regions suggests a selective advantage.

tibia—The larger of the two bones in the lower leg.

total morphological pattern—A concept stressing that the assessment of taxonomic status must be based, not on individual isolated traits, but on a combination of the total pattern.

ulna—One of the two lower arm bones.

uniformitarianism—The doctrine that geological strata can only be interpreted by assuming that they were formed by agencies operating in a uniform way and at a rate comparable with the action of contemporary agencies.

Villafranchian faunal period—Faunal assemblage marking the beginning of the Pleistocene. Includes representatives of the modern genera of horses, elephants, and cattle.

zygomatic arches—Anatomic term referring to the cheekbones.

zygote—A cell formed by the union of two gametes.

Chemistry, Matter, and the Universe, copyright © 1976 by W. A. Benjamin, Inc., Menlo Park, California. *Figures 4-5 and 4-6.* After J. Savage, *Evolution.* Holt, Rinehart and Winston, New York, 1963.

Chapter 5. Courtesy of the American Museum of Natural History. *Figure 5-1.* Courtesy of the American Museum of Natural History.

Chapter 6. Photograph by David Brill, © National Geographic Society, *Figure 6-1.* After John E. Pfeiffer, *The Emergence of Man* (Harper & Row, 1969). *Figure 6-2.* After illustration, "New World and Old World Monkeys," from *The Emergence of Man,* Rev. & Enlarged Edition, by John E. Pfeiffer (Harper & Row, 1972). *Figure 6-3.* After illustration, "Increasing Social Complexity," from *The Emergence of Man,* Rev. & Enlarged Edition, by John E. Pfeiffer (Harper & Row, 1972).

Chapter 7. Reproduced with permission of Dr. Ronald D. Nadler, Yerkes Regional Primate Center. *Figure 7-1.* After R. Yerkes, 1971, *Great Apes, a Study of Anthropoid Life.* Reprint of 1929 edition. Johnson Reprints. *Figure 7-2.* After S. Eimerl and I. DeVore, *The Primates.* Time-Life Books, New York, 1972. *Figure 7-4.* After R. Yerkes, 1971.

Chapter 8. *Figure 8-2.* After J. Buettner-Janusch, *The Origins of Man: Physical Anthropology.* John Wiley & Sons, New York, 1966. *Figure 8-3.* After S. Eimerl and I. DeVore, 1972. *Figure 8-4.* After W. Le Gros Clark, *The Antecedents of Man.* (Harper & Row, 1959). *Figure 8-5.* After J. Buettner-Janusch, 1966. *Figures 8-6, 8-7.* After W. Le Gros Clark, 1959.

Part IV. Photograph by David Brill, © National Geographic Society.

Chapter 9. Courtesy of William M. Bass, The University of Tennessee. Photo by Gerald Holly, *The Tennessean. Figure 9-1.* After J. Downs and H. Bleibtreu, eds., *Human Variation: An Introduction to Physical Anthropology.* Glencoe Press, Beverly Hills, California, 1971. *Figure 9-2.* After R. Moore, *Man, Time, and Fossils.* Alfred A. Knopf, New York, 1961. *Figure 9-3.* After J. Birdsell, *Human Evolution: An Introduction to the New Physical Anthropology.* Rand McNally & Co., Skokie, Illinois, 1972.

Chapter 10. Courtesy of the American Museum of Natural History. *Figures 10-1 and 10-2.* After W. Le Gros Clark, *The Antecedents of Man.* Edinburgh University Press, 1969. *Figure 10-3.* After C. Coon, *The Origin of Race.* Alfred A. Knopf, New York, 1962. *Figure 10-4.* After O. Vlahos, *Human Beginnings.* The Viking Press, New York, 1966. *Figure 10-5.* After J. Pfeiffer, 1969. *Figure 10-6.* After E. Simons, *Primate Evolution, An Introduction to Man's Place in Nature* (The Macmillan Company, New York, 1972) and I. Tattersall, *Man's Ancestors* (Murray, London, 1970). *Figure 10-7.* After E. Simons, 1972, and W. K. Gregory, "On the structure and relations of *Notharctus,* an Ecocene primate," *Mem. Amer. Mus. Nat. Hist.* 3 (2:49). *Figure 10-8.* After J. Pfeiffer, 1969.

Chapter 11. *Figure 11-1.* After B. Kurtén, *Not from the Apes.* Pantheon Books, New York, 1971. *Figure 11-2.* Redrawn from D. Pilbeam, *The Ascent of Man.* The Macmillan Company, New York, 1972. *Figure 11-3.* After E. Simons, 1972. *Figure 11-4.* After E. Simons, 1964, "The early relations of Man." *Scientific American* No. 211.

Chapter 12. Courtesy of the American Museum of Natural History. *Figure 12-1.* After E. Simons, 1964. *Figure 12-2.* After E. Hooton, *Up from the Apes.* The Macmillan Company, New York, 1960. *Figure 12-3.* After B. Kraus, *The Basis of Human Evolution.* Harper & Row, New York, 1964. *Figure 12-4.* After J. Birdsell, 1972. *Figure 12-5.* After D. Pilbeam, 1972. *Figure 12-6.* From W. Howells, *Evolution of the Genus Homo.* copyright © 1973 by Cummings Publishing Company, Menlo Park, California. *Figure 12-7.* From G. Tunnell, *Culture and Biology: Becoming Human.* Burgess Publishing Company, Minneapolis, 1973. *Figure 12-8.* From G. Hewes, *The Origin of Man.* Burgess Publishing Company, Minneapolis, 1973.

Chapter 13. *Figure 13-1.* After H. Tuttle, "Knuckle-walking and the problem of human walking," *Science,* Vol. 166, pp. 953-61, Fig. 8, 21 November 1969. Copyright 1969 by the American Association for the Advancement of Science. *Figure 13-2.* Redrawn from "The antiquity of human walking," by John Napier, *Scientific American,* April 1967. Copyright © 1967 by Scientific American, Inc. All rights reserved. *Figures 13-5 and 13-6.* After D. Pilbeam, 1972. *Figures 13-3 and 13-4.* From Sherwood L. Washburn, *The Study of Human Evolution.* Reprinted by permission. Copyright © 1968 by Oregon State System of Higher Education.

Credits

Chapter 14. Courtesy of P. Andrews and A. C. Walker. *Figures 14-1 and 14-2.* After I. Tattersall, *Ramapithecus.* Burgess Publishing Company, Minneapolis, 1975. *Figure 14-3.* After G. Hewes, 1973. *Figure 14-4.* After B. Kurtén, 1971. *Figures 14-5, 14-6, 14-7, 14-8.* Drawn by H. L. Oyen and O. J. Oyen.

Chapter 15. Courtesy of Richard E. Leakey, National Museums of Kenya. Photo A on page 245 courtesy of Dr. D. Johanson, B and C by David Brill, © National Geographic Society. *Figure 15-1.* After G. Findlay, *Dr. Robert Brook: Paleontologist and Physician, 1866-1951.* A. A. Balkema, Capetown, 1972. *Figure 15-2.* Redrawn from C. L. Brace, *The Stages of Human Evolution.* Prentice-Hall, Inc., Englewood Cliffs, N.J., 1967. *Figure 15-3.* After P. Tobias, "Early man in sub-Saharan Africa," in *The Functional Biology of Primates,* edited by R. Tuttle. Aldine-Atherton, Inc., Chicago, 1972. *Figure 15-4.* After M. D. Leakey, 1967. *Figure 15-6.* After J. Buettner-Janusch, 1966. *Figure 15-7.* After F. Bordes, *The Old Stone Age.* World University Library Series, McGraw-Hill Book Company, New York, 1968. *Figure 15-8.* After J. Bordaz, *Tools of the Old and New Stone Age.* Natural History Press, New York, 1970. *Figure 15-9.* After P. Tobias, *The Brain in Hominid Evolution.* Columbia University Press, New York, 1971. *Figure 15-10.* After M. A. Edey and editors, *The Missing Link.* Time-Life Books, New York, 1972. *Figure 15-11.* After B. Kurtén, 1971. *Figure 15-12.* After C. Coon, 1962. *Figures 15-13 and 15-15.* After W. Le Gros Clark, 1964. *Figure 15-14.* After W. Howells, *Mankind in the Making.* Doubleday & Company, New York, 1967.

Chapter 16. Courtesy of the American Museum of Natural History. *Figure 16-1, 16-3, 16-7.* After *The First Men.* Time-Life Books, New York, 1972. *Figure 16-2.* From A. J. Kelso, 1970 and 1974. *Figure 16-4.* After F. Bordes, 1968. *Figure 16-5.* After J. Pfeiffer, 1969. *Figure 16-6.* After F. Clark Howell and editors, *Early Man.* Time-Life Books, New York, 1970. *Figure 16-8.* Drawn by H. L. Oyen and O. J. Oyen.

Chapter 17. Courtesy of Dr. Ralph S. Solecki. *Figures 17-2 and 17-10.* After C. Brace, H. Nelson, and N. Korn, *Atlas of Fossil Man.* Holt, Rinehart and Winston, New York, 1971. *Figure 17-4.* After C. Brace and A. Montagu, *Man's Evolution: An Introduction to Physical Anthropology.* The Macmillan Company, New York, 1965. *Figure 17-5.* After F. Clark Howell and editors, 1970. *Figure 17-6.* After O. Vlahos, 1966. *Figure 17-7.* After J. Birdsell, 1972. *Figure 17-8.* After D. Pilbeam, 1972, and W. Le Gros Clark, 1964. *Figure 17-9.* After Boule and Vallois, 1957. *Figure 17-11.* After W. Howells, 1967. Photo on page 346 courtesy of W. M. Childers.

Chapter 18. Courtesy of the American Museum of Natural History. *Figures 18-1, 18-3, 18-4.* After F. Clark Howell and editors, 1970. *Figure 18-2.* After T. Prideaux and editors, *Cro-Magnon Man.* Time-Life Books, New York, 1973. *Figure 18-5.* After F. Bordes, 1968.

Chapter 19. Courtesy of the American Museum of Natural History. *Figure 19-1.* From G. Tunnell, 1973. *Figures 19-2 and 19-3.* After J. Buettner-Janusch, 1966.

Part V. Courtesy of South African Information Service.

Chapter 20. *Figure 20-1.* After J. Downs and H. Bleibtreu, *Human Variation: An Introduction to Physical Anthropology.* Glencoe Press, Beverly Hills, California, 1971. *Figure 20-2.* From C. Benjamin Melaca et al., 1971.

Chapter 21. Courtesy of the American Museum of Natural History. *Figure 21-1.* From A. J. Kelso, 1970 and 1974.

Chapter 22. Official U.S. Navy photograph. Photo on page 409 courtesy of WHO.

Chapter 23. Courtesy of Carolina Biological Supply Company. *Figure 23-1.* From Stanley E. Gunstream and John S. Babel, *Explorations in Integrated Biology.* Burgess Publishing Company, Minneapolis, 1967. *Figure 23-2.* After A. Motulsky, Human Biology No. 32, 1960. *Figure 23-4 and 23-6.* After J. Buettner-Janusch, 1966. *Figure 23-5.* From A. J. Kelso, 1970 and 1974.

Chapter 24. Courtesy of Professor Dr. Dr. Hans F. Jürgens, University of Kiel. *Figure 24-1.* After F. Hulse, *The Human Species.* Random House, New York, 1971.

Chapter 25. Courtesy of Carnegie Institute of Washington, Department of Embryology, Davis Division.

Index

Brain, C., 352-53
Breeding population(s), 369-70. *See also* Gene pool
Breuil, Henri, 336
Brno, 339
Broom, Dr. R., 235
BSC, 60-61
Buffon, Georges L. L., 21, 22
Burial(s)
    at Kostenki-Borshevo, 335
    at Lake Mungo, 342
    at Shanidar, 313, 321
    Neanderthal, 313, 320-21
    Upper Paleolithic, 341
Burnett, James (Lord Monboddo), 6
Bushman
    African, 258
    Kalahari, 72-73
    South African, 340, 403, 448

Calcium replacement, 153
Calico, 342-43
Caliper, 391
Callicebus (titi), 122
Callithricidae, 122
Canine(s). *See* Teeth
Canine reduction, 195-96
    tool use hypothesis, 196
Cannibalism, 282
Cap Blanc, 337
Cape Flats, 340
Carbon-14 (C^{14}), 154-55
    dating, 154
Carnivore(s), behavior of, 257
Carnivorous primates, 164
Carpenter, C. R., 82, 113
Castle-Hardy-Weinberg law, 377, 381-84
Catastrophism, theory of, 24
Cave Bear(s), 314
Cave Bear Cult, 314
Cave painting, 335-37
Cayo Santiago, 83, 124
Cebidae, 121
Ceboids, 14
Cenozoic clock, 166
Central American monkeys. *See* Monkeys, New World
Cephalic index, 391
Cercopithecoids, 14, 186
Cerebrum, 147
Ceruloplasmin, 368
Chalicothere(s), 255
Chancelade, 338
Charcoal, and carbon dating, 154-55
Charron, Pierre, 4, 8
"Chellean man," 291
Chemeron, 236, 246
Chenchiawo, 282
Chesowanja, 236
Chimpanzee(s), 4, 92-105, 164
    adaptations for sleeping, 169 n.

communicating with, 101-5
evolution of, 95
modern, 179
predatory behavior of, 98-100
social organization of, 100-101
studies of, 93-105
tool use by, 97-98, 247, 360
China, prehistoric sites in, 278
Chinese *Homo erectus,* 278
Chinji and Nagri, 180, 223
Cholesterol, 361
Chopper tool, 251, 252
Chou Kou Tien, 278, 281-82, 339
Chromosomal aberrations, 372
Chromosome(s), 40-42
Chronological ordering, of fossil remains, 149
Chronological sequence, 149
Chronometric age, of fossil specimens, 154
Clark, Sir W. E. Le Gros, 180
Classification of human populations, 389-93
    modern principles of, 56
Climate(s)
    adaptation to humid, hot, 401-3
    and body size, 407
    and fauna, 151-52
Climatic indicators, 149-51
Climatic niches, 48. *See also* Econiche, Habitat
Climatic stress, responses to, 400-401
Clinal approach, 393
Clinists, 394
Clovis point(s), 344, 348
Cohuna, 341
Cold adaptation, of European Neanderthals, 315-17
Cold injury, and skin color, 410
Collagen, 153, 155
Colobines (colobus monkeys), 133
Colonization, New World, 343-44
Color blindness, 376
Combe Capelle, 338
Combe Grenal, 312
Comparative anatomy, primate, 4, 389
Competition
    results of in adaptation, 51
    rodent-primate, 164
Cooley's anemia (thalassemia), 432-33
Creationist School, 23 n.
Crelin, E., 319
Crocuta crocuta, 151
Cro-Magnon. *See Homo sapiens,* Upper Paleolithic
Cross-dating, 153-56
    fluorine, 153
Crossing-over, in meiosis, 41
Cultural floors, of *Homo erectus,* 293. *See also* Living floors
Cuvier, Georges, 22, 24